GLENCOE FRENCH 1

Bon voyage!

WITH FEATURES BY NATIONAL GEOGRAPHIC

Conrad J. Schmitt • Katia Brillié Lutz

McGraw Hill Glencoe

New York, New York Columbus, Ohio Chicago, Illinois Peoria, Illinois Woodland Hills, California

About the Authors

Conrad J. Schmitt

Conrad J. Schmitt received his B.A. degree magna cum laude from Montclair State University. He received his M.A. from Middlebury College. He did additional graduate work at New York University.

Mr. Schmitt has taught Spanish and French at all levels—from elementary school to university graduate courses. He served as Coordinator of Foreign Languages for the Hackensack, New Jersey, public schools. He also taught Methods of Teaching a Foreign Language at the Graduate School of Education, Rutgers University. Mr. Schmitt was Editor-in-Chief of Foreign Languages and ESL/EFL materials for the School Division of McGraw-Hill and McGraw-Hill International Book Company.

Mr. Schmitt has authored or co-authored more than one hundred books, all published by Glencoe/McGraw-Hill or by McGraw-Hill. He has addressed teacher groups and given workshops in all states of the United States and has lectured and presented seminars throughout the Far East, Latin America, and Canada. In addition, Mr. Schmitt has traveled extensively throughout France, French-speaking Canada, North Africa, French-speaking West Africa, the French Antilles, and Haiti.

Katia Brillié Lutz

Katia Brillié Lutz has her **Baccalauréat** in Mathematics and Science from the Lycée Molière in Paris and her **Licence ès Lettres** in languages from the Sorbonne. She was a Fulbright scholar at Mount Holyoke College.

Ms. Lutz has taught French language at Yale University and French language and literature at Southern Connecticut State College. She also taught French at the United Nations in New York City.

Ms. Lutz was Executive Editor of French at Macmillan Publishing Company. She also served as Senior Editor at Harcourt Brace Jovanovich and Holt Rinehart and Winston. She was a news translator and announcer for the BBC Overseas Language Services in London.

Ms. Lutz is the author of many language textbooks at all levels of instruction.

McGraw Hill Glencoe

The McGraw·Hill Companies

Send all inquiries to:
Glencoe/McGraw-Hill
8787 Orion Place
Columbus, OH 43240-4027

ISBN: 0-07-865630-3 *(Student Edition)*
ISBN: 0-07-865631-1 *(Teacher Wraparound Edition)*

Printed in the United States of America.

6 7 8 9 10 079/055 10 09 08 07

Teacher Reviewers

We wish to express our appreciation to the numerous individuals throughout the United States and the French-speaking world who have advised us in the development of these teaching materials. Special thanks are extended to the people whose names appear below.

Anne-Marie Baumis
Bayside, NY

Claude Benaiteau
Austin, TX

Sr. M. Elayne Bockey, SND
St. Wendelin High School
Fostoria, OH

Linda Burnette
Rockville Junior/Senior High School
Rockville, IN

Linda Butt
Loyola Blakefield
Towson, MD

Betty Clough
Austin, TX

Yolande Helm
Ohio University
Athens, OH

Jan Hofts
Northwest High School
Indianapolis, IN

Kathleen A. Houchens
The Ohio State University
Columbus, OH

Dominique Keith
Lake Forest, CA

Raelene Noll
Delmar, NY

Nancy Price
Fort Atkinson High School
Fort Atkinson, WI

Sally Price
Marysville-Pilchuck High School
Marysville, WA

Bonita Sanders
Eisenhower High School
New Berlin, WI

Deana Schiffer
Hewlett High School
Hewlett, NY

Julia Sheppard
Delaware City Schools
Delaware, OH

James Toolan
Tuxedo High School
Tuxedo, NY

Mary Webster
Romeo High School
Romeo, MI

Marian Welch
Austin ISD
Austin, TX

Richard Wixom
Miller Middle School
Lake Katrine, NY

Brian Zailian
Tamalpais High School
Mill Valley, CA

For the Parent or Guardian

We are excited that your child has decided to study French. Foreign language study provides many benefits for students in addition to the ability to communicate in another language. Students who study another language improve their first language skills. They become more aware of the world around them and they learn to appreciate diversity.

You can help your child be successful in his or her study of French even if you are not familiar with that language. Encourage your child to talk to you about the places where French is spoken. Engage in conversations about current events in those places. The section of their Glencoe French book called **Le monde francophone** on pages xxi–xxxv may serve as a reference for you and your child. In addition, you will find information about the geography of the French-speaking world and links to foreign newspapers at **french.glencoe.com**.

The methodology employed in the Glencoe French books is logical and leads students step by step through their study of the language. Consistent instruction and practice are essential for learning a foreign language. You can help by encouraging your child to review vocabulary each day. As he or she progresses through the text, you will to want to use the study tips on pages H51–H67 to help your child learn French. If you have Internet access, encourage your child to practice using the activities, games, and practice quizzes at **french.glencoe.com**.

Table des matières

La francophonie

Leçons préliminaires

Objectifs

In these preliminary lessons you will learn to:

- ✔ *greet people*
- ✔ *say good-bye to people*
- ✔ *ask people how they are*
- ✔ *ask and tell names*
- ✔ *express simple courtesies*
- ✔ *find out and tell the days of the week*
- ✔ *find out and tell the months of the year*
- ✔ *count from 1 to 30*
- ✔ *find out and tell the time*

CHAPITRE 1 Une amie et un ami

Objectifs

In this chapter you will learn to:

- ✔ *ask or tell what someone is like*
- ✔ *ask or tell where someone is from*
- ✔ *ask or tell who someone is*
- ✔ *describe yourself or someone else*
- ✔ *talk about students from France and Martinique*

CHAPITRE 2 Les cours et les profs

Objectifs

In this chapter you will learn to:

- ✔ *describe people and things*
- ✔ *talk about more than one person or thing*
- ✔ *tell what subjects you take in school and express some opinions about them*
- ✔ *speak to people formally and informally*
- ✔ *talk about French-speaking people in the United States*

CHAPITRE 3 Pendant et après les cours

Objectifs

In this chapter you will learn to:

- ✔ *talk about what you do in school*
- ✔ *talk about what you and your friends do after school*
- ✔ *identify and shop for school supplies*
- ✔ *talk about what you don't do*
- ✔ *tell what you and others like and don't like to do*
- ✔ *discuss schools in France*

CHAPITRE 4 La famille et la maison

Objectifs

In this chapter you will learn to:

- ✔ *talk about your family*
- ✔ *describe your home and neighborhood*
- ✔ *tell your age and find out someone else's age*
- ✔ *tell what belongs to you and others*
- ✔ *describe more people and things*
- ✔ *talk about families and homes in French-speaking countries*

CHAPITRE 5 Au café et au restaurant

Objectifs

In this chapter you will learn to:

- ✔ *order food or a beverage at a café or restaurant*
- ✔ *tell where you and others go*
- ✔ *tell what you and others are going to do*
- ✔ *give locations*
- ✔ *tell what belongs to you and others*
- ✔ *describe more activities*
- ✔ *compare eating habits in the United States and in the French-speaking world*

CHAPITRE 6 La nourriture et les courses

Objectifs

In this chapter you will learn to:

- ✔ *identify more foods*
- ✔ *shop for food*
- ✔ *tell what you or others are doing*
- ✔ *ask for the quantity you want*
- ✔ *talk about what you or others don't have*
- ✔ *tell what you or others are able to do or want to do*
- ✔ *talk about French food-shopping customs*

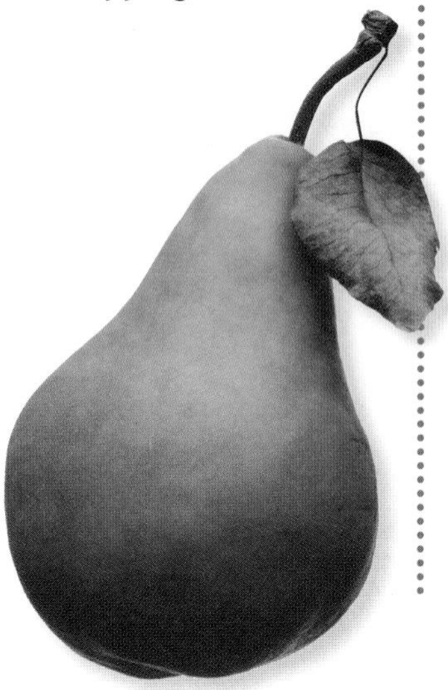

CHAPITRE 7 Les vêtements

Objectifs

In this chapter you will learn to:

- ✔ *identify and describe articles of clothing*
- ✔ *state color and size preferences*
- ✔ *shop for clothing*
- ✔ *describe people's activities*
- ✔ *compare people and things*
- ✔ *express opinions and make observations*
- ✔ *discuss clothes and clothes shopping in the French-speaking world*

AIR FRANCE
le billet électronique
si simple, si pratique

CHAPITRE 8 L'aéroport et l'avion

Objectifs

In this chapter you will learn to:

- *check in for a flight*
- *talk about some services aboard the plane*
- *talk about more activities*
- *ask more questions*
- *talk about people and things as a group*
- *discuss air travel in France*

CHAPITRE 9 La gare et le train

Objectifs

In this chapter you will learn to:

- ✔ *purchase a train ticket and request information about arrival and departure*
- ✔ *use expressions related to train travel*
- ✔ *talk about people's activities*
- ✔ *point out people or things*
- ✔ *discuss an interesting train trip in French-speaking Africa*

CHAPITRE 10 Les sports

Objectifs

In this chapter you will learn to:

- ✔ *talk about team sports and other physical activities*
- ✔ *describe past actions and events*
- ✔ *ask people questions*
- ✔ *discuss what sports are popular in Canada and in French-speaking Africa*

CHAPITRE 11 L'été et l'hiver

Objectifs

In this chapter you will learn to:

- ✔ *describe summer and winter weather*
- ✔ *talk about summer activities and sports*
- ✔ *talk about winter sports*
- ✔ *discuss past actions and events*
- ✔ *make negative statements*
- ✔ *talk about a ski trip in Québec*

CHAPITRE 12 La routine quotidienne

Objectifs

In this chapter you will learn to:

- ✔ *describe your personal grooming habits*
- ✔ *talk about your daily routine*
- ✔ *talk about your family life*
- ✔ *tell some things you do for yourself*
- ✔ *talk about daily activities in the past*
- ✔ *discuss a French family's daily routine*

CHAPITRE 13 Les loisirs culturels

Objectifs

In this chapter you will learn to:

- ✔ *discuss movies, plays, and museums*
- ✔ *tell what you know and whom you know*
- ✔ *tell what happens to you or someone else*
- ✔ *refer to people and things already mentioned*
- ✔ *talk about some cultural activities in Paris*

CHAPITRE 14 La santé et la médecine

Objectifs

In this chapter you will learn to:

- ✔ *explain a minor illness to a doctor*
- ✔ *have a prescription filled at a pharmacy*
- ✔ *tell for whom something is done*
- ✔ *talk about some more activities*
- ✔ *give commands*
- ✔ *refer to people, places, and things already mentioned*
- ✔ *discuss medical services in France*

Literary Companion

Video Companion

Handbook

Guide to Symbols

Throughout **Bon voyage!** you will see these symbols, or icons. They will tell you how to best use the particular part of the chapter or activity they accompany. Following is a key to help you understand these symbols.

Audio Link This icon indicates material in the chapter that is recorded on compact disk.

Recycling This icon indicates sections that review previously introduced material.

Paired Activity This icon indicates sections that you can practice orally with a partner.

Group Activity This icon indicates sections that you can practice together in groups.

Encore Plus This icon indicates additional practice activities that review knowledge from current chapters.

Allez-y! This icon indicates the end of new material in each section and the beginning of the recombination section at the end of the chapter.

Literary Companion This icon appears in the review lessons to let you know that you are prepared to read the literature selection indicated if you wish.

Interactive CD-ROM This icon indicates that the material is also on an Interactive CD-ROM.

Le monde francophone

The French geographer Onésime Reclus first coined the word *francophonie* in 1880 to designate geographical entities where French was spoken. Today, *la francophonie* refers to the collective body of over one hundred million people all over the world who speak French, exclusively or in part, in their daily lives. The term *francophonie* refers to the diverse official organizations, governments, and countries that promote the use of French in economic, political, diplomatic, and cultural exchanges. Politically, French remains the second most important language in the world. In some Francophone nations, French is the official language (France), or the co-official language (Cameroon); in others, it is spoken by a minority who share a common cultural heritage (Andorra). The French language is present in Europe, Africa, the Americas, and Oceania.

Le monde

LE MONDE FRANCOPHONE

Le monde

The areas in color indicate the vast Francophone world.

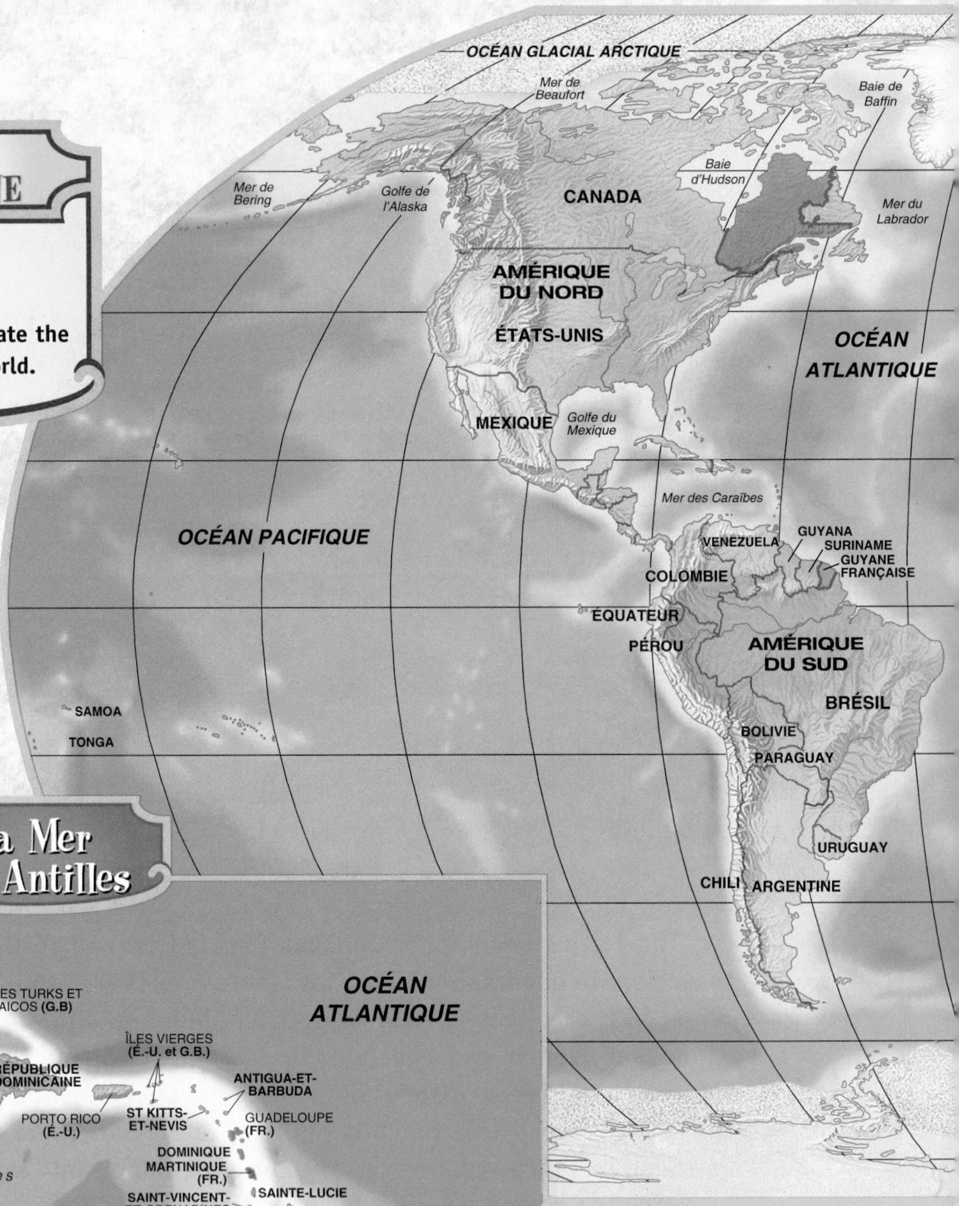

La Mer des Antilles

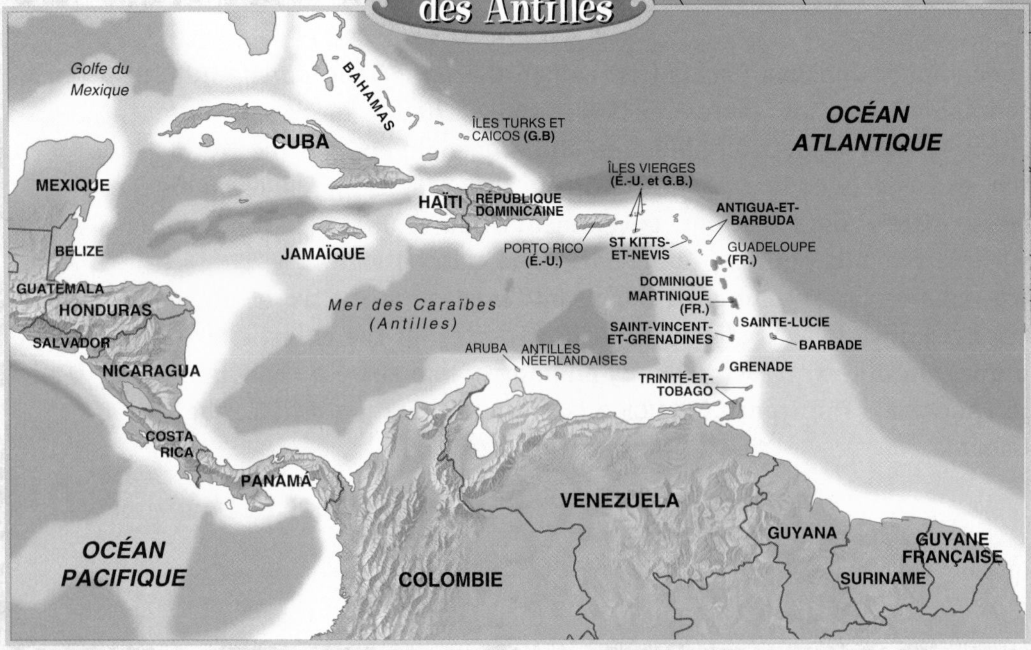

OCÉAN GLACIAL ARCTIQUE
Mer du Groenland
Mer de Norvège
Mer de Barents
Mer de Kara
Mer des Laptev
ISLANDE
Mer du Nord
EUROPE
RUSSIE
ASIE
Mer d'Okhotsk
KAZAKHSTAN
MONGOLIE
GÉORGIE
ARMÉNIE
OUZBÉKISTAN
KIRGHIZISTAN
TURKMÉNISTAN
TADJIKISTAN
CHINE
CORÉE DU NORD
Mer du Japon
JAPON
CORÉE DU SUD
TURQUIE
Mer Méditerranée
TUNISIE
LIBAN
SYRIE
AZERBAÏDJAN
IRAK
ISRAËL
JORDANIE
IRAN
AFGHANISTAN
MAROC
KOWEÏT
BAHREÏN
PAKISTAN
NÉPAL
BHOUTAN
Mer de Chine orientale
ALGÉRIE
SAHARA OCCIDENTAL
LIBYE
ÉGYPTE
QATAR
ARABIE SAOUDITE
ÉMIRATS ARABES UNIS
OMAN
INDE
TAÏWAN
MAURITANIE
BANGLADESH
MYANMAR
LAOS
Mer de Chine méridionale
MALI
NIGER
TCHAD
SOUDAN
ÉRYTHRÉE
YÉMEN
Golfe du Bengale
THAÏLANDE
SÉNÉGAL
BURKINA FASO
AFRIQUE
DJIBOUTI
MARSHALL
GUINÉE
NIGERIA
VIÊT NAM
PHILIPPINES
GHANA
BÉNIN
ÉTHIOPIE
SRI LANKA
CAMBODGE
ÉTATS FÉDÉRÉS DE MICRONÉSIE
RÉPUBLIQUE CENTRAFRICAINE
LIBERIA
TOGO
BRUNEI
PALAU
CÔTE D'IVOIRE
CAMEROUN
SOMALIE
MALAISIE
SÃO TOMÉ ET PRINCIPE
OUGANDA
KENYA
MALDIVES
KIRIBATI
GUINÉE ÉQUATORIALE
GABON
RWANDA
NAURU
CONGO
RÉP. DÉM. DU CONGO
BURUNDI
ÎLES SEYCHELLES
OCÉAN INDIEN
INDONÉSIE
PAPOUASIE-NOUVELLE-GUINÉE
ÎLES SALOMON
TANZANIE
TUVALU
COMORES
ANGOLA
MALAWI
WALLIS-ET-FUTUNA
ZAMBIE
MOZAMBIQUE
Mer de Corail
VANUATU
FIDJI
MADAGASCAR
ÎLE MAURICE
ZIMBABWE
NAMIBIE
OCÉAN ATLANTIQUE
BOTSWANA
RÉUNION
AUSTRALIE
NOUVELLE-CALÉDONIE
AFRIQUE DU SUD
SWAZILAND
LESOTHO
Mer de Tasman
NOUVELLE-ZÉLANDE
ANTARCTIQUE

L'Europe

NORVÈGE
FINLANDE
SUÈDE
ESTONIE
IRLANDE
GRANDE-BRETAGNE
DANEMARK
LETTONIE
RUSSIE
LITUANIE
RUSSIE
PAYS-BAS
BIÉLORUSSIE
BELGIQUE
ALLEMAGNE
POLOGNE
OCÉAN ATLANTIQUE
PARIS
LUXEMBOURG
RÉPUBLIQUE TCHÈQUE
UKRAINE
FRANCE
SLOVAQUIE
SUISSE
AUTRICHE
MOLDAVIE
SLOVÉNIE
HONGRIE
CROATIE
ROUMANIE
BOSNIE-HERZÉGOVINE
SERBIE
PORTUGAL
ESPAGNE
MONACO
YOUGOSLAVIE
Mer Noire
GÉORGIE
ITALIE
MONTÉNÉGRO
BULGARIE
ALBANIE
MACÉDOINE
GIBRALTAR (Brit.)
Mer Méditerranée
GRÈCE
TURQUIE
AFRIQUE
MALTE
CHYPRE
SYRIE
LIBAN

La francophonie

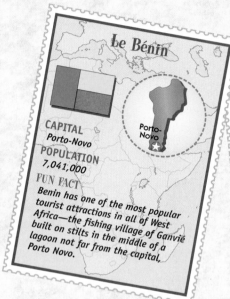

L'Afrique

Le Bénin

CAPITAL
Porto-Novo

POPULATION
7,041,000

FUN FACT
Benin has one of the most popular tourist attractions in all of West Africa—the fishing village of Ganvié built on stilts in the middle of a lagoon not far from the capital, Porto Novo.

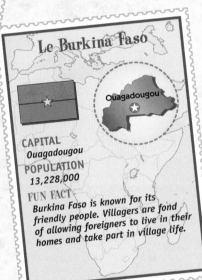

Le Burkina Faso

CAPITAL
Ouagadougou

POPULATION
13,228,000

FUN FACT
Burkina Faso is known for its friendly people. Villagers are fond of allowing foreigners to live in their homes and take part in village life.

L'Algérie

CAPITAL
Algiers

POPULATION
32,818,000

FUN FACT
Algeria is called "the geographic giant" of the Maghreb. It is four times the size of France. Most of the country lies in the Sahara desert.

Le Burundi

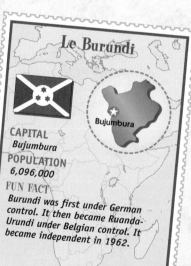

CAPITAL
Bujumbura

POPULATION
6,096,000

FUN FACT
Burundi was first under German control. It then became Ruanda-Urundi under Belgian control. It became independent in 1962.

Le Cameroun

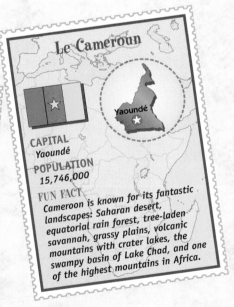

CAPITAL
Yaoundé

POPULATION
15,746,000

FUN FACT
Cameroon is known for its fantastic landscapes: Saharan desert, equatorial rain forest, tree-laden savannah, grassy plains, volcanic mountains with crater lakes, the swampy basin of Lake Chad, and one of the highest mountains in Africa.

Les Comores

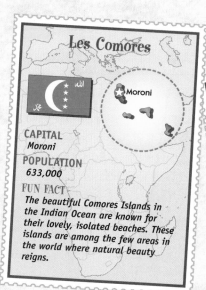

CAPITAL
Moroni

POPULATION
633,000

FUN FACT
The beautiful Comores Islands in the Indian Ocean are known for their lovely, isolated beaches. These islands are among the few areas in the world where natural beauty reigns.

La République Centrafricaine

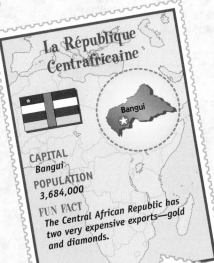

CAPITAL
Bangui

POPULATION
3,684,000

FUN FACT
The Central African Republic has two very expensive exports—gold and diamonds.

La Côte d'Ivoire

CAPITAL
Yamoussoukro

POPULATION
16,962,000

FUN FACT
The Ivory Coast's principal city, Abidjan, is West Africa's most cosmopolitan city and is often referred to as the "Paris of West Africa."

La République du Congo

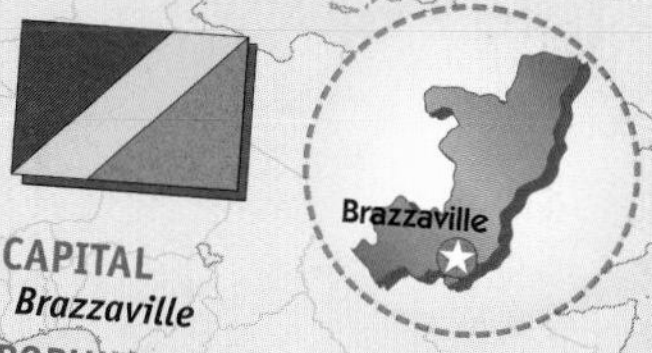

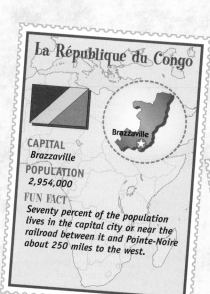

CAPITAL
Brazzaville

POPULATION
2,954,000

FUN FACT
Seventy percent of the population lives in the capital city or near the railroad between it and Pointe-Noire about 250 miles to the west.

La République Démocratique du Congo

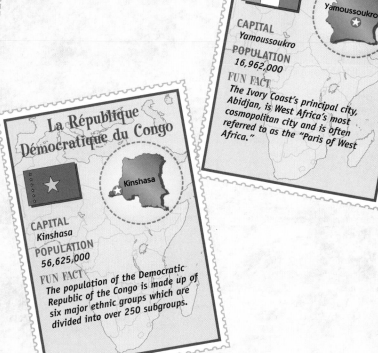

CAPITAL
Kinshasa

POPULATION
56,625,000

FUN FACT
The population of the Democratic Republic of the Congo is made up of six major ethnic groups which are divided into over 250 subgroups.

Le Gabon

CAPITAL
Libreville

POPULATION
1,322,000

FUN FACT
More than three-quarters of the territory of Gabon is covered by forests. Its capital, Libreville (appropriately named), was founded by Catholic missionaries to house liberated slaves.

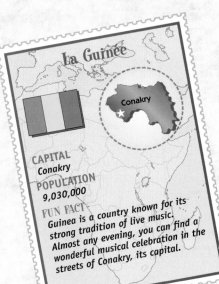

La Guinée

CAPITAL
Conakry

POPULATION
9,030,000

FUN FACT
Guinea is a country known for its strong tradition of live music. Almost any evening, you can find a wonderful musical celebration in the streets of Conakry, its capital.

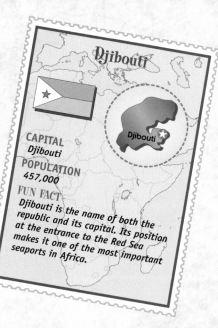

Djibouti

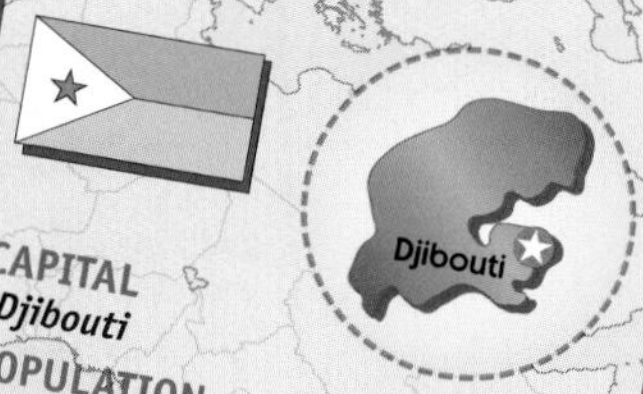

CAPITAL
Djibouti

POPULATION
457,000

FUN FACT
Djibouti is the name of both the republic and its capital. Its position at the entrance to the Red Sea makes it one of the most important seaports in Africa.

Madagascar

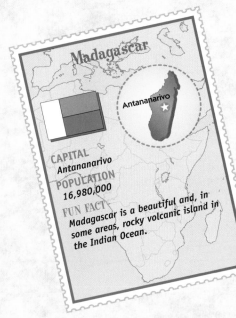

CAPITAL
Antananarivo

POPULATION
16,980,000

FUN FACT
Madagascar is a beautiful and, in some areas, rocky volcanic island in the Indian Ocean.

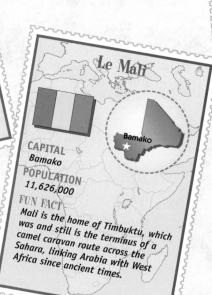

Le Mali

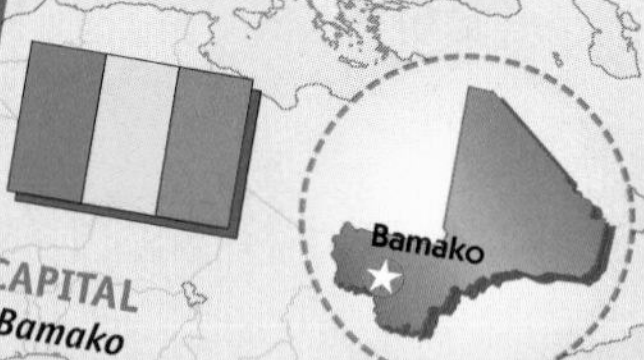

CAPITAL
Bamako

POPULATION
11,626,000

FUN FACT
Mali is the home of Timbuktu, which was and still is the terminus of a camel caravan route across the Sahara, linking Arabia with West Africa since ancient times.

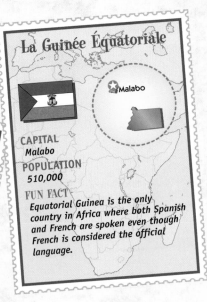

La Guinée Équatoriale

CAPITAL
Malabo

POPULATION
510,000

FUN FACT
Equatorial Guinea is the only country in Africa where both Spanish and French are spoken even though French is considered the official language.

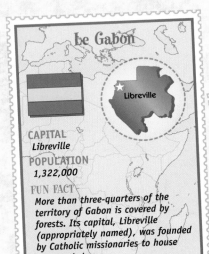

L'île Maurice

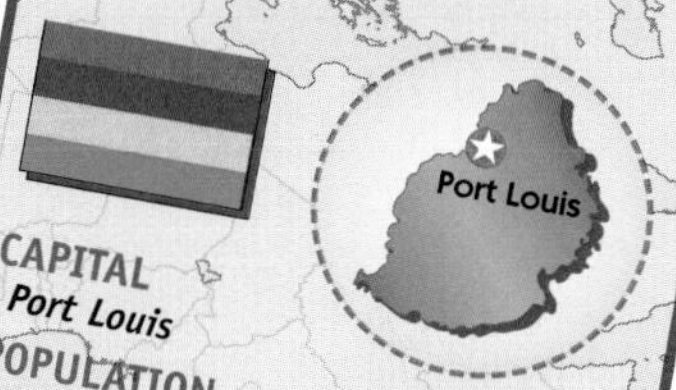

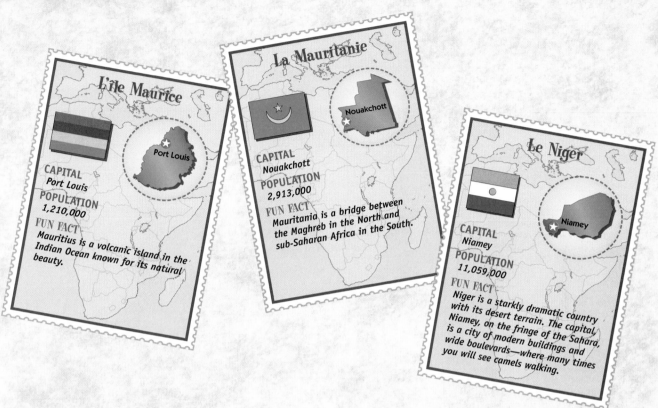

CAPITAL
Port Louis

POPULATION
1,210,000

FUN FACT
Mauritius is a volcanic island in the Indian Ocean known for its natural beauty.

La Mauritanie

CAPITAL
Nouakchott

POPULATION
2,913,000

FUN FACT
Mauritania is a bridge between the Maghreb in the North and sub-Saharan Africa in the South.

Le Niger

CAPITAL
Niamey

POPULATION
11,059,000

FUN FACT
Niger is a starkly dramatic country with its desert terrain. The capital, Niamey, on the fringe of the Sahara, is a city of modern buildings and wide boulevards—where many times you will see camels walking.

Le Maroc

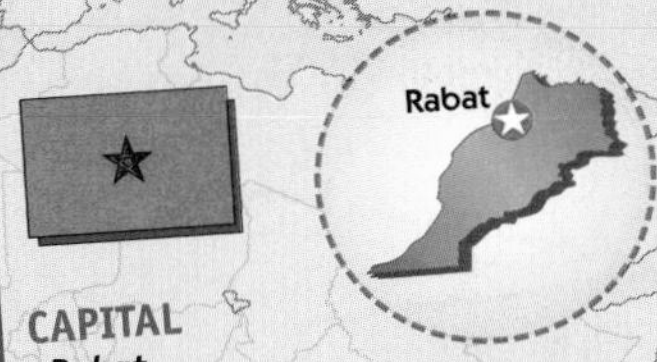

CAPITAL
Rabat

POPULATION
31,689,000

FUN FACT
Morocco is a country of many beautiful, fascinating cities, such as Casablanca, Tangiers, Fez, and Marrakech.

Les Seychelles

CAPITAL
Victoria

POPULATION
86,000

FUN FACT
The Republic of the Seychelles is made up of more than one hundred islands and is a vacationer's paradise. The Seychelles attract people from all over the world.

Le Tchad

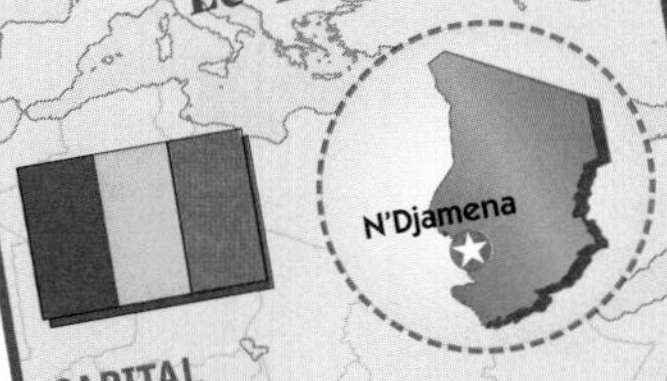

CAPITAL
N'Djamena

POPULATION
9,253,000

FUN FACT
Chad has a lake in the southwest of the country that doubles in size during the rainy season.

Le Rwanda

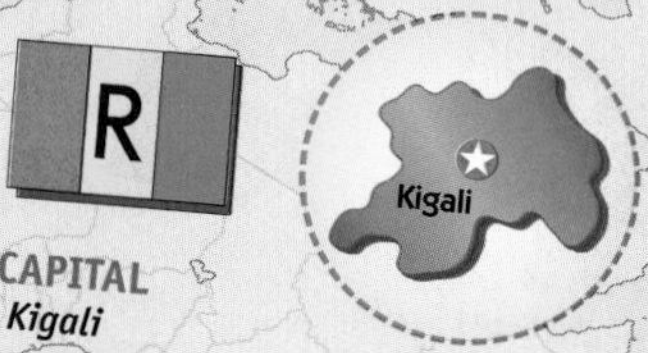

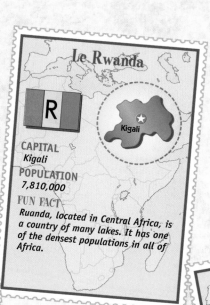

CAPITAL
Kigali

POPULATION
7,810,000

FUN FACT
Ruanda, located in Central Africa, is a country of many lakes. It has one of the densest populations in all of Africa.

La Réunion

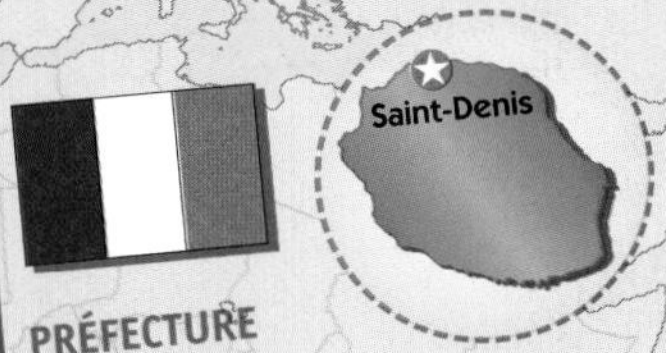

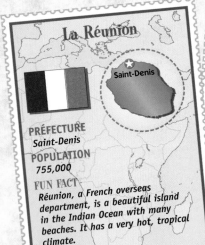

PRÉFECTURE
Saint-Denis

POPULATION
755,000

FUN FACT
Réunion, a French overseas department, is a beautiful island in the Indian Ocean with many beaches. It has a very hot, tropical climate.

Le Sénégal

CAPITAL
Dakar

POPULATION
10,580,000

FUN FACT
Senegal is a country that has a fabulous mix of Afro-French characteristics. More visitors go to Senegal than to any other Western African country.

Le Togo

CAPITAL
Lomé

POPULATION
5,429,000

FUN FACT
Togo is a pencil-thin strip of land whose capital, Lomé, has some of the most beautiful beaches just a block or two from the heart of town.

La Tunisie

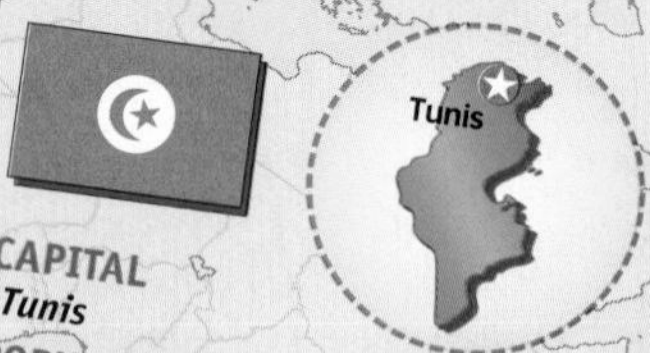

CAPITAL
Tunis

POPULATION
9,925,000

FUN FACT
Tunisia contains Roman archaeological sites second only to Rome itself.

L'Amérique du Nord et du Sud

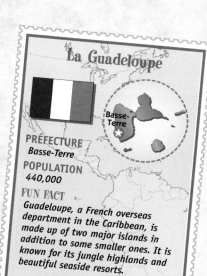

La Guadeloupe

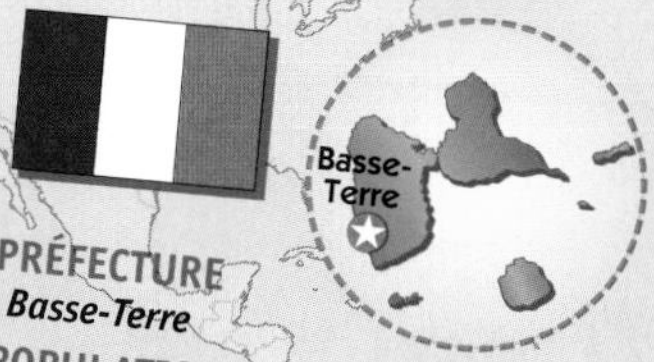

PRÉFECTURE
Basse-Terre

POPULATION
440,000

FUN FACT
Guadeloupe, a French overseas department in the Caribbean, is made up of two major islands in addition to some smaller ones. It is known for its jungle highlands and beautiful seaside resorts.

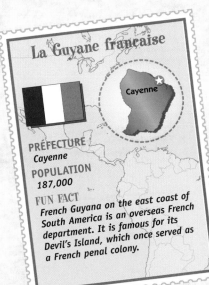

La Guyane française

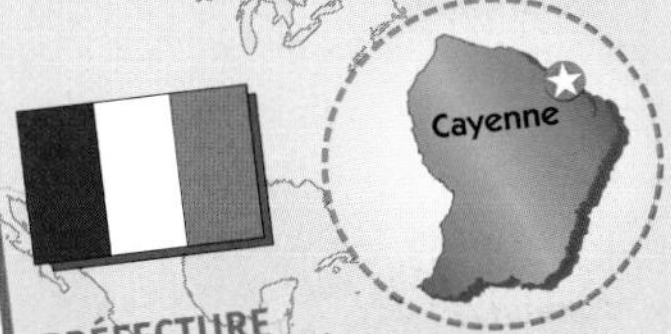

PRÉFECTURE
Cayenne

POPULATION
187,000

FUN FACT
French Guyana on the east coast of South America is an overseas French department. It is famous for its Devil's Island, which once served as a French penal colony.

Haïti

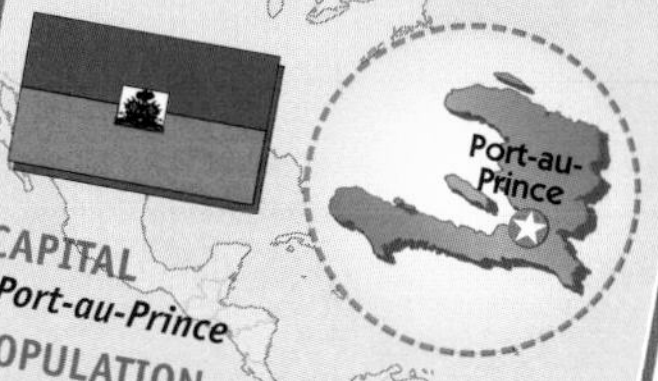

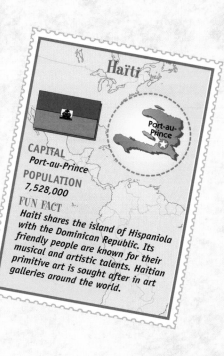

CAPITAL
Port-au-Prince

POPULATION
7,528,000

FUN FACT
Haiti shares the island of Hispaniola with the Dominican Republic. Its friendly people are known for their musical and artistic talents. Haitian primitive art is sought after in art galleries around the world.

La province de Québec

CAPITAL
Québec

POPULATION
7,040,000

FUN FACT
Quebec is the oldest and largest of Canada's provinces. About 90 percent of Quebec's inhabitants are French-speaking.

La Martinique

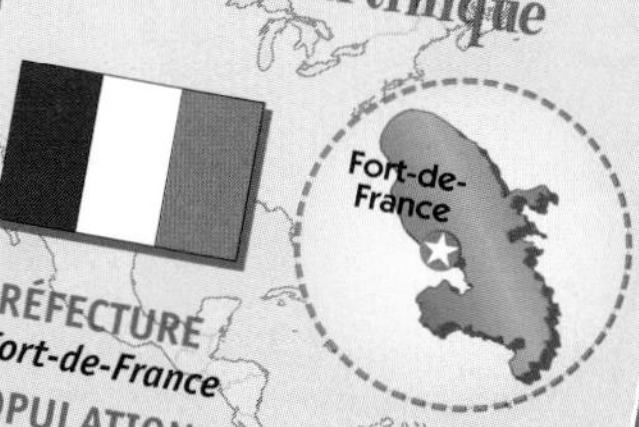

PRÉFECTURE
Fort-de-France

POPULATION
426,000

FUN FACT
Martinique, like Guadeloupe, is a French overseas department in the Caribbean Sea. It is a highly developed island famous for its beautiful, exotic flowers—orchids, hibiscus, and flamingo flowers.

Saint-Pierre-et-Miquelon

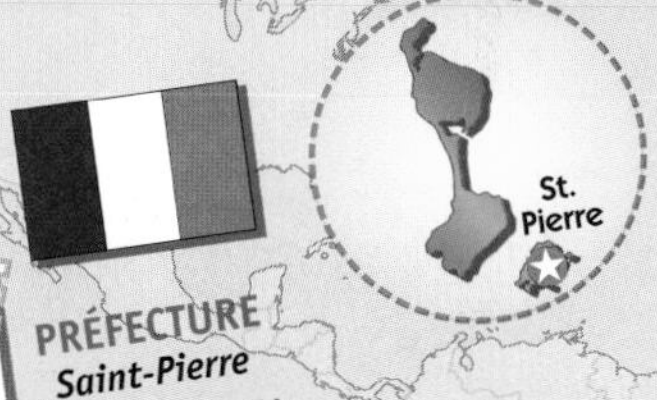

PRÉFECTURE
Saint-Pierre

POPULATION
7,000

FUN FACT
Saint-Pierre and Miquelon are French-speaking islands in the Atlantic Ocean, south of Newfoundland. Many residents work in the cod-fishing industry.

L'Europe

La principauté d'Andorre

CAPITAL
Andorre-la-Vieille

POPULATION
69,000

FUN FACT
Andorra is a co-principality governed by France's president and a Spanish bishop.

La Belgique

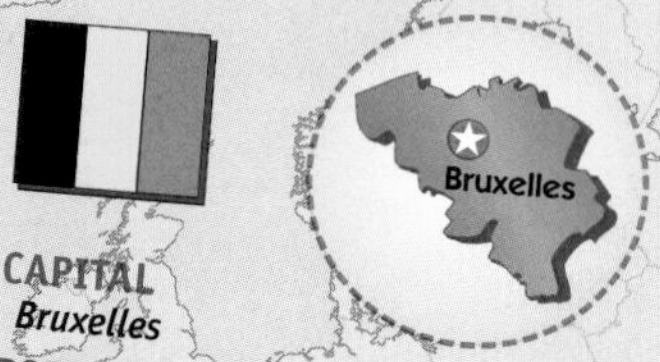

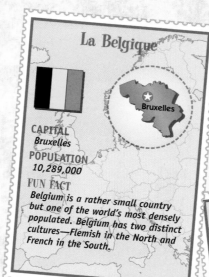

CAPITAL
Bruxelles

POPULATION
10,289,000

FUN FACT
Belgium is a rather small country but one of the world's most densely populated. Belgium has two distinct cultures—Flemish in the North and French in the South.

La France

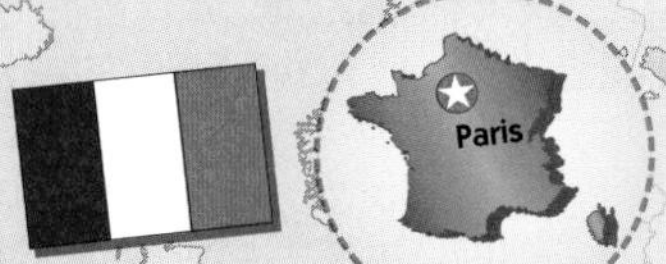

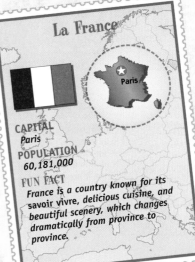

CAPITAL
Paris

POPULATION
60,181,000

FUN FACT
France is a country known for its savoir vivre, delicious cuisine, and beautiful scenery, which changes dramatically from province to province.

La principauté de Monaco

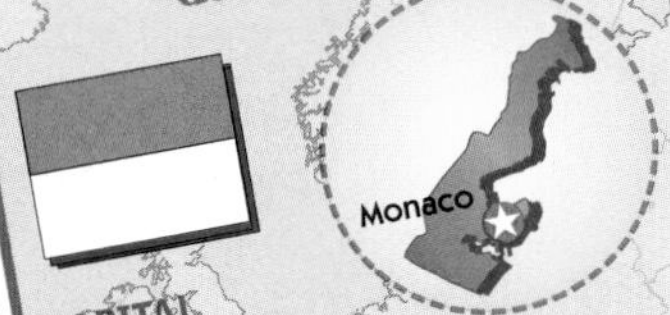

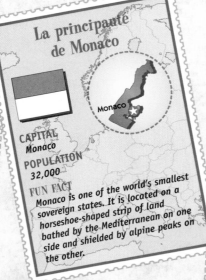

CAPITAL
Monaco

POPULATION
32,000

FUN FACT
Monaco is one of the world's smallest sovereign states. It is located on a horseshoe-shaped strip of land bathed by the Mediterranean on one side and shielded by alpine peaks on the other.

Le grand-duché de Luxembourg

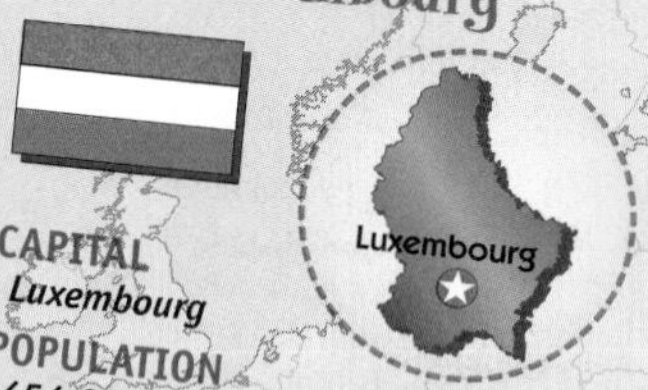

CAPITAL
Luxembourg

POPULATION
454,000

FUN FACT
Luxembourg is smaller than the state of Rhode Island. The native Luxembourgers all speak three languages fluently: Luxembourgish, German, and French.

La Suisse

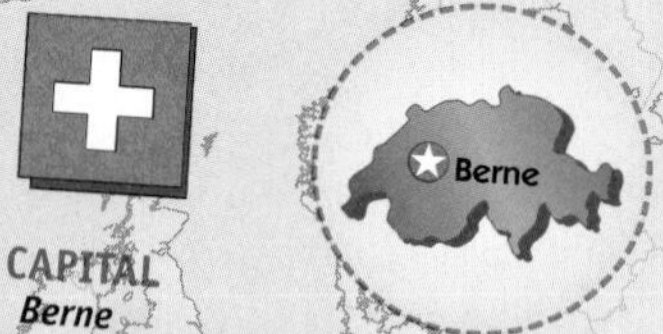

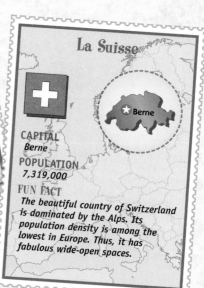

CAPITAL
Berne

POPULATION
7,319,000

FUN FACT
The beautiful country of Switzerland is dominated by the Alps. Its population density is among the lowest in Europe. Thus, it has fabulous wide-open spaces.

L'Océanie

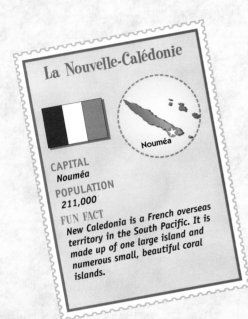

La Nouvelle-Calédonie

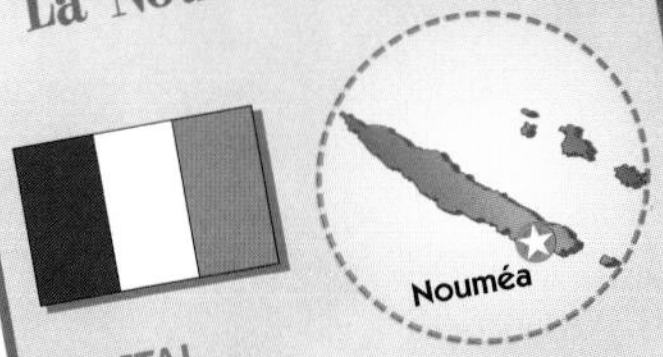

CAPITAL
Nouméa

POPULATION
211,000

FUN FACT
New Caledonia is a French overseas territory in the South Pacific. It is made up of one large island and numerous small, beautiful coral islands.

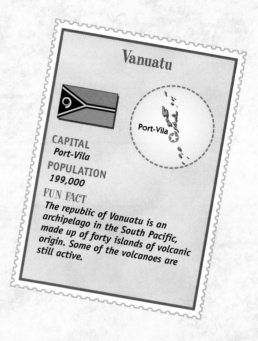

Vanuatu

CAPITAL
Port-Vila

POPULATION
199,000

FUN FACT
The republic of Vanuatu is an archipelago in the South Pacific, made up of forty islands of volcanic origin. Some of the volcanoes are still active.

La Polynésie française

CAPITAL
Papeete

POPULATION
262,000

FUN FACT
French Polynesia is a French overseas territory made up of approximately 130 islands. The islands are known for their volcanic mountains, tropical climate, and beautiful bays and coves.

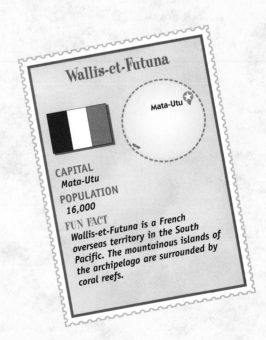

Wallis-et-Futuna

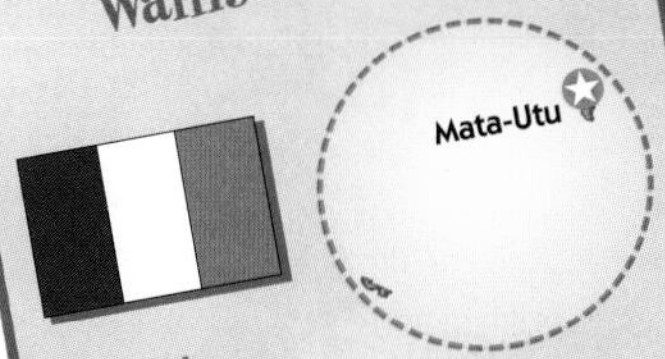

CAPITAL
Mata-Utu

POPULATION
16,000

FUN FACT
Wallis-et-Futuna is a French overseas territory in the South Pacific. The mountainous islands of the archipelago are surrounded by coral reefs.

La France

ANGLETERRE
Mer du Nord
PAYS-BAS
Calais
BELGIQUE
ALLEMAGNE
Manche
Lille
Nord-Pas-de-Calais
Le Havre
Haute-Normandie
Amiens
Caen
Rouen
Picardie
LUXEMBOURG
Brest
Basse-Normandie
Seine
Paris
Marne
Châlons-en-Champagne
Metz
Bretagne
Île-de-France
Meuse
Rennes
Lorraine
Le Mans
Rhine
Champagne-Ardenne
Strasbourg
Orléans
Pays de la Loire
Nantes
Loire
Centre
Alsace
Bourgogne
Besançon
Poitiers
Dijon
Franche-Comté
OCÉAN ATLANTIQUE
Poitou-Charentes
Moulins
SUISSE
Limoges
Clermont-Ferrand
Saône
Limousin
Auvergne
Lyon
Bordeaux
Rhône-Alpes
Grenoble
Garonne
Aquitaine
Rhône
ITALIE
Midi-Pyrénées
Biarritz
Toulouse
Montpellier
Provence-Alpes-Côte d'Azur
Monaco
Nice
Languedoc-Roussillon
MONACO
Marseille
ESPAGNE
Corse
Mer Méditerranée

Paris

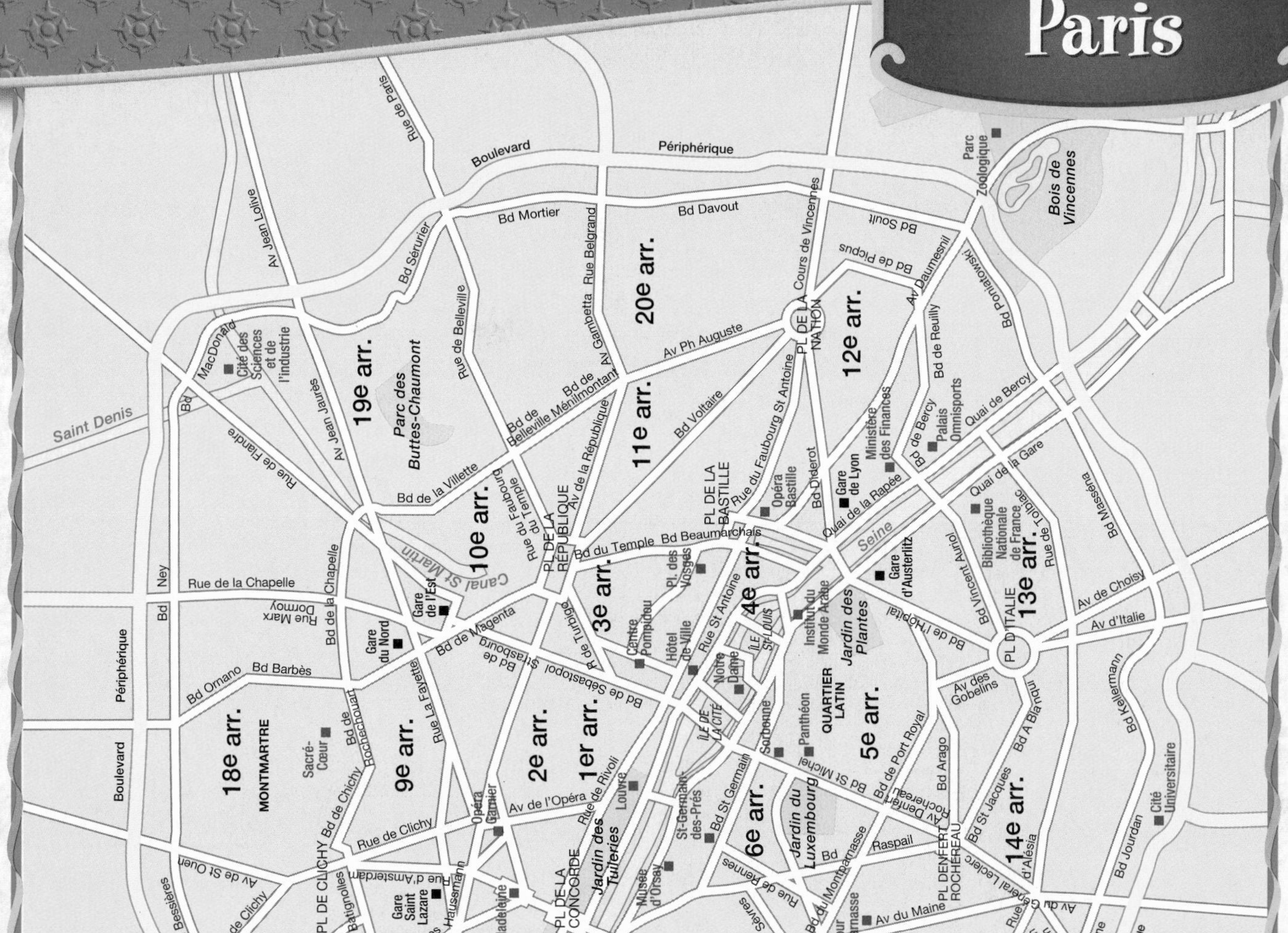

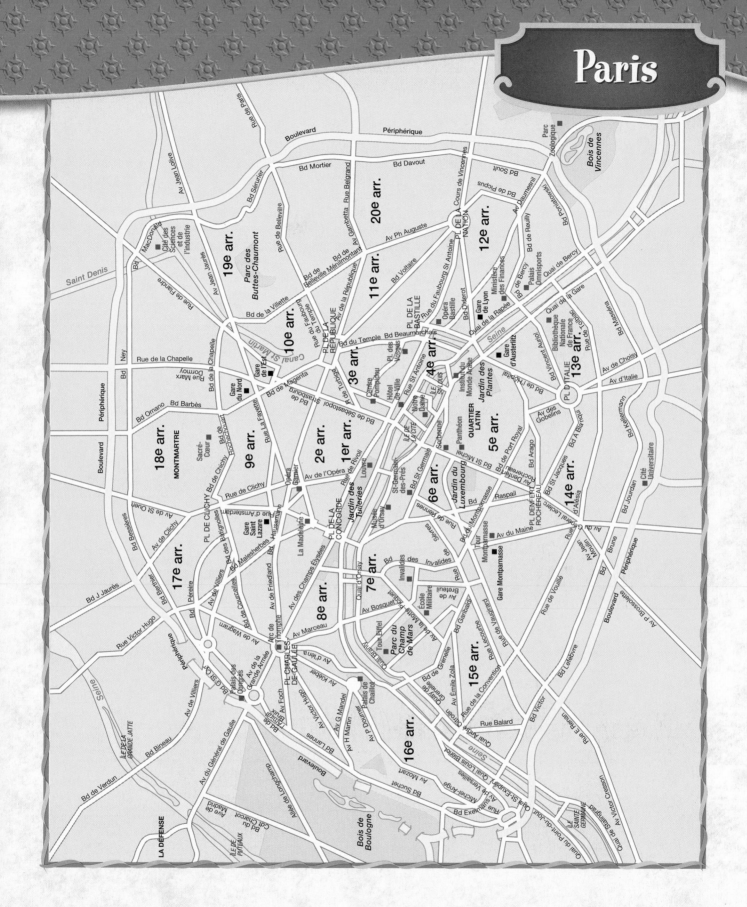

Le Canada

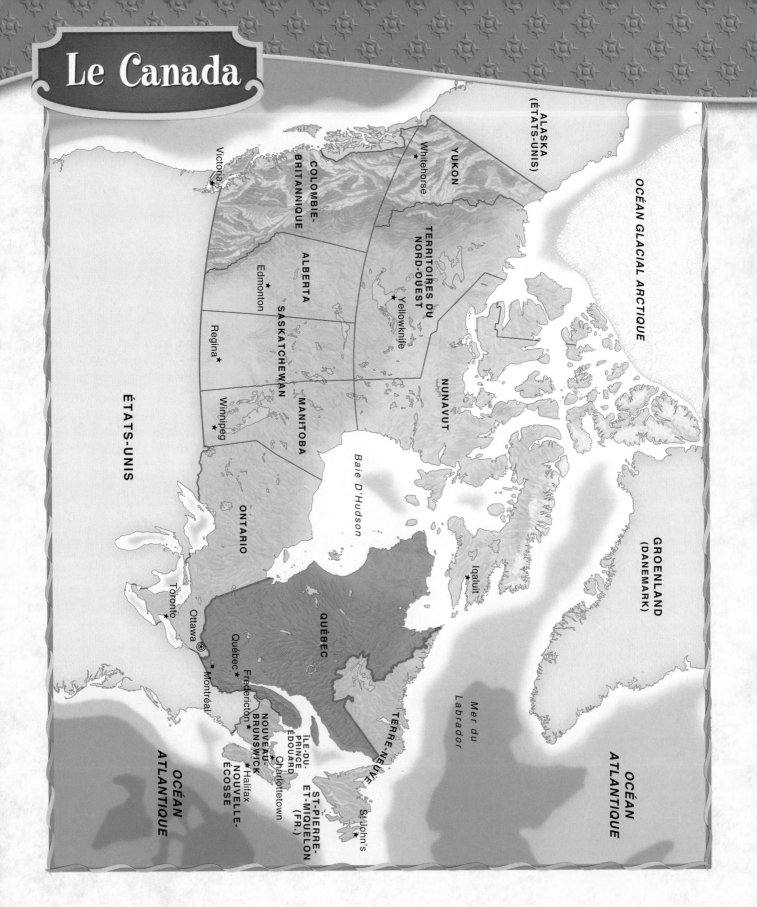

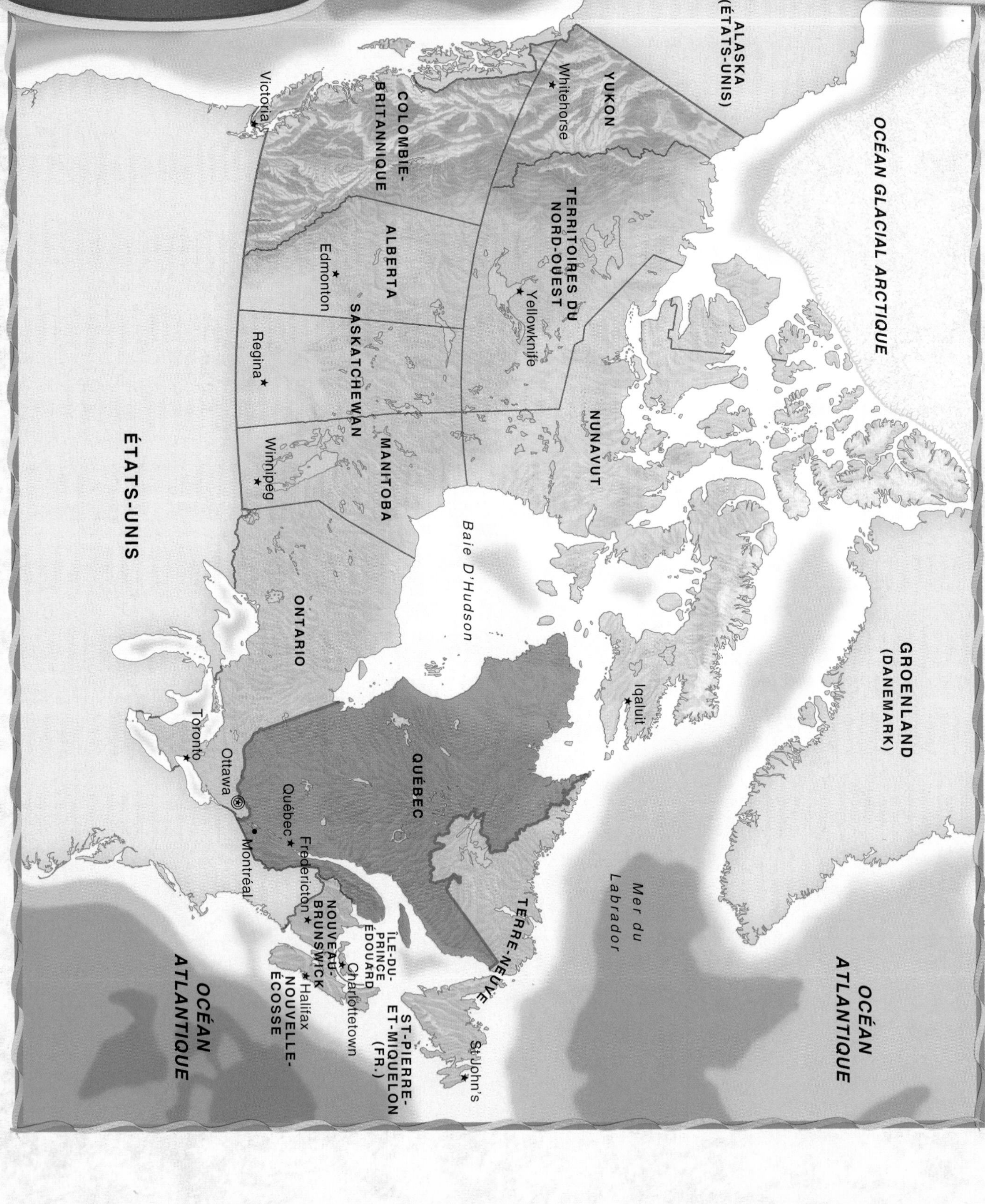
ALASKA
(ÉTATS-UNIS)
YUKON
Whitehorse
COLOMBIE-
BRITANNIQUE
Victoria
TERRITOIRES DU
NORD-OUEST
Yellowknife
ALBERTA
Edmonton
SASKATCHEWAN
Regina
MANITOBA
Winnipeg
NUNAVUT
OCÉAN GLACIAL ARCTIQUE
ÉTATS-UNIS
ONTARIO
Baie D'Hudson
Toronto
Ottawa
QUÉBEC
Québec
Montréal
Iqaluit
GROENLAND
(DANEMARK)
Mer du
Labrador
TERRE-NEUVE
Fredericton
NOUVEAU-
BRUNSWICK
ÎLE-DU-
PRINCE-
ÉDOUARD
Charlottetown
Halifax
NOUVELLE-
ÉCOSSE
ST-PIERRE-
ET-MIQUELON
(FR.)
St John's
OCÉAN
ATLANTIQUE
OCÉAN
ATLANTIQUE

L'Afrique

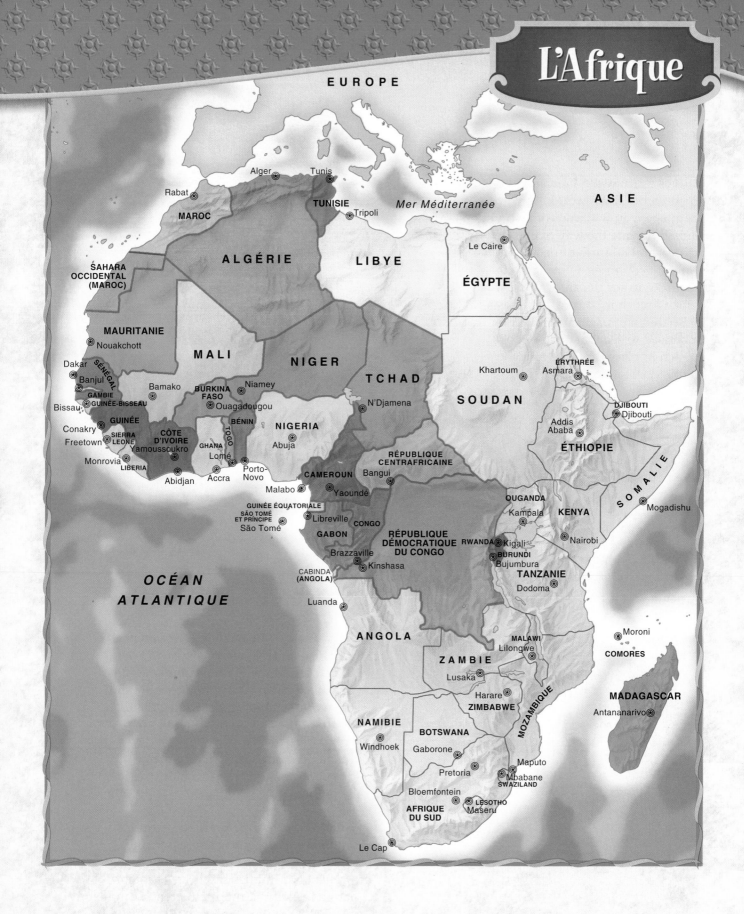

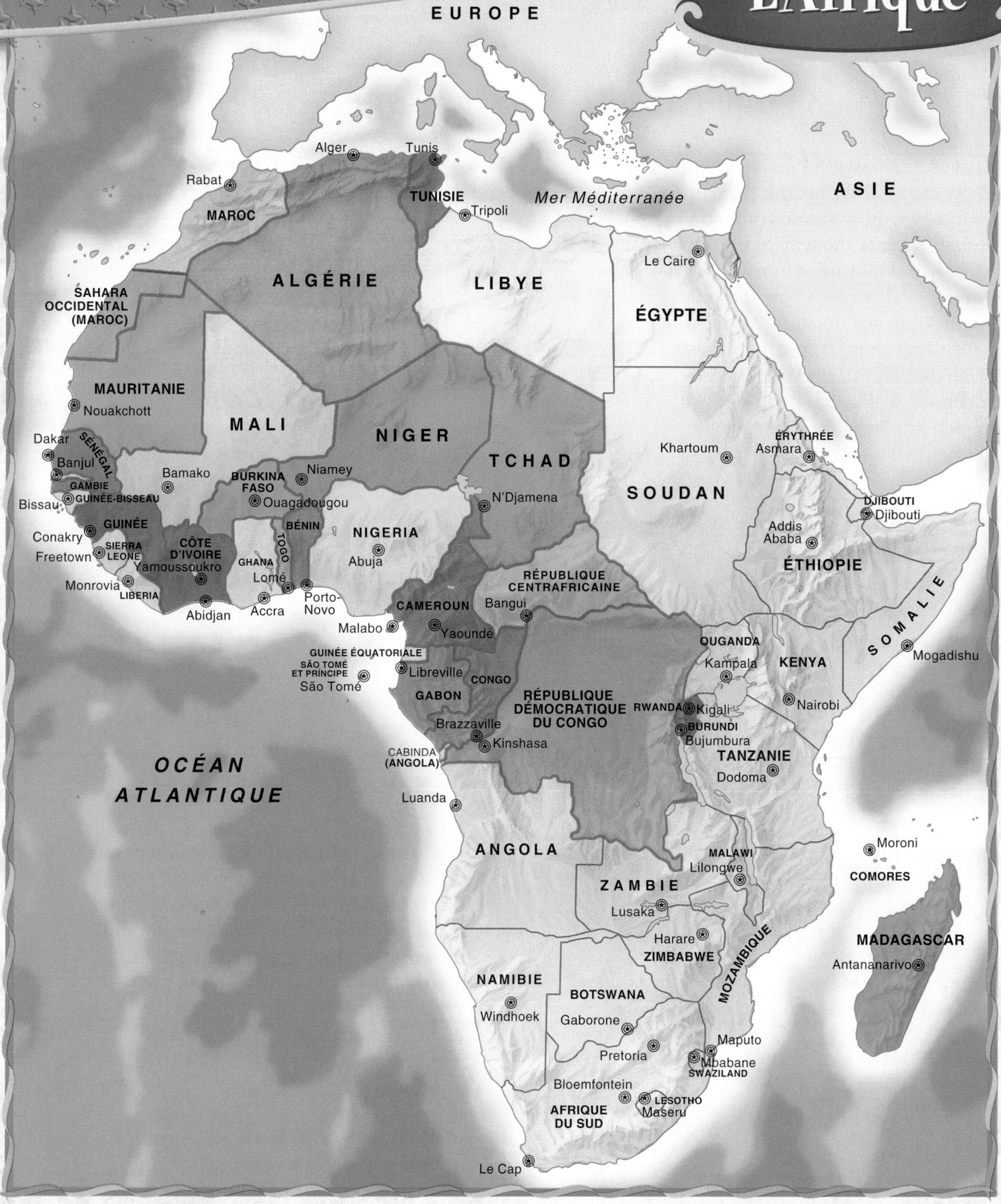
EUROPE
ASIE
Mer Méditerranée
OCÉAN ATLANTIQUE
Alger
Tunis
Rabat
MAROC
TUNISIE
Tripoli
Le Caire
ALGÉRIE
LIBYE
ÉGYPTE
SAHARA OCCIDENTAL (MAROC)
MAURITANIE
Nouakchott
MALI
NIGER
TCHAD
Dakar
SÉNÉGAL
Banjul
GAMBIE
Bissau
GUINÉE-BISSEAU
Bamako
BURKINA FASO
Ouagadougou
Niamey
N'Djamena
Khartoum
ÉRYTHRÉE
Asmara
SOUDAN
DJIBOUTI
Djibouti
Addis Ababa
ÉTHIOPIE
Conakry
GUINÉE
SIERRA LEONE
Freetown
CÔTE D'IVOIRE
Yamoussoukro
GHANA
TOGO
BÉNIN
NIGERIA
Abuja
Monrovia
LIBERIA
Abidjan
Accra
Lomé
Porto-Novo
RÉPUBLIQUE CENTRAFRICAINE
Bangui
CAMEROUN
Yaoundé
Malabo
GUINÉE ÉQUATORIALE
SÃO TOMÉ ET PRINCIPE
São Tomé
Libreville
GABON
CONGO
Brazzaville
Kinshasa
RÉPUBLIQUE DÉMOCRATIQUE DU CONGO
SOMALIE
Mogadishu
OUGANDA
Kampala
KENYA
Nairobi
RWANDA
Kigali
BURUNDI
Bujumbura
TANZANIE
Dodoma
CABINDA (ANGOLA)
Luanda
ANGOLA
Moroni
COMORES
MALAWI
Lilongwe
ZAMBIE
Lusaka
Harare
ZIMBABWE
MOZAMBIQUE
MADAGASCAR
Antananarivo
NAMIBIE
Windhoek
BOTSWANA
Gaborone
Pretoria
Maputo
Mbabane
SWAZILAND
Bloemfontein
LESOTHO
Maseru
AFRIQUE DU SUD
Le Cap

Why Learn French?

The Francophone World

Culture Knowing French will open doors to you around the world. As you study the language, you will also come to understand and appreciate the way of life, customs, values, and cultures of people from many different countries. Look at the map on page xxii to see the areas of the world in which French is spoken, either as a first or second language. You might be surprised to see that people speak French in places as close to home as Haiti, Martinique, Quebec, and Louisiana.

Learning French can be fun and will bring you a sense of accomplishment. You'll be really pleased when you are able to carry on a conversation with a French-speaking person in French. You will also be able to read French literature, keep up with current events in French magazines and newspapers, and understand French films without relying on subtitles. The French language will be a source of enrichment for the rest of your life.

Career Opportunities

Business Your knowledge of French will also be an asset to you in a variety of careers. Many French companies are multinational and have branches around the world, including the United States. Some of the fields in which French companies excel are: clothing and fashion, cosmetics, tourism, agriculture, the automotive and aerospace industries, and technology.

Research France is also a world leader in high-energy physics research and medical genetics. Did you know that French and English are the two major languages of the Internet? French can help you in almost any career path you choose.

Language Link

Another benefit to learning French is that it will improve your English. Once you know another language, you can make comparisons between the two and gain a greater understanding of how languages function. As a result, your use of English will be more effective. You'll also come across many French words that are used in English. Just a few examples are: **rouge, chaise longue, chic, crêpe, à la mode, omelette, chargé d'affaires, déjà vu, détente,** and **laisser faire.** French will also be helpful if you decide to learn yet another language. Once you learn a second language, the learning process for acquiring other languages becomes much easier.

French is a beautiful, rich language that is spoken on many continents. Many people use French on a daily basis as their second language. Whatever your motivation is for choosing to study it, French will expand your horizons and increase your job opportunities. **Vive la langue française! Et bon voyage!**

L'alphabet français

a
***a**mis*

b
***b**é**b**é*

c
***c**irque*

d
***d**eux*

e
*l**e**çon*
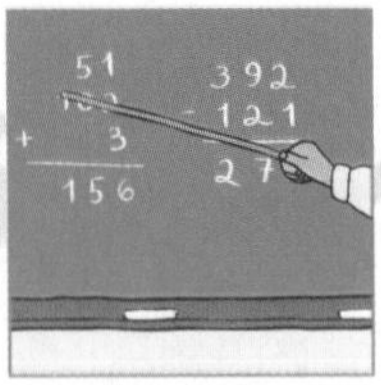

f
***f**enêtre*

g
***g**iraffe*

h
***h**uit*
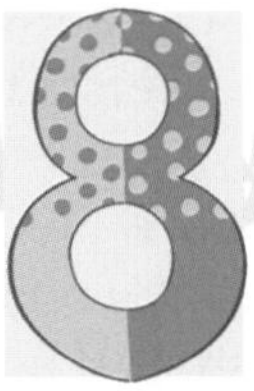

i
***i**gloo*

j
***j**eu*

k
***k**ilo*

l
***l**ivre*

m
***m**aison*

n

***n**ez*

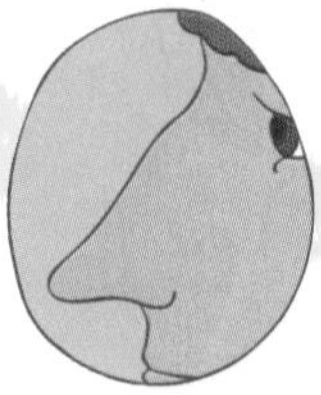

o

***o**live*

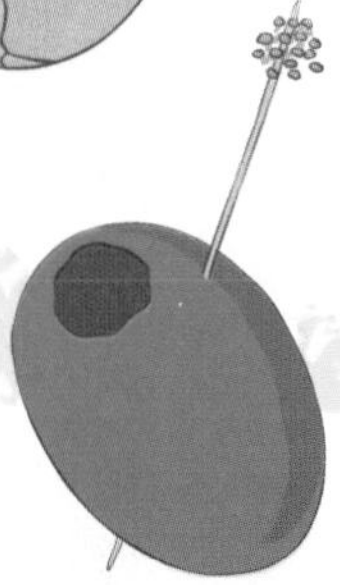

p

***p**ain*

q

***q**uatre*

r

***r**eine*

s

***s**oupe*

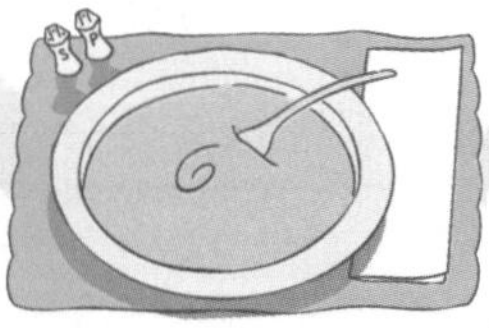

t

***t**able*

u

***u**nivers*

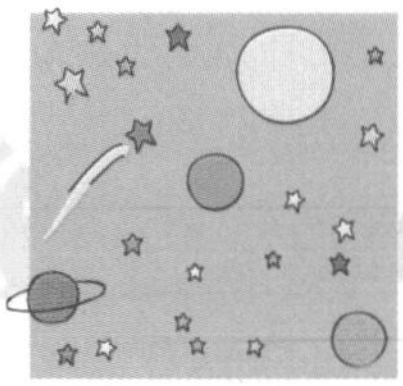

v

***v**iolette*

w

***w**agon*

x

*e**x**tra*

y

***y**eux*

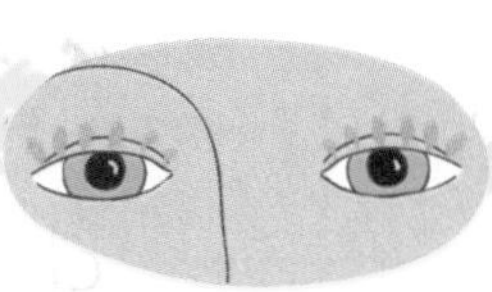

z

***z**èbre*

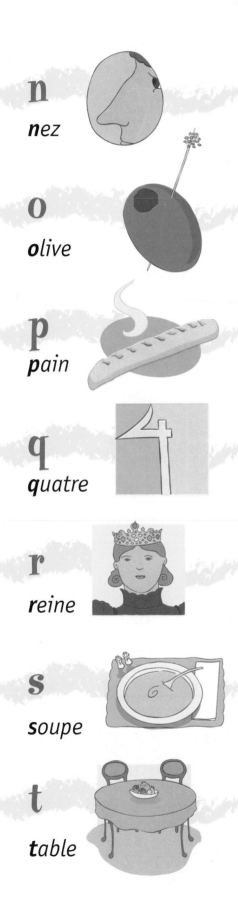

Leçons préliminaires

Bienvenue

Objectifs

In these preliminary lessons you will learn to:

- ✔ *greet people*
- ✔ *say good-bye to people*
- ✔ *ask people how they are*
- ✔ *ask and tell names*
- ✔ *express simple courtesies*
- ✔ *find out and tell the days of the week*
- ✔ *find out and tell the months of the year*
- ✔ *count from 1 to 30*
- ✔ *find out and tell the time*

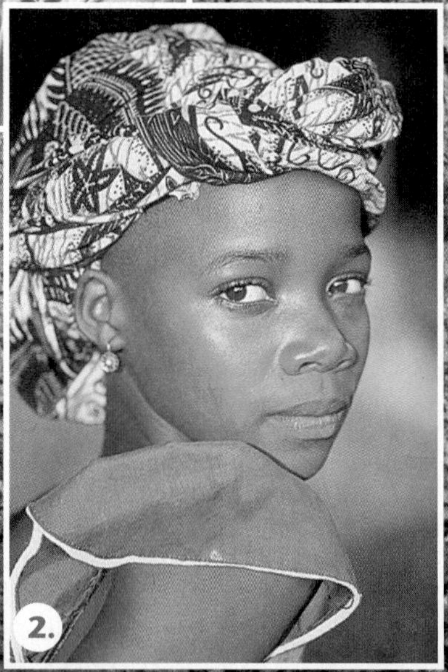

1. Karim Ashour, Tunis, Tunisie
2. Yvonne Senghor, Abidjan, Côte d'Ivoire
3. Jacques Ferrand, Montréal, Canada
4. Thérèse Nguyen, Lyon, France
5. Yves Clémenceau, Fort-de-France, Martinique
6. Ahmed Rashid, Paris, France
7. Vincent Daudet, Rouen, France
8. Élodie Lutz, Strasbourg, France
9. Marie Robert, Marseille, France

5.

6.

7.

8.

9.

Préliminaire A Bonjour!

Greeting people

When someone wants to know how you are doing and asks **Ça va?**, there are several different answers you can give.

Ça va.
Bien, merci.
Ça va très bien.
Pas mal, merci.
comme ci, comme ça
très mal

ç une cédille
makes c sound like an s

1 Salut! = hi (informal)

Get up from your desk. Walk around the classroom. Say hello to each classmate you meet.

2 Ça va?

Work with a classmate. Greet one another and find out how things are going.

More greetings

1. **Salut!** is an informal greeting that you can use with people your own age. When you greet an older person, you may use the following expressions.

Bonjour, monsieur.

Bonjour, madame.

Bonjour, mademoiselle.

2. Note that the titles **monsieur, madame,** and **mademoiselle** are almost always used without the last name of the person.

3 Bonjour!

Draw some figures on the board. Some will represent friends your own age and others will represent older people. Greet each of the figures on the board properly.

4 Salutations

Look at these photographs of young people in France and Martinique. As they greet one another they do some things that are different from what we do when we greet each other. What do you notice in the photographs?

Préliminaire B *Au revoir!*

Saying good-bye

Au revoir, madame.
Au revoir, Christine.

Ciao, Thomas.
À tout à l'heure.
Ciao, Charlotte.

1. A very common expression to use when saying good-bye to someone is **Au revoir.**
2. If you plan to see the person again soon, you can say **À bientôt!** If you plan to see the person very soon, you can say **À tout à l'heure.** If you plan to see the person the next day, you can say **À demain.**
3. An informal expression you often hear is **Ciao.** It comes from Italian and is used in many parts of Europe.

1 Ciao!

Go over to a classmate and say good-bye to him or her.

2 À bientôt!

Work with a classmate. Say **Ciao** to each other and let one another know when you will be getting together again.

3 Au revoir!

Say good-bye to your French teacher. Use **monsieur, madame,** or **mademoiselle,** as appropriate. Then say good-bye to a friend. Use a different expression with each person.

Conversation

4 Salut!

Work with a classmate. Have a conversation in French. Say as much as you can to each other.

5 Bonjour!

Work with a classmate. One of you will pretend to be an older person. Have a conversation. Say as much as you can to each other.

Finding out a person's name

When you want to find out the name of a person who is about the same age as you, you can ask **Tu t'appelles comment?** However, you would not use this expression with an older person. You will learn the more formal forms at a later time.

1 Tu t'appelles comment?

Get up from your desk. Walk around the room. Find out several of your classmates' names. Let them know your name, too.

Conversation

2 Salut!

Have a conversation with a classmate. Find out each other's name, how things are going, and say good-bye to each other.

3 Je m'appelle...

Look at this photograph of young French people introducing each other. Are they doing something that you probably would not do? What is it?

Préliminaire D *La politesse*

Ordering food politely

Expressions of politeness are always appreciated. The following are the French expressions for "please," "thank you," and "you're welcome."

Formal	Informal
S'il vous plaît.	S'il te plaît.
Merci (madame).	Merci.
Je vous en prie.	Je t'en prie.

1 La politesse

With a classmate, practice reading the preceding conversation aloud. Be as animated and as polite as you can.

2 Une limonade, s'il vous plaît.

You are at a café in Canada. Order the following things. Your partner will be the server. Be polite when you order.

un croque-monsieur - grilled ham and cheese sandwich
un croque-madame - grilled ham and cheese with egg

1. 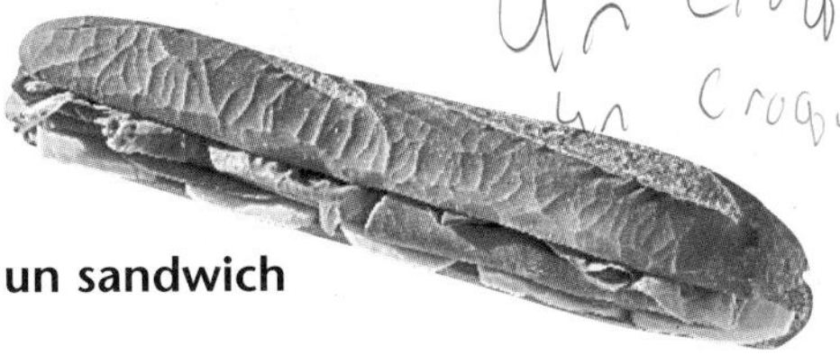
un sandwich

2. 
un coca

desert - fruit peeled

3. 
une limonade

Perrier - sparkling water

4. 
un café

5. 
une pizza

Evian - mineral water

6. 
une saucisse de Francfort, un hot-dog

7. 
une crêpe

Telling the days of the week

To find out and give the day of the week, you say:

C'est quel jour aujourd'hui?
(Aujourd'hui), c'est lundi.
Demain, c'est mardi.

LUNDI	MARDI	MERCREDI	JEUDI	VENDREDI	SAMEDI	DIMANCHE
1	2	3	4	5	6	7
8	9	10	11	12	13	14

1 C'est quel jour?

Answer the following questions in French.

1. C'est quel jour aujourd'hui?
2. Et demain? C'est quel jour?

Telling the months

janvier	mai	septembre
février	juin	octobre
mars	juillet	novembre
avril	août	décembre

Les nombres de 1 à 30

1 un	7 sept	13 treize	19 dix-neuf	25 vingt-cinq
2 deux	8 huit	14 quatorze	20 vingt	26 vingt-six
3 trois	9 neuf	15 quinze	21 vingt et un	27 vingt-sept
4 quatre	10 dix	16 seize	22 vingt-deux	28 vingt-huit
5 cinq	11 onze	17 dix-sept	23 vingt-trois	29 vingt-neuf
6 six	12 douze	18 dix-huit	24 vingt-quatre	30 trente

Finding out and giving the date

Quelle est la date aujourd'hui?
(C'est) le trente et un août.

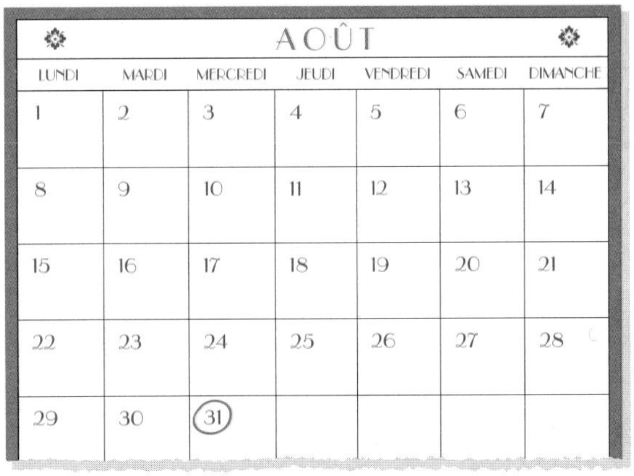
AOÛT
LUNDI MARDI MERCREDI JEUDI VENDREDI SAMEDI DIMANCHE
1 2 3 4 5 6 7
8 9 10 11 12 13 14
15 16 17 18 19 20 21
22 23 24 25 26 27 28
29 30 31

Premier is used for the first day of the month. For other days you use **deux, trois, quatre,** etc.

> **le premier août**
> **le deux septembre**

2 La date, s'il vous plaît.

Answer the following questions in French.

1. Quelle est la date aujourd'hui?
2. Et demain?

le 6 janvier

le 14 juillet à Paris

3 En quel mois?

Each of you will stand up in class and give the date of your birthday in French. Listen carefully and keep a record of how many of you were born in the same month. Then tell in French in which month the greatest number of students were born. In which month were the fewest born?

Telling time

1. To find out the time, you ask:

Il est quelle heure?

2. To give the time on the hour, you say:

1 h
Il est une heure.

2 h
Il est deux heures.

10 h
Il est dix heures.

12 h
Il est midi.

12 h
Il est minuit.

3. To give the time after the hour, you say:

1 h 05
Il est une heure cinq.

3 h 10
Il est trois heures dix.

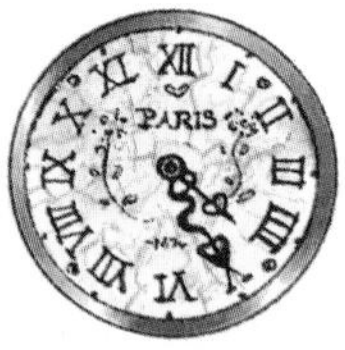

4 h 25
Il est quatre heures vingt-cinq.

4. To give the time before the hour, you say:

4 h 50
Il est cinq heures moins dix.

5 h 40
Il est six heures moins vingt.

9 h 35
Il est dix heures moins vingt-cinq.

5. To express time on the quarter hour and half hour, you say:

2 h 15
Il est deux heures et quart.

6 h 45
Il est sept heures moins le quart.

6 h 30
Il est six heures et demie.

6. If you need to specify whether it is A.M. or P.M., you can use the following expressions.

Il est six heures du matin.

Il est quatre heures de l'après-midi.

Il est onze heures du soir.

1 Il est quelle heure?

Look at each clock and give the time.

1. 

2. 

3. 

4. 

5. 

6. 

Conversation

Salut, Julie. Il est quelle heure, s'il te plaît?
Il est trois heures vingt.

Trois heures vingt! Déjà? Zut! Au revoir!
Au revoir, Vincent. À bientôt!

2 Ciao!

Work with a classmate. Greet each other. Find out the time and react as if you have to get going.

3 Il est quelle heure, s'il te plaît?

Get up from your desk and walk around the room. Go up to a classmate. Greet the person quickly and ask the time. Show your classmate a piece of paper with a time on it. He or she will give you the time.

Leçons préliminaires

Greeting people

Salut!	Ça va?	Bien.
Bonjour!	Pas mal.	Très bien.

Giving titles

Monsieur	Madame	Mademoiselle

Saying good-bye

Au revoir.	À bientôt.
Ciao!	À demain.
À tout à l'heure.	

Finding out a person's name

Tu t'appelles comment?
Je m'appelle…

How well do you know your vocabulary?

- Choose an expression from the list to begin a conversation.
- Have a classmate respond.
- Take turns.

Being courteous

S'il te plaît.	Je t'en prie.
S'il vous plaît.	Je vous en prie.
Merci.	

Telling the days of the week

lundi	jeudi	samedi	C'est quel jour?
mardi	vendredi	dimanche	aujourd'hui
mercredi			demain

Telling the months of the year

Quelle est la date?	avril	août	novembre
janvier	mai	septembre	décembre
février	juin	octobre	
mars	juillet		

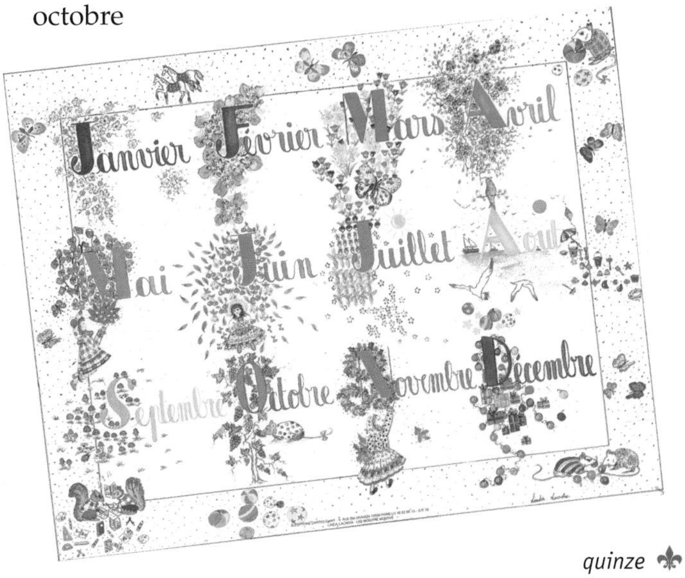

Telling time

Il est quelle heure?	Il est midi.
Il est ____ heure(s).	Il est minuit.
du matin	
de l'après-midi	
du soir	

CHAPITRE 1

Une amie et un ami

Objectifs

In this chapter you will learn to:

- *ask or tell what someone is like*
- *ask or tell where someone is from*
- *ask or tell who someone is*
- *describe yourself or someone else*
- *talk about students from France and Martinique*

Victor Gabriel Gilbert *Enfants jouant au cerceau*

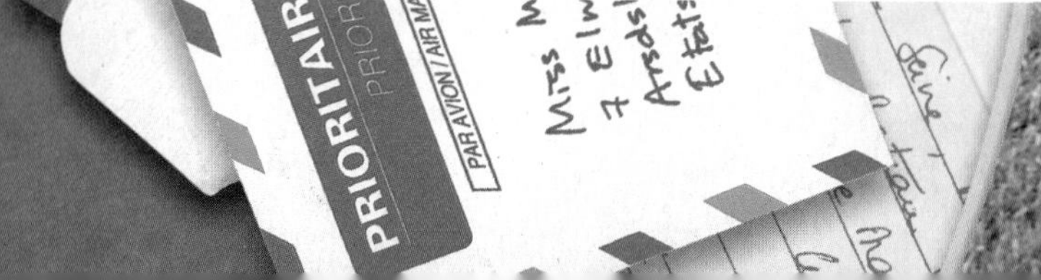

Vocabulaire

Mots 1

Comment est la fille?

How? (description)

C'est qui? who?
C'est Julie Lacroix.
Julie est française.

Elle est d'où, Julie?
Julie est de Paris.

from where?

Comment est le garçon?

C'est qui?
C'est Olivier Charpentier.
Olivier est français aussi.

Il est d'où, Olivier?
Il est de Nice.

Note

Many words in French and English look alike even though they are pronounced differently. These words are called "cognates." You can use the following cognates to describe people.

américain	**intelligent**
blond	**intéressant**
patient	

Here are some words used to express degree.

Il est amusant.
Il est assez amusant.
Il est très amusant.
Il est vraiment amusant.

Quel est le mot?

1 Historiette Une fille française

Inventez une histoire. *(Make up a story.)*

1. Sophie est française ou américaine?
2. Elle est de Paris ou de New York?
3. Elle est brune ou blonde?
4. Elle est amusante?
5. Elle est grande ou petite?

Sophie Legrand

2 Historiette Un garçon français

Inventez une histoire. *(Make up a story.)*

1. Christophe est américain ou français?
2. Il est de Lyon ou de Houston?
3. Il est brun ou blond?
4. Il est amusant?
5. Il est très intelligent?
6. Il est assez patient?

Christophe Gaudin

Bill

Henri

3 Un Français ou un Américain?

Répondez d'après les photos.
(Answer according to the photos.)

1. Qui est américain?
2. Qui est français?
3. Qui est de Paris?
4. Qui est de Los Angeles?
5. Qui est blond?
6. Qui est brun?

4 **Il est... ? Elle est... ?** Look at the following people and say two things about each of them. Then, find out who they are. They are all famous.

5 **C'est qui?** Think of a student in the class. A classmate will ask you questions about the person and try to guess who it is. Take turns.

ENCORE PLUS *For more practice using words from **Mots 1**, do Activity 1 on page H2 at the end of this book.*

Une sœur et un frère

Voilà Nathalie et Luc Simonet.
Nathalie est la sœur de Luc.
Luc est le frère de Nathalie.

Voilà Philippe.
Philippe n'est pas le frère de Nathalie.
Philippe est un ami de Nathalie.

Une école et un collège

Carol est élève dans une école américaine.

Bruno est élève dans un collège français.
Un collège est une école secondaire en France.

Mae est une amie de Mark.
Mae est très sympathique.
Mark est très sympa aussi.

Note

You can also use the following cognates to describe people.

dynamique
énergique
populaire
timide
égoïste
enthousiaste
sociable

Les nombres de 30 à 60

30	trente	35	trente-cinq	40	quarante
31	trente et un	36	trente-six	50	cinquante
32	trente-deux	37	trente-sept	60	soixante
33	trente-trois	38	trente-huit		
34	trente-quatre	39	trente-neuf		

Quel est le mot?

6 **Historiette** Une élève française

Choisissez la bonne réponse. *(Choose the right answer.)*

1. ____ est française.
   a. Céline Dupont b. Thomas Duhamel
2. Céline est élève dans ____.
   a. une école américaine b. un collège français
3. Elle est ____.
   a. de Paris b. de Miami
4. Céline est ____ de Karim.
   a. un ami b. une amie
5. Karim est ____ de Céline.
   a. un ami b. un élève
6. David est ____ de Céline.
   a. la sœur b. le frère
7. Céline est ____ de David.
   a. le frère b. la sœur

7 **Qui est d'où?**

Répondez d'après la carte. *(Answer according to the map.)*

1. Qui est de Bordeaux?
2. D'où est Maïa?
3. Et Olivia, elle est d'où?
4. Et Ahmed, il est d'où?

8 Historiette David Williams, un garçon américain

Inventez une histoire. *(Make up a story.)*

1. Qui est américain, David Williams ou Serge Legrand?
2. D'où est David Williams? Il est de New York ou de Paris?
3. Il est de quelle nationalité? Il est français ou américain?
4. David est élève dans un collège français ou dans une école américaine?
5. Comment est David? Il est timide ou sociable?

Lyon, France

9 Historiette Sophie est vraiment amusante.

Complétez. *(Complete.)*

Sophie Bellecour est de Lyon. Elle est __1__. Elle n'est pas américaine. Sophie est blonde. Elle n'est pas __2__. Elle n'est pas timide. Pas du tout! Elle est très __3__. Elle est très sympa aussi. Elle est __4__ dans un collège à Lyon.

Pascal Denjean

10 Pascal Denjean

Here is a photo of Pascal Denjean. He is a student from Bordeaux. Say a few things about Pascal.

11 Élodie Denjean

The blonde girl in the photo is Élodie Denjean. She is Pascal's sister. She is also a student in Bordeaux. Say a few things about Élodie.

Élodie Denjean

12 Jeu Un nombre secret

Think of a number between 1 and 60. Your partner tries to guess the number you have in mind. Use a hand gesture to indicate whether the number you are thinking of is higher or lower. Continue until your partner guesses the correct number. Take turns.

ENCORE PLUS *For more practice using words from* ***Mots 2****, do Activity 2 on page H3 at the end of this book.*

Les articles au singulier
Talking about a person or a thing

1. A noun is the name of a person, place, or thing. In French, every noun has a gender, either masculine or feminine. Except for people, you cannot tell what the gender of a noun is by just looking at it. You need other clues.

2. Many words that accompany nouns can indicate gender. They are called "gender markers." **Une** and **un** are gender markers. They are indefinite articles and correspond to *a (an)* in English. **Une** accompanies a feminine noun and **un** accompanies a masculine noun.

LES ARTICLES INDÉFINIS

Féminin	Masculin
une amie	un ami
une sœur	un frère
une école	un collège

3. **Le, la,** and **l'** are definite articles and often correspond to *the* in English.

LES ARTICLES DÉFINIS

Féminin	Masculin
la fille	le garçon
la sœur	le frère
l'amie	l'ami

Attention!

Note that the definite articles **le** and **la** are shortened to **l'** when they accompany a noun that begins with a vowel. When pronounced, the vowel sound is dropped. This is called "elision."

l~~a~~ amie → **l'amie**
l~~e~~ ami → **l'ami**

The **n** of the indefinite article **un** is pronounced when it accompanies a noun beginning with a vowel. This is called "liaison."

un‿ami **un‿élève**

Une sœur et un frère

Comment dit-on?

13 Historiette Olivier et Marie

Complétez avec **un** ou **une.** *(Complete with* un *or* une.*)*

Olivier est __1__ garçon très sympa. Olivier est __2__ ami de Christophe. Christophe est __3__ élève très intelligent. Il est élève dans __4__ école secondaire à New York.

Marie est __5__ amie de Christophe. Marie est __6__ élève intelligente aussi. Marie est __7__ fille vraiment amusante.

14 Historiette Brendan Jones et Sabine Morel

Complétez avec **le, la** ou **l'.** *(Complete with* le, la, *or* l'.*)*

__1__ garçon, Brendan Jones, est américain, mais __2__ fille, Sabine Morel, n'est pas américaine. Elle est française. Sabine est __3__ amie de Ludovic Girard et __4__ sœur de Luc Morel. Brendan n'est pas __5__ ami de Sabine; il est de Miami et Sabine est de Strasbourg. Brendan est __6__ ami de Karen Miller et __7__ frère de Melissa Jones. Brendan est élève et Sabine est élève aussi. __8__ école de Brendan est à Miami. __9__ collège de Sabine est à Strasbourg.

Strasbourg, France

L'accord des adjectifs
Describing a person or a thing

1. An adjective is a word that describes a noun. The highlighted words in the following sentences are adjectives.

La fille est blonde. Le garçon est blond aussi.
Jeanne est française. Vincent aussi est français.

2. In French, an adjective must agree with the noun it describes or modifies. Adjectives that end in a consonant such as **blond** and **français** have two forms in the singular. Study the following.

Féminin	Masculin
La fille est blonde.	Le garçon est blond.
La fille est française.	Le garçon est français.
La fille est brune.	Le garçon est brun.
La fille est intelligente.	Le garçon est intelligent.
L'école est grande.	Le collège est grand.

3. Adjectives that end in **e,** such as **énergique** and **sympathique,** are both feminine and masculine.

Féminin	Masculin
Charlotte est très énergique.	Nicolas est très énergique.
Elle est sympathique.	Il est sympathique.

La fille est blonde. Le garçon est brun.

Attention!

When a final consonant is followed by an **e,** you pronounce the consonant. When a word ends in a consonant, you don't pronounce it.

petite	**petit**
française	**français**
intéressante	**intéressant**

Comment dit-on?

15 **Historiette** **Chloé et Adrien Chancel** Répondez d'après le dessin. *(Answer according to the illustration.)*

1. Chloé est française ou américaine?
2. Elle est blonde ou brune?
3. Elle est grande ou petite?
4. Elle est amusante?
5. Adrien est le frère de Chloé?
6. Adrien est blond ou brun?
7. Il est grand ou petit?
8. Il est amusant?
9. Chloé est élève dans un collège français ou dans une école américaine?
10. Et le frère de Chloé, il est élève dans un collège français ou dans une école américaine?

16 **Historiette** **Maïa, Emmanuel et moi** Complétez. *(Complete.)*

1. Maïa est une amie ____ et ____. (amusant, sympathique)
2. Emmanuel est le frère de Maïa. Il est ____ aussi. Il est ____ et très ____! (sympathique, amusant, sociable)
3. Maïa est ____. (français)
4. Et moi, je m'appelle ____ *(your name)*. Je suis ____. Je ne suis pas ____. (américain, français)
5. Je suis élève dans une école ____ ____. (secondaire, américain)
6. Je ne suis pas élève dans un collège ____. (français)

17 **Jeu** **Devinez.** You often hear French teenagers talk about their friends' younger siblings and say something like: **«Oh, la petite sœur de Corinne, elle est vraiment casse-pieds!»** (literally, *a foot-breaker*). Can you guess what expression we use in English?

18 **Un ami idéal ou une amie idéale**

What are some qualities an ideal friend would have? With a classmate, discuss what you think an ideal friend is like.

19 **C'est qui?** Work with a classmate. Say three things that describe someone in the class. First your partner will tell you whether you're describing a boy or a girl. Then, he or she will guess who it is. Take turns.

—brun, grand, amusant
—C'est un garçon. C'est Marc.

Le verbe être au singulier
Identifying people and things

1. The verb *to be* in French is **être.** Study the following forms.

ÊTRE	
je	suis
tu	es
il	est
elle	est

2. You use **je** to talk about yourself.

You use **tu** to address a friend.

You use **il** to talk about a boy or a man.

You use **elle** to talk about a girl or woman.

3. You also use **il/elle** when referring to things.

Le collège? Il est grand.
L'école? Elle est petite.

Comment dit-on?

20 Historiette Sylvie Latour Voici une photo de Sylvie Latour. Décrivez Sylvie d'après les indications. *(Here is a photo of Sylvie Latour. Describe Sylvie using the cues.)*

1. canadienne
2. blonde
3. amusante et intelligente
4. sociable
5. de Montréal

21 En France Répétez la conversation. *(Repeat the conversation.)*

Salut! Tu es l'ami américain de Sandrine Valois, n'est-ce pas?
Oui, je m'appelle Matt, Matt Porter.
Tu es de New York?
Oui, je suis de New York.

22 Historiette Matt Porter Parlez de Matt. *(Say all you can about Matt.)*

23 Pardon! Répondez d'après le modèle. *(Answer according to the model.)*

Je suis de Paris.
Pardon, tu es d'où?

1. Je suis de Nice.
2. Je suis d'Antibes.
3. Je suis de Lille.
4. Je suis de Strasbourg.

24 **Je suis...** Donnez des réponses personnelles. *(Give your own answers.)*

Je m'appelle __1__ *(name)*. Je suis de __2__ *(place)*. Je suis __3__ *(nationality)*. Je suis __4__ *(occupation)*.

25 **Une interview** Posez des questions à un(e) ami(e). *(Ask a friend the following questions.)*

1. Tu es français(e) ou américain(e)?
2. Tu es d'où?
3. Tu es élève dans une école secondaire?
4. Tu es sociable ou timide?

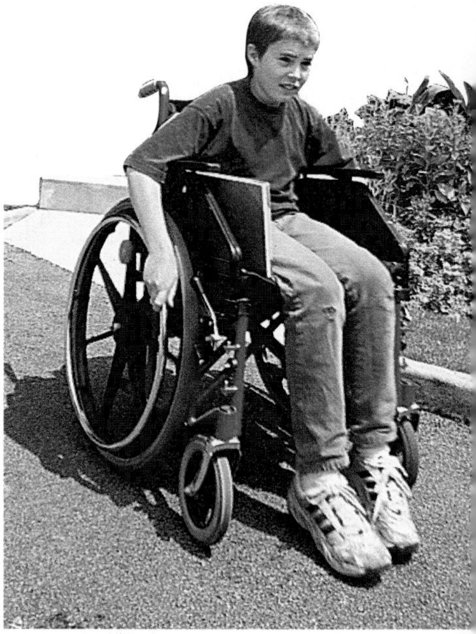

Rémi Tonon

26 **Rémi** Voici une photo de Rémi Tonon. Il est de Nîmes. Posez des questions à Rémi d'après le modèle. *(Ask Rémi questions according to the model. Your partner will answer as Rémi.)*

français →
—Rémi, tu es français?
—Oui, je suis français.

1. de Nîmes
2. élève dans un collège de Nîmes
3. sociable
4. intelligent

27 **Historiette** **Antoine Delcourt** Complétez. *(Complete.)*

Voici Antoine Delcourt. Il __1__ français. Il est de Marseille. Moi aussi, je __2__ de Marseille. Marseille __3__ un port important en France. Antoine __4__ élève dans un collège à Marseille. Le collège est assez grand.

Et toi, tu __5__ français(e) ou américain(e)? Tu __6__ d'où? Tu __7__ élève dans une école secondaire? L'école __8__ petite?

Marseille, France

La négation
Making a sentence negative

To make a sentence negative in French, you put **ne... pas** around the verb. Note that **ne** becomes **n'** before a vowel.

Affirmatif	Négatif
Je suis américain.	Je ne suis pas français.
Tu es amusant.	Tu n'es pas timide.
Il est sociable.	Il n'est pas égoïste.
Elle est de Lyon.	Elle n'est pas de Paris.

LYCÉE HENRI

Lycée Henri IV, Paris

Comment dit-on?

28 Non, Justine n'est pas américaine.
Mettez à la forme négative. *(Change to the negative.)*

1. Justine est américaine.
2. Elle est de San Francisco.
3. Et moi, je suis français(e).
4. Je suis de Paris.
5. Je suis élève dans un collège à Paris.

29 Tu es français(e)? Donnez des réponses personnelles. *(Give your own answers.)*

1. Tu es français(e)?
2. Tu es de Lyon?
3. Tu es timide?
4. Tu es l'ami(e) de Justine?

30 Un petit ami ou une petite amie A classmate will pretend that he or she has a new boyfriend or girlfriend. Ask as many questions as you can to find out who it is.

ENCORE PLUS *For more practice using the verb* ***être****, do Activity 3 on page H4 at the end of this book.*

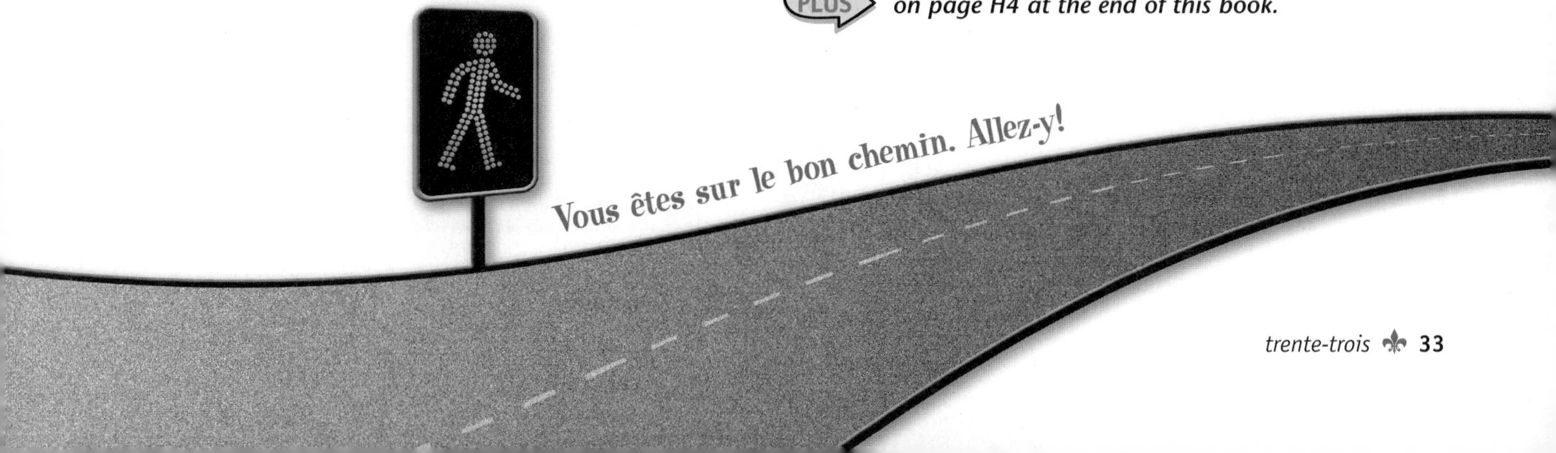
Vous êtes sur le bon chemin. Allez-y!

Conversation

Il est d'où, Luc?

Sophie: Luc, tu es de Paris, non?
Luc: Non. Je ne suis pas de Paris.
Sophie: Tu es d'où, alors?
Luc: Je suis de Cannes.
Sophie: Tu es de Cannes… sur la Côte d'Azur?
Luc: Oui.
Sophie: C'est super, la Côte d'Azur!

Vous avez compris?

Répondez. *(Answer.)*

1. Luc est de Paris?
2. Il est d'où?
3. Où est Cannes?
4. Comment est la Côte d'Azur?

Parlons un peu plus

A **Au café** You've just met a student your own age at a café in Antibes, near Cannes. Have a conversation to get to know each other better.

Antibes, France

B **Jeu** **Tu es... !**
Play a guessing game. Think of someone in the class. Pretend you are this person and describe yourself. Your classmates have to guess who you are.

Prononciation

L'accent tonique

1. In English, you stress certain syllables more than others. In French, you pronounce each syllable evenly. Compare the following pairs of English and French words.

   timid / **timide** *patient* / **patient**
   popular / **populaire** *American* / **américain**
   sociable / **sociable**

2. Repeat the following sentences. Notice how each word is linked to the next so that the sentence sounds like one long word.

   Élisabeth est l'amie de Nathalie.
   Paul est le frère de Nathalie.
   Il est très sympathique.

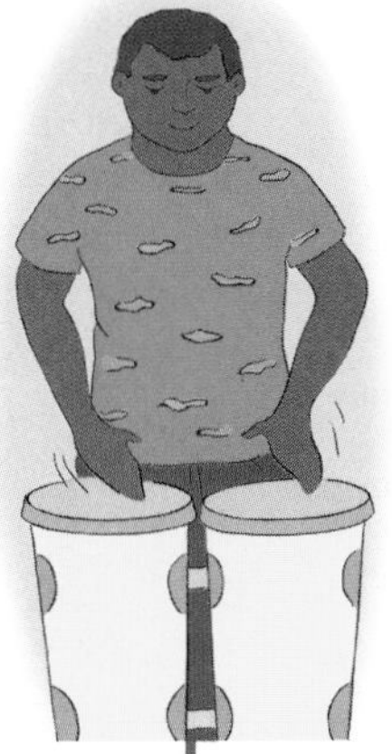

Le Québec

Lectures culturelles

Reading Strategy

Cognates

Words that look alike and have similar meanings in French and English are called "cognates." Look for cognates whenever you read in French. Recognizing cognates can help you figure out the meaning of many words in French and will help you understand what you read.

Un garçon et une fille

Un Parisien

Nicolas Martin est français. Il est de Paris, la capitale de la France. Nicolas est un garçon sympa. Il est très intelligent aussi. Nicolas est élève dans un lycée à Paris, le lycée Henri IV. Un lycée est aussi une école secondaire en France, mais après[1] le collège. Le lycée Henri IV à Paris est une école excellente.

[1] après *after*

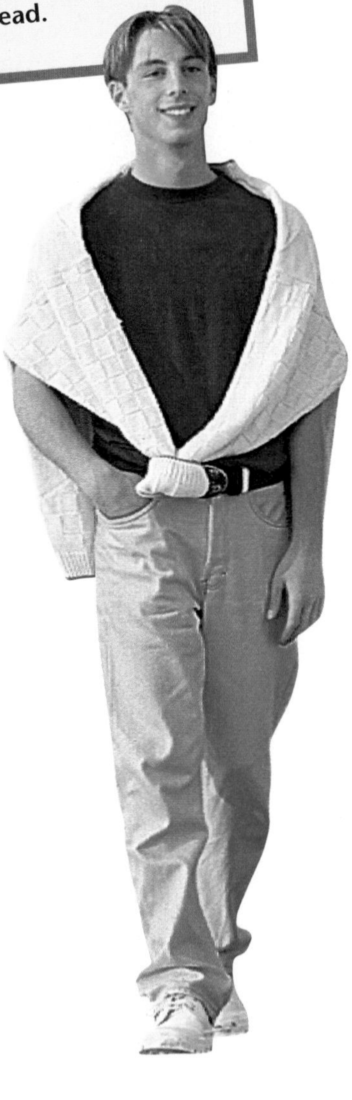

Lycée Henri IV, Paris

La Polynésie française

Tahiti

Haïti

La Martinique

La France

La Suisse

La Belgique

Une Martiniquaise

Valérie Boucher est française aussi. Elle est de Fort-de-France, la ville[2] principale de la Martinique. La Martinique est une île[3] française dans la mer des Caraïbes (la mer des Antilles). Valérie est élève dans un lycée à Fort-de-France—le lycée Bellevue. Le lycée Bellevue est une école excellente.

[2] ville *city* [3] île *island*

Fort-de-France, Martinique

La Tunisie

Le Maroc

Vous avez compris?

A Un Parisien Répondez. *(Answer.)*

1. Nicolas Martin est de quelle nationalité?
2. Il est d'où?
3. Quelle est la capitale de la France?
4. Comment est Nicolas?
5. Il est élève où?

B Une Martiniquaise Vrai ou faux? *(True or false?)*

1. Valérie Boucher est espagnole.
2. Elle est de Pointe-à-Pitre.
3. La Martinique est une île portugaise.
4. Valérie est élève dans une école américaine.

Le Sénégal

Lecture supplémentaire 1

Le français en Afrique

Bonjour! Je m'appelle Diane Koffi. Je suis d'Abidjan. Abidjan est la ville principale de la Côte d'Ivoire. La Côte d'Ivoire est un pays[1] d'Afrique Occidentale[2]. C'est un pays francophone[3].

Moi, je m'appelle Karim Ashour. Je suis tunisien. Je suis de Tunis, la capitale de la Tunisie. La Tunisie est un pays nord-africain sur la mer Méditerranée. La langue officielle de la Tunisie est l'arabe. Le français est la deuxième[4] langue.

[1] pays *country*
[2] Occidentale *Western*
[3] francophone *French-speaking*
[4] deuxième *second*

Abidjan, Côte d'Ivoire

Tunis, Tunisie

Vous avez compris?

A Diane Complétez. *(Complete.)*

1. Diane Koffi est d'____.
2. Abidjan est la ville principale de la ____.
3. La Côte d'Ivoire est un pays d'____ Occidentale.

B Karim Vrai ou faux? *(True or false?)*

1. Karim Ashour est une fille.
2. Karim est algérien.
3. Karim est de Tunis.
4. Tunis est la capitale de la Tunisie.
5. La Tunisie est en Europe.
6. La langue officielle de la Tunisie est le français.

Lecture supplémentaire 2

Un artiste français

Henri de Toulouse-Lautrec est un peintre français. Il est d'Albi, une petite ville dans le sud de la France. La famille d'Henri est noble et assez riche.

Le jeune Henri est très petit. Il est boiteux[1]. Le petit garçon souffre de beaucoup de[2] fractures. Mais le jeune Henri possède un grand talent. Il adore la peinture[3].

Un sujet favori de Toulouse-Lautrec est la vie[4] parisienne.

Un autre sujet favori de Toulouse-Lautrec est le cirque. Le clown est très amusant, n'est-ce pas?

[1] boiteux *lame*
[2] beaucoup de *many*
[3] peinture *painting*
[4] vie *life*

Albi, France

Vous avez compris?

A Un peintre français

Répondez. *(Answer.)*

1. Qui est Toulouse-Lautrec?
2. Il est d'où?
3. Comment est la famille Toulouse-Lautrec?
4. Comment est le jeune Henri?
5. Il souffre de beaucoup de fractures?
6. Il adore la peinture?
7. Il adore le cirque?

B Stratégie de lecture

Trouvez les mots apparentés dans la lecture. *(Find the following cognates in the reading.)*

1. family
2. talent
3. rich
4. subject
5. possess
6. favorite
7. circus
8. painter

La Belgique

La Tunisie

Le Mali

CONNEXIONS

Les sciences sociales

La géographie

Geography is the study of the earth. It deals with all the earth's features, such as mountains, rivers, and seas. It is also the study of where people live and how the earth's features affect their lives. It is a subject that has interested human beings since the earliest of times.

Look at the map of France. Notice how many geographical terms you are able to recognize in French. See how easy it is to read about geography in French.

Le Rhône à Avignon

La Seine à Paris

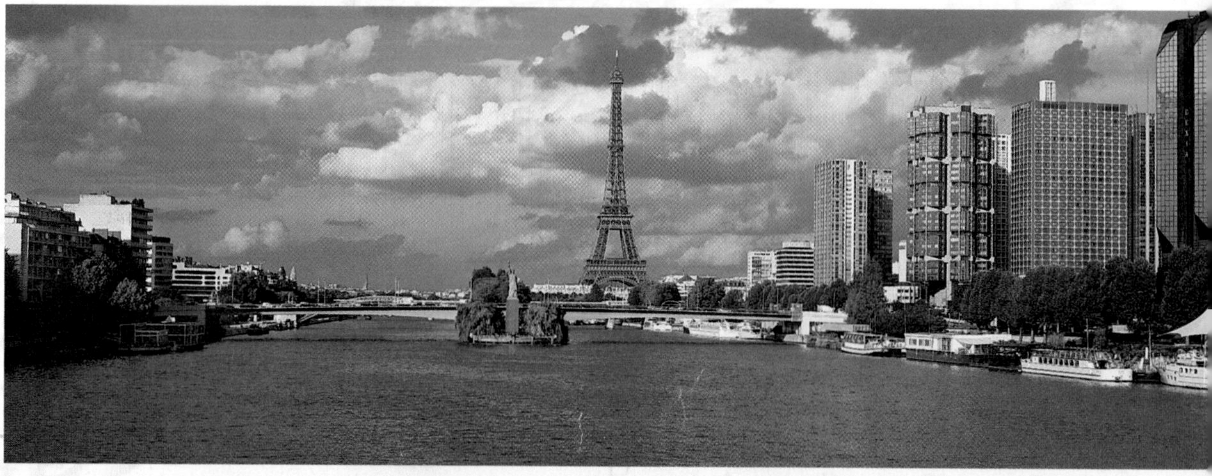

ville = city
pays = country
fleuve = river
nord = north
sud = south

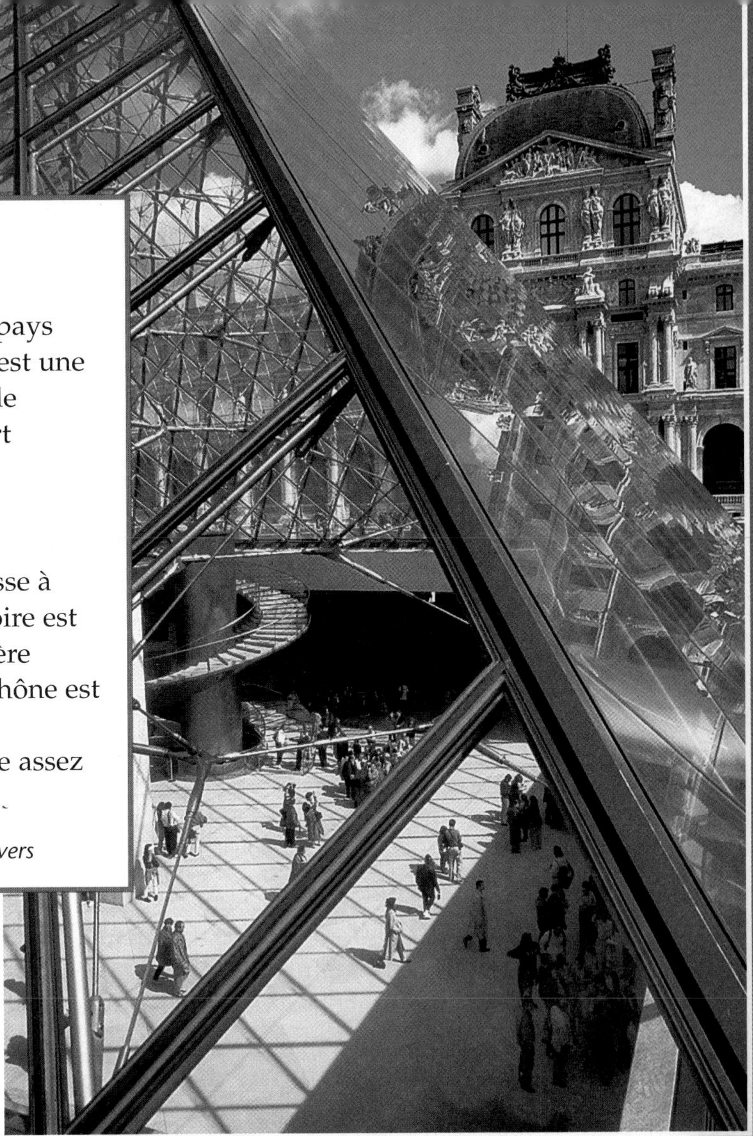

Musée du Louvre, Paris

La France

Villes

La France est en Europe. La France est un pays important dans le monde[1]. La capitale, Paris, est une ville culturelle. Lille, dans le nord, est une ville industrielle. Marseille, dans le sud, est un port important sur la mer Méditerranée.

Fleuves

Il y a[2] cinq fleuves[3] en France. La Seine passe à Paris. La Seine est un fleuve très calme. La Loire est un fleuve très long. Le Rhin forme une frontière naturelle entre la France et l'Allemagne. Le Rhône est un fleuve important: c'est une grande source d'énergie électrique. La Garonne est un fleuve assez violent.

[1] monde *world* [2] Il y a *There are* [3] fleuves *rivers*

La Loire à Orléans

Vous avez compris?

Un peu de géographie

Vrai ou faux? *(True or false?)*

1. La France est un continent.
2. Paris est une ville industrielle.
3. Lille est dans le sud de la France.
4. Marseille est un port.
5. La Seine est un fleuve violent.
6. La Loire est un fleuve très long.
7. Un fleuve forme une frontière naturelle entre la France et l'Allemagne.

C'est à vous

Use what you have learned

PARLER 1

Un ami

✔ *Describe a male friend and answer questions about him*

Work with a classmate. Here's a picture of Vincent Terrier, a friend of yours from Paris, France. Say as much as you can about him. Answer any questions your partner may have about Vincent.

PARLER 2

Une élève

✔ *Ask a female friend questions and tell her about yourself*

Jeanne Marin (a classmate) is a new girl in your school. She is from Montreal, Canada. You want to get to know her better and help her feel at home. Find out as much as you can about her. Tell Jeanne about yourself, too.

Jeanne Marin

Saint-Tropez, France

PARLER 3

Dis donc, c'est qui?

✔ *Ask someone questions about another person*

You and a friend (a classmate) are at a sidewalk café in Saint-Tropez, on the French Riviera. You see an attractive girl or boy sitting a few tables away. It just so happens that your friend knows the person. Ask your friend as many questions as you can to find out about the boy or girl you're interested in.

ÉCRIRE

4 Un ami français

✔ Write a postcard to a friend about yourself

Here's a postcard you just received from a new pen pal. First read his message. Then answer it. Give Christophe similar information about yourself.

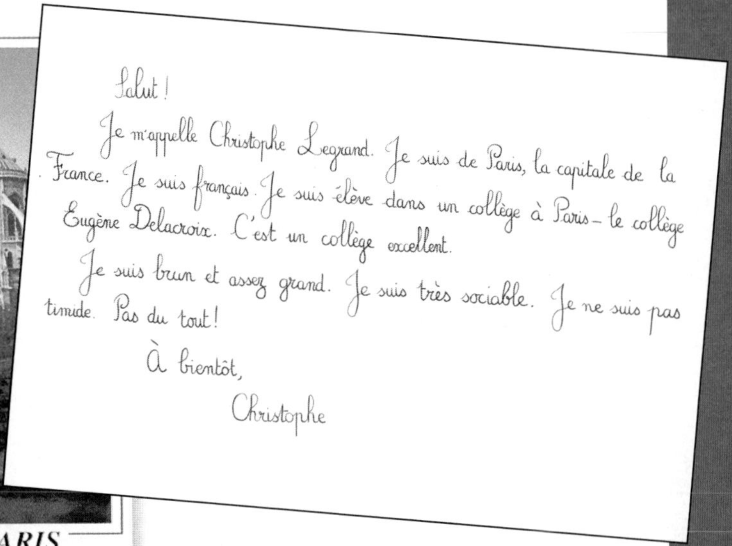

Salut!

Je m'appelle Christophe Legrand. Je suis de Paris, la capitale de la France. Je suis français. Je suis élève dans un collège à Paris—le collège Eugène Delacroix. C'est un collège excellent.

Je suis brun et assez grand. Je suis très sociable. Je ne suis pas timide. Pas du tout!

À bientôt,

Christophe

Writing Strategy

Freewriting One of the easiest ways to begin any kind of personal writing is simply to begin—to let your thoughts flow and write the first thing that comes to mind. Sometimes as you think of one word, another word you know will come to mind. If you get stuck, take several minutes to think of another word or phrase you have already learned. Brainstorming and freewriting are often methods for generating ideas when writing about yourself.

ÉCRIRE

5 Moi

On a piece of paper, write down as much as you can about yourself in French. Your teacher will collect the descriptions and choose students to read them to the class. You'll all try to guess who's being described.

Assessment

Paris, France

Vocabulaire

To review **Mots 1**, turn to pages 18–19.

1 Répondez d'après la photo. *(Answer according to the photo.)*

1. Jeanne est française ou américaine?
2. Elle est de Paris ou de Boston?
3. Elle est blonde ou brune?

To review **Mots 2**, turn to pages 22–23.

2 Choisissez. *(Choose.)*

4. Guillaume est ____ dans un collège français.
   a. ami **b.** élève
5. Guillaume est ____ de Françoise.
   a. le frère **b.** la sœur

Structure

3 Complétez avec «un» ou «une». *(Complete with* un *or* une.*)*

6. Sylvie est élève dans ____ collège français.
7. Sylvie est ____ fille très sympa.
8. Paul est ____ ami de Sylvie.
9. Paul est ____ garçon sympa aussi.

To review these gender markers, turn to page 26.

4 Complétez avec «le», «la» ou «l'». *(Complete with* le, la, *or* l'.*)*

10. ____ fille, Sylvie, est de Lyon.
11. Jean-Pierre est ____ frère de Sylvie.
12. ____ école de Sylvie est grande.

To review agreement of adjectives, turn to page 28.

5 Complétez. *(Complete.)*

13. C'est une école assez ____. (petit)
14. Martine est une fille très ____. (dynamique)
15. Le garçon ____ est amusant. (américain)
16. Robert est un élève ____. (intelligent)

6 Complétez avec «être». *(Complete with* être.*)*

17. Dominique, tu ____ français?
18. Oui, je ____ de Bordeaux.
19. La fille blonde, elle ____ américaine?
20. Non, elle ____ canadienne.

To review the verb **être**, turn to page 30.

7 Répondez au négatif. *(Answer in the negative.)*

21. Alain Gérard est américain?
22. Il est timide?
23. Alain est le frère de Julie?

To review making a sentence negative, turn to page 33.

Culture

8 Choisissez. *(Choose.)*

24. Un lycée est ____ secondaire en France.
    a. un collège **b.** un élève **c.** une école
25. La ville principale de la Martinique est ____.
    a. Bellevue **b.** Fort-de-France **c.** Paris

To review this cultural information, turn to pages 36–37.

Grand-Rivière, Martinique

On parle super bien!

Tell all you can about this illustration.

Vocabulaire

Identifying a person or thing

un garçon
une fille
un ami
une amie
un(e) élève
un frère
une sœur
une école
un collège
être

Describing a person

petit(e)
grand(e)
brun(e)
blond(e)
amusant(e)
patient(e)
intelligent(e)
intéressant(e)
sympa(thique)
timide
énergique
égoïste
dynamique
populaire
sociable
enthousiaste

Stating nationality

français(e)
américain(e)

Finding out information

Qui?
D'où?
Comment?
C'est qui?
De quelle nationalité?

Expressing degrees

assez
très
vraiment

Other useful words

voilà
aussi
secondaire

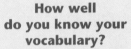

How well do you know your vocabulary?

- Choose five words that describe a good friend.
- Use these words to write several sentences about him or her.

VIDÉOTOUR

Épisode 1

In this video episode, Vincent and Chloé, each hoping to get a great shot of **le Sacré-Cœur**, bump into each other on the steps below the church. See page 526 for more information.

CHAPITRE 2

Les cours et les profs

Objectifs

In this chapter you will learn to:

- *describe people and things*
- *talk about more than one person or thing*
- *tell what subjects you take in school and express some opinions about them*
- *speak to people formally and informally*
- *talk about French-speaking people in the United States*

Pierre Bonnard *Écriture de fille*

FRANCE ÉCONOMIQUE
MDI
ROYAUME-UNI
BELGIQUE
ALLEMAGNE
MANCHE
LUXEMBOURG
Le Havre
Lille
Rennes
Nancy
Strasbourg
St-Nazaire
Dijon
Bordeaux
Toulouse
Bayonne
ANDORRE
ESPAGNE
L'Europe :

Vocabulaire
Mots 1

Les élèves et les profs

Karine et Stéphanie sont françaises.
Pierre et Alexandre sont français aussi.

Les quatre copains sont de Rouen.
Ils sont élèves dans le même lycée.
Ils sont tous très sympathiques.

Comment sont les cours?

la salle de classe
la classe
les élèves

Le cours de français est facile.
La prof n'est pas trop stricte. Juste un peu.

Mais les cours de sciences sont vraiment difficiles. Toi, tu es d'accord ou pas?
Non, je ne suis pas d'accord. Pour moi, les cours de sciences sont très faciles.

Quel est le mot?

Rennes, France

1 Historiette

Deux copines françaises

Inventez une histoire. *(Make up a story.)*

1. Léa et Touria sont françaises ou américaines?
2. Elles sont copines?
3. Elles sont de Rennes?
4. Elles sont élèves dans le même lycée?
5. Le lycée est à Rennes?
6. Elles sont dans la salle de classe?

2 Historiette

Deux copains français

Inventez une histoire. *(Make up a story.)*

1. Paul et Jamal sont français ou américains?
2. Ils sont copains?
3. Ils sont amusants?
4. Ils sont sympathiques?
5. Ils sont de Rennes?
6. Ils sont élèves dans le même lycée?

Des lycéens de Rennes

FRENCH Online

For more information about Rennes and other cities in France, go to the Glencoe French Web site: french.glencoe.com

3 Le cours de français

Donnez des réponses personnelles. *(Give your own answers.)*

1. Qui est le/la prof de français?
2. Il/Elle est sympa?
3. Il/Elle est strict(e)?
4. Il/Elle est de quelle nationalité?
5. Le cours de français est facile ou difficile?
6. Pour toi, les cours de sciences sont faciles ou difficiles?

4 **Le prof idéal ou la prof idéale** Work with a classmate. Share ideas as to what you look for in an ideal teacher. Let your classmate know whether you agree with him or her. You may want to use some of the following words.

intéressant | sympathique | patient | strict
intelligent | amusant | enthousiaste | dynamique

Un cours de français aux États-Unis

ENCORE PLUS *For more practice using words from **Mots 1**, do Activity 4 on page H5 at the end of this book.*

Vocabulaire Mots 2

Les matières

Les sciences naturelles

la biologie
la chimie
la physique

Les mathématiques (Les maths)

l'algèbre
la géométrie
la trigonométrie
le calcul

Les langues

le français
l'italien
l'espagnol
l'allemand
l'anglais
le latin

Les sciences sociales

l'histoire
la géographie
l'économie

D'autres matières

la littérature
l'informatique
la gymnastique
la musique
le dessin

En cours de français

Salut les copains! Nous sommes américains. Nous sommes de New York. Et vous, vous êtes américains aussi, n'est-ce pas?

M. Boursier est le prof de français. Maintenant, nous sommes en cours de français.

Nous sommes tous très forts en français!
C'est pas vrai! Vous êtes très mauvais!
France

Les nombres de 70 à 100

70 soixante-dix	80 quatre-vingts	90 quatre-vingt-dix
71 soixante et onze	81 quatre-vingt-un	91 quatre-vingt-onze
72 soixante-douze	82 quatre-vingt-deux	92 quatre-vingt-douze
73 soixante-treize	83 quatre-vingt-trois	93 quatre-vingt-treize
74 soixante-quatorze	84 quatre-vingt-quatre	94 quatre-vingt-quatorze
75 soixante-quinze	85 quatre-vingt-cinq	95 quatre-vingt-quinze
76 soixante-seize	86 quatre-vingt-six	96 quatre-vingt-seize
77 soixante-dix-sept	87 quatre-vingt-sept	97 quatre-vingt-dix-sept
78 soixante-dix-huit	88 quatre-vingt-huit	98 quatre-vingt-dix-huit
79 soixante-dix-neuf	89 quatre-vingt-neuf	99 quatre-vingt-dix-neuf
		100 cent

Quel est le mot?

Un cours de chimie à Paris

5 Sciences ou langues? Vrai ou faux?
(True or false?)

1. La chimie est une science.
2. L'histoire et la géographie sont des mathématiques.
3. Le calcul est une langue.
4. Le latin et l'espagnol sont des langues.
5. Pour vous, le français est un cours obligatoire.

6 Des cours faciles et difficiles Donnez des réponses personnelles. *(Give your own answers.)*

1. Le cours de français est facile ou difficile?
2. Pour toi, quels sont les cours faciles?
3. Quels sont les cours difficiles?
4. Tu es fort(e) en français?
5. Tu es fort(e) en sciences?
6. Tu es très fort(e) en quelle matière?
7. Tu es assez mauvais(e) en quelle matière?

7 Historiette Des élèves américains
Inventez une histoire. *(Make up a story.)*

1. Les élèves sont de quelle nationalité?
2. Ils sont élèves dans une école secondaire américaine?
3. Ils sont en cours de français?
4. Le cours de français est facile ou difficile?
5. Les élèves sont forts en français?

8 C'est quel cours? Identifiez le cours. *(Identify the course.)*

1. la littérature, la grammaire anglaise
2. la conversation, la culture française
3. un poème, une pièce de théâtre, une fable
4. un microbe, un animal, une plante, un microscope
5. un cercle, un rectangle, un triangle, un parallélogramme
6. un piano, un violon, un concert, un opéra
7. les montagnes, les villes, les villages, les capitales, les océans
8. la peinture, la sculpture, les statues, les artistes
9. une disquette, un moniteur, un microprocesseur, un bit

9 **Comment est la classe?** With a classmate, look at the illustration. Take turns asking each other questions about it. Use the following question words: **qui, où, quel cours, à quelle heure, comment.**

LUGAGNE-DELPON Olivier
257 r Lecourbe 15e.......................01 45 58 96 30
LUGAGNE DELPON Paul
4 r Chevert 7e.......................01 44 05 55 31
LUGAGNE-DELPONT Véronique
15 r Marie et Louise 10e.......................01 43 41 37 85
LUGAN Benoît
34 pl Marché St-Honoré 1e........01 42 97 55 05
» **Bernard et Gabrielle**
5 bd Grenelle 15e.......................01 45 75 47 83
» **Bruno et Stéphanie** Bat A2
64 r Compans 19e.......................01 40 18 13 57
» **Hermann**
11 r Vasco de Gama 15e.............01 45 55 44 35
» **Jacques** 75 av Ledru Rollin 12e......01 43 47 84 57

10 **Le numéro de téléphone** Look at this page from the Paris phone book with a classmate. Give a telephone number. Your classmate will tell whose number it is. Then reverse roles.

11 **Jeu** **Quelle matière?**
Work with a classmate. Think of a school subject and use whatever means necessary (voice, hands, drawings) to help your partner guess which subject it is.

Un cours de dessin à Paris

ENCORE PLUS *For more practice using words from **Mots 2**, do Activity 5 on page H6 at the end of this book.*

Le pluriel: articles, noms et adjectifs
Talking about more than one person or thing

1. The articles you know **(un/une, le/la/l')** are singular markers. The plural forms of these articles are plural markers. Study the following.

LES ARTICLES INDÉFINIS

Masculin		Féminin	
Singulier	Pluriel	Singulier	Pluriel
un garçon	des garçons	une fille	des filles
un‿(n)ami	des‿(z)amis	une amie	des‿(z)amies
un collège	des collèges	une école	des‿(z)écoles

LES ARTICLES DÉFINIS

Masculin		Féminin	
Singulier	Pluriel	Singulier	Pluriel
le garçon	les garçons	la fille	les filles
l'ami	les‿(z)amis	l'amie	les‿(z)amies
le collège	les collèges	l'école	les‿(z)écoles

2. In French, you form the plural of most nouns by adding an **s.** This **s,** however, is not pronounced. It is the article **les** or **des** that lets you know the noun is plural: **un prof → des prof~~s~~; la prof → les prof~~s~~.**

3. When a noun is plural, any adjective that describes or modifies it must also be in the plural. You form the plural of most adjectives in French by adding an **s.** The **s** is not pronounced.

Singulier	Pluriel
La classe est petite.	Les classes sont petites.
La prof est patiente.	Les profs sont patientes.
Le lycée est grand.	Les lycées sont grands.
Le prof est intéressant.	Les profs sont intéressants.

Note: You do not add an **s** if the word already ends in **s.**

un cours **des cours**

Comment dit-on?

12 **Ils sont comment?** Mettez au pluriel.
(Put in the plural.)

—Le garçon est blond.
—Les garçons sont blonds.

1. La fille est blonde.
2. Le garçon est brun.
3. La sœur de Valentin est amusante.
4. Le frère de Stéphane est égoïste.
5. Le prof est intéressant.
6. Le cours est assez difficile.
7. La salle de classe est petite.
8. L'ami de Paul est vraiment sympathique.
9. L'élève est très intelligent.
10. L'ami de Valérie est amusant.

Deux lycéennes de Yerres, France

13 **Pour toi...** Citez... *(Name . . .)*

Pour moi, deux matières très intéressantes sont ____ et ____.

1. deux matières très intéressantes
2. deux cours très intéressants
3. deux écoles excellentes
4. deux élèves sociables
5. deux professeurs stricts
6. deux filles très intelligentes
7. deux garçons très sympas
8. deux élèves fort(e)s en géographie
9. deux élèves assez mauvais(es) en musique

14 **En commun** Inventez des points communs. *(Make up what these people have in common.)*

Caroline et Marie →
Elles sont amusantes, fortes en algèbre...

1. Laurent et Christian
2. Isabelle et Sandrine
3. Romain et Christophe
4. Marine et Nathalie
5. Loïc et Mathias

15 **Comme moi** Work with a classmate. Tell your partner what you and your friends have in common. Your partner will agree or disagree.

Sue et Jennifer sont sociables... comme moi.
Moi, je ne suis pas d'accord. Elles ne sont pas sociables du tout!

Les vrais amis sont amis pour la vie

Le verbe être au pluriel
Talking about more than one

1. You have already learned the singular forms of the verb **être.** Now study the plural forms.

ÊTRE

Singulier	Pluriel
je suis	nous sommes
tu es	vous ‿z êtes
il/elle est	ils/elles sont

2.

You use **nous** when referring to yourself and another person or other people.

You use **vous** when talking to two or more people.

You use **ils** when referring to two or more males or to a group of males and females.

You use **elles** when referring to two or more females.

Savez-vous que... ?

You also use **ils/elles** when referring to things.

Les cours? Ils sont très faciles.

Les salles? Elles sont petites.

Comment dit-on?

16 **Vous êtes d'où?** Répétez la conversation. *(Repeat the conversation.)*

17 **Historiette** **Ils sont américains.** Complétez d'après la conversation. *(Complete according to the conversation.)*

Les deux garçons __1__ américains. Ils ne __2__ pas de New York. Ils __3__ de Boston. Boston __4__ une grande ville américaine.

Les deux filles ne __5__ pas américaines. Elles __6__ françaises. Elles __7__ de Toulouse. Toulouse __8__ une grande ville française.

18 **À vous** Répondez en utilisant **nous.** *(Choose a partner and answer for both of you using* nous.*)*

1. Vous êtes américain(e)s?
2. Vous êtes d'où?
3. Vous êtes élèves dans une école secondaire?
4. Vous êtes dans la classe de quel professeur?
5. Vous êtes fort(e)s en français?

ENCORE PLUS

For more practice using the verb être, do Activity 6 on page H7 at the end of this book.

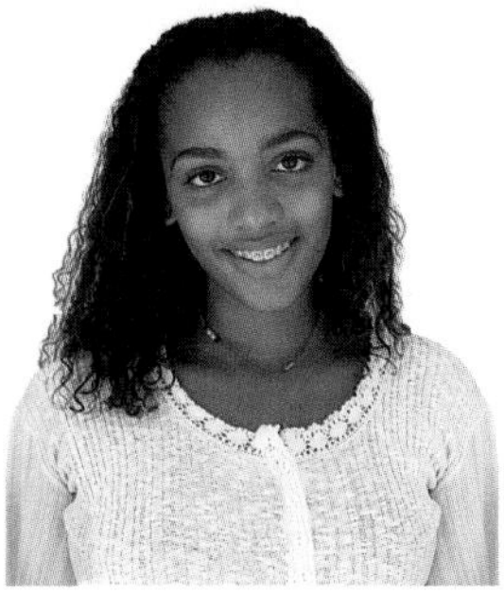

19 **Des questions** Posez des questions et répondez d'après le modèle. *(Ask and answer questions according to the model.)*

américaine / française →
—Vous êtes américaines ou françaises?
—Nous sommes françaises.

1. martiniquaise / américaine
2. petit / grand
3. sociable / timide
4. brune / blonde

20 **Historiette** **L'ami de Christophe**
Complétez en utilisant **être.** *(Complete with* être.*)*

Je __1__ un ami de Christophe. Christophe __2__ très sympa et très amusant. Nous __3__ français, Christophe et moi. Nous __4__ de Cancale, un petit village breton (en Bretagne). Cancale __5__ vraiment très pittoresque.

Nous __6__ élèves dans un collège. Où __7__ le collège? À Dinard. Tous les deux, nous __8__ forts en anglais. La prof d'anglais, Mlle Fielding, __9__ anglaise. Elle __10__ de Liverpool. Elle __11__ assez stricte et le cours d'anglais n'__12__ pas facile. Mais les élèves de Mlle Fielding __13__ très intelligents!

Dinard, Bretagne

21 **Vous êtes américains?** Complétez la conversation. *(Complete the conversation.)*

—Vous __1__ américains, n'est-ce pas?
—Oui, nous __2__ américains. Nous __3__ de __4__.
—Vous __5__ élèves dans une école secondaire?
—Oui, et nous __6__ très forts en français.
—Vraiment? Qui __7__ le/la prof de français?
—C'est __8__.
—Il/Elle __9__ comment?
—Il/Elle __10__ __11__.

22 **Tous les deux** Work with a classmate. Discuss things you have in common.
—Nous sommes sympathiques, intelligent(e)s, fort(e)s en…

Tu et vous
Talking to people formally or informally

1. As you already know, there are two ways to say *you* in French: **tu** and **vous.** You use **tu** when talking to a friend, a person your own age, or a family member.

Éric, tu es trop timide!

Maman, tu es d'accord?

2. You use **vous** when talking to two or more people.

Vous deux, vous êtes d'accord?

3. You also use **vous** when talking to an older person, a person whom you do not know very well, or anyone to whom you wish to show respect.

Monsieur, s'il vous plaît! Vous êtes le professeur de musique?

Comment dit-on?

23 **Vous êtes français?** Regardez les photos et posez la question.
(Ask the people in the photographs if they are French.)

1. 

2. 

3. 

4. 

5. 

6. 

24 **D'autres questions** Ask the same people other questions. You may want to use some of the following words or expressions: **d'où, de quelle nationalité, d'accord, patient, fort en.**

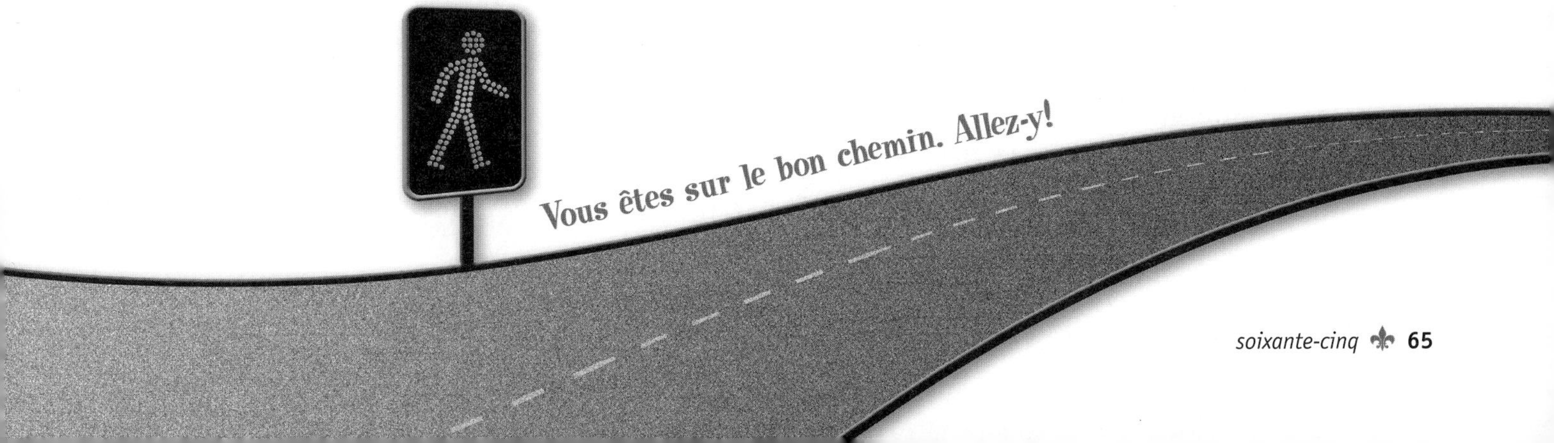
Vous êtes sur le bon chemin. Allez-y!

Conversation

Quel prof?

Paul: Vous êtes dans la classe de Mme Martin?
Anne: Non, nous sommes dans la classe de M. Lepic.
Paul: M. Lepic?
Anne: Ben oui, le prof de maths.
Paul: Ah oui. Comment il est?
Anne: Un peu strict, mais sympa.
Paul: Oui, mais toi et Samuel, vous êtes forts en maths.
Anne: Ben, toi aussi.
Paul: Moi? Je suis très mauvais en maths. Je suis complètement nul!

Vous avez compris?

Répondez. *(Answer.)*

1. Anne et Samuel sont dans la classe de Mme Martin?
2. Ils sont dans la classe de quel professeur?
3. Qui est M. Lepic?
4. Il est comment?
5. Samuel et Anne sont forts en maths?
6. Et Paul, il est fort en maths?

Parlons un peu plus

A **D'accord ou pas?** Make a chart like the one below. List all your classes and rate them. Then compare your chart with that of a classmate.

—Pour moi, le cours de français n'est pas difficile. Tu es d'accord?
—Oui, je suis d'accord. / Non, je ne suis pas d'accord. Pour moi, le cours de français est très difficile.

Cours	Pas difficile	Assez difficile	Très difficile
le français	✓		
l'algèbre			✓

B **Jeu** **Quel cours?** Work with a classmate. He or she gives you one word about a class. Guess what class it is. If you're wrong, your partner will give you another hint until you can guess the class. Take turns.

Prononciation

Les consonnes finales

1. In French, you do not usually pronounce the final consonant you see at the end of a word. Repeat the following.

petit	**grand**	**intéressant**	**français**
amusant	**intelligent**	**patient**	**blond**

2. You also do not pronounce the final **s** you add to a word to make it plural. This is why a singular noun and its plural sound alike. Repeat the following pairs of words and then the sentences.

un copain → des copains	**une copine → des copines**
le garçon → les garçons	**la fille → les filles**

Tous les copains de Vincent sont sympathiques.
Les cours de maths sont très difficiles.

intelligent

Le Québec

Lectures culturelles

Reading Strategy

Using titles

Always look at titles and subtitles before you begin to read. They will help you figure out what a reading selection is about. Having an idea of what a reading is about will help you guess the meaning of unfamiliar words and therefore understand better as you read.

Deux copains haïtiens

Une plage près de Port-au-Prince, Haïti

Le français aux États-Unis

L'influence haïtienne

Bonjour! Nous sommes Abélard Jean-Baptiste et Nicole Jolicœur. Nous sommes élèves dans une école secondaire à Miami. Et pour nous, le cours de français est vraiment très facile! Pour nous, le français n'est pas une langue étrangère[1]. Nous sommes haïtiens. Nous sommes de Port-au-Prince, la capitale d'Haïti. En Haïti, il y a[2] deux langues—le français et le créole. Le créole est une langue à base de français, d'espagnol et de divers dialectes africains.

L'influence canadienne

Et nous? Nous sommes Antonine Gagnon et Donald Maillet. Nous sommes de Montpelier dans le Vermont. Comme beaucoup de personnes de la Nouvelle-Angleterre[3], nous sommes d'origine canadienne. Et pour nous, le français n'est pas une langue étrangère. Le français est la langue maternelle des Canadiens français.

Deux amis de Montpelier

[1] étrangère *foreign*
[2] il y a *there are*
[3] Nouvelle-Angleterre *New England*

La Polynésie française

Tahiti

Haïti

La Martinique

La France

La Suisse

La Belgique

La Tunisie

Le Maroc

Le Mali

Le Sénégal

L'influence «cajun»

Bonjour! Ici Alice Richard et Pierre Doucet. Nous sommes de Louisiane. Nous sommes cajuns. Nous les Cajuns, nous sommes des descendants des Acadiens. Les Acadiens sont les Français expulsés[4] de l'est du Canada par les Anglais.

L'influence cajun est assez forte en Louisiane. Il y a même[5] deux langues officielles en Louisiane—l'anglais et le français.

[4] expulsés *expelled* [5] même *even*

Deux élèves de Louisiane

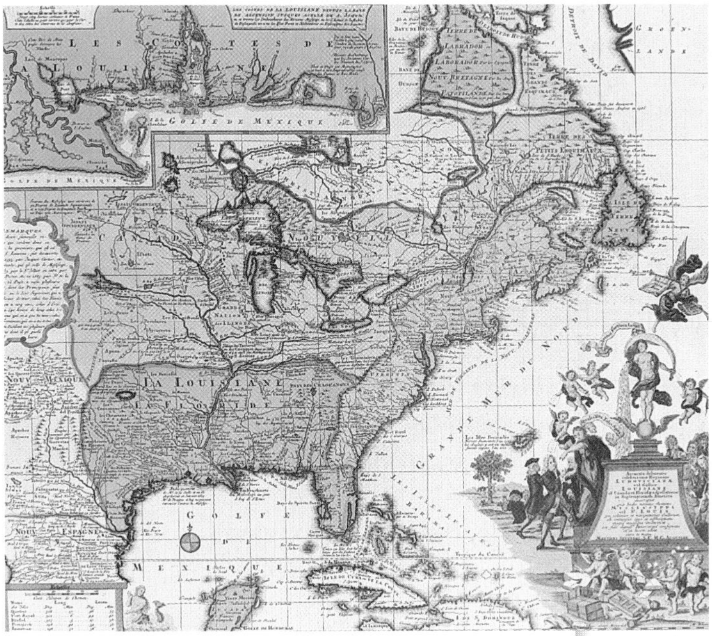

Vous avez compris?

A Les Haïtiens

Répondez. *(Answer.)*

1. Abélard Jean-Baptiste et Nicole Jolicœur sont d'où?
2. Pour Abélard et Nicole, le français est facile?
3. Ils sont de quelle nationalité?
4. Le créole est à base de quelles langues?

B Les descendants des Canadiens français Répondez. *(Answer.)*

1. D'où sont Antonine et Donald?
2. Montpelier est dans quel état?
3. Il y a beaucoup de personnes d'origine canadienne en Nouvelle-Angleterre?
4. Quelle est la langue maternelle des Canadiens français?

C Les Cajuns Répondez. *(Answer.)*.

1. Qui sont les Cajuns?
2. Quelles sont les deux langues officielles en Louisiane?

Lecture supplémentaire 1

La scolarité en France

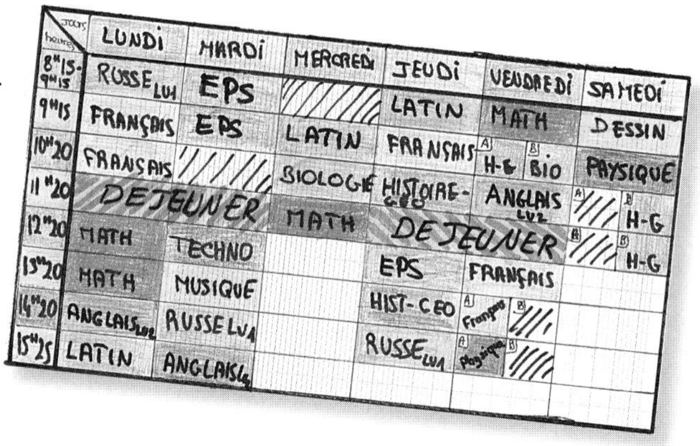

jours / heures	LUNDI	MARDI	MERCREDI	JEUDI	VENDREDI	SAMEDI
8h15-9h15	RUSSE LV1	EPS	///	LATIN	MATH	DESSIN
9h15	FRANÇAIS	EPS	LATIN	FRANÇAIS	A H-G / B BIO	PHYSIQUE
10h20	FRANÇAIS	///	BIOLOGIE	HISTOIRE-GÉO	ANGLAIS LV2	A /// / B H-G
11h20	DEJEUNER	DEJEUNER	MATH	DEJEUNER	DEJEUNER	A /// / B H-G
12h20	MATH	TECHNO		EPS	FRANÇAIS	
13h20	MATH	MUSIQUE		HIST-GÉO	A Français / B ///	
14h20	ANGLAIS LV2	RUSSE LV1		RUSSE LV1	A Physique / B ///	
15h25	LATIN	ANGLAIS LV2				

Le collège en France est une école secondaire. Les élèves sont des collégiens. Le collège est obligatoire pour quatre ans.

Après[1] le collège, le lycée est aussi une école secondaire, mais pour trois ans. Les élèves sont des lycéens. Il y a[2] deux diplômes d'études secondaires—un diplôme professionnel après deux ans et le baccalauréat après trois ans. Le baccalauréat ou «le bac» est nécessaire pour entrer à l'université.

Voici l'emploi du temps de Louise Belleroche. Elle est en troisième, l'équivalent de *ninth grade*. Il y a combien de[3] cours en troisième en France?

[1] Après *After* [2] Il y a *There are* [3] combien de *how many*

Lycée Pasteur, Neuilly, France

Vous avez compris?

A La scolarité Vrai ou faux? *(True or false?)*

1. En France un collège est une petite université.
2. Le collège n'est pas obligatoire.
3. Le lycée est une école secondaire.
4. Le «bac» est un diplôme universitaire.
5. Le «bac» est nécessaire pour entrer à l'université.

B L'emploi du temps de Louise Répondez. *(Answer.)*

1. Il y a combien de cours?
2. Le cours de maths est quels jours? À quelle heure?
3. Et le cours d'anglais?
4. Et le cours de français?
5. Et le cours de biologie?
6. Et le cours d'histoire/géographie?
7. Et le cours de dessin?

Lecture supplémentaire 2

Un message

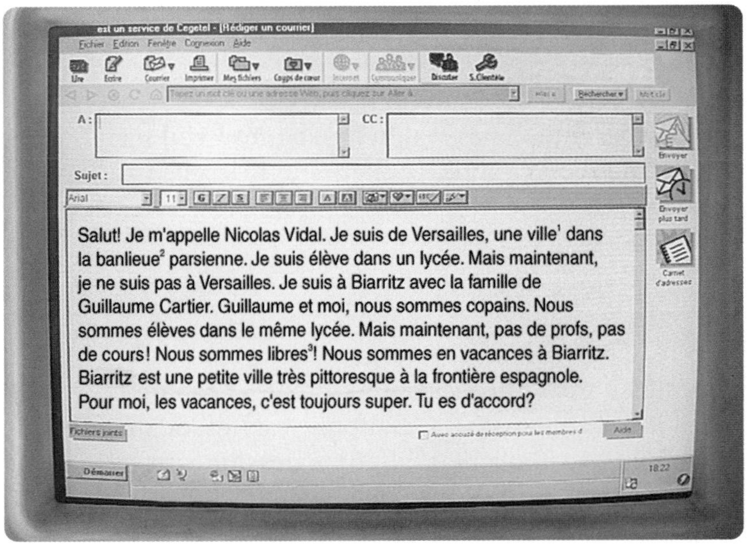
Salut! Je m'appelle Nicolas Vidal. Je suis de Versailles, une ville[1] dans la banlieue[2] parisienne. Je suis élève dans un lycée. Mais maintenant, je ne suis pas à Versailles. Je suis à Biarritz avec la famille de Guillaume Cartier. Guillaume et moi, nous sommes copains. Nous sommes élèves dans le même lycée. Mais maintenant, pas de profs, pas de cours! Nous sommes libres[3]! Nous sommes en vacances à Biarritz. Biarritz est une petite ville très pittoresque à la frontière espagnole. Pour moi, les vacances, c'est toujours super. Tu es d'accord?

[1] ville *town* [2] banlieue *suburbs* [3] libres *free*

Biarritz, France

Versailles, France

Vous avez compris?

A Deux copains Répondez. *(Answer.)*

1. D'où est Nicolas?
2. Où est Versailles?
3. Où est Nicolas maintenant?
4. Il est à Biarritz avec qui?
5. Les deux garçons sont copains?
6. Les deux copains sont en vacances? Où?

B Un peu de géographie

Vrai ou faux? *(True or false?)*

1. Versailles est sur la Côte d'Azur.
2. Versailles est dans la banlieue parisienne.
3. Biarritz est aussi dans la banlieue parisienne.
4. Biarritz est à la frontière espagnole.
5. Biarritz est en Espagne.
6. Biarritz est en France.

La Belgique
La Tunisie
Le Maroc
Le Mali

CONNEXIONS

Les sciences naturelles

La biologie, la physique et la chimie

Sciences are an important part of the school curriculum. If you like science, it would be fun to be able to read some scientific material in French. You will see how easy it is. It's easy because you already have some background in science from your science courses. In addition, many scientific terms are cognates.

La biologie

La biologie est l'étude des organismes vivants. En biologie, il y a trois catégories importantes: l'anatomie, la zoologie et la botanique. L'anatomie est l'étude du corps humain. La zoologie est l'étude des animaux et la botanique est l'étude des plantes.

La botanique est l'étude des plantes.

La zoologie est l'étude des animaux.

La physique et la chimie

La physique est l'étude de la matière et de l'énergie. La chimie est l'étude des caractéristiques des éléments.

Les savants

Dans un laboratoire, le savant (le biologiste, le chimiste ou le physicien) observe et analyse des phénomènes scientifiques. Le biologiste, par exemple, observe et analyse des microbes[1], des cellules, des bactéries et des virus à l'aide d'un microscope.

[1] microbes *germs*

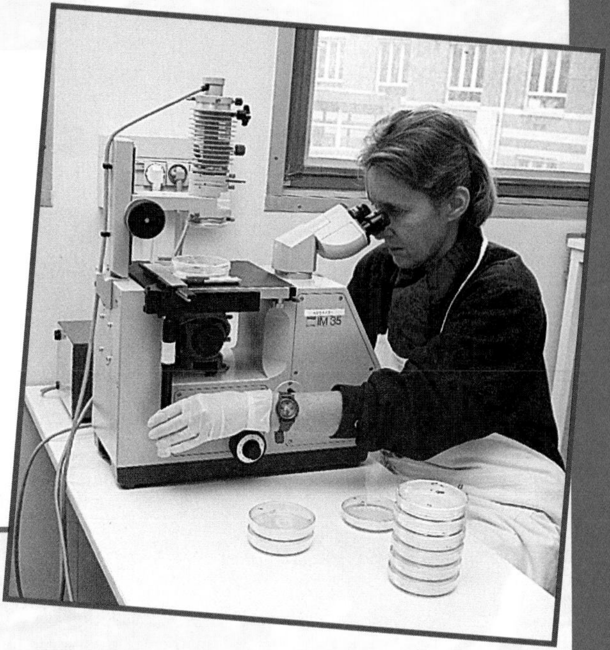

Une biologiste

Vous avez compris?

A Des termes scientifiques

Préparez une liste. *(Make a list of scientific terms you recognize in the reading.)*

Des élèves dans un laboratoire à Paris

B C'est quelle science?

Répondez. *(Answer.)*

1. l'étude des animaux
2. l'étude des plantes
3. l'étude de la matière et de l'énergie
4. l'étude du corps humain

C Stratégie de lecture

Note that the words in each of the following groups are all related to one another. If you know the meaning of one word, you can guess the meanings of the others. Can you figure them all out?

1. la biologie, un(e) biologiste, biologique
2. analyser, une analyse, analytique
3. un microbe, microbien
4. une bactérie, bactérien
5. un virus, viral

Use what you have learned

L'école internationale de Paris

PARLER 1

Nous

✔ *Describe yourself and someone else*

Work with a classmate. You are at an international student gathering in France. You and your partner introduce yourselves to the other students. Try to get to know one another better. You may use the following as a guide:

- say who you are
- give your nationality
- tell where you're from
- give the name of your school
- describe some of your qualities or faults

PARLER 2

L'école idéale

✔ *Talk about school*

Work with a classmate. Describe what for each of you is an ideal school. Say as much as you can about the teachers, classes, and students. Determine whether or not you share the same opinions.

Lycée Janson de Sailly, Paris

ÉCRIRE

3 Un message

✔ Write about your classes and friends

You answer an e-mail message from a student in France who wants to know about your life in the United States. Give him or her as many details as possible about your classes and your friends.

Collège de Montois, Noyen-sur-Seine

Writing Strategy

Keeping a journal There are many kinds of journals you can keep, each having a different purpose. One type of journal is the kind in which you write about daily events and record your thoughts and impressions about these events. It's almost like "thinking aloud." By keeping such a journal, you may find that you discover something new that you were not aware of.

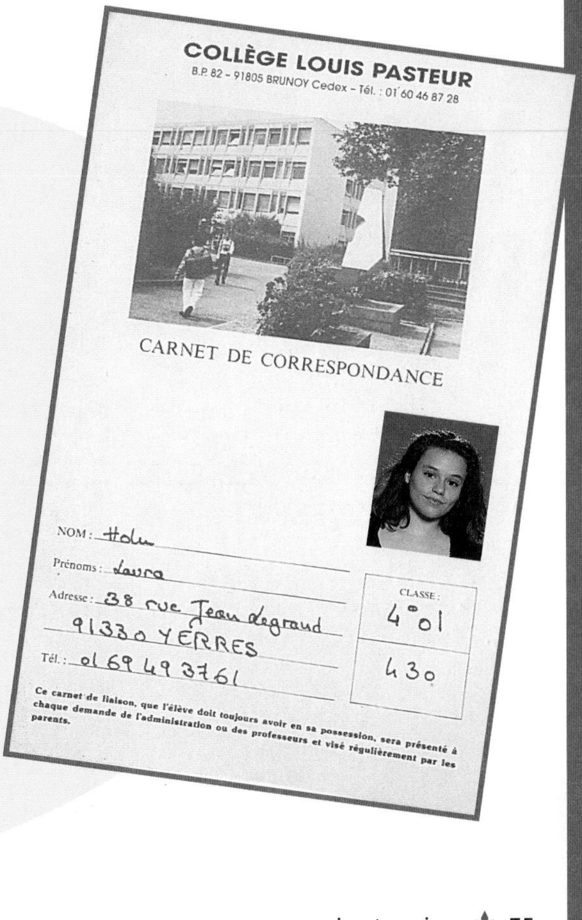

COLLÈGE LOUIS PASTEUR
B.P. 82 – 91805 BRUNOY Cedex – Tél. : 01 60 46 87 28

CARNET DE CORRESPONDANCE

NOM : Holu
Prénoms : Laura
Adresse : 38 rue Jean Legraud
91330 YERRES
Tél. : 01 69 49 37 61

CLASSE : 4°01
430

Ce carnet de liaison, que l'élève doit toujours avoir en sa possession, sera présenté à chaque demande de l'administration ou des professeurs et visé régulièrement par les parents.

ÉCRIRE

4 Les cours et les professeurs

You've been in school for about a month. You've had a chance to get to know what your courses are like and to become familiar with your teachers. Create a journal entry about school. Try to write about your classes, the days and times of each, what the class is like, who the teacher is, and what he or she is like. When you have finished, reread your journal entry. Did you discover anything about your courses or your teachers that you hadn't thought of before?

Assessment

Vocabulaire

To review **Mots 1**, turn to pages 50–51.

1 Choisissez. *(Choose.)*

1. Christophe et Julien sont amis. Ils sont ____.
   a. frères **b.** sœurs **c.** copains
2. Les deux garçons sont ____ dans un lycée français.
   a. élèves **b.** profs **c.** cours
3. Le cours de français n'est pas difficile. Le cours de français est ____.
   a. strict **b.** facile **c.** comique
4. La prof n'est pas très stricte. Juste ____.
   a. difficile **b.** d'accord **c.** un peu

To review **Mots 2**, turn to pages 54–55.

2 Vrai ou faux? *(True or false?)*

5. L'algèbre et la musique sont des sciences naturelles.
6. L'économie est une langue.
7. Pour les élèves américains, l'anglais est un cours obligatoire.
8. L'allemand est une science sociale.

Structure

To review plural articles, nouns, and adjectives, turn to page 58.

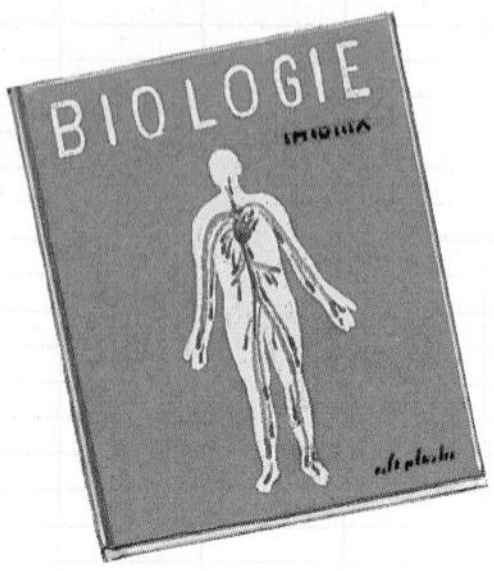

3 Mettez au pluriel. *(Put in the plural.)*

9. Le copain de Lucie est amusant.
   ____ copain__ de Lucie sont amusant__.
10. La sœur de Monique est intelligente.
    ____ sœur__ de Monique sont intelligente__.
11. L'ami de Frédéric est français.
    ____ ami__ de Frédéric sont français__.
12. Le prof de biologie est strict.
    ____ prof__ de biologie sont strict__.
13. La fille brune est américaine.
    ____ fille__ brune__ sont américaine__.

4 Complétez avec «être».
(Complete with être.*)*

14. Nous ____ élèves dans une école secondaire américaine.
15. Ils ____ élèves dans un lycée français.
16. Vous ____ élèves où?
17. Les élèves de Madame Fauvet ____ intelligents.
18. Qui ____ le prof de géométrie?

To review the verb ***être****, turn to page 60.*

Culture

5 Choisissez. *(Choose.)*

19. En Haïti, il y a deux langues—le français et ____.
 a. l'anglais **b.** le créole **c.** l'espagnol
20. Il y a beaucoup d'influence «cajun» en ____.
 a. Nouvelle-Angleterre **b.** Haïti **c.** Louisiane

To review this cultural information, turn to pages 68–69.

La Nouvelle-Orléans, Louisiane

On parle super bien!

Tell all you can about this illustration.

Vocabulaire

Identifying a person or thing

un professeur
un(e) prof
un copain
une copine
un lycée
une salle de classe
un cours
une classe
une matière

Identifying school subjects

les sciences naturelles
- la biologie
- la chimie
- la physique

les mathématiques, les maths *(f. pl.)*
- l'algèbre *(f.)*
- la géométrie
- la trigonométrie
- le calcul

les langues *(f. pl.)*
- le français
- l'espagnol *(m.)*
- l'italien *(m.)*
- l'allemand *(m.)*
- l'anglais *(m.)*
- le latin

les sciences sociales
- l'histoire *(f.)*
- la géographie
- l'économie *(f.)*

d'autres matières
- la littérature
- l'informatique *(f.)*
- la gymnastique
- la musique
- le dessin

Describing teachers, students, and courses

facile
difficile
strict(e)
intéressant(e)
fort(e)
mauvais(e)

Agreeing and disagreeing

Tu es d'accord?
Oui, je suis d'accord.
Non, je ne suis pas d'accord.
C'est vrai.
Ce n'est pas vrai. C'est pas vrai.

Other useful words and expressions

en cours de (français, maths, etc.)
même
tous
trop
juste un peu

How well do you know your vocabulary?

- **Choose your favorite school subject. Choose words to describe this subject.**
- **Use these words to describe the subject and your teacher.**

VIDÉOTOUR

Épisode 2

In this video episode, you will see Vincent at the lycée Louis-le-Grand, interviewing students about their teachers and courses. See page 527 for more information.

CHAPITRE 3

Pendant et après les cours

Objectifs

In this chapter you will learn to:

- *talk about what you do in school*
- *talk about what you and your friends do after school*
- *identify and shop for school supplies*
- *talk about what you don't do*
- *tell what you and others like and don't like to do*
- *discuss schools in France*

Pierre Auguste Renoir *La lecture*

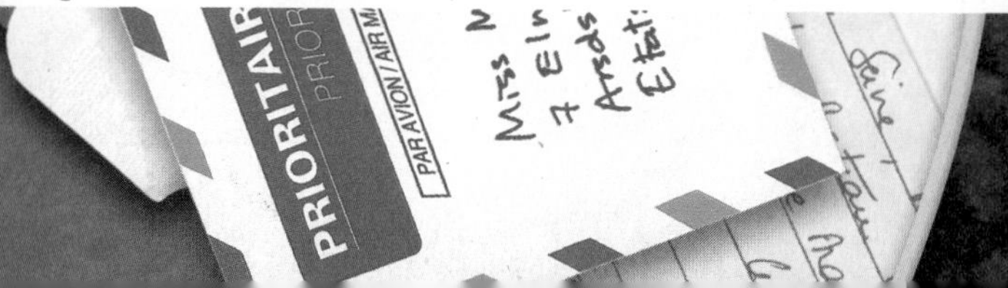

Une journée à l'école

Patrick habite près de Paris.
Il habite rue Saint-Paul.
Patrick quitte la maison.

Le matin, Patrick arrive à l'école.
À quelle heure?
Il arrive à l'école à huit heures.
Il passe la journée à l'école.

Le prof parle.
Les élèves écoutent bien.
Les élèves étudient.

Les élèves regardent une vidéo (un DVD).
Deux élèves écoutent des CD.

Moi, je n'aime pas du tout les examens. Je déteste les examens.
la main

Vincent passe un examen.
Il n'aime pas les examens.

Sophie lève la main.
Elle pose une question.

Note
The expression **passer un examen** is an example of a false cognate **(un faux ami).** It means "to take an exam," not "to pass an exam."

la cantine

Les élèves déjeunent à la cantine.
Ils déjeunent à midi (12 h).

jouer
la cour

Pendant la récré(ation) les élèves jouent dans la cour.
Il y a beaucoup d'élèves dans la cour.
Ils rigolent.
Ils parlent entre les cours.

Note
The popular word **rigoler** means "to joke around." **Tu rigoles!** means "You don't mean it!" or "You're joking!"

Quel est le mot?

1 Historiette Un élève parisien

Inventez une histoire. *(Make up a story.)*

1. Fabien est de Paris?
2. Il habite rue Jacob?
3. Il quitte la maison à quelle heure?
4. Il passe la journée où?
5. Il déjeune à la cantine?

Un lycéen français

2 Toujours des questions Répondez. *(Answer.)*

Le matin, les élèves arrivent à l'école à huit heures.

1. Qui arrive à l'école?
2. Ils arrivent où?
3. Ils arrivent à quelle heure?
4. Ils arrivent à l'école le matin ou à midi?

Les élèves déjeunent à la cantine à midi.

5. Qui déjeune?
6. Les élèves déjeunent où?
7. Ils déjeunent à la cantine à quelle heure?

3 Historiette En classe Complétez. *(Complete.)*

En classe la prof __1__ et les élèves __2__. Anne est une élève excellente. Elle __3__ beaucoup. Sophie est dans la même classe. Elle __4__ la main et __5__ une question.

Vincent __6__ un examen. Les examens sont difficiles. Vincent n'__7__ pas les examens. Il __8__ les examens.

4 **Pardon!** Préparez une petite conversation d'après le modèle. *(Prepare a short conversation according to the model.)*

Sandrine regarde un DVD.
Pardon? Qu'est-ce qu'elle regarde?

1. Sandrine regarde une vidéo.
2. Sandrine écoute un CD.
3. Sandrine lève la main.
4. Sandrine pose une question.
5. Sandrine passe un examen.
6. Sandrine adore les vidéos.

5 **Historiette** **Dans la cour** Répondez. *(Answer.)*

1. Les élèves sont dans la cour?
2. Ils sont dans la cour pendant la récréation?
3. Ils parlent entre les cours?
4. Ils jouent où?
5. Ils rigolent avec les copains?
6. Ils déjeunent dans la cour?

6 **En classe** With a classmate, look at the illustration. Take turns saying as much as you can about it.

ENCORE PLUS

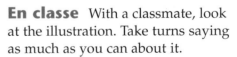

For more practice using words from* Mots 1, *do Activity 7 on page H8 at the end of this book.

Des fournitures scolaires

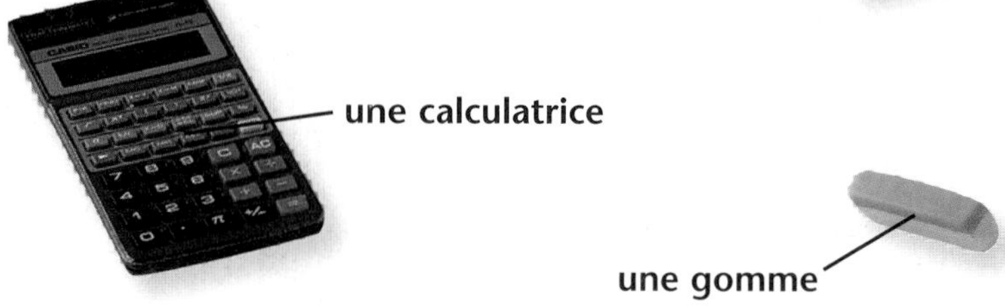

Qu'est-ce que c'est?
C'est un cahier.

Après les cours

Le sac à dos, c'est combien, s'il vous plaît?
Vingt dollars cinquante.
la caisse
payer
un magasin

Lucette travaille après les cours.
Elle travaille dans une papeterie.
Combien d'heures par semaine?
Dix heures.

Sylvain regarde un sac à dos.
Il demande combien coûte le sac à dos.
Il achète le sac à dos.
Il paie à la caisse.

Les nombres de 100 à 1 000

100	cent	400	quatre cents
101	cent un	500	cinq cents
102	cent deux	600	six cents
200	deux cents	700	sept cents
220	deux cent vingt	800	huit cents
300	trois cents	900	neuf cents
350	trois cent cinquante	1 000	mille

Après les cours, Patrick ne travaille pas.
Il rentre à la maison l'après-midi.
Il rentre chez lui.

Il écoute la radio.
Il parle un peu au téléphone.

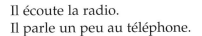

Quel est le mot?

7 **Des fournitures scolaires** Préparez une liste de fournitures scolaires. *(Make a list of school supplies.)*

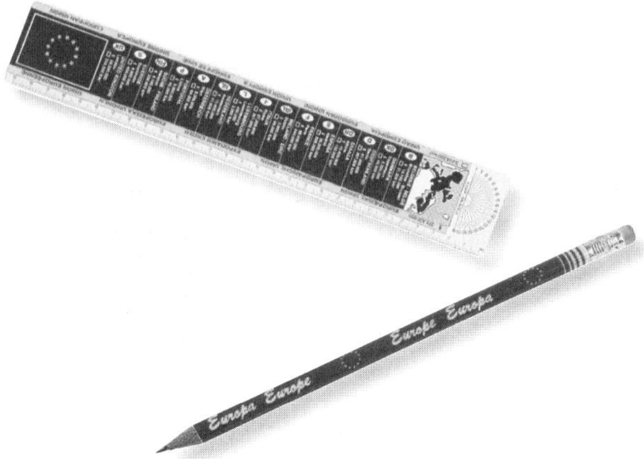

8 **Historiette Loïc est français.**
Répondez d'après l'indication.
(Answer according to the cues.)

1. Loïc est français ou américain? (français)
2. Il habite où? (près de Paris)
3. Il travaille après les cours? (non)
4. Il rentre chez lui après les cours? (oui)
5. Qu'est-ce qu'il écoute? (la radio)
6. Qu'est-ce qu'il regarde? (une vidéo)
7. Il parle au téléphone? (oui)
8. Avec qui? (les copains)

Une papeterie, Montréal, Canada

9 **Historiette Dans une papeterie** Inventez une histoire. *(Make up a story.)*

1. Catherine est canadienne?
2. Elle travaille après les cours?
3. Elle travaille combien d'heures par semaine?
4. Elle travaille dans une papeterie?
5. Où est la papeterie?
6. Qu'est-ce qu'il y a dans une papeterie?
7. Il y a beaucoup d'élèves dans la papeterie?
8. Un garçon paie à la caisse?
9. Un cahier coûte combien?

10 **Historiette** **À la papeterie** Choisissez la bonne réponse. *(Choose the correct completion.)*

1. Sandrine ____ dans une papeterie.
   a. étudie **b.** habite **c.** travaille
2. Elle ____ à un client au téléphone.
   a. écoute **b.** parle **c.** paie
3. Les élèves ____ des fournitures scolaires dans la papeterie.
   a. travaillent **b.** rentrent **c.** regardent
4. Un garçon ____ un cahier.
   a. regarde **b.** joue **c.** rentre
5. Il ____ une calculatrice pour le cours de maths.
   a. passe **b.** quitte **c.** achète
6. La calculatrice ____ six dollars canadiens.
   a. paie **b.** habite **c.** coûte
7. Le garçon ____ à la caisse.
   a. quitte **b.** coûte **c.** paie

11 **Pour la rentrée des classes** Work with a classmate. It's back-to-school time and you're buying the school supplies below. Take turns being the customer and the salesperson.

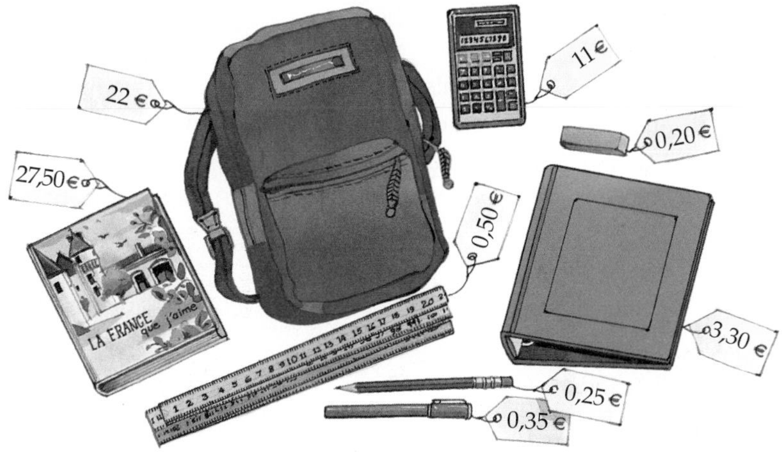

12 **Jeu** **Qu'est-ce que c'est?** Work with a classmate. Have your partner close his or her eyes. Hand your partner a school supply. Have your partner guess what it is. Take turns.

ENCORE PLUS *For more practice using words from **Mots 2**, do Activity 8 on page H9 at the end of this book.*

Structure

Les verbes réguliers en -er au présent
Talking about people's activities

1. A word that expresses an action or a state is a verb. **Parler** (*to speak*), **écouter** (*to listen to*), and **aimer** (*to like*) are verbs in the infinitive form. They are called regular verbs because they all follow a regular pattern. Their infinitives end in **-er.**

2. French verbs change endings with each subject. To form the stem to which the endings are added, you drop the **-er** from the infinitive.

Infinitive	Stem
parler	parl-
écouter	écout-
aimer	aim-

3. You add the ending for each subject to the stem. Note that, although the endings for the **je, tu, il,** and **ils** forms are spelled differently, they are pronounced the same.

			PARLER		AIMER	
je	parl	-e	je	parle	j'	aime
tu	parl	-es	tu	parles	tu	aimes
il/elle	parl	-e	il/elle	parle	il/elle	aime
nous	parl	-ons	nous	parlons	nous$_{z}$	aimons
vous	parl	-ez	vous	parlez	vous$_{z}$	aimez
ils/elles	parl	-ent	ils/elles	parlent	ils$_{z}$/elles$_{z}$	aiment

4. You will see and hear the word **on** a great deal. **On** has several meanings, such as "we," "they," and "people." **On** always takes the **il/elle** form of the verb. In spoken French, people use **on** more often than **nous.**

   On parle français en France.
   On travaille beaucoup.
   On$_{n}$arrive à l'école le matin.

Attention!

There is elision when **je** or **ne** is followed by a verb that begins with a vowel or silent **h.**

J'habite à Paris. **Je n'habite pas à Lyon.**
J'aime les maths. **Je n'aime pas les sciences.**

There is a liaison with all plural subject pronouns and a verb that begins with a vowel or silent **h.** The **s** on the pronoun is pronounced as a **z.**

nous$_{z}$étudions **vous$_{z}$aimez** **ils$_{z}$habitent**

Comment dit-on?

Bonjour !
LA CARTE DE FRANCE

Un cours de français aux États-Unis

13 **Historiette Un Américain**
Inventez une histoire. *(Make up a story.)*

1. Kevin est français ou américain?
2. Il habite à Paris ou à Chicago?
3. Il parle anglais ou français?
4. Il étudie quelle langue?
5. Il parle beaucoup en classe?
6. Il travaille bien à l'école?

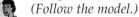

14 **Historiette Les élèves ou les profs?** Suivez le modèle. *(Follow the model.)*

—Qui arrive à l'école le matin?
—Les élèves et les profs arrivent à l'école.

1. Qui parle en classe?
2. Qui écoute quand le prof parle?
3. Qui écoute des cassettes?
4. Qui passe des examens?
5. Qui étudie beaucoup?
6. Qui lève la main?
7. Qui pose des questions?
8. Qui rigole dans la cour?

15 **Aux États-Unis** Un(e) élève français(e) pose des questions à un(e) élève américain(e). *(You are a French student. Ask a classmate about life in the United States.)*

On arrive à l'école à quelle heure?
On arrive à l'école à huit heures.

1. On arrive à l'école à quelle heure?
2. On quitte l'école à quelle heure?
3. On travaille beaucoup à l'école?
4. On aime beaucoup les examens?
5. On travaille après les cours?
6. On écoute des CD?
7. On regarde la télé?
8. On parle au téléphone?

16 **Tu parles français?** Répétez la conversation. *(Repeat the conversation.)*

Sue: Tu n'es pas français, toi?
Luc: Non, je ne suis pas français.
Sue: Mais tu parles français!
Luc: Bien sûr que je parle français.
Sue: Et comment ça, si tu n'es pas français?
Luc: Mais je suis belge.
Sue: Ah, c'est vrai. On parle français en Belgique.

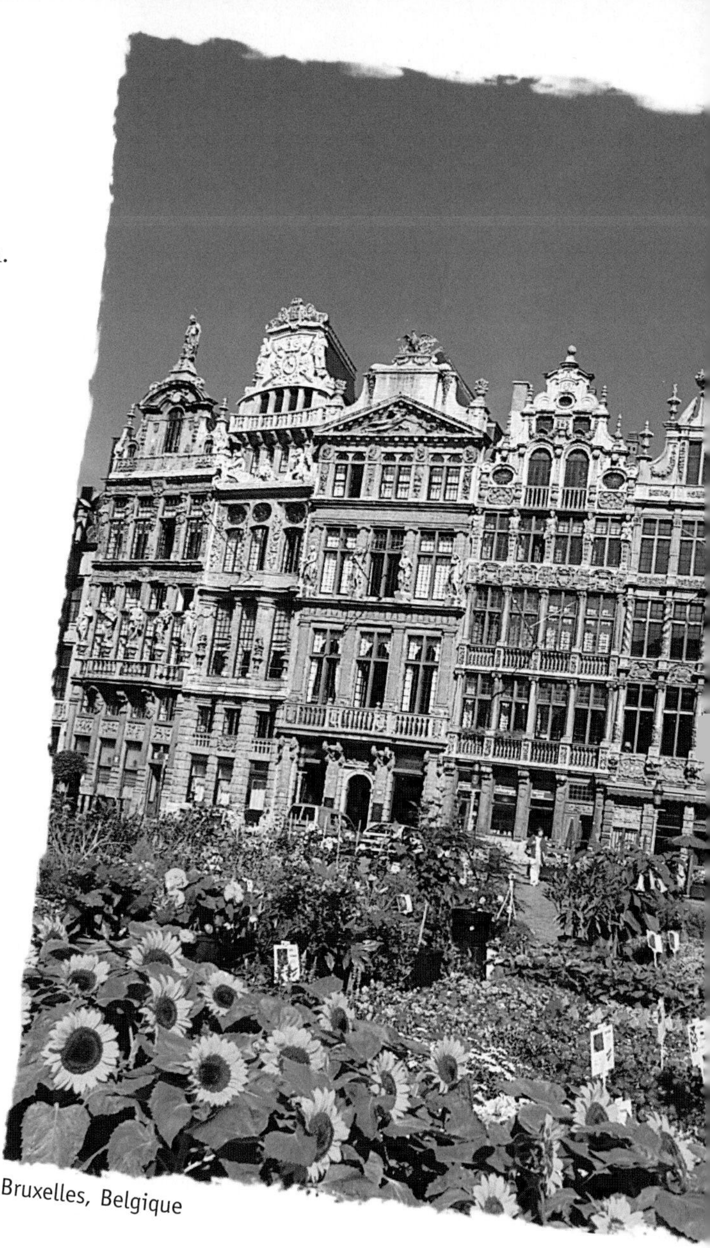

Bruxelles, Belgique

17 **Historiette** **À votre tour!** Donnez des réponses personnelles. *(Give your own answers.)*

1. Tu habites dans quelle ville?
2. Tu quittes la maison à quelle heure le matin?
3. Tu arrives à l'école à quelle heure?
4. Est-ce que tu parles français avec les copains?
5. Tu aimes quelles matières?
6. Tu aimes quels profs?
7. Tu détestes quelles matières?
8. Tu travailles après les cours?
9. Tu parles beaucoup avec les copains au téléphone?
10. Tu regardes la télé?

18 **Pardon?** Posez des questions d'après le modèle. *(Ask questions according to the model.)*

Nous écoutons des CD.
Pardon? Qu'est-ce que vous écoutez?

1. Nous détestons les examens.
2. Nous regardons la télé.
3. Nous regardons des magazines.
4. Nous écoutons la radio.
5. Nous aimons l'école.
6. Nous étudions l'espagnol.

19 **Nous tous** Donnez des réponses personnelles en utilisant **nous.** (*Give answers about you and your classmates. Use* nous.)

1. Vous arrivez à l'école à quelle heure le matin?
2. Vous quittez l'école à quelle heure l'après-midi?
3. Vous passez combien d'heures à l'école?
4. Vous aimez les cours?
5. Vous écoutez bien quand le professeur parle en classe?
6. Vous aimez ou vous détestez les examens?

20 **Historiette** **À l'école** Complétez. (*Complete.*)

Nous __1__ (arriver) à l'école à sept heures et demie. Et vous, vous __2__ (arriver) à quelle heure? Avant les cours, j'__3__ (aimer) parler un peu avec les copains. On __4__ (rigoler). Mais en classe, non! On __5__ (travailler) beaucoup. Moi, j'__6__ (écouter) bien quand les profs __7__ (parler). Et toi, tu __8__ (travailler) beaucoup aussi? Tu __9__ (passer) des examens? Tu __10__ (aimer) les examens ou pas?

21 **Une journée typique** Work with a classmate. Tell each other about a typical school day. Find out what activities you have in common.

22 **Tu travailles ou pas?** Get together in small groups and find out who works after school in your group. Find out where, how many hours a week, etc. Here are some words you may want to use.

un restaurant
un fast-food
une station-service
un magasin
un supermarché

ENCORE PLUS *For more practice using -**er** verbs in the present, do Activity 9 on page H10 at the end of this book.*

La négation des articles indéfinis
Talking about what you don't do

In the negative, the indefinite articles **un, une,** and **des** change to **de** (or **d'**).

Affirmatif	Négatif
Julie regarde un CD.	Éric ne regarde pas de CD.
Julie regarde une vidéo.	Éric ne regarde pas de vidéo.
Julie regarde des photos.	Éric ne regarde pas de photos.

Attention!

Note the elision with **de.**
Je suis content: pas d'examen aujourd'hui!

Comment dit-on?

23 **En classe** Répondez que non. *(Answer with* non.*)*

1. Tu écoutes un CD?
2. Tu regardes une vidéo?
3. Tu poses des questions?
4. Tu écoutes des cassettes?
5. Tu passes un examen aujourd'hui?

24 **Historiette Dans une papeterie**
Répondez d'après les indications. *(Answer according to the cues.)*

1. René est dans une papeterie? (oui)
2. Il regarde un feutre et un cahier? (oui)
3. Il achète un stylo-bille? (non)
4. Il achète un feutre? (oui)
5. Il achète un DVD? (non)
6. Il achète une vidéo? (oui)

25 **J'achète ou je n'achète pas.** Work with a classmate. Take turns telling what you buy or don't buy.

Verbe + infinitif
Discussing likes and dislikes

1. In French when the verbs **aimer, adorer,** and **détester** are followed by another verb, the second verb is in the infinitive form.

   Il aime rigoler.
   J'adore écouter la radio.
   On déteste travailler.

2. In a negative sentence, the **ne... pas** goes around the first verb.

   Vous n'aimez pas travailler?

Comment dit-on?

26 **Tu aimes travailler?** Posez les questions suivantes à un copain ou une copine. *(Ask a classmate the following questions.)*

—Tu aimes travailler?
—Bien sûr. J'aime beaucoup travailler./ Non, pas du tout. Je déteste travailler.

1. Tu aimes regarder la télé?
2. Tu aimes écouter la musique?
3. Tu aimes étudier?
4. Tu aimes rigoler?
5. Tu aimes parler au téléphone?

27 **On aime ou on n'aime pas!** Work with a classmate. Tell some things you like and don't like to do.

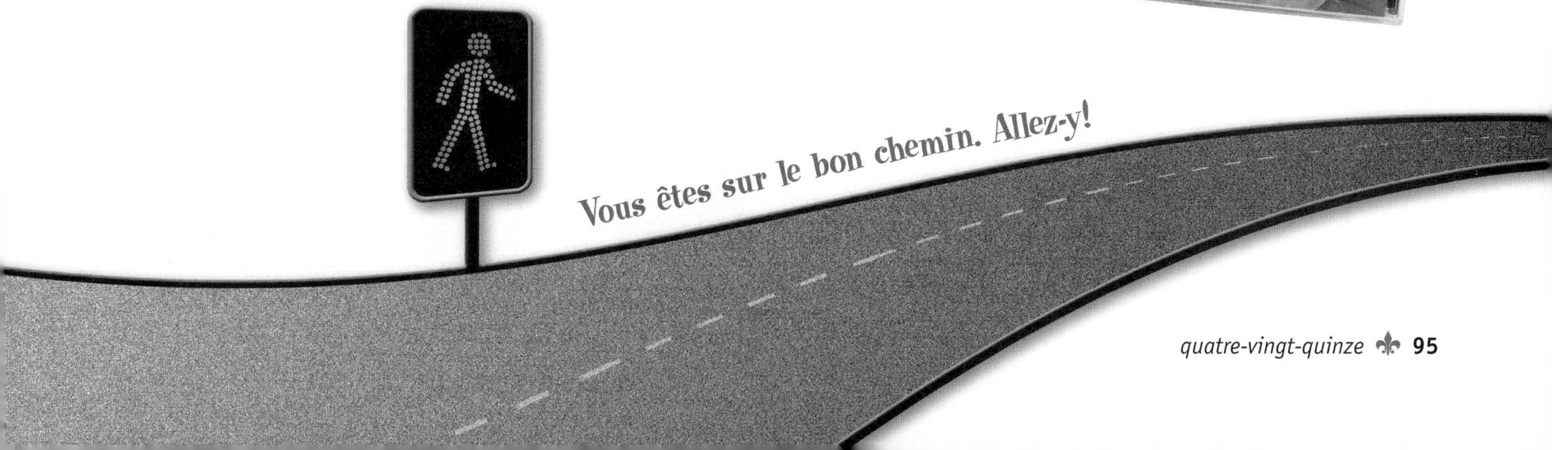

Conversation

Un élève français aux États-Unis

Carol: En France, tu arrives à quelle heure à l'école le matin?
Cédric: Moi, j'arrive à l'école vers sept heures et demie.
Carol: Et les cours commencent à quelle heure?
Cédric: À huit heures. J'aime parler un peu avec les copains avant la classe.
Carol: Et tu quittes l'école à trois heures?
Cédric: À trois heures! Tu rigoles! En France on quitte l'école à cinq heures.
Carol: À cinq heures! C'est pas vrai!
Cédric: Si, c'est vrai.

Vous avez compris?

Répondez. *(Answer.)*

1. En France, Cédric arrive à l'école à quelle heure?
2. Cédric parle avec une amie américaine ou française?
3. Les cours de Cédric commencent à quelle heure?
4. Cédric quitte l'école à quelle heure?
5. Et Carol, elle quitte l'école à quelle heure?

Parlons un peu plus

A **Comparaisons** With a classmate, look at the illustrations. Then compare your own daily school habits with those of the students in the illustrations.

1. 
2. 

3. 
4. 
5. 

B **Jeu** **Les nombres** Give some numbers in a mathematical pattern but leave one out. Your partner will guess what the missing number is. Take turns. Use the model as a guide.

—deux cents, quatre cents, ____, huit cents
—six cents

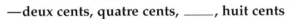

Prononciation

Les sons /é/ et /è/

élève

1. There is an important difference in the way French and English vowels are pronounced. When you say the French word **des,** your mouth is tense, in one position. You can repeat the sound **/é/** many times without moving your mouth at all. But when you pronounce the English word *day,* your mouth is relaxed and you actually say two vowel sounds.
2. Listen to the word **élève.** It has two distinct vowel sounds. The sound **/é/** is "closed" and the sound **/è/** is "open." This describes the positions of the mouth for each sound. Repeat the following.

Le son /é/:	**la télé**	**l'école**	**la journée**	**parler**	**écoutez**
Le son /è/:	**après**	**la cassette**	**vous êtes**	**le collège**	

Après l'école, les élèves aiment écouter des cassettes.
Elles aiment regarder la télé.

Le Québec

Lectures culturelles

Reading Strategy

Using pictures and photographs

Before you begin to read, look at the pictures, photographs, or any other visuals that accompany a reading. By doing this, you can often tell what the reading selection is about before you actually read it.

Une journée avec Jacqueline

Jacqueline est une élève française. Elle habite rue Jacob à Paris. La rue Jacob est dans le Quartier latin, tout près de[1] la Sorbonne. La Sorbonne est une université célèbre[2] à Paris. Le Quartier latin est un quartier très fréquenté par les étudiants d'université et les lycéens.

[1] tout près de *very near*
[2] célèbre *famous*

Une librairie, boulevard Saint-Michel, Paris

La Sorbonne, Paris

La Polynésie française

Tahiti

Haïti

La Martinique

La France

La Suisse

La Belgique

Jacqueline est élève au lycée Louis-le-Grand. Le matin, elle quitte la maison à sept heures et demie. Les cours commencent à huit heures. Jacqueline passe la journée au lycée. Comme tous[3] les lycéens, Jacqueline travaille beaucoup, à Louis-le-Grand et à la maison. À la récréation, Jacqueline retrouve[4] des copains dans la cour. Ils parlent et ils rigolent un peu. À midi, ils déjeunent à la cantine. Ils ne rentrent pas à la maison pour déjeuner.

Jacqueline quitte le lycée à cinq heures de l'après-midi. Et vous, vous quittez l'école à quelle heure?

[3] Comme tous *Like all*
[4] retrouve *meets, gets together with*

Lycée Louis-le-Grand, Paris

18 kins Louis's
Louis IX Saint

La Tunisie

Le Maroc

Vous avez compris?

A Une élève française Répondez. *(Answer.)*

1. Qui est Jacqueline?
2. Elle habite où?
3. Jacqueline quitte la maison à quelle heure?
4. Les cours commencent à quelle heure?
5. Elle retrouve des copains où?
6. À midi, elle rentre chez elle pour déjeuner?
7. Elle déjeune avec qui?
8. Elle quitte le lycée à quelle heure?

B Paris Trouvez les informations dans la lecture. *(Find the information in the reading.)*

1. la rue où Jacqueline habite
2. le nom d'une université célèbre à Paris
3. un quartier de Paris fréquenté par les étudiants et les lycéens
4. le nom du lycée de Jacqueline

Le Mali

Le Sénégal

Lecture supplémentaire 1

Qui travaille?

Antoine est canadien. Il est québécois. Il est de Montréal, la deuxième ville francophone du monde après Paris. Après les cours, il travaille dans une papeterie pour gagner un peu d'argent[1]. Il travaille dix heures par semaine. La papeterie où il travaille est dans le centre commercial[2] «Place de la Cathédrale». C'est un très grand centre commercial souterrain[3].

Le centre commercial «Place de la Cathédrale»

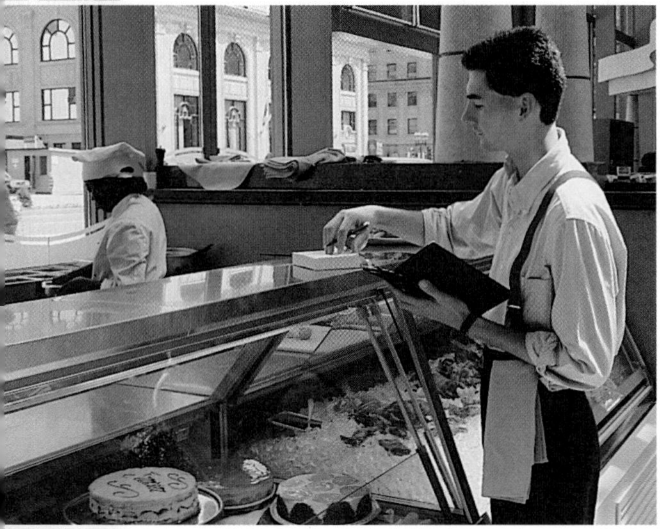

Un restaurant fast-food, Montréal

Aux États-Unis et au Québec aussi, un grand nombre d'élèves travaillent après les cours. Ils travaillent dans un magasin, dans un supermarché ou dans un restaurant fast-food (de restauration rapide). Ils gagnent de l'argent pour acheter des CD, des cassettes, un blue jean. En France, non. Très peu de collégiens ou de lycéens travaillent après les cours. C'est assez rare. Certains travaillent, mais seulement pendant les vacances. Mais… ils sont à l'école jusqu'à cinq heures de l'après-midi!

[1] gagner un peu d'argent *to earn a little money*
[2] centre commercial *mall*
[3] souterrain *underground*

Vous avez compris?

Au Québec Exprimez d'une autre façon. *(Express another way.)*

1. Antoine est *du Canada.*
2. Montréal est la *seconde* ville francophone du monde.
3. Antoine travaille après *l'école.*
4. C'est un *immense* centre commercial.
5. Aux États-Unis, *beaucoup* d'élèves travaillent.
6. *Pas beaucoup* de lycéens français travaillent après les cours.

GRAFFITI
RESTO·CITÉ
• Situé au cœur de la ville et de la vie des gens de Québec
• Fine cuisine du marché italo-française
• Déjeuner-dîner le dimanche
• Décor chaleureux, verrière et salon privé
• Stationnement

Lecture supplémentaire 2

Un groupe de rap–Manau

Quand les collégiens ou les lycéens français rentrent à la maison l'après-midi, qu'est-ce qu'ils écoutent? Eh bien, ils écoutent la même musique que les élèves américains. Ils écoutent du rap, par exemple.

Manau, c'est un groupe de rap très populaire chez les collégiens français. Et Manau n'est pas un groupe de rap ordinaire. C'est un groupe de rap «celtique». Les instruments de musique sont la cornemuse[1], le violon, la harpe… Les chansons[2] de Manau parlent de mythes et légendes celtes avec des druides et des dolmens.

Les deux garçons du groupe, Cédric et Martial, sont copains. Le musicien, c'est Cédric: Cédric est le compositeur de la musique. Et le texte, c'est Martial: Martial est l'auteur des paroles[3].

Les deux garçons sont de la région parisienne. Mais les mères[4] de Cédric et Martial sont de Bretagne. Comme beaucoup de Bretons, elles sont d'origine celtique. Le nom du premier[5] album de Manau? *Panique Celtique!*

[1] cornemuse *bagpipes*
[2] chansons *songs*
[3] paroles *words*
[4] mères *mothers*
[5] premier *first*

FRENCH Online

For more information about music in the Francophone world, go to the Glencoe French Web site: french.glencoe.com

Un dolmen près de Carnac, Bretagne

Vous avez compris?

Un groupe de rap Vrai ou faux? *(True or false?)*

1. Les collégiens français n'écoutent pas la même musique que les élèves américains.
2. Manau, c'est un groupe de rap ordinaire.
3. Les chansons de Manau parlent de l'école.
4. Cédric et Martial sont de Bretagne.

La Belgique

La Tunisie

Le Maroc

Le Mali

CONNEXIONS

La technologie

L'ordinateur

Some years ago computers began to revolutionize the way people conduct their lives. They have changed the way we view the world. Computers have a place in our homes, in our schools, and in the world of business.

If you are interested in computers, you may want to familiarize yourself with some basic computer vocabulary in French. Then read the information about computers on the next page.

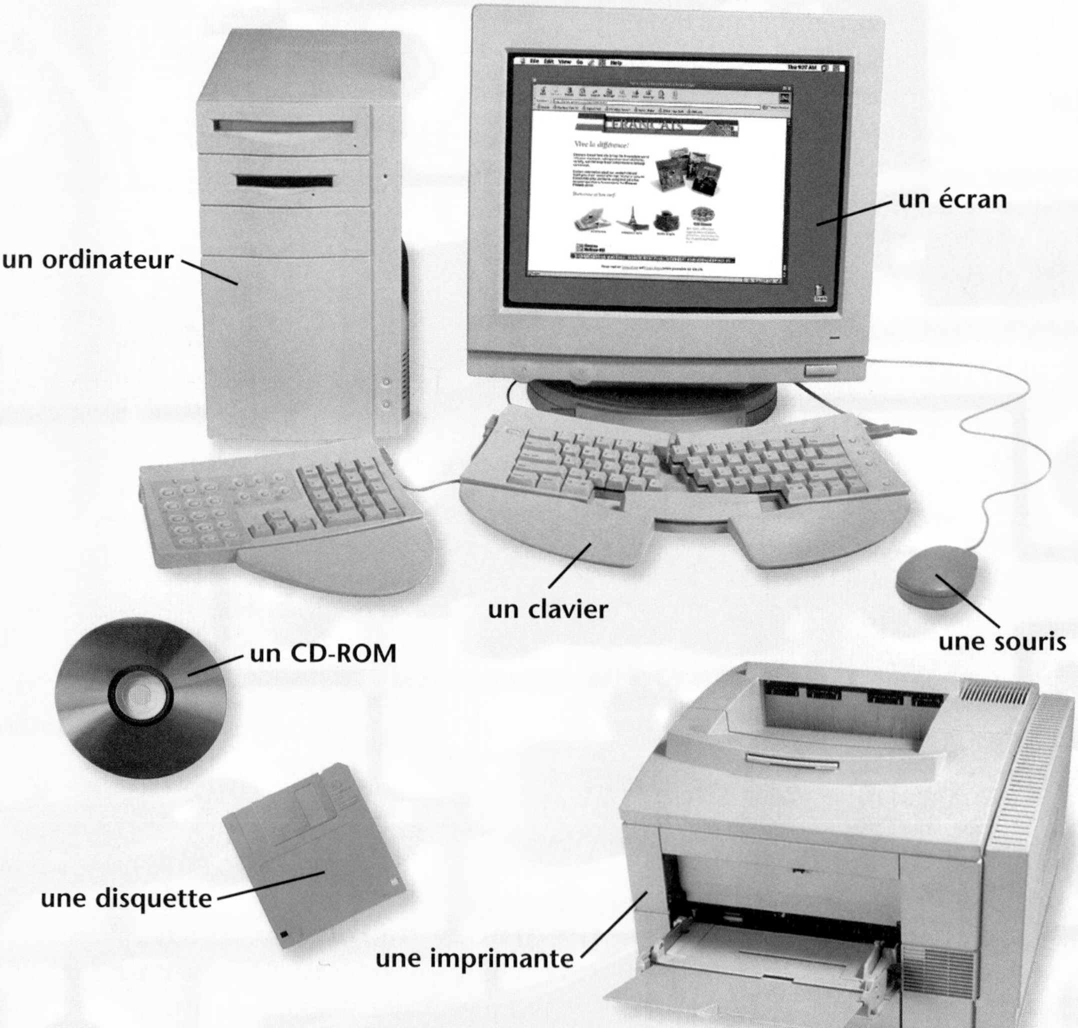

L'ordinateur travaille!

Le hardware et le software

Un ordinateur exécute très rapidement les instructions d'un programme. Le hardware, c'est la partie électronique de l'ordinateur. Le software, c'est la partie programmation de l'ordinateur. Les logiciels sont des programmes. Un programme ou un logiciel est un groupe d'instructions. Un document est un fichier. L'ordinateur stocke des données[1]. On sauvegarde les documents importants sur une disquette ou un CD.

Internet

Quand on est connecté à Internet par cable ou satellite, la connexion est pratiquement instantanée. Les satellites transmettent l'information vingt fois plus vite que le modem. Et l'ADSL transmet l'information de cinquante à cent cinquante fois plus vite que le modem. De jour en jour, grâce aux progrès de la technologie, les communications deviennent[2] plus faciles et plus rapides. C'est un fait, le monde[3] entier est connecté! Le nombre des sites est infini. On télécharge[4] des informations sur l'histoire, l'économie, l'art, la musique et toutes sortes de domaines intéressants. Quand on navigue sur Internet, on est capable d'envoyer[5] un e-mail, parler avec des amis sur d'autres continents… Il n'y a pas de limites!

[1] données *data*
[2] deviennent *become*
[3] monde *world*
[4] télécharge *download*
[5] envoyer *to send*

Vous avez compris?

A En français, s'il vous plaît. Trouvez les mots suivants dans la lecture. *(Find the following words in the reading.)*

1. hardware
2. software
3. program
4. file
5. modem
6. surf the net
7. e-mail
8. connection
9. site
10. save

B Une page Web Look at the monitor on page 102. If you have access to the Internet either at home or at school, go to french.glencoe.com

C'est à vous

Use what you have learned

PARLER

1 Dans une papeterie

✔ Identify and shop for school supplies

With a classmate, take turns playing the parts of a student and a salesperson in a stationery store. Here are a few exchanges you may want to use.

—Où sont les ______, s'il vous plaît?
—Là-bas.
—Merci.
—______, c'est combien?
—______ euros.
—On paie à la caisse?
—Non, ici.

Une papeterie, Évry, France

PARLER

2

Au café

✔ Talk about school life in the United States

You're seated at a café in Provins. You're chatting with a French student (your partner). He or she has some questions about school life in the United States. Have a conversation. Be sure to answer his or her questions.

Un café, Provins, France

ÉCRIRE

3

Une journée typique

✔ Write about a typical school day

You can now go back to the e-mail you sent your new friend on page 75 and add more details about what a typical school day is like in the United States.

Writing Strategy

Preparing for an interview An interview is one way to gather information for a story or a report. A good interviewer should think about what he or she hopes to learn from the interview and prepare the questions ahead of time. The interview questions should be open-ended. Open-ended questions cannot be answered by "yes" or "no." They give the person being interviewed more opportunity to "open up" and speak freely.

PARLER

4

ÉCRIRE

Interview avec Charles Bauchart

Your first assignment for the school newspaper is to write an article about a new exchange student, Charles Bauchart, from Fort-de-France in Martinique. To prepare for your interview with him, write down as many questions as you can. Ask him about himself, his school, and his friends in Martinique. After you have prepared your questions, conduct the interview with a partner who plays the role of Charles. Write down your partner's answers. Then organize your notes and write your article.

Vocabulaire

To review **Mots 1**, turn to pages 82–83.

1 Choisissez. *(Choose.)*

1. Sandrine ____ la maison à sept heures et demie.
   a. quitte **b.** arrive **c.** habite
2. Les élèves passent ____ à l'école.
   a. la cantine **b.** la prof **c.** la journée
3. Leïla pose une ____.
   a. rue **b.** question **c.** maison
4. Vincent ____ des cassettes.
   a. écoute **b.** quitte **c.** passe
5. Le prof ____ et les élèves écoutent bien.
   a. travaille **b.** regarde **c.** parle

To review **Mots 2**, turn to pages 86–87.

2 Identifiez. *(Identify.)*

6. 

7. 

8. 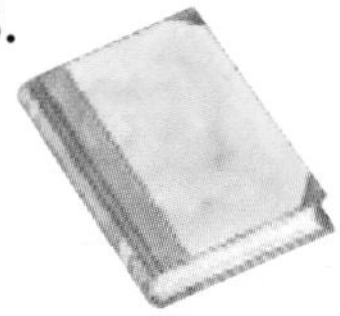

9. 

10. 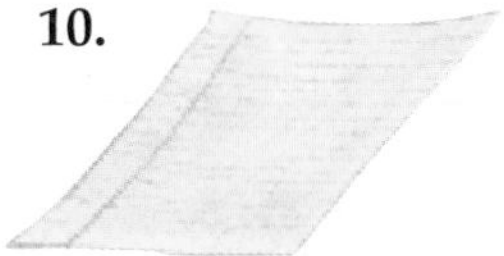

Structure

To review **-er** verbs in the present tense, turn to page 90.

3 Complétez. *(Complete.)*

11. Les élèves ____ à l'école le matin. (arriver)
12. Nous ____ entre les cours. (parler)
13. Je ____ à la cantine avec les copains. (déjeuner)
14. Luc ____ la télé après les cours. (regarder)
15. Tu ____ beaucoup à la maison? (travailler)
16. On ____ français en France. (parler)

4 Mettez à la forme négative.

(Make each sentence negative.)

17. Sandrine achète un crayon à la papeterie.
18. Elle regarde une calculatrice.
19. Ils achètent des livres.
20. Les élèves passent un examen aujourd'hui.

To review indefinite articles in the negative, turn to page 94.

5 Choisissez. *(Choose.)*

21. On aime ____ la télé.
    a. regardent **b.** regarder **c.** regarde
22. Je déteste ____.
    a. travailler **b.** travaille **c.** travaillons

To review the use of verbs with infinitives, turn to page 95.

Culture

6 Vrai ou faux? *(True or false?)*

Une rue du Quartier latin, Paris

To review this cultural information, turn to pages 98–99.

23. La Sorbonne est une université célèbre à Paris.
24. La Sorbonne est dans le Quartier latin.
25. En France, les élèves quittent le lycée à trois heures de l'après-midi.

On parle super bien!

Tell all you can about this illustration.

Vocabulaire

Getting to school

une maison
une rue
quitter
habiter
arriver

Discussing classroom activities

passer la journée
parler
écouter
regarder
étudier
lever la main
poser une question
passer un examen

How well do you know your vocabulary?

- Identify the words and expressions that describe what you do at school and after school. Make two lists.
- Use as many words as you can from one of your lists to write a story about either your school activities or what you do after school.

Discussing recess and lunch activities

la récré(ation)
la cour
la cantine
jouer
rigoler
déjeuner

Discussing afterschool activities

rentrer à la maison
écouter la radio
parler au téléphone
travailler

Identifying school supplies

Qu'est-ce que c'est?
des fournitures *(f. pl.)* scolaires
un cahier
un bloc-notes
un crayon
un stylo-bille
un feutre
une gomme
une règle
un livre
un classeur
une calculatrice
une feuille de papier
un sac à dos
une cassette
une vidéo, un DVD
un CD

Shopping for school supplies

un magasin
une papeterie
la caisse
acheter
payer
demander
coûter
C'est combien?
Ça coûte combien?

Other useful words and expressions

aimer
détester
après
pendant
entre
chez
le matin
l'après-midi
À quelle heure?
combien de (d')
beaucoup de (d')

VIDÉOTOUR

Épisode 3

In this video episode, you will join Amadou and Christine after school. See page 528 for more information.

CHAPITRE 4

La famille et la maison

Objectifs

In this chapter you will learn to:

- *talk about your family*
- *describe your home and neighborhood*
- *tell your age and find out someone else's age*
- *tell what belongs to you and others*
- *describe more people and things*
- *talk about families and homes in French-speaking countries*

Pierre Auguste Renoir *Madame Charpentier et ses enfants*

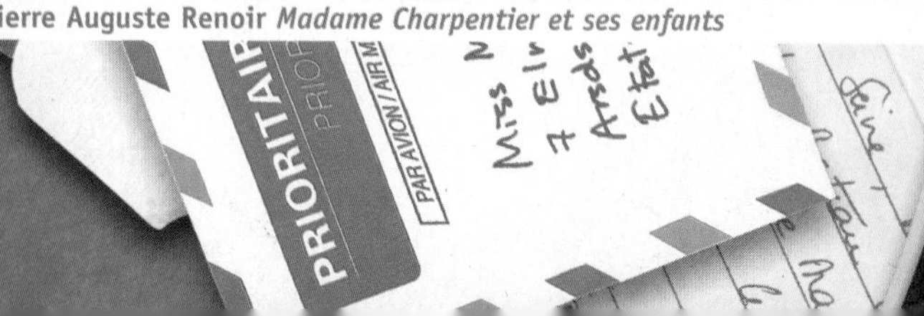

Vocabulaire

Mots 1

Médor

le chien

Voici la famille Morel.
M. et Mme Morel ont deux enfants—un fils et une fille.
Les Morel ont un chien.
Leur chien est adorable.
La famille Morel n'a pas de chat.

Lucie

le chat

L'anniversaire de Marie

Tu as quel âge, Marie?
un cadeau
un gâteau
une bougie
Moi? J'ai quinze ans. Aujourd'hui, c'est mon anniversaire.

C'est quand, l'anniversaire de Marie?
C'est le deux août.
Tout le monde a un cadeau pour Marie.
Il y a beaucoup de cadeaux.

Marie donne une fête pour son anniversaire. Elle invite ses amis et ses cousins.

Note

In French, some of the words for family members are cognates. Can you guess who these family members are?

une tante **un oncle**
une cousine **un cousin**
une nièce **un neveu**

Here are some words for other family members.

une belle-mère *stepmother*
un beau-père *stepfather*
une demi-sœur *half sister*
un demi-frère *half brother*

Quel est le mot?

Marie et Blaise Senghor habitent à Paris.

1 Historiette La famille Senghor

Inventez une histoire. *(Make up a story.)*

1. Madame Senghor est la femme de Monsieur Senghor?
2. Monsieur Senghor est le mari de Madame Senghor?
3. La famille Senghor est française?
4. M. et Mme Senghor ont deux enfants? Ils ont un fils et une fille?
5. Les enfants ont quel âge?
6. Quelle est la date de l'anniversaire de la fille?
7. Il y a combien de personnes dans la famille Senghor?
8. Les Senghor ont un chien ou un chat?

2 Historiette L'anniversaire de Francine

Répondez d'après les indications. *(Answer according to the cues.)*

1. Elle a quel âge, Francine? (quinze ans)
2. C'est quand, son anniversaire? (aujourd'hui)
3. Quelle est la date aujourd'hui? (le deux août)
4. Qu'est-ce que Francine donne pour son anniversaire? (une fête)
5. Elle invite qui à la fête? (ses amis et ses cousins)
6. Qu'est-ce que tout le monde a pour Francine? (beaucoup de cadeaux)
7. Il y a un gâteau pour Francine? (oui)
8. Le gâteau a des bougies? (oui, quinze)

3 La famille

Complétez. *(Complete.)*

1. Le frère de mon père est mon ____.
2. La sœur de mon père est ma ____.
3. Le frère de ma mère est mon ____.
4. La sœur de ma mère est ma ____.
5. Le fils de mon oncle et de ma tante est mon ____.
6. La fille de mon oncle et de ma tante est ma ____.
7. Le père de ma mère est mon ____.
8. Et la mère de mon père est ma ____.

Ma grand-mère habite à Paris.

4 **Moi** Choisissez la bonne réponse. *(Choose the correct answer.)*

1. Moi, je suis ____ de mes grands-parents.
   a. le petit-fils **b.** la petite-fille
2. Je suis ____ de mes parents.
   a. le fils **b.** la fille
3. Je suis ____ de mon oncle.
   a. le neveu **b.** la nièce
4. Je suis ____ de mes cousins.
   a. le cousin **b.** la cousine

Une noce à la campagne

5 **Une famille** This country wedding, *Une noce à la campagne,* was painted by le Douanier Rousseau in 1905. Give the people names and decide who they are in relation to one another.

6 **Une fête d'anniversaire** With a classmate describe some things that take place at a typical birthday party. You may want to use some of the following words.

arriver

écouter

donner

danser

préparer

inviter

regarder

ENCORE PLUS *For more practice using words from **Mots 1,** do Activity 10 on page H11 at the end of this book.*

Vocabulaire Mots 2

La maison

La vieille maison est très belle.
Il y a un jardin autour de la maison.
De la terrasse on a une vue du jardin.

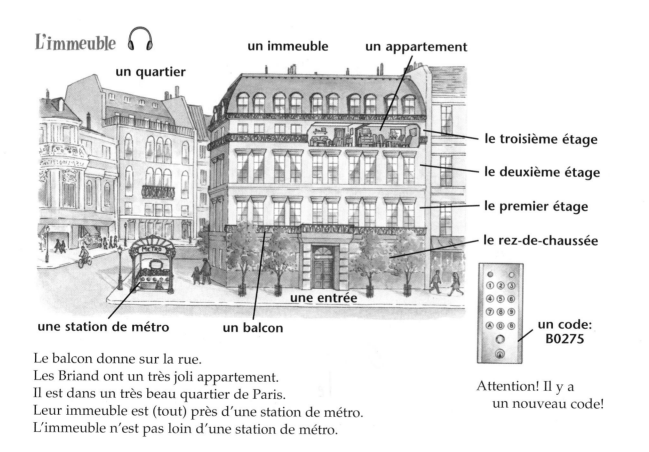

L'immeuble

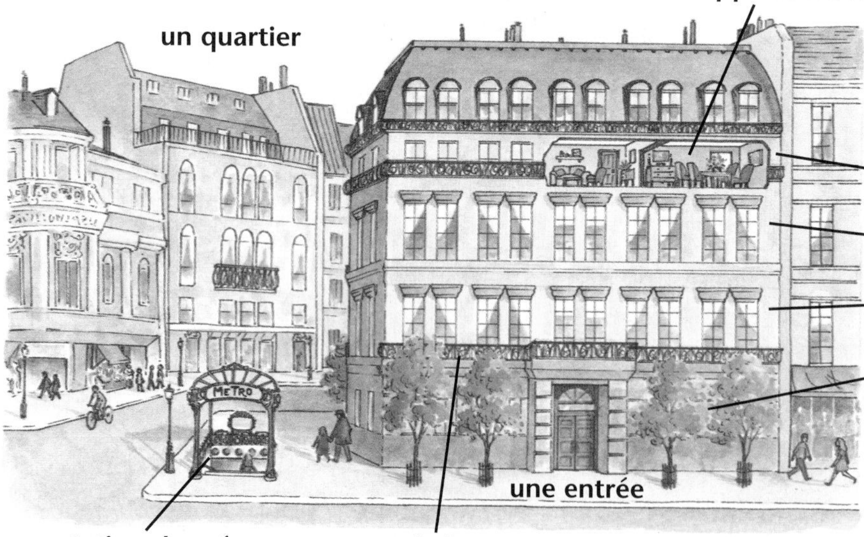

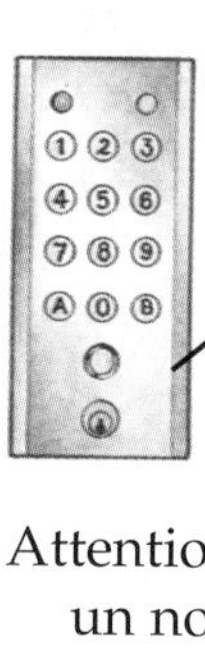

Le balcon donne sur la rue.
Les Briand ont un très joli appartement.
Il est dans un très beau quartier de Paris.
Leur immeuble est (tout) près d'une station de métro.
L'immeuble n'est pas loin d'une station de métro.

Attention! Il y a un nouveau code!

Les voisins sont dans la cour.

Les Briand montent toujours en ascenseur. Ils montent au troisième étage.

Les pièces de la maison

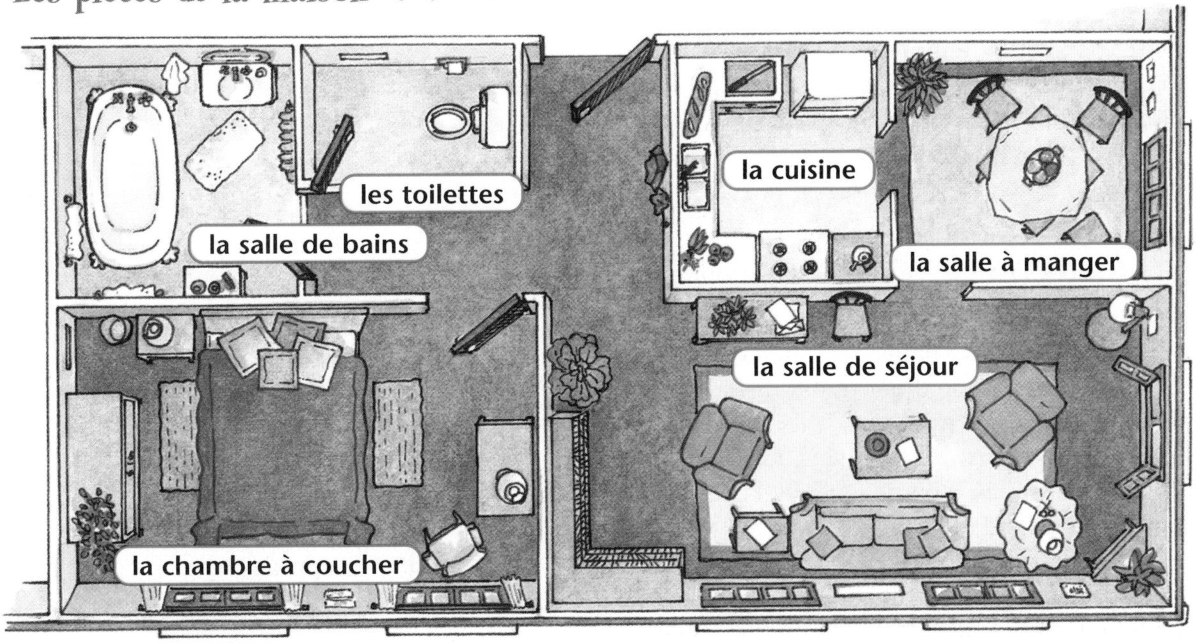

Quel est le mot?

La maison de Claude Monet, Giverny

7 Historiette La maison de Monet

Historiette La maison de Monet Répondez que **oui.** *(Answer* oui.*)*

1. Monet est un artiste célèbre?
2. Il a une jolie maison?
3. Sa maison est grande?
4. Il y a un jardin autour de sa maison?
5. C'est un très beau jardin?
6. Il y a des arbres et des fleurs dans le jardin?

FRENCH Online

For more information about French painters, go to the Glencoe French Web site: french.glencoe.com

8 Historiette L'appartement des Lapeyre

Inventez une histoire. *(Make up a story.)*

1. La famille Lapeyre a un appartement dans un vieil immeuble à Paris?
2. Leur appartement est dans un beau quartier de Paris?
3. L'appartement est au rez-de-chaussée ou au troisième étage?
4. Leur balcon donne sur la rue ou sur la cour?
5. Il y a six pièces dans l'appartement de la famille Lapeyre?
6. Quelles pièces?
7. Les Lapeyre montent toujours à pied ou en ascenseur?
8. L'immeuble est près d'une station de métro ou loin d'une station de métro?
9. Il y a un code pour entrer dans l'immeuble?

9 Quelle pièce?

Quelle pièce? Choisissez la bonne réponse. *(Choose the correct answer.)*

1. On regarde la télé dans ____.
   a. la salle de bains **b.** la salle à manger **c.** la salle de séjour
2. On prépare le dîner dans ____.
   a. la salle à manger **b.** la cuisine **c.** la chambre à coucher
3. On parle avec ses voisins dans ____.
   a. la salle de bains **b.** la cour **c.** la chambre à coucher
4. On dîne dans ____.
   a. la salle à manger **b.** la salle de séjour **c.** la chambre à coucher
5. On a une belle vue ____.
   a. du balcon **b.** de l'étage **c.** de l'ascenseur

10 **Historiette** **Chez moi** Donnez des réponses personnelles.
(Give your own answers.)

1. Tu habites quelle rue?
2. Tu habites dans un appartement ou dans une maison privée?
3. Il y a combien de pièces dans l'appartement ou la maison?
4. Il y a combien de chambres à coucher?
5. Il y a un jardin ou un balcon?
6. La maison ou l'immeuble a un garage?
7. Il y a une voiture dans le garage?

11 **Quelle maison pour nous?** Work with a classmate. Your families plan to spend a month in France. Read the following real estate ads and discuss which house or apartment is good for your family.

Appartement

dans un bel immeuble, cinq pièces, deux chambres à coucher, une grande cuisine moderne, bien situé au centre-ville, près d'une station de métro

Très jolie villa

avec jardin et terrasse, vue sur l'océan, huit pièces, quatre chambres à coucher, garage pour deux voitures, située dans une rue très calme, loin de la ville

Petit bungalow

dans un vieux quartier, beaucoup de charme, trois pièces, une chambre à coucher, vingt minutes de la ville de Caen.

ENCORE PLUS *For more practice using words from **Mots 2,** do Activity 11 on page H12 at the end of this book.*

Structure

Le verbe avoir au présent
Telling what you and others have

1. Study the following forms of the irregular verb **avoir** *(to have).*

AVOIR	
j' ai	nous z avons
tu as	vous z avez
il/elle/on n a	ils z /elles z ont

2. You also use the verb **avoir** to express age.

Tu as quel âge?
Moi? J'ai quatorze ans.

3. The expression **il y a** means "there is" or "there are."

Il y a un jardin autour de la maison.
Il n'y a pas de fleurs dans le jardin.

Rappelez-vous que...

Un, une, and **des** become **de (d')** after a negative.
J'ai une sœur mais Marc n'a pas de sœur.

Comment dit-on?

12 Historiette **Les Binand**

Inventez une histoire.
(Make up a story.)

1. Suzanne Binand a un frère?
2. Guillaume a une sœur?
3. Monsieur et Madame Binand ont deux enfants?
4. La famille Binand a un appartement à Paris?
5. Ils ont un chat?

Deux amis, Narbonne, France

13 **Tu as un frère?** Répétez la conversation. *(Repeat the conversation.)*

Flore: Tu as un frère?
Rémi: Non, je n'ai pas de frère, mais j'ai une sœur.
Flore: Tu as une sœur? Elle a quel âge?
Rémi: Elle a quatorze ans.
Flore: Et toi, tu as quel âge?
Rémi: Moi, j'ai seize ans.
Flore: Et… vous avez un chien?
Rémi: Non, on n'a pas de chien. Mais on a un petit chat.

14 **Rémi** Complétez d'après la conversation. *(Complete according to the conversation.)*

1. Rémi n'____ pas ____ frère.
2. Il ____ une sœur.
3. Sa sœur ____ quatorze ans.
4. Rémi ____ seize ans.
5. Rémi et sa sœur n'____ pas ____ chien.
6. Mais ils ____ un petit chat adorable.

15 **Historiette** **Ma famille** Donnez des réponses personnelles. *(Give your own answers.)*

1. Tu as des frères? Tu as combien de frères?
2. Tu as des sœurs? Tu as combien de sœurs?
3. Tu as un chien ou un chat?
4. Tu as des amis?
5. Tu as des cousins?
6. Tu as combien de cousins?
7. Tu as une grande famille ou une petite famille?
8. Tu as quel âge?

Un père et son fils

16 **Dans mon sac à dos** Préparez une conversation d'après le modèle. *(Make up a conversation according to the model.)*

—Tu as des livres dans ton sac à dos?
—Oui, j'ai des livres dans mon sac à dos. /
Non, je n'ai pas de livres dans mon sac à dos.

17 **Qu'est-ce que vous avez?** Préparez une conversation d'après le modèle. *(Make up a conversation according to the model.)*

une maison ou un appartement →
—Vous avez une maison ou un appartement?
—Nous avons ____.

1. une grande famille ou une petite famille
2. une grande voiture ou une petite voiture
3. un chien ou un chat
4. un PC ou un Mac

18 **Historiette** **La famille Ghez** Complétez avec **avoir.**
(Complete with avoir.*)*

La famille Ghez ____1____ un bel appartement à Nice. Leur appartement ____2____ six pièces. Leur appartement ____3____ un balcon. Le balcon donne sur la mer Méditerranée. Du balcon les Ghez ____4____ une très belle vue sur la mer.

Il y a quatre personnes dans la famille Ghez. Halima a dix-sept ans et son frère, Ahmed, ____5____ quinze ans. Halima et Ahmed ____6____ un petit chat adorable.

Et toi, tu ____7____ un chien ou un chat? Tu ____8____ une petite ou une grande famille? Vous ____9____ un appartement ou une maison?

Moi, j'____10____ quinze ans et j'____11____ un chien adorable. J'adore mon petit chien.

Les adjectifs possessifs
Telling what belongs to you and others

1. You use a possessive adjective to show possession or ownership. Like other adjectives, a possessive adjective must agree with the noun it modifies.

2. The adjectives **mon** *(my)*, **ton** *(your)*, and **son** *(his/her)* each have three forms. The adjectives **notre** *(our)*, **votre** *(your)*, and **leur** *(their)* each have two forms.

SINGULIER		PLURIEL	
Masculin	Féminin	Masculin	Féminin
mon frère	ma sœur	mes frères	mes sœurs
ton frère	ta sœur	tes frères	tes sœurs
son frère	sa sœur	ses frères	ses sœurs
notre frère	notre sœur	nos frères	nos sœurs
votre frère	votre sœur	vos frères	vos sœurs
leur frère	leur sœur	leurs frères	leurs sœurs

3. **Son, sa,** and **ses** can mean "his" or "her." The adjective agrees with the item owned, not the owner.

   C'est le chien de Paul. **C'est son chien.**
   C'est le chien de Marie. **C'est son chien.**

4. You use **mon, ton,** or **son** before a feminine singular noun that begins with a vowel or silent **h.**

   son‿n‿amie et mon‿n‿amie

Une famille d'origine marocaine, Saint-André, France

Attention!

Liaison occurs with **mon, ton,** and **son,** as well as with all plural possessive adjectives.

mon‿n‿oncle **nos‿z‿amis**
ton‿n‿ami **vos‿z‿amis**
son‿n‿école **leurs‿z‿amis**

Comment dit-on?

19 **Historiette Ta famille et chez toi** Donnez des réponses personnelles. *(Give your own answers.)*

1. Où est ta maison ou ton appartement?
2. Ta maison ou ton appartement a combien de pièces?
3. Ta maison est grande ou petite? Ton appartement est grand ou petit?
4. C'est quand, ton anniversaire? Tu as quel âge?
5. Quel âge a ton frère, si tu as un frère?
6. Quel âge a ta sœur, si tu as une sœur?

Un beau chalet, Suisse

20 **J'ai une question pour toi.**
Suivez le modèle. *(Follow the model.)*

—Où est __ta__ maison?
—Ma maison est dans la rue Jacob.

1. Qui est ____ amie?
2. Qui est ____ ami?
3. Où habitent ____ grands-parents?
4. ____ frère a quel âge?
5. ____ sœur a quel âge?
6. Où est ____ maison ou ____ appartement?
7. Tu aimes ____ cours de français?
8. ____ prof est sympa?

21 **Oui!** Suivez le modèle. *(Follow the model.)*

—Le frère de Marine est dans sa chambre?
—Oui, son frère est dans sa chambre.

1. Le père de Marine est dans la cuisine?
2. La sœur de Marine est blonde?
3. La sœur de Thomas est à Paris?
4. La maison de Thomas est jolie?
5. L'appartement de Marine est beau?
6. Les cousins de Thomas sont élèves?
7. Les grands-parents de Thomas ont un chien?

22 Historiette Notre école

Donnez des réponses personnelles.
(Give your own answers.)

1. Votre école est grande ou petite?
2. Votre école est près ou loin de votre maison?
3. Votre école a combien d'élèves?
4. Vos cours sont faciles ou difficiles?
5. Vos profs sont intéressants ou pas?
6. Vos classes sont grandes ou petites?

La Techno Parade, Paris

23 Historiette Leur maison

Complétez. *(Complete.)*

Fabien et Christophe sont frères. Ils sont dans __1__ chambre. Ils écoutent __2__ disques. __3__ collection de CD est surtout de la techno. __4__ amies, Catherine et Émilie, aiment aussi la techno. Fabien et Christophe, __5__ deux amies et __6__ copains écoutent souvent de la techno. Mais __7__ parents n'aiment pas du tout la techno.

24 Votre famille

Votre famille Draw your own family tree and say as many things as you can about your family to your classmates.

ENCORE PLUS *For more practice using **avoir** and possessive adjectives, do Activity 12 on page H13 at the end of this book.*

D'autres adjectifs
Describing more people and things

1. Most French adjectives follow the noun. Some common ones, such as **petit** and **grand,** come before the noun. The adjectives **beau** *(beautiful),* **nouveau** *(new),* and **vieux** *(old)* also come before the noun. These adjectives have several forms. Pay careful attention to both the spelling and the pronunciation of these adjectives.

SINGULIER

Féminin	Masculin (Voyelle)	Masculin (Consonne)
une belle maison	un bel appartement	un beau quartier
une nouvelle maison	un nouvel appartement	un nouveau quartier
une vieille maison	un vieil appartement	un vieux quartier

PLURIEL

Féminin	Masculin (Voyelle)	Masculin (Consonne)
de belles maisons	de beaux$_{z}$appartements	de beaux quartiers
de nouvelles maisons	de nouveaux$_{z}$appartements	de nouveaux quartiers
de vieilles maisons	de vieux$_{z}$appartements	de vieux quartiers

2. In formal French, **de** is used instead of **des** with a plural adjective that precedes the noun. In informal French, people use **des.**

Attention!

Liaison occurs with **beaux, nouveaux,** and **vieux** when they come before a word beginning with a vowel or silent **h.** The **x** is pronounced as a **z.**

mes nouveaux$_{z}$amis
les vieux$_{z}$appartements

De belles maisons, Montréal, Canada

Comment dit-on?

25 Historiette **Le bel appartement des Texier** Complétez. *(Complete.)*

1. Les Texier ont un ____ appartement dans un ____ immeuble dans un ____ quartier de la ville. (beau, vieux, beau)
2. Il y a de ____ et de ____ quartiers à Montréal. (nouveau, vieux)
3. L'appartement des Texier a de très ____ pièces. (beau)
4. Il a de ____ pièces et un très ____ balcon. (grand, beau)
5. De l'appartement il y a une très ____ vue sur la ville. (beau)
6. Les Texier ont une ____ voiture. (nouveau)
7. Leur ____ voiture est ____. (nouveau, beau)

Attention!

You have just learned that the plural of **beau** and **nouveau** is spelled with an **x**. Almost all words in French that end in **(e)au** or **eu** are spelled with **x**, not **s**, in the plural.

un cadeau	**des cadeaux**
un beau château	**de beaux châteaux**
mon neveu	**mes neveux**

Mettez au pluriel. *(Write in the plural.)*

1. Il a un très beau cadeau pour son neveu.
   Il a de très ____ ____ pour ses ____.
2. Le beau gâteau est aussi pour son neveu.
   Les ____ ____ sont aussi pour ses ____.
3. Il visite un beau château avec son neveu.
   Il visite de ____ ____ avec ses ____.

26 **Comme qui?** Work with a classmate. Take turns saying whom you and your family members take after. You may wish to use the following words.

Je suis intelligent(e) comme ma mère.
Mon frère est enthousiaste comme notre père.

petit · amusant · blond · sympa · grand · beau · brun

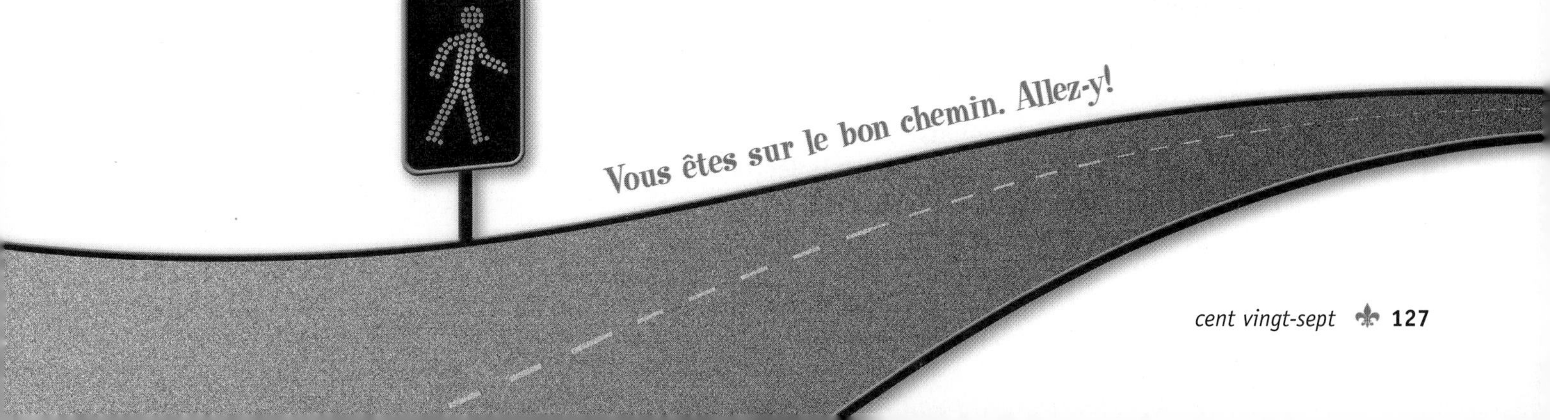
Vous êtes sur le bon chemin. Allez-y!

Conversation

Ma nouvelle adresse

Vincent: Tu as ma nouvelle adresse?
Charlotte: Ta nouvelle adresse? Non! Tu habites où maintenant?
Vincent: 21, avenue de la Bourdonnais.
Charlotte: Ah, avenue de la Bourdonnais. C'est dans le 7e tout près de la tour Eiffel, non?
Vincent: Oui. De notre balcon on a une très belle vue sur la tour Eiffel.
Charlotte: Génial!

Vous avez compris?

Répondez. *(Answer.)*

1. Vincent parle à qui?
2. Charlotte a la nouvelle adresse de Vincent?
3. Quelle est sa nouvelle adresse?
4. Où est l'avenue de la Bourdonnais?
5. Est-ce que l'appartement de Vincent a un balcon?
6. De son balcon il a une vue sur la tour Eiffel?

Parlons un peu plus

A **Appartement ou maison?** Work with a classmate. Pretend you live in Rouen. One of you lives in a house, the other lives in an apartment. Decide who lives where. Then describe your house or apartment.

B **Jeu** **Qui est qui?** Work with a classmate. Write down the first names of some of your family members. Exchange lists and then ask each other who's who.

C'est qui, Paul?
C'est mon oncle. C'est le frère de ma mère.

Prononciation

Le son /ã/

1. There are three nasal vowel sounds in French: **/ã/** as in **cent, /õ/** as in **sont,** and **/ẽ/** as in **cinq.** They are called "nasal" because some air passes through the nose when they are pronounced. In this chapter, you will practice only the sound **/ã/** as in **cent.**
2. Repeat the following. Notice that there is no **/n/** sound after the nasal vowel.

Jean	**cent**	**grand**	**amusant**
français	**parent**	**fantastique**	

Voilà les grands-parents, les parents et les enfants.
Jean-François est fantastique. Il est français, grand, amusant.

les parents et les enfants

Lectures culturelles

Reading Strategy

Visualizing

As you are reading, try to visualize or make a mental picture of what is being described. Allow your mind to freely develop an image. This will help you remember what you read. It may also help you identify with what you are reading.

Où habitent les Français?

Maisons et appartements

Beaucoup de Français qui habitent en ville habitent dans un appartement. Il y a des appartements de toutes sortes: des studios, de petits appartements, de grands appartements. Pour les gens qui n'ont pas beaucoup d'argent il y a des H.L.M.[1] (Habitations à Loyer Modéré). Les H.L.M. sont généralement à l'extérieur des villes, à la périphérie ou en banlieue[2]. En banlieue, il y a aussi de petites maisons individuelles—des pavillons.

[1] H.L.M. *low-income housing*
[2] en banlieue *in the suburbs*

Des H.L.M.

Des pavillons de la banlieue parisienne

la Polynésie française

Tahiti

Haïti

La Martinique

La famille Duval

Les Duval habitent à Paris. Leur appartement est dans un vieil immeuble dans le premier arrondissement. Les Duval habitent dans un très beau quartier.

L'immeuble où habitent les Duval a six étages. Les Duval habitent au cinquième. Ils ont un appartement de quatre pièces: une salle de séjour, une salle à manger et deux chambres à coucher. Il y a aussi, bien sûr, une cuisine, une salle de bains, des toilettes et même une petite entrée. La salle de séjour et la salle à manger donnent sur la rue. La cuisine et les chambres à coucher donnent sur la cour. De leur balcon, les Duval ont une très belle vue sur le musée du Louvre.

Un bel appartement à Paris

Vous avez compris?

A Le logement Vrai ou faux? *(True or false?)*

1. Beaucoup de Français habitent dans des appartements.
2. Il y a beaucoup de maisons individuelles dans les villes françaises.
3. Les H.L.M. sont pour les gens qui n'ont pas beaucoup d'argent, qui ne sont pas très riches.
4. Les H.L.M. sont toujours au centre-ville.
5. Le Louvre est dans le deuxième arrondissement.

B La famille Duval Répondez. *(Answer.)*

1. Où habitent les Duval?
2. Où est leur appartement?
3. Il y a combien d'étages dans l'immeuble?
4. Ils habitent au cinquième?
5. Quelles pièces donnent sur la rue?
6. Quelles pièces donnent sur la cour?
7. Du balcon de l'appartement, il y a une vue sur quel musée parisien?

Lecture supplémentaire 1

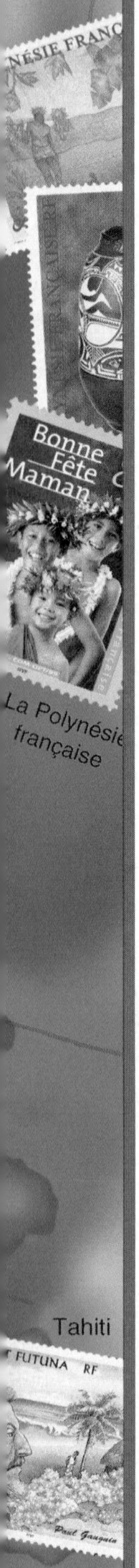

Le logement dans d'autres pays

Dakar, Sénégal

En Afrique

Dans les grandes villes modernes de l'Afrique Occidentale comme Abidjan ou Dakar il y a beaucoup de grands immeubles où les Ivoiriens et les Sénégalais habitent dans de très beaux appartements de grand standing. Mais dans les petits villages de la brousse[1], les gens habitent dans des petites maisons avec un toit de chaume. Voilà une maison typique de la brousse.

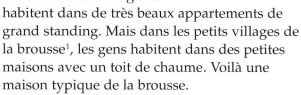

Une maison avec un toit de chaume, Sénégal

À la Martinique

La Martinique est une belle île francophone dans la mer des Antilles (la mer des Caraïbes). La Martinique est un département français d'outre-mer[2]. Beaucoup de Martiniquais habitent dans des maisons en bois[3]. Les couleurs des maisons martiniquaises sont très belles.

[1] brousse *bush*
[2] d'outre-mer *overseas*
[3] en bois *wooden*

Vous avez compris?

Le monde francophone Donnez les informations suivantes. *(Give the following information.)*

1. deux grandes villes africaines
2. une région rurale dans beaucoup de pays africains
3. un département français d'outre-mer
4. une île où il y a beaucoup de maisons multicolores en bois

Une maison en bois, Pointe-à-Pitre, Guadeloupe

Lecture supplémentaire 2

Les noms de famille

En France les noms de famille ont des origines très variées. Certains évoquent une caractéristique physique: **Legrand, Lebrun, Petit.**

D'autres sont des noms de profession.

D'autres sont des noms d'endroits.

D'autres encore sont des termes géographiques.

Quel est votre nom de famille?
Il signifie quelque chose de spécial?

Vous avez compris?

Noms de famille américains Can you think of some American family names for each of the above categories? Can you think of any other categories for American family names?

CONNEXIONS

Les Beaux-Arts

Art et histoire

Art and history are often closely connected. Looking at a beautiful painting brings us much enjoyment. It can also teach us a great deal about the period in which the artist produced it. A portrait, for example, shows us how people looked and dressed at the time.

Today many families keep a photo album. Prior to the invention of photography many families had a portrait done. This was particularly true of the royal families, and King Louis XVI and his queen, Marie-Antoinette, were no exception.

Marie-Antoinette à la rose

La portraitiste de Marie-Antoinette

Élisabeth Vigée-Lebrun est née[1] à Paris en 1775 (mille sept cent soixante-quinze). Elle étudie l'art auprès de son père, l'artiste Louis Vigée. La jeune Élisabeth a beaucoup de talent et en très peu de temps[2] elle a du succès. Élisabeth Vigée-Lebrun est la portraitiste de Marie-Antoinette.

Marie-Antoinette

Voici un portrait de Marie-Antoinette avec ses quatre enfants. La reine est une mère dévouée. Elle adore ses enfants.

[1] née *born*
[2] en très peu de temps *in a short time*

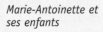

Marie-Antoinette et ses enfants

Versailles

Versailles

La famille royale habite dans le grand palais à Versailles. Mais Marie-Antoinette n'aime pas beaucoup la vie[3] au grand palais. Elle a un petit palais—le Petit Trianon. Pas loin du Petit Trianon Marie-Antoinette a un petit hameau où elle aime passer du temps. Le hameau est un petit village avec des maisonnettes (petites maisons) avec un toit de chaume. Là, Marie-Antoinette aime passer du temps avec les gens[4] simples.

La Révolution

Pendant la Révolution la famille royale est séparée et emprisonnée. Louis XVI et Marie-Antoinette sont guillotinés. *Les adieux de Louis XVI* est un tableau de l'artiste J.-J. Hauer de l'époque révolutionnaire.

[3] vie *life* [4] gens *folks, people*

Le hameau de Marie-Antoinette

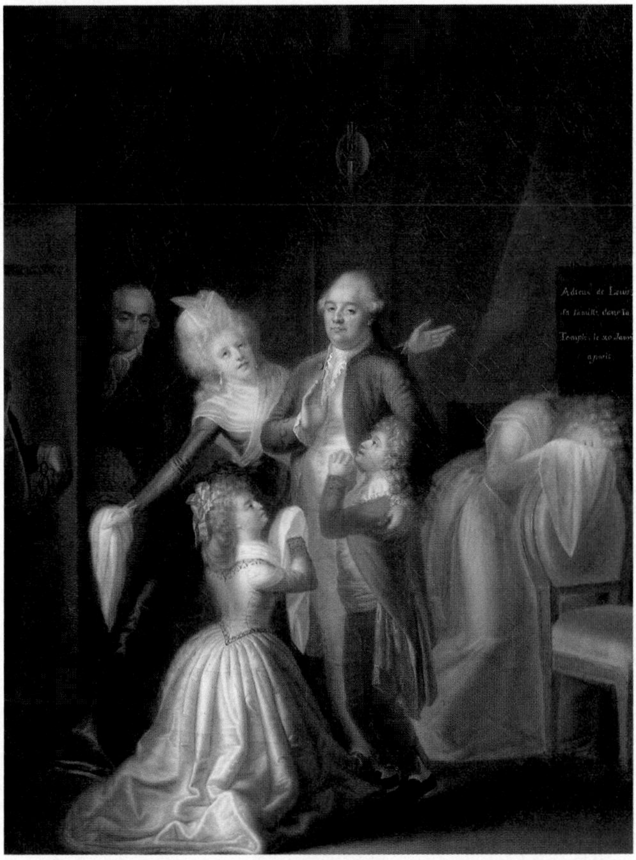

Les adieux de Louis XVI

Vous avez compris?

La famille royale Donnez les informations suivantes. *(Give the following information.)*

1. le nom de la portraitiste de Marie-Antoinette
2. le nom du mari de Marie-Antoinette
3. la résidence officielle de la famille royale
4. le nom du petit palais de Marie-Antoinette
5. la destinée de la famille royale

C'est à vous

Use what you have learned

PARLER

1 Belle résidence

✔ Describe a home or apartment

You are trying to sell one of the apartments or houses listed in the ads. Say as much as you can to convince your client (your classmate) to buy one.

CHAUSSON IMMOBILIER
• 33, av. de Foix - 09120 VARILHE
Tél. : 05.61.60.79.80 - Fax : 05.61.60.86
Près VARILHES : (09) **MAISON** campagne, 5 pièces, salle d'eau, wc, grandes dépendances (bergerie, étable, chai) aménageables. Cour, jardin. Proximité toutes commodités.

Région PAMIERS : (09) **NID D'AIGLE** rénové, cuisine campagnarde, séjour-salon cheminée 65 m², bureau, 4 chambres, salle de bains, wc. Tout confort. Grande dépendance. Site isolé avec très bel environnement.

Dans station thermale des **PYRÉNÉES :** près station de ski, **MAISON** de maître, 12 pièces, bon état, maison de gardien, garage, boxes à chevaux. Terrain 8 ha. Situation exceptionnelle.

PARLER

2 L'immeuble

✔ Talk about families and where they live

With a classmate, look at the apartment building. A different family lives on each floor. University students live in the garrets under the roof. Give each family and student a name. Say as much as you can about them and their lodgings.

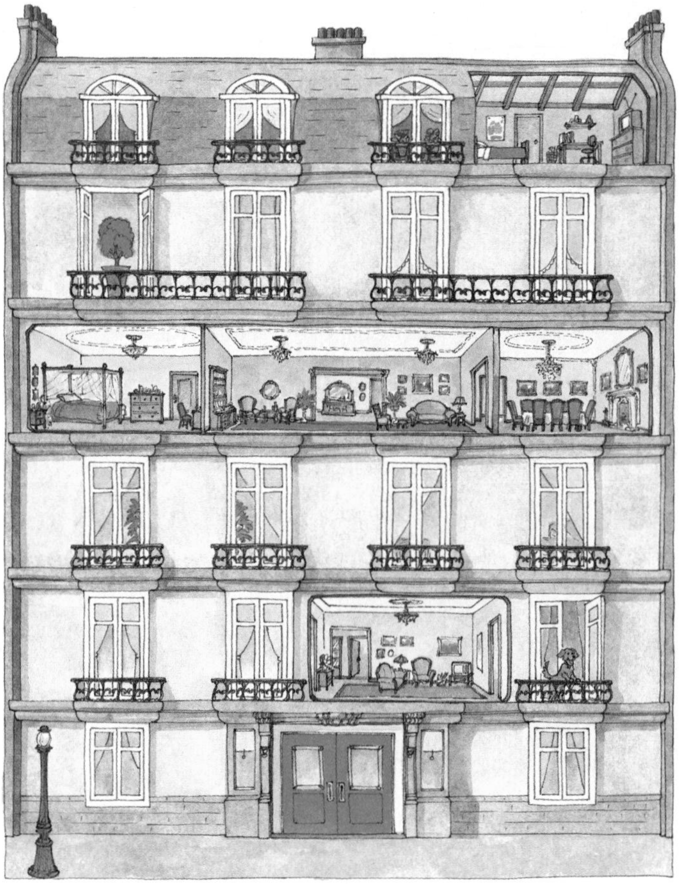

ÉCRIRE

3 Quinze ans

✔ *Invite a friend to a birthday party*

A good friend will soon be fifteen. Write an invitation to his or her birthday party. You may wish to use the well-known French expression R.S.V.P.—**Répondez, s'il vous plaît.**

ÉCRIRE

4 Ma famille et moi

✔ *Describe yourself and your family*

You plan to spend next year as an exchange student in Toulouse, France. You have to write a letter about yourself and your family to the agency in your community that selects the exchange students. Your letter must be in French. Make your description as complete as possible.

Writing Strategy

Ordering details There are several ways to order details when writing. The one you choose depends upon your purpose for writing. When describing a physical place, it is sometimes best to use spatial ordering. This means describing things as they actually appear—from left to right, from back to front, from top to bottom, or any other logical order that works.

ÉCRIRE

5 La maison de mes rêves

Write a description of your dream house. Be as complete as you can.

Un château à Rocamadour, France

Assessment

Vocabulaire

*To review **Mots 1**, turn to pages 112–113.*

1 Complétez. *(Complete.)*

1. Mes parents sont ma ____ et mon ____.
2. Les parents de mes parents sont mes ____.
3. La sœur de ma mère est ma ____.
4. Le frère de mon père est mon ____.
5. Les enfants de mes oncles et de mes tantes sont mes ____ et mes ____.

*To review **Mots 2**, turn to pages 116–117.*

2 Identifiez. *(Identify.)*

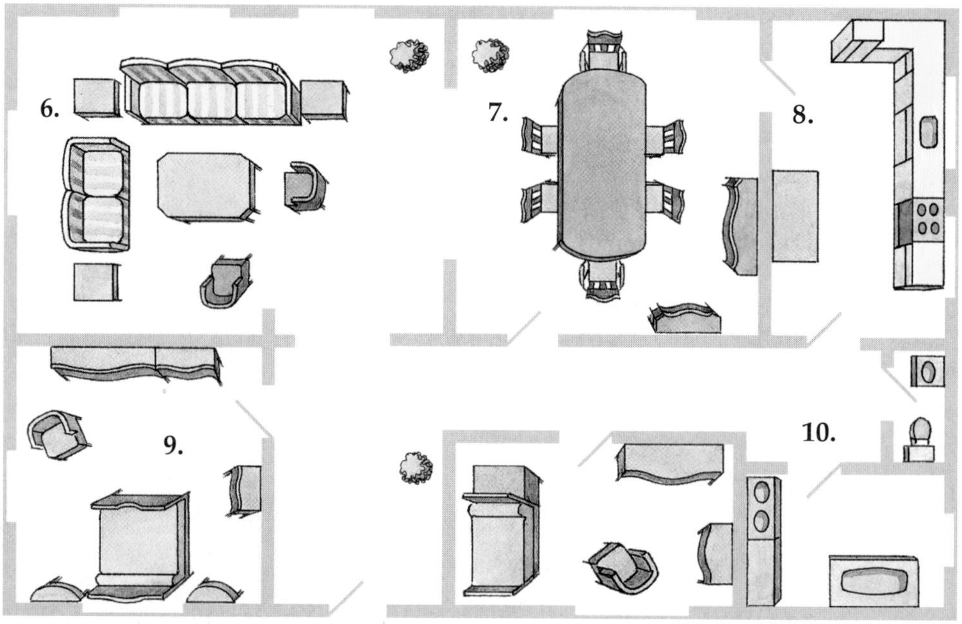

Structure

*To review the verb **avoir**, turn to page 120.*

3 Complétez avec «avoir». *(Complete with* avoir.*)*

11. J'____ une petite famille.
12. Marc aussi ____ une petite famille.
13. Sa sœur ____ seize ans.
14. Les parents de Marc et sa sœur ____ un appartement à Paris.
15. Vous ____ une maison ou un appartement?
16. Et toi, tu ____ une petite ou une grande famille?

4 Choisissez. *(Choose.)*

17. Où est la voiture de Serge? ____ voiture est dans le garage?
 a. Sa b. Son c. Ses
18. Où est ____ maison?
 a. ta b. ton c. tes
19. ____ anniversaire est le 4 novembre.
 a. Ma b. Mon c. Mes
20. Paul et Marc sont les frères de Sandrine? Oui, ce sont ____ frères.
 a. leurs b. son c. ses

To review possessive adjectives, turn to page 123.

5 Complétez. *(Complete.)*

21. Il y a de très ____ maisons dans notre ____ quartier. (vieux, beau)
22. Nous avons un ____ appartement avec de ____ pièces. (nouveau, beau)

To review these adjectives, turn to page 126.

Culture

6 Vrai ou faux? *(True or false?)*

23. Les pavillons sont de petites maisons en banlieue.
24. Les H.L.M. sont généralement à l'extérieur des villes.
25. Beaucoup de Français qui habitent en ville habitent dans une maison privée.

To review this cultural information, turn to pages 130–131.

Des H.L.M.

On parle super bien!

Tell all you can about this illustration.

Vocabulaire

Identifying family members

la famille
les parents *(m. pl.)*
le père
la mère
le mari
la femme
le fils
la fille
l'enfant *(m. et f.)*
le frère
la sœur
les grands-parents *(m. pl.)*
le grand-père
la grand-mère
les petits-enfants *(m. pl.)*
le petit-fils
la petite-fille
l'oncle
la tante
le neveu
la nièce
le/la cousin(e)
un chat
un chien

Talking about family affairs or events

un anniversaire
un cadeau
un gâteau
une bougie
une fête
donner
inviter
avoir… ans
Quel âge… ?

How well do you know your vocabulary?

- Find the sixteen cognates.
- Use as many of them as you can to write a story.

Identifying the rooms of a house

une pièce
une salle de séjour
une cuisine
une salle à manger
une chambre à coucher
une salle de bains
des toilettes *(f. pl.)*

Talking about a home and the neighborhood

une maison
un appartement
un immeuble
un quartier
une station de métro
une terrasse
un jardin
un arbre
une fleur
un garage
une voiture
un balcon
une vue
le rez-de-chaussée
un étage
un escalier
un ascenseur
une entrée
un code
une cour
un(e) voisin(e)
beau, belle
nouveau, nouvelle
vieux, vieille
premier, première
deuxième
troisième
(tout) près de
loin de
donner sur
monter
 à pied
 en ascenseur

Other useful words and expressions

une journée
tout le monde
autour de (d')
il y a
C'est (pas) rigolo.

VIDÉOTOUR

Épisode 4

In this video episode, you will accompany Christine and Madame Séguin on a trip to Giverny. See page 529 for more information.

Conversation

Un anniversaire

Sandrine: Bonjour, Christophe. Ça va?
Christophe: Oui, ça va. Et toi?
Sandrine: Pas mal. Qu'est-ce que tu as dans ton sac?
Christophe: J'ai un cadeau pour ma sœur. C'est son anniversaire aujourd'hui.
Sandrine: Ta sœur Mélanie? Elle a quel âge?
Christophe: Elle a seize ans. Et Sandrine, tu as ma nouvelle adresse?
Sandrine: Ta nouvelle adresse? Tu n'habites pas rue de l'Odéon?
Christophe: Non, maintenant on habite dans le 5e, tout près de la station de métro Maubert-Mutualité.

Le boulevard Haussmann, Paris

La station de métro Maubert-Mutualité

Vous avez compris?

Répondez. *(Answer.)*

1. Sandrine parle à qui?
2. Qu'est-ce qu'il y a dans son sac?
3. C'est l'anniversaire de qui?
4. C'est quand, son anniversaire?
5. Elle a quel âge?
6. Qui a une nouvelle adresse?
7. Il habite où maintenant?
8. Il habite près de quelle station de métro?

Structure

Les verbes au présent

1. Review the forms of regular **-er** verbs.

PARLER	je parle, tu parles, il/elle/on parle, nous parlons, vous parlez, ils/elles parlent
AIMER	j'aime, tu aimes, il/elle/on‿n‿aime, nous‿z‿aimons, vous‿z‿aimez, ils‿z‿/elles‿z‿aiment

2. Review the irregular verbs you have learned so far.

ÊTRE	je suis, tu es, il/elle/on‿n‿est, nous sommes, vous‿z‿êtes, ils/elles sont
AVOIR	j'ai, tu as, il/elle/on‿n‿a, nous‿z‿avons, vous‿z‿avez, ils‿z‿/elles‿z‿ont

3. Review the placement of **ne (n')... pas** when expressing a negative idea.

Je ne travaille pas.
Il n'habite pas à Paris.

1 Historiette Flore habite à Paris.

Inventez une histoire. *(Make up a story.)*

1. Flore habite à Paris?
2. Elle quitte la maison à quelle heure le matin?
3. Et toi, tu habites où?
4. Le matin, tu arrives à l'école à quelle heure?
5. Tu parles français ou anglais à l'école?
6. Et Flore, qu'est-ce qu'elle parle?
7. Flore quitte le collège à cinq heures de l'après-midi?
8. Tes copains et toi, vous quittez l'école à quelle heure?
9. Vous travaillez après les cours?
10. Les élèves français travaillent après les cours?

2 Historiette Une famille

Complétez. *(Complete.)*

1. Bonjour. Moi, je ____ français. Je ____ de Paris. (être)
2. Ma famille n'____ pas très grande. Nous ____ quatre. (être)
3. J'____ une sœur. (avoir)
4. Ma sœur ____ dix ans et moi, j'____ dix-sept ans. (avoir)
5. Et vous, vous ____ quel âge? (avoir)
6. Vous ____ américain(e) ou français(e)? (être)

Une famille française avec leur chat

Les articles et les adjectifs

1. Review the following forms of the indefinite and definite articles.

un garçon	**une fille**	
des copains	**des_z écoles**	
le garçon	**la fille**	**l'ami(e)**
les copains	**les_z écoles**	**les_z ami(e)s**

2. Adjectives that end in a consonant have four forms.

Le garçon est brun.	**Les garçons sont bruns.**
La fille est brune.	**Les filles sont brunes.**

3. Adjectives that end in **e** have only two forms, singular and plural.

un ami sympathique	**des amis sympathiques**
une amie sympathique	**des amies sympathiques**

Deux copains sympathiques à Paris

3 Historiette La famille de Valentin

Complétez avec **un, une** ou **des.** *(Complete with* un, une, *or* des.*)*

Valentin a une grande famille. Il a __1__ père et __2__ mère. Il a __3__ frères et __4__ sœurs? Oui, il a trois frères et quatre sœurs. Il a aussi sept cousins, mais __5__ seule cousine. Il a __6__ chien, Tifou, et __7__ chat, Pompon.

Valentin et sa famille habitent dans __8__ grande maison à Pontchartrain. Valentin est élève dans __9__ lycée de la région. Valentin est __10__ élève excellent.

4 C'est qui?

Complétez avec **le, la, l'** ou **les.** *(Complete with* le, la, l', *or* les.*)*

1. Guillaume est ____ ami de Loïc.
2. Joanne est ____ sœur de Guillaume.
3. Mais Joanne n'est pas ____ amie de Loïc.
4. Justine et Mélanie sont ____ amies de Joanne et Guillaume.
5. Marc et Jean-Paul aussi sont ____ amis de Joanne et Guillaume.
6. Guillaume est ____ frère de Joanne et Christelle.
7. Christelle est ____ cousine de Loïc.

5 **Sa sœur aussi** Répondez d'après le modèle. *(Answer according to the model.)*

—Il est très intelligent.
—Sa sœur aussi est très intelligente.

1. Il est content.
2. Il est amusant.
3. Il est sympathique.
4. Il est énergique.
5. Il est très intéressant.
6. Il est brun.

Les adjectifs possessifs

1. Review the forms of the possessive adjectives. The adjectives **mon, ton,** and **son** have three forms.

mon ‿ₙappartement	ma maison	mes ‿z appartements	mes maisons
ton ‿ₙappartement	ta maison	tes ‿z appartements	tes maisons
son ‿ₙappartement	sa maison	ses ‿z appartements	ses maisons

2. The adjectives **notre, votre,** and **leur** have two forms—singular and plural.

notre appartement	notre maison	nos ‿z appartements	nos maisons
votre appartement	votre maison	vos ‿z appartements	vos maisons
leur appartement	leur maison	leurs ‿z appartements	leurs maisons

3. Remember that you use **mon, ton, son** before a feminine singular noun that begins with a vowel or silent **h: mon‿n adresse, mon‿n amie.**

La salle à manger de la maison de Monet à Giverny

6 **Qui?** Complétez. *(Complete.)*

Julien a un frère, Paul, et une sœur, Magali. __1__ parents ont donc trois enfants. __2__ trois enfants sont Julien, __3__ frère et __4__ sœur.

—Julien, __5__ frère a quel âge?

—Euh… __6__ frère a quinze ans et __7__ sœur a neuf ans.

—Julien et Paul, comment est __8__ prof de musique?

—Qui? __9__ prof de musique? Il est très sympa. Beaucoup de __10__ profs sont sympas.

École nationale de musique et de danse, Yerres

7 **Un(e) ami(e)** Work with a classmate. Each of you will tell about a friend. Describe your friend, some things he or she does, and where he or she lives.

8 **Une conversation** Have a conversation with a classmate. Talk about your school, classes, family, and house.

LITERARY COMPANION *You may wish to read the adaptation of* **La petite Fadette**, *a novel by George Sand. You will find this literary selection on page 504.*

1. Champ de coquelicots en Provence
2. Quart de finale de la coupe de l'UEFA à Lens, dans le Nord
3. La cité médiévale de Carcassonne, dans le Languedoc
4. La Promenade des Anglais et l'hôtel Negresco à Nice, sur la Côte d'Azur
5. Fillette musulmane à Marseille
6. L'Hôtel du Palais à Biarritz, au Pays Basque
7. Homme en costume traditionnel de l'Auvergne

1

3

2

4

5

6

NATIONAL GEOGRAPHIC

REFLETS de la France

7

8. Paons dans le parc du château de Valençay, dans la vallée de la Loire
9. Fillette en costume traditionnel au festival d'Obernai, en Alsace
10. Le Mont-Saint-Michel, en Normandie
11. Un TGV (un Train à Grande Vitesse)
12. Coureurs cyclistes du Tour de France à Vitré, en Bretagne
13. Rosace de la cathédrale Notre-Dame de Reims, en Champagne
14. Jeune écolier et cycliste, en Normandie

8

9

10

11

12

NATIONAL GEOGRAPHIC

REFLETS de la France

CHAPITRE 5

Au café et au restaurant

Objectifs

In this chapter you will learn to:

- *order food or a beverage at a café or restaurant*
- *tell where you and others go*
- *tell what you and others are going to do*
- *give locations*
- *tell what belongs to you and others*
- *describe more activities*
- *compare eating habits in the United States and in the French-speaking world*

Vincent Van Gogh *Terrasse du café le soir*

Mère Catherine
CHEZ EUGENE
STATIONNE
GÉNANT

Vocabulaire

Mots 1

À la terrasse d'un café

Karim va au café avec Maïa.
Les deux copains y vont ensemble.
Ils trouvent une table libre.

Le serveur arrive.
Il donne la carte à Karim.
Maïa regarde la carte.

Vous désirez?
Un coca, s'il vous plaît.
Et pour moi, une limonade.

Karim prend un coca.
Maïa prend une limonade.
Ils commandent une boisson (une consommation).

un citron pressé

un café (un express)

un jus d'orange

un jus de pomme

un crème

des tartines de pain beurré

un croissant

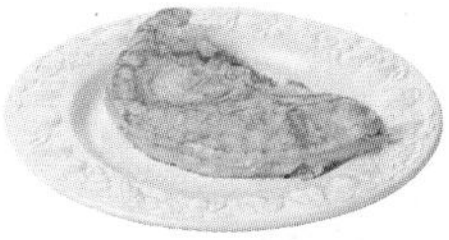
une omelette nature

une omelette aux fines herbes

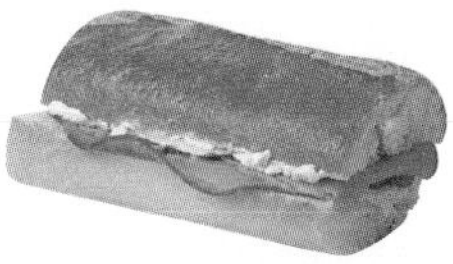
un sandwich au jambon

un croque-monsieur

un sandwich au fromage

une salade verte

des frites

une soupe à l'oignon

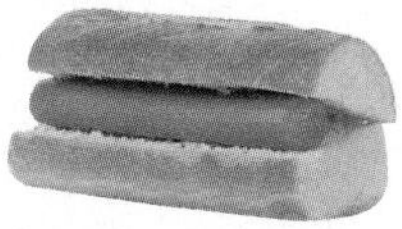
une saucisse de Francfort, un hot-dog

une crêpe

une glace au chocolat

une glace à la vanille

Quel est le mot?

1 Historiette **On va au café.**

Répondez d'après les indications.
(Answer according to the cues.)

1. Pierre va où? (au café)
2. Il va au café avec qui? (Chantal)
3. Ils vont au café quand? (après les cours)
4. Les deux copains y vont ensemble? (oui)
5. Qu'est-ce qu'ils trouvent? (une table libre)
6. Qui arrive? (le serveur)
7. Il donne la carte à qui? (à Chantal)
8. Qu'est-ce que les amis commandent? (une boisson)
9. Chantal prend une limonade? (oui)
10. Qu'est-ce que Pierre prend? (un coca)

Un café, Nice

2 **Tu as faim ou soif?** Suivez les modèles.

(Follow the models.)

une salade →
Moi, j'ai faim. Je voudrais quelque chose à manger.

un coca →
Moi, j'ai soif. Je voudrais quelque chose à boire.

1. un citron pressé
2. un petit crème
3. une omelette nature
4. une limonade
5. une glace à la vanille
6. un jus d'orange
7. un croque-monsieur
8. une crêpe

3 Historiette **Un beau café**

Répondez d'après le dessin.
(Answer according to the illustration.)

1. C'est la terrasse d'un café ou l'intérieur d'un café?
2. Il y a beaucoup de tables occupées?
3. Il y a une table libre?
4. Qui travaille dans le café?
5. Magali a soif. Qu'est-ce qu'elle commande?
6. Rémi a faim. Qu'est-ce qu'il commande?

4 **À la terrasse d'un café** Suivez le modèle.
(Follow the model.)

Client: Monsieur, s'il vous plaît!
Serveur: Oui, vous désirez?
Client: Une glace au chocolat, s'il vous plaît.

1. 
2. 
3. 
4. 
5. 
6. 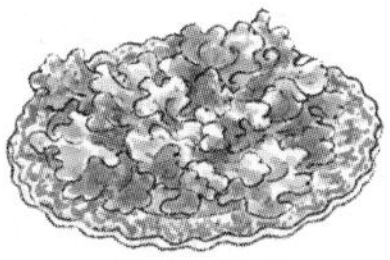
7. 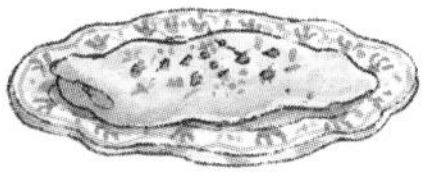

5 **J'aime ça.** Work with a classmate. Tell what snack foods and beverages you like or don't like.

6 **Au café** Work in small groups. You're in a café in Honfleur, in Normandy. One of you will be the server. Have a conversation from the time you enter the café until you leave. You will get a table, order, and talk about your friends, family, and school. The waiter will have to interrupt once in a while.

Honfleur, Normandie

7 **Jeu** **Devinette** French people often tell you: **J'ai une faim de loup!** Can you guess whether it means they are very hungry or not? You also hear: **Elle mange comme un oiseau.** Can you guess whether it means she eats a lot or very little? Are there similar expressions in English? What are they?

ENCORE PLUS *For more practice using words from* ***Mots 1****, do Activity 13 on page H14 at the end of this book.*

Vocabulaire

Mots 2

Le couvert

Au restaurant

Vous aimez votre steak comment?
À point, s'il vous plaît.
Monsieur, s'il vous plaît! Je n'ai pas de serviette.

Alexandre prend un steak frites.

Alexandre va au restaurant.
Il ne va pas au restaurant tout seul.
Il y va avec des copains.
Ils n'y vont pas en voiture.
Ils ne prennent pas le bus.
Ils y vont à pied.

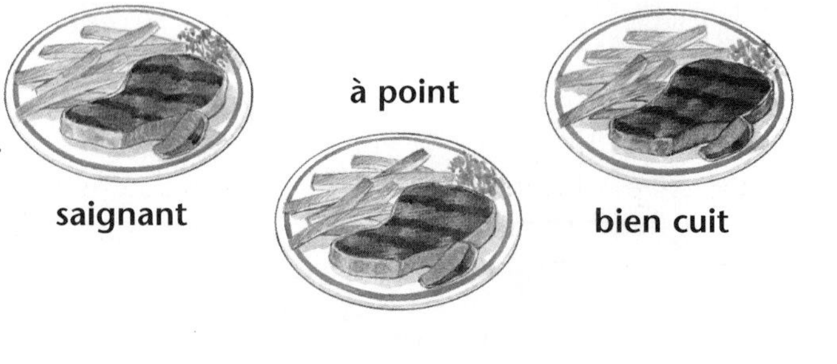

Alexandre n'invite pas ses copains.
Chacun paie pour soi.

Le service est compris.
Mais Alexandre laisse tout de même un petit pourboire.
Il laisse un peu d'argent pour le serveur.

Note

Here are some common time expressions. They range from "always" to "very seldom."

Au café...
Il y va toujours.
Il y va souvent.
Il y va quelquefois.
Il y va très peu.

Les trois repas de la journée

le petit déjeuner

On prend le petit déjeuner le matin.

le déjeuner

On déjeune entre midi et deux heures.

le dîner

On dîne le soir.

Quel est le mot?

8 **Historiette** Au restaurant

Inventez une histoire. *(Make up a story.)*

1. Laurène va au restaurant?
2. Elle prend le bus pour aller au restaurant?
3. Elle a faim?
4. Elle regarde la carte?
5. Elle commande un steak frites?
6. Elle aime son steak comment?
7. Pour le dessert, elle prend une glace? À quel parfum? Au chocolat ou à la vanille?
8. Après le déjeuner, Laurène demande l'addition?
9. Le service est compris ou pas?
10. Laurène laisse un pourboire pour le serveur?
11. Elle laisse un peu d'argent ou beaucoup d'argent?

Laurène regarde la carte.

Un serveur

9 **Historiette** Un dîner au resto

Choisissez. *(Choose.)*

1. Loïc ne va pas au restaurant ____. Il y va avec des copains.
   a. ensemble **b.** au cinquième **c.** tout seul
2. Ils n'y vont pas en voiture. Ils ne prennent pas le métro. Ils y vont ____.
   a. ensemble **b.** à pied **c.** après les cours
3. Loïc ____ un steak frites.
   a. prend **b.** laisse **c.** prépare
4. Après le dîner, Loïc demande ____.
   a. la carte **b.** le pourboire **c.** l'addition
5. Dans les restaurants en France, le service est ____.
   a. occupé **b.** compris **c.** libre
6. Le service est excellent et Loïc ____ un pourboire.
   a. laisse **b.** prend **c.** commande
7. Mais Loïc n'invite pas ses copains. ____ paie pour soi.
   a. L'addition **b.** Chacun **c.** Le serveur

10 Madame, s'il vous plaît!

Madame, s'il vous plaît! Demandez à la serveuse.
(Tell the waitress what you need.)

Une serviette, s'il vous plaît, madame!

1. 
2. 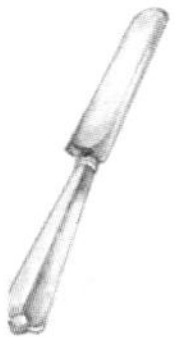
3. 
4. 
5. 

11 Les repas

Les repas Vrai ou faux? *(True or false?)*

1. On dîne le matin.
2. En France, on déjeune entre midi et deux heures.
3. On prend une tartine et un grand crème pour le dîner.
4. On prend un croque-monsieur pour le déjeuner.
5. On prend une soupe à l'oignon pour le dessert.
6. Une fourchette, c'est pour la soupe.
7. Une assiette, c'est pour le café.
8. Une nappe, c'est pour la soupe.

12 Au restaurant

Au restaurant Work with a classmate. Take turns asking each other questions about the illustration. Answer each other's questions.

13 Qu'est-ce que tu manges?

Qu'est-ce que tu manges? With a classmate, take turns finding out what each of you eats for breakfast and lunch.

ENCORE PLUS *For more practice using words from **Mots 2**, do Activity 14 on page H15 at the end of this book.*

Structure

Le verbe aller au présent
Telling and finding out where people go

1. The verb **aller** *(to go)* is an irregular verb. Study the following forms.

ALLER			
je	vais	nous‿allons	
tu	vas	vous‿allez	
il/elle/on	va	ils/elles	vont

Je vais au café, mais mes parents vont au restaurant.
Tu vas au restaurant avec des copains?
Vous y allez en bus?

2. If you do not mention the place you are going to, you must put the word **y** before the verb **aller. Y** refers to a place already mentioned. **Aller** cannot stand alone.

Tu vas au café?
Oui, j'y vais et Laurent y va aussi.

Savez-vous que... ?

The expression **On y va!** means "Let's get going." As a question, it means "Should we go?"

3. As you already know, the verb **aller** is also used to express how you feel.

Ça va?	**Oui, ça va bien, merci.**
Comment tu vas?	**Très bien, merci. Et toi?**
Vous allez bien?	**Oui, je vais bien, merci. Et vous?**

Café de Flore, Paris

Comment dit-on?

14 **Au restaurant!** Répétez la conversation avec un copain ou une copine. *(Repeat the conversation with a classmate.)*

15 **On va au Flore.** Complétez d'après la conversation. *(Complete according to the conversation.)*

1. Marie ____ bien.
2. Où ____ Paul?
3. Il ____ au Café de Flore.
4. Il n'y ____ pas tout seul.
5. Son amie Marie y ____ aussi.
6. Les deux copains y ____ ensemble.
7. Ils n'y ____ pas en voiture.
8. Ils y ____ à pied.

16 Historiette **Oui, j'y vais.** Donnez des réponses personnelles.
(Give your own answers.)

1. Tu vas souvent ou très peu au restaurant?
2. Tu y vas seul(e) ou avec ta famille?
3. Tu vas quelquefois dans un restaurant chinois ou italien?
4. Tu vas toujours dans le même restaurant?
5. Tu vas quelquefois au restaurant avec des copains?

17 Historiette **À l'école** Donnez des réponses personnelles.
(Give your own answers.)

1. Tes copains et toi, vous allez à l'école?
2. Vous allez à quelle école?
3. Vous allez à l'école à quelle heure?
4. Vous y allez comment—à pied, en car scolaire ou en voiture?
5. Après les cours, vous allez au café?

Honfleur, Normandie

18 **On dîne au restaurant.** Complétez la conversation. *(Complete the conversation.)*

Anne: Ce soir, je dîne au restaurant.
Jean: Ah oui? Où est-ce que tu __1__?
Anne: Au Vieux Honfleur.
Jean: Excellente idée! On y __2__ ensemble.
Anne: Mais, euh… je n'y __3__ pas toute seule.
Jean: Ah bon, tu y __4__ avec qui?
Anne: Euh… avec Olivier.
Jean: Vous y __5__ à quelle heure?
Anne: Mais tu es bien indiscret!

Aller + infinitif
Telling what's going to happen

1. You use **aller** + an infinitive to express what is going to take place in the near future.

   Demain on va avoir un examen.
   Les élèves vont étudier.
   Je vais passer l'examen.
   L'examen va être difficile, c'est sûr!

2. To make a sentence negative, you put **ne... pas** around the conjugated form of **aller.**

   Tu ne vas pas aller au café?
   Moi, je ne vais pas regarder la télé.

Comment dit-on?

tonight demain — tomorrow

19 **Ce soir!** Donnez des réponses personnelles. *(Give your own answers.)*

1. Ce soir, tu vas regarder la télé?
2. Tu vas téléphoner à un copain ou une copine?
3. Tu vas préparer le dîner?
4. Tu vas aller en classe?
5. Tu vas inviter tes professeurs au restaurant?

20 **Absurdités** Mettez à la forme négative. *(Make the sentences negative.)*

1. Nous allons en classe pendant le week-end.
2. Les chiens et les chats vont à l'école.
3. Demain le prof de maths va parler français.
4. Vous allez déjeuner pendant le cours de géographie.
5. Ce soir, je vais parler au téléphone avec Elvis Presley.

21 **Quand?** Work with a classmate. Tell each other some things you like to do. Then tell when you are going to do them—**ce soir, demain, demain matin, la semaine prochaine.**

Les contractions avec à et de
Expressing direction and possession

1. The preposition **à** can mean "to," "in," or "at." **À** is contracted with **le** and **les** to form one word—**au, aux.** Note that liaison occurs when **aux** is followed by a vowel.

à + le = au	Je vais au lycée.
à + les = aux	Le prof parle aux‿élèves.
à + la = à la	Tu vas à la cantine?
à + l' = à l'	Vous allez à l'école à pied?

Savez-vous que... ?

À is used in many food expressions.

une soupe à l'oignon
une omelette aux fines herbes

2. The preposition **de** can mean "of," "from," or "about." **De** contracts with **le** and **les** to form one word—**du, des.** Liaison occurs when **des** is followed by a vowel.

de + le = du	Il y a une belle vue du balcon.
de + les = des	On parle toujours des‿amis.
de + la = de la	Il arrive de la cantine.
de + l' = de l'	Je rentre de l'école.

3. The preposition **de** also indicates possession or ownership.

Le lycée de Vincent est à Paris.
C'est la voiture du professeur de Vincent.
Minou est le chat des voisins de Vincent.

Comment dit-on?

22 **Tu vas où?** Donnez des réponses personnelles. *(Give your own answers.)*

1. Quel est le nom de ton école?
2. Tu vas à l'école à quelle heure?
3. Tu vas au cours de français le matin ou l'après-midi?
4. Tu vas au cours d'anglais à quelle heure?
5. Tu aimes parler aux profs?
6. Tu aimes parler des profs aussi?
7. Tu habites près de l'école ou loin de l'école?
8. Tu rentres de l'école à quelle heure?
9. Comment est-ce que tu rentres de l'école?

23 Historiette Je n'y vais pas. Complétez avec à. *(Complete with* à.*)*

Ce soir, je ne vais pas __1__ (le concert). Je ne vais pas __2__ (le parc). Je ne vais pas __3__ (le collège). Je ne vais pas __4__ (le restaurant). Je ne vais pas parler __5__ (les copains). Je ne vais pas __6__ (l'anniversaire) de Julie. Je vais aller où, alors? Je vais rentrer __7__ (la maison). Pourquoi? Je suis fatigué(e)!

24 Au café Suivez le modèle. *(Follow the model.)*

une tarte aux fruits / une tarte aux pommes →
—Qu'est-ce que tu vas prendre?
—Je vais prendre une tarte.
—Une tarte aux fruits ou une tarte aux pommes?
—Oh, je vais prendre une tarte ____.

1. un sandwich au jambon / un sandwich au fromage
2. une omelette au fromage / une omelette aux fines herbes
3. une soupe à la tomate / une soupe à l'oignon
4. une glace au chocolat / une glace à la vanille
5. une crêpe au chocolat / une crêpe aux fruits

25 Le dîner des copains Combinez d'après le modèle. *(Combine according to the model.)*

c'est la voiture / les parents de Vincent →
C'est la voiture des parents de Vincent.

1. je vais à la table / les amis de Marc
2. ils sont à la terrasse / le café
3. nous regardons la carte / le restaurant
4. c'est le coca / l'amie de Marc
5. voilà le pourboire / la serveuse

Cellia Saubry *Coin de rue*

Le verbe prendre au présent
Describing more activities

1. The verb **prendre,** "to take," also means "to have" when used with foods. It is an irregular verb. Pay particular attention to both its spelling and pronunciation.

PRENDRE			
je	prends	nous	prenons
tu	prends	vous	prenez
il/elle/on	prend	ils/elles	prennent

Je prends le car scolaire pour aller à l'école.
Les voisins ne prennent pas l'ascenseur.
Je vais prendre un coca.

2. The verbs **apprendre** *(to learn)* and **comprendre** *(to understand)* are conjugated the same way as **prendre.**

On apprend beaucoup à l'école.
Vous comprenez le français, n'est-ce pas?

Les deux amis apprennent l'anglais.

Comment dit-on?

26 **Historiette** **Alexandre** Inventez une histoire. *(Make up a story.)*

1. Alexandre prend le car scolaire pour aller à l'école?
2. En classe, il prend des notes quand le professeur parle?
3. Il comprend bien le français?
4. Il apprend beaucoup de choses au cours de français?

Ils prennent leur petit déjeuner.

27 À l'école Donnez des réponses personnelles. *(Give your own answers.)*

1. Tu prends ton petit déjeuner à la maison ou à la cafétéria de l'école?
2. À l'école, tu prends l'escalier ou l'ascenseur pour monter au premier étage?
3. À la cafétéria de l'école, qu'est-ce que tu prends quand tu as soif?
4. Qu'est-ce que tu prends quand tu as faim?

28 Toujours à l'école Répondez. *(Answer.)*

1. La majorité des élèves prennent le car scolaire pour aller à l'école?
2. Les élèves prennent l'escalier ou l'ascenseur pour monter au premier étage?
3. En cours de français, tout le monde comprend bien quand le professeur parle?
4. Vous apprenez beaucoup de choses en cours de français?

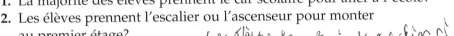

29 Au pluriel! Mettez au pluriel. *(Make the sentences plural.)*

1. Je prends le car scolaire pour aller à l'école.
2. Je prends l'ascenseur pour monter au quatrième étage.
3. Tu prends le bus, le métro ou la voiture?
4. Tu prends beaucoup de notes en classe?
5. L'élève est très intelligent et il apprend beaucoup de choses.
6. Elle comprend bien la leçon.
7. Son copain prend un coca au café.
8. Et moi, je prends une glace au chocolat.

ENCORE PLUS *For more practice using the verbs **aller** and **prendre**, do Activity 15 on page H16 at the end of this book.*

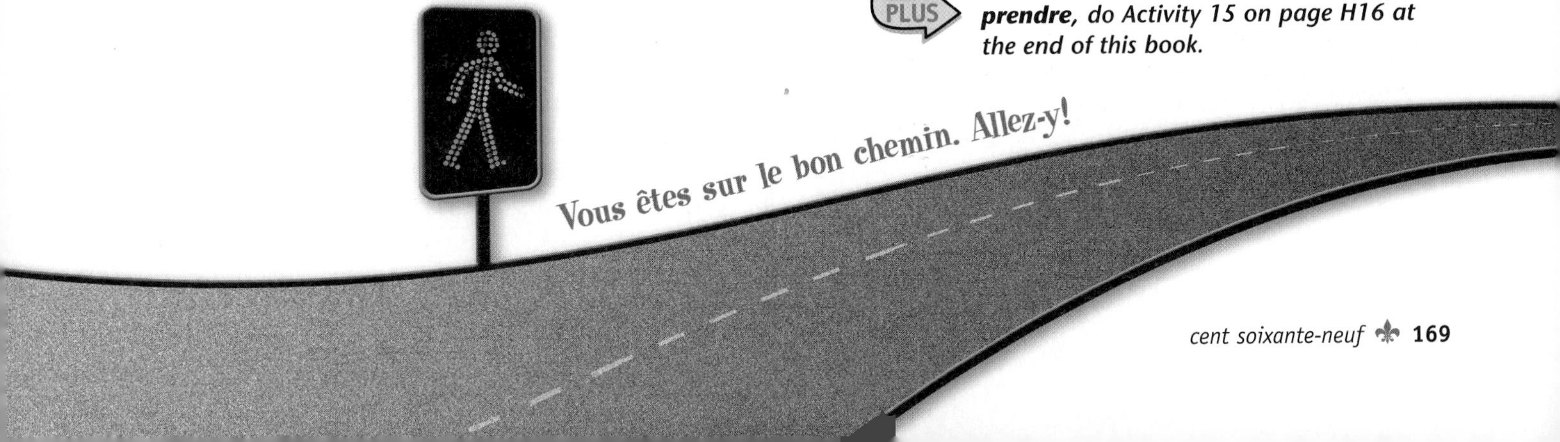
Vous êtes sur le bon chemin. Allez-y!

Conversation

Au restaurant

Claire: Tu as faim?
Loïc: Oui. J'ai hyper faim! Je vais prendre un bon steak frites.
Serveur: Vous désirez?
Loïc: Un steak frites, s'il vous plaît. Saignant.
Serveur: Et pour vous, mademoiselle?
Claire: Ben, un steak aussi, mais pas de frites. Une salade verte.
Serveur: Et vous aimez votre steak comment?
Claire: À point, s'il vous plaît.
(Après le dîner)
Loïc: L'addition, s'il vous plaît!
Serveur: Oui, monsieur, j'arrive!
Claire: On laisse quelque chose? Il est sympa, le serveur.
Loïc: Oh, écoute, le service est compris.

Vous avez compris?

Répondez. *(Answer.)*

1. Où sont Claire et Loïc?
2. Loïc a faim?
3. Qu'est-ce qu'il va prendre?
4. Et Claire, qu'est-ce qu'elle va prendre?
5. Qu'est-ce qu'elle commande avec le steak?
6. Claire et Loïc prennent leur steak comment?
7. Après le dîner, qui demande l'addition?
8. À votre avis *(In your opinion)*, est-ce qu'ils vont laisser un pourboire?

Parlons un peu plus

On commande? You and your friend are at a restaurant. Look at the menu and try to decide what to order. Then order. Another one of your classmates will be the server.

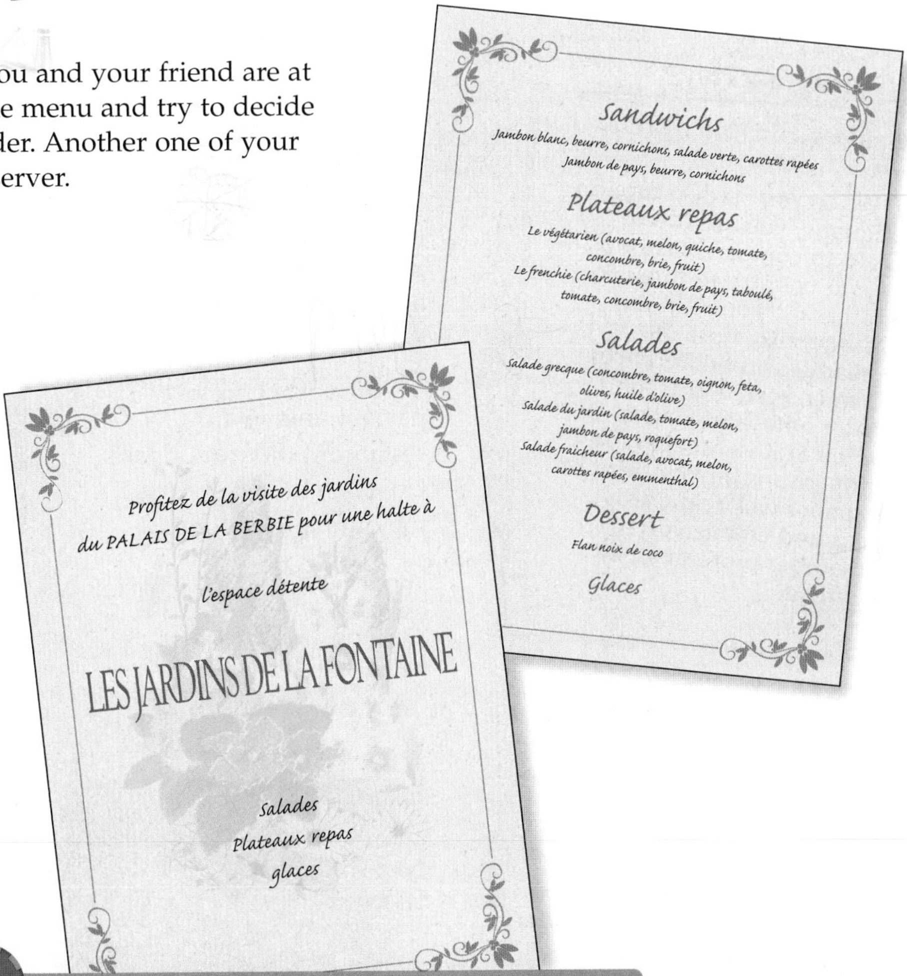
Sandwichs
Jambon blanc, beurre, cornichons, salade verte, carottes rapées
Jambon de pays, beurre, cornichons
Plateaux repas
Le végétarien (avocat, melon, quiche, tomate, concombre, brie, fruit)
Le frenchie (charcuterie, jambon de pays, taboulé, tomate, concombre, brie, fruit)
Salades
Salade grecque (concombre, tomate, oignon, feta, olives, huile d'olive)
Salade du jardin (salade, tomate, melon, jambon de pays, roquefort)
Salade fraîcheur (salade, avocat, melon, carottes rapées, emmenthal)
Dessert
Flan noix de coco
Glaces
Profitez de la visite des jardins du PALAIS DE LA BERBIE pour une halte à
l'espace détente
LES JARDINS DE LA FONTAINE
Salades
Plateaux repas
glaces

Prononciation

Le son /r/

The French sound **/r/** is very different from the American /r/. When you say **/r/**, the back of your tongue should almost completely block the air going through the back of your throat. Repeat the following words and sentences.

le verre	**toujours**	**la voiture**	**le pourboire**
la carte	**la tartine**	**la cuillère**	**la fourchette**
pour	**les crêpes**	**le serveur**	**le croque-monsieur**
boire	**les frites**	**le croissant**	

Le serveur arrive avec un verre de jus d'orange.
Je voudrais laisser un pourboire pour la serveuse.

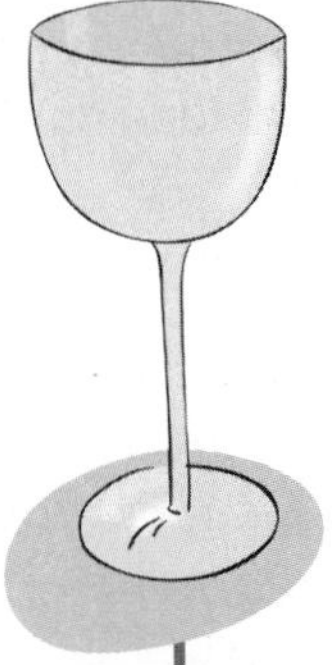

verre

Le Québec

Lectures culturelles

Reading Strategy

Making comparisons while reading

When you study a foreign language, you are often asked to compare customs in your country to those in another. As you read the passage, take note of similarities and differences between restaurants in France and those in the United States. Making these comparisons in your head or on paper will help clarify ideas and enable you to remember more of what you read.

Au restaurant? Vraiment?

Ce soir, Valentin va dîner dans un petit restaurant du coin[1]. Il invite ses deux amis Ahmed et Julie. Ils vont aller tous ensemble au restaurant.

Les copains arrivent au restaurant. Ils trouvent une table libre et ils prennent leur place. Tango prend sa place aussi, sous[2] la table. Sous la table? Oui. Mais qui est Tango? C'est le chien de Julie. Il est très bien élevé[3], Tango. Julie ne laisse pas Tango seul à la maison. Tango accompagne Julie partout, même au restaurant. Pourquoi pas? Un chien bien élevé est toujours le bienvenu[4]!

[1] du coin *local*
[2] sous *under*
[3] bien élevé *well-behaved*
[4] le bienvenu *welcome*

Haïti La Martinique

Le serveur arrive. Les amis regardent la carte et ils commandent. Après le dîner, Valentin demande l'addition. Le serveur arrive et donne l'addition à Valentin. Valentin regarde l'addition et paie. D'habitude chacun paie pour soi, mais aujourd'hui, c'est exceptionnel. Valentin paie pour tout le monde parce qu'il invite ses copains. En France, «inviter», c'est «payer»!

Vous avez compris?

A Valentin va au restaurant? Vrai ou faux? *(True or false?)*

1. Valentin va au restaurant tout seul.
2. Les copains entrent dans le restaurant et demandent une table au serveur.
3. Tango est un chien bien élevé.
4. Tango aussi va au restaurant.
5. Ahmed et Julie demandent l'addition.
6. Les trois amis paient l'addition.

B Des différences culturelles In this reading, there are some interesting cultural differences between France and the United States. What are they?

La France · La Suisse · La Belgique · La Tunisie · Le Maroc · Le Mali · Le Sénégal

Lecture supplémentaire 1

Les repas en France

La façon de manger en France change assez vite[1]. Pour le petit déjeuner, ça ne change pas vraiment; on prend toujours le petit déjeuner à la maison. C'est toujours un petit déjeuner rapide et frugal: une tartine de pain beurré et un bol de café, de thé ou de chocolat. Quelquefois, les enfants mangent des céréales.

On déjeune entre midi et deux heures. Mais le déjeuner n'est plus[2] le repas principal parce que les enfants déjeunent à la cantine de l'école. Les parents déjeunent à la cafétéria de leur entreprise[3] ou dans un restaurant près de l'entreprise.

Le dîner est maintenant le repas principal pour beaucoup de Français. Un des parents (ou les deux) prépare le dîner dans la cuisine et la famille dîne ensemble. Souvent on mange des produits surgelés[4]. En France, il y a des plats surgelés excellents. Le dîner est un moment important pour la famille; c'est le seul moment de la journée où on est ensemble.

[1] vite *fast*
[2] n'est plus *is no longer*
[3] entreprise *firm*
[4] surgelés *frozen*

Un restaurant aux Champs-Élysées

Vous avez compris?

Les repas Répondez. *(Answer.)*

1. En France, comment est le petit déjeuner?
2. Qu'est-ce qu'on prend pour le petit déjeuner?
3. On déjeune à quelle heure?
4. On déjeune où?
5. Quel est le repas principal?
6. Qu'est-ce qu'on prépare souvent pour le dîner?
7. Le dîner est un moment important pour la famille? Pourquoi?

Un dîner en famille

Lecture supplémentaire 2

La Belgique

La Tunisie

Le Maroc

Le Mali

Les goûts changent.

Beaucoup de Français sont de vrais gourmets. Ils aiment manger bien. La cuisine française est excellente. Elle est célèbre dans le monde entier. Les Français continuent à apprécier leur cuisine mais ils apprécient aussi les plats d'autres pays[1]. La cuisine asiatique est très populaire: la cuisine chinoise, la cuisine thaïlandaise et aussi la cuisine vietnamienne. En France, il y a beaucoup de restaurants vietnamiens. La cuisine vietnamienne ressemble un peu à la cuisine chinoise. Il y a aussi beaucoup de restaurants algériens, tunisiens et marocains où la spécialité est toujours le couscous.

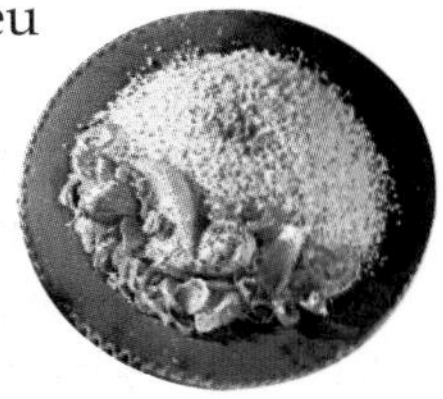

Comme aux États-Unis, il existe en France des chaînes de restaurants et des chaînes de fast-food. Certaines sont américaines, d'autres sont européennes. Elles sont françaises ou belges, par exemple, comme *Léon de Bruxelles.* Sa spécialité: les moules[2] frites, c'est-à-dire[3] des moules avec toutes sortes de sauces et des frites. C'est un plat traditionnel en Belgique.

Et la pizza? La pizza est très appréciée en France! Tout le monde aime la pizza!

[1] pays *countries*
[2] moules *mussels*
[3] c'est-à-dire *that is to say*

Au restaurant *Léon de Bruxelles*

Les aliments préférés des jeunes de 7 à 14 ans sont:
le steak frites (51%), les hamburgers (51%), la pizza (49%), les gâteaux (37%), les spaghettis ou raviolis (32%), les sandwichs (17%).
71% des Français indiquent qu'ils préfèrent la cuisine française aux cuisines étrangères.

Vous avez compris?

Au restaurant en France Vrai ou faux? *(True or false?)*

1. Les Français aiment manger bien.
2. Les Français n'apprécient pas leur cuisine.
3. La cuisine asiatique est très populaire en France.
4. Les restaurants asiatiques en France sont toujours des restaurants chinois.
5. Le couscous est une spécialité vietnamienne.
6. *Léon de Bruxelles* est une chaîne de restaurants belge en France.
7. Les Français n'aiment pas du tout la pizza.

CONNEXIONS

Les mathématiques

L'arithmétique

When we go shopping or out to eat, it is often necessary to do some arithmetic. We either have to add up the bill ourselves or check the figures someone else has done for us. In a café or restaurant we may want to figure out what we should leave for a tip, even if **le service est compris.**

We almost never do arithmetic in a foreign language. We normally do arithmetic in the language in which we learned it. However, it is fun to know some basic arithmetical terms in case we have to discuss a problem concerning a bill, for example, with a French-speaking person.

Before we learn some of these arithmetical terms in French, let's look at some differences in numbers. Note how the numbers 1 and 7 are written in French.

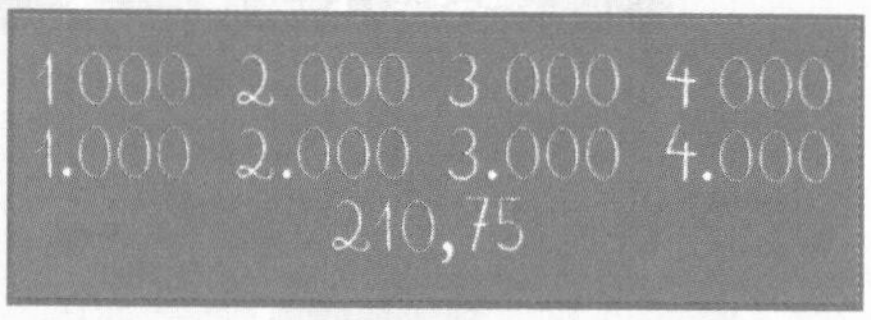

Note also that the thousands are indicated by a space or a period and the decimals are indicated by a comma.

L'arithmétique

additionner	+	soustraire	−
multiplier	×	diviser	÷

Pour additionner:

Deux plus deux, ça fait quatre.

$2 + 2 = 4$

Pour soustraire:

Quatre moins deux, ça fait deux.

$4 - 2 = 2$

Pour multiplier:

Deux fois deux, ça fait quatre.

$2 \times 2 = 4$

Pour diviser:

Quatre divisé par deux, ça fait deux.

$4 \div 2 = 2$

Dix pour cent (%) de 200 euros, c'est 20 euros.

Vous avez compris?

A Ça fait combien? Faites les opérations suivantes à voix haute. *(Solve the following problems aloud.)*

1. $2 + 2 =$
2. $14 + 6 =$
3. $30 - 8 =$
4. $20 - 4 =$
5. $4 \times 4 =$
6. $8 \times 3 =$
7. $27 \div 9 =$
8. $80 \div 10 =$

B L'addition, s'il vous plaît! You went out to a restaurant with three friends. This is your bill. Do the following.

1. Add up to see if the total is correct.
2. Add 10 percent, even though the tip is included.
3. Calculate how much each of you owes.

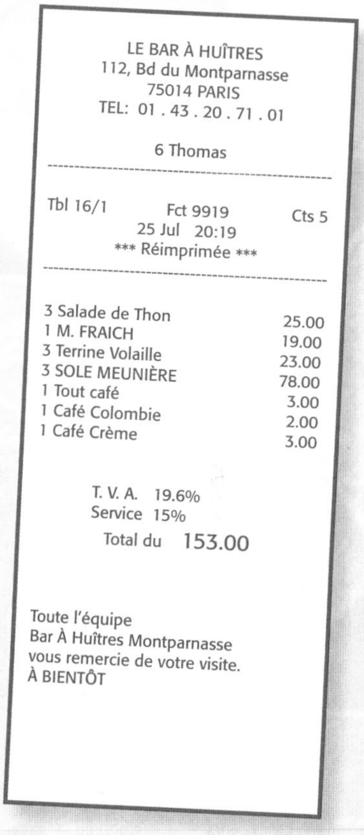

LE BAR À HUÎTRES
112, Bd du Montparnasse
75014 PARIS
TEL: 01 . 43 . 20 . 71 . 01

6 Thomas

Tbl 16/1 Fct 9919 Cts 5
25 Jul 20:19
*** Réimprimée ***

3 Salade de Thon	25.00
1 M. FRAICH	19.00
3 Terrine Volaille	23.00
3 SOLE MEUNIÈRE	78.00
1 Tout café	3.00
1 Café Colombie	2.00
1 Café Crème	3.00

T. V. A. 19.6%
Service 15%
Total du 153.00

Toute l'équipe
Bar À Huîtres Montparnasse
vous remercie de votre visite.
À BIENTÔT

C Comment compter sur ses doigts Here are three different ways people count on their fingers. Which one is yours? With a classmate, choose a way that is not yours and show each other numbers. Take turns figuring out which number it is.

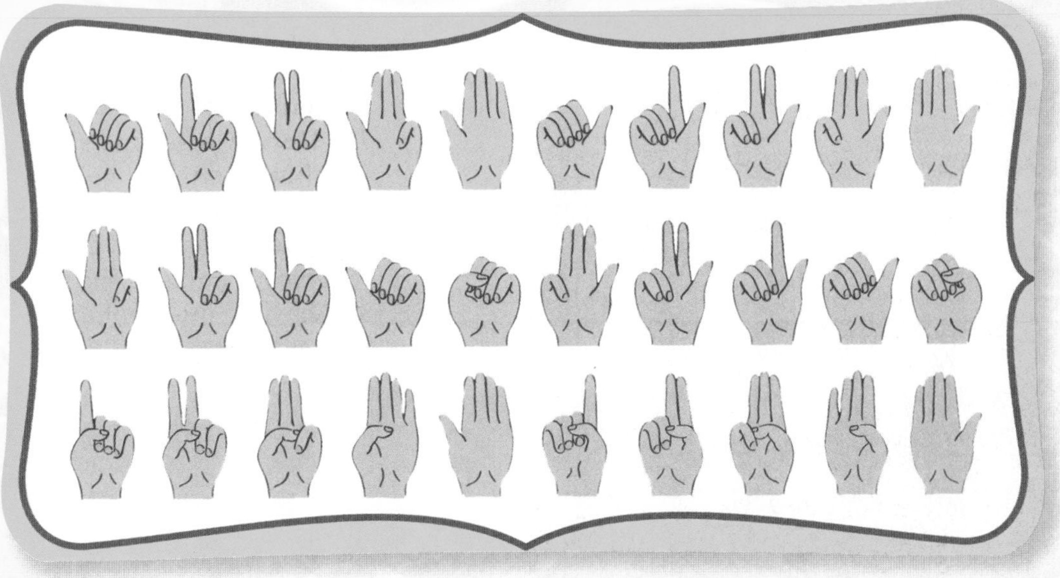

Use what you have learned

PARLER

1 Au café

✔ *Order something to eat or drink in a café*

Work with a classmate. One of you is the customer and the other is the server. You order from the menu provided.

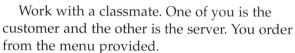

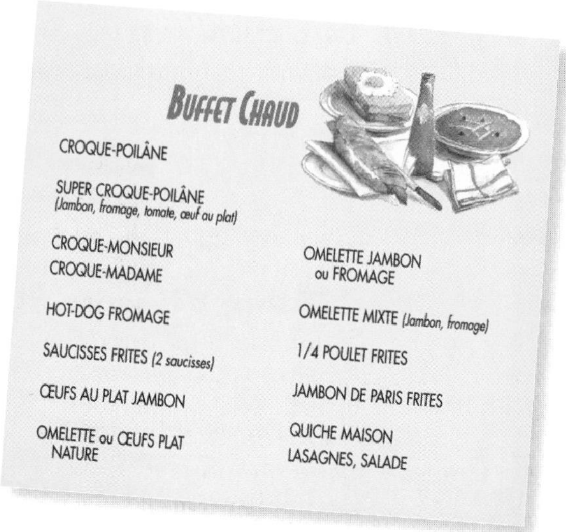
BUFFET CHAUD

CROQUE-POILÂNE

SUPER CROQUE-POILÂNE (Jambon, fromage, tomate, œuf au plat)

CROQUE-MONSIEUR

CROQUE-MADAME

HOT-DOG FROMAGE

SAUCISSES FRITES (2 saucisses)

ŒUFS AU PLAT JAMBON

OMELETTE ou ŒUFS PLAT NATURE

OMELETTE JAMBON ou FROMAGE

OMELETTE MIXTE (Jambon, fromage)

1/4 POULET FRITES

JAMBON DE PARIS FRITES

QUICHE MAISON

LASAGNES, SALADE

PARLER ÉCRIRE

2 À la terrasse des Deux Magots

✔ *Talk about school and teachers as you order food and drinks*

Work in groups of three or four. You're all friends sitting on the **terrasse** of the famous café **Les Deux Magots** in Paris, watching the world go by. You talk about many things—school, teachers, friends, etc. One of you will play the role of the waiter. You have to interrupt the conversation once in a while to take the orders and serve.

ÉCRIRE

3 La carte

✔ *Plan a menu*

Write a menu in French for your school cafeteria.

Élodie prend le déjeuner à la cantine.

Writing Strategy

Visualizing Many writers have a mental picture of what they want to write before they actually begin to write. The mental picture helps organize what they want to say. It also helps them visualize what they want to describe in their writing. Closing your eyes and visualizing what you want to write can make the writing experience more pleasant. When writing in a foreign language, you also have to restrict your mental picture to what you know how to say.

ÉCRIRE

4 Un restaurant

You have been asked to write a short article about a visit to a restaurant. Look at this illustration. Pretend this is the mental picture you have of the restaurant you are going to write about. Look at it for several minutes and then write a paragraph about it.

Assessment

Vocabulaire

1 Choisissez. *(Choose.)*

To review **Mots 1**, turn to pages 154–155.

1. Après les cours, Michel et Chantal vont au _____.
   a. café **b.** ensemble
2. Ils trouvent _____ à la terrasse.
   a. une table libre **b.** une tartine
3. Le serveur _____ la carte à Chantal.
   a. regarde **b.** donne
4. Chantal a soif. Elle commande quelque chose à _____.
   a. manger **b.** boire
5. Michel a faim. Il prend _____.
   a. un jus d'orange **b.** une tartine de pain beurré

Deux amis au café

2 Choisissez. *(Choose.)*

To review **Mots 2**, turn to pages 158–159.

6. À midi, Henri va _____ au restaurant.
   a. dîner **b.** déjeuner **c.** payer
7. Il _____ le métro.
   a. prend **b.** commande **c.** laisse
8. Henri aime son steak _____.
   a. à pied **b.** à point **c.** ensemble
9. Après le déjeuner, Henri _____ l'addition.
   a. demande **b.** invite **c.** laisse
10. Dans les restaurants en France _____ est compris.
    a. le verre **b.** l'addition **c.** le service

Structure

Au centre de Paris, près de l'Opéra
Angle 14, rue Favart - 9, rue d'Amboise
75002 - Paris - France
Tél : 01 42 96 36 89 - Fax : 01 47 03 97 31
Métro - Richelieu-Drouot

3 Complétez avec «aller».
(Complete with the verb aller.*)*

11. Nous _____ à l'école en voiture?
12. Laurent, tu _____ au café?
13. Vous _____ bien, madame?

*To review the verb **aller**, turn to page 162.*

4 Choisissez. *(Choose.)*

14. Je vais _____ au café avec mes copains.
    a. déjeune **b.** déjeuner
15. Ils vont _____ un pourboire pour le serveur.
    a. laisser **b.** laissent

*To review the use of **aller** + an infinitive, turn to page 165.*

5 Complétez avec «à» ou «de».
(Complete with à *or* de.*)*

16. Les amis vont _____ café.
17. Vincent rentre _____ école à cinq heures.
18. C'est la voiture _____ père de Marie.
19. Le prof donne un examen _____ élèves.

*To review the forms of **à** and **de**, turn to page 166.*

6 Complétez avec «prendre».
(Complete with the verb prendre.*)*

20. Les copains _____ le métro.
21. Vous _____ le petit déjeuner à la maison?
22. Pour monter à l'appartement, on _____ l'ascenseur.
23. Tu _____ un sandwich à midi?

*To review the verb **prendre**, turn to page 168.*

Culture

7 Complétez. *(Complete.)*

24. Les copains _____ une table libre au restaurant.
25. Claire paie pour tout le monde. Elle _____ ses copains.

To review this cultural information, turn to pages 172–173.

On parle super bien!

Tell all you can about this illustration.

Vocabulaire

Getting along in a café or restaurant

un café
la terrasse d'un café
une table
  occupée
  libre
un serveur
une serveuse

la carte
l'addition *(f.)*
l'argent *(m.)*
le pourboire
aller
trouver une table
commander

inviter
payer
laisser
prendre
déjeuner
dîner
avoir faim

avoir soif
Vous désirez?
je voudrais
quelque chose
  à manger
  à boire
Le service est compris.

Identifying snacks and beverages

une boisson
une consommation
un coca
une limonade
un café
un express
un crème
un citron pressé
un jus de pomme

un jus d'orange
une tartine de pain
  beurré
un croissant
un sandwich
  au jambon
  au fromage
un croque-monsieur

un steak
  saignant
  à point
  bien cuit
des frites *(f. pl.)*
une soupe à l'oignon
une omelette
  nature
  aux fines herbes

une saucisse de
  Francfort, un
  hot-dog
une salade verte
une glace
À quel parfum?
  au chocolat
  à la vanille
une crêpe

Identifying a place setting

le couvert
un verre
une tasse

une fourchette
un couteau
une cuillère

une assiette
une nappe
une serviette

How well do you know your vocabulary?

- Choose words for specific foods you enjoy.
- Create a menu using these words.

Identifying meals

un repas
le petit déjeuner
le déjeuner
le dîner

Other useful words and expressions

tout(e) seul(e)
toujours
souvent

quelquefois
peu

VIDÉOTOUR

Épisode 5

In this video episode, you will join Chloé and Christine at a café. See page 530 for more information.

CHAPITRE 6

La nourriture et les courses

Objectifs

In this chapter you will learn to:

- *identify more foods*
- *shop for food*
- *tell what you or others are doing*
- *ask for the quantity you want*
- *talk about what you or others don't have*
- *tell what you or others are able to do or want to do*
- *talk about French food-shopping customs*

Paul Cézanne *Nature morte au panier*

OFFICE
DU
TOURISME

Vocabulaire

Mots 1

À la boulangerie-pâtisserie

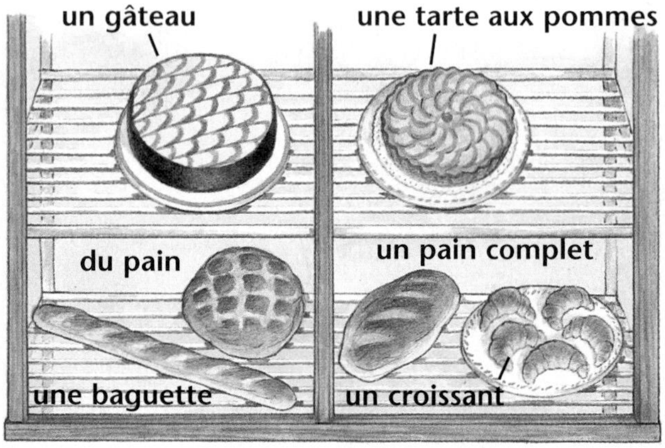

À la crémerie

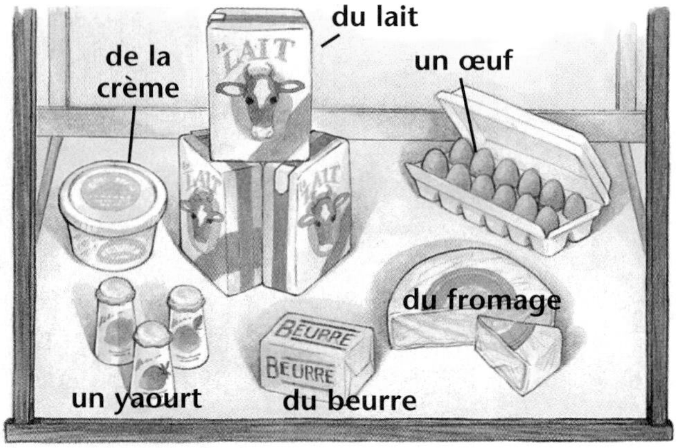

la fromagerie = cheese store

À la boucherie

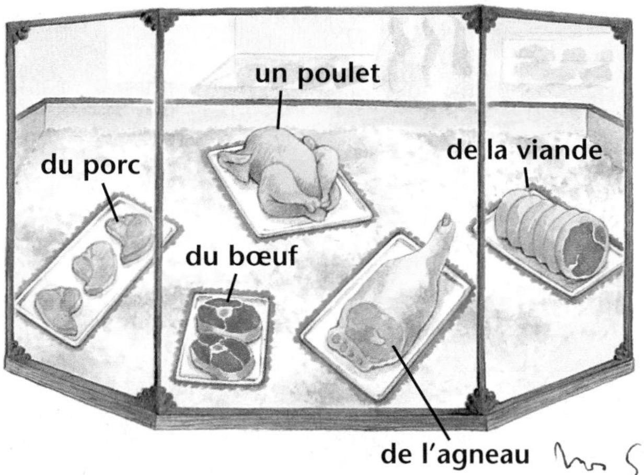

un sommelier

À la poissonnerie

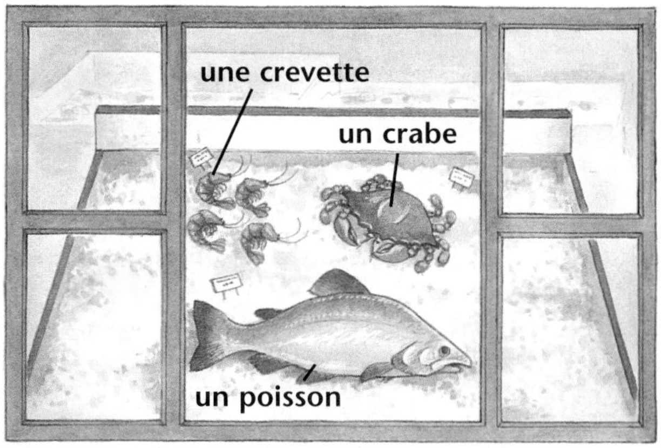

À la charcuterie

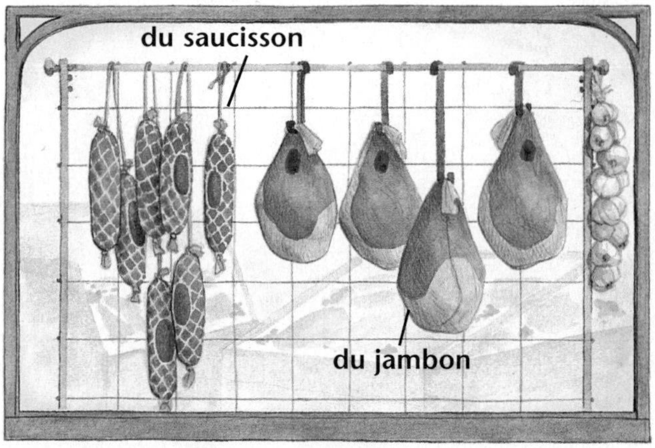

À l'épicerie

un sac

Paul fait les courses.
Il va à la boulangerie.
Il va chercher du pain.

Je voudrais une baguette, s'il vous plaît.
Ah, je regrette, il n'y a plus de baguettes.

Paul est à la boulangerie.
Il veut acheter une baguette.
Il n'y a plus de baguettes.

Bon, alors un pain complet.
Et avec ça?
C'est tout, merci.

Il ne peut pas acheter de baguette.
Il achète un pain complet.

Quel est le mot?

Une crémerie, Montgeron, France

1 Historiette À la crémerie

Inventez une histoire. *(Make up a story.)*

1. Madame Cadet va chercher du beurre. Elle va à la crémerie ou à la boucherie?
2. Elle veut acheter aussi du lait. Elle va à la crémerie?
3. Elle veut des œufs aussi?
4. Elle peut acheter du fromage à la crémerie?
5. Elle va acheter des yaourts pour le dessert?

2 Historiette On fait les courses.

Répondez d'après les indications. *(Answer according to the cues.)*

1. Qui fait les courses? (Élodie)
2. Elle fait les courses quand? (le samedi matin)
3. Elle a un sac? (oui)
4. Elle va au supermarché? (non)
5. Elle va où? (à la boulangerie)
6. Qu'est-ce qu'elle va acheter à la boulangerie? (du pain)
7. Elle veut une baguette? (oui)
8. Il n'y a plus de baguettes? (non)
9. Alors, qu'est-ce qu'elle achète? (un pain complet)

3 À l'épicerie

Complétez d'après la photo. *(Complete according to the photo.)*

On va acheter du __1__, des __2__, de la __3__, du __4__, de l'__5__, du __6__ et du __7__.

4 **On va où?** Complétez. *(Complete.)*

1. Pour acheter un poulet, du bœuf, du porc et de l'agneau, on va ____.
2. Pour acheter du lait, on va ____.
3. Pour acheter des croissants et un gâteau, on va ____.
4. Pour acheter de la viande, on va ____.
5. Pour acheter du saucisson et du jambon, on va ____.
6. Pour acheter de la crème et des œufs, on va ____.
7. Pour acheter du poisson et des crevettes, on va ____.
8. Pour acheter des yaourts, on va ____.
9. Pour acheter une tarte aux pommes, on va ____.
10. Pour acheter des crabes, on va ____.

Une poissonnerie, Paris

5 **Les courses** You're living in Arles with a French family. You offered to do the grocery shopping. Your host gives you this list. Find out from your French brother or sister (your partner) where you go for each item.

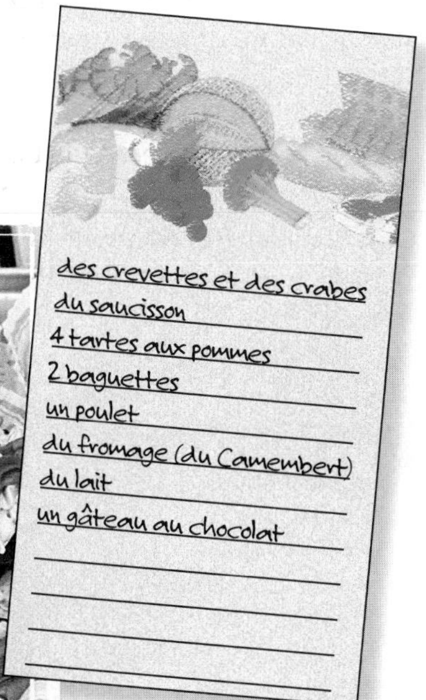

ENCORE PLUS *For more practice using words from **Mots 1**, do Activity 16 on page H17 at the end of this book.*

Au marché

Il est bon, mon melon!

Elle est bonne, ma salade!

C'est combien, les carottes?
Un euro le kilo.
Alors, un kilo, s'il vous plaît.
Vous voulez autre chose?

Oui, une livre de tomates et c'est tout.
Alors ça fait deux euros cinquante.

Ariane est au marché.
Elle veut acheter des légumes.
Elle va chez la marchande de fruits et légumes.

un kilo = 1 000 (mille) grammes
une livre = 500 (cinq cents) grammes

€1 = $1.40

Julien et son frère sont au supermarché.
Julien veut acheter de l'eau minérale et du lait.
Il achète une bouteille d'eau minérale et un litre de lait.

Note

Many words for foods in French are cognates.

un fruit	**une carotte**
une banane	**une tomate**
une orange	**un oignon**

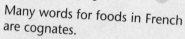

un paquet de légumes surgelés Frozen

un pot de moutarde

un litre de lait

250 grammes de beurre

une boîte de petits pois
une boîte de conserve Box/can

une bouteille d'eau minérale

une tranche de jambon

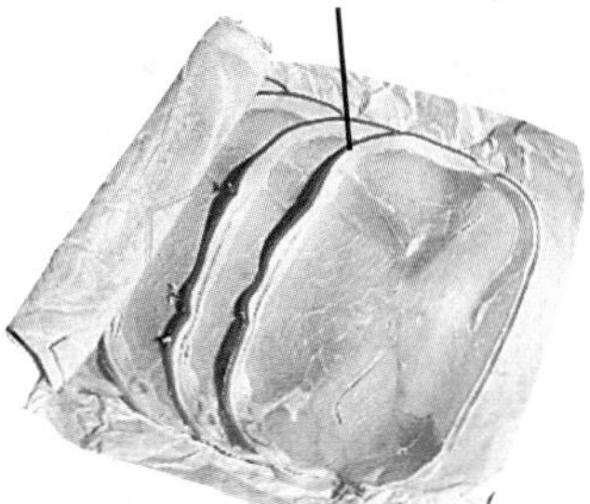

un pot de confiture

une douzaine d'œufs

Quel est le mot?

6 **Fruit(s) ou légume(s)?** Identifiez d'après le modèle. *(Identify according to the model.)*

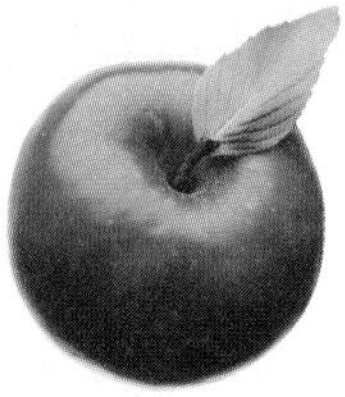

C'est une pomme. C'est un fruit.

1. 

2. 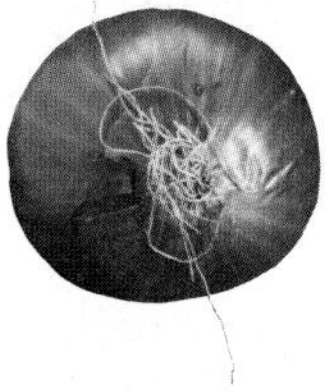

3. 

4. 

5. 

6. 

7. 

8. 

7 **Historiette** **Mathilde va au marché.** Complétez. *(Complete.)*

Mathilde veut préparer une grande salade. Elle va au marché. Elle va chez la __1__. Elle achète une __2__, des __3__ et des __4__. La marchande demande: «Vous voulez autre chose?» Mathilde répond: «Non, merci, __5__.» Elle donne de l'argent à la __6__.

8 **Historiette** **Martin va au supermarché.** Complétez. *(Complete.)*

Martin veut acheter de la moutarde, de l'eau minérale, une boîte de petits pois et un paquet de légumes surgelés. Pour acheter tout ça, il va au supermarché. Au supermarché, il prend un chariot. Il achète deux __1__ d'eau minérale, un __2__ de carottes surgelées et trois __3__ de sardines. Et autre chose aussi—un __4__ de moutarde. Martin va à la caisse. Ça __5__ combien, les bouteilles d'eau minérale, le paquet de carottes surgelées, les __6__ de sardines et le __7__ de moutarde? Ça fait onze euros cinquante.

9 **C'est combien, s'il vous plaît?** Conversez d'après le modèle.
(Make up a conversation according to the model.)

—C'est combien, la boîte de petits pois?
—Un euro quatorze.

1. 

2. 

3. 

4. 

5. 

6. 

10 **Pourquoi pas?** Conversez d'après le modèle.
(Make up a conversation according to the model.)

Tu veux des épinards?
Des épinards? Non.
Pourquoi?
Parce que je n'aime pas ça.

1. Tu veux du saucisson?
2. Tu veux des fraises?
3. Tu veux des haricots verts?
4. Tu veux des petits pois?
5. Tu veux de la confiture de fraises?
6. Tu veux du poisson?

Carnet
eau minérale
jambon
fraises
œufs
lait
beurre
frites surgelées

11 **À l'épicerie** You're in a grocery store in Paris. You want to buy the items on the list. Tell the clerk (your partner) how much you want of each item and find out how much it costs.

ENCORE PLUS *For more practice using words from **Mots 2**, do Activity 17 on page H18 at the end of this book.*

Structure

Le verbe faire au présent
Telling and finding out what people do

1. The verb **faire** *(to do, to make)* is an irregular verb. Study the following forms.

FAIRE			
je	fais	nous	faisons
tu	fais	vous	faites
il/elle/on	fait	ils/elles	font

2. You will use the verb **faire** a great deal in French. **Faire** is used in many expressions that take a different verb in English. Such expressions that cannot be translated directly from one language to another are called "idiomatic expressions." **Faire les courses** *(to go grocery shopping)* and **faire ses devoirs** *(to do homework)* are examples of idiomatic expressions. The following are some others.

   Maman prépare un bon dîner. Elle aime beaucoup faire la cuisine.
   Les copains vont faire un pique-nique.
   Moi, je fais de l'allemand et ma sœur fait de l'espagnol.

Comment dit-on?

12 On fait les courses.
Répétez la conversation.
(Repeat the conversation.)

Éric: Salut, Anne! Ça va?
Anne: Ça va. Qu'est-ce que tu fais?
Éric: Je fais les courses.
Anne: Ben, moi aussi. Je vais au marché de la rue Dejean. On fait nos courses ensemble?
Éric: Merci, mais j'ai beaucoup de choses différentes à acheter. Je vais aller au supermarché.
Anne: Ben, je vais avec toi. C'est dans la même direction.
Éric: D'accord.

Rue Dejean, Paris

13 **Qu'est-ce qu'ils font?** Complétez et répondez d'après la conversation.
(Complete and answer according to the conversation.)

1. Qu'est-ce qu'il ____, Éric?
2. Qu'est-ce qu'elle ____, Anne?
3. Qu'est-ce qu'ils ____, Anne et Éric?
4. Est-ce qu'ils ____ les courses ensemble?

14 **Et toi?** Donnez des réponses personnelles.
(Give your own answers.)

1. Tu fais quelquefois la cuisine chez toi?
2. Tu fais tes études dans un lycée français ou dans une école secondaire américaine?
3. Tu fais tes devoirs devant la télévision?
4. Tu fais du français?

15 **À chacun son travail** Suivez le modèle. *(Follow the model.)*

Moi, je fais le dîner. Et vous deux, qu'est-ce que vous faites?
Nous aussi, on fait le dîner.

1. Moi, je fais les courses.
2. Moi, je fais la cuisine.
3. Moi, je fais le déjeuner.
4. Moi, je fais les sandwichs.
5. Moi, je fais le gâteau.

16 **Historiette** **Mon copain Hugo** Complétez. *(Complete.)*

Hugo et moi, on est copains. Il est très intelligent. Hugo __1__ du russe. Moi aussi, je __2__ du russe. Nous __3__ du russe ensemble. Hugo et moi, nous __4__ quelquefois nos devoirs ensemble.

Hugo et son amie Marie __5__ de l'histoire avec Madame Delcourt. Qu'est-ce qu'ils __6__ au cours d'histoire? Ils apprennent beaucoup de nouvelles choses. Vous __7__ du français, n'est-ce pas? Vous __8__ du français avec qui?

17 **Nous sommes gentils.** Get together with a classmate. Discuss the things you do to help around the house. Decide who is the most helpful.

ENCORE PLUS *For more practice using the verb **faire**, do Activity 18 on page H19 at the end of this book.*

Le partitif et l'article défini
Talking about all or some

1. In French, you use the definite article **(le, la, l', les)** when talking about something in a general sense.

Les enfants aiment le lait.	*Children like milk.*
Je déteste les œufs.	*I hate eggs.*
Je n'aime pas la salade.	*I don't like lettuce.*

2. The partitive expresses an unspecified amount. English uses "some," "any," or no word at all to express the partitive.

Do you have (any) toast?
Yes, I do. Would you like (some) jam with your toast?

3. In French, you use **de** + the definite article to express the partitive. Remember that **de** contracts with **le** and **les** to form one word, **du** and **des.**

de + le = du	Tu as du lait et du beurre?
de + les = des	Je vais acheter des fruits et des légumes.
de + la = de la	Je voudrais de la crème.
de + l' = de l'	Je voudrais de l'eau.

4. Study the following chart. It contrasts the use of a noun in the general sense with the partitive.

General Sense	Partitive
J'aime le poulet.	Je voudrais du poulet.
J'aime la viande.	Je voudrais de la viande.
J'aime l'eau minérale.	Je voudrais de l'eau minérale.
J'aime les pommes.	Je voudrais des pommes.

Note that verbs indicating likes and dislikes are followed by the definite article. All other verbs are followed by the partitive.

Il déteste la viande.	**Elle va acheter de la viande.**
J'adore le fromage.	**Tu prends du fromage?**

24 **Je voudrais...** Conversez d'après le modèle.
(Make up a conversation according to the model.)

Je voudrais du jambon, s'il vous plaît.
Je regrette, mais il n'y a plus de jambon.

1. Je voudrais de l'eau minérale, s'il vous plaît.
2. Je voudrais de la glace à la vanille, s'il vous plaît.
3. Je voudrais des croissants, s'il vous plaît.
4. Je voudrais des fraises, s'il vous plaît.
5. Je voudrais du fromage, s'il vous plaît.

25 **Juliette fait les courses.** Répondez d'après le modèle.
(Answer according to the model.)

—Elle va acheter du poisson à la boucherie?
—Non, elle ne va pas acheter de poisson à la boucherie. Elle va acheter de la viande.

1. Elle va acheter du pain à la boucherie?
2. Elle va acheter du fromage à la boulangerie?
3. Elle va acheter des légumes à la charcuterie?
4. Elle va acheter de la viande à la crémerie?
5. Elle va acheter des œufs chez le marchand de fruits et légumes?

Une charcuterie, Conques, France

26 **Je n'aime pas ça!**
Répondez d'après le modèle.
(Answer according to the model.)

—Tu as de la confiture?
—Non, je n'ai pas de confiture. Je n'aime pas la confiture.

1. Tu as du saucisson?
2. Tu as du fromage?
3. Tu as du café?
4. Tu as de la limonade?
5. Tu as des épinards?
6. Tu as des sardines?

27 Historiette Au supermarché Complétez. *(Complete.)*

Quand je vais au supermarché, je n'achète pas __1__ fruits. Je n'aime pas __2__ fruits du supermarché. J'achète __3__ fruits au marché, chez le marchand de fruits et légumes. Je n'achète pas __4__ café au supermarché. Je n'achète pas __5__ viande. Je n'achète pas __6__ légumes, pas __7__ oignons. Qu'est-ce que j'achète au supermarché? J'achète seulement __8__ boîtes de conserve, __9__ bouteilles d'eau minérale, __10__ sel, __11__ poivre, __12__ vinaigre et __13__ huile.

28 Dans le frigidaire

Work with a classmate. Ask him or her for something you'd like to eat or drink. Your partner will check to see whether or not it's in the refrigerator. Use the model as a guide.

—Tu as de la glace au chocolat? J'adore la glace au chocolat.
—Je regrette, il n'y a plus de glace au chocolat.

29 Un sandwich extraordinaire

Work with a classmate. Discuss what would be a great sandwich. You may (or may not) want to use some of the following ingredients.

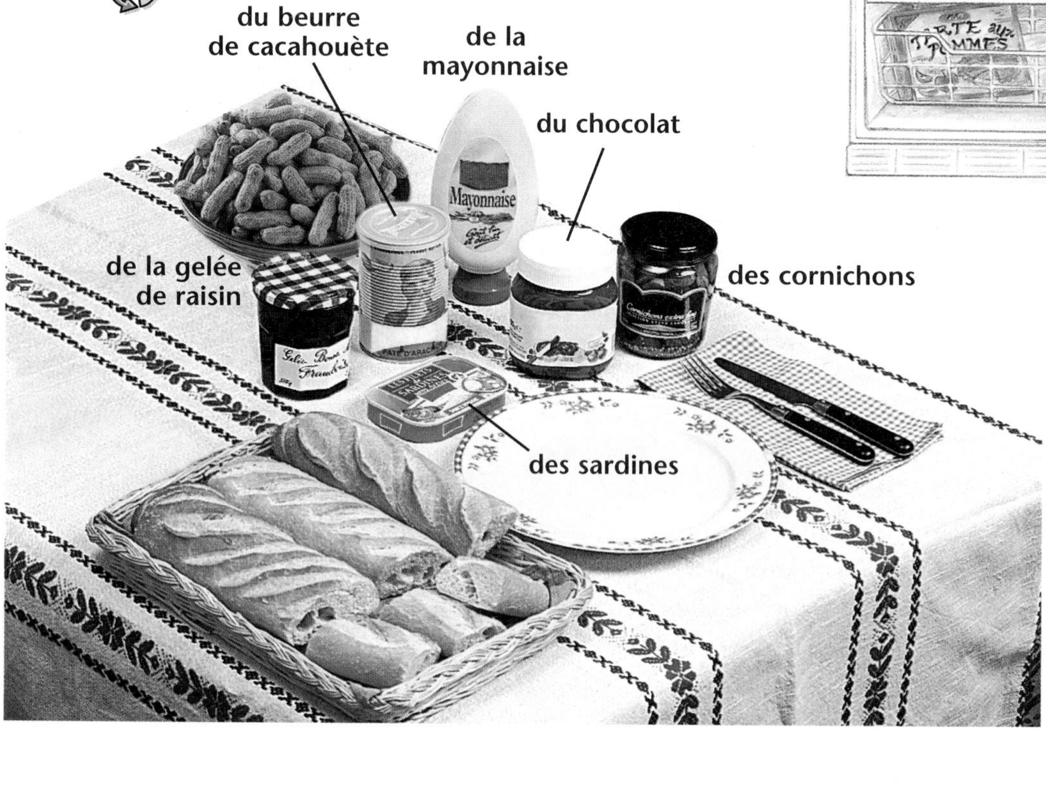

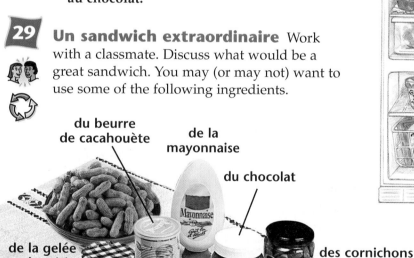

Attention!

Pay special attention to the spelling and pronunciation of the following adjectives that double the consonant in the feminine.

Féminin	Masculin
bonne(s)	**bon(s)**
canadienne(s)	**canadien(s)**
gentille(s)	**gentil(s)**
quelle(s)	**quel(s)**

Complétez. *(Complete.)*

1. Tu fais de la ____ cuisine? (bon)
2. Tu fais de ____ sandwichs? (bon)
3. Tu as des amis ____ et ____? (canadien, vietnamien)
4. Tu as des amies ____? (tunisien)
5. Tu aimes les filles qui sont ____? (gentil)
6. Tu aimes ____ profs? (quel)

Les verbes pouvoir et vouloir

Telling what one can do or wants to do

1. Study the forms of the verbs **pouvoir** *(to be able to)* and **vouloir** *(to want).*

POUVOIR		VOULOIR	
je	peux	je	veux
tu	peux	tu	veux
il/elle/on	peut	il/elle/on	veut
nous	pouvons	nous	voulons
vous	pouvez	vous	voulez
ils/elles	peuvent	ils/elles	veulent

Savez-vous que... ?

Je voudrais is a polite form of **je veux.** It means "I would like."

Je voudrais une livre de haricots verts, s'il vous plaît.

Michel ne peut pas aller au marché à pied.
Il veut acheter des légumes et des fruits.
Vous voulez manger maintenant?
Vous pouvez si vous voulez.

2. In the negative, you put **ne... pas** around the verbs **pouvoir** and **vouloir.**

Je ne veux pas manger de frites.
Ils ne peuvent pas aller au restaurant ce soir.

ex 30-33

p 202-203

Comment dit-on?

30 **Je veux bien, mais je ne peux pas.** Conversez d'après le modèle. *(Make up a conversation according to the model.)*

—Tu veux aller au restaurant?
—Je veux bien, mais je ne peux pas.

1. Tu veux aller au café?
2. Tu veux dîner avec Caroline?
3. Tu veux travailler après l'école?
4. Ta sœur veut faire les courses?
5. Elle veut aller au marché?
6. Elle veut préparer le dîner?
7. Elle veut inviter des amis?

Un marché, Saint-Rémy-de-Provence, France

31 **Si vous voulez, vous pouvez.** Conversez d'après le modèle. *(Make up a conversation according to the model.)*

Nous voulons travailler.
Si vous voulez travailler, vous pouvez travailler.

1. Nous voulons manger maintenant.
2. Nous voulons inviter des amis.
3. Nous voulons aller au restaurant.
4. Nous voulons commander de la pizza.
5. Nous voulons regarder le film.
6. Nous voulons écouter nos CD.

32 **Historiette** **Pas assez d'argent** Complétez avec **pouvoir** ou **vouloir.** *(Complete with* pouvoir *or* vouloir.*)*

Pierre et son frère ont faim. Ils ___1___ aller dans un restaurant où ils ___2___ dîner rapidement. Ils ___3___ commander deux hamburgers chacun, mais ils ne ___4___ pas. Pierre insiste, mais son frère ne ___5___ pas: «Pas question! On n'a pas assez d'argent! Tu ___6___ commander seulement un hamburger aujourd'hui.»

33 **Qui peut préparer le dîner?** Complétez. *(Complete.)*

Marie: Je voudrais bien faire le dîner ce soir, mais vraiment, je ne ___1___ (pouvoir) pas.
Julien: Tu ne ___2___ (pouvoir) pas? Pourquoi?
Marie: Je ___3___ (être) très fatiguée! Je ___4___ (être) vraiment crevée.
Julien: On ___5___ (pouvoir) aller au restaurant, si tu ___6___ (vouloir).
Marie: Oh, je ne ___7___ (vouloir) pas aller au restaurant ce soir.
Julien: On ___8___ (pouvoir) faire des sandwichs.
Marie: Oui, ou… toi, tu ___9___ (pouvoir) faire le dîner.
Julien: Je ___10___ (vouloir) bien, mais ce n'___11___ (être) pas une très bonne idée.
Marie: Pourquoi?
Julien: Parce que je ___12___ (faire) très mal la cuisine!

34 **Pourquoi pas?** Work with a classmate. Tell each other some things you or you and your friends want to do but can't. When possible, give reasons.

ENCORE PLUS *For more practice using the verbs **pouvoir** and **vouloir**, do Activity 19 on page H20 at the end of this book.*

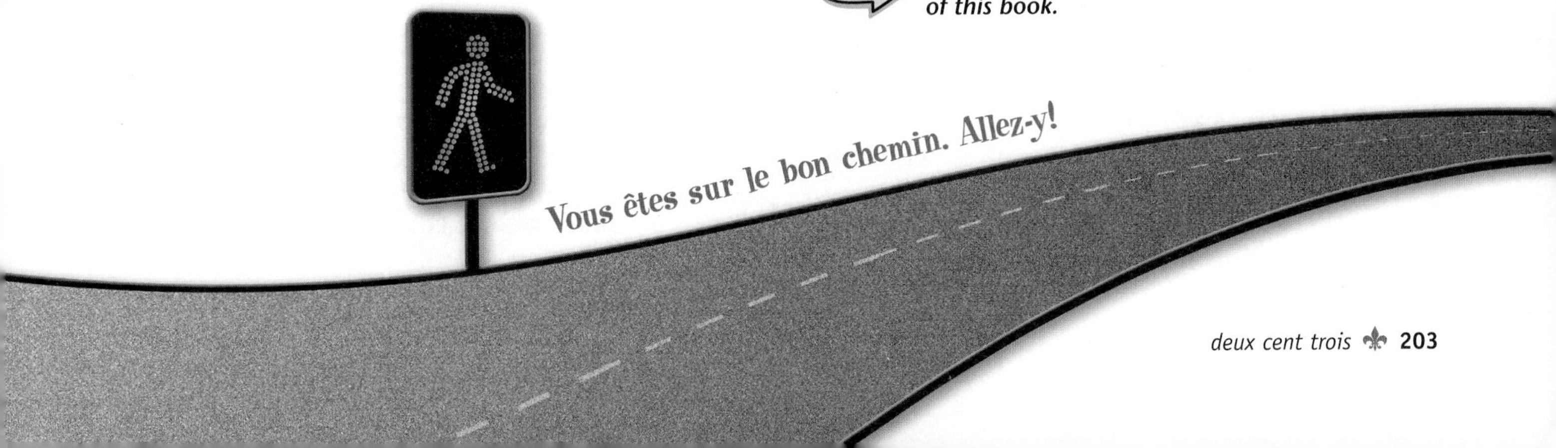
Vous êtes sur le bon chemin. Allez-y!

Conversation

Au marché

Marchand: Et maintenant, je suis à vous, madame. Comment allez-vous ce matin?
Mme Brun: Très bien, merci. Et vous?
Marchand: Oh, comme ci, comme ça! Enfin... Qu'est-ce que vous désirez aujourd'hui?
Mme Brun: Je voudrais des haricots verts et des carottes. C'est combien, les haricots verts?
Marchand: Quatre euros le kilo. Et ils sont bons!
Mme Brun: Alors, un kilo, s'il vous plaît, et une livre de carottes.
Marchand: Et avec ça, madame?
Mme Brun: C'est tout, merci. Ça fait combien?
Marchand: Alors, un kilo de haricots verts, une livre de carottes... Ça fait quatre euros cinquante.
Mme Brun: Voilà, monsieur.
Marchand: Merci, madame. Et à samedi prochain.

Vous avez compris?

Répondez. *(Answer.)*

1. Mme Brun fait ses courses?
2. Le marchand va bien?
3. Mme Brun fait ses courses au supermarché?
4. Elle parle au marchand de légumes?
5. Qu'est-ce qu'elle veut acheter?
6. Elle veut des haricots verts?
7. Ça fait combien, les haricots verts et les carottes?

Parlons un peu plus

Qu'est-ce qu'on va manger? Work with a classmate. Prepare a menu in French for tomorrow's meals—**le petit déjeuner, le déjeuner et le dîner.** Based on your menus, prepare a shopping list. Be sure to include the quantities you need.

Une poissonnerie, Abidjan, Côte d'Ivoire

Prononciation

Les sons /œ́/ et /œ̀/

1. Listen to the difference in the vowel sounds in **peut** and **peuvent.** The sound /œ́/ in **peut** is a closed vowel sound and the sound /œ̀/ in **peuvent** is an open vowel sound. Repeat the following words with the sound /œ́/.

   il peut **il veut** **des œufs** **deux**

2. Repeat the following words with the sound /œ̀/.

   ils peuvent **ils veulent** **un œuf**
   leur sœur **du beurre**

3. Now repeat the following pairs of words. Be sure to distinguish between the two vowel sounds.

   il peut / ils peuvent
   il veut / ils veulent

4. Now repeat the following sentences.

   Elle veut faire les courses, mais ils ne veulent pas.
   Elle veut du beurre et des œufs.
   Leur sœur est sérieuse.

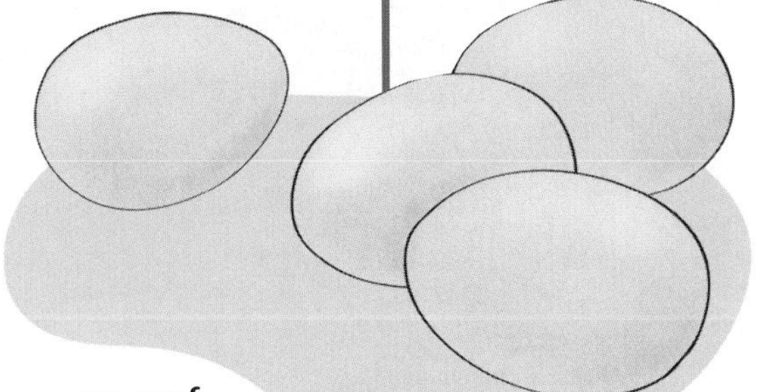
un œuf
des œufs

Lectures culturelles

Reading Strategy

Guessing meaning from context

It's easy to understand words you have already studied. There are also ways to understand words you are not familiar with. One way is to use the context—the way these words are used in the sentence or reading—to help you guess the meanings of those words you don't know.

Les courses

C'est aujourd'hui mardi. À dix heures du matin, comme tous les matins, excepté le lundi quand les magasins sont fermés[1], Mme Lelong quitte son appartement. Elle a son sac et elle va faire les courses. Elle fait les courses dans différents petits magasins. Elle achète du pain tous les jours. Elle va à la boulangerie où elle achète une baguette. Si elle veut de la viande, elle va à la boucherie. Si elle veut du poisson, elle peut aller à la poissonnerie, mais elle est très loin. Pour un pot de confiture ou une bouteille d'eau minérale, l'épicerie n'est pas loin.

Après le déjeuner, si elle n'a pas assez de pain pour le soir, elle peut acheter une autre baguette. Mais pas avant 16 heures. Les petits magasins sont fermés tous les jours de 13 heures à 16 heures, et bien sûr le dimanche!

[1] fermés *closed*

Un marchand de fruits, Paris

Une boulangerie-pâtisserie, Paris

La Polynésie française

Haïti

La Martinique

Une boucherie, Domme, France

Une boulangerie, Paris

Les Français aiment bien aller chez les petits commerçants du quartier—l'épicier, le boucher, le boulanger, etc. Leurs prix sont un peu plus chers[2] qu'au supermarché, mais la qualité de leurs produits est très bonne. Il y a aussi le côté humain[3]. Les Français aiment bavarder (converser) un peu avec le marchand ou la marchande. On trouve ça sympa.

[2] Leurs prix sont un peu plus chers *Their prices are a little more expensive*
[3] côté humain *human dimension*

Vous avez compris?

A Madame Lelong Répondez. *(Answer.)*

1. Mme Lelong quitte son appartement à quelle heure?
2. Qu'est-ce qu'elle prend pour faire ses courses?
3. Elle fait ses courses où?
4. Elle va où pour acheter du pain?
5. Si elle veut de la viande, elle va où?
6. Si elle veut du poisson, elle peut aller où?
7. Qu'est-ce qu'elle achète à l'épicerie?
8. Quand est-ce que les petits magasins sont fermés?

B Stratégie de lecture Reread the Reading Strategy on page 206. You don't know the meaning of the word **commerçants.** Using the suggestion given in the Reading Strategy, can you figure out the meaning of this word?

C Les petits commerçants Expliquez. *(Explain.)*

1. Qui sont les petits commerçants du quartier?
2. Comment est la qualité de leurs produits?
3. En général, comment sont leurs prix?
4. Qu'est-ce que les Français aiment faire avec les commerçants?

Lecture supplémentaire 1

Les grandes surfaces

Beaucoup de Français font leurs courses dans les petits magasins de leur quartier. Mais beaucoup d'autres Français—surtout les gens[1] qui travaillent ou qui n'habitent pas en ville—font leurs courses dans les grandes surfaces.

Les grandes surfaces sont de grands supermarchés ou hypermarchés. Ils sont généralement situés à la périphérie des villes. Il y a toujours un grand parking parce que les clients y vont en voiture.

Un hypermarché, Nantes

Dans un hypermarché on peut tout acheter: de la nourriture, mais aussi des vêtements[2], des bicyclettes, des livres, des disques et même des ordinateurs[3]. Les clients prennent des chariots pour transporter leurs achats[4]. Les grandes chaînes ont pour nom Leclerc et Carrefour.

[1] gens *people*
[2] vêtements *clothes*
[3] ordinateurs *computers*
[4] achats *purchases*

L'intérieur d'un hypermarché

Vous avez compris?

Les courses Vrai ou faux? *(True or false?)*

1. Les supermarchés et les hypermarchés sont des grandes surfaces.
2. Les grandes surfaces sont situées surtout au centre des villes.
3. Les clients vont presque toujours à pied dans les grandes surfaces.
4. Dans un hypermarché on peut acheter toutes sortes de marchandises.

Lecture supplémentaire 2

La Belgique

Les marchés

Dans les villes et les villages de France, il y a toujours un marché. Dans les grandes villes, il y a des marchés permanents et temporaires. Les marchés temporaires ont lieu[1] en général deux fois par semaine, le mercredi ou le jeudi et le samedi. Ils ont lieu dans la rue ou sur une place.

Les marchés existent dans les autres pays francophones. Voici un très joli marché à Dakar. Et voici un marché à Fort-de-France. Les fruits et les légumes ont l'air[2] très bons, n'est-ce pas? Ils sont délicieux!

[1] ont lieu *take place* [2] ont l'air *look*

Sarlat-la-Canéda, Dordogne

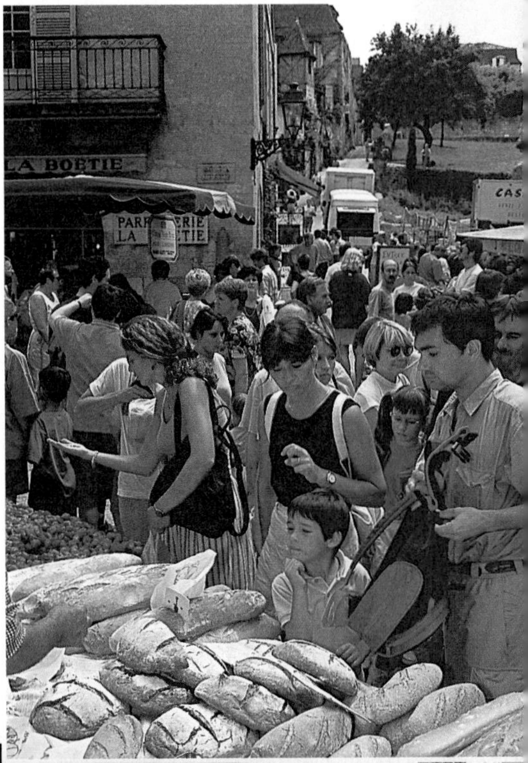

Dakar, Sénégal

Fort-de-France, Martinique

Maroc

Le Mali

Vous avez compris?

Les marchés Complétez. *(Complete.)*

1. Dans les villes et les villages de France, il y a toujours un ____.
2. Les marchés peuvent être temporaires ou ____.
3. Ils peuvent avoir lieu dans ____ ou ____.
4. Ils ont lieu le ____ ou le ____ et le ____.
5. Il y a aussi des marchés dans ____.

CONNEXIONS

Les mathématiques

Les conversions

When you travel in many of the French-speaking countries, or almost anywhere in Europe, you need to make many mathematical conversions. The metric system, rather than the English system, is used for distance, weights, and measures.

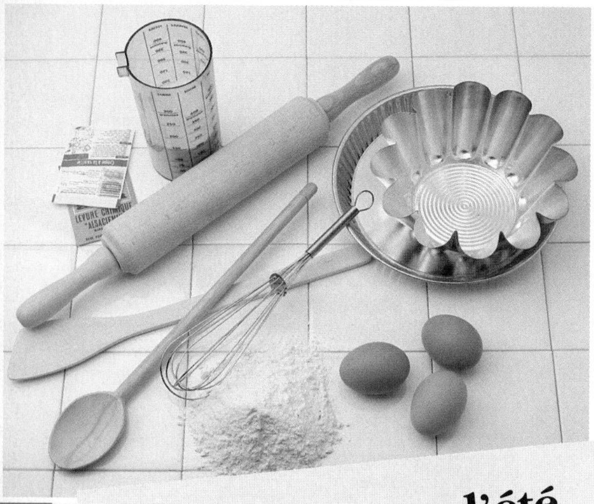

soupe d'été

Je trouve sympa de présenter la soupe avec tous ces petits morceaux de légumes. Parfois, je la sers accompagnée de croûtons de pain à l'ail et de gruyère coupé en dés. On se régale tous. Au menu, j'ai prévu une salade crue (pour la vitamine C) avec un œuf dur (pour les éléments bâtisseurs: les protéines). 1 œuf, cela peut remplacer 50 g de viande ou de poisson.

LES USTENSILES

- 1 planche à découper
- 1 cocotte
- 1 couteau de cuisine en acier inoxydable
- 1 cuillère à soupe
- 1 cuillère en bois

LES INGREDIENTS POUR 4 PERSONNES

- Pommes de terre : 250 g — 3 moyennes
- Courgettes : 250 g — 2 moyennes
- Tomates : 3 moyennes
- Oignons : 2
- Huile : 1 cuillerée à soupe
- Eau : 1 litre

Le système métrique

Le système métrique est un système décimal: il a pour base 10. Les mesures ont pour base le mètre et les poids ont pour base le gramme. Pour les liquides, la base est le litre. Les unités supérieures et inférieures sont formées avec les préfixes suivants:

kilo = × 1 000	**un kilogramme = 1 000 grammes**
hecto = × 100	**un hectomètre = 100 mètres**
déca = × 10	**un décalitre = 10 litres**
déci = ÷ 10	**un décimètre = 1 mètre ÷ 10**
centi = ÷ 100	**un centilitre = 1 litre ÷ 100**
milli = ÷ 1 000	**un milligramme = 1 gramme ÷ 1 000**

Un kilogramme (un kilo) est équivalent à environ[1] deux livres[2]. Une livre est équivalente à un peu moins[3] d'un demi-kilo. Un mile américain est équivalent à environ un kilomètre et demi. Un litre est équivalent à environ un quart américain.

[1] environ *about*
[2] livres *pounds*
[3] un peu moins *a little less*

Vous avez compris?

Poids et mesures

Vrai ou faux? *(True or false?)*

1. Le système anglais de poids et mesures a pour base 10.
2. Les poids ont comme unité de base le litre.
3. Il y a 1 000 grammes dans un kilo.
4. Un kilo est l'équivalent d'environ deux livres anglaises.
5. Une livre américaine est l'équivalent de 500 grammes.
6. On mesure les liquides en quarts en France.
7. En France, on mesure les liquides en litres.

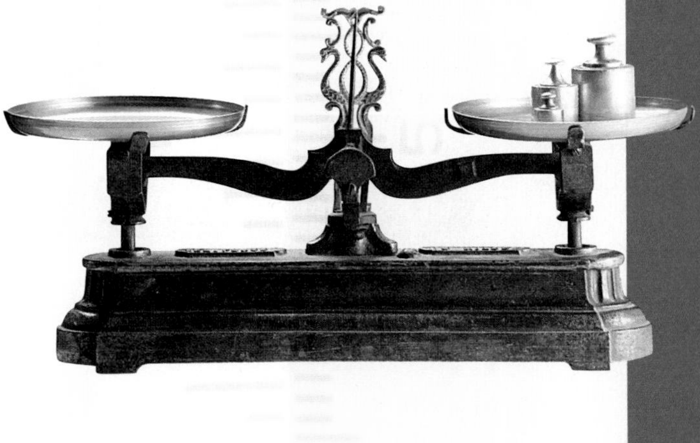

C'est à vous

Use what you have learned

PARLER

1

Au marché

✔ *Buy food from a vendor at the market*

Work with a classmate. You are spending a semester studying in Belgium. You are going to prepare a dinner for your Belgian family. Decide what you need to buy at the market and in what quantities. Then have a conversation with your classmate, who will be the vendor at the market.

PARLER

2

Je veux bien, mais je ne peux pas parce que...

✔ *Talk about what you want to do but can't*

Work in groups of three or four. Tell some things you want to do but can't do because you are going to do something else. Tell what you are going to do.

PARLER

3

ÉCRIRE

Jeu Une compétition

✔ *Express quantities*

Compete with a classmate. You each have two minutes. See which one of you can make up the most phrases using the following words.

un kilo de | une livre de | un litre de | une bouteille de | une boîte de | six tranches de | un paquet de

ÉCRIRE

4 Une publicité

✓ *Write an advertisement for a supermarket*

Using these French supermarket ads as a guide, write similar food advertisements in French for your local supermarket. Choose any four foods you like to advertise.

Writing Strategy

Ordering ideas You can order ideas in a variety of ways when writing. Therefore, you must be aware of the purpose of your writing in order to choose the best way to organize your material. When describing an event, it is logical to put the events in the order in which they happen. Using a sensible and logical approach helps readers develop a picture in their minds.

Un supermarché, Dakar, Sénégal

ÉCRIRE

5 On fait les courses.

Your class is planning a French meal. Describe the trip you take with your class to the local market or supermarket to buy the ingredients. Tell what you buy, whom you buy it from, and how much everything costs.

Assessment

Vocabulaire

To review ***Mots 1****, turn to pages 186–187.*

1 Identifiez. *(Identify each item.)*

1. 

2. 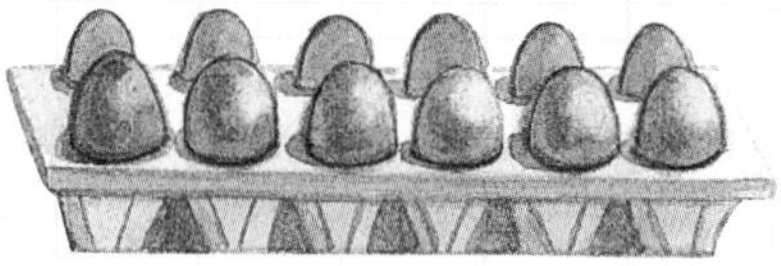

3. 

4. 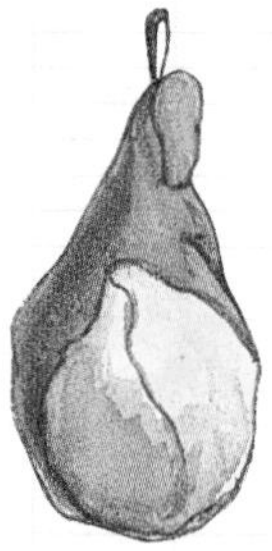

To review ***Mots 2****, turn to pages 190–191.*

2 Choisissez. *(Choose.)*

5. Une pomme et une poire sont des ____.
   a. fraises **b.** légumes **c.** fruits
6. C'est ____, un kilo de carottes?
   a. comment **b.** combien **c.** un marchand
7. Il va acheter ____ de moutarde.
   a. un paquet **b.** une boîte **c.** un pot
8. Je voudrais six ____ de jambon, s'il vous plaît.
   a. bouteilles **b.** tranches **c.** litres

Structure

To review the verb ***faire****, turn to page 194.*

3 Complétez avec «faire». *(Complete with* faire.*)*

9. Je ____ les courses le matin.
10. Mon frère ____ du latin.
11. Vous ____ vos devoirs?
12. Les élèves ne ____ pas la cuisine.

4 Choisissez. *(Choose.)*

13. Moi, j'aime beaucoup ____ lait.
 a. le **b.** du **c.** de
14. Je voudrais ____ eau.
 a. d' **b.** de l' **c.** du
15. Il va acheter ____ fruits et ____ légumes.
 a. des **b.** de **c.** les

To review the partitive and the definite article, turn to pages 196, 198.

5 Récrivez au négatif. *(Rewrite the sentences in the negative.)*

16. Je vais acheter du pain.
17. Je voudrais de la crème.

6 Récrivez les phrases. *(Rewrite the sentences.)*

18. Les carottes sont très bonnes.
 Le poisson ____.
19. Tu veux quel sandwich?
 Tu veux ____ salade?

To review these special adjectives, turn to page 201.

7 Complétez. *(Complete.)*

20. Je ____ faire le travail. (pouvoir)
21. Vous ____ aller au restaurant? (vouloir)
22. Tu ____ aller au marché. (pouvoir)
23. Ils ____ parler au prof. (vouloir)

To review the verbs **pouvoir** and **vouloir**, turn to page 201.

Culture

8 Répondez. *(Answer.)*

24. Beaucoup de magasins sont fermés quel jour en France?
25. On peut aller où pour acheter un pot de confiture ou une bouteille d'eau minérale?

To review this cultural information, turn to pages 206–207.

On parle super bien!

Tell all you can about this illustration.

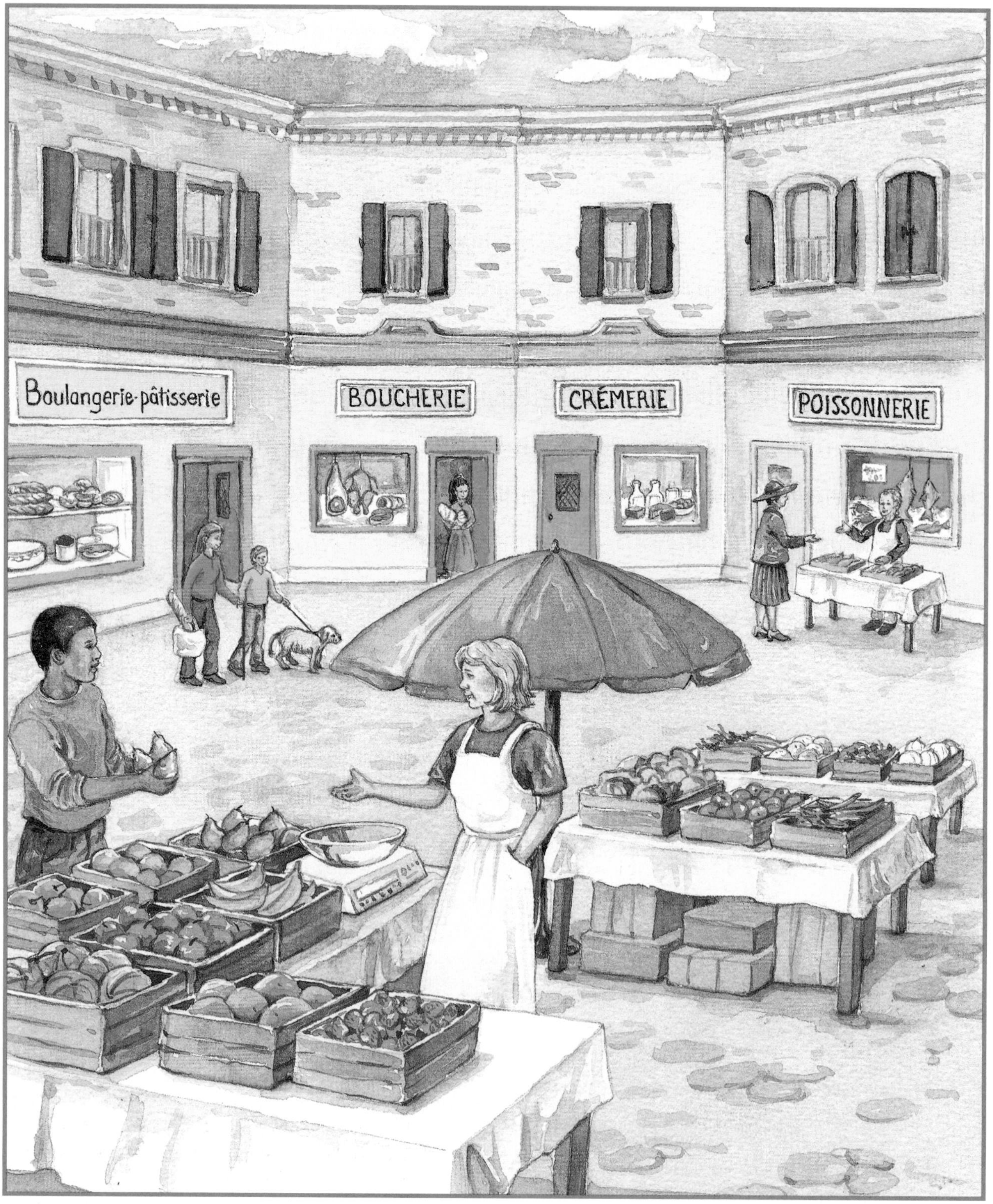

Vocabulaire

Shopping for food

faire les courses *(f. pl.)*
une boulangerie
une pâtisserie
une crémerie
une boucherie
une poissonnerie
une charcuterie
une épicerie
un marché
un supermarché
le/la marchand(e)
un sac
surgelé(e)

Identifying some food

du pain
un pain complet
un croissant
une baguette
une tarte aux pommes
de la crème
du lait
du beurre
du fromage
de la confiture
un œuf
un yaourt
un poulet
de la viande
du bœuf
de l'agneau *(m.)*
du porc
du jambon
du saucisson
du poisson
une crevette
un crabe
du sel
du poivre
de l'huile *(f.)*
du vinaigre
de l'eau minérale
de la moutarde
un fruit
une banane
une pomme
une orange
une poire
une fraise
un melon
une tomate
un légume
une salade
une carotte
une pomme de terre
des haricots verts
des épinards *(m. pl.)*
des petits pois *(m. pl.)*
un oignon

How well do you know your vocabulary?

- **Choose two foods that you like from the list.**
- **Tell how you buy each, for example, *une douzaine, une bouteille,* etc.**

Identifying quantities

un paquet
un pot
un gramme
un kilo(gramme)
une livre
un litre
une douzaine
une boîte
une bouteille
une tranche

Other useful words and expressions

aller chercher
il n'y a plus de
je regrette
C'est combien?
Ça fait combien?
bon(ne)
Vous voulez autre chose?
Et avec ça?
C'est tout.
Pourquoi?
parce que

VIDÉOTOUR

Épisode 6

In this video episode, you will join Manu and Vincent as they do their food shopping. See page 531 for more information.

CHAPITRE 7

Les vêtements

Objectifs

In this chapter you will learn to:

- *identify and describe articles of clothing*
- *state color and size preferences*
- *shop for clothing*
- *describe people's activities*
- *compare people and things*
- *express opinions and make observations*
- *discuss clothes and clothes shopping in the French-speaking world*

Un tissu de la Côte d'Ivoire

Vocabulaire *Mots 1*

Les vêtements sport

un short

un pull

un t-shirt

des sandales

une paire de chaussures

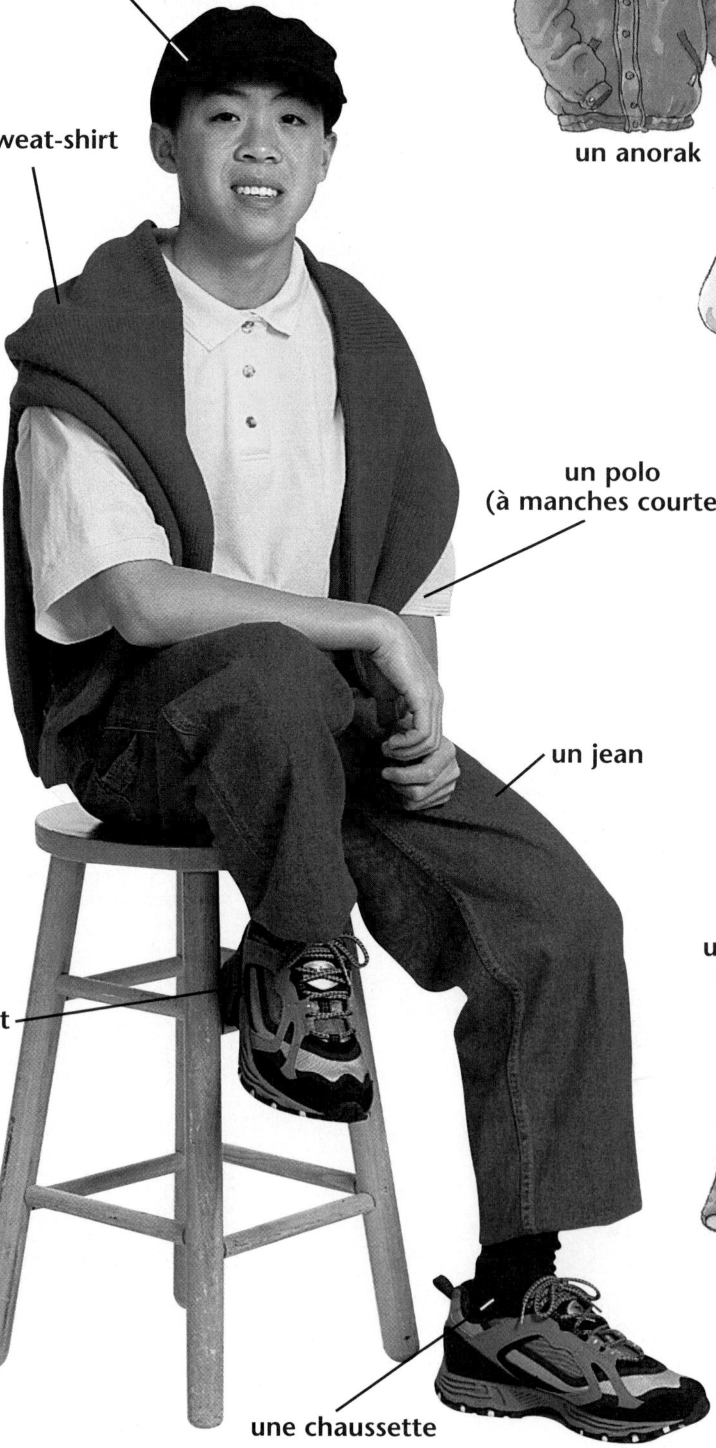

un anorak

un blouson

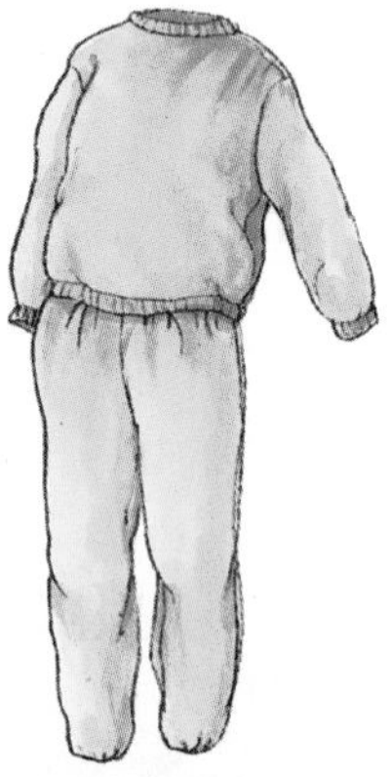

un survêtement

un manteau

Les vêtements pour hommes

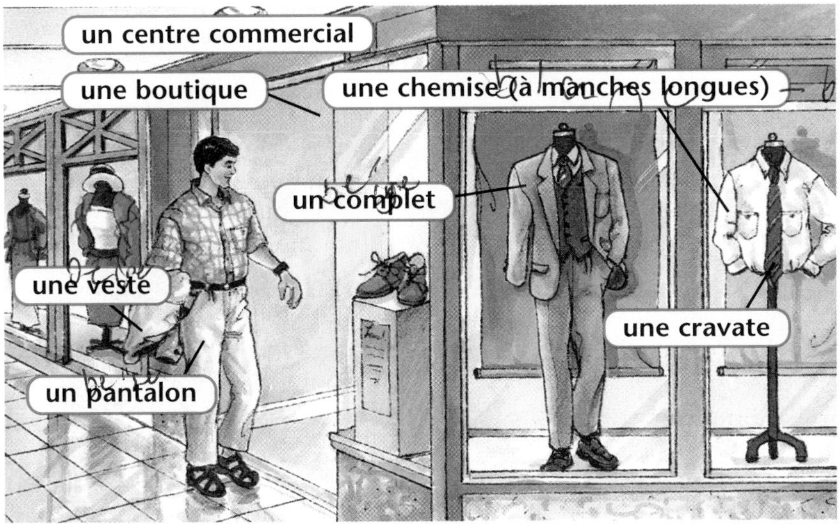

Marc porte des sandales.
Il voit des chaussures dans la vitrine.
Il entre dans la boutique.

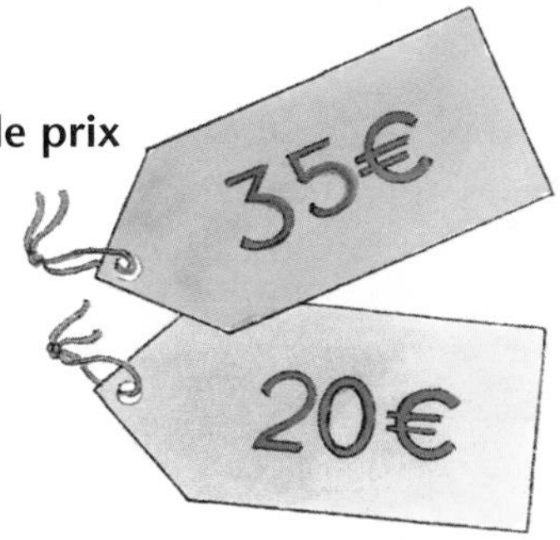

Les prix sont moins chers quand il y a des soldes.

Les vêtements pour femmes

Johanne va au grand magasin.
Elle voit beaucoup de chemisiers.
Elle voit des chemisiers au rayon des vêtements pour femmes.
Tous les chemisiers sont en solde!

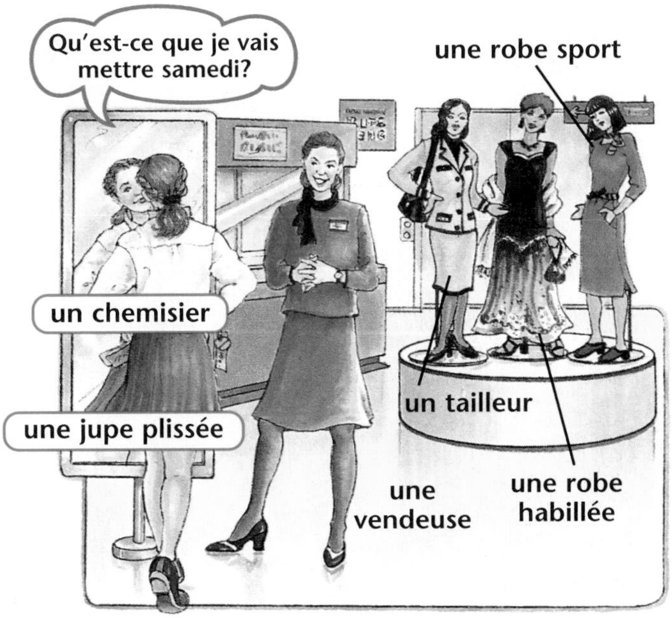

Quel est le mot?

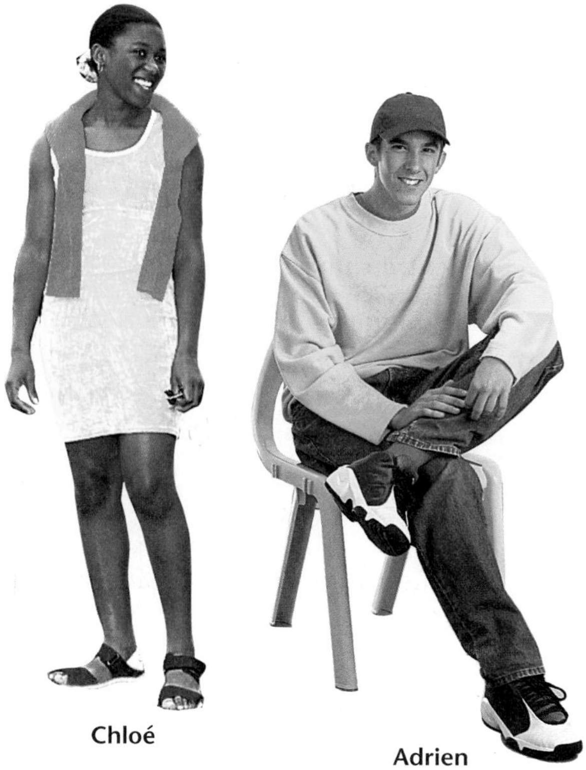

Chloé

Adrien

1 Chloé et Adrien
Répondez d'après les photos. *(Answer according to the photos.)*

1. Qu'est-ce que Chloé porte?
2. Et Adrien? Qu'est-ce qu'il porte?

2 Qu'est-ce qu'on va mettre?
Répondez. *(Answer.)*

1. Ce soir M. Ben Azar va aller dans un restaurant chic. Qu'est-ce qu'il va mettre?
2. Qu'est-ce que sa femme va mettre?
3. Qu'est-ce que tu portes à l'école?
4. Qu'est-ce que tu portes à la maison?
5. Qu'est-ce qu'on porte en juillet et en août?
6. Qu'est-ce qu'on porte en décembre et janvier?
7. Qu'est-ce qu'une femme porte quand elle va travailler?
8. Qu'est-ce qu'un homme porte quand il va au travail?

La vitrine d'une boutique, Paris

3 Sport ou habillé?
Identifiez. *(Tell whether each item is casual or formal.)*

1. des baskets
2. un tailleur
3. un jean
4. un complet
5. un blouson
6. une cravate
7. un polo à manches courtes
8. une chemise à manches longues
9. un survêtement
10. une jupe plissée

4 Historiette **Au rayon des chemisiers** Inventez une histoire.

(Make up a story.)

1. Mélanie entre dans un grand magasin ou dans une boutique?
2. La boutique est dans une rue ou dans un centre commercial?
3. Il y a des soldes aujourd'hui?
4. Il y a des chemisiers dans la vitrine?
5. Elle va au rayon des chemisiers?
6. Elle voit beaucoup de chemisiers?
7. Elle parle à la vendeuse?
8. Elle veut un chemisier à manches courtes ou à manches longues?
9. Elle veut un chemisier habillé ou sport?
10. Les chemisiers sont en solde?
11. Les vêtements sont moins chers quand ils sont en solde?

5 C'est qui?

Work with a classmate. One of you describes what someone in the class is wearing and the other has to guess who it is. Take turns.

6 Mon ensemble favori

Work with a classmate. Discuss what you consider an ideal outfit for school. Tell what you like to wear and what you don't like to wear. See if you are on the same wavelength.

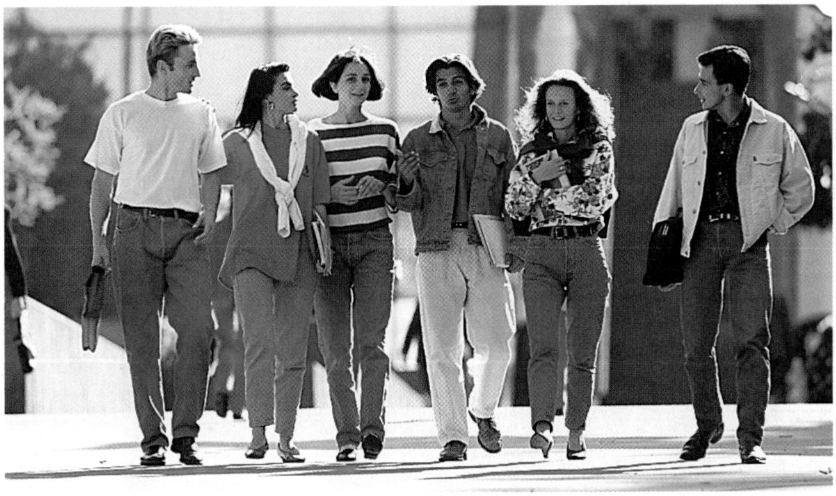

Des jeunes habillés sport

ENCORE PLUS *For more practice using words from **Mots 1,** do Activity 20 on page H21 at the end of this book.*

On fait des courses.

Il est joli, le pantalon vert. Tu ne trouves pas?
Si, j'aime beaucoup!
le shopping

Vous faites quelle pointure?
Je fais du 38.

une cabine d'essayage

Ça va, le pantalon?
Non, il est trop grand. Il est trop large. Je voudrais la taille au-dessous.
Vous faites quelle taille?
Je fais du 38.

Non, il est trop petit. Il est trop serré. Je voudrais la taille au-dessus.
essayer

Julien essaie le pantalon.

pourpre - purple
violet

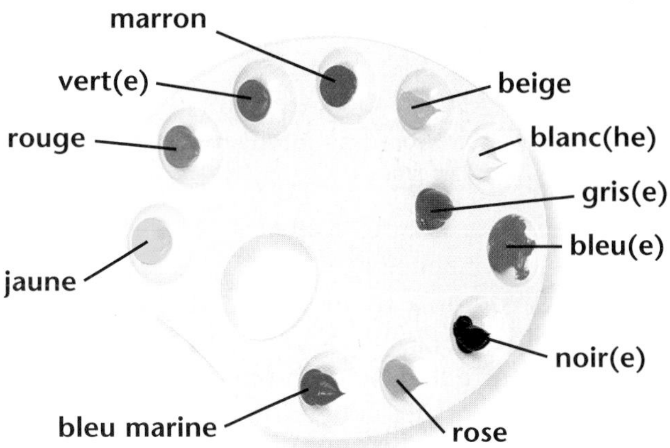

De quelle couleur est la jupe?
Elle est verte.

Et les chaussures?
Elles sont marron.

Note

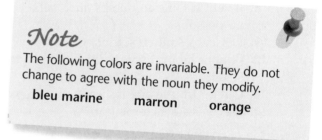

The following colors are invariable. They do not change to agree with the noun they modify.

bleu marine **marron** **orange**

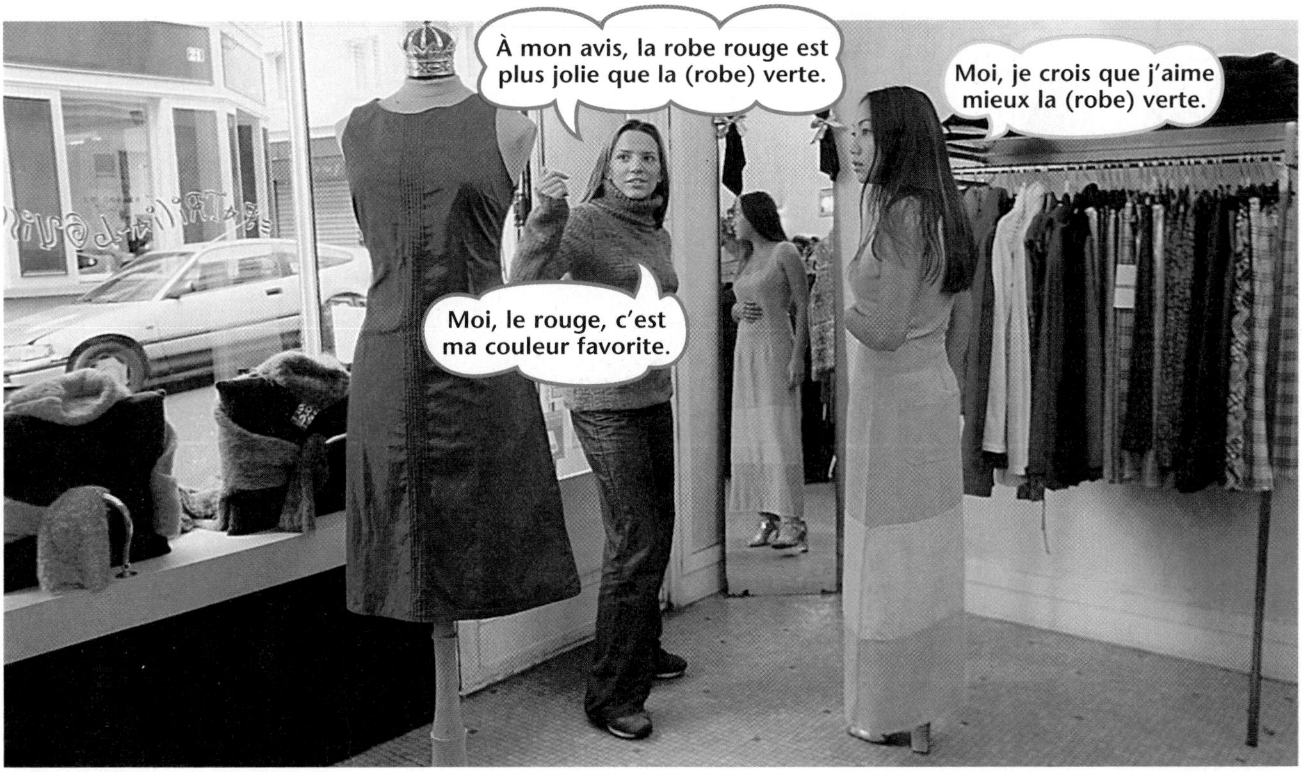

À mon avis, la robe rouge est plus jolie que la (robe) verte.
Moi, je crois que j'aime mieux la (robe) verte.
Moi, le rouge, c'est ma couleur favorite.

Quel est le mot?

Rayon des vêtements pour hommes, Galeries Lafayette, Paris

7 **Historiette Olivier fait des courses.** Inventez une histoire. *(Make up a story.)*

1. Olivier fait des courses?
2. Il veut acheter un blue jean?
3. Il voit un jean qu'il aime dans la vitrine?
4. Il entre dans le grand magasin?
5. Il fait quelle taille?
6. Il va essayer le jean?
7. Il est comment, le pantalon—grand, petit, juste à sa taille?
8. Il veut la taille au-dessus ou la taille au-dessous?
9. Les jeans sont en solde?
10. Ils sont moins chers quand ils sont en solde?
11. Olivier trouve que les jeans sont chers?
12. Olivier va acheter le jean?

8 **Ta couleur favorite** Donnez des réponses personnelles. *(Give your own answers.)*

1. De quelle couleur est ton blouson favori?
2. De quelle couleur est ton jean favori?
3. De quelle couleur est ta chemise favorite ou ton chemisier favori?
4. Qu'est-ce que tu portes aujourd'hui? De quelle couleur sont tes vêtements?

9 **Mes préférences** Donnez des réponses personnelles. *(Give your own answers.)*

1. Tu aimes mieux les vêtements sport ou habillés?
2. Les baskets ou les chaussures?
3. Les chemises ou les chemisiers à manches longues ou à manches courtes?
4. Les vêtements un peu serrés ou larges?
5. Les couleurs sombres ou les couleurs claires?
6. Les vêtements chers ou pas chers?

10 De petits problèmes Répondez. *(Answer.)*

1. Les chaussures sont trop petites ou trop grandes?

2. La jupe est trop longue ou trop courte?

3. Le pantalon est un peu serré ou un peu large?

4. Les manches sont trop longues ou trop courtes?

5. Le tailleur est joli ou pas?

11 Les couleurs Complétez d'après la couleur. *(Complete with the color.)*

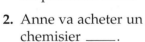

1. Aurélien va acheter un pantalon ____.

2. Anne va acheter un chemisier ____.

3. Fred va acheter une chemise ____.

4. Justine va acheter une robe ____.

5. Mélodie va acheter une jupe ____.

6. Cyril va acheter des chaussures ____.

12 Jeu Qui porte une jupe bleue?

Study the clothing of all the students in the next row for several minutes. Then turn your back to that row. One of your classmates will mention an item of clothing and ask you who is wearing it. If you don't remember, your classmates can help you out by giving hints such as: **La personne est blonde. Elle est très amusante.**

ENCORE PLUS *For more practice using words from **Mots 2**, do Activity 21 on page H22 at the end of this book.*

Structure

Le verbe mettre au présent
Describing people's activities

1. Study the forms of the verb **mettre** *(to put, to put on)* in the present tense.

METTRE			
je	mets	nous	mettons
tu	mets	vous	mettez
il/elle/on	met	ils/elles	mettent

FRENCH Online

For more information about shopping for clothing in the Francophone world, go to the Glencoe French Web site: french.glencoe.com

2. Note that **mettre** has various meanings.

Il met une chemise et une cravate pour aller au travail.
Les serveurs mettent la table au restaurant.
On met la télévision pour regarder un film.

Comment dit-on?

13 **Qu'est-ce qu'on met?**
Répondez. *(Answer.)*

1. Tu mets un survêtement quand tu fais du jogging?
2. Tu mets la table pour le dîner?
3. Ton père met la télé le matin pendant le petit déjeuner?
4. Ta mère met la radio pour écouter les informations?
5. Tes copains mettent une cravate pour aller à l'école?
6. Tes copines mettent une jupe plissée pour aller à l'école?

Des amis devant l'école

14 Dans le sac à dos

Complétez avec **mettre** d'après les dessins. *(Complete with* mettre *according to the illustrations.)*

1. Qu'est-ce qu'ils ____ dans leur sac à dos?
   Ils ________________.

2. Qu'est-ce que tu ____ dans ton sac à dos?
   Je ________________.

3. Qu'est-ce que vous ____ dans votre sac à dos?
   On ________________.

15 Qu'est-ce que vous mettez?

Work with a classmate. Compare what you wear on different occasions.

- pour aller à l'école
- quand vous allez dîner chez des amis de vos parents
- pour aller au cinéma le samedi soir
- pour aller à un mariage
- pour aller dans un restaurant chic

Attention!

Pay particular attention to the spelling and pronunciation of the following adjectives. Note that the final consonant sound is pronounced in the feminine forms but not in the masculine forms.

FÉMININ	MASCULIN
sérieuse(s)	sérieux
longue(s)	long(s)
favorite(s)	favori(s)
blanche(s)	blanc(s)

Note that all forms of cher—chère(s), cher(s)—sound alike.

Complétez et prononcez.
(Complete and pronounce aloud.)

1. sérieux
   un élève ____ et une élève ____
2. long
   une jupe ____ et un manteau ____
3. favori
   mon pull ____ et ma robe ____
4. blanc
   une chemise ____ et un chemisier ____
5. long
   des pantalons ____ et des manches ____

ENCORE PLUS
*For more practice using the verb **mettre**, do Activity 22 on page H23 at the end of this book.*

Le comparatif des adjectifs
Comparing people and things

1. When you compare two or more people or things, you use **plus (+)... que, moins (−)... que,** and **aussi (=)... que.** Study the following chart.

Le jean est plus cher que le pantalon.
Le jean est aussi cher que le pantalon.
Le jean est moins cher que le pantalon.

Les sandales sont moins confortables que les baskets.
Mais elles sont plus confortables que les chaussures.

Attention!

Note the liaison with **plus** and **moins.**
plus ‿z **intéressant(e)**
moins ‿z **élégant(e)**

2. You use the stress pronouns **moi, toi, lui, elle, nous, vous, eux,** and **elles** after **que (qu')** when comparing people.

Elle est plus sympa que moi.
Elle est aussi sympa que lui.
Elle est moins sympa que vous.

Il est aussi intelligent que moi.
Mais il est plus intelligent qu'eux.

Comment dit-on?

16 **À mon avis** Donnez des réponses personnelles. *(Give your own answers.)*

1. Le français, c'est plus difficile ou plus facile que les maths?
2. Le professeur de français est plus strict, moins strict ou aussi strict que les autres professeurs?
3. Le football américain est plus amusant ou moins amusant que le basket-ball?
4. Ton école secondaire est plus grande ou moins grande que ton école primaire?
5. Ta classe de français est aussi grande ou plus petite que ta classe de sciences?

17 Plus ou moins que l'autre

Répondez d'après les dessins. Suivez le modèle. *(Answer according to the illustrations.)*

—Le blouson bleu est aussi grand que le blouson noir?
—Oui, le blouson bleu est aussi grand que le blouson noir.

1. Le blouson bleu est aussi cher que le blouson noir?
2. Le blouson bleu est moins beau que le blouson noir?
3. La jupe jaune est moins chère que la jupe grise?
4. La jupe grise est plus courte que la jupe jaune?

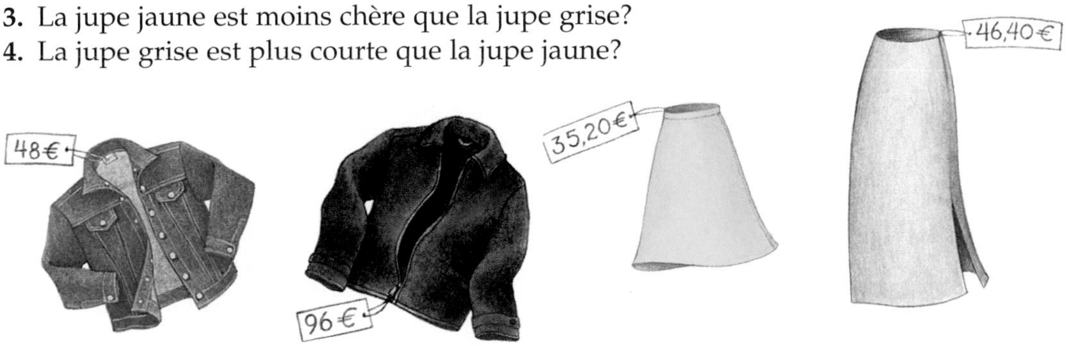

18 Ma famille et mes copains

Donnez des réponses personnelles. *(Give your own answers.)*

1. Ta sœur, elle est plus petite ou plus grande que toi? Tu es plus grand(e) ou plus petit(e) qu'elle?
2. Tu es plus patient(e) ou moins patient(e) que ton frère? Il est plus patient ou moins patient que toi?
3. Tes grands-parents sont aussi stricts que tes parents? Ils sont vraiment moins stricts qu'eux?
4. Tes copains sont plus sociables que toi? Tu es plus timide qu'eux?

19 Comparaisons

Work with a classmate. Compare people you know. You may want to use the following words.

grand · petit · sociable · intéressant · dynamique

amusant · beau · sympa · sérieux

Les verbes voir et croire
Seeing and believing

Study the forms of the verbs **voir** *(to see)* and **croire** *(to believe).*

VOIR		CROIRE	
je	vois	je	crois
tu	vois	tu	crois
il/elle/on	voit	il/elle/on	croit
nous	voyons	nous	croyons
vous	voyez	vous	croyez
ils/elles	voient	ils/elles	croient

Savez-vous que... ?

When **voir** and **croire** are followed by a clause, you must use **que (qu')**.

Je vois que vous êtes content.

Je crois qu'il est content aussi.

Comment dit-on?

20 **À votre avis** Répondez que oui. *(Answer* yes.*)*

1. Vos parents croient que vous êtes intelligents?
2. Votre professeur de français croit que vous travaillez bien?
3. Vos camarades de classe croient que vous êtes sympathiques?
4. Vos grands-parents croient que vous êtes adorables?

21 **Dans une boutique**
Répondez que oui. *(Answer* yes.*)*

1. Tu vois des choses que tu aimes dans la vitrine?
2. Tu crois qu'on peut entrer dans la boutique?
3. Tu crois que tu vas acheter le pantalon noir?
4. Tu crois qu'ils vont avoir ta taille?
5. Tu vois le prix?

22 **Vraiment?** Conversez d'après le modèle.
(Make up a conversation according to the model.)

—Il va bientôt arriver.
—Vous croyez?

1. Il va bientôt téléphoner.
2. Il va bientôt payer.
3. Il va bientôt rentrer.
4. Il va bientôt acheter une maison.

23 **Des opinions différentes!** Complétez avec **croire.** *(Complete with* croire.*)*

1. Il ____ que tout est moins cher pendant les soldes. Et vous, vous ____ ça aussi?
2. Julien ____ que l'examen va être facile, mais nous, on ____ qu'il va être difficile.
3. Tu ____ que les chats sont plus intelligents que les chiens, mais moi, je ____ que les chiens sont plus intelligents que les chats.
4. Alice ____ que Paris est près de Nice, mais nous, nous ____ que c'est loin de Nice.
5. Moi, je ____ que la cousine de Sandra est française, mais mes copains ____ qu'elle est italienne.

Attention!

Pay particular attention to the spelling of verbs that end in -yer.

ESSAYER	**j'essaie**	**nous essayons**
	tu essaies	**vous essayez**
	il essaie	**ils essaient**
PAYER	**je paie**	**nous payons**
	tu paies	**vous payez**
	il paie	**ils paient**

Complétez. *(Complete.)*

1. Vous ____ où? (payer)
2. On ____ à la caisse. (payer)
3. Je ____ parce que j'invite. (payer)
4. Il va ____ la chemise? (essayer)
5. Non, mais il ____ le pantalon. (essayer)

ENCORE PLUS *For more practice using the verbs* ***voir*** *and* ***croire****, do Activity 23 on page H24 at the end of this book.*

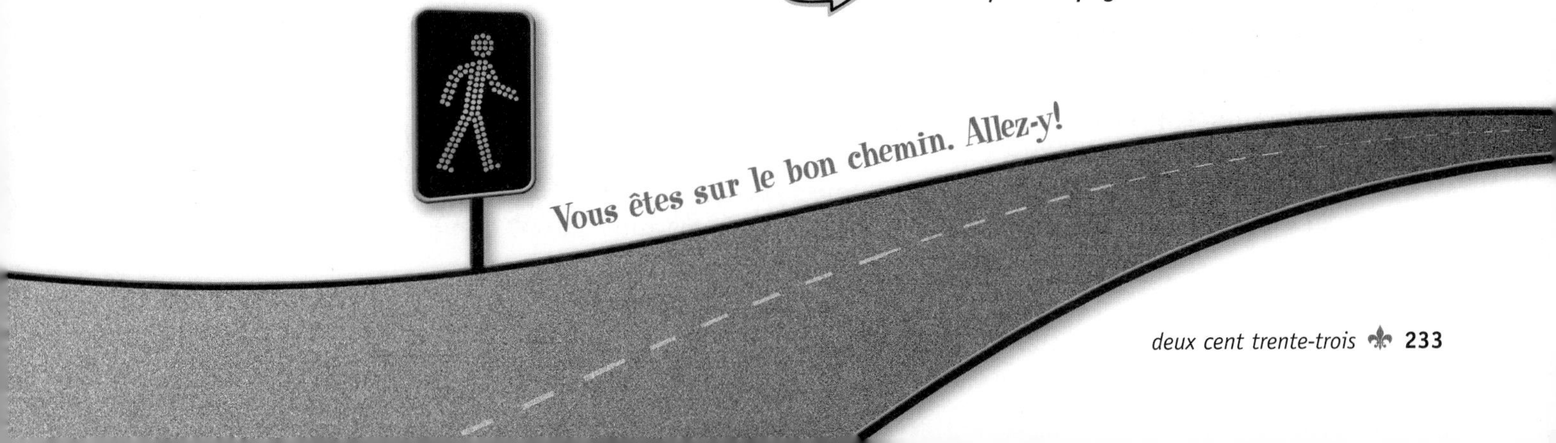
Vous êtes sur le bon chemin. Allez-y!

Conversation

Dans une petite boutique

Vendeur: Bonjour, monsieur. Vous voulez voir quelque chose?
Fabien: Bonjour. Oui, je voudrais un jean, s'il vous plaît.
Vendeur: Oui, vous faites quelle taille?
Fabien: Je fais du 36.
Vendeur: Voilà un 36. La cabine d'essayage est juste là.
(Fabien essaie le jean dans la cabine d'essayage.)
Vendeur: Ça va, la taille?
Fabien: Pas vraiment. Je crois que c'est un peu petit.
Vendeur: Vous voulez la taille au-dessus?
Fabien: Oui, je veux bien.
(Fabien essaie l'autre jean.)
Fabien: Ah oui, c'est bien.
Vendeur: Vous désirez autre chose?
Fabien: Oui, un polo bleu marine ou blanc.
Vendeur: Vous avez de la chance. Ils sont en solde.

Vous avez compris?

Répondez. *(Answer.)*

1. À qui parle Fabien?
2. Qu'est-ce qu'il veut voir?
3. Il fait quelle taille?
4. Où est-ce qu'il essaie son jean?
5. Le jean est trop grand ou trop petit?
6. Il veut la taille au-dessus ou la taille au-dessous?
7. Il veut acheter autre chose?

Parlons un peu plus

A **Au magasin** Work with a classmate. Take turns playing the role of the salesperson and the customer in the following situations.

- **Au rayon des vêtements pour hommes** You want to buy a shirt as a gift for your father or a friend. They have his size but not the color you want.
- **Au rayon des chaussures** You are looking for a pair of brown shoes. The ones the salesperson shows you are quite expensive.

B **Jeu** **Qu'est-ce qu'il/elle porte?** Have one student leave the room while others choose a classmate to describe. The student who left comes back in and has to guess which classmate the others have chosen by asking questions about his or her clothes.

Prononciation

Les sons **/sh/** et **/zh/**

It is important to make a distinction between the sounds **/sh/** as in **chat** and **/zh/** as in **joli.** Put your fingers on your throat. When you say the sound **/zh/** as in **joli,** you should feel a vibration, but not when you say **/sh/** as in **chat.** Repeat the following words with the sound **/sh/.**

acheter	**chaussure**	**chemise**
chemisier	**achat**	**short**

Now repeat the following words with the sound **/zh/.**

large	**jupe**	**orange**
beige	**joli**	

Now repeat the following sentences that combine both sounds.

J'achète toujours mes chaussures au marché.
Le t-shirt jaune est joli, mais le short orange est moins cher.

chemise orange

Lectures culturelles

Reading Strategy

Scanning for specific information

Scanning for specific information means reading to find out certain details without concerning yourself with the other information in the passage. Some examples of scanning are searching a television listing to find out when certain programs are on or reading an ad to find out something specific, such as a store's hours.

On fait des courses où, à Paris?

Chez les grands couturiers[1]

Les noms des grands couturiers français—Yves Saint-Laurent, Dior, Cardin, Givenchy, Coco Chanel—sont célèbres dans le monde entier. On peut voir les boutiques élégantes des grands couturiers dans l'avenue Montaigne ou dans la rue du Faubourg-Saint-Honoré. C'est là que les gens aisés (riches) vont acheter leurs vêtements et accessoires.

Rue du Faubourg-Saint-Honoré, Paris

Magasin de la Samaritaine, Paris

Les petites boutiques et les grands magasins

Mais la plupart (la majorité) des Parisiens ne font pas leurs achats chez les grands couturiers. Partout à Paris, il y a de petites boutiques qui sont beaucoup moins chères que les boutiques des grands couturiers. Il y a aussi des grands magasins. À Paris, les grands magasins du Printemps et des Galeries Lafayette sont les plus renommés (célèbres). Il y a aussi des chaînes de magasins bon marché[2] comme le Prisunic.

Dans les grands magasins, on peut aller d'un rayon à un autre. Il y a souvent des articles en promotion[3] et deux fois par an il y a des soldes—début janvier et début juillet.

[1] grands couturiers *designers*
[2] bon marché *inexpensive*
[3] en promotion *on special*

Les marchés aux puces[4]

Les adolescents aiment bien aller aux puces. Ils y vont pendant le week-end parce que les marchés aux puces sont fermés[5] pendant la semaine.

Les marchés aux puces sont de grands marchés où on trouve de tout—des vêtements, de la nourriture, des tables, des chaises, etc. On peut trouver un vêtement ou un accessoire avec la griffe[6] d'un grand couturier très bon marché… ou très cher!

[4] marchés aux puces *flea markets*
[5] fermés *closed*
[6] griffe *label*

Marché aux puces, Saint-Ouen, Paris

Vous avez compris?

A Des informations Donnez les informations suivantes. *(Give the following information.)*

1. les noms de quelques grands couturiers français
2. les noms de quelques rues très élégantes à Paris
3. là où la plupart des Parisiens vont faire leurs achats
4. le nom d'un grand magasin parisien assez élégant
5. le nom d'une chaîne de magasins aux prix plus modestes
6. là où les adolescents aiment faire leurs achats

B Les achats Vrai ou faux? *(True or false?)*

1. La plupart des Parisiens font leurs achats chez les grands couturiers.
2. Les petites boutiques sont plus chères que les boutiques des grands couturiers.
3. Les Galeries Lafayette, c'est le nom d'un grand magasin à Paris.
4. Les grands magasins n'ont pas de soldes.
5. On va souvent au marché aux puces le lundi.
6. On peut acheter beaucoup de marchandises différentes dans un marché aux puces.

Marché aux puces, Nice

Lecture supplémentaire 1

Les vêtements

En Afrique du Nord

Dans les pays du Maghreb (le Maroc, l'Algérie et la Tunisie), beaucoup de gens[1] vont dans les souks pour acheter leurs vêtements. Un souk est un grand marché, souvent situé dans la médina, le vieux quartier d'une ville arabe. Dans les pays du Maghreb, beaucoup d'hommes portent un pull et un jean. Beaucoup de femmes portent une jupe et un chemisier. Mais on voit souvent des vêtements plus traditionnels. On voit des hommes qui portent une djellaba, par exemple. En Tunisie, beaucoup de femmes ont un sifsari. Le sifsari est un type de voile[2]. Le sifsari n'a pas de signification religieuse.

Deux hommes en djellaba, Tunisie

Un souk, Marrakech, Maroc

En Afrique Occidentale

Dans les pays d'Afrique Occidentale, les femmes portent souvent un boubou. Un boubou est une longue tunique ample. Les boubous sont très jolis. Les hommes aussi portent un boubou. Ils portent un boubou par-dessus[3] un pantalon et une chemise.

[1] gens *people*
[2] voile *veil*
[3] par-dessus *on top of, over*

Deux femmes en boubou, Sénégal

Vous avez compris?

Quel est le mot? Identifiez le mot. *(Identify the word.)*

1. un marché arabe
2. le vieux quartier d'une ville arabe
3. un vêtement masculin des pays du Maghreb
4. un type de voile tunisien
5. un vêtement porté par les hommes et les femmes en Afrique Occidentale

Lecture supplémentaire 2

Les tailles Clothing size

En France et dans les autres pays d'Europe, les pointures et les tailles ne sont pas les mêmes qu'aux États-Unis. Voici des tableaux qui indiquent les correspondances.

FEMMES					
Chaussures					
États-Unis	6	7	8	9	
France	36	37	38	39	
Robes, Tailleurs, Pulls, Chemisiers					
États-Unis	6	8	10	12	14
France	38	40	42	44	46

HOMMES					
Chaussures					
États-Unis	9	10	11	12	
France	40	41	42	43	
Chemises					
États-Unis	14½	15	15½	16	16½
France	37	38	39	40	41

Si vous trouvez des chaussures que vous aimez et que vous voulez acheter, vous allez demander quelle pointure?

Si vous voyez une chemise ou un chemisier que vous voulez acheter, vous allez demander quelle taille?

Vous avez compris?

Moi Donnez des réponses personnelles.
(Give your own answers.)

1. Vous êtes en France. Vous voulez des chaussures. Vous faites quelle pointure?
2. Vous voulez une chemise ou un chemisier. Quelle est votre taille?

CONNEXIONS

Les lettres

La poésie

A poem is a literary piece most often written in verse. The poet uses images, meter, rhythm, and sounds to evoke or suggest ideas, sensations, and emotions in the reader. Many poets say a great deal in very few words. The poem we are about to read by the French poet Apollinaire is an example.

Apollinaire (1880–1918)

Guillaume Apollinaire a une vie[1] bohème. Sa poésie reflète sa vie. Il visite beaucoup de pays européens. Les mouvements intellectuels et artistiques de son époque intéressent Apollinaire. C'est une période (avant la guerre[2] de 1914) très riche en idées. Les poètes et les artistes peintres échangent leurs nouvelles idées. Apollinaire discute ses idées avec son bon ami, le peintre Picasso.

Apollinaire est un des premiers grands poètes modernes français. Certains de ses poèmes sont des calligrammes. Le poème a la forme de l'objet que le poète décrit[3]. Le poème «La cravate» est un exemple de calligramme.

[1] vie *life*
[2] guerre *war*
[3] décrit *describes*

Pablo Picasso

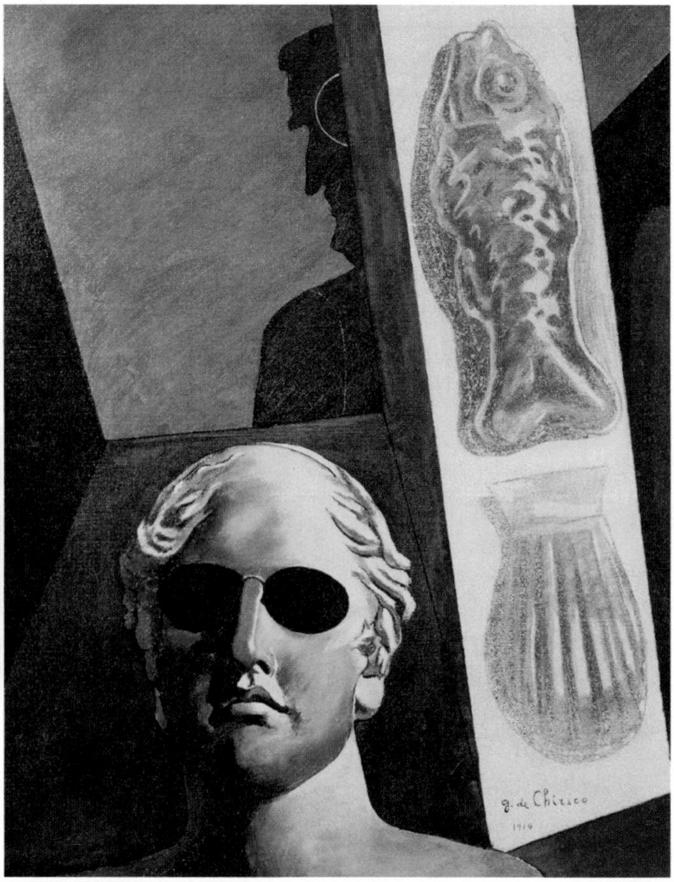

Giorgio de Chirico *Guillaume Apollinaire*

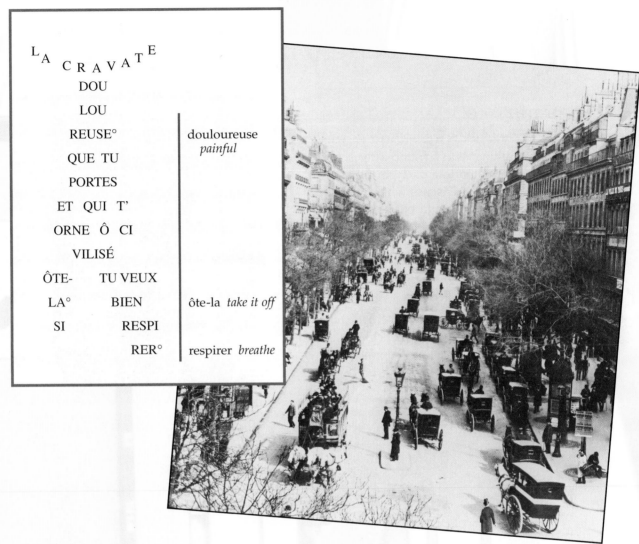

LA CRAVATE
DOU
LOU
REUSE°
QUE TU
PORTES
ET QUI T'
ORNE Ô CI
VILISÉ
ÔTE- TU VEUX
LA° BIEN
SI RESPI
RER°

douloureuse *painful*

ôte-la *take it off*

respirer *breathe*

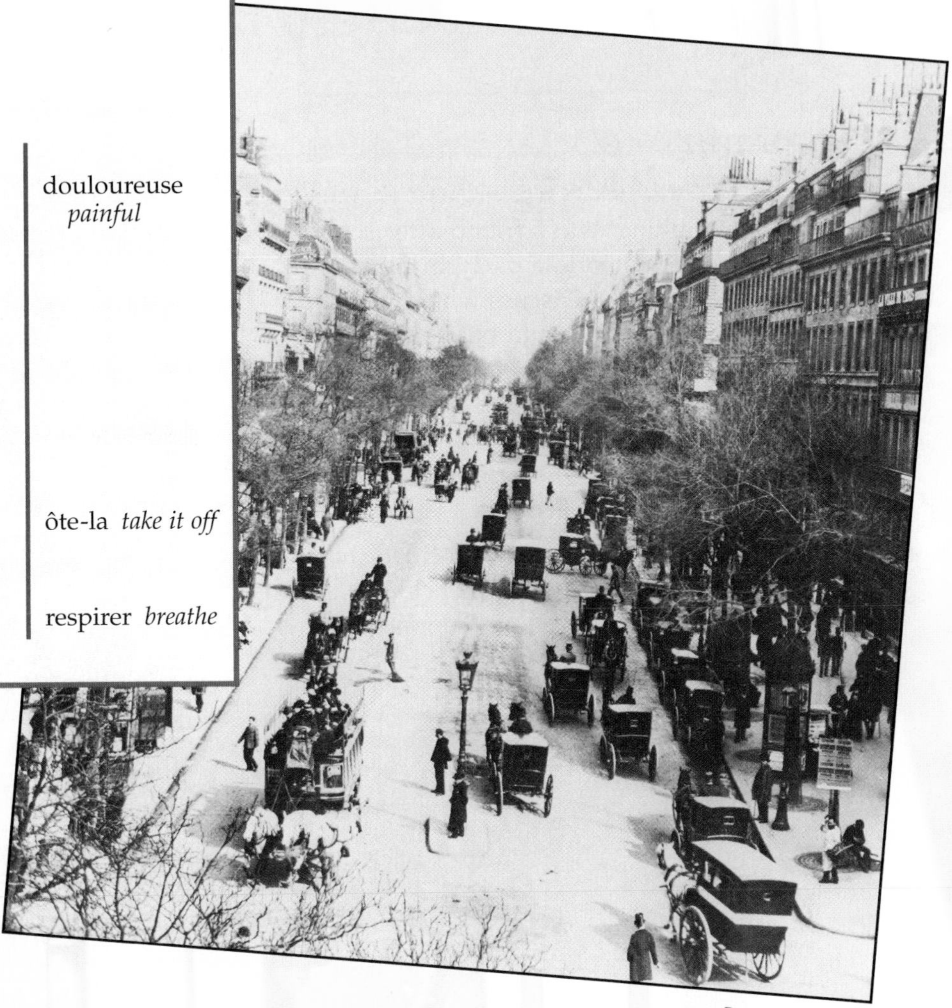

Paris vers 1900

Vous avez compris?

A Mes idées Répondez. *(Answer.)*

1. Si tu es un garçon, tu aimes mettre une cravate?
2. Si tu es une fille, tu trouves que c'est une bonne idée d'obliger un garçon à porter une cravate?
3. Apollinaire aime les cravates?
4. Il croit qu'on peut bien respirer si on porte une cravate?
5. Il croit que l'homme civilisé porte une cravate?

B Explication du texte Explain in English Apollinaire's ideas and tell whether you agree with him.

C'est à vous

Use what you have learned

PARLER 1

Une fête

✔ Identify and describe articles of clothing

You are talking with a friend after school. You are both invited to a party, but you don't know what to wear. Discuss what kind of a party it is and what would be appropriate.

PARLER 2

Un nouveau look

✔ State your color and style preferences in clothes

You and your partner have decided that you are going to change your style of clothes. Discuss what the new "you" is going to look like.

Des amies à Ouagadougou, Burkina Faso

PARLER 3 ÉCRIRE

Des cadeaux

✔ Shop for clothing

You have just spent a few weeks in France and want to buy some gifts for family and friends back home. Make a list of what you want to buy. Go to different stores to buy the items you want. With a classmate, take turns being the customer and salesperson at the stores where you are purchasing the items on your list.

ÉCRIRE

4 On commande des vêtements.

✔ *Order clothing from a catalogue and give color preferences and size*

You want to order from the catalogue to the right. Write a letter stating which items you want, what color, what size.

REVUE DE DETAILS
NEWS MODE
Repéré aux quatre coins de la mode, tout ce qui nous plaît. De la tête aux pieds.

Coloris: noir, beige.
Tailles: du 36 au 40 pour la femme; du 40 au 45 pour l'homme.
modèle femme du 36 au 40 76,07€
modèle homme du 40 au 45 76,07€

l'une 15,23€
Chemise 77% viscose, 23% polyester.
Coloris assortis.
Du 37/38 au 43/44.

l'une 15,23€
Cravate 100% soie.
Coloris assortis.

(1) Robe en velours (150€, 5 tailles, 8 coloris).
(2) Veste sur jupe en taffetas de soie (75€, 3 tailles, 5 coloris (veste) et 150€, du 36 au 42, en noir ou bronze (jupe)).

ÉCRIRE

5 Le catalogue

✔ *Write descriptions of clothing*

Write five descriptions for an online clothing catalogue. Describe the items, tell the sizes they come in, the colors, the occasions they could be worn for, and the prices.

Writing Strategy

Clustering Most writers brainstorm ideas before they begin to write. The next logical step is to "cluster" these ideas. This is done by writing down your main ideas and drawing a box around each one. Then draw a line indicating which ideas are connected to each other. Once you do this, it is easy to add other details to each cluster of ideas. When beginning to write, sort out your clusters and present each in a logical and organized paragraph.

Quel est leur look?

ÉCRIRE

6 Le look de ton école

Write a note to your French friend describing **le look** at your school. Tell him or her what boys and girls usually wear to school and what types of clothing and colors are "in" **(à la mode).**

Assessment

Vocabulaire

To review **Mots 1**, *turn to pages 220–221.*

1 Identifiez. *(Identify.)*

1. 
2. 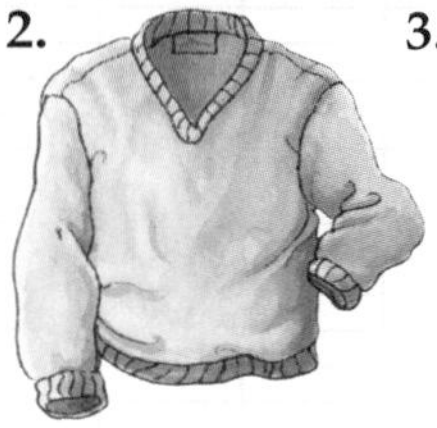
3. 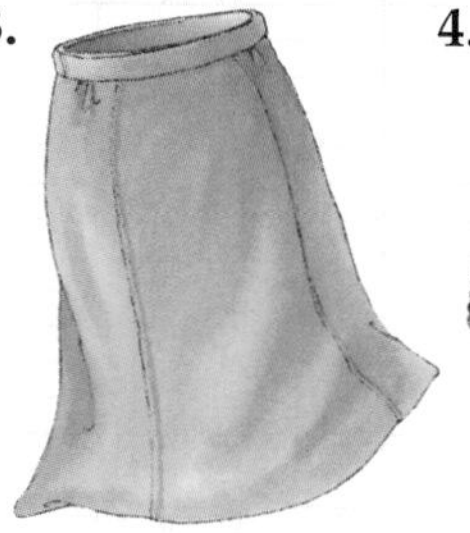
4. 

To review **Mots 2**, *turn to pages 224–225.*

2 Complétez. *(Complete.)*

5. —_____, le pantalon?
   —Non, il est trop grand.
6. —Vous faites quelle ____?
   —Je fais du 38, pour les chemises.
7. —De quelle ____ est la jupe?
   —Elle est grise.
8. —Le jean est trop petit.
   —Je voudrais la taille ____.

Structure

To review the verb **mettre**, *turn to page 228.*

3 Complétez avec «mettre». *(Complete with* mettre.*)*

9. Les garçons ne ____ pas de cravate pour aller à l'école.
10. Après le dîner je ____ la télé.
11. Qu'est-ce que vous ____ quand vous faites du jogging?
12. Qu'est-ce que tu ____ dans ton sac à dos?

To review the forms of these adjectives, turn to page 229.

4 Complétez. *(Complete.)*

13. C'est ma boutique ____. (favori)

14–15. La chemise est ____ et le pantalon est ____ aussi. (blanc)

16. Elle met une robe ____. (long)

5 Complétez. *(Complete.)*

To review the comparative of adjectives, turn to page 230.

17. —Jean est très sympa.
—Oui. Mais il n'est pas ____ sympa ____ toi.

18. —Ce jean ne coûte pas cher.
—Non, il est ____ cher ____ les autres.

19. —Les deux frères sont très intelligents.
—C'est vrai. Paul est ____ intelligent ____ Loïc.

6 Récrivez chaque phrase. *(Rewrite each sentence.)*

To review the verbs **voir** and **croire**, turn to page 232.

20. Je crois que oui.
Vous ____.

21. Elle voit de jolies chaussures dans la vitrine.
Elles ____.

22. Vous voyez ça?
Tu ____?

Culture

7 Vrai ou faux? *(True or false?)*

To review this cultural information, turn to pages 236–237.

23. Les boutiques des grands couturiers sont très chères.

24. Un grand magasin a beaucoup de rayons différents.

25. On trouve les marchés aux puces dans les quartiers élégants de Paris.

La boutique d'un grand couturier, Paris

On parle super bien!

Tell all you can about this illustration.

Vocabulaire

Identifying articles of clothing

les vêtements *(m. pl.)*
un jean
un short
une casquette
un pull
une veste
un pantalon
un t-shirt
une sandale
un sweat-shirt
un polo
un manteau
un anorak
un blouson
un survêtement
une basket
une chaussure
une chaussette

Identifying men's clothing

une chemise
une cravate
un complet

How well do you know your vocabulary?

- Choose words that describe an outfit you would like to have.
- Describe your shopping trip to look for the outfit.

Identifying women's clothing

une jupe plissée
un chemisier
une robe
un tailleur

Shopping

une boutique
un centre commercial
un grand magasin
une vitrine
une cabine d'essayage
un vendeur
une vendeuse
un rayon
des soldes *(m. pl.)*
le prix
cher (chère)
faire des courses
essayer
entrer (dans)
porter
trouver
mettre

Describing clothes

large
serré(e)
habillé(e)
sport
joli(e)
favori(te)
à manches
longues
courtes
la pointure
la taille
au-dessus
au-dessous

Identifying colors

De quelle couleur?
blanc(he)
brun(e)
vert(e)
noir(e)
gris(e)
bleu(e)
jaune
rouge
beige
rose
bleu marine
marron
orange

Other useful words and expressions

Vous faites quelle taille?
Je fais du 40.
en solde
à mon avis
voir
croire

VIDÉOTOUR

Épisode 7

In this video episode, you will visit a boutique with Chloé and Christine. See page 532 for more information.

Révision

Conversation

Faire la cuisine!

Julie: Tu vas préparer le déjeuner?
Miéna: Moi? Préparer le déjeuner? Tu rigoles! Je déteste faire la cuisine.
Julie: Tu veux aller au resto, alors?
Miéna: Non, je ne peux pas. Je n'ai pas le temps. Je vais manger une tranche de pizza.
Julie: Tu n'as pas le temps d'aller au resto? Pourquoi?
Miéna: Je veux acheter quelque chose pour samedi. Je vais à une fête chez une amie.
Julie: Qu'est-ce que tu vas acheter?
Miéna: Je crois que je vais acheter une robe.
Julie: Près de chez moi, il y a des soldes dans une petite boutique sympa.
Miéna: Merci, mais je vais aller aux Galeries. Je trouve toujours quelque chose là.

Galeries Lafayette, Paris

Vous avez compris?

Répondez. *(Answer.)*

1. Miéna va préparer le déjeuner?
2. Elle aime faire la cuisine?
3. Elle veut aller déjeuner au restaurant?
4. Elle ne peut pas aller au restaurant?
5. Qu'est-ce qu'elle va manger?
6. Qu'est-ce qu'elle veut acheter?
7. Elle va où samedi?
8. Elle va aller dans quel magasin?

Structure

Les verbes irréguliers au présent

1. Review the following irregular verbs.

ALLER	je vais, tu vas, il/elle/on va, nous‿allons, vous‿allez, ils/elles vont
PRENDRE	je prends, tu prends, il/elle/on prend, nous prenons, vous prenez, ils/elles prennent
FAIRE	je fais, tu fais, il/elle/on fait, nous faisons, vous faites, ils/elles font
POUVOIR	je peux, tu peux, il/elle/on peut, nous pouvons, vous pouvez, ils/elles peuvent
VOULOIR	je veux, tu veux, il/elle/on veut, nous voulons, vous voulez, ils/elles veulent
METTRE	je mets, tu mets, il/elle/on met, nous mettons, vous mettez, ils/elles mettent
CROIRE	je crois, tu crois, il/elle/on croit, nous croyons, vous croyez, ils/elles croient
VOIR	je vois, tu vois, il/elle/on voit, nous voyons, vous voyez, ils/elles voient

2. Note that for all the preceding verbs except **aller,** the three singular forms sound alike. For all these verbs except **faire,** the **nous** and **vous** stems are the same.

1 **Historiette On fait des courses.** Répondez d'après les indications. *(Answer according to the cues.)*

1. Tu vas aller où? (aux Galeries Lafayette)
2. Qu'est-ce que tu vas faire? (acheter un cadeau)
3. Qu'est-ce que tu veux acheter? (une chemise blanche)
4. C'est pour qui, la chemise? (mon père)
5. Il fait quelle taille? (du 39)
6. Tu vois un chemisier pour ta mère? (oui)
7. Qui met le chemisier dans un sac? (le vendeur)

Galeries Lafayette, Paris

2 **Historiette À l'école** Mettez au pluriel. *(Make the sentences plural.)*

1. Je vais à l'école.
2. Je prends le car pour aller à l'école.
3. Je veux poser une question.
4. L'élève peut poser des questions.
5. Sandrine croit qu'elle a la bonne réponse.
6. Elle prend ses cahiers.

Des pâtisseries

Les contractions au et du

The prepositions **à** and **de** contract with **le** to form **au** and **du,** and with **les** to form **aux** and **des.**

à + le = au	**Il va au collège.**
à + les = aux	**Le prof parle aux élèves.**
de + le = du	**Il rentre du collège.**
de + les = des	**Il parle des élèves.**

3 **Où?** Répondez d'après les indications. *(Answer according to the cues.)*

1. On achète des tartes où? (pâtisserie)
2. Et du saucisson? (charcuterie)
3. Et de l'eau minérale? (épicerie)
4. Et du poisson? (marché)
5. On parle à qui au marché? (marchands)

4 **D'où?** Complétez en utilisant **de** + un article défini. *(Answer with* de + *a definite article.)*

1. Mon frère rentre ____ lycée.
2. Mon autre frère rentre ____ collège.
3. Ma sœur rentre ____ école.
4. Mon autre sœur rentre ____ cantine.
5. Nous parlons tous ____ professeurs.

Le partitif

1. Remember that the partitive, "some," "any," is expressed in French by **de** + the definite article. **De** contracts with **le** to form **du** and with **les** to form **des.** In the negative, **du, de la, de l',** and **des** all become **de** or **d'.**

Je veux de l'argent.	**Je ne veux pas d'argent.**
J'ai des croissants.	**Je n'ai pas de croissants.**

2. Remember that **un** and **une** also become **de** or **d'** after a negative expression.

Tu veux un couteau?	**Tu ne veux pas de couteau?**
J'ai une serviette.	**Je n'ai pas de serviette.**

5 **Dans le chariot** Dites ce qu'il y a dans le chariot. *(Tell what is in the cart.)*

6 **Pas dans le chariot** Dites ce qu'il n'y a pas dans le chariot de l'Activité 5. *(Tell what is not in the cart in Activity 5.)*

7 **J'ai faim** Répondez d'après le modèle.
(Answer according to the model.)

—Tu veux du poisson?
—Non, je ne veux pas de poisson. Je n'aime pas le poisson!

1. Tu veux du bœuf?
2. Tu veux des œufs?
3. Tu veux des carottes à la crème?
4. Tu veux du poulet?
5. Tu veux de la salade?
6. Tu veux du gâteau au chocolat?

Le comparatif

1. You use the comparative to compare two people or two items.

    Aurélie est plus (aussi, moins) sportive que son frère.
    Le pantalon est plus (aussi, moins) cher que le jean.

2. You use the stress pronouns **moi, toi, lui, elle, nous, vous, eux,** and **elles** after **que (qu')** when comparing people.

    Il est moins sympa qu'elle (que toi, qu'eux).

Marie est plus fatiguée que sa sœur.

8 **Cyril et moi** Répondez d'après le modèle.
(Answer according to the model.)

Cyril est très sérieux. →
—Il est plus sérieux que moi?
—Non, il est aussi sérieux que toi.

1. Cyril est très timide.
2. Cyril est très grand.
3. Cyril est très amusant.
4. Cyril est très patient.
5. Cyril est très beau.
6. Cyril est très sympathique.

9 **Christelle et moi** Remplacez Cyril par Christelle dans l'Activité 8. *(Replace* Cyril *with* Christelle *in Activity 8.)*

10 **Au restaurant** With a classmate, make up a conversation between a waiter or a waitress and a customer.

Un restaurant, Paris

11 **Qu'est-ce que tu fais?** Work with a classmate. Ask each other questions about the things you do or want to do. Use the following words in the conversation.

prendre, vouloir, pouvoir, croire, faire, aller

12 **Des courses** Work with a classmate. Each of you will make up a grocery list. Exchange lists. Then tell each other where you are going to go and what you are going to do.

Literary Companion *You may wish to read the poem «Dors mon enfant», by Elolongué Epanya Yondo, who was born in Cameroun and studied in Paris. This poem is found on page 510.*

1. Maisons du pays Dogon au Mali
2. Masque sénoufo de la Côte d'Ivoire
3. Danse rituelle et tambourinaires du Burundi
4. Une petite fille du Mali
5. Dakar, la capitale du Sénégal
6. Youssou N'Dour, le célèbre chanteur pop du Sénégal
7. Un griot raconte aux jeunes du village l'histoire de leurs ancêtres

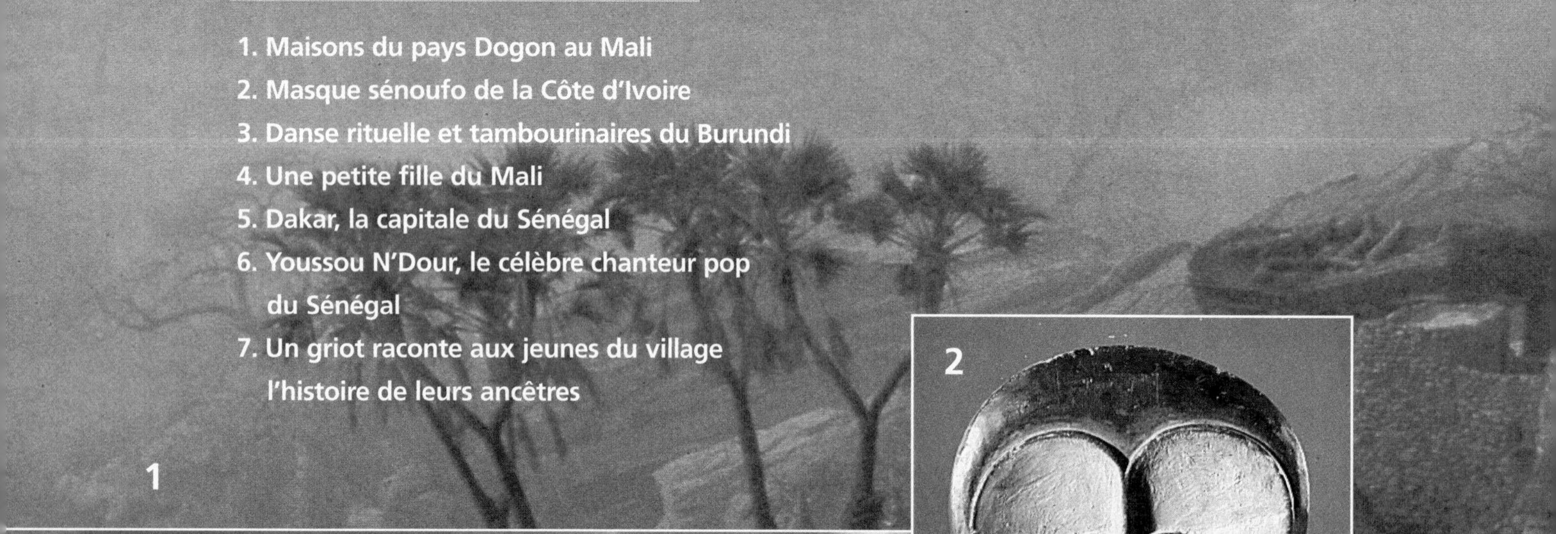

6

Reflets de l'Afrique

7

8. Baobab à Madagascar
9. Cueillette du thé au Burundi
10. Mosquée à Djenné, au Mali
11. Abidjan en Côte d'Ivoire
12. Match de la Coupe d'Afrique des Nations au Burkina Faso
13. Femme adioukrou en Côte d'Ivoire
14. Marchande de pain à Cotonou, au Bénin

9

8

10

11

12

13

NATIONAL GEOGRAPHIC

REFLETS de l'Afrique

14

CHAPITRE 8

L'aéroport et l'avion

Objectifs

In this chapter you will learn to:

- *check in for a flight*
- *talk about some services aboard the plane*
- *talk about more activities*
- *ask more questions*
- *talk about people and things as a group*
- *discuss air travel in France*

René Magritte *La grande famille*

Vocabulaire Mots 1

À l'aéroport

Maintenant Justine est dans le hall de l'aéroport.
Elle fait enregistrer ses bagages.
L'agent vérifie son billet.

Justine choisit une place dans l'avion.
Elle demande une place côté couloir.

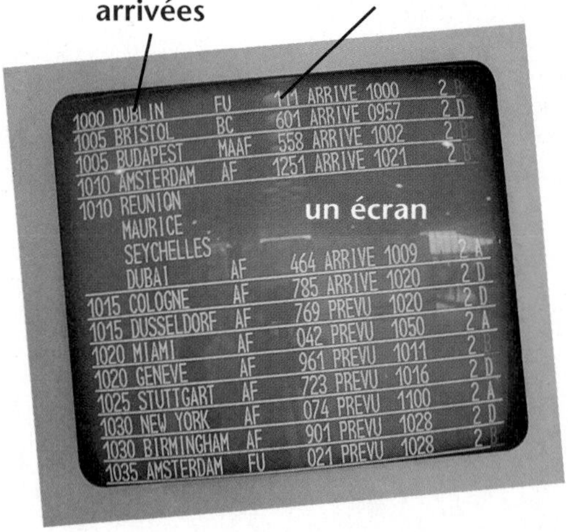

L'avion a du retard.
L'avion n'est pas à l'heure.

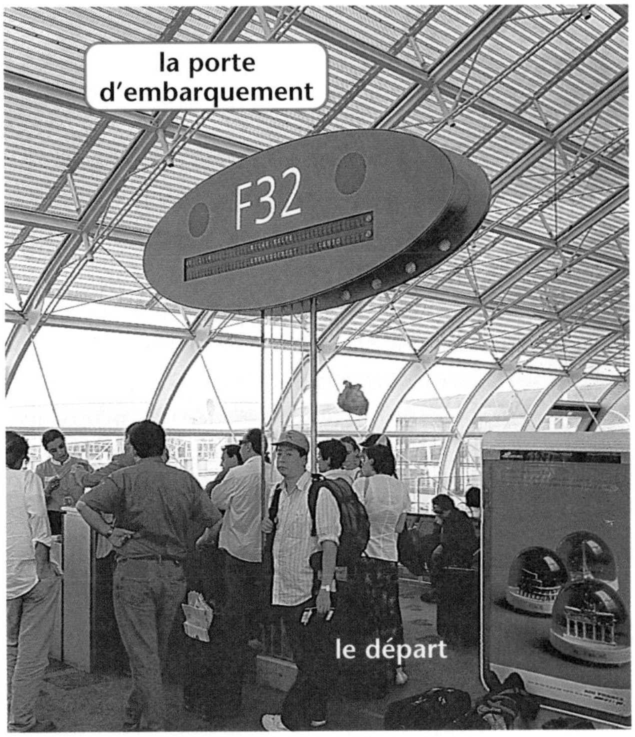

L'avion part de la porte 32.

L'avion atterrit.

L'avion décolle.

Justine aime voyager.
Elle fait un voyage à Montréal.
Avant le voyage elle fait sa valise.

> un vol à destination de Paris = un vol qui va à Paris
> un vol en provenance de Lyon = un vol qui arrive de Lyon
> un vol intérieur = un vol entre deux villes du même pays (Paris–Lyon)
> un vol international = un vol entre deux villes de pays différents (Paris–Rome)

Quel est le mot?

1 Historiette Un voyage à Genève

Inventez une histoire.

1. Laurence aime voyager?
2. Elle fait un voyage à Genève?
3. Elle fait ses valises avant de partir pour l'aéroport?
4. Elle est au comptoir de la compagnie aérienne?
5. L'agent vérifie son billet et son passeport?
6. Laurence a beaucoup de bagages à main?
7. Elle fait enregistrer ses bagages?
8. Elle choisit une place dans l'avion?
9. Elle veut une place côté couloir ou côté fenêtre?
10. Elle a sa carte d'embarquement?
11. Elle va à la porte d'embarquement?

Laurence part pour Genève.

2 Historiette À l'aéroport

Répondez d'après les indications.

1. Les passagers sont où? (à l'aérogare 2)
2. Leur avion part à quelle heure? (à onze heures trente)
3. Il part de quelle porte? (trente-deux)
4. Qu'est-ce que les passagers regardent pour vérifier la porte et l'heure du départ? (l'écran)
5. Leur avion va partir à l'heure ou va avoir du retard? (va partir à l'heure)
6. Les passagers vont passer par où? (le contrôle de sécurité)
7. Qu'est-ce qu'on annonce? (le départ du vol)
8. Les passagers vont d'Abidjan à Dakar. Ils prennent un vol intérieur? (non, international)
9. L'avion est sur la piste? (oui)
10. Il va décoller ou atterrir? (décoller)
11. L'avion va atterrir à Paris? (non, à Dakar)
12. C'est un vol à destination ou en provenance de Dakar? (à destination)

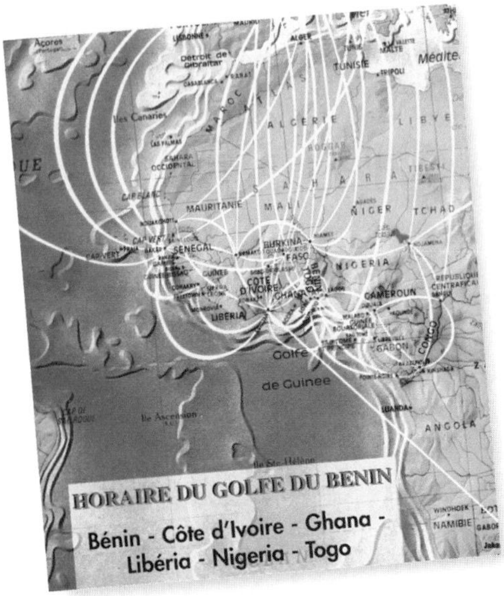

3 **À l'aéroport** Work with a classmate. You're checking in at the airport for your flight to Fort-de-France in Martinique. Have a conversation with the airline agent (your partner) at the ticket counter.

Aéroport Charles-de-Gaulle, Roissy

4 **Un vol** Work with a classmate. Look at the illustration. You are a passenger on this flight. Tell as much as you can about your experience at the airport.

ENCORE PLUS *For more practice using words from **Mots 1**, do Activity 24 on page H25 at the end of this book.*

Vocabulaire Mots 2

À bord

Le personnel de bord:
le pilote
le steward
l'hôtesse de l'air

C'est un vol non-fumeurs.

la cabine

Il faut mettre vos bagages sous le siège devant vous ou dans le coffre à bagages.

L'hôtesse de l'air fait une annonce.

Le steward sert des boissons à bord.
On sert un repas.

Vous ne finissez pas votre repas?
Non, merci. Je n'ai plus faim.

On ramasse les plateaux.

Un passager sort ses bagages du coffre à bagages.
Une passagère dort.
Une autre remplit sa carte de débarquement.

Quel est le mot?

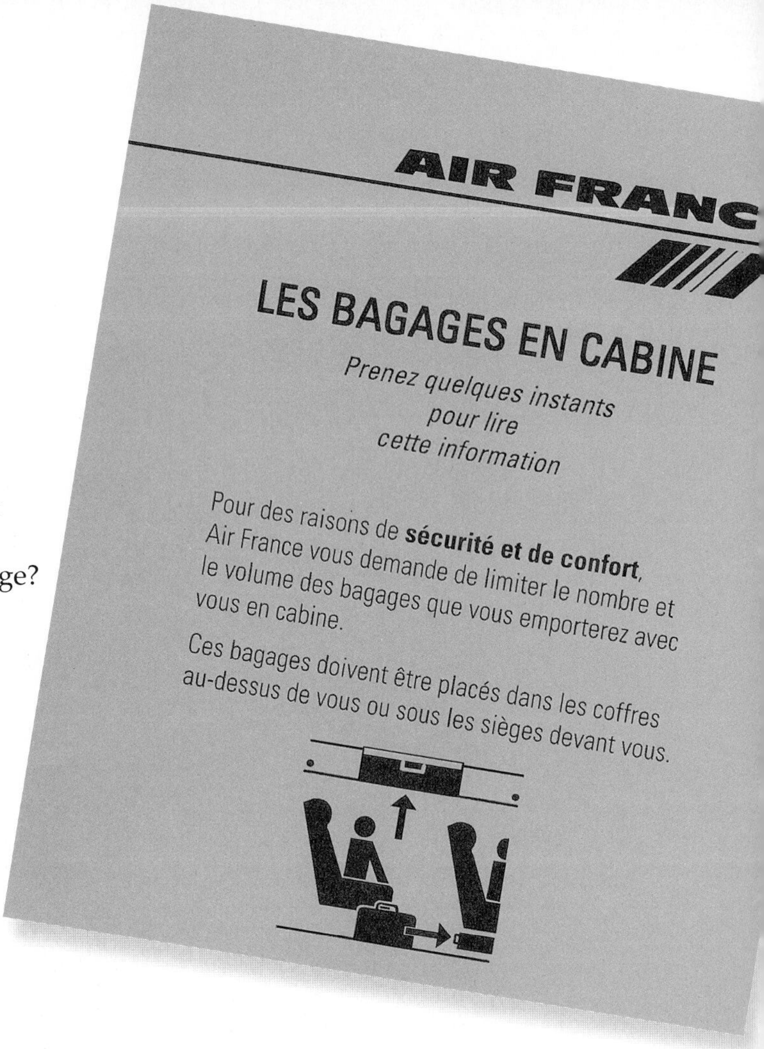
AIR FRANC
LES BAGAGES EN CABINE
Prenez quelques instants
pour lire
cette information
Pour des raisons de **sécurité et de confort**, Air France vous demande de limiter le nombre et le volume des bagages que vous emporterez avec vous en cabine.
Ces bagages doivent être placés dans les coffres au-dessus de vous ou sous les sièges devant vous.

5 Historiette À bord de l'avion

Inventez une histoire.

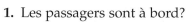

1. Les passagers sont à bord?
2. Le personnel de bord fait des annonces?
3. Il faut attacher sa ceinture de sécurité avant le décollage?
4. Il faut mettre ses bagages à main sous le siège?
5. On peut mettre des bagages dans le coffre à bagages?
6. Après le décollage, on sert le dîner?
7. Qui sert le dîner, le steward ou le pilote?
8. On peut fumer pendant le vol?

L'avion décolle.

6 Antonymes Trouvez le contraire.

1. atterrir	**a.** mettre
2. l'embarquement	**b.** à destination de
3. une hôtesse de l'air	**c.** l'atterrissage
4. en provenance de	**d.** le débarquement
5. un vol intérieur	**e.** un steward
6. embarquer	**f.** un vol international
7. l'arrivée	**g.** décoller
8. sortir	**h.** débarquer
9. le décollage	**i.** le départ

7 À bord Vrai ou faux?

1. Il faut passer par le contrôle de sécurité avant le vol.
2. On peut laisser ses bagages à main dans le couloir pendant le vol.
3. Il faut attacher sa ceinture de sécurité avant le décollage et l'atterrissage.
4. Il faut faire ses valises après le vol.
5. L'hôtesse de l'air ou le steward ramasse les plateaux après le repas.
6. Le pilote sert un repas et des boissons pendant le vol.
7. L'hôtesse de l'air fait une annonce.
8. Le steward dort pendant le vol.
9. Il faut remplir sa carte de débarquement.

8 Une carte d'embarquement

This is a boarding card for a flight you are about to take. Tell a classmate (your partner) all you can about your flight based on the information on the card.

9 Arrivées

Work with a classmate. Look at this arrival screen at Charles-de-Gaulle airport. Give as much information about the flights as you can, then ask each other questions about them.

Aéroport Charles-de-Gaulle, Roissy

ENCORE PLUS *For more practice using words from* ***Mots 2****, do Activity 25 on page H26 at the end of this book.*

Structure

Les verbes en -ir au présent
Describing people's activities

1. A second group of regular verbs in French has infinitives that end in **-ir.** Verbs like **finir** *(to finish)* and **choisir** *(to choose)* are regular **-ir** verbs. They have two different stems, one for the singular and one for the plural. Study the following chart.

			FINIR		CHOISIR	
je	fin	-is	je	finis	je	choisis
tu	fin	-is	tu	finis	tu	choisis
il/elle/on	fin	-it	il/elle/on	finit	il/elle/on	choisit
nous	fin + iss	-ons	nous	finissons	nous	choisissons
vous	fin + iss	-ez	vous	finissez	vous	choisissez
ils/elles	fin + iss	-ent	ils/elles	finissent	ils/elles	choisissent

2. Other verbs that belong to this group are **atterrir** and **remplir.**

Ils remplissent une carte de débarquement.
L'avion atterrit à l'heure.

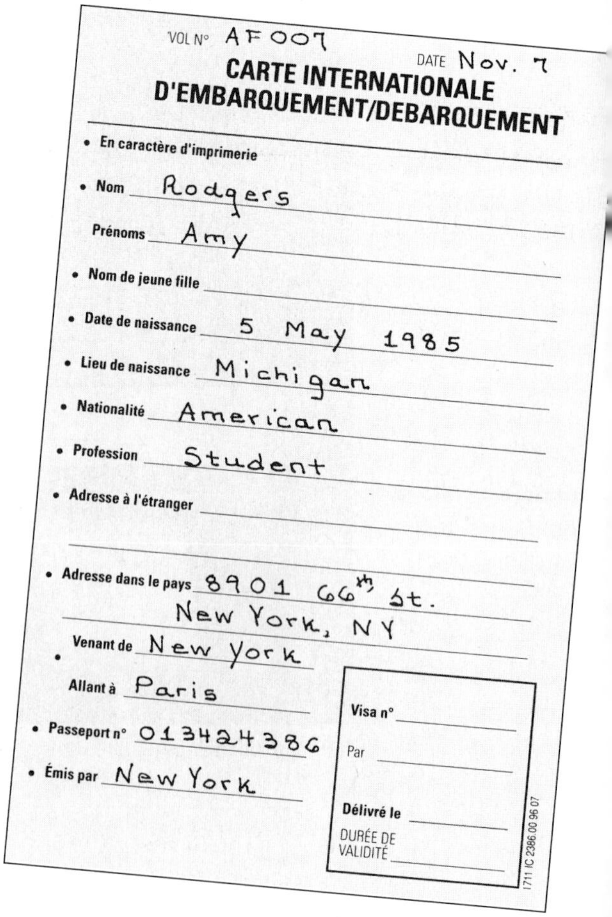
VOL N° AF007 DATE Nov. 7
CARTE INTERNATIONALE D'EMBARQUEMENT/DEBARQUEMENT
• En caractère d'imprimerie
• Nom Rodgers
Prénoms Amy
• Nom de jeune fille
• Date de naissance 5 May 1985
• Lieu de naissance Michigan
• Nationalité American
• Profession Student
• Adresse à l'étranger
• Adresse dans le pays 8901 66th St. New York, NY
• Venant de New York
Allant à Paris
• Passeport n° 013424386
• Émis par New York
Visa n°
Par
Délivré le
DURÉE DE VALIDITÉ
1711 IC 2386.00 96 07

Comment dit-on?

10 Historiette Un vol pour Paris

Répondez d'après les indications.

1. Madame Lauzier choisit quelle compagnie? (Air France)
2. Elle choisit quelle classe? (la classe économique)
3. Elle choisit une place côté couloir ou côté fenêtre? (côté fenêtre)
4. Elle finit tout son repas? (non)
5. Son avion atterrit à quelle heure? (à midi)
6. Il atterrit à quel aéroport? (à Charles-de-Gaulle)
7. Qu'est-ce qu'elle remplit avant l'arrivée? (une carte de débarquement)

11 Historiette Au restaurant Donnez des réponses personnelles.

1. En général, tu choisis des restaurants chers ou pas chers?
2. Tu choisis la spécialité de la maison?
3. Tu choisis de la viande ou du poisson?
4. Tu finis ton repas par un dessert ou du fromage?
5. Tu choisis un gâteau ou une glace?
6. Tu finis toujours tout sur ton assiette?

12 Un bon dîner Mettez au pluriel d'après le modèle.

Je choisis du bœuf et tu choisis du poisson.
Nous choisissons du bœuf et vous choisissez du poisson.

1. Je choisis un petit restaurant et tu choisis un restaurant gastronomique.
2. Je choisis un steak bien cuit et tu choisis un steak à point.
3. Je remplis mon assiette et tu remplis ton assiette.
4. Je finis mon repas par une tarte et tu finis ton repas par des crêpes Suzette.
5. Je finis mon repas par un crème et tu finis ton repas par un express.

13 Un autre vol Complétez avec **choisir** ou **remplir**.

1. Les passagers ____ un vol Air France?
2. Ils ____ une place côté fenêtre ou côté couloir?
3. Ils ____ le poulet ou le poisson pour le dîner à bord?
4. Ils ____ leur carte de débarquement pendant le vol?

ENCORE PLUS *For more practice using* ***-ir*** *verbs, do Activity 26 on page H27 at the end of this book.*

Quel et tout
Describing people and things as a group

1. You use the interrogative adjective **quel** with a noun when you want to ask "what" or "which." Note that all forms of **quel** are pronounced the same even though they are spelled differently.

	Masculin	Féminin
Singulier	quel vol quel avion	quelle compagnie quelle hôtesse
Pluriel	quels vols quels avions	quelles compagnies quelles hôtesses

2. You use **tout(e)** with the definite articles **le, la,** and **l'** to express "the whole" or "the entire." You use **tous** and **toutes** with **les** to express "all" or "every."

	Masculin	Féminin
Singulier	tout le personnel	toute la compagnie
Pluriel	tous les stewards	toutes les hôtesses

Toute la classe fait le voyage. *The whole class is taking the trip.*
Tous les élèves prennent le même vol. *All the students are taking the same flight.*
Il y a un vol tous les jours. *There is a flight every day.*

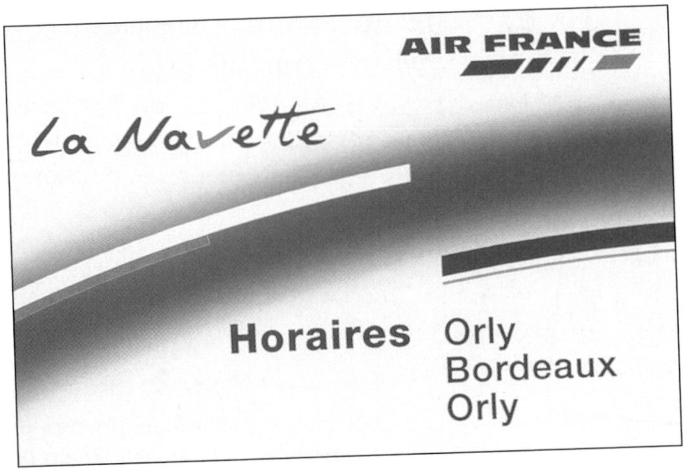

Rappelez-vous que...

The expression **tout le monde** means "everyone."
Tout le monde veut aller en France.

Comment dit-on?

14 **Quels cours?** Répondez d'après le modèle.

—Tu aimes quels cours?
—Moi? J'aime tous les cours.

1. Tu aimes quelles matières?
2. Tu aimes quelles langues?
3. Tu aimes quelles sciences?
4. Tu aimes quels livres?
5. Tu aimes quels CD?
6. Tu aimes quels profs?

AIR FRANCE
faire du ciel le plus bel endroit de la terre
le billet électronique
si simple, si pratique

15 **Quel vol?** Complétez avec **quel** et puis répondez.

1. Tu fais un voyage? ____ voyage?
2. Ton avion part à ____ heure?
3. Ton avion part de ____ porte?
4. Pendant le vol, tu vas regarder ____ film?
5. Tu vas écouter ____ cassettes?
6. Tu aimes ____ livres?

16 **Tous les vols pour quelle ville?**
Complétez avec **tout.**

1. ____ les places sont occupées.
2. ____ l'avion est classe économique. Il n'y a pas de première classe.
3. ____ la cabine est non-fumeurs.
4. C'est vrai. Maintenant ____ les vols sont non-fumeurs.

17 **Dans l'avion** Complétez et puis répondez.

1. ____ le personnel parle ____ langues? (tout, quel)
2. ____ les stewards servent ____ boissons et ____ repas? (tout, quel, quel)
3. ____ les hôtesses font ____ annonces? (tout, quel)
4. ____ les passagers font enregistrer ____ bagages? (tout, quel)
5. ____ les vols ont ____ destination? (tout, quel)

18 **Toute la famille** Get together with a classmate. Tell each other some things that your whole family often does together. Compare notes and see if both your families do many of the same things.

Les verbes sortir, partir, dormir et servir
Describing more activities

The verbs **sortir, partir, dormir**, and **servir** all follow the same pattern—the consonant sound in the infinitive is heard in the plural forms but not in the singular forms. Study the following.

SORTIR		PARTIR		DORMIR		SERVIR	
je	sors	je	pars	je	dors	je	sers
tu	sors	tu	pars	tu	dors	tu	sers
il/elle/on	sort	il/elle/on	part	il/elle/on	dort	il/elle/on	sert
nous	sortons	nous	partons	nous	dormons	nous	servons
vous	sortez	vous	partez	vous	dormez	vous	servez
ils/elles	sortent	ils/elles	partent	ils/elles	dorment	ils/elles	servent

Savez-vous que... ?

Sortir means "to go out" or "to leave."

Je sors de l'école à trois heures.

With a direct object, it means "to take out."

Je sors mes livres de mon sac à dos.

Comment dit-on?

19 Historiette Un vol Paris–Abidjan

Inventez une histoire.

1. M. Kuti va prendre l'avion. Il sort son billet?
2. Il sort son passeport?
3. Son avion part de quelle porte?
4. Son avion part à quelle heure?
5. À bord, on sert des boissons?
6. On sert un repas?
7. M. Kuti dort un peu pendant le vol?

M. Kuti part pour Abidjan.

20 Historiette Qui part?

Donnez des réponses personnelles.

1. Tu pars pour l'école à quelle heure le matin?
2. Tu sors de la maison à quelle heure le matin?
3. Quand tu arrives à l'école, qu'est-ce que tu sors de ton sac à dos?
4. Quelquefois, tu dors un peu en classe?
5. Le week-end, tu sors avec tes copains? Qu'est-ce que vous faites?

FRENCH Online

For more information on air travel in the Francophone world, go to the Glencoe French Web site: french.glencoe.com

21 On part demain. Répétez la conversation.

Valérie: Demain, on part pour Tunis, Marie et moi!
Philippe: Vous partez à quelle heure?
Valérie: On part à onze heures.
Philippe: Et vous partez de quel aéroport?
Valérie: D'Orly. C'est la première fois que je pars d'Orly.
Philippe: Ah oui?
Valérie: Oui, en général, nous partons toujours de Charles-de-Gaulle.

22 **Après la conversation** Complétez d'après la conversation.

1. Valérie et Marie ____ pour Tunis.
2. Elles ____ en avion.
3. Leur avion ____ à onze heures.
4. Il ____ d'Orly.
5. En général, Valérie ____ d'Orly ou de Charles-de-Gaulle?

Port El Kantaoui, Tunisie

23 **Historiette** **Un petit voyage** Complétez.

1. Vous ____ quand? (partir)
2. Votre avion ____ à quelle heure? (partir)
3. Vous ____ pendant le vol? (dormir)
4. Vos copains ____? (dormir)
5. Après votre arrivée à Paris, vous ____ tout de suite? (sortir)
6. Et vos amis, ils ____ aussi ou ils ____? (sortir, dormir)

24 **Un travail** Work with a classmate. You've got a part-time job working at your local airport because you speak French. Help each of the following passengers.

- A passenger is leaving on flight 125 for Chicago. He doesn't know if it's leaving on time. Help him out.
- Another passenger is confused. He doesn't know his flight number to New York. Let him know what it is and also what time it leaves.
- An older passenger doesn't have his glasses. They are in his suitcase. He asks you to tell him what his seat number is.
- Another passenger is in a real hurry. She wants to know what gate to go to for her flight to Los Angeles. Tell her.

Fort-de-France, Martinique

Attention!

A masculine adjective or noun that ends in **-al** changes to **-aux** in the plural.

un journal → **des journaux**

un vol international → **des vols internationaux**

but

une ville internationale → **des villes internationales**

Complétez.

La Martinique est une île __1__ (tropical) dans la mer des Caraïbes. Sa ville __2__ (principal) est Fort-de-France. À Fort-de-France, il y a plusieurs petits parcs __3__ (municipal). L'aéroport __4__ (international) est près de la ville. Tous les jours, il y a des vols __5__ (international) qui décollent et atterrissent. Il y a des vols __6__ (international) à destination de Paris et de beaucoup de villes des États-Unis comme Miami et New York.

Vous êtes sur le bon chemin. Allez-y!

Conversation

On part pour Toulouse.

Départ à destination de Toulouse, vol Air France numéro 6106. Embarquement immédiat, porte 24.

Cécile: C'est notre vol. On y va?
Pierre: D'accord. Tu sors les cartes d'embarquement?
Cécile: Mais moi, je n'ai pas les cartes d'embarquement!
Pierre: Tu n'as pas les cartes d'embarquement! Ben, elles sont où alors?
Cécile: Dans ton sac?
Pierre: Ah, oui. Voilà! On part de la porte 24.
Cécile: On a quelles places?
Pierre: 10A et 10B.
Cécile: Ah, c'est bien. C'est à l'avant de la cabine. On va pouvoir sortir vite.

Vous avez compris?

Répondez.

1. Où sont Cécile et Pierre?
2. Qu'est-ce qu'on annonce?
3. Quel est le numéro de leur vol?
4. Ils vont où?
5. Ils partent de quelle porte?
6. Qui a les cartes d'embarquement?
7. Ils ont quelles places?
8. Pourquoi c'est bien d'avoir des places à l'avant de la cabine?

Parlons un peu plus

A **Tu vas où?** You're at the airport waiting for your flight. You strike up a conversation with the person sitting next to you (your partner). Find out information about each other's flight.

B **Un billet pour Nice** Work with a classmate. You want to fly from New York to Nice. Call the airline to get a reservation. Your partner will be the reservation agent. Before you call, think about the information you will need to give or get from the agent: date of departure, departure time, arrival time in Nice, flight number, price.

Cap Ferrat, près de Nice, France

Prononciation

Le son /l/ final

1. The names Michelle and Nicole were originally French names, but today many American girls also have these names. When you hear French people say the names Michelle and Nicole, the final /l/ sound is much softer than in English. Say "Michelle" and "Nicole" in French. Repeat the following words.

il	**vol**	**animal**	**elle**	**école**
salle	**décolle**	**journal**	**quel**	**ville**

2. Now repeat the following sentences.

C'est un vol international spécial.
Quelle est la ville principale?
Mademoiselle Michelle, elle est très belle.

Il décolle.

Lectures culturelles

Reading Strategy

Recognizing text organization

Before you read a passage, try to figure out how the text is organized. If you can follow the organization of a text, you will understand the main ideas more quickly and be able to look for certain ideas and information more easily.

On va en France.

C'est le mois d'avril et toute la classe de Madame Cadet va passer les vacances de Pâques[1] en France. Ils sont maintenant dans le hall de l'aérogare 1 de l'aéroport international JFK à New York. Ils sont au comptoir d'Air France. Ils vont prendre le vol 007. L'agent vérifie leurs billets et leurs passeports. Il donne toutes les cartes d'embarquement à Madame Cadet.

Les falaises d'Étretat, Normandie

Mont-Saint-Michel, Normandie

Les élèves passent par le contrôle de sécurité. Leur avion part de la porte A. Il part à l'heure. Il ne va pas avoir de retard. Après le décollage, le personnel de bord sert des boissons et un repas. Après le repas, il y a un film. Beaucoup de personnes ne regardent pas le film; elles dorment. Mais pas les élèves de Madame Cadet. Ils ne dorment pas. Ils parlent de leur voyage. Ils vont passer quelques jours à Paris et ensuite[2] ils vont en Normandie. Là, ils vont visiter le Mont-Saint-Michel. Avant l'arrivée à Paris, tout le monde remplit une carte de débarquement.

[1] Pâques *Easter* [2] ensuite *then*

À huit heures du matin, après un vol agréable, l'avion atterrit à l'aéroport Charles-de-Gaulle à Roissy. Charles-de-Gaulle est un des deux aéroports de Paris. D'abord, il faut passer au contrôle des passeports. Ensuite les formalités de douane[3] sont très simples et quarante minutes après l'atterrissage, les élèves de Madame Cadet sont dans l'autocar (le bus) qui fait la navette[4] entre l'aéroport et Paris. Tout le monde est très fatigué après le long vol. Vous croyez qu'ils vont dormir? Pas question! Le premier jour à Paris, on ne dort pas. On va visiter la belle ville de Paris.

[3] douane *customs*
[4] fait la navette *makes the run*

L'île de la Cité, Paris

Un car Air France, aéroport Charles-de-Gaulle

Tunisie

Le Maroc

Le Mali

Le Sénégal

Vous avez compris?

A Un voyage en France Vrai ou faux?

1. Toute la classe de Madame Cadet va à Montréal.
2. À l'aéroport, l'agent de la compagnie aérienne donne toutes les cartes d'embarquement à un des élèves de Madame Cadet.
3. L'avion pour Paris va avoir du retard.
4. Les passagers servent un bon repas après le décollage.
5. Beaucoup de passagers dorment pendant le vol.
6. Le Mont-Saint-Michel est à Paris.
7. Les formalités de douane sont très compliquées en France.
8. Quand les élèves de Madame Cadet arrivent à Paris, ils vont dormir.

B Des informations Cherchez les informations.

1. Quel est le nom d'un aéroport à New York?
2. Quel est le nom d'un des aéroports de Paris?
3. Quel est le numéro du vol des élèves de Madame Cadet?
4. Leur avion part de quelle porte?
5. Quelle est la destination de leur vol?
6. Ils arrivent à Paris à quelle heure?

Lecture supplémentaire 1

Le décalage horaire

Les gens qui voyagent beaucoup souffrent souvent du décalage horaire. Le décalage horaire, qu'est-ce que c'est? C'est la différence entre l'heure d'une ville—New York, par exemple—et une autre ville comme Paris. Quand il est minuit à New York, il est six heures du matin à Paris. Les voyageurs souffrent du décalage horaire parce que quand c'est l'heure de dormir dans une ville, c'est l'heure de travailler dans une autre.

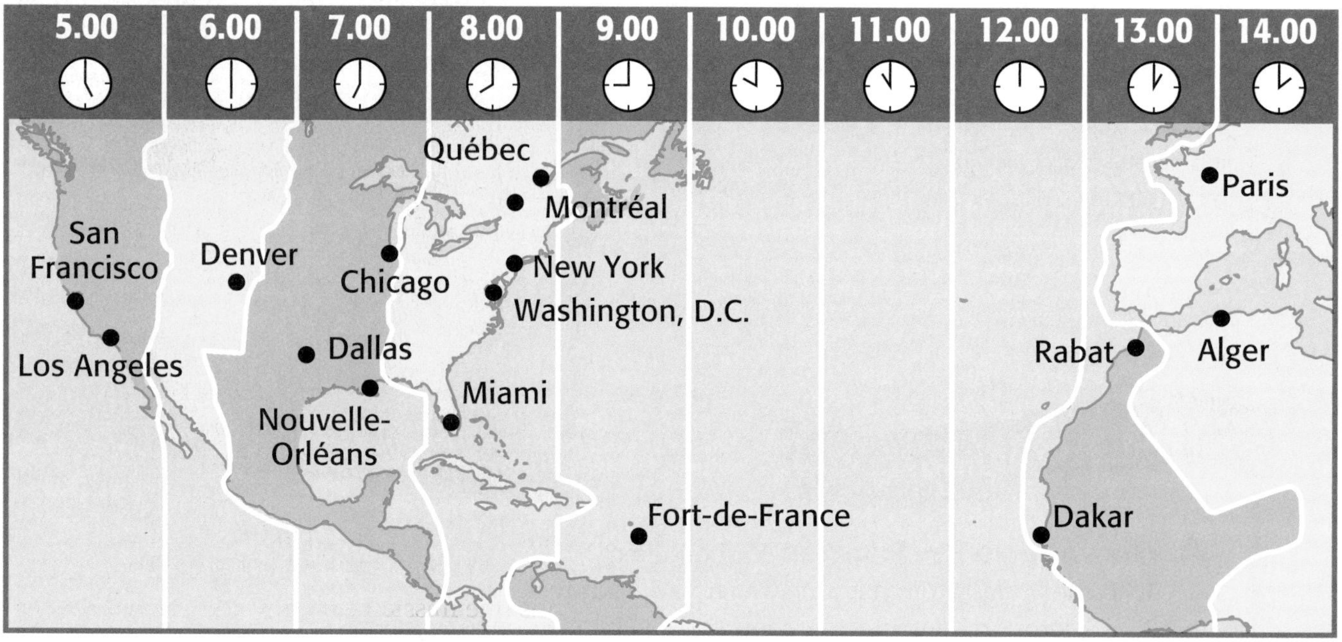

Vous avez compris?

Le décalage horaire Regardez la carte et répondez.

1. Quand il est midi à Washington, D.C., il est quelle heure à Paris?
2. Et à Dakar?
3. Et à Alger?
4. Et à Québec?
5. Et à Los Angeles?
6. Et à la Nouvelle-Orléans?

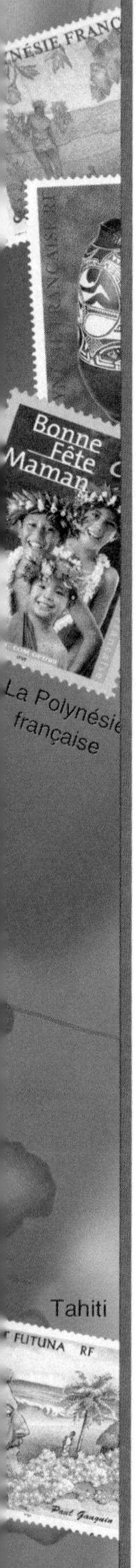

La Polynésie française

Tahiti

Lecture supplémentaire 2

Un pilote écrivain

Antoine de Saint-Exupéry (1900–1944) est un écrivain (un auteur) français célèbre. Mais c'est aussi un homme d'action. Il est né[1] à Lyon en 1900. Pendant son service militaire, il apprend à piloter un avion. Il est pilote de ligne entre Toulouse et Dakar en Afrique. Il est aussi chef de l'Aéropostale (la poste par avion) à Buenos Aires. Il participe aux premiers vols France-Amérique.

Le Petit Prince est son livre le plus connu[2]. Il est connu dans le monde entier. Ses autres romans[3] reflètent sa carrière de pilote. *Courrier sud* parle de ses vols Toulouse–Dakar. *Vol de nuit* parle de trois pilotes basés à Buenos Aires. L'un d'eux est en difficulté dans le ciel[4] noir d'Amérique du Sud. *Terre des hommes* évoque le souvenir[5] de ses camarades disparus, comme Jean Mermoz, le grand aviateur français.

Antoine de Saint-Exupéry

Le 13 juillet 1944, Saint-Exupéry disparaît aussi. Il disparaît dans une mission aérienne militaire au-dessus de la mer Méditerranée. Il reste[6] pour la légende le courageux, le charmant, l'exceptionnel «Saint-Ex».

[1] est né *was born*
[2] le plus connu *best-known*
[3] romans *novels*
[4] ciel *sky*
[5] souvenir *memory*
[6] reste *remains*

Vous avez compris?

Saint-Exupéry Identifiez.

1. le nom de l'écrivain
2. la ville où il est né
3. une ville d'Amérique du Sud où il travaille
4. le nom d'un grand aviateur français

CONNEXIONS

Les sciences physiques

Le climat et le temps

We often speak about the weather, especially when we are traveling. Weather can have a very positive or negative effect on our trip. When planning a vacation, for example, it's a good idea to take into account the climate of the area we are going to visit. When we talk about weather or climate, we must remember that there is a big difference between the two. Weather is the condition of the atmosphere for a short period of time. Climate refers to the weather that prevails in one area over a long period of time.

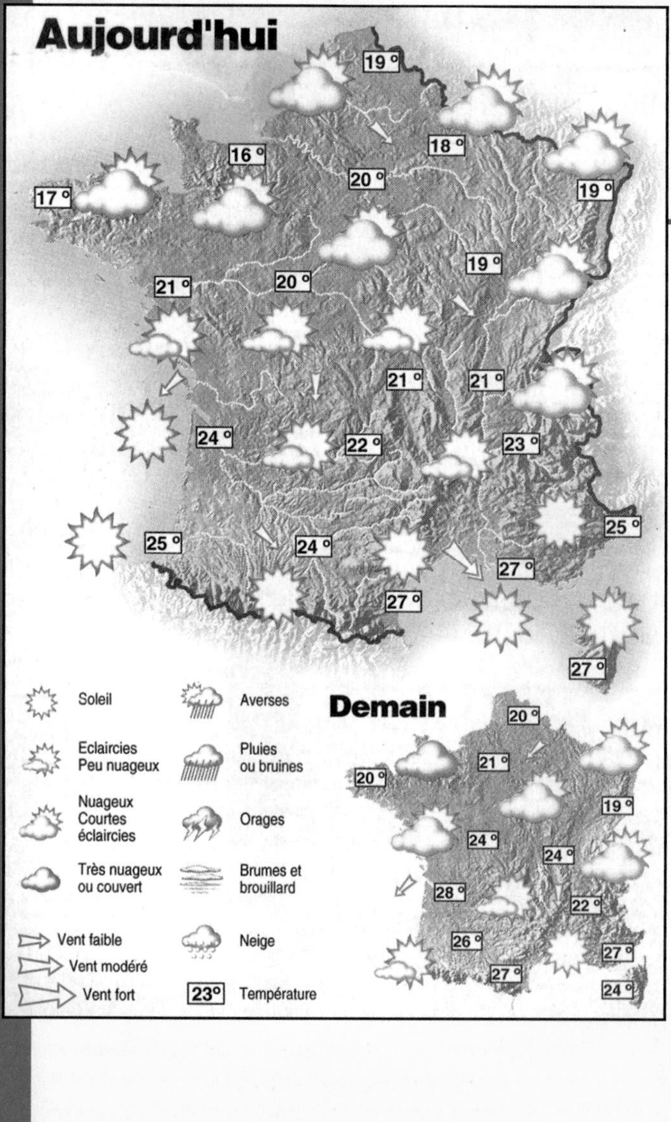

Différence entre climat et temps[1]

Il y a une grande différence entre le climat et le temps. Le temps est la condition de l'atmosphère pendant une courte période. Le temps peut changer très vite. Il peut changer plusieurs fois dans une seule journée.

Le climat, c'est le temps qu'il fait chaque année dans le même endroit[2], dans la même région.

[1] temps *weather* [2] endroit *place*

Des champs de lavande, Digne, Provence

Val-d'Isère, France

Zones climatiques

Dans le monde francophone, il y a beaucoup de zones climatiques. La France, par exemple, a un climat tempéré. Dans une région où le climat est tempéré, il y a quatre saisons: l'été, l'automne, l'hiver, le printemps. Le temps change à chaque saison.

Beaucoup de pays francophones en Afrique sont dans des zones tropicales. Le Bénin et la Côte d'Ivoire, par exemple, sont des pays tropicaux. Ils sont tout près de l'équateur. Là il fait chaud[3] toute l'année et les pluies[4] sont abondantes. Il y a deux saisons—la saison des pluies et la saison sèche[5]. Les saisons varient d'une région à l'autre.

[3] il fait chaud *it's hot* [4] pluies *rains* [5] sèche *dry*

Un village de la brousse, Bénin

Vous avez compris?

Explication du texte

Expliquez en anglais.

1. What's the difference between weather and climate?
2. What is a characteristic of an area with a temperate climate?
3. What is a characteristic of a tropical climate?

C'est à vous

Use what you have learned

PARLER

1 Tu vas où?

✔ *Talk about a plane trip*

You just got to the airport and unexpectedly ran into a friend (your partner). Exchange information about the trip and flight each of you is about to take.

PARLER / ÉCRIRE

2 On fait un voyage?

✔ *Plan a plane trip to a French-speaking destination*

Go to a travel agency in your community. Get some travel brochures and plan a plane trip. Tell all about your trip.

ÉCRIRE

3 Un voyage en avion

✔ *Write about airport activities and services aboard the plane*

You have a French pen pal who is going to visit you this winter. This will be his or her first flight. Write your pen pal a letter and explain all the things he or she is going to experience before and during the flight.

Writing Strategy

Answering an essay question When writing an answer to an essay question, first read the question carefully and determine how to structure your answer. Then restate the essay question in a single statement in your introduction. Next, support the statement with facts, details, and reasons. Finally, close with a conclusion that summarizes your answer.

ÉCRIRE

4

Un concours

In order to win an all-expense-paid trip to the French-speaking country of your choice, you have to write an essay in French and send it to the company sponsoring the trip. Read the following essay questions and then write your answers. You really want to go, so be sure to plan your answers carefully and check your work.

Tu veux aller dans quel pays?
Tu vas y aller comment?
Qu'est-ce que tu veux faire là-bas?
Qu'est-ce que tu veux apprendre?

Lac Léman, Genève, Suisse

Fès, Maroc

Paris, France

Assessment

Vocabulaire

To review **Mots 1**, turn to pages 260–261.

1 Vrai ou faux?

1. Un bagage à main est une très grande valise.
2. Avant un voyage on fait ses valises.
3. Un vol intérieur est un vol entre deux pays.
4. Les passagers partent d'une porte d'embarquement.
5. L'avion atterrit dans le hall de l'aéroport.

To review **Mots 2**, turn to pages 264–265.

2 Identifiez.

8.

9.

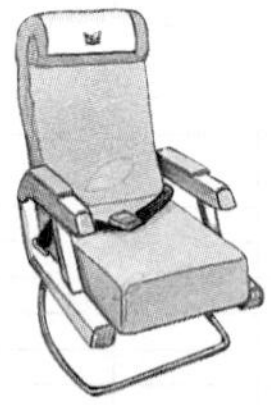

10.

Structure

To review **-ir** verbs, turn to page 268.

3 Complétez.

11. Je ____ mon dîner. (finir)
12. Les passagers ____ leur carte de débarquement. (remplir)
13. Il ____ sa place dans l'avion. (choisir)
14. Nous ____ nos devoirs. (finir)
15. L'avion ____ à l'heure. (atterrir)

To review **quel**, turn to page 270.

4 Complétez avec «quel».

16. —C'est ____ vol?
    —C'est le vol pour Paris.
17. —Tu voyages avec ____ compagnie aérienne?
    —Air France.
18. —Il parle de ____ hôtesses?
    —Des hôtesses d'Air France.

5 Complétez pour indiquer *the whole* ou *every*.

19. ____ classe va faire le voyage.
20. ____ vols n'arrivent pas à la même heure.

To review the use of **tout** with definite articles, turn to page 270.

6 Récrivez chaque phrase.

21. Je sers le dîner.
    Ils ________.
22. Vous sortez?
    Tu ________?
23. Ils partent demain.
    Elle ________.

To review these **-ir** verbs, turn to page 272.

Culture

7 Vrai ou faux?

24. Charles-de-Gaulle est le nom d'un aéroport près de Paris.
25. Le Mont-Saint-Michel est un monument célèbre à Paris.

To review this cultural information, turn to pages 278–279.

Mont-Saint-Michel

On parle super bien!

Tell all you can about this illustration.

Vocabulaire

Getting around an airport

un aéroport
une aérogare
un avion
un hall
un comptoir
une compagnie aérienne
un passager
une passagère
un bagage à main
une valise
un billet
un passeport

le numéro du vol
une porte d'embarquement
une carte d'embarquement
une place
  côté couloir
  côté fenêtre
un départ
une arrivée
une piste
le contrôle de sécurité

un vol
  intérieur
  international
  non-fumeurs
  à destination de
  en provenance de
une annonce
un pays
une ville

Aboard the plane

à bord
la cabine
un siège
le couloir

une ceinture de sécurité
un coffre à bagages
un plateau
une carte de débarquement

How well do you know your vocabulary?

- Choose a word from the list.
- Have a classmate give a related word: **annonce, annoncer.**

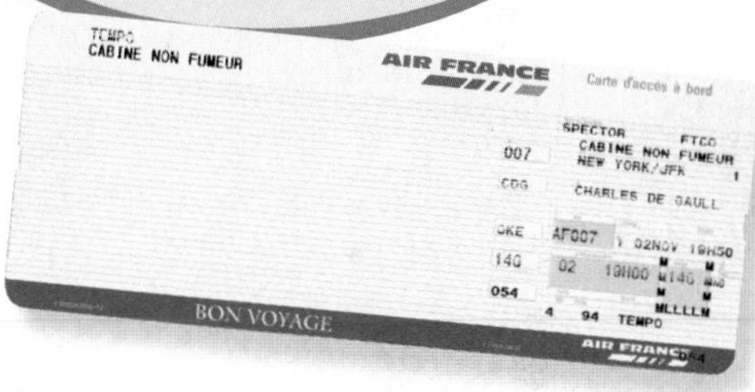

Identifying airline personnel

un agent
le personnel de bord
un pilote

un steward
une hôtesse de l'air

Describing activities at the airport and aboard the plane

voyager
faire un voyage
faire une annonce
finir
choisir
remplir
atterrir

partir
sortir
dormir
servir

passer par
vérifier
décoller
attacher

ramasser
être à l'heure
avoir du retard
(faire) enregistrer

Other useful words and expressions

sous
il faut
faire ses valises

VIDÉOTOUR

Épisode 8

In this video episode, Christine has an unusual "adventure" at the airport. See page 533 for more information.

CHAPITRE 9

La gare et le train

Objectifs

In this chapter you will learn to:

- *purchase a train ticket and request information about arrival and departure*
- *use expressions related to train travel*
- *talk about people's activities*
- *point out people or things*
- *discuss an interesting train trip in French-speaking Africa*

Claude Monet *La locomotive*

MONTREUX

À la gare

On vend des journaux et des magazines au kiosque.

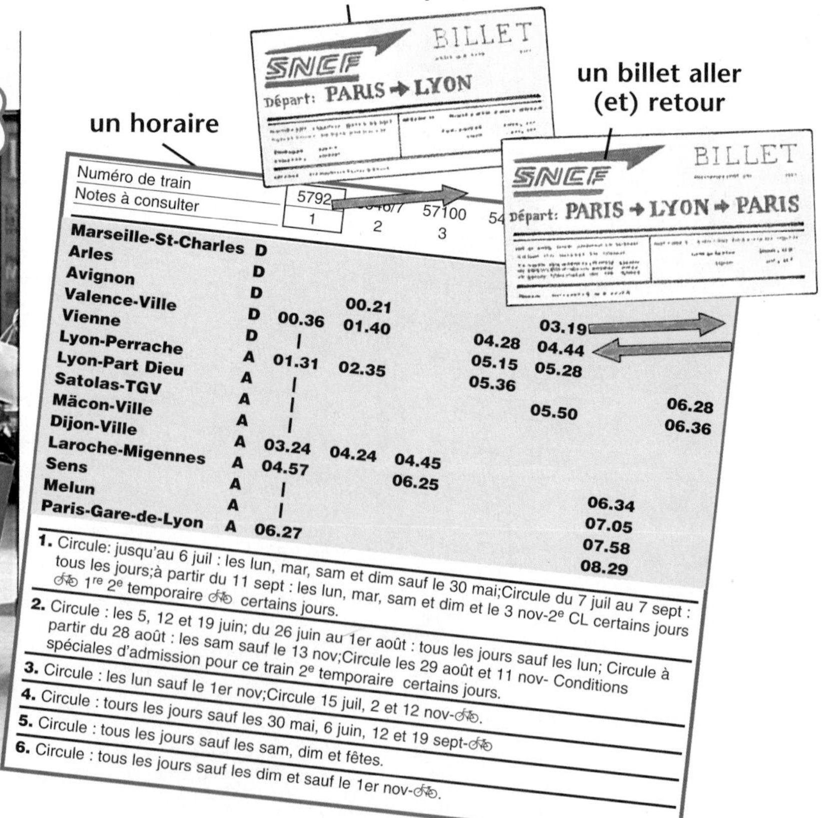

On vend les billets au guichet.
Les passagers font la queue au guichet.

SNCF
la société
Nationale
des Chemins
de fer

Les voyageurs attendent le train.
On attend le train sur le quai.

On annonce le départ du train.
Un voyageur n'arrive pas à entendre l'annonce.

Marie est en retard.
Elle n'est pas en avance.

Quel est le mot?

1 Historiette Un voyage en train

Inventez une histoire.

1. Les voyageurs sont à la gare?
2. Ils attendent le train dans la salle d'attente?
3. On vend des billets où?
4. Où est-ce que M. Merlin prend son billet?
5. Il va faire Paris–Lyon–Paris. Il veut un billet aller-retour ou un aller simple?
6. Avant de prendre son billet, il fait la queue au guichet?
7. Les voyageurs peuvent consulter l'horaire pour vérifier l'heure du départ de leur train?
8. On annonce les départs à la gare?
9. M. Merlin arrive à comprendre l'annonce?
10. Il prend un chariot?
11. Il met ses bagages sur le chariot?
12. Son train part à l'heure ou en retard?

Gare de Lyon, Paris

2 Historiette Ton voyage en train

Donnez des réponses personnelles.

1. Tu fais un voyage en train? Tu vas où?
2. Tu arrives à la gare en avance?
3. Tu prends ton billet?
4. Tu achètes un billet aller-retour ou un aller simple?
5. Tu voyages en première ou en seconde?
6. Tu consultes l'horaire?
7. Ton train part à quelle heure?
8. Ton train part de quelle voie?
9. Tu vas acheter un journal ou un magazine? Où?
10. Tu vas prendre un café au buffet de la gare?

Gare de Lyon, Paris

3 On attend le train. Choisissez la bonne réponse.

1. On vend des journaux, des magazines et des cartes postales ____.
   a. au guichet b. au kiosque c. sur le quai
2. On ____ le train dans la salle d'attente.
   a. attend b. prend c. entend
3. Les voyageurs ____ l'annonce du départ de leur train.
   a. mettent b. entendent c. font
4. On fait ____ au guichet pour prendre son billet.
   a. l'annonce b. le quai c. la queue
5. Le train part ____.
   a. de la voie b. du chariot c. du kiosque
6. Il faut ____ son billet avant d'aller sur le quai.
   a. vendre b. faire c. composter

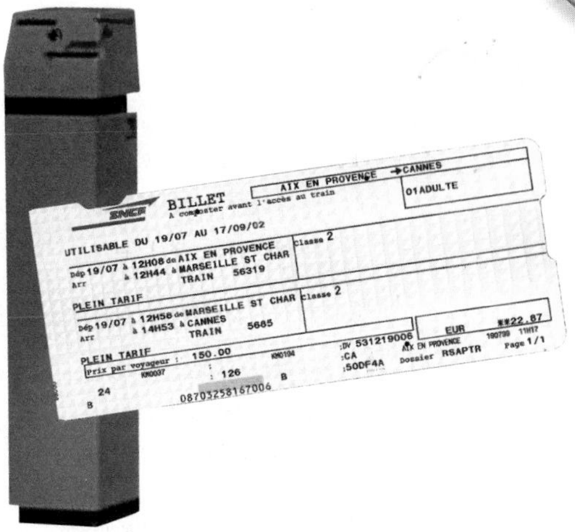

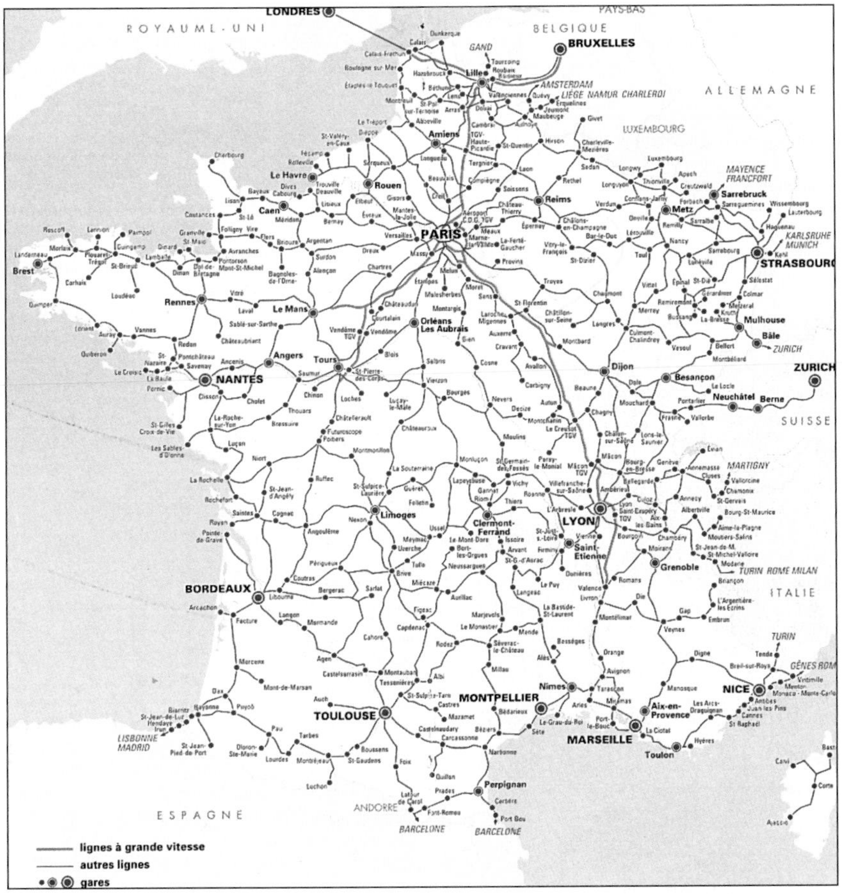

4 La SNCF (La Société nationale des chemins de fer français)

You're in France and you want to visit one of the cities on the map. A classmate will be the ticket agent. Get yourself a ticket and ask the agent any questions you have about your train trip.

FRENCH Online

For more information on la SNCF, go to the Glencoe French Web site: french.glencoe.com

ENCORE PLUS

*For more practice using words from **Mots 1**, do Activity 27 on page H28 at the end of this book.*

Vocabulaire Mots 2

Un voyage en train

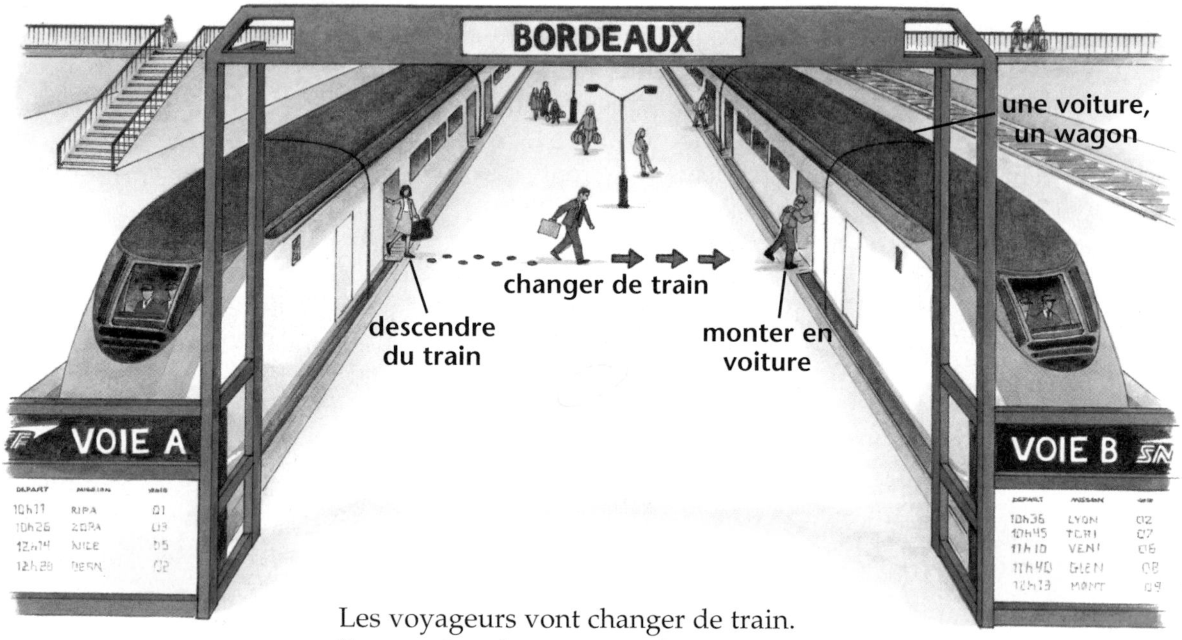

Les voyageurs vont changer de train.
Ils attendent la correspondance.
Ils ont une correspondance à Bordeaux.

Dans le train

La plupart des voyageurs sont assis.
Il y a quelques voyageurs debout.
Sylvain lit un livre.
Sa copine Christine écrit des cartes (postales).

Le contrôleur contrôle les billets.
Romain a une question.
Le contrôleur répond à sa question.

Jean et Thouria attendent un ami devant la gare.
Ils vont tous les trois à La Rochelle.
Jean et Thouria attendent depuis quarante-cinq minutes!
Jean dit qu'il commence à perdre patience.

Quel est le mot?

5 **Historiette** **De Paris à Avignon** Répondez d'après les indications.

1. Pour aller à Avignon, on change de train? (non)
2. Qui monte en voiture? (les voyageurs)
3. Qui contrôle les billets? (le contrôleur)
4. Presque toutes les places sont occupées? (oui)
5. La plupart des voyageurs sont assis? (oui)
6. Il y a quelques voyageurs debout? (oui)
7. Qu'est-ce que le contrôleur contrôle? (les billets)
8. Les voyageurs descendent où? (à Avignon)

6 **Historiette** **Aïcha prend le train.** Complétez avec le mot ou l'expression qui convient.

descend	**lit**	**écrit**	**monte**	**attendre**
contrôle	**rater**	**dit**	**snack-bar**	**arrêt**

1. Aïcha fait un voyage en train. Elle ____ en voiture.
2. Le contrôleur ____ son billet.
3. Elle ____ un article dans un magazine.
4. Elle n'____ pas de cartes postales.
5. Elle a faim. Elle va au ____.
6. Aïcha ____ au contrôleur qu'elle va à Aix-en-Provence.
7. Il répond: «Il faut changer de train à Marseille. C'est le prochain ____.»
8. Elle ____ du train à Marseille.
9. À Marseille, elle va ____ sa correspondance pour Aix-en-Provence.
10. Elle ne va pas ____ le train pour Aix-en-Provence.

Aix-en-Provence, France

ENCORE PLUS *For more practice using words from* ***Mots 2****, do Activity 28 on page H29 at the end of this book.*

7 Toujours des questions! Répondez.

1. Le train pour Lyon part de la voie numéro 5 à six heures trente.
   C'est le train ou l'avion qui part pour Lyon?
   Le train va où?
   Il part de quelle voie?
   Il part à quelle heure?
2. Sandrine va à Nantes et elle ne trouve pas sa place dans le train.
   Qui va à Nantes?
   Où est Sandrine?
   Qu'est-ce qu'elle ne trouve pas?

Nantes, France

8 L'horaire Look at the information on this schedule. Take turns with a classmate asking and answering questions about it.

MARSEILLE - ARLES - TARASCON - AVIGNON

SEMAINE

	•	◉		◉	◉	•	◉	◉	◉	•	•		◉	◉	◉	◉	◉	◉	◉	◉	•	◉	◉	◉		◉	◉	•	◉	◉	•	
		CAR			TGV																			CAR		TGV						TGV
			28	3		29		30			31	32							12						33	34			14	35		36
Marseille-St-Charles			05.29		06.12	06.31	06.35	06.51			08.27	08.36	08.47	09.08	10.59		11.36	12.09			13.18	14.03	14.36		15.24			16.12		16.26	16.40	16.57
Miramas			06.00			07.04	07.15	·	07.40		09.11	09.11	·	·	11.33		·	12.42			14.04	·	·		15.59			16.51		·	17.27	·
Arles		06.05	06.17		06.57	07.21	07.32	07.39	08.00		09.28	09.28	09.35	·	11.51		·	12.59	13.23		14.24	14.52	15.21	15.30	16.17	16.45		17.08		·	17.49	·
Arles (Le Trébon)		·	·		·	·	·	·	·		·	·	·	·	·		·	·	·		·	·		·	·	·		·		·	·	·
Arles (Car. St-Gabriel)		·	·		·	·	·	·	·		·	·	·	·	·		·	·	·		·	·		·	·	·		·		·	·	·
Tarascon	05.06	06.25	·	07.25	·	07.31	·	07.48	·	08.42	·	·	09.44	·	·	12.16	·	13.08	·	13.52	·	·		15.50	·	·	16.54	17.21	18.02	·	·	·
Tarascon (Pl.Condamine)	·	·	·	·	·		·		·	·	·	·		·	·	·	·		·	·	·	·		·	·	·	·		·	·	·	·
Graveson (Maillane)	·	·	·	·	·		·		·	·	·	·		·	·	·	·		·	·	·	·		·	·	·	·		·	·	·	·
Graveson (Bon-Accueil)	·	·	·	·	·		·		·	·	·	·		·	·	·	·		·	·	·	·		·	·	·	·		·	·	·	·
Graveson (La Roque)	·	·	·	·	·		·		·	·	·	·		·	·	·	·		·	·	·			·	·	·	·		·	·	·	·
Rognonas (Emb.Gare)	·	·	·	·	·		·		·	·	·	·		·	·	·	·		·	·	·	·		·	·	·	·		·	·	·	·
Rognonas (Pl.Mairie)	·	·	·	·	·		·		·	·	·	·		·	·	·	·		·	·	·	·		·	·	·	·		·	·	·	·
Avignon (Gambetta)	·	·	·	·	·		·		·	·	·	·		·	·	·	·		·	·	·	·		·	·	·	·		·	·	·	·
Avignon	05.18	06.55	06.33	07.40	07.13		07.50		08.16	08.55	09.45	09.45		10.11	12.09	12.29	12.41		13.42	14.04	14.42	15.10		16.20	16.34	17.03	17.10		18.14	17.30	18.07	17.57

La desserte détaillée entre Marseille et Miramas figure sur la fiche horaire Marseille - Miramas via Rognac et Port de Bouc.

Voir aussi Fiche horaire Marseille - Salon - Cavaillon - Avignon.

• Du lundi au vendredi.
◉ Du lundi au samedi.

ⓘ Certains trains périodiques ne figurent pas sur ce document horaire.
CAR Desserte assurée par autocar. Tarification SNCF.
ⓘ TGV : réservation obligatoire.
ⓘ Horaires en italiques : train soumis à des conditions d'emprunt, ou à supplément; renseignements dans les gares.
ⓘ Ces horaires sont donnés sous réserve de toute modification.

3 Ne circule
12 Ne circule
14 Ne circule
17 Circule les
circule aus
24 Circule du
26 Ne circule
27 Circule les

9 Jeu Les phrases Play a game with a classmate. See who can make up the most sentences using the following words. The time limit is two minutes.

le quai · aller-retour · le contrôleur · l'annonce · assis · le train · le billet · la correspondance · debout

Structure

Les verbes en -re au présent
Describing more activities

1. Another group of regular verbs in French has infinitives that end in **-re.** Some verbs that belong to this group are: **vendre, attendre, descendre, répondre, entendre, perdre.**

	VENDRE	ATTENDRE
je vend -s	je vends	j' attends
tu vend -s	tu vends	tu attends
il/elle/on vend —	il/elle/on vend	il/elle/on‿attend (n)
nous vend -ons	nous vendons	nous‿attendons (z)
vous vend -ez	vous vendez	vous‿attendez (z)
ils/elles vend -ent	ils/elles vendent	ils‿/elles‿attendent (z)

2. **Descendre** can have several meanings. When used alone, it means "to go down" or "to get off." When used with a direct object, it means "to take down."

Ils descendent du train.
Ils descendent les bagages sur le quai.

Savez-vous que... ?

The verb **répondre** is followed by **à.**
Il répond à la question du contrôleur.
Il répond à l'employé.

La gare, Dakar, Sénégal

Comment dit-on?

10 **Historiette** **Les voyageurs** Répondez que oui.

1. Les voyageurs attendent le train?
2. Ils attendent le train dans la salle d'attente?
3. Ils perdent patience?
4. Ils entendent l'annonce du départ de leur train?
5. Ils descendent du train?

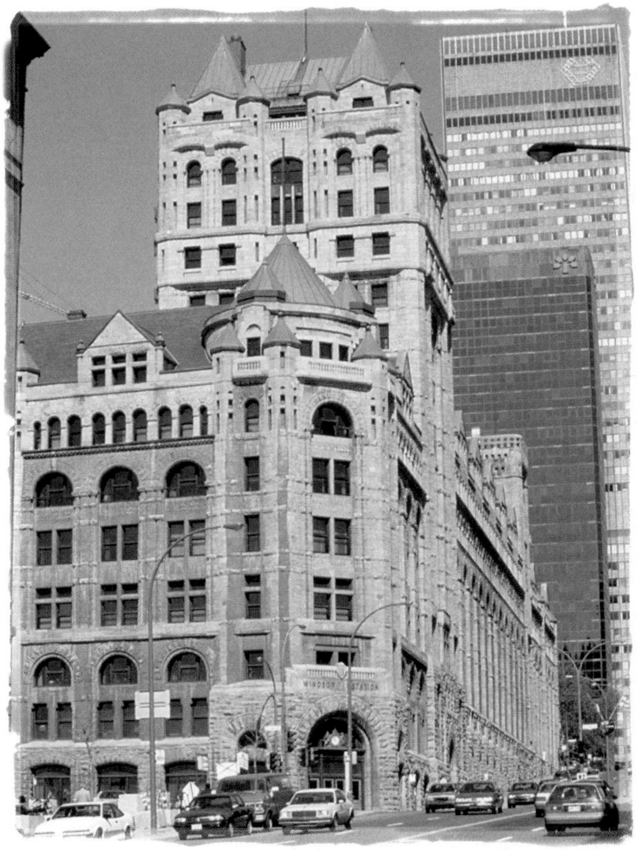

La gare Windsor, Montréal

11 **Historiette** **Un voyage à Montréal**
Répondez que oui.

1. Tu es à la gare de Grand Central à New York?
2. Tu attends le train pour Montréal?
3. Tu attends depuis une heure?
4. Tu perds patience?
5. Tu entends l'annonce du départ de ton train?
6. Tu vas sur le quai?
7. Quand tu descends du train à Montréal, tu es fatigué(e)?

12 **Le train** Complétez.

1. —Vous ____ depuis combien de temps? (attendre)
   —Nous ____ depuis cinq minutes. C'est tout! (attendre)
2. —Vous allez à Rennes?
   —Oui.
   —Vous ____ au prochain arrêt, alors. (descendre)
   —Ah bon? Merci.
   —Hé, les copains! On ____ au prochain arrêt! (descendre)

13 Historiette **Dans la salle d'attente** Complétez.

Les voyageurs __1__ (attendre) le train dans la salle d'attente. Marc __2__ (attendre) le train pour Saint-Malo. Ah, voilà son ami, Luc.

Marc: Salut, Luc! Quelle surprise! Tu __3__ (attendre) un train?

Luc: Oui, j'__4__ (attendre) le train pour Saint-Malo.

Marc: Pas vrai? Moi aussi je vais à Saint-Malo.

Les deux garçons __5__ (entendre) l'annonce du départ de leur train. Il part de la voie numéro 5. Ils vont sur le quai. Les voyageurs qui arrivent __6__ (descendre) leurs bagages du train. Ils __7__ (descendre) leurs bagages sur le quai. Le contrôleur crie: «En voiture, s'il vous plaît!» et tout le monde qui part monte dans le train. Le contrôleur demande aux garçons où ils vont. Luc __8__ (répondre) au contrôleur. Il __9__ (répondre): «À Saint-Malo».

Saint-Malo, Bretagne, France

14 À la gare

Work with a classmate. Pretend you are at a train station somewhere in France. Take turns asking and answering questions about your wait at the train station. You may want to use the following expressions: **attendre le train, entendre l'annonce du départ, prendre un billet, faire la queue, aller au kiosque, prendre un café au buffet de la gare.**

Les adjectifs démonstratifs
Pointing out people and things

1. You use the demonstrative adjectives to point out people or things. In English, the demonstrative adjectives are "this," "these," "that," and "those." However, in French there is only one set of demonstrative adjectives. Study the following forms.

	Masculin		Féminin	
	Consonne	Voyelle	Consonne	Voyelle
Singulier	ce train	cet‿horaire	cette voiture	cette annonce
Pluriel	ces trains	ces‿horaires	ces voitures	ces‿annonces

2. The word **-là** is often attached to the noun following the demonstrative adjectives for emphasis.

—C'est un magazine super.
—Ce magazine-là! Tu rigoles! Il est horrible!

Un ancien wagon-restaurant

Comment dit-on?

15 Tu parles de qui ou de quoi? Suivez le modèle.

Tu parles d'une fille? De quelle fille?
De cette fille-là.

1. Tu parles d'un garçon? De quel garçon?
2. Tu parles d'une copine? De quelle copine?
3. Tu parles d'un copain? De quel copain?
4. Tu parles des élèves? De quels élèves?
5. Tu parles des filles? De quelles filles?
6. Tu parles d'un train? De quel train?
7. Tu parles d'un horaire? De quel horaire?
8. Tu parles des journaux? De quels journaux?
9. Tu parles d'un arrêt? De quel arrêt?
10. Tu parles d'une carte? De quelle carte?

16 À Grenoble ou à Chamonix? Complétez avec **ce, cet, cette** ou **ces.**

Christine: __1__ train va à Grenoble?
Contrôleur: Non, il va à Chamonix.
Christine: Et tous __2__ voyageurs, alors, ils ne prennent pas __3__ train?
Contrôleur: Non, ils attendent le train pour Grenoble.
Christine: Il va partir de __4__ quai aussi?
Contrôleur: Oui, mais pas de __5__ voie. De la voie numéro 2.

Chamonix-Mont-Blanc, France

17 Historiette Au kiosque

Répondez d'après les photos.

1. Ce kiosque est dans une gare ou dans la rue?
2. Qu'est-ce qu'on vend dans ce kiosque?
3. Combien coûtent ces cartes postales?
4. Ces journaux sont français ou américains?

Gare de l'Est, Paris

18 Au kiosque

You want to buy several items but you don't know how much they cost. Ask the vendor (your partner) how much they cost. Then make sure the addition is correct when he or she asks you for the sum you owe. You may want to use the following words.

- du chewing-gum
- un livre
- un journal
- un magazine
- une carte postale
- des kleenex

Les verbes dire, écrire et lire
Describing more activities

Study the forms of the irregular verbs **dire** *(to say)*, **écrire** *(to write)*, and **lire** *(to read)*.

DIRE	ÉCRIRE	LIRE
je dis	j' écris	je lis
tu dis	tu écris	tu lis
il/elle/on dit	il/elle/on écrit	il/elle/on lit
nous disons	nous écrivons	nous lisons
vous dites	vous écrivez	vous lisez
ils/elles disent	ils/elles écrivent	ils/elles lisent

Comment dit-on?

19 **Historiette** **Christine et Juliette** Remplacez **Christine** par **Christine et Juliette.**

Christine est dans le train. Elle lit. Elle dit que le livre qu'elle lit est très intéressant. Christine a aussi des cartes postales à écrire. Elle écrit ses cartes postales. Elle dit que ses amis, eux, n'écrivent pas. Ils lisent les cartes postales de Christine? Bien sûr qu'ils lisent ses cartes postales!

20 **Petites conversations** Suivez le modèle.

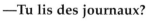

lire des journaux →
—Tu lis des journaux?
—Oui, je lis des journaux.

1. lire le journal local
2. lire beaucoup de livres
3. lire des magazines
4. écrire des lettres aux copains
5. écrire des cartes
6. dire toujours que oui

ENCORE PLUS *For more practice using these verbs, do Activity 29 on page H30 at the end of this book.*

21 Oui ou non? Répondez.

1. Tes amis et toi, vous dites toujours des choses sérieuses?
2. Vous dites quelquefois des choses stupides?
3. Vous dites des choses amusantes?
4. Vous lisez beaucoup de livres?
5. Vous lisez beaucoup de poèmes?
6. Vous écrivez beaucoup de lettres?

La Conciergerie, Paris, France

Une jolie baie, Tahiti

22 Tout le monde Complétez.

1. (dire) Lui, il ____ toujours des choses stupides. Il ____ des bêtises. Ses amis ____ des bêtises aussi. Et vous, vous ____ quelquefois des bêtises aussi?
2. (dire) Lui, il ____ que oui. Ses amis ____ que oui. Et vous, qu'est-ce que vous ____?
3. (écrire) Lui, il ____ toujours des lettres. Mais ses amis n'____ pas de lettres. Ils ____ quelquefois des cartes postales. Et vous, vous ____ des lettres ou des cartes postales?
4. (lire) Lui, il ____ toujours des magazines. Ses amis ne ____ pas de magazines. Ils ____ des livres. Et vous? Vous ____ des magazines ou des livres?

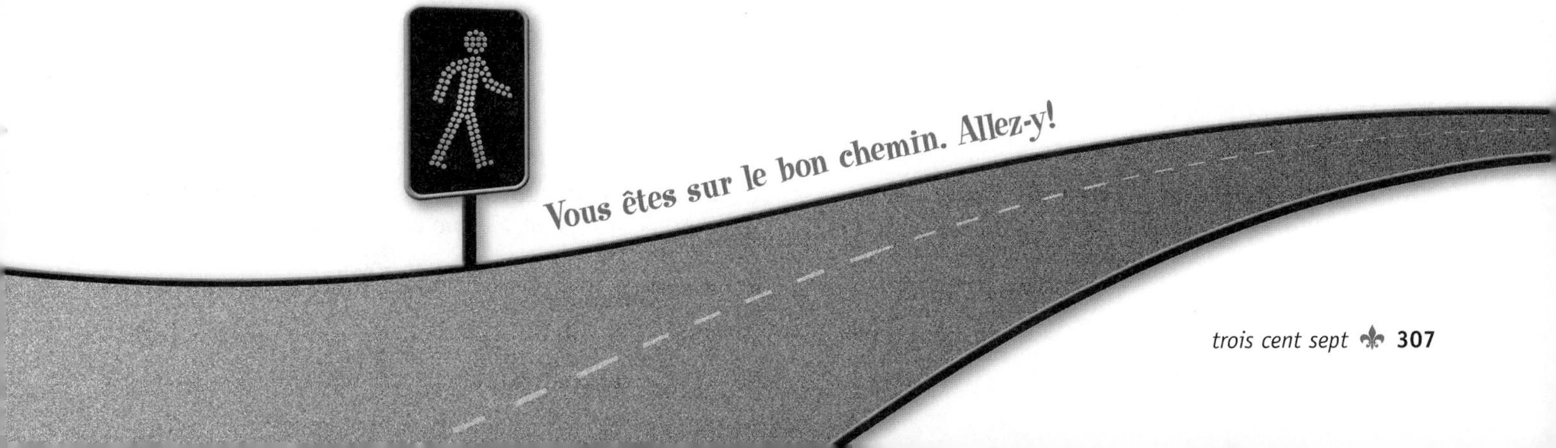
Vous êtes sur le bon chemin. Allez-y!

Conversation

Au guichet

Employé: Bonjour.
Voyageuse: Bonjour, monsieur. Un billet pour Nice, s'il vous plaît.
Employé: Aller-retour ou aller simple?
Voyageuse: Aller-retour en seconde, tarif étudiant, s'il vous plaît.
Employé: Vous avez votre carte?
Voyageuse: Oui, voilà… C'est combien?
Employé: Alors, tarif étudiant, c'est trente euros.
Voyageuse: Le prochain train part à quelle heure?
Employé: À dix heures trente, voie numéro 12.
Voyageuse: Merci, monsieur. Au revoir.

Vous avez compris?

Répondez.

1. La voyageuse est à la gare?
2. Elle parle à un employé de la gare?
3. Elle veut aller où?
4. Elle prend un billet aller-retour ou aller simple?
5. Elle est étudiante?
6. Elle a sa carte d'étudiante?
7. Elle a une réduction?
8. Le billet coûte combien?
9. Le prochain train part à quelle heure?
10. Il part de quelle voie?

Parlons un peu plus

Réservation: 3615 3616 AF -www.airfrance.fr					
Jours	Dép.	Arr.	Nº Vol	Corr.	Validité
PARIS					
→ Madison (WI)					-6:00
1234567	16.00 C	21.05	AF380/AF8737(DL)	CVG	29/10-23
→ Madrid					+1:00
1234567	07.15 F	09.15 1	AF1000	→	29/10-24
1234567	09.40 F	11.40 1	AF1300	→	29/10-24
1234567	10.45 F	12.45 1	AF1500	→	29/10-24
1234567	12.45 F	14.45 1	AF1600	→	29/10-24
1234567	14.15 F	16.15 1	AF1700	→	29/10-24
1234567	15.30 F	17.30 1	AF1800	→	29/10-24
1234567	16.30 F	18.30 1	AF1900	→	29/10-24
1234567	17.35 F	19.35 1	AF2000	→	29/10-24
1234567	19.20 F	21.20 1	AF2100	→	29/10-24
12345-7	20.00 F	22.00 1	AF2200	→	29/10-23
→ Malaga					+1:00
1234567	10.25 W	12.45	AF3408	→	29/10-24

A **On va à Madrid.** You and a classmate are spending a semester in Paris. You will be going to Madrid for a couple of days. One of you is going to fly, and the other is going to take the train. Compare your trips: time of departure, how long the trip takes, and what you have to do the day you leave.

TRAINHOTEL Francisco de Goya

HORAIRES

	TRAIN 409		TRAIN 407
PARIS-AUSTERLITZ	19.47	MADRID-CHAMARTIN	19.00
POITIERS	22.18	VALLADOLID	21.20
VITORIA/GASTEIZ	04.12	BURGOS	22.19
BURGOS	05.21	VITORIA/GASTEIZ	23.29
VALLADOLID	06.19	POITIERS	05.45
MADRID-CHAMARTIN	08.58	PARIS-AUSTERLITZ	08.29

Circulation quotidienne

B **Renseignements** You're at the information desk at one of the Paris train stations. You need some information. Have a conversation with the SNCF agent (your partner). You may wish to use the following expressions: **à quelle heure, le prochain train, quelle voie, quel quai, voyager en seconde, c'est combien, changer de train, attendre la correspondance.**

Prononciation

Les sons /õ/ et /ẽ/

1. Listen to the difference between the nasal sound **/ã/** as in **cent** and the two other nasal sounds, **/õ/** as in **son** and **/ẽ/** as in **cinq: cent / son / cinq.** Repeat the following words with the sounds **/õ/** and **/ẽ/**.

annonce	**non**	**bon**	**son**	**correspondance**
cinq	**copain**	**train**	**pain**	**vingt**

2. Now repeat the following sentences.

On annonce le train dans combien de temps?
Nous attendons des copains.

son train

Lectures culturelles

Reading Strategy

Thinking while reading

Good readers always think as they read. They read the title and look at the visuals to determine the topic of the passage. They predict, create visual images, check for understanding, and pay close attention to each sentence in the reading.

Un voyage intéressant

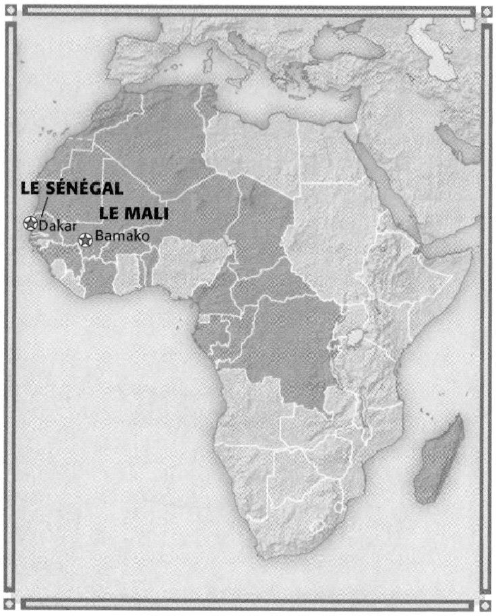

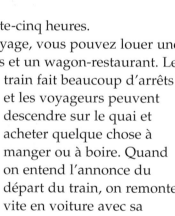

Vous dites que vous voulez faire un voyage intéressant en train. J'ai une bonne idée. Vous pouvez prendre le train de Bamako à Dakar. Deux fois par semaine, il y a un train entre ces deux villes. Les trains partent dans les deux sens (directions) tous les mercredis et les samedis matins.

Vous aimez lire? Pas de problème! Vous avez beaucoup de cartes postales à écrire à vos amis? Pas de problème non plus! Vous avez trente heures pour lire tous les livres que vous voulez et écrire beaucoup de cartes postales! Quand je dis trente heures, c'est d'après l'horaire. En réalité, le train est toujours en retard et c'est plutôt[1] un voyage de trente-cinq heures.

Si vous voulez dormir pendant le voyage, vous pouvez louer une couchette[2]. Il y a des wagons-couchettes et un wagon-restaurant. Le train fait beaucoup d'arrêts et les voyageurs peuvent descendre sur le quai et acheter quelque chose à manger ou à boire. Quand on entend l'annonce du départ du train, on remonte vite en voiture avec sa nourriture et le voyage continue.

[1] plutôt *more*
[2] louer une couchette *reserve a berth*

Le train qui fait Bamako–Dakar

La Polynésie française
Haïti
La Martinique

La France

Le Sahara, Mali

La Belgique

Le Maroc

Le Mali

Où sont Bamako et Dakar? Bamako est la capitale du Mali. Le Mali est le pays francophone le plus grand d'Afrique Occidentale. Le Sahara couvre 60% du pays et il y a très peu de pluie[3]. Dakar est la capitale du Sénégal. Dakar est une très grande ville moderne sur l'océan Atlantique. C'est aussi un port important.

[3] pluie *rain*

Un marché, Mali

Vous avez compris?

A Bamako–Dakar Choisissez la bonne réponse.

1. Il y a un train entre Bamako et Dakar ____.
   a. une fois par semaine b. deux fois par semaine
2. Les trains partent ____.
   a. le matin b. l'après-midi
3. Les trains partent ____.
   a. le mardi et le dimanche b. le mercredi et le samedi
4. Le voyage entre Bamako et Dakar dure trente heures d'après ____.
   a. les contrôleurs b. l'horaire
5. Le train arrive presque toujours ____.
   a. en retard b. à l'heure
6. Beaucoup de voyageurs achètent quelque chose à manger ____.
   a. dans les gares b. au wagon-couchette

B Un peu de géographie Choisissez la bonne réponse.

1. a. Le Sahara est un grand lac.
   b. Le Sahara est un grand désert.
2. a. Le Sénégal est un pays désertique.
   b. Le Mali est un pays désertique.
3. a. Bamako est la capitale du Mali.
   b. Bamako est la capitale du Sénégal.
4. a. Il y a très peu de pluie à Dakar.
   b. Il y a très peu de pluie à Bamako.

Le Sénégal

Lecture supplémentaire

La SNCF
(La Société[1] nationale des chemins de fer français)

Erica Saunders est une élève américaine. Elle passe ses vacances d'été en France. En ce moment elle est à la gare de Lyon à Paris. Elle va prendre le train pour Avignon. Tous les trains qui partent de cette gare vont vers le sud. Le train est un moyen de transport très populaire en France. Il y a six gares à Paris. Erica va au guichet et prend son billet. Elle veut un aller-retour en seconde. Elle a de la chance parce qu'il n'y a pas de queue.

Munie de[2] son billet, Erica va sur le quai et monte dans le train. Avant d'aller sur le quai, elle composte son billet—elle passe son billet dans une machine. Ça indique où elle commence son voyage. C'est très important. Si on ne composte pas son billet, on paie une amende[3]. Erica n'attend pas longtemps. Il est 10 h 11 et le train part. Comme toujours le train part exactement à l'heure. En France, le service de la SNCF est excellent. Il y a très peu de retards.

[1] société *company*
[2] Munie de *With*
[3] amende *fine*

Gare de Lyon, Paris

Si Erica a faim pendant le voyage, elle peut aller au snack-bar. Là on offre de la restauration rapide—un sandwich, une pizza ou une boisson, par exemple.

Pendant le voyage, Erica lit un guide sur Avignon. Le guide répond à toutes ses questions. Elle apprend qu'Avignon est une ville de culture et de fête. Elle va visiter le célèbre palais des Papes. Elle a de la chance, parce qu'en juillet, il y a un grand festival de théâtre qui a lieu[4] dans la cour du palais… et dans toute la ville. Elle veut voir aussi le pont d'Avignon qui traverse le Rhône. Ce pont célèbre date du douzième siècle. Là, elle va chanter «Sur le pont d'Avignon». Tous les élèves américains qui font du français apprennent cette chanson.

[4] a lieu *takes place*

Palais des Papes, Avignon, France

Le Maroc

Le Mali

Vous avez compris?

On va à Avignon. Répondez.

1. Qui est Erica Saunders?
2. Elle est où, en ce moment?
3. Elle va aller où?
4. Elle prend quel type de billet?
5. Le train part à quelle heure?
6. Comment est le service de la SNCF?
7. Si Erica a faim, elle peut manger où?
8. Qu'est-ce qu'elle lit pendant le voyage?
9. Qu'est-ce qu'elle veut voir à Avignon?
10. Qu'est-ce qu'il y a à Avignon pendant le mois de juillet?

CONNEXIONS

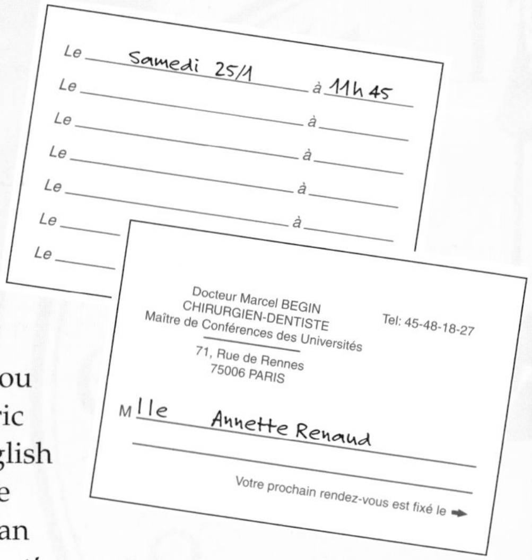

Les mathématiques

Des conversions—les horaires

When traveling through the French-speaking countries, you will need to make some mathematical conversions. The metric system is used for weights and measures rather than the English system, which we use in the United States. For schedules, the twenty-four-hour clock is used, rather than our A.M./P.M. system of indicating time. Let's learn to make some of these conversions.

Arman *L'heure de tous*

L'heure

Il y a deux façons[1] de dire l'heure. Il y a l'heure de la conversation normale: la journée est divisée[2] en deux fois douze heures—de une heure du matin à midi et de une heure de l'après-midi à minuit. Mais il y a aussi l'heure officielle. C'est l'heure des horaires de train, d'avion, de manifestations culturelles. C'est aussi l'heure qu'on utilise quand on prend rendez-vous[3] chez le dentiste, par exemple.

[1] façons *ways*
[2] divisée *divided*
[3] prend rendez-vous *make an appointment*

Pour l'heure officielle, la journée est divisée en 24 heures, de zéro heure à 23 heures. Étudiez le tableau suivant.

HORAIRES		CONVERSATION
0.25	zéro heure vingt-cinq	minuit vingt-cinq
8.15	huit heures quinze	huit heures et quart du matin
12.00	douze heures	midi
14.00	quatorze heures	deux heures de l'après-midi
16.40	seize heures quarante	cinq heures moins vingt de l'après-midi
22.00	vingt-deux heures	dix heures du soir
23.50	vingt-trois heures cinquante	minuit moins dix

Vous voulez prendre rendez-vous chez le dentiste pour 3 h de l'après-midi. C'est quelle heure en langage officiel? Votre train part à 21 h 35. C'est quelle heure en langage courant?

Les distances

Pour mesurer la distance, le système métrique utilise le mètre et non le *yard* ni le *mile* comme en anglais. Le mètre est un peu plus d'un *yard*. Un kilomètre (1 000 mètres) est équivalent à 0,621 *mile*—un peu plus d'un demi-*mile*.

Vous avez compris?

A L'heure Read the departure board on page 314 and give the departure times of the trains in conversational French.

B Les distances Read these road signs. Give the approximate distance in miles to each town.

C'est à vous

Use what you have learned

PARLER

1 Le train, l'autocar ou l'avion?

✔ *Discuss train, bus, and plane travel*

Work in groups of three or four. Discuss the advantages **(les avantages)** and disadvantages **(les inconvénients)** of train, bus **(autocar),** or plane travel. In your discussion, include such things as speed, price, location of terminals, and anything else you consider important.

Le bus, Dakar

L'aéroport, Saint-Barthélemy, les Antilles

La gare, Québec

Un bouchon, place d'Italie, Paris

PARLER

2 Qu'est-ce qu'on va faire?

✔ *Discuss what to do if you miss your train*

You and a classmate are on a bus on the way to **la gare de l'Est** in Paris. There's an awful traffic jam **(un bouchon).** You know you are going to miss your train. Discuss your predicament and decide what you are going to do.

ÉCRIRE

3 Dans la gare

✔ *Write a paragraph using expressions related to train travel*

Look at the photograph and write a paragraph about it.

La gare Saint-Charles, Marseille

Writing Strategy

Writing a descriptive paragraph Your goal in writing a descriptive paragraph is to enable the reader to visualize a scene. To achieve this, you must select and organize details that create an impression. Using a greater number of specific nouns and vivid, descriptive adjectives will make your writing livelier.

ÉCRIRE

4 Un voyage fabuleux

Write about a trip you want to take. It can be a real or imaginary trip. Describe how you'll go and when. Describe in great detail how you'll get there. Describe all the things you have to do. Continue by writing about what you are going to see and do when you get there. Try to make your readers understand what it is about the place that makes you like it so much.

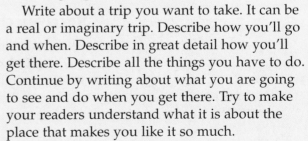

Assessment

Vocabulaire

To review **Mots 1**, *turn to pages 292–293.*

1 Répondez.

1. Qu'est-ce qu'on vend au kiosque?
2. Les voyageurs attendent le train où?
3. Qu'est-ce qu'on regarde pour vérifier l'heure du départ ou de l'arrivée d'un train?
4. On vend les billets de train où?

To review **Mots 2**, *turn to pages 296–297.*

2 Complétez d'après le dessin.

5. La plupart des voyageurs sont assis.
6. Trois voyageurs sont debout.
7. Une passagère écrit ____.
8. Un autre passager lit ____.

Structure

To review **-re** *verbs in the present, turn to page 300.*

3 Récrivez chaque phrase.

9. Ils attendent le train.
   Il attend le train.
10. Tu entends l'annonce?
    Vous ____________?
11. Tout le monde perd patience.
    Je ____________.
12. Qu'est-ce qu'elle vend?
    Qu'est-ce qu'elles ____________?
13. On descend au prochain arrêt.
    Tu ____________.

4 Complétez avec «ce».

14. ____ train va à Bordeaux.
15. ____ carte postale est très jolie.
16. Notre train part de ____ voie ou de la voie 5?
17. ____ voitures sont assez vieilles.

To review demonstrative adjectives, turn to page 303.

5 Complétez.

18. J'____ des cartes postales. (écrire)
19. Ils ____ beaucoup. (lire)
20. Vous ____ que oui ou que non? (dire)
21. Vous ____ beaucoup de lettres. (écrire)
22. Tu ____ quel livre? (lire)

*To review **dire**, **écrire**, and **lire**, turn to page 306.*

Culture

6 Vrai ou faux?

23. Il y a un train deux fois par semaine entre Bamako et Dakar.
24. Ce train arrive toujours à l'heure.
25. Dakar, la capitale du Sénégal, est une très grande ville moderne sur la mer Mediterranée.

To review this cultural information, turn to pages 310–311.

La gare, Dakar, Sénégal

On parle super bien!

Tell all you can about this illustration.

Vocabulaire

Getting around a train station

une gare
un train
un quai
une voie
la correspondance
un horaire
un guichet
un billet
un aller simple
un aller (et) retour
en seconde
en première
un chariot
un kiosque
un journal
un magazine
une carte (postale)
une salle d'attente
un buffet

Describing activities at a train station

faire la queue
attendre
descendre
vendre
monter (en voiture)
composter
partir
changer (de)
rater

On board the train

une voiture
un wagon
assis(e)
debout
un voyageur
une voyageuse
un contrôleur
contrôler les billets
lire
dire
écrire
répondre
un snack-bar
un arrêt
au prochain arrêt

How well do you know your vocabulary?

- Choose five words from the vocabulary list.
- Use the words in original sentences to tell a story.

Other useful words and expressions

arriver à + infinitif
être en avance
être en retard
perdre patience
la plupart des
quelques
depuis

VIDÉOTOUR

Épisode 9

In this video episode, Amadou and Chloé set out on a train trip to Lille. Or at least they try to. See page 534 for more information.

CHAPITRE 10

Les sports

Objectifs

In this chapter you will learn to:

- *talk about team sports and other physical activities*
- *describe past actions and events*
- *ask people questions*
- *discuss sports in Canada and in French-speaking Africa*

Robert Delaunay *Les coureurs*

Aquarel
CREDIT
LYONNAIS
250

Vocabulaire

Mots 1

Le foot(ball)

Le gardien arrête le ballon.
Il bloque le ballon.
Le ballon n'entre pas dans le but.

Une équipe de foot a onze joueurs.

Pour jouer au football, on a besoin d'un ballon.
Et c'est tout!

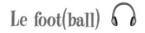

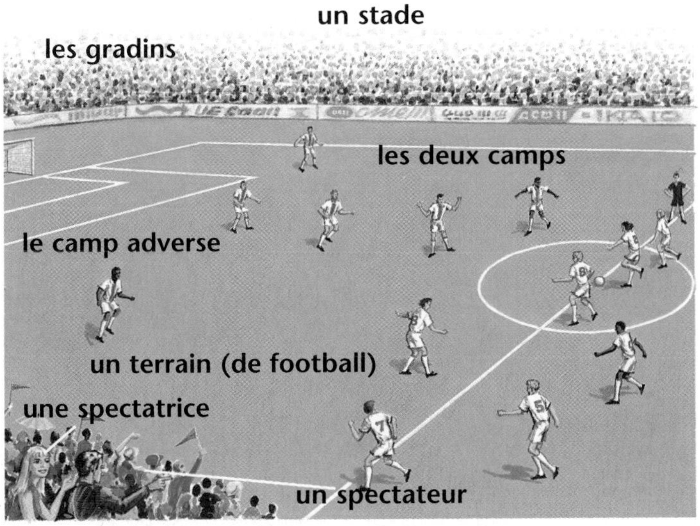

Le stade est comble.
Il y a beaucoup de monde.
Les gradins sont pleins.

Une joueuse passe le ballon à l'autre.

Hier Auxerre a joué contre Lyon.
Le match a opposé Lyon et Auxerre.
Ils ont joué au foot(ball).
Lafitte a donné un coup de pied dans le ballon.
Auxerre a gagné par 3 à 2.
Lyon a perdu.

Sissoko a envoyé le ballon dans le but.
Il a marqué un but.
Il a égalisé le score—2 à 2.

Quel est le mot?

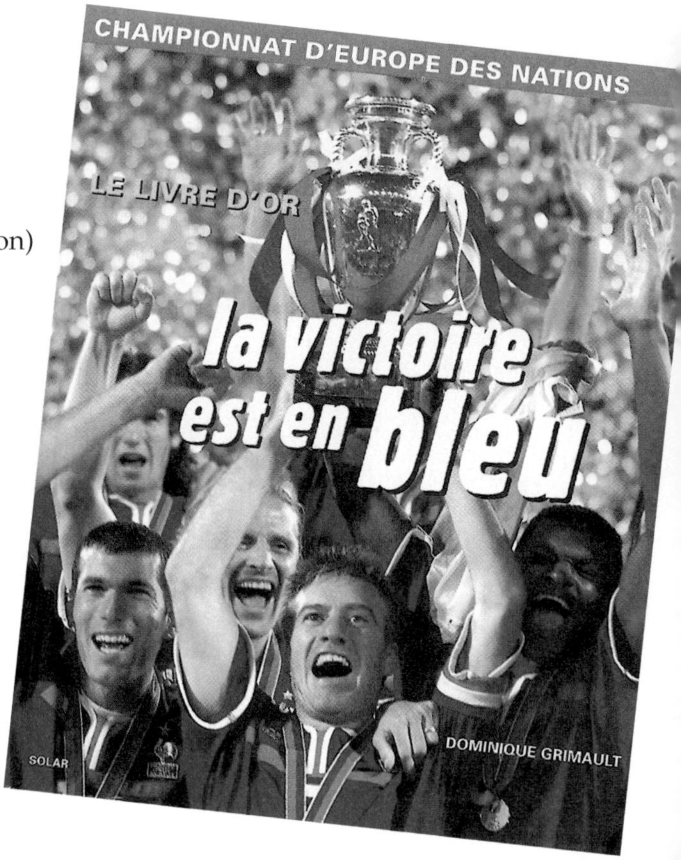

1 **Historiette Un match de foot** Répondez d'après les indications.

1. On a besoin de quoi pour jouer au foot? (un ballon)
2. Dans un match de foot, il y a combien d'équipes? (deux)
3. Chaque équipe a combien de joueurs? (onze)
4. Il y a combien de joueurs sur le terrain? (vingt-deux)
5. Dans un match, il y a combien de camps? (deux)
6. Le match est divisé en quoi? (en deux mi-temps)
7. Chaque mi-temps dure combien de minutes? (quarante-cinq minutes)
8. Qui garde le but? (le gardien de but)
9. Qu'est-ce que chaque équipe veut faire? (marquer des buts)
10. Qui bloque ou arrête le ballon? (le gardien de but)

Des fanas de foot

2 **Historiette Le stade est comble.** Inventez une histoire.

1. Il y a beaucoup de spectateurs dans le stade aujourd'hui?
2. Les gradins sont pleins ou il y a beaucoup de places libres?
3. Le stade est comble?
4. Il y a beaucoup de monde dans le stade?
5. Le foot, c'est un sport d'équipe ou un sport individuel?

3 **Auxerre contre Lyon** Répondez que oui.

1. Hier, Lyon a joué contre Auxerre?
2. Lafitte a donné un coup de tête dans le ballon?
3. Lafitte a passé le ballon à Sissoko?
4. Sissoko a marqué un but?
5. Sissoko a égalisé le score?
6. L'arbitre a sifflé?
7. Il a déclaré un penalty contre Lyon?
8. Auxerre a gagné le match?
9. Lyon a perdu le match?

4 **Un match de foot** Work with a classmate. Take turns describing the soccer game in the illustration.

ENCORE PLUS *For more practice using words from* ***Mots 1****, do Activity 30 on page H31 at the end of this book.*

D'autres sports d'équipe

Le basket(-ball)

Une joueuse a dribblé le ballon.
Elle a dribblé le ballon jusqu'au demi-cercle.

Le joueur a lancé le ballon dans le panier.
Il a réussi un beau panier.

Le volley(-ball)

Un joueur a servi.

Un autre joueur a renvoyé le ballon.
Le ballon ne doit pas toucher le sol.

Le cyclisme

Le coureur roule vite.
Pendant la course, les coureurs boivent de l'eau.

L'athlétisme

Khalil (Numéro 27) a gagné la course.
Leblanc (N° 10) a perdu la course.

Khalil a reçu la coupe.
C'est la première fois qu'il reçoit la coupe.

Note

The following expressions are often used to express past events:

hier
avant-hier
la semaine dernière
l'année dernière

Quel est le mot?

Un match de basket

5 Historiette Un match de basket

Répondez.

1. Le basket-ball est un sport individuel ou collectif (d'équipe)?
2. Il y a cinq ou onze joueurs dans une équipe de basket?
3. Pendant un match de basket, les joueurs dribblent le ballon ou donnent un coup de pied dans le ballon?
4. Un joueur dribble le ballon jusqu'au demi-cercle ou jusqu'au sol?
5. Un joueur de basket lance le ballon dans le panier ou dans le filet?

6 Historiette Le volley-ball Vrai ou faux?

1. Une équipe de volley-ball a onze joueurs.
2. Un joueur sert.
3. Un joueur du camp adverse renvoie le ballon.
4. Quand il renvoie le ballon, le ballon peut toucher le filet.
5. On renvoie le ballon par-dessus le filet.
6. Le ballon doit toucher le sol.

7 Historiette Une course cycliste Choisissez.

1. Un vélo est ___.
   a. une bicyclette **b.** une voiture **c.** un stade
2. ___ roule à vélo.
   a. Un spectateur **b.** Un coureur cycliste **c.** Un joueur
3. Dans une course internationale, chaque équipe ___.
   a. reçoit une coupe **b.** représente son pays **c.** roule
4. Le gagnant de la course est ___.
   a. la coupe **b.** le champion **c.** le coureur
5. Dans une course cycliste, les coureurs roulent sur ___.
   a. des gradins **b.** un terrain **c.** une piste
6. Pendant la course les coureurs boivent ___.
   a. du vinaigre **b.** du café **c.** de l'eau

8 **C'est quel sport?** Choisissez.

1. Le joueur a dribblé le ballon très vite.
2. Le joueur a donné un coup de tête dans le ballon.
3. La joueuse a réussi un beau panier.
4. La coureuse française a gagné.
5. Le gardien de but a arrêté le ballon.
6. La joueuse américaine a renvoyé le ballon par-dessus le filet.
7. Un joueur a servi.

9 **Jeu** **C'est quel sport?** Work with a classmate. Give him or her some information about a sport. He or she has to guess the sport you're talking about. Take turns.

10 **Mon équipe favorite** Work with a classmate. Find out each other's favorite team. Explain why it is your favorite team. You may like to know that "baseball" is the same word in French: **le base-ball.**

Fabien Barthez, gardien de but de l'équipe de France

Henry Rodriguez, les Expos de Montréal

FRENCH Online

For more information about team sports in the Francophone world, go to the Glencoe French Web site: french.glencoe.com

ENCORE PLUS *For more practice using words from* ***Mots 2****, do Activity 31 on page H32 at the end of this book.*

Structure

Le passé composé des verbes réguliers
Describing past actions

1. You use the **passé composé** to express an action that began and was completed in the past. To form the **passé composé,** you use the present tense of the verb **avoir** and the past participle. Study the forms of the past participle of regular verbs.

-er → é		-ir → i		-re → u	
parler	parlé	finir	fini	perdre	perdu
jouer	joué	choisir	choisi	vendre	vendu

2. Study the forms of the **passé composé.**

JOUER	CHOISIR	PERDRE
j' ai joué	j' ai choisi	j' ai perdu
tu as joué	tu as choisi	tu as perdu
il/elle/on a joué	il/elle/on a choisi	il/elle/on a perdu
nous avons joué	nous avons choisi	nous avons perdu
vous avez joué	vous avez choisi	vous avez perdu
ils/elles ont joué	ils/elles ont choisi	ils/elles ont perdu

Hier soir, j'ai téléphoné à un copain.
Après j'ai regardé un match de foot.
Mon copain aussi a regardé le match.
Malheureusement, notre équipe a perdu.

3. In the **passé composé, n'... pas** goes around the verb **avoir.**

Tu n'as pas regardé la télé?
Non, parce que je n'ai pas fini mes devoirs.

Savez-vous que... ?

When you talk about playing a sport, you use **jouer à.**

Ils ont joué au football.
Mais moi, j'ai joué au base-ball.

Comment dit-on?

11 Participes passés Donnez le participe passé des verbes suivants.

1. habiter
2. parler
3. écouter
4. travailler
5. remplir
6. réussir
7. servir
8. dormir
9. perdre
10. vendre
11. attendre
12. répondre

12 Historiette Hier Donnez des réponses personnelles.

1. Hier matin, tu as quitté la maison à quelle heure?
2. Tu as rigolé un peu avec les copains avant les cours?
3. Tu as parlé au prof de français?
4. Tu as passé un examen?
5. Tu as répondu à toutes les questions?
6. Tu as quitté l'école à quelle heure?
7. Tu as attendu le bus pour rentrer à la maison?

13 Historiette La fête de Chloé Complétez au passé composé.

Samedi dernier, Chloé __1__ (donner) une fête. Elle __2__ (téléphoner) à tous ses copains. Tous ses copains __3__ (répondre) au téléphone. Chloé __4__ (inviter) tous ses amis à la fête. Tous, ils __5__ (accepter) son invitation. Yves et moi, nous __6__ (préparer) des sandwichs, mais c'est Chloé qui __7__ (acheter) la nourriture et les boissons. À la fête, on __8__ (écouter) de la musique, on __9__ (danser). On __10__ bien __11__ (rigoler).

Paris-Saint-Germain contre Metz

14 Historiette Un match de foot
Inventez des réponses.

1. Tu as regardé un match de foot à la télé hier soir?
2. Auxerre a joué contre Lyon?
3. L'année dernière, qui a gagné la coupe? Lyon?
4. Mais hier soir, Lyon a perdu?
5. L'arbitre a puni un joueur lyonnais?
6. Il a déclaré un penalty contre Lyon?
7. Les spectateurs ont applaudi?

15 **Un voyage en avion** Répondez que non.

1. Tu as voyagé l'année dernière?
2. Tu as voyagé sur Air France?
3. Tu as choisi classe économique?
4. Tu as choisi une place côté couloir?
5. L'avion a décollé à l'heure?
6. Et il a atterri à l'heure?
7. Tu as voyagé avec un copain ou une copine?
8. Tu as attendu longtemps tes bagages?
9. La compagnie aérienne a perdu tes bagages?

16 **Historiette** **Un voyage en train** Mettez au passé composé.

J'attends le train. Ma copine Alice et moi, nous voyageons ensemble. Nous attendons le train dans la salle d'attente. J'achète un magazine au kiosque. Ma copine choisit un livre. Nous entendons l'annonce du départ de notre train. Nous trouvons la voiture numéro 11. Nous montons nos bagages dans le train. Nous trouvons nos places réservées occupées par deux personnes très désagréables! Que faire? Nous laissons nos places à ces personnes!

17 **Le voyage d'Alice** Relisez l'Activité 16 et posez des questions à Alice et sa copine sur leur voyage. Suivez le modèle.

Vous avez voyagé ensemble?

Stade de France, Paris

18 **La semaine dernière** Work with a classmate. Ask each other what you did last week. Answer each other's questions. Talk about the things you both did. You can also talk about some things your friends did. Here are some words you may wish to use: **regarder, parler, jouer, quitter, étudier, acheter, voyager, écouter, travailler, préparer, gagner, servir, dormir, attendre, perdre, répondre à.**

ENCORE PLUS *For more practice using regular verbs in the* ***passé composé****, do Activity 32 on* *page H33 at the end of this book.*

Qui, qu'est-ce que, quoi
Asking questions

1. You use **qui** in questions when asking about a person.

Qui va gagner?	**Paul.**
Tu as invité qui?	**Nathalie.**

2. You use **qu'est-ce que (qu')** or **quoi** to ask "what." **Qu'est-ce que (qu')** goes at the beginning of a sentence and **quoi** at the end.

Qu'est-ce que tu regardes?
Tu regardes quoi? } **Un match de foot.**

3. After a preposition, you use **qui** for people and **quoi** for things.

Tu vas aller au match avec qui?	**Avec Loïc.**
On joue au foot avec quoi?	**Avec un ballon.**
Tu as besoin de quoi?	**D'un ballon.**

Savez-vous que… ?

Qu'est-ce que tu as? can mean "What's the matter (with you)?"

Comment dit-on?

19 **Qui ça?** Posez des questions avec **qui.**

1. *Marie* parle au téléphone.
2. Elle parle à *son copain Julien.*
3. Elle invite *Julien* à un match de football.
4. *Julien* veut aller au match.
5. *Ézédine* va jouer.
6. *Ézédine* est un très bon joueur.
7. Julien parle souvent d'*Ézédine.*

20 **Comment? Qu'est-ce que tu fais?** Posez des questions d'après le modèle.

J'écoute la radio.
Comment? Qu'est-ce que tu écoutes?

1. Je lis le journal.
2. Je regarde la télé.
3. Je fais des exercices.
4. J'écris une carte postale.
5. Nous voulons le journal.
6. Nous mettons la table.
7. Nous préparons le petit déjeuner.

21 **Mini-conversations** Posez des questions et répondez d'après le modèle.

marquer un but →
—Qu'est-ce que les joueurs ont marqué?
—Ils ont marqué un but.

1. lancer le ballon
2. dribbler le ballon
3. envoyer le ballon
4. perdre le match
5. gagner la coupe
6. égaliser le score

Le garçon dribble le ballon.

22 **On a besoin de quoi?** Conversez d'après le modèle.

—J'ai besoin d'un verre pour boire de l'eau.
—Qu'est-ce que tu dis? Tu as besoin de quoi?

1. J'ai besoin d'une télé pour regarder des vidéos.
2. J'ai besoin d'un ballon pour jouer au basket.
3. J'ai besoin d'un billet pour prendre le train.
4. J'ai besoin d'un stylo-bille pour écrire des cartes postales.
5. J'ai besoin d'un oignon pour faire la salade.

23 **Je n'ai pas bien entendu.** Posez des questions.

1. Il aime bien *Marie.*
2. Il parle souvent de *Marie.*
3. Il parle à *Marie* maintenant.
4. Il invite Marie à *une fête.*
5. Il parle à Marie de *la fête.*

24 **Jeu** **Beaucoup de questions** Work with a classmate. Play a guessing game. Ask as many questions as you can. See who can answer the most questions.

Les verbes boire, devoir et recevoir
Describing more activities

Study the forms of the irregular verbs **boire** *(to drink)*, **devoir** *(to owe)*, and **recevoir** *(to receive)*.

BOIRE		DEVOIR		RECEVOIR	
je	bois	je	dois	je	reçois
tu	bois	tu	dois	tu	reçois
il/elle/on	boit	il/elle/on	doit	il/elle/on	reçoit
nous	buvons	nous	devons	nous	recevons
vous	buvez	vous	devez	vous	recevez
ils/elles	boivent	ils/elles	doivent	ils/elles	reçoivent

Vous buvez de l'eau ou de la limonade?
Je dois beaucoup d'argent à mes parents.
Cet enfant reçoit toujours trop de cadeaux.

Savez-vous que... ?

When **devoir** is followed by another verb, it means "must" or "to have to."
Elle doit étudier parce qu'elle doit passer un examen demain.

Comment dit-on?

25 Historiette Un match de volley-ball Répondez.

1. Pendant un match de volley-ball, les joueurs reçoivent le ballon?
2. Ils doivent renvoyer le ballon?
3. Le ballon doit toucher le sol?
4. Il doit passer par-dessus le filet?
5. Après le match, les joueurs boivent de l'eau?

Elles jouent au volley-ball.

26 **Moi** Donnez des réponses personnelles.

1. Tu dois boire beaucoup d'eau?
2. Tu bois de l'eau?
3. Qu'est-ce que tu bois quand tu as soif?
4. Tu dois de l'argent à tes amis?
5. Tu dois de l'argent à tes parents?
6. Tu reçois de l'argent pour ton anniversaire?
7. Tu reçois des cadeaux?

À CONSOMMER SANS MODÉRATION

C'est au cours des repas que nous consommons près de 70% de ce que nous buvons. Mais où placer les autres pauses boisson? L'idéal est de commencer par boire un verre d'eau avant le petit déjeuner pour bien drainer notre organisme. Un autre avant de passer à table remet à neuf le palais et permet de mieux jouir du goût des aliments. Enfin, un petit dernier avant de se coucher évite la trop grande concentration des urines. C'est tout? Mais non! Un verre toutes les deux heures, même sans avoir spécialement soif, cela fait du bien.

27 **Pardon?** Suivez le modèle.

Je bois beaucoup d'eau.
Pardon? Je n'ai pas bien entendu. Qu'est-ce que vous buvez?

1. Je bois beaucoup d'eau minérale.
2. Je dois boire beaucoup d'eau.
3. Je reçois le ballon.
4. Je dois renvoyer le ballon.

28 **Qu'est-ce que je dois faire?** Work with a classmate. Discuss some things you should or must do. Tell if you can do them or not. If you can't, try to explain why.

Le marathon de Paris

ENCORE PLUS *For more practice using **boire, devoir,** and **recevoir,** do Activity 33 on page H34 at the end of this book.*

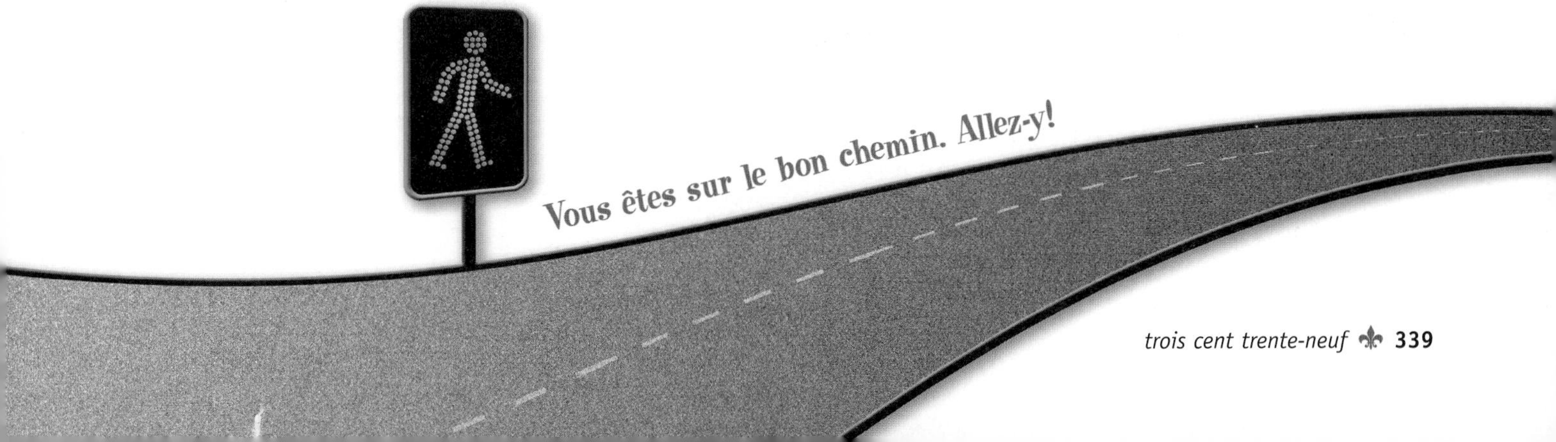
Vous êtes sur le bon chemin. Allez-y!

Conversation

On a gagné!

Jean: Tu as regardé la télé hier soir?
Rémi: Ben, bien sûr. J'ai regardé France–Brésil, comme tout le monde!
Jean: On a gagné, mais tout juste, hein! Un–zéro.
Rémi: Oui, heureusement que Lafitte a marqué à la dernière minute.
Jean: Les Brésiliens ne doivent pas être contents!
Rémi: Ça, c'est sûr! Marcos a bien arrêté tous les ballons mais…
Jean: Il n'a pas bloqué le dernier!
Rémi: Remarque, le match d'avant, les Brésiliens ont réussi à égaliser à deux secondes de la fin!

Vous avez compris?

Répondez.

1. À qui parle Rémi?
2. Qu'est-ce qu'ils ont regardé hier?
3. Qui a gagné le match?
4. Qui a marqué le but pour la France?
5. Qui est Marcos?
6. Qu'est-ce qu'il n'a pas bloqué?
7. Dans le match précédent qui a égalisé le score?

Parlons un peu plus

J'AIME PAS LE SPORT!
J'AIME PAS ME FATIGUER!
J'AIME RIEN!

A **Je ne suis pas très fana de...** Work with a classmate. Tell him or her what sport you don't like to play. Tell what sport or sports you like. Then ask your classmate questions to find out what sports he or she does or doesn't like.

B **Un match de foot** You are at a soccer game with a friend (your classmate). He or she has never been to a soccer game before and doesn't understand the game. Your friend has a lot of questions. Answer his or her questions and explain the game. You may want to use some of the following words: **jouer, recevoir, donner un coup de pied, donner un coup de tête, marquer, perdre, gagner, devoir, passer, arrêter, bloquer.**

Prononciation

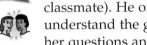

Liaison et élision

- You know that liaison or elision occurs when certain words are followed by a vowel. Some liaisons are obligatory, some are optional.
- Liaison is obligatory with plural subject pronouns, plural articles, plural possessive and demonstrative adjectives, and plural adjectives preceding the noun. Repeat the following.

ils z ont	**les z équipes**	**des z amateurs**
mes z amis	**ces z arbitres**	**de bonnes z équipes**

- Elision is always obligatory. It occurs with **le** and **la,** with **je,** the negative **ne,** and **que.** Repeat the following.

l'arbitre	**Je n'aime pas ça.**	**Qu'est-ce qu'il fait?**
l'équipe	**j'attends**	

- Now repeat the following pairs of sentences.

Vous z avez perdu. / Vous n'avez pas perdu.
J'ai fini. / Je n'ai pas fini.

des z arbitres

Lectures culturelles

Reading Strategy

Using background knowledge

When assigned a reading, look at the titles and the visuals to determine what the reading is about. Spend a few minutes thinking about what you already know about the topic. If you do this, the reading will be easier to understand and you will be able to figure out unfamiliar words.

Le hockey et le basket-ball

Au Québec

Le hockey est un sport très apprécié au Québec. Le hockey ressemble un peu au football, sauf[1] qu'on joue sur de la glace. Il y a deux équipes de cinq joueurs et deux gardiens de but. Un match de hockey est divisé en trois périodes de vingt minutes. Chaque joueur pousse le palet avec une crosse et essaie de mettre le palet dans le but de l'équipe adverse. Comme au football, on fait des passes à ses coéquipiers[2] pour essayer de marquer des buts.

[1] sauf *except*
[2] coéquipiers *teammates*

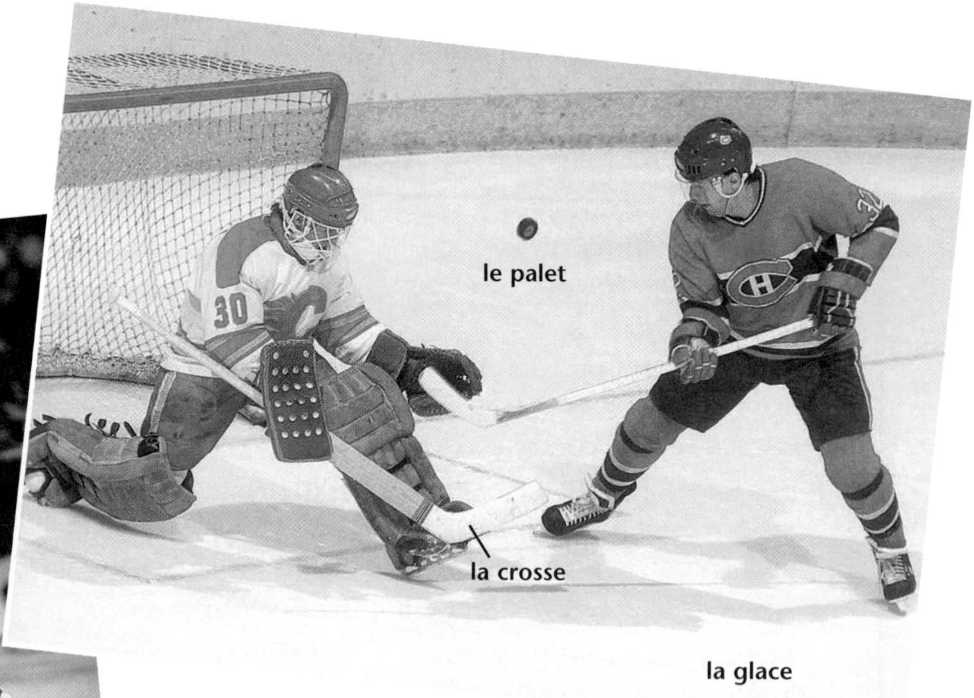

Les Canadiens de Montréal contre les Calgary Flames

Turner Stevenson, les Canadiens de Montréal

En Afrique

Dans les pays d'Afrique Occidentale, le sport numéro un, c'est le football, comme en France. Mais le deuxième sport, c'est le basket-ball. Une équipe de basket-ball est composée de cinq joueurs. Chaque joueur veut prendre possession du ballon. Il essaie de lancer le ballon dans le panier de l'équipe adverse. On joue au basket-ball avec les mains uniquement. On ne peut pas marcher[3] avec le ballon dans les mains. Il faut dribbler le ballon.

Et toi, quel est ton sport favori? Tu es fana de foot, de basket ou de hockey? Tu aimes mieux les sports d'équipe ou les sports individuels?

Tu préfères participer ou être spectateur (spectatrice)?

[3] marcher *walk*

Un match de basket: Sénégal contre Canada

Vous avez compris?

A Le hockey Répondez.

1. Quel est un sport très apprécié au Québec?
2. On joue au hockey sur quoi?
3. On joue au hockey avec quoi?
4. Il y a combien de joueurs dans une équipe de hockey?
5. Qu'est-ce qu'un joueur de hockey essaie de faire?
6. Qu'est-ce qu'il fait à ses coéquipiers?

B Le basket-ball Vrai ou faux?

1. Le basket-ball est très apprécié dans les pays d'Afrique Occidentale.
2. C'est le sport le plus populaire.
3. Une équipe de basket-ball a onze joueurs.
4. Un joueur de basket-ball essaie de lancer le ballon dans le panier de l'équipe adverse.
5. On joue au basket avec les mains et les pieds.

Un joueur de basket du Cameroun

Lecture supplémentaire

Le Tour de France

Un sport très apprécié

Un des sports les plus appréciés en France, c'est le cyclisme. Et l'événement sportif le plus populaire, c'est le Tour de France. Le Tour de France a lieu[1] tous les ans au mois de juillet. C'est une course cycliste sur un long circuit de routes françaises, tout autour du pays et quelquefois dans d'autres pays. Des coureurs cyclistes de tous les pays du monde participent au Tour de France.

Qu'est-ce que le Tour de France?

Le Tour de France est divisé en plusieurs étapes[2]. On va d'une ville à l'autre. On part le matin et on arrive le soir. Le Tour de France dure trois semaines. On donne au gagnant une coupe et le droit[3] de porter le maillot[4] jaune. Il reçoit aussi une somme d'argent.

On a organisé le premier Tour de France en 1903. C'est Maurice Garin qui a gagné le premier Tour de France. Il a fait 2 397 kilomètres en six étapes. Depuis 1903, 21 Français ont gagné le Tour de France.

Tour de France

Lance Armstrong a gagné!

En 1999, il y a un miracle. Un Américain, Lance Armstrong, gagne le Tour de France. Le miracle, ce n'est pas qu'un Américain gagne le Tour de France. Non, un autre Américain, Greg LeMond, a gagné le Tour de France trois fois. Pourquoi un miracle? Parce que trois ans avant, à l'âge de 25 ans, Lance Armstrong a

[1] a lieu *takes place*
[2] étapes *laps*
[3] droit *right*
[4] maillot *jersey*

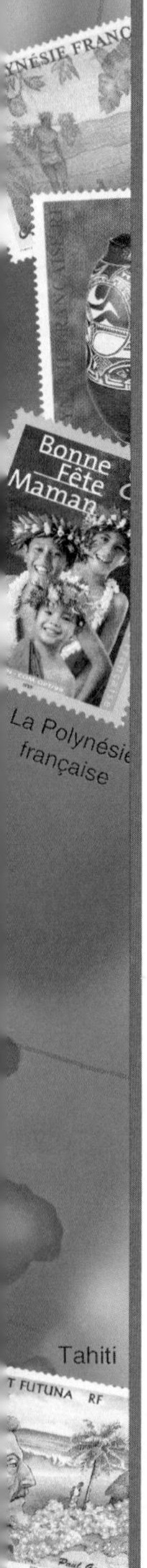

le cancer. Après deux opérations et quatre traitements de chimiothérapie et beaucoup de courage et de volonté[5] de sa part, le jeune Armstrong est guéri[6] et il recommence sa carrière de coureur cycliste.

Depuis cent ans, les Français appellent le vélo, «la petite reine»[7]. Ils disent que c'est la petite reine qui choisit toujours le nouveau roi du Tour de France. Pour six années, de 1999 jusqu'à 2004, elle a choisi son roi—Lance Armstrong. Et pour lui, comme pour tout le monde, c'est un vrai miracle!

[5] volonté *willpower*
[6] guéri *cured*
[7] reine *queen*

Tour de France

Lance Armstrong

La Belgique

Le Maroc

Le Mali

Vous avez compris?

A Une course cycliste Vrai ou faux?

1. Le cyclisme n'est pas très apprécié en France.
2. Le Tour de France est une course cycliste.
3. Le Tour de France a lieu au mois de décembre.
4. Tous les cyclistes qui participent au Tour de France sont français.
5. Le Tour de France est divisé en deux mi-temps.
6. Pendant le Tour de France, les cyclistes roulent la nuit—de minuit à six heures.
7. Le gagnant du Tour de France reçoit une coupe et une somme d'argent.

B Un miracle Répondez.

1. Qui a gagné le Tour de France trois fois?
2. Il est de quelle nationalité?
3. Qui est le deuxième Américain qui a gagné le Tour de France?
4. Il a quel âge quand il apprend qu'il a le cancer?
5. Armstrong a recommencé à faire du vélo après combien d'opérations?
6. Quelles sont les qualités de Lance Armstrong?
7. D'après les Français, qui est la petite reine qui choisit le gagnant du Tour de France?
8. C'est une personne?
9. Elle a choisi qui de 1999 jusqu'à 2004?

CONNEXIONS

Les sciences naturelles

L'anatomie

Staying in good physical condition is important for all athletes. To do so, they have to know how to care for their bodies. They also have to know something about their bone structure to avoid injuries. Athletes should have some basic knowledge of anatomy. Anatomy is the branch of science that studies the structures of humans and animals.

Before reading this selection on anatomy, study the diagrams of the human body.

le squelette

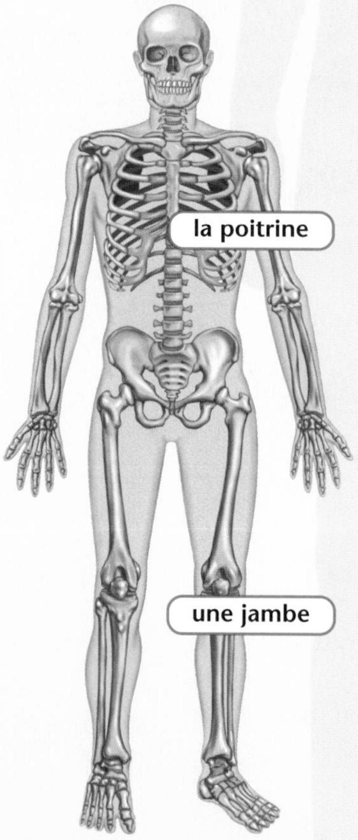

Le corps humain

Le squelette

Le squelette humain a en tout 206 os. Il y a 32 os dans chaque bras et 31 os dans chaque jambe. Il y a plus de 600 muscles dans le corps humain. Certains muscles sont attachés à un os. Ils peuvent être attachés directement à l'os ou par l'intermédiaire d'un tendon.

En plus des muscles squelettiques, il y a de nombreux muscles internes. Le cœur, par exemple, est un muscle.

Le cerveau et le système nerveux

Le cerveau est bien protégé par la boîte cranienne[1]. Le cerveau est

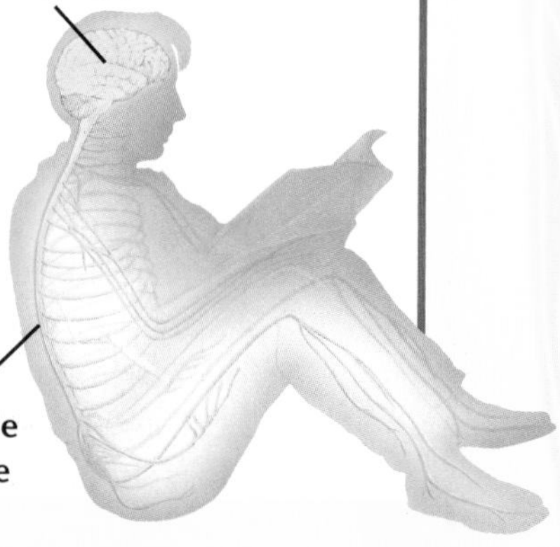

[1] boîte crânienne *skull*

composé de deux hémisphères. Le tronc cérébral relie[2] le cerveau à la moelle épinière. Le tronc cérébral contient les centres nerveux qui contrôlent les fonctions automatiques telles que le rythme cardiaque et la respiration[3].

Le cœur et les poumons

Le cœur est un organe musculaire. C'est le principal organe de la circulation du sang. Le cœur est situé plus ou moins au centre de la poitrine. Les poumons sont situés de part et d'autre[4] du cœur. Le poumon est le principal organe de l'appareil respiratoire. L'air arrive dans chaque poumon par une bronche. Le sang arrive par l'artère pulmonaire. Quand il arrive, l'air est chargé de gaz carbonique. Quand le sang ressort[5] par les veines pulmonaires, il est purifié et enrichi en oxygène.

Il n'y a pas de doute, le corps humain est une machine extraordinaire!

[2] relie *connects*
[3] respiration *breathing*
[4] de part et d'autre *on each side*
[5] ressort *leaves*

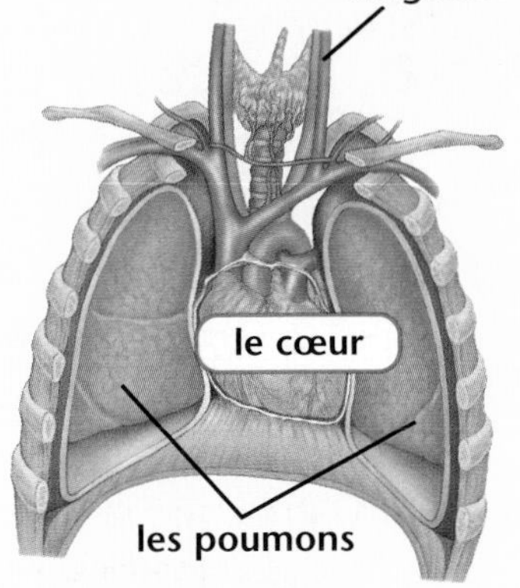

le bras

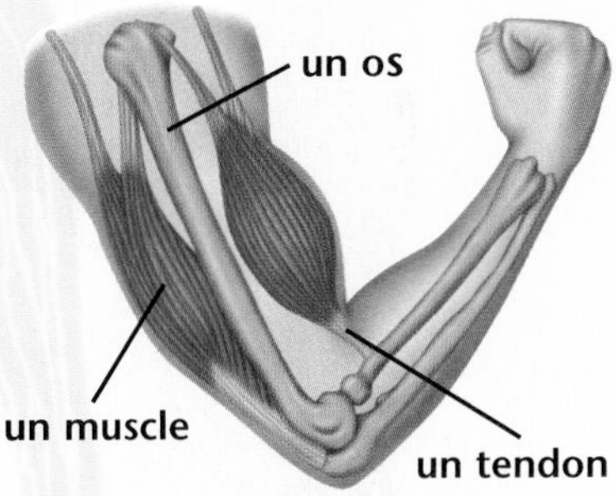

Vous avez compris?

A Les mots apparentés Trouvez les mots apparentés dans la lecture.

B Des informations Identifiez.

1. le nombre d'os dans chaque bras
2. le nombre de muscles dans le corps humain
3. ce qui attache un muscle à un os
4. un muscle interne très important, un muscle vital
5. ce qui protège le cerveau
6. ce qui relie le cerveau à la moelle épinière
7. ce qui contrôle les fonctions automatiques du corps humain
8. l'organe vital situé au centre de la poitrine
9. l'organe principal de l'appareil respiratoire
10. là où le sang est purifié et enrichi en oxygène

Use what you have learned

PARLER

1

Je suis fana de...

✔ Describe your favorite sport

Work with a classmate. Each of you will name a sport you really like and give a description of that sport.

Elles jouent au foot.

La France est victorieuse.

PARLER

2

Une interview du capitaine

✔ Ask someone questions about his or her team

You have to interview the captain of one of the school's sports teams (your classmate) for a French television station. Find out as much information as possible from him or her. Then reverse roles.

PARLER

3

Jeu Devinette

✔ Describe your favorite sports hero and ask questions about your classmates' favorites

Think of your favorite sports hero. Tell a classmate something about him or her. Your classmate will ask you three questions about your hero before guessing who it is. Then reverse roles and guess who your classmate's hero is.

ÉCRIRE 4 Reportage

✔ *Write a description of a sporting event*

Work in groups of three. One of you is the captain of one of the school's teams. The other two are sports reporters for a French newspaper. The two reporters will prepare an interview with the captain about the team's last game. The reporters will edit the information they get from the interview and write their report for tomorrow's paper. The report can be in the present tense.

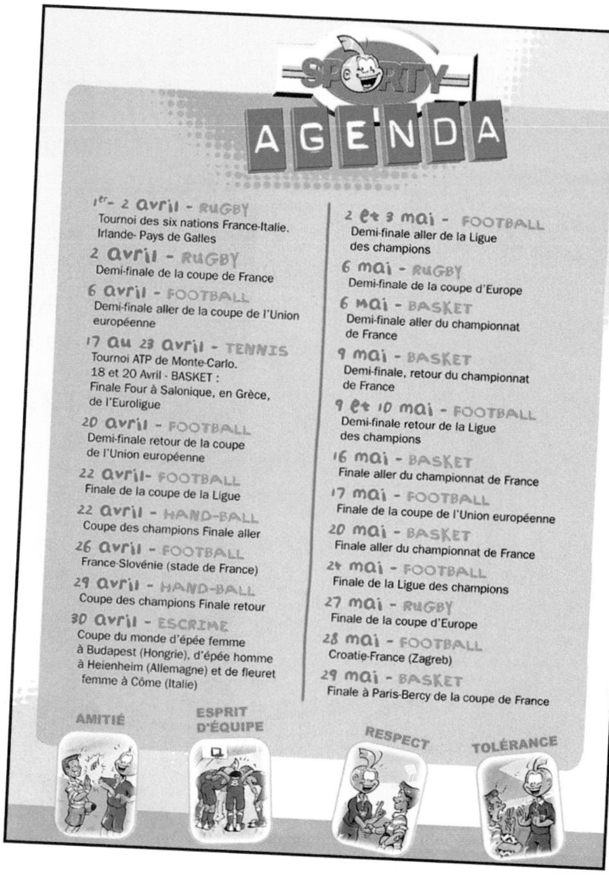

ÉCRIRE 5 Calendrier sportif

✔ *Post a schedule of sporting events*

Your French class has a Web site. Prepare your school's schedule of sporting events for the coming month in French to post at your site.

Writing Strategy

Gathering information If your writing projects deal with a subject you are not familiar with, you may need to gather information before you begin to write. Some of your best sources are the library, the Internet, and people who know something about the topic. Even if you plan to interview people about the topic, it may be necessary to do some research in the library or on the Internet to acquire enough knowledge to prepare good interview questions.

ÉCRIRE 6 La Coupe du Monde

Many of you already know that the World Cup is a soccer championship. Try to give a description of the World Cup as best you can in French. If you are not familiar with it, you will need to do some research. It might be interesting to take what you know or find out about the World Cup and compare it to the World Series in baseball. Gather information about both these championships and write a report in French.

Assessment

Vocabulaire

To review **Mots 1,** turn to pages 324–325.

1 Complétez.

1–2. Il y a onze ____ dans une ____ de foot.
3. Le gardien veut arrêter ou ____ le ballon.
4. Le stade est comble. Les ____ sont pleins.
5. Le joueur peut donner un coup de ____ ou un coup de tête dans le ballon.

2 Identifiez.

To review **Mots 2,** turn to pages 328–329.

6.

7.

8.

9.

10.

Structure

To review the **passé composé** of regular verbs, turn to page 332.

3 Récrivez au passé composé.

11. Je joue au foot.
12. Ils regardent le match à la télé.
13. Elle réussit un beau panier.
14. Notre équipe ne perd pas.
15. Vous finissez la course?

4 Complétez.

16. —Tu as invité ____?
 —Nathalie.
17. —____ tu as regardé à la télé?
 —La course cycliste.
18. —Pour jouer, tu as besoin de ____?
 —D'un ballon et d'un filet.

To review asking questions, turn to page 335.

5 Complétez au présent.

19. Tu ____ des cadeaux. (recevoir)
20. Je ____ beaucoup d'eau. (boire)
21. Elle ____ passer l'examen. (devoir)
22. Vous ____ combien d'argent? (recevoir)
23. Ils ____ faire attention. (devoir)

To review **boire**, **devoir**, and **recevoir** in the present, turn to page 337.

Culture

6 Identifiez.

24. un sport populaire qui est très apprécié au Québec
25. le deuxième sport dans les pays d'Afrique Occidentale

To review this cultural information, turn to pages 342–343.

Un match de hockey

On parle super bien!

Tell all you can about this illustration.

Vocabulaire

Describing a sports event

un stade
des gradins *(m. pl.)*
un spectateur
une spectatrice
un terrain
une piste
un match
un joueur

une joueuse
une équipe
le camp (adverse)
un arbitre
un penalty
le score
un(e) gagnant(e)
une coupe

jouer (à)
lancer
servir
envoyer
renvoyer
passer
recevoir
égaliser

gagner
perdre
siffler
beaucoup de monde
comble
plein
contre

Describing a soccer game

le foot(ball)
un ballon
marquer un but
un gardien de but

un coup
 de pied
 de tête
un but

bloquer
arrêter

How well do you know your vocabulary?

- **Choose a sport from the list.**
- **Ask classmates to give a word associated with the sport you chose.**

Describing a basketball game

le basket(-ball)
un panier
un demi-cercle

dribbler
réussir un beau panier

Describing a volleyball game

le volley(-ball)
un filet

le sol

Describing a bicycle race

un vélo
une bicyclette

un coureur cycliste
une coureuse cycliste

le cyclisme
une course

rouler vite

Describing a track event

l'athlétisme *(m.)*
une piste

un coureur
une coureuse

Expressing the past

hier
hier matin
hier soir

avant-hier
la semaine dernière
l'année dernière

une fois

Other useful words and expresssions

par-dessus

VIDÉOTOUR

Épisode 10

In this video episode, Manu entertains the crowd with his narration of an exciting game. See page 535 for more information.

CHAPITRE 11

L'été et l'hiver

Objectifs

In this chapter you will learn to:

- *describe summer and winter weather*
- *talk about summer activities and sports*
- *talk about winter sports*
- *discuss past actions and events*
- *make negative statements*
- *talk about a ski trip in Quebec*

Maurice Utrillo *Montmartre sous la neige*

Vocabulaire
Mots 1

À la plage

Fabien a passé la journée à la plage.
Il a apporté sa crème solaire et sa serviette.
À la plage, il faut faire attention.
Il faut mettre de la crème solaire.
Il ne faut pas rester trop longtemps au soleil.

Caroline a pris un bain de soleil.
Elle a bronzé.
Elle a mis de la crème solaire.
Elle n'a pas attrapé de coup de soleil.

Des activités d'été

faire de la planche à voile

faire du ski nautique

faire du surf

faire une promenade

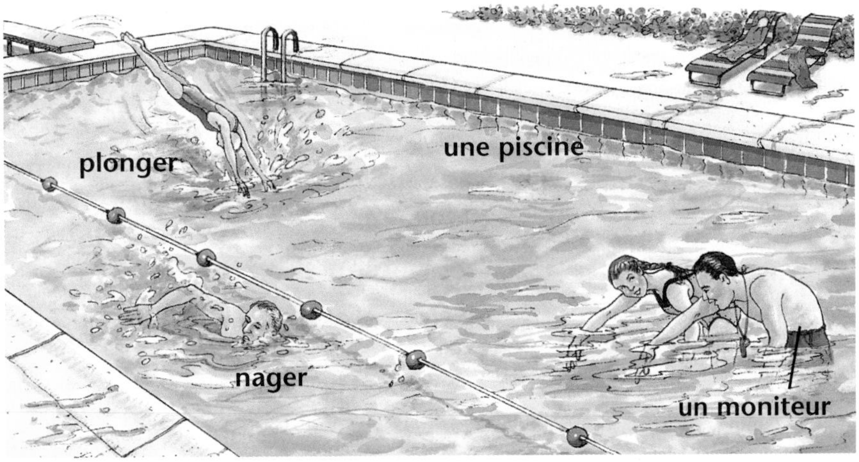

Cécile a plongé dans la piscine.
Laure a pris des leçons de natation.
Elle a appris à nager.

Le printemps

Il fait quel temps au printemps?

Il fait beau.
De temps en temps, il y a des nuages.

Il y a du vent.
Il pleut.
Il fait mauvais.

L'été

En été il fait chaud.
Il fait du soleil.

Quel est le mot?

1 Historiette À la plage

Inventez une histoire.

1. Juliette a passé la journée à la plage?
2. Elle a beaucoup nagé?
3. Elle a pris un bain de soleil?
4. Elle a apporté de la crème solaire?
5. Elle a fait attention? Elle a mis de la crème solaire?
6. Elle a mis aussi des lunettes de soleil?
7. Elle a bronzé?
8. Elle a fait du ski nautique?
9. Elle a fait une promenade sur la plage?
10. Elle a fait de la planche à voile aussi?

Nice, France

De la crème solaire et des lunettes de soleil

2 Historiette En été

Donnez des réponses personnelles.

1. En été, tu aimes aller à la plage?
2. Tu vas dans quelle station balnéaire?
3. Tu vas à la plage quand il pleut?
4. Tu aimes nager dans la mer ou dans une piscine?
5. Tu aimes plonger?
6. Qu'est-ce que tu mets pour nager?
7. Il faut mettre de la crème solaire quand on va à la plage?
8. Et toi, tu mets de la crème solaire?
9. Tu bronzes facilement ou tu attrapes des coups de soleil?
10. Tu mets des lunettes de soleil quand tu vas à la plage?
11. Tu apportes ta serviette?

Il faut étudier
It is necessary one must

3 Historiette Au bord de la mer Complétez.

1. Au bord de la mer, on va à la ____ pour nager et bronzer.
2. Il y a beaucoup de plages et de stations balnéaires sur la ____ Méditerranée.
3. Il y a de grandes ____ sur la mer ou sur l'océan, surtout quand il y a du ____.
4. Beaucoup de gens aiment prendre un ____ de soleil sur la plage.
5. Il faut mettre de la ____ si on ne veut pas attraper de coup de soleil.
6. Quand on va nager, on met un ____.
7. Quand il fait chaud à la plage, il ne faut pas ____ trop longtemps au soleil.
8. On peut faire du ____ ou du ____ sur la mer quand il fait beau.
9. Quand il fait mauvais, il y a souvent des ____ dans le ciel.
10. À Biarritz, sur l'océan Atlantique, il y a souvent des ____ qui font du surf.

Une leçon de natation

4 Qu'est-ce qu'elle a appris?

Répondez d'après la photo.

1. Jeanne a appris à nager?
2. Elle a pris des leçons de natation?
3. Elle a appris à nager dans la mer ou dans une piscine?
4. Elle a compris toutes les instructions de la monitrice?

5 On va à la plage.

Work with a classmate. You are going to spend a day or two at the beach. Go to the store to buy some things you need for your beach trip. One of you will be the salesperson and the other will be the shopper. Take turns.

6 Des vacances parfaites

Plan a great summer vacation. Tell your classmate where you want to go and why. Tell him or her what you do there. Then find out your classmate's summer plans.

Une jolie baie, Tahiti

7 Le temps au printemps ou en été

With a classmate describe the spring or summer weather where you live. Which season do you prefer? Tell why.

ENCORE PLUS

*For more practice using words from **Mots 1**, do Activity 34 on page H35 at the end of this book.*

Vocabulaire Mots 2

Une station de sports d'hiver

Les skieurs ont descendu la piste verte.
La piste verte, c'est pour les débutants.

Marie est débutante.
Elle n'a jamais fait de ski.
Elle tombe tout le temps.

Ce matin, elle a pris sa première leçon.
Elle a eu un très bon moniteur.

Les filles font du patin à glace avec leur mère.

L'automne

En automne il ne fait pas froid.
Il fait frais.

L'hiver

Il fait quel temps en hiver?

Il fait froid.

Il neige.

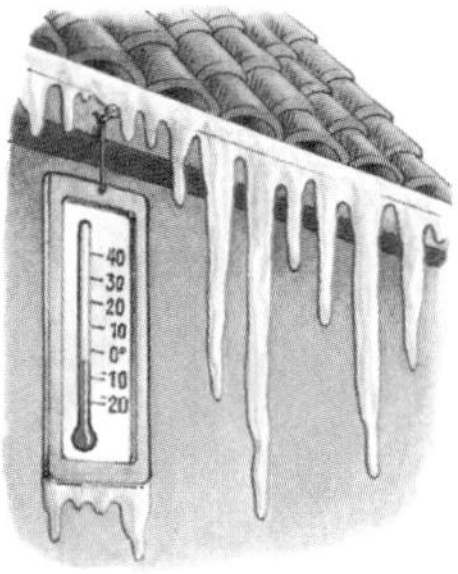

Il gèle.

Quel est le mot?

8 Historiette Dans une station de sports d'hiver

Répondez d'après les indications.

1. Les stations de sports d'hiver sont très fréquentées en quelle saison? (en hiver)
2. Quel temps fait-il en hiver à la montagne? (froid)
3. Il y a quelles catégories de pistes dans une station de sports d'hiver? (pour les skieurs débutants, pour les skieurs moyens et pour les skieurs experts)
4. Les skieurs ont fait du ski où? (sur la piste verte)
5. Qu'est-ce qu'ils ont pris pour monter au sommet de la montagne? (un télésiège)
6. Ils ont descendu quelle piste? (la piste noire)
7. Qu'est-ce qu'il y a sur les pistes noires? (beaucoup de bosses)
8. Les bosses, c'est dangereux pour les débutants? (oui, très)
9. Après le ski, ils ont mis leurs patins? (oui)
10. Ils ont fait du patin à glace où? (à la patinoire)

9 On fait du ski. Répondez d'après les dessins.

1. C'est une station balnéaire ou une station de sports d'hiver?
2. C'est une plage ou une montagne?
3. C'est la neige ou la mer?
4. C'est le sommet de la montagne ou la vallée?
5. C'est quelle saison? L'automne ou l'hiver?
6. C'est une piste ou une piscine?
7. C'est une skieuse ou une nageuse?
8. Elle fait du ski alpin ou du ski de fond?
9. Elle skie bien ou elle tombe souvent?

10 Historiette Leçons de ski

Inventez une histoire.

1. Christine a appris à faire du ski?
2. Qui a appris à Christine à faire du ski?
3. Elle a eu un très bon moniteur?
4. Christine a mis un anorak de quelle couleur?
5. Elle a mis des gants, une écharpe et un bonnet?
6. Elle a mis ses chaussures de ski et ses skis?
7. Elle a pris le télésiège?
8. Elle a descendu quelle piste?
9. Il a fait très froid? Il a neigé? Il a gelé?

11 Qu'est-ce qu'on fait?

A French exchange student (a classmate) asks you what the weather is like in your town in the summer and in the winter and what people do during these seasons. Answer his or her questions, giving as much information as possible.

12 Dans une station de sports d'hiver

Have a conversation with a classmate. Tell as much as you can about what people do at a ski resort. Find out which one of you knows more about skiing. If skiing is a sport that is new to you, tell whether you think you would like to ski.

13 Dans quelle ville?

With a classmate, look at this weather map that appeared in a Paris newspaper. You are both in Paris and you want to take a short side trip. Since you both have definite preferences concerning weather, use the map to help make a decision. Choose what city you want to go to, tell why, and explain what you are going to do there.

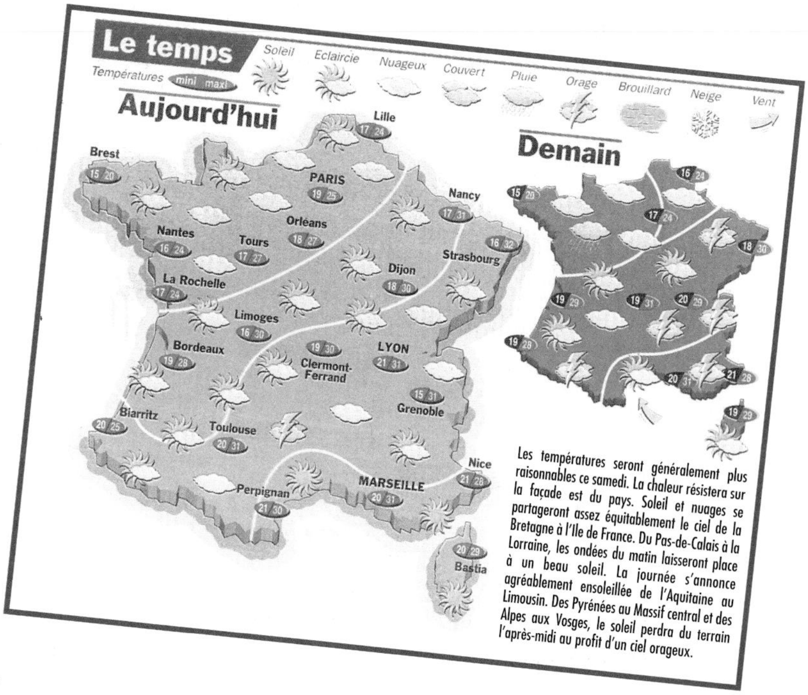

ENCORE PLUS

*For more practice using words from **Mots 2**, do Activity 35 on page H36 at the end of this book.*

Structure

Le passé composé des verbes irréguliers
Describing more past actions

1. You have already learned that the past participles of regular verbs end in the sounds **/é/, /i/,** and **/ü/.** The past participles of most irregular verbs also end in the sounds **/i/** or **/ü/,** even though they are not spelled the same way.

Infinitif → participe passé /i/		Infinitif → participe passé /ü/	
dire	dit	avoir	eu
écrire	écrit	croire	cru
		voir	vu
mettre	mis	boire	bu
permettre	permis	devoir	dû
		pouvoir	pu
prendre	pris	lire	lu
apprendre	appris	recevoir	reçu
comprendre	compris	vouloir	voulu

J'ai pris des leçons de natation.
J'ai appris à nager.
J'ai eu un bon moniteur.

Tu as lu son livre?
Il a écrit un livre?
Tu as compris ce qu'il a dit?

2. The verbs **être** and **faire** have irregular past participles.

être → été	faire → fait

J'ai fait un voyage à Megève l'année dernière.
J'ai été content d'apprendre à faire du ski.

Une classe de ski

Comment dit-on?

14 Historiette Gilles a fait du ski.

Répondez que oui.

1. Gilles a mis son anorak?
2. Son ami a dit «Bonne chance» à Gilles?
3. Son ami a déjà fait du ski aujourd'hui?
4. Gilles a bien fait du ski?
5. Il a eu un accident?
6. Après l'accident, il a lu un livre pour les débutants?

Une vue de la ville de Québec

15 Ce matin

Donnez des réponses personnelles.

1. Tu as pris ton petit déjeuner à quelle heure ce matin?
2. Qu'est-ce que tu as bu au petit déjeuner?
3. Est-ce que tu as lu le journal ce matin? Et tes parents?
4. Est-ce que tu as reçu une lettre?
5. Est-ce que tu as vu tes copains avant les cours?
6. Est-ce que tu as dit bonjour à ton prof de français?

16 Qu'est-ce que tu as dit?

Complétez d'après le modèle.

—J'____ que j'____ ce que j'____.

—J'ai dit que j'ai lu ce que j'ai écrit.

1. Il ____ qu'il ____ ce qu'il ____.
2. Nous ____ que nous ____ ce que nous ____.
3. Tu ____ que tu ____ ce que tu ____.
4. J'____ que j'____ ce que j'____.
5. Vous ____ que vous ____ ce que vous ____.
6. Elles ____ qu'elles ____ ce qu'elles ____.

17 Historiette À Chamonix

Complétez au passé composé.

Laurent aime beaucoup le ski. Son ami Étienne et lui ____1____ (décider) d'aller faire du ski. Ils ____2____ (prendre) le Guide Michelin et ____3____ (lire) la description de plusieurs stations. Finalement, ils ____4____ (choisir) Chamonix. Ils ____5____ (avoir) de la chance. Les parents de Laurent ____6____ (permettre) aux deux garçons de prendre leur voiture. La voiture, c'est plus pratique que le train! Alors les deux copains ____7____ (mettre) leurs skis sur la voiture et… en route! Mais la voiture, ça n'est pas toujours plus pratique que le train: il y ____8____ (avoir) une avalanche et la route ____9____ (être) bloquée pendant dix heures!

Chamonix, France

18 L'été dernier

Your classmate wants to know what you did last summer. Tell him or her several things you did, using some of the verbs below. Then reverse roles.

recevoir · prendre · écrire · voir · bronzer · nager · lire · pouvoir · boire · mettre · faire

*For more practice using irregular verbs in the **passé composé**, do Activity 36 on page H37 at the end of this book.*

Les mots négatifs
Making negative statements

1. You already know the negative expressions **ne... pas** and **ne... plus.** Study the following negative expressions that function the same way as **ne... pas** and **ne... plus.**

Affirmatif	Négatif
Elle voit quelque chose.	Elle ne voit rien.
Elle voit quelqu'un.	Elle ne voit personne.
Il lit toujours.	Il ne lit jamais.
Il lit souvent.	Il ne lit jamais.
Il lit quelquefois.	Il ne lit jamais.
Il lit encore.	Il ne lit plus.

Rappelez-vous que...

Un, une, des, du, de la, de l' change to **de (d')** after **pas** and other negative expressions.
Il n'a pas d'amis.
Il ne fait jamais de sport.
Elle n'écrit plus de lettres.

2. With the exception of **personne,** the negative words go around the verb **avoir** in the **passé composé. Personne** goes after the past participle.

Je n'ai jamais dit ça!
On n'a plus parlé de ça. *mais* **Je n'ai vu personne.**
On n'a rien dit. **Et je n'ai parlé à personne!**

Comment dit-on?

19 **Le matin, en haut de la montagne** Répondez que non.

Il voit quelque chose?
Non, il ne voit rien.

1. Il dit quelque chose?
2. Il entend quelque chose?
3. Il regarde quelque chose?
4. Il voit quelqu'un?
5. Il regarde quelqu'un?
6. Il parle à quelqu'un?
7. Il attend quelqu'un?

De la planche à voile à la Martinique

20 Elle ne fait jamais de sport.

Répondez d'après le modèle.

—Jeanne adore nager.
—Elle dit ça, mais elle ne nage jamais!

1. Jeanne adore faire du surf.
2. Elle adore aller à la plage.
3. Elle adore faire de la planche à voile.
4. Elle adore faire du sport.
5. Elle adore jouer au tennis.
6. Elle adore faire du ski nautique.

21 C'est fini! Répondez que non.

1. Ta grand-mère travaille encore?
2. Ta sœur joue encore au foot?
3. Tu écris encore à ton amie Marie?
4. Tes amis et toi, vous allez encore en vacances à Chamonix?
5. Tes amis sont encore à Paris?

22 Non, non et non!

Répondez que non.

1. Tu as dit quelque chose?
2. Il a vu quelque chose?
3. Ils ont acheté quelque chose?
4. Ils ont appris quelque chose?
5. Ils ont toujours fait du sport?
6. Il a vu quelqu'un?
7. Ils ont entendu quelqu'un?
8. Tu as téléphoné à quelqu'un?

23 L'été

Work with a classmate. Tell him or her some things you like to do in the summer. For some reason, you didn't get to do these things last summer. Tell what you didn't do.

Une piscine, Paris

Le passé composé avec être
Describing more past actions

1. Certain verbs form their **passé composé** with **être** instead of **avoir.** Many verbs that are conjugated with **être** express motion to or from a place.

arriver	**Il est arrivé.**
entrer	**Il est entré.**
monter	**Il est monté.**
descendre	**Il est descendu.**
aller	**Il est allé.**
partir	**Il est parti.**
sortir	**Il est sorti.**
rentrer	**Il est rentré.**

Rappelez-vous que...

Ne... pas goes around the verb **avoir** in the **passé composé.** It also goes around the verb **être** in the **passé composé.**
Il n'est pas arrivé.

2. The past participle of verbs conjugated with **être** must agree with the subject in number (singular and plural) and in gender (masculine and feminine). Note that when **on** means **nous,** the past participle agreement is the same as for **nous.** Study the following forms.

Masculin		Féminin	
je	suis parti	je	suis partie
tu	es parti	tu	es partie
il	est parti	elle	est partie
on	est parti(s)	on	est partie(s)
nous	sommes partis	nous	sommes parties
vous	êtes parti(s)	vous	êtes partie(s)
ils	sont partis	elles	sont parties

On - one
they
people
we

Note that since all the past participles of the verbs above end in a vowel, there is no difference in sound.

3. Although the following verbs do not express motion to or from a place, they are also conjugated with **être.**

rester	**Il est resté huit jours.**	*He stayed a week.*
tomber	**Il est tombé.**	*He fell.*
naître	**Elle est née en France.**	*She was born in France.*
mourir	**Elle est morte en 2003.**	*She died in 2003.*

Comment dit-on?

Un téléphérique, Grenoble

24 Historiette Un voyage à Grenoble

Répondez que oui.

1. Carine est allée à Grenoble?
2. Elle est arrivée à la gare de Lyon à 10 h?
3. Elle est allée sur le quai?
4. Elle est montée dans le train?
5. Le train est parti à l'heure?
6. Le train est arrivé à Grenoble à l'heure?
7. Carine est descendue du train à Grenoble?
8. Elle est sortie de la gare?

25 Historiette À l'école. Donnez des réponses personnelles.

1. Tu es allé(e) à l'école ce matin?
2. Tu es arrivé(e) à quelle heure?
3. Tu es entré(e) immédiatement?
4. Tu es sorti(e) de l'école à quelle heure hier?
5. Tu es rentré(e) chez toi à quelle heure?

Villefranche, Côte d'Azur

26 Historiette Au bord de la mer

Mettez au passé composé.

Michel et sa sœur vont au bord de la mer. Ils partent à l'heure. Ils montent dans l'autocar. Ils arrivent à Villefranche. Ils descendent de l'autocar. Ils vont à la plage. La sœur de Michel va nager. Elle sort de l'eau. Tous les deux, ils vont au café. Ils rentrent chez eux très tard.

27 Qui est sorti? Donnez des réponses personnelles.

1. Le mois dernier, vous êtes allés au cinéma, tes copains et toi?
2. Vous y êtes allés comment? En voiture? En bus?
3. Qu'est-ce que vous avez vu comme film?
4. Vous êtes partis tous ensemble?
5. Vous êtes arrivés en retard?
6. Vous êtes allés manger et boire quelque chose après le film?
7. À quelle heure est-ce que vous êtes rentrés chez vous?

28 Une excursion
Complétez en utilisant le passé composé.

Mathieu: Tu __1__ (aller) en Normandie avec Laure. C'est ça?
Thérèse: C'est ça. Nous __2__ (aller) au Mont-Saint-Michel.
Mathieu: Vous avez aimé?
Thérèse: Nous avons adoré! Nous __3__ (monter) à la basilique. Heureusement, nous __4__ (arriver) avant tous les touristes!
Mathieu: Vous __5__ (sortir) sur la terrasse?
Thérèse: Oui. Superbe, la vue! Mais des cars entiers de touristes __6__ (arriver), alors nous __7__ (partir). Nous __8__ (rentrer) à l'hôtel.

Mont-Saint-Michel, Normandie

Saint-Jean-de-Luz, Pays Basque

29 Être ou ne pas être
Donnez des réponses personnelles.

1. Tu es né(e) quel jour?
2. Tu es né(e) à l'hôpital? Dans quel hôpital?
3. Ta mère est restée combien de jours à l'hôpital?
4. Tes parents sont nés où?
5. Et tes grands-parents, ils sont nés où?
6. Ta grand-mère est morte? Et ton grand-père?

30 À Saint-Jean-de-Luz
Work with a classmate. You both went to Saint-Jean-de-Luz, on the Atlantic Ocean, near the Spanish border, but you did not go together. Ask each other what you did there. Find out as much as you can about each other's trip.

ENCORE PLUS
*For more practice using the **passé composé** with **être**, do Activity 37 on page H38 at the end of this book.*

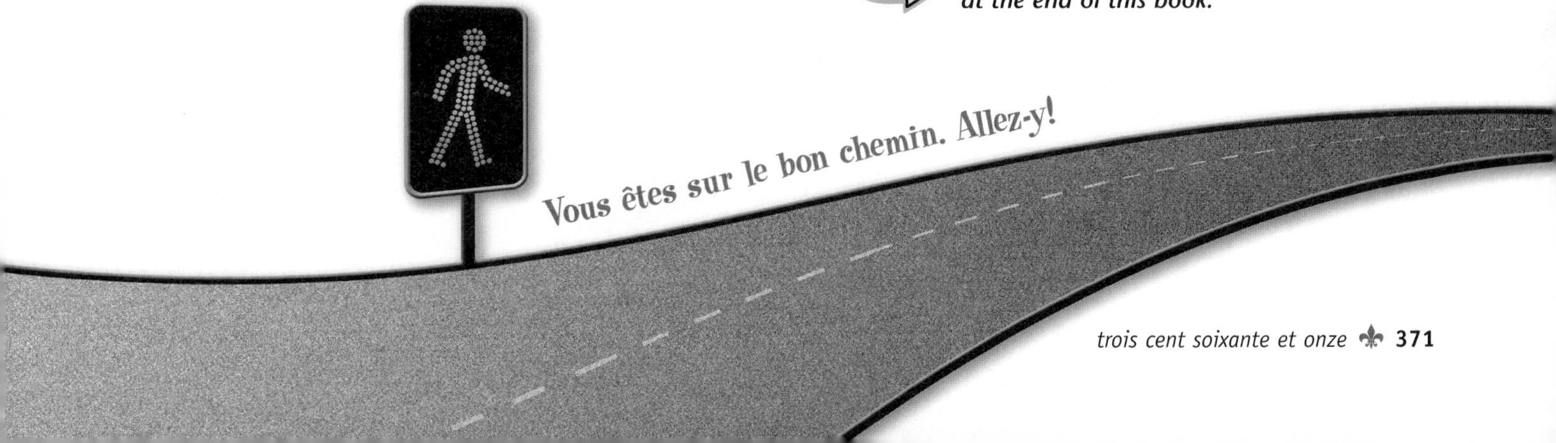
Vous êtes sur le bon chemin. Allez-y!

Conversation

À la plage

Laurène: Qu'est-ce que tu as fait hier?
Marine: Je suis allée à la plage.
Laurène: Tu as eu de la chance. Il a fait très beau hier!
Marine: Oui, mais je suis arrivée à la plage, j'ai regardé dans mon sac et… pas de maillot!
Laurène: Ben, qu'est-ce que tu as fait, alors?
Marine: Je suis allée dans l'eau.
Laurène: Sans maillot!
Marine: Oui, mais en blue-jean! Et toi, qu'est-ce que tu as fait?
Laurène: Absolument rien. Je n'ai rien fait et je n'ai vu personne.

Vous avez compris?

Répondez.

1. Marine est allée où hier?
2. Il a fait beau?
3. Elle a pris son maillot?
4. Elle a nagé?
5. Elle est allée dans l'eau sans maillot?
6. Elle est allée dans l'eau comment?
7. Et Laurène, qu'est-ce qu'elle a fait hier?
8. Elle a vu quelqu'un?

Parlons un peu plus

A **Quel temps fait-il?** Work with a classmate. Pretend that one of you lives in Montreal and the other lives in Fort-de-France in Martinique. Compare what it's like on a typical day in February. Tell some things you do in February.

B **À Tahiti** Work with a classmate. Pretend you spent a week on the beach in Tahiti. Tell your partner about your vacation and answer any questions he or she may have.

Martinique
Les Plages

Vauclin / Plage de Macabou : Entrée payante, plage aménagée, sable blanc et raisiniers bord de mer, tables pour pique-nique.

Plage du Diamant / Plage de la Dizac : Plage sauvage, très ventilée, beaucoup de vagues. Littoral ombragé et aménagé. Baignade avec prudence.

Anses d'Arlets / Plage de Grande Anse et Petite Anse : Jolies plages de sable blanc, très ensoleillées. Mer très calme, peu ventée, restaurants à proximité.

Sainte-Luce : Plage de Corps de Garde et de Gros Raisin, plages animées et aménagées, tables et bancs, sable blanc.

L'Anse Céron / L'Anse Couleuvre : Belle plage aménagée et typique. Sable noir. En continuant le petit chemin pittoresque, à un kilomètre de marche, vous arriverez à l'Anse Couleuvre, plage déserte de dable noir. Eaux profondes.

Plage du Carbet / Anse Turin : Grande plage de sable noir, eaux profondes.

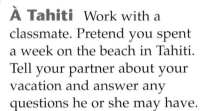

Prononciation

Le son /y/

1. The sound /y/ occurs in two positions: final, and between two vowel sounds. Repeat the following.

fille	**soleil**	**travaille**	**taille**
bouteille	**maillot**	**travailler**	**billet**

2. Now repeat the following sentences.

J'ai un vieux maillot.
On ne travaille pas bien au soleil.

un soleil en maillot

Le Québec

Lectures culturelles

Reading Strategy

Summarizing

When reading an informative passage, we try to remember what we read. Summarizing helps us to do this. The easiest way to summarize is to begin to read for the general sense and take notes on what you are reading. It is best to write a summarizing statement for each paragraph and then one for the entire passage.

Un petit voyage au Canada

En février, pendant les huit jours de vacances d'hiver, les élèves de Madame Lebrun sont allés au Canada, avec Madame Lebrun, bien sûr. Ils ont pris le train à New York et sont descendus à Montréal. Ils ont passé trois jours à Montréal. Montréal est la deuxième ville francophone après Paris. Les élèves de Madame Lebrun ont été très contents parce qu'ils ont pu pratiquer leur français. Et ils ont tout compris!

Après trois jours à Montréal, ils sont partis pour le parc du Mont-Tremblant. Le Mont-Tremblant est une station de sports d'hiver tout près de la jolie ville de Québec. Ils sont arrivés au parc à midi. Ils ont mis leurs skis et sont montés au sommet de la montagne en télésiège. De là-haut, quelle vue superbe on a sur les montagnes et les vallées couvertes de neige! Tu n'as jamais vu de montagnes couvertes de neige? Il n'y a rien de plus beau!

Vieux-Port à Montréal

Mont-Tremblant, Québec

Une rue résidentielle, Montréal

Haïti

La Martinique

Skis aux pieds et bâtons en mains, ils ont commencé à descendre la piste. Ils ont choisi une piste verte. Au Québec, les pistes vertes sont les pistes faciles pour débutants. Après trois heures sur les pistes, ils sont allés à la patinoire où ils ont fait du patin à glace.

À neuf heures du soir, un des élèves a dit: «Moi, je n'ai jamais été aussi fatigué!» Ça a été le signal de la retraite vers les dortoirs[1]. Ils ont tous dormi comme des souches[2]!

[1] dortoirs *dormitories*
[2] souches *tree stumps*

Vous avez compris?

A Au Canada Répondez.

1. La classe de Madame Lebrun est allée où?
2. Ils y sont allés quand?
3. Ils y sont allés comment?
4. Ils ont pratiqué leur français où?
5. Après trois jours à Montréal, ils sont partis pour où?
6. Qu'est-ce que le Mont-Tremblant?
7. C'est près de quelle ville?
8. Ils y sont arrivés à quelle heure?
9. Ils sont montés jusqu'où?
10. Qu'est-ce qu'ils ont vu du sommet?

B Les vacances d'hiver Vrai ou faux?

1. Les élèves ont eu un mois de vacances.
2. Ils ont pris le train pour aller à Montréal.
3. Montréal est une petite ville.
4. Les élèves sont montés à skis au sommet de la montagne.
5. Pour faire du ski, ils ont mis des patins.
6. Ils ont pris la piste rouge pour les très bons skieurs.
7. Ils ont fait aussi du patin à glace.

Lecture supplémentaire 1

Les grandes vacances

Le mois d'août, c'est le mois des grandes vacances en France. Beaucoup de Français quittent la ville et vont à la montagne, à la campagne[1] ou au bord de la mer.

En été, quand le soleil brille dans le ciel bleu, il est fabuleux de passer la journée à la plage. La France est un pays de plages merveilleuses. Il y a plus de mille kilomètres de côtes et des stations balnéaires tout le long de ces côtes—sur la Manche au nord; sur l'océan Atlantique à l'ouest; sur la mer Méditerranée au sud.

Étretat, Normandie

Cannes, Côte d'Azur

Biarritz, Pays Basque

Vous voulez passer une petite semaine sur une belle plage en France? Vous voulez rentrer chez vous bien bronzé(e)(s)? Vous allez aller où?

[1] campagne *countryside*

Vous avez compris?

Au bord de la mer Identifiez.

1. le mois des grandes vacances en France
2. la mer qui sépare l'Angleterre de la France
3. l'océan à l'ouest de la France
4. la mer au sud de la France

Lecture supplémentaire 2

Le carnaval

«Bonhomme Carnaval», Québec

La neige arrive au Québec fin novembre et reste jusqu'au mois d'avril. Les jours sont courts, froids, mais très beaux. Le soleil brille souvent dans le ciel bleu et la neige scintille[1].

En février, les Québécois sortent de chez eux pour célébrer le carnaval. Des milliers de visiteurs vont à Québec à cette époque pour célébrer le carnaval. Pendant les dix jours de festivités, il y a un grand défilé de chars[2]. On construit un magnifique palais de glace et il y a un concours[3] de sculptures de glace.

Toutes ces festivités sont orchestrées par un gigantesque bonhomme de neige appelé «Bonhomme Carnaval».

[1] scintille *sparkles*
[2] défilé de chars *float parade*
[3] concours *contest*

Le palais de glace, Québec

La Belgique

Tunisie

Le Maroc

Le Mali

Vous avez compris?

Au Québec et à Québec Décrivez.

1. un jour d'hiver au Québec
2. le carnaval de Québec
3. «Bonhomme Carnaval»

CONNEXIONS

Les Beaux-Arts

La peinture

One may know a great deal or just a little about art. But almost everyone has at least some interest in art. How often have we heard, "I may not know anything about art, but I certainly know what I like"?

There is no doubt that France has produced many of the world's greatest artists. Do you recognize the names of these famous French artists: Renoir, Monet, Manet, Degas, Seurat, Boudin, Gauguin?

In 1874, two of these painters, Monet and Renoir, were among a group of artists who held a famous exhibition of their works in Paris. The critics laughed at their works and called the artists "Impressionists" to mock one of Monet's paintings entitled ***Impression, soleil levant***. Today, paintings by the Impressionists are among the most admired works in the history of art.

Claude Monet *La pie*

Claude Monet *La route sous la neige à Honfleur*

Les impressionnistes

On dit que les impressionnistes sont les peintres de la vie moderne. Ils ont peint la vie quotidienne[1] des gens (personnes) simples. Pour eux, tous les sujets sont bons. Ils ont peint des parcs, des gares, des usines[2]. Beaucoup de peintres impressionnistes ont préféré quitter leur atelier[3] pour aller peindre en plein air. Les scènes d'été et les scènes d'hiver sont des sujets favoris de plusieurs impressionnistes.

Voici deux tableaux de paysages d'hiver de Claude Monet—*La pie* et *La route sous la neige à Honfleur.*

[1] vie quotidienne *daily life*
[2] usines *factories*
[3] atelier *studio*

Eugène Boudin *La plage de Trouville*

Voici maintenant des scènes de plage. Eugène Boudin a peint *La plage de Trouville.*

Ce tableau *Sur la plage* a été peint par l'ami de Monet, Édouard Manet.

Georges Seurat a peint *Les baigneurs à Asnières.* Asnières est dans la banlieue[4] parisienne sur la Seine. Au fond, on voit les cheminées des usines de Clichy. Il fait très chaud et les ouvriers[5] font un petit plongeon dans la Seine.

[4] banlieue *suburbs*
[5] ouvriers *workers*

Édouard Manet *Sur la plage*

Georges Seurat *Les baigneurs à Asnières*

Vous avez compris?

A Un peu de géographie Find all the places mentioned where these artists painted.

B Mon tableau favori Pick your favorite painting, describe it, and explain why it is your favorite.

Use what you have learned

PARLER

1 La mer ou la montagne?

✔ Talk about summer or winter vacations

Work with a classmate. Tell him or her where you like to go on vacation. Tell what you do there and some of the reasons you enjoy it so much. Take turns.

Mont-Blanc, Chamonix

Dans les Alpes

PARLER

2 Des vacances merveilleuses

✔ Talk about vacation activities

Work with a classmate. Pretend you each had a million dollars. You went on a dream vacation. Take turns describing what you did.

PARLER

3 Le ski

✔ Talk about skiing

You're having a hot chocolate on the terrace of a chalet near the slopes of Pralognan-la-Vanoise in the French Alps. You make friends with a French skier (your classmate). Find out as much as you can about each other's skiing habits and abilities.

ÉCRIRE

4 Une carte postale

✔ Write about a summer or winter vacation destination

Look at these postcards. Choose one. Pretend you spent a week there. Write the postcard to a friend.

Saint-Malo, Bretagne

Mont-Tremblant, Québec

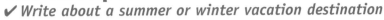

Writing Strategy

Comparing and contrasting Before you begin to write a comparison of people, places, or things, you must be aware of how they are alike or different. When you compare, you are emphasizing similarities; when you contrast, you are emphasizing differences. Making a diagram or a list of similarities and differences is a good way to organize your details before you begin to write.

ÉCRIRE

5 En été et en hiver

A summer day in most parts of the world is quite different from a winter day. Write a paragraph comparing how you spend a vacation day in the summer in comparison to the way you spend a vacation day in the winter. Because of the weather, many of your activities are probably quite different. Not everything is different, however. Describe some things you do whether it's summer or winter.

Assessment

Vocabulaire

To review **Mots 1**, turn to pages 356–357.

1 Complétez.

1. Au bord de la mer, on va à la ____.
2. Il faut mettre de la ____ quand on prend un bain de soleil.
3. Laure apprend à nager. Elle a un très bon ____.
4. Elle apprend à nager dans une ____.
5. Quand il fait mauvais, il y a souvent des nuages dans le ____.
6. Il y a beaucoup de stations balnéaires sur la ____ Méditerranée.

To review **Mots 2**, turn to pages 360–361.

2 Identifiez.

7.

8.

9.

10.

3 Répondez.

11. Il fait quel temps en hiver?
12. Qui tombe souvent—un skieur débutant ou un bon skieur?

Structure

To review irregular verbs in the **passé composé**, turn to page 364.

4 Complétez au passé composé.

13. Il ____ des leçons de natation. (prendre)
14. Il ____ un très bon moniteur. (avoir)
15. Elles ____ un maillot de bain. (mettre)
16. J'____ une carte postale. (écrire)
17. Tu ____ le match? (voir)

5 **Donnez le contraire.**

18. Il joue toujours au foot.
19. Il entend quelque chose.
20. Il regarde quelqu'un.

To review negative statements, turn to page 367.

6 **Récrivez au passé composé.**

21. Elles arrivent à la plage.
22. Il part.
23. Anne et Marie, vous sortez?

*To review the **passé composé** with **être**, turn to page 369.*

Culture

7 **Vrai ou faux?**

24. On peut pratiquer le français au Québec parce que les Québécois parlent français.
25. Il y a beaucoup de stations de sports d'hiver dans la ville de Montréal.

To review this cultural information, turn to pages 374–375.

Le ski alpin

On parle super bien!

Tell all you can about this illustration.

Vocabulaire

How well do you know your vocabulary?

- Choose one of the seasons from the list.
- Have a classmate make up a sentence that tells something about that season.

Going to the beach

une station balnéaire
au bord de la mer
la mer
une plage
une vague
des lunettes *(f. pl.)* de soleil
de la crème solaire
un maillot de bain
une serviette

Describing summer activities

nager
plonger
prendre un bain de soleil
bronzer
attraper un coup de soleil
faire du surf
faire du ski nautique
faire de la planche à voile
faire une promenade
la natation
une leçon de natation
un moniteur, une monitrice
une piscine
un surfeur, une surfeuse

Going to a ski resort

une station de sports d'hiver
une montagne
un sommet
un skieur, une skieuse
un(e) débutant(e)
un télésiège
une piste
une bosse
le ski alpin
le ski de fond
un ski
une chaussure de ski
un bâton
une patinoire
la glace
le patin à glace
un patin
un gant
un bonnet
une écharpe
un anorak

Describing winter activities

faire du ski
monter en télésiège
descendre une piste
tomber
faire du patin à glace

Describing weather and seasons

le temps
le printemps
l'été *(m.)*
l'automne *(m.)*
l'hiver *(m.)*
Il fait quel temps… ?
au printemps
en été
en automne
en hiver
Il fait beau.
Il fait mauvais.
Il fait chaud.
Il fait froid.
Il fait frais.
Il fait du soleil.
Il pleut.
Il neige.
Il gèle.
le vent
le ciel
le soleil
un nuage

Other useful words and expressions

la journée
passer
faire attention
apporter
rester
longtemps
de temps en temps
tout le temps

VIDÉOTOUR

Épisode 11

In this video episode, Christine experiences "almost firsthand" the wonderful world of skiing. See page 536 for more information.

Révision

Conversation

En vacances

Anne: Tu es arrivé à Nice quand?
Loïc: Je suis arrivé ce matin.
Anne: Tu as pris le train ou l'avion?
Loïc: J'ai pris le train—le TGV.
Anne: Et maintenant qu'est-ce que tu vas faire?
Loïc: Absolument rien! Je ne vais rien faire. Je vais passer toute la journée à la plage et lire tous les magazines sportifs que je n'ai jamais le temps de lire.

Promenade des Anglais, Nice

Vous avez compris?

Répondez.

1. Loïc est arrivé à Nice quand?
2. Qu'est-ce qu'il a pris, le train ou l'avion?
3. Il a pris le TGV?
4. Qu'est-ce que Loïc va faire à Nice?
5. Il va passer toute la journée où?
6. Qu'est-ce qu'il veut lire?

Structure

Les verbes au présent

1. Review the following regular **-ir** and **-re** verbs.

FINIR	je finis, tu finis, il/elle/on finit, nous finissons, vous finissez, ils/elles finissent
VENDRE	je vends, tu vends, il/elle/on vend, nous vendons, vous vendez, ils/elles vendent

2. Review these other **-ir** verbs.

SORTIR	je sors, tu sors, il/elle/on sort, nous sortons, vous sortez, ils/elles sortent
PARTIR	je pars, tu pars, il/elle/on part, nous partons, vous partez, ils/elles partent
DORMIR	je dors, tu dors, il/elle/on dort, nous dormons, vous dormez, ils/elles dorment
SERVIR	je sers, tu sers, il/elle/on sert, nous servons, vous servez, ils/elles servent

3. Review the following irregular verbs.

ÉCRIRE	j'écris, tu écris, il/elle/on‿n‿écrit, nous‿z‿écrivons, vous‿z‿écrivez, ils‿z‿/elles‿z‿écrivent
LIRE	je lis, tu lis, il/elle/on lit, nous lisons, vous lisez, ils/elles lisent
DIRE	je dis, tu dis, il/elle/on dit, nous disons, vous dites, ils/elles disent

RECEVOIR	je reçois, tu reçois, il/elle/on reçoit, nous recevons, vous recevez, ils/elles reçoivent
DEVOIR	je dois, tu dois, il/elle/on doit, nous devons, vous devez, ils/elles doivent
BOIRE	je bois, tu bois, il/elle/on boit, nous buvons, vous buvez, ils/elles boivent

1 Historiette **Un voyage en train** Complétez au présent.

Nous ___1___ (partir) en voyage. Maman ___2___ (attendre) devant le guichet. Elle ___3___ (choisir) deux places en seconde. Maman ___4___ (sortir) de l'argent et achète les billets. Nous ___5___ (attendre) le train sur le quai. Le train ___6___ (partir) à l'heure. Je ___7___ (sortir) les billets de mon sac à dos. Je ___8___ (donner) les billets au contrôleur. Nous ___9___ (aller) au snack-bar. Je ___10___ (choisir) un sandwich au jambon. Maman aussi ___11___ (prendre) un sandwich au jambon. Le serveur ___12___ (servir) Maman en premier. Nous ___13___ (finir) notre sandwich. Nous commandons un express; nous ___14___ (boire) notre express. Nous retournons à notre place. Nous ___15___ (dormir) un peu… Et nous arrivons à Toulon. Tous les voyageurs ___16___ (descendre) du train. Nous ___17___ (descendre) aussi. Enfin, nous sommes en vacances!

2 **Qu'est-ce que tu fais?** Donnez des réponses personnelles.

1. Tu lis tous les magazines que tu reçois?
2. Tu écris des articles dans le journal de l'école?
3. Tu dis toujours quels sont tes projets à tes amis?
4. Tu reçois quelquefois des e-mails de tes amis?
5. Tu dois aller voir tes grands-parents de temps en temps?

3 **Qu'est-ce qu'il fait?**

Refaites l'Activité 2 en remplaçant **tu** par **il,** et puis répondez.

4 **Qu'est-ce que vous faites?**

Refaites l'Activité 2 en remplaçant **tu** par **vous,** et puis répondez.

Les adjectifs

1. Review the adjectives **quel, ce,** and **tout.**

Quel groupe? Ce groupe? Oui, tout le groupe.	Quels garçons? Ces garçons? Oui, tous les garçons.	Quelle classe? Cette classe? Oui, toute la classe.	Quelles filles? Ces filles? Oui, toutes les filles.

2. Remember that you use **cet** before a singular masculine noun that begins with a vowel or a silent **h: cet‿ami, cet‿horaire.**

5 Quels sont tes favoris? Répondez.

1. Toutes les classes sont intéressantes?
   Tu aimes cette classe aussi?
   Quelle classe est vraiment ta favorite?
2. Tu trouves tous les sports intéressants?
   Tu aimes ce sport?
   Quel est ton sport favori?
3. Tous les joueurs de cette équipe sont bons?
   Cette équipe gagne tous les matchs?
   Tous les spectateurs aiment ce sport?
   On parle de quel sport?

Ils jouent au foot.

6 Les sports

Complétez d'après les indications.

1. Tu parles de ____ équipe et de ____ match? (quel)
2. Je parle de ____ équipe, de ____ match et de ____ arbitre. (ce)
3. J'aime ____ les sports, mais pas ____ les équipes. (tout)
4. Voilà ____ les joueurs de l'équipe. (tout)
5. ____ trois joueurs sont excellents. C'est pourquoi ____ équipe gagne toujours. (ce)

Les verbes au passé composé

1. The **passé composé** expresses an action begun and completed at a specific time in the past. You form the **passé composé** by using the present tense of **avoir** and the past participle. Review the regular **-er, -ir,** and **-re** verbs.

PARLER		CHOISIR		ATTENDRE	
j'	ai parlé	j'	ai choisi	j'	ai attendu
tu	as parlé	tu	as choisi	tu	as attendu
il/elle/on	a parlé	il/elle/on	a choisi	il/elle/on	a attendu
nous	avons parlé	nous	avons choisi	nous	avons attendu
vous	avez parlé	vous	avez choisi	vous	avez attendu
ils/elles	ont parlé	ils/elles	ont choisi	ils/elles	ont attendu

2. Review the verbs that have an irregular past participle.

devoir	**dû**	**recevoir**	**reçu**	**dire**	**dit**
boire	**bu**	**avoir**	**eu**	**écrire**	**écrit**
croire	**cru**				
voir	**vu**	**prendre**	**pris**	**être**	**été**
lire	**lu**	**apprendre**	**appris**	**faire**	**fait**
pouvoir	**pu**	**comprendre**	**compris**		
vouloir	**voulu**	**mettre**	**mis**		

Aéroport Charles-de-Gaulle, Roissy

7 **Historiette** **En voyage** Répondez.

1. Tu as fait tes valises?
2. Tu as pris ton billet et ton passeport?
3. À l'aéroport, tu as fait enregistrer tes bagages?
4. Tu as choisi ta place?
5. Tu as fait bon voyage?

8 **Historiette C'est passé.** Complétez en utilisant le passé composé.

1. Ils ___ ce que vous ___. (croire, dire)
2. Elle ___ des leçons de natation et elle ___ toutes les instructions de son moniteur. (prendre, comprendre)
3. Nous ___ une lettre de Marianne mais nous n'___ pas ___ à sa lettre. (recevoir, répondre)
4. Il ___ des courses. Il ___ tout ce qu'il ___ dans un grand sac. (faire, mettre, acheter)
5. Chez elle, elle ___ un verre d'eau et elle ___ son journal. (boire, lire)
6. J'___ très contente de voir Sébastien, mais je n'___ pas ___ sortir avec lui. (être, vouloir)

Le passé composé avec être

1. Many verbs that express motion to or from a place are conjugated with **être** in the **passé composé.** Such verbs are: **aller, descendre, rentrer, entrer, sortir, monter, arriver,** and **partir.**

MASCULIN		FÉMININ	
ALLER	DESCENDRE	ALLER	DESCENDRE
je suis allé	je suis descendu	je suis allée	je suis descendue
tu es allé	tu es descendu	tu es allée	tu es descendue
il est allé	il est descendu	elle est allée	elle est descendue
on est allé(s)	on est descendu(s)	on est allée(s)	on est descendue(s)
nous sommes allés	nous sommes descendus	nous sommes allées	nous sommes descendues
vous êtes allé(s)	vous êtes descendu(s)	vous êtes allée(s)	vous êtes descendue(s)
ils sont allés	ils sont descendus	elles sont allées	elles sont descendues

Note that the past participle of verbs conjugated with **être** agrees with the subject.

2. The verbs **rester, tomber, naître,** and **mourir** are also conjugated with **être.**

Il est resté huit jours.
Elle est tombée.
Elle est née le 20 décembre.
Son grand-père est mort le 2 janvier.

9 Historiette **À l'école** Répondez.

1. Tu es allé(e) à l'école à quelle heure ce matin?
2. Tu es sorti(e) de la maison à quelle heure?
3. Quand tu es entré(e) dans la classe de français, tu as dit bonjour au professeur?
4. Tu es resté(e) à l'école après les cours?
5. Tu es allé(e) où après les cours?
6. Tu es rentré(e) chez toi vers quelle heure?

10 Historiette **En train** Refaites les phrases avec le sujet indiqué.

1. Ils sont allés à Genève. (elles)
2. Les voyageurs sont descendus du train. (la voyageuse)
3. Elle est sortie de la gare. (il)
4. Il a cherché un taxi. (elle)
5. Elles sont rentrées à neuf heures du soir. (nous)

Genève, Suisse

Les mots négatifs

Review the negative words. Pay particular attention to their placement.

Je ne vais pas au café.
Je ne vais jamais au café.
Je ne vais plus au café.

Je ne suis pas allé(e) au café.
Je ne suis jamais allé(e) au café.
Je ne suis plus allé(e) au café.

Je ne vois rien et je n'ai rien vu.
Je ne vois personne et je n'ai vu personne.

LITERARY COMPANION *You may wish to read the adaptation of* La Chanson de Roland. *You will find this literary selection on page 512.*

11 **Non.** Répondez que non.

1. Tu vois quelqu'un?
2. Tu entends quelqu'un?
3. Tu vois quelque chose?
4. Tu veux quelque chose?
5. Tu vas encore au café?
6. Tu arrives toujours en retard?
7. Tu as vu quelque chose?
8. Tu as dit quelque chose?
9. Tu as vu quelqu'un?
10. Tu as attendu quelqu'un?

12 **Enquête sur les saisons** You want to know if your partner prefers summer or winter. On a separate sheet of paper, make a chart like the one to the right. Fill it out for both seasons. Compare your chart with your partner's and try to guess which season your partner prefers by asking questions about his or her choices.

	L'hiver	L'été
Vêtements		
Activités	le ski	le ski nautique
Équipement		
Nourriture		

13 **Un match** Work with a classmate. Discuss the last sports event you saw.

14 **On y va comment?** Look at these train and plane schedules. You want to go from Paris to London. With a classmate decide how you are going to get there and discuss your choice. Then tell what you are going to do there.

Réservation : 0 820 820 820

PARIS CDG 2 +0:00

Jours	Dép.	Arr.	N°Vol	Corr. Validité
→ Londres "City"				
12345--	07.30 F	07.35	AF1680(WX)	→ 30/10-23/03
12345--	08.40 F	08.45	AF1880(VM)	→ 30/10-23/03
12345--	12.00 F	12.05	AF2180(WX)	→ 30/10-23/03
12345--	15.25 F	15.30	AF2580(WX)	→ 30/10-23/03
12345--	17.45 F	17.50	AF1080(VM)	→ 30/10-23/03
12345--	18.55 F	19.00	AF1180(WX)	→ 30/10-23/03
→ Londres Heathrow				+0:00
1234567	07.00 F	07.10 2	AF1070	→ 29/10-24/03
123456-	07.30 F	07.50 2	AF2670	→ 30/10-24/03
1234567	08.00 F	08.25 2	AF1170	→ 29/10-24/03
12345--	09.00 F	09.25 2	AF1270	→ 30/10-23/03
1234567	10.00 F	10.20 2	AF1370	→ 29/10-24/03
------7	11.00 F	11.10 2	AF1470	→ 29/10-18/03
12345-7	12.00 F	12.15 2	AF1570	→ 29/10-23/03
1234567	13.00 F	13.10 2	AF1670	→ 29/10-24/03
1234567	15.00 F	15.10 2	AF1870	→ 29/10-24/03
1234567	16.00 F	16.10 2	AF1970	→ 29/10-24/03
1234567	17.00 F	17.10 2	AF2070	→ 29/10-24/03
1234567	18.00 F	18.10 2	AF2170	→ 29/10-24/03
1234567	19.00 F	19.20 2	AF2270	→ 29/10-24/03
1234567	19.30 F	19.50 2	AF2570	→ 29/10-24/03
1234567	20.00 F	20.20 2	AF2370	→ 29/10-24/03

CDG

Jours	Dép.	Arr.	N°Vol	Corr. Validité
← Londres "City"				LCY
12345--	08.10	10.15 F	AF1681(WX)	→ 30/10-23/03
12345--	09.55	12.00 F	AF1881(VM)	→ 30/10-23/03
12345--	12.40	14.45 F	AF2181(WX)	→ 30/10-23/03
12345--	16.05	18.10 F	AF2581(WX)	→ 30/10-23/03
12345--	18.25	20.30 F	AF1081(VM)	→ 30/10-23/03
12345--	19.35	21.40 F	AF1181(WX)	→ 30/10-23/03
← Londres Heathrow				LHR
1234567	06.55 2	09.05 F	AF2471	→ 29/10-24/03
1234567	08.15 2	10.25 F	AF1071	→ 29/10-24/03
123456-	08.45 2	10.55 F	AF2671	→ 30/10-24/03
1234567	09.15 2	11.25 F	AF1171	→ 29/10-24/03
12345--	10.15 2	12.25 F	AF1271	→ 30/10-23/03
1234567	11.15 2	13.25 F	AF1371	→ 29/10-24/03
------7	12.15 2	14.25 F	AF1471	→ 29/10-18/03
12345-7	13.05 2	15.15 F	AF1571	→ 29/10-23/03
1234567	14.00 2	16.10 F	AF1671	→ 29/10-24/03
1234567	16.00 2	18.10 F	AF1871	→ 29/10-24/03
1234567	17.00 2	19.10 F	AF1971	→ 29/10-24/03
1234567	18.00 2	20.10 F	AF2071	→ 29/10-24/03
1234567	19.15 2	21.25 F	AF2171	→ 29/10-24/03
1234567	20.15 2	22.25 F	AF2271	→ 29/10-24/03
1234567	20.45 2	22.55 F	AF2571	→ 29/10-24/03

1. La ville de Québec vue du Saint-Laurent
2. La porte Saint-Louis à Québec
3. Le complexe Desjardins à Montréal
4. La chute Montmorency à l'est de la ville de Québec
5. Bateau de pêche dans la baie de Gaspé
6. Skieurs à Sainte-Agathe-des-Monts dans les Laurentides
7. Marionnettes sur le Vieux-Port à Montréal

1

2

3

4

5

6

NATIONAL GEOGRAPHIC

REFLETS
du Canada

7

8. Le Rocher Percé en Gaspésie
9. Détail d'un totem au musée McCord d'histoire canadienne à Montréal
10. Tours et la basilique Notre-Dame de Montréal
11. Intérieur de la basilique Notre-Dame de Montréal
12. Course de canots sur le Saint-Laurent au carnaval de Québec
13. Jeune fille de Montréal
14. Kayaks dans le parc du Mont-Tremblant dans les Laurentides

8

9

10

11

12

13

NATIONAL GEOGRAPHIC

REFLETS du Canada

14

CHAPITRE 12

La routine quotidienne

Objectifs

In this chapter you will learn to:

- *describe your personal grooming habits*
- *talk about your daily routine*
- *talk about your family life*
- *tell some things you do for yourself*
- *talk about daily activities in the past*
- *discuss a French family's daily routine*

Edgar Degas *Toilette matinale*

Vocabulaire Mots 1

La routine

tôt tard

Elle se lève tôt.
Elle ne se lève pas tard.

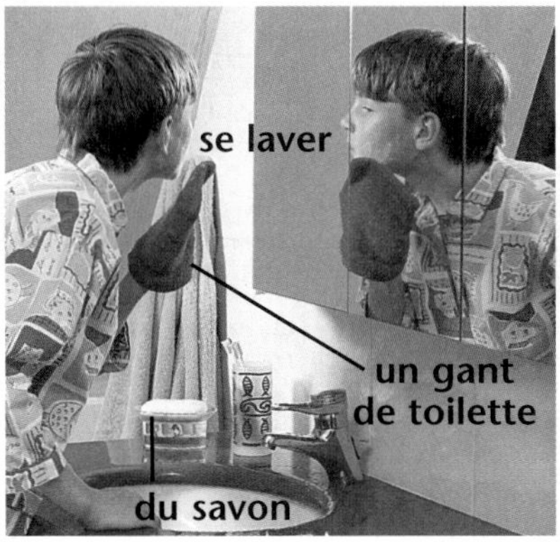

Il se lave la figure.

du shampooing

un peigne

une brosse

Une fille se peigne.
L'autre se brosse les cheveux.

se laver (se brosser) les dents

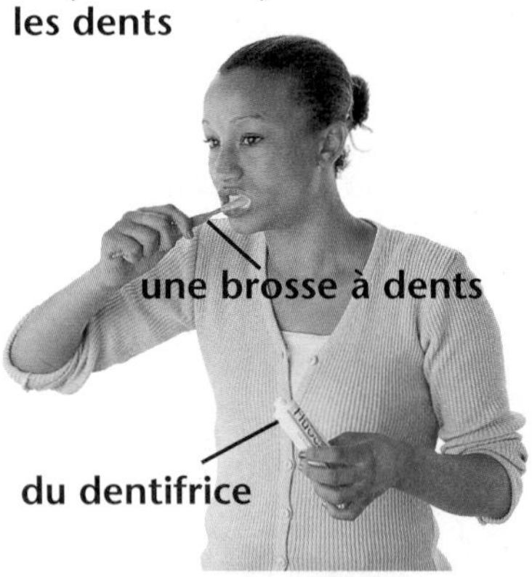

se maquiller

s'habiller

Elle s'appelle Mélanie.
Mélanie se réveille.
Elle se lève tout de suite.

D'abord, elle se lave.

Ensuite elle se lave les dents.

Enfin elle prend son petit déjeuner.

Elle se dépêche.

Quel est le mot?

1 Historiette La matinée de Guillaume

Inventez des réponses.

1. Le matin Guillaume se réveille à six heures? Il se lève tôt ou tard?
2. Il se lève tout de suite?
3. D'abord, il va dans la salle de bains pour se laver?
4. Il se lave la figure avec un gant de toilette?
5. Ensuite, il se lave les dents avec une brosse à dents et du dentifrice?
6. Il prend un bain ou une douche?
7. Il se regarde dans la glace quand il se rase?
8. Il s'habille dans sa chambre à coucher?
9. Enfin, il prend son petit déjeuner avant d'aller à l'école?
10. Il se dépêche? Pourquoi?

Guillaume se rase.

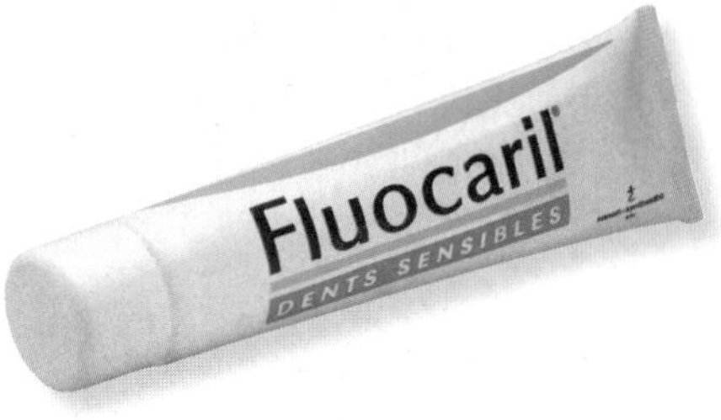

2 Dans quelle pièce? Complétez.

1. On se brosse les dents dans ____.
2. On se couche dans ____.
3. On prend une douche dans ____.
4. On se maquille dans ____.
5. On dort dans ____.
6. On prend son petit déjeuner dans ____.

3 **Qu'est-ce qu'il faut?** Choisissez la bonne réponse.

1. Pour se laver les dents il faut ____.
   a. de la crème **b.** du dentifrice **c.** du déodorant
2. Pour se laver la figure et les mains, il faut ____.
   a. du déodorant **b.** du dentifrice **c.** du savon
3. Pour se raser il faut ____.
   a. un rasoir **b.** une brosse à dents **c.** un peigne
4. Pour se peigner il faut ____.
   a. du shampooing **b.** un peigne **c.** du savon
5. Pour se laver les cheveux il faut ____.
   a. du déodorant **b.** du shampooing **c.** du savon
6. Pour se brosser les cheveux il faut ____.
   a. une brosse **b.** un peigne **c.** une brosse à dents

4 **Pendant la journée** Work with a classmate. Each of you will choose a family member and tell each other about that person's daily activities.

mon père   mon cousin   ma mère

ma sœur   ma cousine   mon frère

Une famille fait les courses, Yerres, France.

ENCORE PLUS *For more practice using words from* ***Mots 1****, do Activity 38 on page H39 at the end of this book.*

Vocabulaire
Mots 2

Chez les Moulin

Avant le dîner, Christophe met la table.

Après le dîner, Mélanie débarrasse la table.
Et Maman fait la vaisselle.

M. Moulin a mis (a allumé) la télé.

M. Moulin a zappé pour éviter les publicités.
Il a changé de chaîne.
Il a regardé son émission favorite.
Mélanie a fait ses devoirs après le dîner.

Après l'émission M. Moulin a éteint la télé.

Mélanie a fait ses devoirs.
Elle n'a pas pu regarder le film à la télé.
Elle a enregistré le film.

Quel est le mot?

5 Historiette Chez les Fauvet

Répondez d'après les indications.

1. Qui a mis la table? (Paul)
2. Qui a servi le dîner? (Mme Fauvet)
3. Qui a débarrassé la table? (M. Fauvet)
4. Qui a fait la vaisselle? (Sophie)
5. Où est-ce qu'elle a mis les assiettes, les verres et les couverts? (dans le lave-vaisselle)
6. Après le dîner, qui a mis la télé? (M. Fauvet)
7. Qu'est-ce qu'ils ont regardé à la télé? (leur émission favorite)
8. Ils ont zappé pour éviter les publicités? (oui)
9. Qui a éteint la télé? (M. Fauvet)
10. Qui est sorti après le dîner? (Sophie)
11. Elle s'est bien amusée? (oui)
12. Elle a fait ses devoirs avant de sortir? (oui)

Ils regardent la télé.

6 Quel est le mot? Complétez.

1. L'évier, le frigidaire et le lave-vaisselle se trouvent dans la ____.
2. On rince la vaisselle dans l'____, et ensuite, on met les verres, les assiettes et les couverts dans le ____.
3. Avant le dîner, on ____ la table.
4. Après le dîner, on ____ la table.
5. Quand on veut regarder la télévision, on ____ la télévision.
6. M. Fauvet n'arrive pas à trouver une émission qu'il aime. Il change souvent de ____.
7. On peut changer de chaîne avec une ____.
8. Si on n'est pas à la maison pour regarder un film, on peut ____ le film sur une cassette vidéo.
9. Pour enregistrer un film à la télé il faut avoir un ____.

7 **Historiette Chez moi** Donnez des réponses personnelles.

1. Tu rentres à la maison vers quelle heure?
2. Qui prépare le dîner chez toi?
3. Qui met la table?
4. Qui sert le dîner?
5. Qui débarrasse la table?
6. Qui fait la vaisselle?
7. Qu'est-ce que vous faites après le dîner?
8. Tu fais tes devoirs avant de regarder la télévision?

8 **Chez nous** Work with a classmate. Share information about what you usually do when you return home after school. Decide if much of your routine is the same.

9 **En famille** Work with a classmate. Ask each other questions about the illustration. Answer each other's questions.

ENCORE PLUS *For more practice using words from* ***Mots 2****, do Activity 39 on page H40 at the end of this book.*

Structure

Les verbes réfléchis au présent
Telling what people do for themselves

1. Compare the following pairs of sentences.

Paul regarde le bébé.

Paul se regarde.

Anne couche le bébé.

Anne se couche.

In the sentences on the left, one person performs the action and another receives the action. In the sentences on the right, the person performs the action and also receives the action. For this reason, the pronoun **se** must be used. **Se** refers to the subject or doer of the action and is called a "reflexive" pronoun. It indicates that the action of the verb is reflected back to the subject.

2. Each subject pronoun has its corresponding reflexive pronoun. Study the following.

SE LAVER		S'HABILLER	
je	me lave	je	m'habille
tu	te laves	tu	t'habilles
il/elle/on	se lave	il/elle/on	s'habille
nous	nous lavons	nous	nous z habillons
vous	vous lavez	vous	vous z habillez
ils/elles	se lavent	ils/elles	s'habillent

3. The reflexive pronoun cannot be separated from the verb. In the negative, **ne** comes before the reflexive pronoun and **pas** comes after the verb.

Je me réveille mais je ne me lève pas tout de suite.
On ne se lave jamais les dents avant le dîner.
Je ne me lave plus les cheveux tous les jours.

4. When a reflexive verb follows another verb, the reflexive pronoun agrees with the subject.

Je ne veux pas me lever tôt.
Vous allez vous coucher tard.

Les lavages publics du Banco, Abidjan, Côte d'Ivoire

Comment dit-on?

10 **La matinée de Jean-Marc** Répétez la conversation.

11 **Historiette** **C'est malin!** Répondez d'après la conversation.

1. Jean-Marc se lève à quelle heure?
2. Il se lave?
3. Il se lave les dents?
4. Il se rase?
5. Il s'habille?
6. Qu'est-ce qu'il fait en une demi-heure?

Les deux sœurs se maquillent.

12 Historiette Caroline et Stéphanie

Remplacez **Caroline** par **Caroline et Stéphanie.**

1. Caroline se réveille à sept heures.
2. Caroline se lève tout de suite.
3. Caroline se lave les dents.
4. Caroline se lave les mains et la figure.
5. Caroline se brosse les cheveux.
6. Caroline s'habille.
7. Caroline se maquille.

13 Historiette Le matin

Donnez des réponses personnelles.

1. Tu te lèves à quelle heure le matin?
2. Tu vas dans la salle de bains?
3. Tu te laves?
4. Tu te laves les mains et la figure?
5. Tu prends une douche ou un bain?
6. Tu te laves les cheveux avec du shampooing?
7. Tu te peignes?
8. Tu te regardes dans la glace quand tu te peignes?

14 Historiette Ma famille

Remplacez **on** par **nous.**

Je m'appelle Christian. Dans la famille on se réveille tôt. On ne se lave pas le matin parce qu'on se lave le soir. Ensuite on s'habille. On prend notre petit déjeuner tous ensemble. Après, on se lave les dents. Et on se dépêche d'aller, moi à l'école, mes parents au travail.

15 Ta famille

Posez des questions à Christian. Utilisez le paragraphe de l'Activité 14 comme guide. Vous pouvez utiliser les sujets suivants.

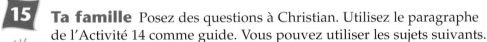

tu — tes parents — ta famille — vous

16 Historiette Dimanche

Donnez des réponses personnelles.

1. Tu vas te réveiller à quelle heure dimanche?
2. Tu vas t'habiller avant de prendre le petit déjeuner?
3. Tu vas sortir avec des amis?
4. Vous allez vous habiller comment?
5. Tu vas te coucher tard?

ENCORE PLUS

For more practice using reflexive verbs, do Activity 40 on page H41 at the end of this book.

17 **Je me réveille et...** Work in groups of three or four. Tell the order of your daily activities from morning to night. Do you all do everything in the same order? What's the most common routine? Who has the oddest routine? Describe it.

AMICO

18 **Jeu** **J'ai quelque chose.** You have something you use routinely. Tell a classmate what it is. He or she will guess what you use it for.

J'ai du dentifrice.
Tu te laves les dents.

Attention!

1. Note the changes in pronunciation and spelling of the following verbs.

SE LEVER	**nous nous levons**
je me lève	**vous vous levez**
tu te lèves	**ils se lèvent**
il se lève	
S'APPELER	**nous nous appelons**
je m'appelle	**vous vous appelez**
tu t'appelles	**ils s'appellent**
il s'appelle	

The verbs **se promener** and **acheter** have the same spelling changes as **se lever.**

2. Note the spelling of the **nous** form of verbs that end in **-ger** and **-cer: nous mangeons, nous nageons, nous voyageons, nous commençons.**

Répondez d'après le modèle.

— Je me lève à six heures!
— Nous aussi, nous nous levons à six heures.

1. Je me lève à cinq heures.
2. Je me promène un peu dans le parc.
3. Je nage dans la piscine.
4. J'achète un café et un croissant.
5. Je commence à manger mon croissant dans la rue.
6. Je mange tout mon croissant dans la rue.

Les verbes réfléchis au passé composé
Telling what people did for themselves

1. You form the **passé composé** of reflexive verbs with the verb **être.** Note the agreement of the past participle with reflexive verbs.

SE LAVER

Masculin		Féminin	
je	me suis lavé	je	me suis lavée
tu	t'es lavé	tu	t'es lavée
il	s'est lavé	elle	s'est lavée
on	s'est lavé(s)	on	s'est lavée(s)
nous	nous sommes lavés	nous	nous sommes lavées
vous	vous êtes lavé(s)	vous	vous êtes lavée(s)
ils	se sont lavés	elles	se sont lavées

2. Note that when a part of the body follows a reflexive verb, there is no agreement.

Agreement	No agreement
Marie s'est lavée.	Marie s'est lavé les mains.
Nous nous sommes brossés.	Nous nous sommes brossé les cheveux.

3. In the negative sentence, you put the negative words around the reflexive pronoun and the verb **être.**

Je ne me suis pas levée tard.
Mes amis ne se sont jamais amusés chez Paul.

Comment dit-on?

Papa va se réveiller?
Il s'est déjà réveillé.

19 **Déjà fait** Répondez d'après le modèle.

1. Papa va se lever?
2. Papa va se laver?
3. Papa va se peigner?
4. Papa va s'habiller?

20 **Maman** Refaites l'Activité 19 en remplaçant **Papa** par **Maman.**

21 **Historiette** **Tôt** Donnez des réponses personnelles.

1. Tu t'es réveillé(e) tôt ce matin?
2. Tu t'es levé(e) tout de suite ou tu t'es rendormi(e)?
3. Tu as pris une douche ou tu t'es lavé seulement la figure et les mains?
4. Tu t'es habillé(e) avant ou après le petit déjeuner?
5. Tu t'es peigné(e) ou tu t'es brossé les cheveux ce matin?
6. Tu t'es lavé les dents après le petit déjeuner?
7. Tu t'es bien amusé(e) à l'école?
8. Tu t'es couché(e) à quelle heure hier soir?

22 **Nous et vous** Complétez au passé composé.

1. Ce matin, ma sœur et moi, nous ____ à sept heures. Et vous, vous____ à quelle heure? (se réveiller)
2. Nous ____ tard. Vous ____ tard? (se lever)
3. Nous ____. Vous ____ aussi? (se dépêcher)
4. Nous ____ très vite. Vous ____ vite aussi? (s'habiller)

Elles se dépêchent.

23 **Mes cousins** Mettez au pluriel.

1. Il s'est levé.
2. Il s'est lavé.
3. Il s'est rasé.
4. Il s'est habillé.
5. Elle s'est levée tard.
6. Elle s'est maquillée.
7. Elle s'est vite habillée.
8. Elle s'est dépêchée.

24 **Historiette** **Ce matin** Inventez une histoire.

1. Tu t'es levé(e) à quelle heure ce matin?
2. Et ton frère, il s'est levé à quelle heure?
3. Vous vous êtes tous habillés avant le petit déjeuner?
4. Vous vous êtes lavé les dents après le petit déjeuner?
5. Tes parents se sont dépêchés pour aller au travail?

25 **Qu'est-ce qu'elle a fait?** Complétez.

1. Elle s'est levé__ ce matin à six heures.
2. Elle s'est lavé__ la figure.
3. Elle s'est lavé__ les dents.
4. Elle s'est amusé__ à l'école.
5. Elle s'est couché__ de bonne heure.

26 **Ce matin** Work with a classmate. Tell each other what you did this morning from the time you woke up until you left for school.

27 **On s'est bien amusé(e)s.** Choose one of the illustrations. Describe it. A classmate will tell which one you're describing and let you know whether the people had fun. Take turns.

1.

2.

3.

28 **Une journée extraordinaire!** Work with a classmate. Imagine that yesterday was really a great day. Tell each other what happened.

ENCORE PLUS For more practice using reflexive verbs, do Activity 41 on page H42 at the end of this book.

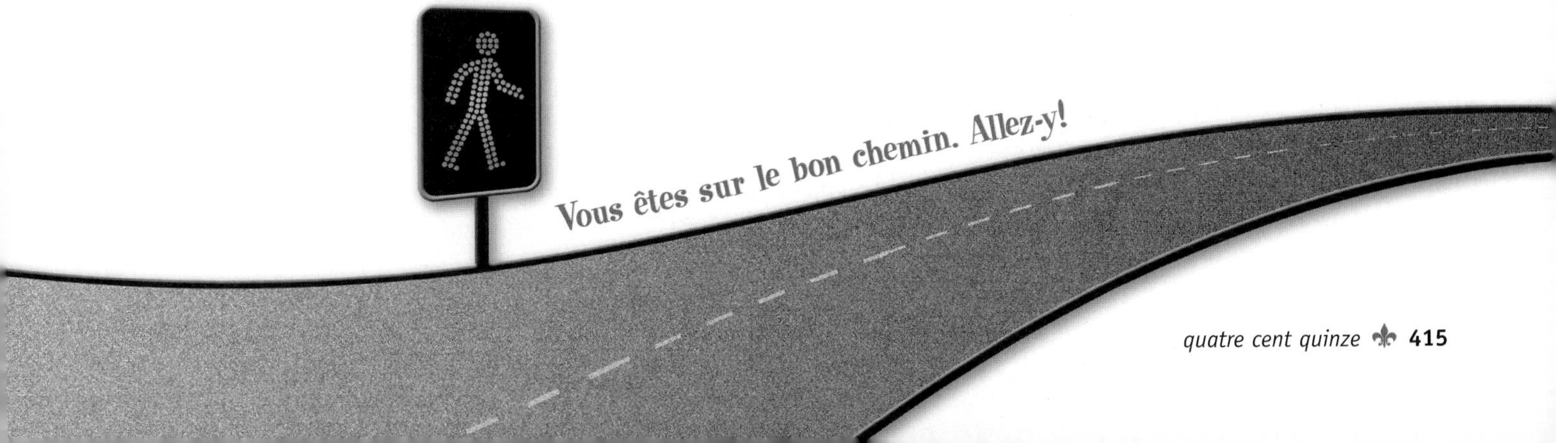
Vous êtes sur le bon chemin. Allez-y!

Conversation

Quelle interro?

Thomas: Tu n'as pas l'air très réveillée, ce matin.
Magali: Ben, non, je n'ai pas assez dormi.
Thomas: Tu t'es couchée à quelle heure?
Magali: À trois heures du matin.
Thomas: À trois heures du mat! Ça va pas, non? Qu'est-ce que tu as fait? Tu n'as pas pu éteindre la télé, c'est ça?
Magali: La télé? Tu rigoles! L'interrogation de maths, plutôt.
Thomas: L'interro de maths? Quelle interro de maths?

Vous avez compris?

Répondez.

1. Magali a assez dormi hier soir?
2. Elle s'est couchée à quelle heure?
3. Elle a regardé la télévision?
4. Qu'est-ce qu'elle a fait?
5. Et Thomas, il a étudié ses maths?

Parlons un peu plus

A **Je suis fatigué(e)!** Neither you nor your classmate look too good this morning. You both got to bed really late. Tell each other why.

B **Une journée horrible!** Work with a classmate. Imagine that yesterday was a really bad day. Tell each other what happened.

Prononciation

Les sons /s/ et /z/

1. It is important to make a distinction between the sounds /s/ and /z/. After all, you would not want to confuse **poisson** and **poison!** Repeat the following words with the sound /s/ as in **assez** and /z/ as in **raser.**

/s/		/z/	
assez	**dessert**	**désert**	**télévision**
classe	**séjour**	**maison**	**zapper**
vaisselle	**boisson**	**raser**	**cousin**
salle	**savon**	**cousine**	

2. Now repeat the following sentences.

Son cousin choisit le dessert et les boissons.
La télévision est dans la salle de séjour.
La salle de classe est assez grande.

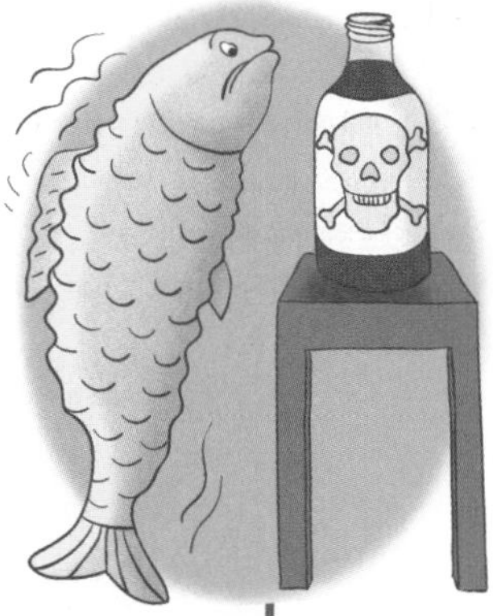

poisson **poison**

Lectures culturelles

Reading Strategy

Skimming

There are several ways to read an article or a passage—each one with its own purpose. Skimming means reading quickly in order to find out the general idea of a passage. To skim means to read without paying careful attention to small details, noting only information about the main theme or topic. Sometimes a reader will skim a passage only to decide whether it's interesting enough to read in detail.

La famille Ben Amar

Les Ben Amar habitent à Saint-Quentin-en-Yvelines. C'est une ville nouvelle dans la banlieue[1] parisienne. Les Ben Amar sont des Français d'origine algérienne. En France, il y a beaucoup de gens originaires des pays du Maghreb, c'est-à-dire des trois pays francophones d'Afrique du Nord—le Maroc, l'Algérie et la Tunisie. Aujourd'hui, la deuxième religion en France, c'est la religion musulmane.

Le matin

Dans la famille Ben Amar, il y a six personnes: M. Ben Amar, sa femme et leurs quatre enfants. Ce matin, comme d'habitude, les Ben Amar se sont levés entre six heures et six heures et demie. Ils se sont lavés, peignés, habillés et ils ont pris leur petit déjeuner. Ils sont partis de chez eux vers sept heures et demie. M. Ben Amar est allé à l'usine[2] où il travaille comme contremaître[3]. Ahmed et Halima vont au collège et Aïcha est à l'école primaire. Le petit Jamal a deux ans. Il ne peut pas encore aller à l'école maternelle. Il passe la journée chez sa grand-mère qui habite dans le même immeuble. Comme beaucoup de femmes françaises, Mme Ben Amar travaille à l'extérieur. Tout est assez cher et la famille a besoin de deux salaires. Mme Ben Amar est assistante sociale[4]. Et Mima est toujours contente de garder son petit Jamal.

Les Ben Amar rentrent déjeuner? Non, ils ne rentrent pas chez eux à midi. M. et Mme Ben Amar déjeunent là où ils travaillent et les enfants déjeunent à la cantine de leur école. Le petit Jamal déjeune avec sa grand-mère.

[1] banlieue *suburbs*
[2] usine *factory*
[3] contremaître *supervisor*
[4] assistante sociale *social worker*

Une famille d'origine algérienne

Mima avec son petit-fils

Haïti

La Martinique

Tahiti

la Polynésie française

Le soir

Saint-Quentin-en-Yvelines, près de Paris

Le soir, les enfants rentrent de l'école vers cinq heures. Ils vont chez leur grand-mère. Ils mangent une tartine de confiture ou des petits gâteaux faits par Mima et ils font leurs devoirs. Vers sept heures et demie, leurs parents rentrent. Ce soir, Mima a préparé un bon couscous pour toute la famille. Après le dîner, Ahmed débarrasse la table, Halima aide sa mère à faire la vaisselle et M. Ben Amar regarde la télévision. Ce soir, il y a un bon film égyptien à 22 h 30. Les films égyptiens sont excellents et M. et Mme Amar aiment bien voir de temps en temps un film en arabe.

Un bon couscous

Vous avez compris?

A Les Ben Amar Lisez rapidement le texte et trouvez les informations suivantes.

1. le nom de la petite ville où les Ben Amar habitent
2. les noms des pays du Maghreb
3. la deuxième religion en France
4. le nombre d'enfants dans la famille
5. leurs prénoms respectifs
6. l'heure où les Ben Amar se lèvent
7. comment les enfants appellent leur grand-mère

B La journée des Ben Amar Décrivez.

1. le travail de M. Ben Amar
2. le travail de Mme Ben Amar
3. le travail de la grand-mère
4. le dîner des Ben Amar
5. la soirée des Ben Amar

Lecture supplémentaire

Le petit déjeuner

La Polynésie française

Tout le monde se réveille le matin, se lève, se lave, s'habille et… prend son petit déjeuner. On commence la journée par un bon petit déjeuner. Mais le petit déjeuner n'est pas le même partout[1].

Aux États-Unis

Aux États-Unis, on boit souvent un verre de jus de fruit—du jus d'orange, par exemple. Ensuite on mange des céréales ou des œufs—des œufs brouillés[2], des œufs sur le plat avec du bacon, des saucisses ou du jambon et du pain grillé. Avec ça, on boit du café ou du chocolat ou même un verre de lait. C'est un vrai petit déjeuner américain, mais ce n'est pas un petit déjeuner français. En France, on ne mange jamais d'œufs ni de bacon au petit déjeuner.

[1] partout *everywhere*
[2] brouillés *scrambled*

Un petit déjeuner américain—des œufs sur le plat

Tahiti

En France

Un petit déjeuner typiquement français, c'est du pain, des croissants ou des brioches avec un bol de café au lait (le lait est chaud.) Les enfants boivent souvent du chocolat chaud. On mange souvent des tartines. Une tartine, c'est une tranche de pain beurré avec de la confiture.

Une tartine

Un croissant et une brioche

Du droî

Des olives

Des figues et des raisins secs

Au Maghreb

En Tunisie, les enfants mangent souvent du droî pour le petit déjeuner. Le droî est de la farine de sorgho[3] cuite à l'eau bouillante[4]. On mange le droî chaud avec un peu de sucre. Les adultes mangent aussi quelquefois du droî, mais souvent ils mangent des tartines comme en France. À la campagne, on mange quelquefois des figues et des raisins secs blancs.

En Algérie, on mange des tartines et du café au lait comme en France, mais à la campagne, on mange quelquefois du fromage, des olives, du pain et de la soupe.

[3] farine de sorgho *sorghum flour*
[4] cuite à l'eau bouillante *cooked in boiling water*

Vous avez compris?

Un petit déjeuner excellent Décrivez.

1. un petit déjeuner américain
2. un petit déjeuner français
3. un petit déjeuner tunisien
4. un petit déjeuner algérien

CONNEXIONS

Les sciences

L'écologie

Ecology is a subject of great interest to people around the world. No one wants to wake up each morning and breathe polluted air or drink contaminated water. Unfortunately, however, much of what we do in our daily life has a negative impact on our environment. The way we dispose of waste litters fields and pollutes waterways. Factories and vehicles belch smoke and fumes that pollute the air. We are all aware that urgent and dramatic steps must be taken to avert future disasters.

L'air pollué, Lyon

L'air pur, Pays Basque

L'écologie

L'écologie, c'est l'équilibre entre les êtres vivants[1] et la nature. Le terme est maintenant synonyme de survie[2] pour beaucoup d'êtres humains à cause de problèmes écologiques très graves.

La pollution de l'air

L'air que nous respirons est souvent pollué. Le plus souvent, il est pollué par des émissions de gaz qui s'échappent des voitures

[1] êtres vivants *living beings*
[2] survie *survival*

et des camions[3]. Il est pollué aussi par la fumée qui se dégage des cheminées des usines qui brûlent[4] des substances chimiques.

La pollution de l'eau

La contamination de l'eau de nos lacs, de nos rivières et de nos mers est catastrophique dans certaines régions. Les accidents de pétroliers font que des millions de litres de pétrole se déversent[5] dans les mers et les océans. Dans les zones industrielles les usines déversent des déchets[6] industriels dans les rivières. Beaucoup de ces déchets sont toxiques et peuvent causer des maladies[7] très graves.

Le recyclage

De nos jours, il y a de grandes campagnes de recyclage. Grâce au recyclage, nous pouvons utiliser à nouveau des déchets de verre, de papier, de métal et même de plastique.

[3] camions *trucks*
[4] brûlent *burn*
[5] se déversent *are spilled*
[6] déchets *wastes*
[7] maladies *illnesses*

Le naufrage d'un pétrolier, Bretagne

Conteneurs pour le recyclage

Vous avez compris?

A En français, s'il vous plaît.

Trouvez l'équivalent des mots suivants dans la lecture.

1. ecology
2. ecological problems
3. chemical substances
4. air pollution
5. toxic wastes
6. recycling

B Discussion Répondez.

1. L'air est pollué là où vous habitez?
2. Il y a beaucoup d'usines près de chez vous?
3. Il y a beaucoup de voitures, d'autocars et de camions qui passent?
4. Vous recyclez? Qu'est-ce que vous recyclez? Le papier, le carton *(cardboard)*, le verre… ?

C'est à vous

Use what you have learned

PARLER

1 Ma famille

✔ Compare your family life to someone else's

Work with a classmate. Find out about some family habits in your respective homes: who does what chores, what you do after dinner, etc. Compare your findings.

Vincent Van Gogh *La chambre de Vincent à Arles*

PARLER

2 Pas la même chose

✔ Talk about your weekday and weekend routines

Most people like a change of pace on the weekend. Talk with a classmate about things that students do or don't do during the week. Your partner will say how that differs on the weekend and why. Take turns.

Pendant la semaine, on se lève tôt.
Pendant le week-end, on se lève plus tard.

PARLER

3 Quel jour!

✔ Talk about an atypical day

You have a set routine but sometimes you just can't stick to it. That was the case yesterday. Have a conversation with a friend. Use the model as a guide.

—D'habitude je me lève à sept heures.
—Tu t'es levé(e) à quelle heure hier?
—Je me suis levé(e) à dix heures et demie.

ÉCRIRE

4 Une journée typique

✔ *Write about your daily routine*

Your Tunisian pen pal is curious about your daily routine. Write him or her an e-mail describing all the activities you do on a typical day, from the time you wake up to the time you go to bed.

Halima est de Kairouan en Tunisie.

Writing Strategy

Taking notes Taking notes gives you a written record of important information you may need for later use. When taking notes from a lecture, write down key words and phrases as you continue to focus on what the speaker is saying. When the speaker has finished, go back over your notes as soon as possible, highlighting the most important points and adding details to make them as complete as possible. If necessary, rewrite your notes, organizing them so they will be of utmost use to you.

ÉCRIRE

5 Un job d'été

You are working in Quebec this summer. You are going to help take care of two small children. The children's parents give you many instructions about the children's routine and activities. Since you probably will not remember all they are telling you, you jot down notes. Take your notes and organize them to describe each child's day. Then write down your responsibilities—what it is you have to do.

Assessment

Vocabulaire

1 Identifiez.

1. 

2. 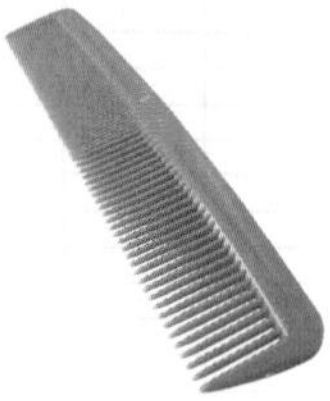

3. 

4. 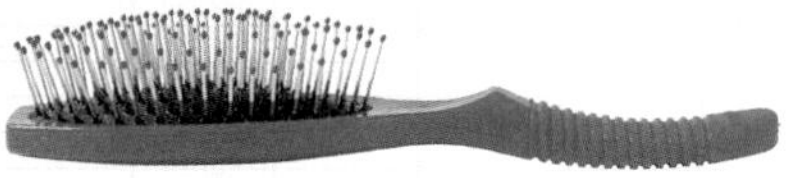

5. 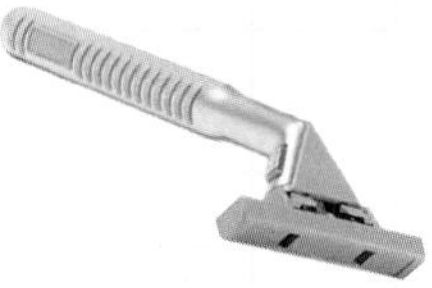

To review **Mots 1**, *turn to pages 400–401.*

2 Mettez en ordre.

6. ____	**a.** se laver
7. ____	**b.** se réveiller
8. ____	**c.** se coucher
9. ____	**d.** se lever

To review **Mots 2**, *turn to pages 404–405.*

3 Choisissez.

10. Après le dîner, il ____ la table.
a. met **b.** débarrasse **c.** fait

11. Il lave les assiettes, les verres, etc. Il fait ____.
a. le lave-vaisselle **b.** la vaisselle **c.** l'évier

12. Il ____ pour éviter les publicités.
a. allume la télé **b.** fait ses devoirs **c.** zappe

13. Après son émission favorite, il a ____ la télé.
a. éteint **b.** regardé **c.** mis

Structure

To review reflexive verbs in the present, turn to pages 408–409.

4 Complétez au présent.

14. Il ____ la figure. (se laver)
15. Elles ____ les cheveux. (se brosser)
16. Nous ____ beaucoup. (s'amuser)
17. Je ____ à onze heures. (se coucher)
18. Éric, tu ____ tous les matins? (se raser)

5 Récrivez.

19. Tu t'appelles comment?
    Vous ____________?
20. Nous nous levons tôt.
    Je ____________.

To review verbs with spelling changes, turn to page 412.

6 Complétez au passé composé.

21. Elle _____. (se laver)
22. Elles _____ les cheveux. (se laver)
23. Mes amis _____. (s'amuser)

*To review reflexive verbs in the **passé composé**, turn to page 413.*

Culture

7 Identifiez.

24. les pays du Maghreb
25. la deuxième religion en France

To review this cultural information, turn to pages 418–419.

Un marché, Alger, Algérie

FRENCH Online

For more information on the Maghreb, go to the Glencoe French Web site: french.glencoe.com

On parle super bien!

Tell all you can about this illustration.

Vocabulaire

Doing daily activities

la routine	se laver	s'habiller
prendre un bain	se brosser	s'amuser
prendre une douche	se raser	se dépêcher
se réveiller	se maquiller	se coucher
se lever	se peigner	

Identifying grooming articles

du savon	une brosse à dents	un rasoir
un gant de toilette	du dentifrice	un peigne
du shampooing	une glace	une brosse

Identifying more parts of the body

la figure
les cheveux *(m. pl.)*
les dents *(f. pl.)*

Identifying household appliances

un évier	une télé(vision)
un lave-vaisselle	une télécommande
un frigidaire, un réfrigérateur	un magnétoscope

How well do you know your vocabulary?

- **Choose an expression from the list that describes something you do as part of your daily routine.**
- **Ask a classmate to give words related to that particular daily activity.**

Discussing home activities

mettre la table	mettre la télévision	zapper	une émission
débarrasser la table	allumer	changer de chaîne	une publicité
faire la vaisselle	éteindre		une chaîne
faire ses devoirs	enregistrer		

Other useful words and expressions

s'appeler	d'abord	tout de suite
tôt	ensuite	
tard	enfin	

VIDÉOTOUR

Épisode 12

In this video episode, you will join Vincent as he "coaches" Manu through his morning routine. See page 537 for more information.

CHAPITRE 13

Les loisirs culturels

Objectifs

In this chapter you will learn to:

- *discuss movies, plays, and museums*
- *tell what you know and whom you know*
- *tell what happens to you or someone else*
- *refer to people and things already mentioned*
- *talk about some cultural activities in Paris*

Des statues béninoises du seizième siècle

Vocabulaire

Mots 1

Au cinéma

Pierre est devant le guichet.
La prochaine séance est à treize heures.

Qui joue dans ce film?
On joue un film étranger au Rex.
Le film est en V.O. (version originale).
On le voit avec des sous-titres.
Dans un autre cinéma, le film est doublé.
On peut le voir en français.

Qu'est-ce que tu veux voir?
Ça m'est égal.

Qu'est-ce qu'on joue au Rex?
Je ne sais pas. On peut regarder dans *l'Officiel des Spectacles.*
Les places coûtent combien?

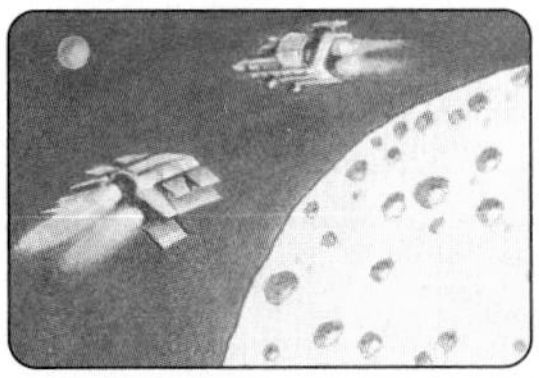
un film de science-fiction

un film d'horreur

un film policier

un documentaire

un dessin animé

un film d'amour

un film d'aventures

Au théâtre

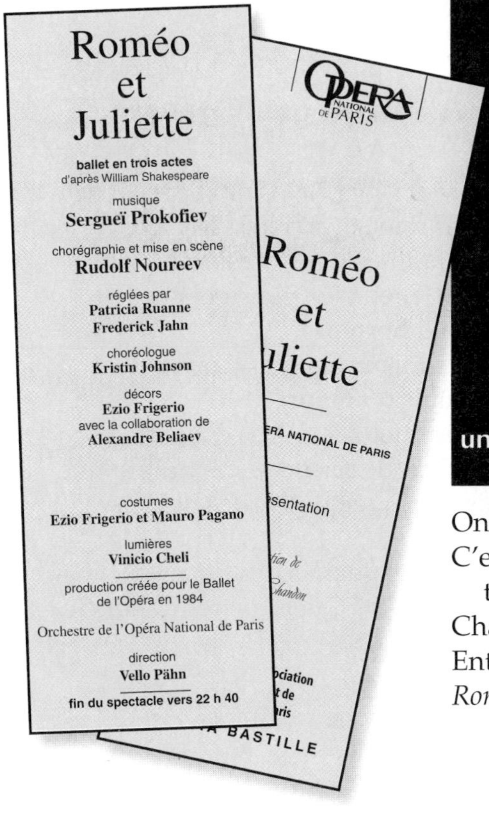
Roméo et Juliette

ballet en trois actes
d'après William Shakespeare

musique
Sergueï Prokofiev

chorégraphie et mise en scène
Rudolf Noureev

réglées par
Patricia Ruanne
Frederick Jahn

choréologue
Kristin Johnson

décors
Ezio Frigerio
avec la collaboration de
Alexandre Beliaev

costumes
Ezio Frigerio et Mauro Pagano

lumières
Vinicio Cheli

production créée pour le Ballet
de l'Opéra en 1984

Orchestre de l'Opéra National de Paris

direction
Vello Pähn

fin du spectacle vers 22 h 40

On va monter *Roméo et Juliette.*
C'est une pièce de théâtre en trois actes.
Chaque acte a deux scènes.
Entre deux actes, il y a un entracte.
Roméo et Juliette est aussi un ballet.

Voici d'autres genres de pièces:
- une tragédie
- une comédie
- un drame
- une comédie musicale

Quel est le mot?

Le cinéma Champollion, Paris

1 Fana de cinéma ou pas?

Donnez des réponses personnelles.

1. Tu vas souvent au cinéma?
2. Qu'est-ce que tu aimes comme films?
3. Quel est ton acteur préféré? Et ton actrice préférée? Il/Elle est très connu(e)?
4. Il y a un cinéma près de chez toi?
5. La première séance est à quelle heure?
6. Où est-ce que tu achètes les billets?
7. Tu fais souvent la queue devant le guichet?
8. Dans la salle de cinéma, tu aimes mieux une place près de l'écran ou loin de l'écran?
9. Si tu vas voir un film étranger, tu aimes mieux voir le film doublé ou en version originale avec des sous-titres?

2 Historiette Au cinéma Complétez.

Ce soir, on __1__ un très bon film au Wepler. C'est un film étranger. Il n'est pas doublé. Il y a des __2__. Le film est en __3__ originale. La prochaine __4__ est à quelle heure? Les __5__ coûtent combien?

Les garçons louent un DVD.

3 Tu aimes mieux quels genres de film?

Donnez des réponses personnelles.

1. Tu aimes mieux (préfères) les documentaires ou les westerns?
2. Tu aimes mieux les films policiers ou les films d'horreur?
3. Tu aimes mieux les films comiques ou les films d'amour?
4. Tu aimes mieux les films d'aventures ou les films de science-fiction?
5. Tu vas voir quelquefois des dessins animés?
6. Tu loues quelquefois des films en vidéo ou DVD? Quels genres de film?

4 Des pièces et des films Complétez.

1. Au lycée les élèves ____ une pièce tous les ans.
2. On voit un film au cinéma. On voit une pièce au ____.
3. Une ____ a des actes et les actes sont divisés en ____.
4. Entre deux actes, il y a un ____.
5. Un ____ joue le rôle de Roméo.
6. Une ____ joue le rôle de Juliette.
7. Dans une comédie musicale, les ____ chantent et les ____ dansent.

5 Historiette Au théâtre Donnez des réponses personnelles.

1. Tu aimes le théâtre?
2. Tu vas souvent au théâtre?
3. Il y a un théâtre là où tu habites?
4. Ton école a un club d'art dramatique?
5. Tu es membre de ce club?
6. Le club monte combien de pièces par an?
7. Cette année, le club va monter quelle pièce?
8. C'est quel genre de pièce?
9. Il y a combien d'actes?
10. Il y a combien d'entractes?

6 Mon film préféré Find out what a classmate's favorite movies are and why. Then find out which movies he or she dislikes and why. Take turns.

ENCORE PLUS
*For more practice using words from **Mots 1**, do Activity 42 on page H43 at the end of this book.*

Au musée

Une exposition de peinture et sculpture

Le musée n'est pas ouvert le mardi.
Il est ouvert tous les jours sauf le mardi.

Quel est le mot?

7 **Un peu de culture** Répondez d'après les dessins.

1. C'est un musée ou un théâtre?

2. Le musée est ouvert ou fermé?

3. Elle est peintre ou sculpteur?

4. C'est un tableau ou une statue?

8 **Historiette** Au musée

Inventez des réponses.

1. Michel sait comment s'appelle le peintre?
2. Il connaît le peintre personnellement?
3. Il connaît l'œuvre du peintre?
4. Annick sait dans quel musée il y a une exposition de Monet?
5. Elle trouve ses tableaux extraordinaires?
6. Elle connaît le musée de l'Orangerie?
7. Elle le visite souvent?
8. Elle sait que le musée est fermé le mardi?
9. Le musée de l'Orangerie est ouvert tous les jours sauf le mardi?

Claude Monet *Le bassin aux nymphéas*

9 **L'art français** Work with a classmate. Discuss together what you have learned so far about French art and French artists. Find out who appreciates art more and who knows more about art.

Paul Cézanne *Pommes et oranges*

Tours et crypte archéologique
de **Notre-Dame** **–12 ans : gratuit**

Rue de Cloître, Paris 4e. **M°**: Cité, ou **RER C**: St. Michel. Tours: **tél**: 01 44 32 16 72, groupes: 01 44 32 16 72. **Horaires**: 9h30-19h30 du 1.04 au 30.09; 10h-17h du 1.10 au 31.03. Fermeture des caisses 45mn plus tôt. Crypte: **tél**: 01 43 29 83 51. **Horaires**: 9h30-18h du 1.04 au 30.09; 10h-16h30 du 1.10 au 31.03.
Du haut des tours: une vue exceptionnelle sur la cathédrale et la ville. . . Dans la crypte archéologique: l'histoire de Paris de l'époque gallo-romaine au XIXe s.

Musée de l'**Ordre de la Libération** **–12 ans : gratuit**

Hôtel national des Invalides, 51 bis, boulevard de Latour-Maubourg, Paris 7e. **Tél**: 01 47 05 35 15. **M°**: Invalides. **Horaires**: 10h-17h.
Musée de la France Libre, de la Résistance et de la Déportation.

Musée d'**Orsay** **– 18 ans : gratuit**

1, rue de Bellechasse, Paris 7e. **Tél**: 01 40 49 48 14 . **M°**: Solférino, ou **RER C**: Musée d'Orsay. **Horaires**: 10h-18h, nocturne le jeudi jusqu' à 21h45. Le dimanche, et du 20.06 au 20.09: 9h-18h. Fermé le lundi.
Peintures impressionnistes et ensemble de la création artistique de 1848 à 1914.

10 **Renseignements** You're in Paris and you'd like to visit one of the museums listed in the brochure on the left. Call the museum and find out from the museum employee (your partner) where it's located, what time it opens and closes, what day it's closed, and how much a ticket costs. Your partner can use the information in the brochure to answer your questions.

ENCORE PLUS *For more practice using words from **Mots 2**, do Activity 43 on page H44 at the end of this book.*

Structure

Les verbes savoir et connaître
Telling whom and what you know

1. Study the following present-tense forms of the verbs **savoir** and **connaître,** both of which mean "to know."

SAVOIR		CONNAÎTRE	
je	sais	je	connais
tu	sais	tu	connais
il/elle/on	sait	il/elle/on	connaît
nous	savons	nous	connaissons
vous	savez	vous	connaissez
ils/elles	savent	ils/elles	connaissent

Note the **passé composé** of these verbs: **j'ai su, j'ai connu.**

2. You use **savoir** to indicate that you know a fact or that you know something by heart.

Tu sais à quelle heure la séance commence?
Tu sais le numéro de téléphone de Philippe?

3. You use **savoir** + infinitive to indicate that you know how to do something.

Tu sais danser le tango?
Il ne sait pas nager.

4. **Connaître** means "to know" in the sense of "to be acquainted with." You can use **connaître** only with nouns—people, places, and things. Compare the meanings of **connaître** and **savoir** in the sentences below.

Je sais comment elle s'appelle. Nathalie.	**Je connais bien Nathalie.**
Je sais où elle habite. À Grenoble.	**Je connais bien Grenoble.**
Je sais le nom de l'auteur. Victor Hugo.	**Je connais son œuvre.**

Grenoble, France

Comment dit-on?

11 **Qu'est-ce que tu sais?** Donnez des réponses personnelles.

1. Tu sais où habite ton ami(e)? Il/Elle habite dans quelle ville?
2. Tu connais bien cette ville?
3. Tu sais où on peut bien manger pour pas cher?
4. Tu sais le nom de l'auteur de *Hamlet?*
5. Tu connais les pièces de Shakespeare?
6. Tu connais *Hamlet?*

12 **On sait tout!** Complétez.

1. Moi, je ____ où se trouve le théâtre.
2. Paul, tu ____ quel est le numéro de téléphone?
3. Nous ne ____ pas l'adresse exacte.
4. Nos amis ____ à quelle heure la pièce commence.
5. Vous ____ quelle pièce on joue en ce moment à la Comédie-Française?
6. Il faut demander à Julie. Elle ____ tout.

13 **Qu'est-ce que tu connais?** Complétez.

1. Je ____ bien la France.
2. Les élèves de Mme Benoît ____ bien la peinture française.
3. Mais ils ne ____ pas très bien la littérature française.
4. Tu ____ la culture française?
5. Et Paul, il ____ la peinture française contemporaine?
6. Vous ____ les sculptures de Rodin?
7. Nous ____ des impressionnistes comme Monet, Manet et Renoir.
8. Tu ____ l'œuvre du peintre Edgar Degas?
9. Oui, je ____ son œuvre. J'adore ses danseuses.

Edgar Degas *Deux danseuses en scène*

14 **Tu le/la connais bien!** Work with a classmate. Think of someone in the class whom you know quite well. Tell your partner some things you know about this person. Don't say who it is. Your partner will guess. Take turns.

ENCORE PLUS

*For more practice using **savoir** and **connaître**, do Activity 44 on page H45 at the end of this book.*

Les pronoms me, te, nous, vous
Telling who does what for whom

1. The pronouns **me, te, nous,** and **vous** are object pronouns.

Marie t'invite au théâtre?	**Oui, elle m'invite au théâtre.**
Elle te parle au téléphone?	**Oui, elle me parle au téléphone.**
Le prof vous regarde?	**Oui, il nous regarde.**
Il vous explique la leçon?	**Oui, il nous explique la leçon.**

2. The object pronoun **me, te, nous,** or **vous** always comes right before the verb it is linked to.

Il	me parle.
Il ne	me parle pas.
Il veut	me parler.
Il ne veut pas	me parler.

Comment dit-on?

15 Historiette **Une invitation**

Répondez que oui.

1. Jean te téléphone?
2. Il te parle longtemps?
3. Il t'invite au cinéma?
4. Il te demande quel film tu veux voir?
5. Il te paie la place?
6. Après le film il t'invite au café?

Une conversation au café

16 Historiette **En classe** Répondez que oui.

1. En classe, la prof vous parle, à toi et aux autres élèves?
2. Elle vous apprend à lire et écrire en français?
3. Elle vous explique la grammaire?
4. Elle vous présente le vocabulaire?
5. Elle vous donne beaucoup de devoirs?
6. Elle vous donne trop de devoirs?
7. Elle vous parle toujours en français?

17 **Au rayon des chemisiers** Complétez avec **me** ou **vous.**

Je suis au rayon des chemisiers des Galeries Lafayette. La vendeuse __1__ parle. Elle __2__ demande:

La vendeuse: Vous désirez?
Moi: Je voudrais ce chemisier, s'il __3__ plaît. Je fais du 40.
La vendeuse: Je __4__ donne quelle couleur?
Moi: Qu'est-ce que vous __5__ proposez?
La vendeuse: Je ne sais pas. En bleu marine, il __6__ plaît?
Moi: Oui, il __7__ plaît.
La vendeuse: Mais je __8__ suggère d'essayer un 38.
Moi: D'accord. Je peux __9__ payer par carte de crédit?
La vendeuse: Mais bien sûr, mademoiselle!

18 **Pourquoi ça?** Répondez d'après le modèle.

Il me regarde!
Il te regarde? Pourquoi?

1. Il me pose des questions!
2. Il me parle!
3. Il me téléphone!
4. Il me dit son numéro de téléphone!
5. Il me donne son adresse!

JOYEUX ANNIVERSAIRE!

19 **Historiette** **C'est ton anniversaire.**
Inventez une histoire.

1. Tes copains vont te téléphoner le jour de ton anniversaire?
2. Ils vont te voir?
3. Ils vont t'inviter au cinéma ou au concert?
4. Ils vont te dire «Joyeux anniversaire!» ?
5. Ils vont te faire un gâteau?
6. Ils vont te donner des cadeaux?

Les pronoms le, la, les
Referring to people and things already mentioned

1. You have already learned to use **le, la, l',** and **les** as definite articles. These words are also used as direct object pronouns. A direct object receives the action of the verb. A direct object pronoun can replace either a person or a thing.

Singulier	Je connais ce film.	Je le connais.
	Je connais cet acteur.	Je le connais.
	J'admire cet acteur.	Je l'admire.
	Je connais cette pièce.	Je la connais.
	Je connais cette actrice.	Je la connais.
	J'admire cette actrice.	Je l'admire.
Pluriel	Je connais les tableaux de Monet.	Je les connais.
	Je connais les pièces de Molière.	Je les connais.
	Je connais ces actrices.	Je les connais.
	J'admire ces acteurs.	Je les‿z admire.

2. Just as with the pronouns **me, te, nous, vous,** the pronouns **le, la, l',** and **les** come right before the verb they are linked to.

Je le vois.
Je ne le vois pas.
Je veux le voir.
Je ne veux pas le voir.

Attention!

Note the elision and liaison with the direct object pronouns.
Vous l'admirez. **Vous les‿z admirez.**

Opéra Garnier, Paris

Comment dit-on?

20 **Contacts** Répondez d'après le modèle.

Tu vois toujours Mélanie?
Oui, je la vois de temps en temps.

1. Tu vois toujours Sylvie?
2. Tu vois toujours tes copains tunisiens?
3. Tu vois toujours Marc?
4. Tu vois toujours tes cousines de Lyon?
5. Tu vois toujours tes professeurs de l'année dernière?

21 **En version originale** Complétez.

Paul: On va voir le film doublé ou en V.O.?
Annick: On va __1__ voir en V.O.
Paul: Tu connais l'actrice principale?
Annick: Tu rigoles! Bien sûr que je ne __2__ connais pas, mais je sais qui c'est!
Paul: Tu comprends l'espagnol?
Annick: Oui, je __3__ comprends un peu.
Paul: Tu __4__ comprends assez bien pour comprendre le film?
Annick: Non, mais il y a des sous-titres. Alors je __5__ lis quand je ne comprends pas les dialogues.

22 Tout est très beau!

Répondez d'après le modèle.

—Tu vois la statue?

—Oui, je la trouve très belle.

1. Tu vois le théâtre?
2. Tu vois les tableaux?
3. Tu vois l'acteur?
4. Tu vois l'actrice?
5. Tu vois les sculptures?

Jean-Antoine Houdon *Molière*

23 Tout n'est pas très beau.

Refaites l'Activité 22 d'après le modèle.

—Tu vois la statue?

—Oui, mais je ne la trouve pas très belle.

Pierre Auguste Renoir *Bal du moulin de la Galette*

ENCORE PLUS *For more practice using pronouns, do Activity 45 on page H46 at the end of this book.*

24 **Demain** Répondez d'après le modèle.

—Tu as vu ce film?
—Non, mais je vais le voir demain.

1. Tu as vu cette pièce?
2. Tu as vu cette exposition?
3. Tu as vu ces sculptures de Rodin?
4. Tu as vu ces tableaux?
5. Tu as vu l'exposition des tableaux de Gauguin?

Auguste Rodin *Le penseur*

25 **Devinettes** Devinez ce que c'est.

1. On le présente quand on va dans un pays étranger.
2. On le prend pour voyager très loin.
3. On les lave avant de manger.
4. On les lave avec une brosse à dents.
5. On la remplit avant de débarquer.
6. On l'écoute attentivement en classe.

26 **Jeu** Encore des devinettes Work in groups and make up riddles similar to those in Activity 25. Ask other groups your riddles. The group that guesses the most riddles wins.

27 **L'artiste** Have some fun. Pretend you are an artist. Draw something. Have a classmate give a critique of your artwork. Take turns.

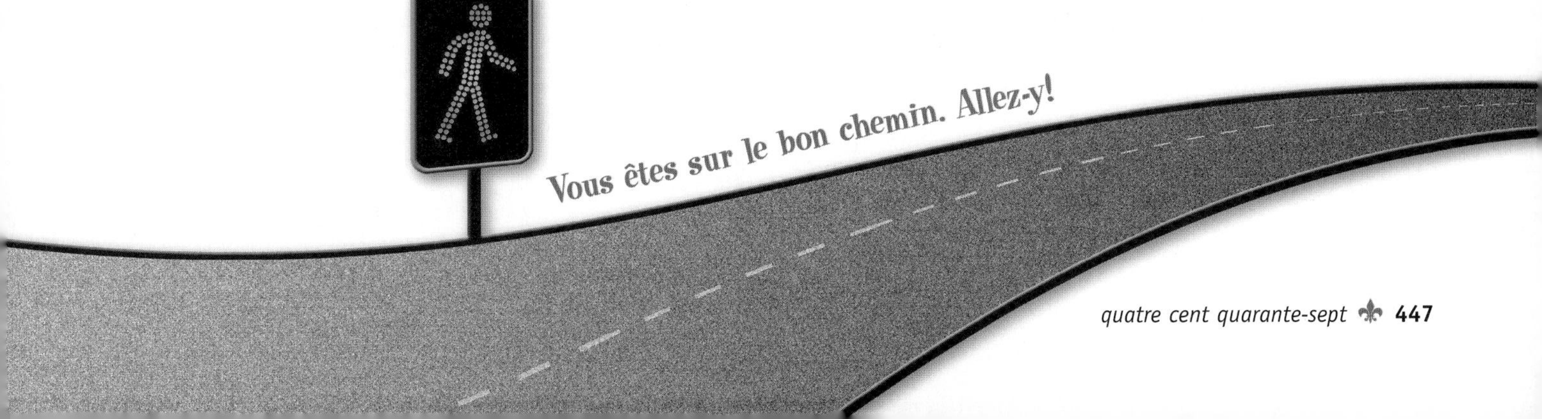
Vous êtes sur le bon chemin. Allez-y!

Conversation

On va au cinéma?

Bruno: Qu'est-ce que tu veux faire?
Léa: Je ne sais pas, moi. Aller au cinéma.
Bruno: Qu'est-ce que tu veux voir?
Léa: Ça m'est égal. Comme tu veux. Qu'est-ce qu'il y a de bien?
Bruno: Attends. Je vais te dire… *(Il prend* l'Officiel des Spectacles, *il l'ouvre et il le lit…)* Il y a un film avec Ricki Dean.
Léa: Ah non, pas Ricki Dean. Je le déteste, ce type. Il est parfaitement ridicule et il ne le sait même pas!
Bruno: Il y a un film espagnol au Ciné-Élysées. Ça t'intéresse?
Léa: Oui, un film espagnol, ça me dit. On va pouvoir travailler notre espagnol.
Bruno: Alors, il faut se dépêcher. La prochaine séance est à seize heures.

Vous avez compris?

Répondez.

1. Qu'est-ce que Léa veut faire?
2. Qui a *l'Officiel des Spectacles*?
3. Qui le lit?
4. Léa aime Ricki Dean? Pour quelle raison?
5. Bruno et Léa vont voir quel film?
6. Pourquoi est-ce que Léa veut voir un film espagnol?
7. Ils vont aller à quelle séance?

Parlons un peu plus

On va au cinéma? Look at the movie guide. Decide which movie you'd like to see and invite a classmate to see it with you. Tell your partner when and where the movie is playing, whether it is dubbed or in the original language with subtitles. Discuss whether or not you both want to see the movie or figure out an alternative.

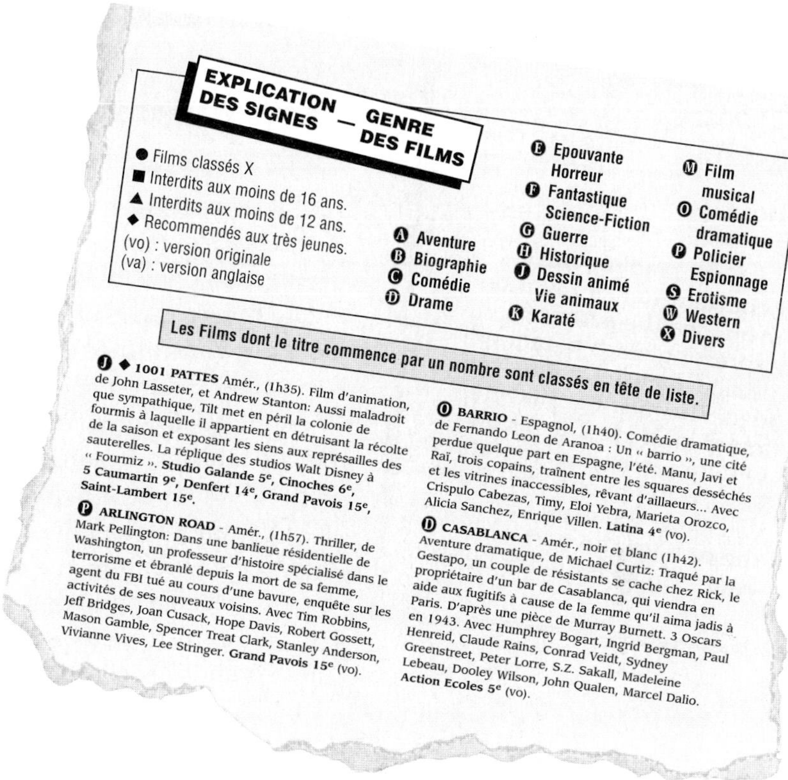

EXPLICATION DES SIGNES — GENRE DES FILMS

● Films classés X
■ Interdits aux moins de 16 ans.
▲ Interdits aux moins de 12 ans.
◆ Recommendés aux très jeunes.
(vo) : version originale
(va) : version anglaise

A Aventure
B Biographie
C Comédie
D Drame
E Epouvante Horreur
F Fantastique Science-Fiction
G Guerre
H Historique
J Dessin animé Vie animaux
K Karaté
M Film musical
O Comédie dramatique
P Policier Espionnage
S Erotisme
W Western
X Divers

Les Films dont le titre commence par un nombre sont classés en tête de liste.

J ◆ **1001 PATTES** Amér., (1h35). Film d'animation, de John Lasseter, et Andrew Stanton: Aussi maladroit que sympathique, Tilt met en péril la colonie de fourmis à laquelle il appartient en détruisant la récolte de la saison et exposant les siens aux représailles des sauterelles. La réplique des studios Walt Disney à « Fourmiz ». **Studio Galande 5e, Cinoches 6e, 5 Caumartin 9e, Denfert 14e, Grand Pavois 15e, Saint-Lambert 15e.**

P **ARLINGTON ROAD** - Amér., (1h57). Thriller, de Mark Pellington: Dans une banlieue résidentielle de Washington, un professeur d'histoire spécialisé dans le terrorisme et ébranlé depuis la mort de sa femme, agent du FBI tué au cours d'une bavure, enquête sur les activités de ses nouveaux voisins. Avec Tim Robbins, Jeff Bridges, Joan Cusack, Hope Davis, Robert Gossett, Mason Gamble, Spencer Treat Clark, Stanley Anderson, Vivianne Vives, Lee Stringer. **Grand Pavois 15e** (vo).

O **BARRIO** - Espagnol, (1h40). Comédie dramatique, de Fernando Leon de Aranoa : Un « barrio », une cité perdue quelque part en Espagne, l'été. Manu, Javi et Raï, trois copains, traînent entre les squares desséchés et les vitrines inaccessibles, rêvant d'aillaeurs... Avec Crispulo Cabezas, Timy, Eloi Yebra, Marieta Orozco, Alicia Sanchez, Enrique Villen. **Latina 4e** (vo).

D **CASABLANCA** - Amér., noir et blanc (1h42). Aventure dramatique, de Michael Curtiz: Traqué par la Gestapo, un couple de résistants se cache chez Rick, le propriétaire d'un bar de Casablanca, qui viendra en aide aux fugitifs à cause de la femme qu'il aima jadis à Paris. D'après une pièce de Murray Burnett. 3 Oscars en 1943. Avec Humphrey Bogart, Ingrid Bergman, Paul Henreid, Claude Rains, Conrad Veidt, Sydney Greenstreet, Peter Lorre, S.Z. Sakall, Madeleine Lebeau, Dooley Wilson, John Qualen, Marcel Dalio. **Action Ecoles 5e** (vo).

Prononciation

Le son /ü/

1. To say the sound **/ü/**, first say the sound **/i/**, then round your lips. Repeat the following words.

   une statue **une sculpture** **une peinture**
   une voiture **un musée**

2. The sound **/ü/** also occurs in combination with other vowels. Repeat the following words.

   aujourd'hui **depuis** **je suis** **huit**

3. Now repeat the following sentences.

   Tu as vu ces statues?
   C'est une sculpture très connue?
   Le musée est rue Sully depuis huit ans.

une statue

Le Québec

Lectures culturelles

Reading Strategy

Identifying the main idea

When reading, it is important to identify the main idea the author is expressing. Each paragraph usually discusses a different idea. The main idea is often found in the first or second sentence in each paragraph. First, skim the passage. Once you know the main idea of the passage, go back and read it again more carefully.

Les loisirs culturels en France

Les musées

Les musées en France sont toujours très fréquentés par les Français et par les touristes qui visitent la France. Tu connais les impressionnistes? Tu apprécies leurs tableaux? Alors il faut aller au musée d'Orsay. Le musée d'Orsay est une ancienne gare qui a été transformée en musée. C'est le musée du dix-neuvième siècle[1]. On trouve des tableaux, des sculptures, des meubles[2], tout du dix-neuvième siècle. Il y a une exposition permanente de tableaux des impressionnistes.

Si tu es fana d'art moderne, tu vas beaucoup aimer le centre Pompidou. Là, il y a toujours des expositions d'art moderne. Il y a aussi une vue extraordinaire sur Paris.

Mais la perle des musées français, c'est le Louvre. Au Louvre, tu peux admirer des tableaux et des sculptures de grands artistes de tous les siècles.

Le premier dimanche de chaque mois, l'entrée des musées nationaux est gratuite. Les autres dimanches, elle est demi-tarif[3]. C'est pourquoi les musées sont toujours combles le dimanche.

1 siècle *century*
2 meubles *furniture*
3 demi-tarif *half-price*

Centre Pompidou

Musée d'Orsay

La Polynésie française

Tahiti

Haïti

La Martinique

La France
La Suisse

Opéra Garnier

Le ballet et l'opéra

Si tu aimes la danse classique, il faut aller voir un ballet à l'opéra Garnier.

Si tu aimes l'opéra, il faut aller à l'opéra Bastille. On a inauguré le nouvel opéra sur la place de la Bastille en 1989 pour commémorer le bicentenaire de la Révolution française de 1789. Tu préfères l'architecture de quel opéra? De l'ancien opéra Garnier ou du nouvel opéra Bastille? L'architecture, c'est un art aussi, tu sais.

Le théâtre

Tu connais les grands auteurs dramatiques du dix-septième siècle: Racine, Corneille, Molière? Si tu as envie[4] d'aller voir une de leurs pièces, tu peux aller à la Comédie-Française, le plus vieux théâtre national du monde.

[4] as envie *feel like*

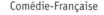

Opéra Bastille

Comédie-Française

La Tunisie

Vous avez compris?

A Les musées Répondez.

1. Qui fréquente les musées français?
2. Tu connais quelques peintres impressionnistes?
3. Tu apprécies leurs tableaux?
4. Tu connais leur œuvre?
5. Il y a une exposition permanente des impressionnistes dans quel musée?
6. Quel est le musée d'art moderne?
7. Quel est un autre musée très célèbre à Paris?
8. Qu'est-ce qu'il y a dans ce musée?
9. Les musées sont presque toujours combles le dimanche. Pourquoi?

B D'autres loisirs Répondez.

1. Tu es à Paris et tu veux voir un ballet. Tu vas où?
2. Tu veux voir un opéra. Tu vas où?
3. Tu veux voir une tragédie de Racine ou une comédie de Molière. Tu vas où?

Le Mali

Le Sénégal

Lecture supplémentaire

La musique africaine

Quand on parle de musique africaine, on parle de deux sortes de musique—la musique traditionnelle et la musique moderne pop. Il y a une grande différence entre les deux.

Un griot

La musique traditionnelle

La musique traditionnelle est la musique de la brousse[1], des villages ruraux. Cette musique traditionnelle accompagne toutes les activités de la vie quotidienne ainsi que[2] les événements mémorables de la vie sociale. Il y a de la musique pour les femmes, par exemple, de la musique pour les jeunes, pour les chasseurs[3], etc. À toutes ces festivités, les griots, des poètes musiciens, racontent des histoires et jouent de la musique. Tous les instruments de musique sont souvent faits à la main par les griots eux-mêmes[4].

Un musicien joue du kora, Gambie

La musique moderne

La musique pop africaine est devenue[5] très populaire au-dehors des pays africains, surtout en Europe. La première fois que vous l'entendez, vous pensez que c'est un mélange de rythmes latins et afro-américains des États-Unis comme le rock et le jazz. C'est vrai. Pourquoi? Parce que la musique africaine est à l'origine de la musique latino-américaine et de la musique afro-américaine d'aujourd'hui.

[1] brousse *brush*
[2] ainsi que *as well as*
[3] chasseurs *hunters*
[4] eux-mêmes *themselves*
[5] est devenue *has become*

Youssou N'Dour

Le chanteur sénégalais Youssou N'Dour a un très grand succès. Il est né dans le quartier pauvre de la Médina à Dakar. Il est fils et petit-fils de griots, les poètes musiciens en Afrique. C'est lui le plus grand interprète de la musique «fusion pop». C'est une fusion d'un rythme africain, le m'balax, avec des rythmes de reggae, de rock et de jazz.

Vous avez compris?

La musique africaine Vrai ou faux?

1. La musique traditionnelle d'Afrique, c'est la musique des grandes villes cosmopolites.
2. La musique traditionnelle varie selon l'événement.
3. Les griots sont des poètes et des musiciens.
4. Les griots jouent toujours de la guitare électrique.
5. La musique moderne africaine est très populaire en Europe.
6. Le rock et le jazz ont influencé la musique africaine.
7. Youssou N'Dour est un chanteur sénégalais très connu.
8. La musique latino-américaine est une fusion de musique africaine avec du reggae, du rock et du jazz.

CONNEXIONS

Les Beaux-Arts

La musique

Like painting and literature, music is a form of art. Think of all the times you hear music each day. Music has been an integral part of the daily lives of people since the beginning of recorded history.

Before reading some general information about music, let's take a look at some of the many cognates that exist in the language of music.

un ballet

un orchestre symphonique

un opéra

une fanfare

un chœur

The names of many musical instruments are also cognates.

un piano	**un saxophone**	**une trompette**
une guitare	**une flûte**	**une clarinette**
un accordéon	**un violon**	**une harpe**

La musique

Les instruments musicaux

On peut classifier les instruments musicaux en quatre groupes principaux—les instruments à cordes, les instruments à vent, les instruments à percussion et les instruments à clavier.

Un orchestre ou une fanfare

Quelle est la différence entre un orchestre et une fanfare? Une fanfare n'a pas d'instruments à cordes. Il n'y a pas de violons, par exemple. Et dans une fanfare, il n'y a pas de flûtes ni de hautbois[1]. Les fanfares qui jouent de la musique pendant les événements sportifs et qui participent aux défilés[2] sont plus populaires aux États-Unis qu'en France.

[1] hautbois *oboes* [2] défilés *parades*

L'opéra *Carmen*

L'orchestre symphonique

Un orchestre symphonique est un grand orchestre composé d'instruments de tous les groupes musicaux. Une symphonie est une composition musicale pour orchestre. Une symphonie est en général une composition ambitieuse qui dure de vingt à quarante-cinq minutes.

L'opéra

Un opéra est une composition dramatique sans dialogue parlé. Dans un opéra, les acteurs chantent; ils ne parlent jamais. Ils chantent des airs d'une beauté extraordinaire. L'orchestre les accompagne. L'histoire est en général très tragique. Un opéra comique est un opéra avec des dialogues parlés. Un opéra comique n'est pas nécessairement très amusant. Un opéra bouffe est un opéra dont l'histoire est une comédie. *Carmen* de Georges Bizet et *Dialogue des Carmélites* de Francis Poulenc sont deux opéras français très célèbres.

La musique populaire

Il y a toutes sortes de musique populaire. Il y a des groupes de jazz, de rock et de rap, par exemple. De nos jours, le rap et la musique techno sont très populaires. Les chansons populaires ont souvent des thèmes romantiques. Il y a toujours une relation intime entre la musique populaire et la danse.

La chanteuse Céline Dion

Vous avez compris?

A Des instruments Nommez.

1. un instrument à cordes
2. quelques instruments à vent

B Vous le savez? Répondez.

1. Quelle est la différence entre un orchestre et une fanfare?
2. Qu'est-ce qu'un opéra?
3. Quels sont quelques types de musique populaire?

C'est à vous

Maison du Roi, Bruxelles, Belgique

Use what you have learned

PARLER

1 Pour t'amuser

✔ *Discuss movies, plays, and museums*

Work with a classmate. Pretend you're on vacation in Brussels in Belgium. You meet a Belgian teenager (your partner) who's interested in what you do for fun in your free time. Tell him or her about your leisure activities. Then your partner will tell you about what he or she does.

PARLER

2 Une journée au musée

✔ *Ask and answer questions about a museum visit*

Work in groups of three or four. Pretend that one or two of you spent the day at a museum last Saturday. Other friends have some questions. Describe your museum visit and be sure to answer all their questions.

Musée du Louvre

ÉCRIRE

3 Une affiche

✔ *Make a poster for a play*

Prepare a poster in French for your school play. Give all the necessary information to advertise **le spectacle.**

ÉCRIRE

4 Des renseignements, s'il vous plaît.

✔ *Write for information about cultural events*

You're going to spend a month in the French city of your choice. Write a letter or an e-mail to the tourist office **(le syndicat d'initiative)** asking for information about cultural events during your stay. Be sure to mention your age, what kind of cultural activities you like, and the dates of your stay.

Une colonne Morris, Paris

Les Grandes Heures du Parlement

L'Assemblée nationale présente dans l'aile du Midi du Château de Versailles un musée qui vous permet de découvrir la salle des séances du Congrès du Parlement, troisième hémicycle de la République, dans laquelle vous assisterez à un spectacle audiovisuel sur les grands débats de la Nation.

Sur le pourtour de cette salle, vous revivrez deux cents ans d'histoire parlementaire et vous vous familiariserez avec le travail au quotidien du député. Vous découvrirez l'activité internationale du Parlement français et ses liens avec les différents parlements du monde.

Prix d'entrée

Individuel:visite libre avec audioguide
Tarif normal: 4€ - Tarif réduit 3€ - Gratuit pour les scolaires

Group de 30 personnes au plus: visite commentée
Tarif normal: 40€ - Tarif réduit 30€ - Gratuit pour les scolaires

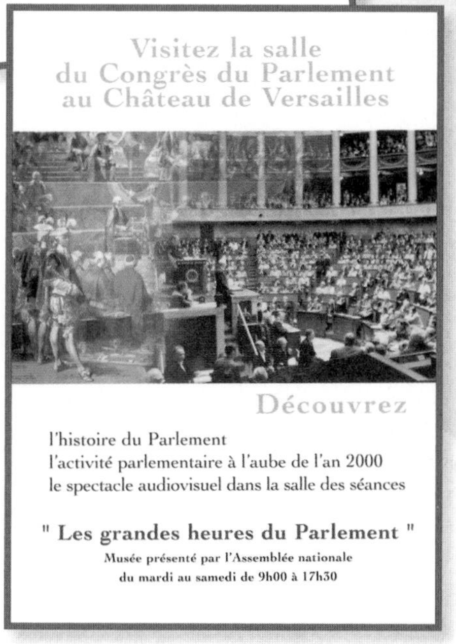

Visitez la salle
du Congrès du Parlement
au Château de Versailles
Découvrez
l'histoire du Parlement
l'activité parlementaire à l'aube de l'an 2000
le spectacle audiovisuel dans la salle des séances
" Les grandes heures du Parlement "
Musée présenté par l'Assemblée nationale
du mardi au samedi de 9h00 à 17h30

Writing Strategy

Persuasive writing Persuasive writing is writing that encourages a reader to do something or to accept an idea. Newspaper and magazine advertisements, as well as certain articles, are examples of persuasive writing. As you write, present a logical argument to encourage others to follow your line of thinking. Your writing should contain sufficient evidence to persuade readers to "buy into" what you are presenting. Explain how your evidence supports your argument; end by restating your argument.

ÉCRIRE

5 Un reportage

Your local newspaper has asked you to write an article to attract French-speaking readers to a cultural event taking place in your community. You can write about a real or fictitious event. You have seen the event and you really liked it. Tell why as you try to convince or persuade your readers to go see it.

Vocabulaire

1 Choisissez.

To review **Mots 1**, turn to pages 432–433.

1. On joue des films où?
   - **a.** dans une séance
   - **b.** dans une salle de cinéma
   - **c.** dans un théâtre
2. Qui joue dans un film?
   - **a.** des acteurs et des actrices
   - **b.** des sous-titres
   - **c.** des joueurs
3. Une pièce de théâtre est divisée en quoi?
   - **a.** en version originale
   - **b.** en entractes
   - **c.** en actes et en scènes
4. Le film est doublé?
   - **a.** Oui, il y a deux films.
   - **b.** Non, il est en V.O.
   - **c.** Oui, il y a des sous-titres.
5. Qu'est-ce que *l'Officiel des Spectacles?*
   - **a.** un magazine
   - **b.** une place
   - **c.** un film

2 Identifiez.

To review **Mots 2**, turn to pages 436–437.

6.

7.

8.

9.

10.

Structure

3 Récrivez.

11. Je sais le numéro.
    Vous __________.
12. Vous connaissez mon ami?
    Il ________________?

To review the verbs ***savoir*** *and* ***connaître,*** *turn to page 440.*

4 Complétez avec «savoir» ou «connaître».

13. Je ____ son numéro de téléphone.
14. Vous ____ où il habite, non?
15. Je ____ très bien l'œuvre de cet artiste.
16. Tu ____ Paris?
17. Ils ____ danser le tango.

5 Répondez avec un pronom.

To review the object pronouns, turn to pages 442–444.

18. Il te parle au téléphone? Oui, ____.
19. Tu invites Jean? Oui, ____.
20. Tu vas inviter sa petite amie aussi? Oui, ____.
21. Le prof vous donne beaucoup de devoirs? Oui, ____.
22. Tu vois la petite fille? Oui, ____.
23. Tu connais les pièces de Molière? Oui, ____.

Culture

6 Identifiez.

24. un musée à Paris
25. un auteur français dramatique du dix-septième siècle

To review this cultural information, turn to pages 450–451.

Musée du Louvre, Paris

On parle super bien!

Tell all you can about this illustration.

Vocabulaire

Discussing a movie

un cinéma
une salle de cinéma
un guichet
une place
une séance
un écran

un film comique
policier
d'horreur
de science-fiction
d'aventures
d'amour

un documentaire
un dessin animé
étranger
en V.O.
doublé
avec des sous-titres

jouer un film
louer une vidéo

Describing a play

un théâtre
une pièce
un acteur
une actrice
un chanteur
une chanteuse

un danseur
une danseuse
une scène
un acte
un entracte
une tragédie

une comédie
un drame
monter une pièce
chanter
danser

How well do you know your vocabulary?

- **Choose the name of a cultural event or artistic profession.**
- **Have a classmate tell you his or her favorite in the category you chose.**

Describing a museum visit

un musée
une exposition
un tableau
une sculpture
une statue

une œuvre
une peinture
un(e) peintre
un sculpteur *(m. et f.)*

Other useful words and expressions

connaître
savoir
ouvert
fermé

célèbre
connu
sauf
ça (m')est égal

VIDÉOTOUR

Épisode 13

In this video episode, you will join Chloé and Vincent as they experience some cultural wonders. See page 538 for more information.

CHAPITRE 14

La santé et la médecine

Objectifs

In this chapter you will learn to:

- *explain a minor illness to a doctor*
- *have a prescription filled at a pharmacy*
- *tell for whom something is done*
- *talk about some more activities*
- *give commands*
- *refer to people, places, and things already mentioned*
- *discuss medical services in France*

Édouard Vuillard *Le docteur Viau dans son cabinet*

DES FRANCS
BOURGEOIS
PHARMACIE
Essayez
si vous êtes
un homme !
BASIC
HOMME
HERBORISTERIE
DIETETIQUE
EST

Vocabulaire
Mots 1

On est malade.

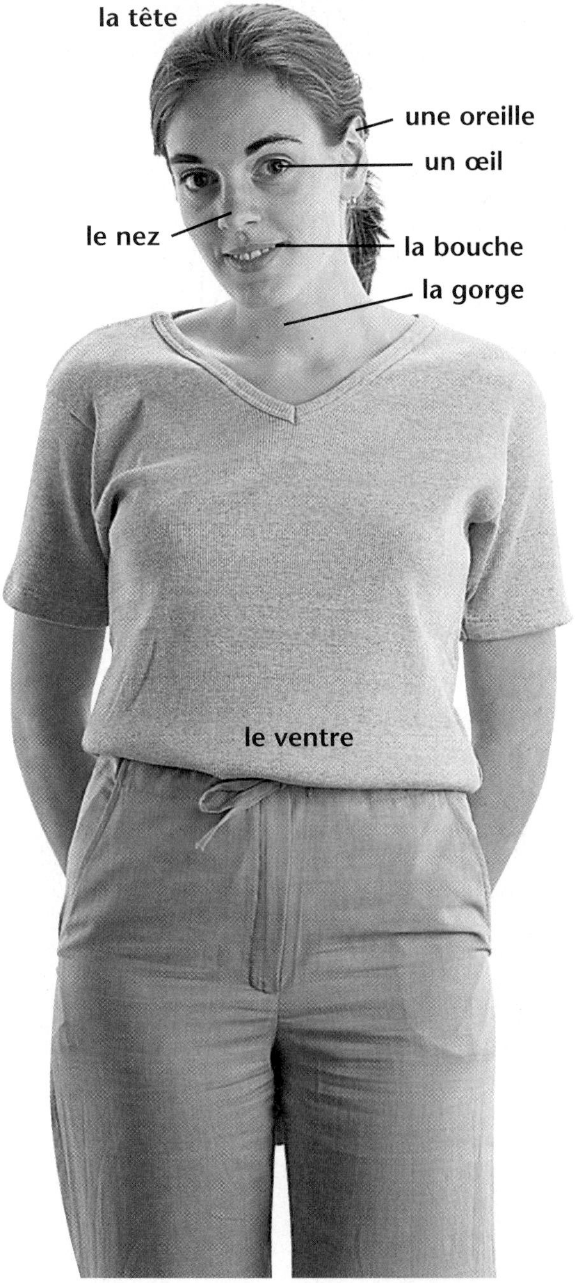

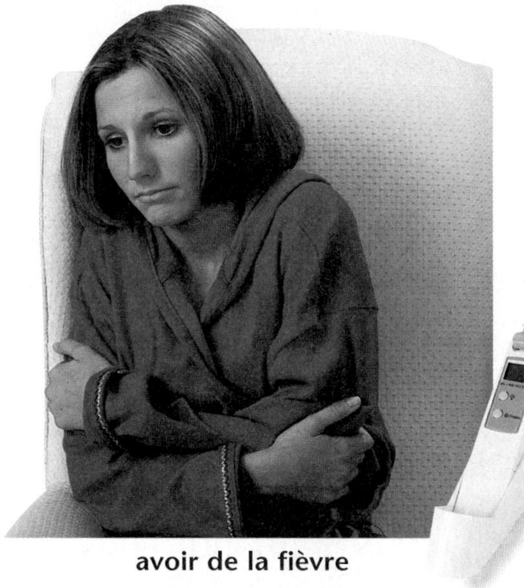
avoir de la fièvre

Paul a un rhume.
Il est enrhumé.
Il éternue.
Il a besoin d'un kleenex ou d'un mouchoir.

David tousse.

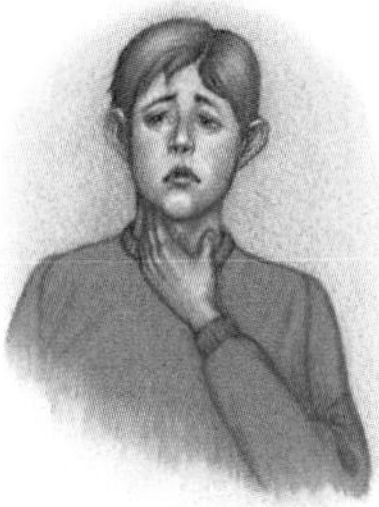

Christophe a très mal à la gorge.
Il a une angine.

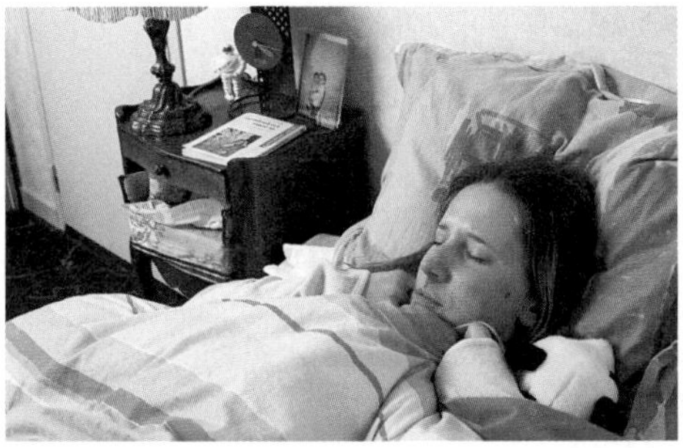

La pauvre Miriam, qu'est-ce qu'elle a?
Elle a la grippe.
Elle a de la fièvre.
Elle a des frissons.

Martin n'est pas en bonne santé.
Il est en mauvaise santé.
Il est très malade, le pauvre.
Il ne se sent pas bien. Il se sent très mal.

Elle a mal à la tête.

Note

Study the following cognates related to health and medicine:

allergique	**un sirop**
bactérien(ne)	**de l'aspirine**
viral(e)	**une infection**
une allergie	**de la pénicilline**
un antibiotique	**la température**

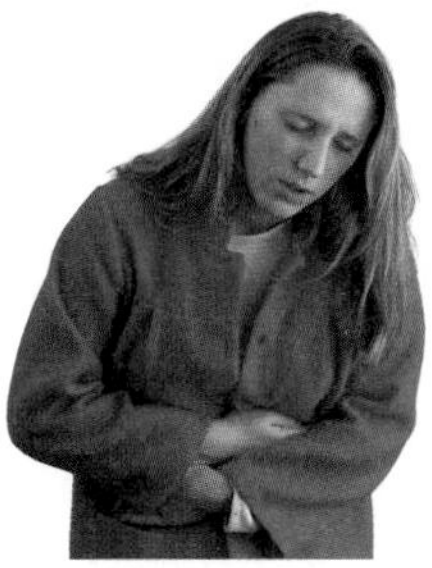

Elle a mal au ventre.

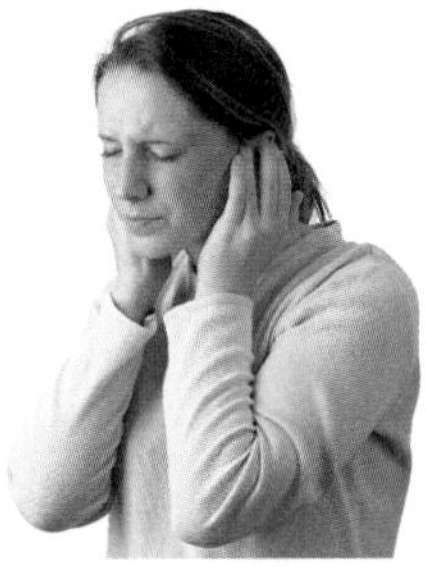

Elle a mal aux oreilles.

Elle a le nez qui coule.

Elle a les yeux qui piquent.

Elle a la gorge qui gratte.

Quel est le mot?

1 Qu'est-ce que c'est?

Identifiez.

2 Historiette Qu'est-ce qu'il a?

Inventez une histoire.

1. David est malade?
2. Il ne se sent pas bien?
3. Qu'est-ce qu'il a?
4. Il a de la fièvre et des frissons?
5. Il a la gorge qui gratte?
6. Il a les yeux qui piquent et le nez qui coule?
7. Il a mal à la tête?
8. Il a mal au ventre?
9. Il a mal aux oreilles?

3 Historiette La santé Donnez des réponses personnelles.

1. Tu es en bonne santé ou en mauvaise santé?
2. Quand tu es enrhumé(e), tu as le nez qui coule?
3. Tu as les yeux qui piquent?
4. Tu as la gorge qui gratte?
5. Tu tousses?
6. Tu éternues?
7. Qu'est-ce qu'on te dit quand tu éternues?
8. Tu as mal à la tête?
9. Tu ne te sens pas bien?
10. Tu as de la fièvre quand tu as un rhume?
11. Et quand tu as la grippe, tu as de la fièvre?
12. Quand tu as de la fièvre, tu as quelquefois des frissons?

4 **On a mal.** Complétez.

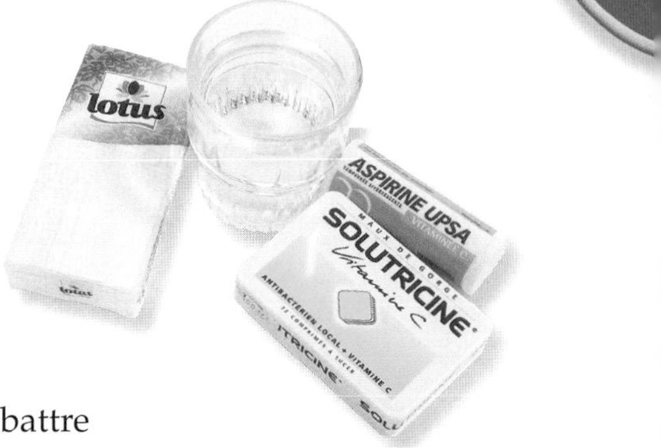

1. On prend de l'aspirine quand on a mal à la ____.
2. Si on a très mal à la gorge, on a une ____.
3. La ____ est un antibiotique.
4. L'aspirine et les antibiotiques sont des ____.
5. On ne peut pas prendre de pénicilline quand on est ____ à la pénicilline.
6. Si on a une température de 40° Celsius, on a de la ____.
7. Quand on est toujours malade, on est en ____.
8. On donne des antibiotiques comme la pénicilline pour combattre des infections bactériennes, pas des infections ____.
9. Quand on a le nez qui coule, on a besoin d'un ____ ou d'un ____.
10. Quand on a un rhume, on ____ et on ____.
11. Quand on est enrhumé ou quand on écoute la musique trop fort, on a mal aux ____.

5 **Qu'est-ce que tu as?** Work with a classmate. Ask him or her what the matter is. Your classmate will tell you. Then suggest something he or she can do to feel better. Take turns.

6 **Devinette** Have some fun! Work with a classmate and look at the following illustrations and French sayings. Together come up with some English equivalents.

Je ne suis pas dans mon assiette aujourd'hui.

Tu vas vite être sur pied.

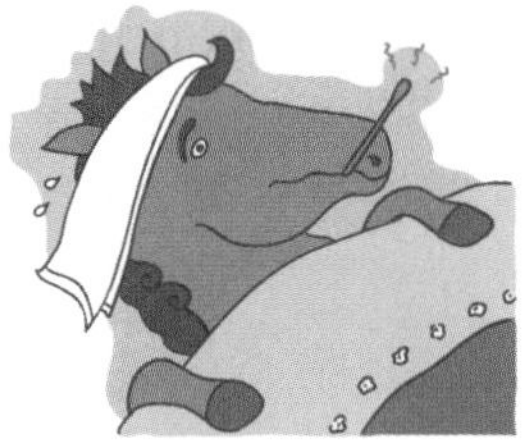

Il a une fièvre de cheval.

Ça fait mal. Aïe aïe aïe!

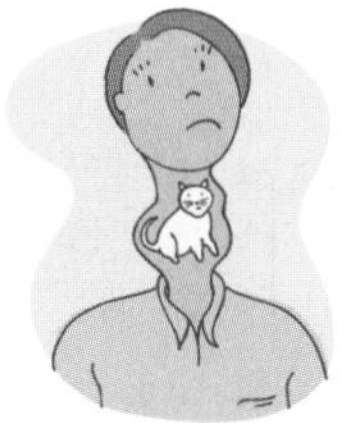

J'ai un chat dans la gorge.

ENCORE PLUS *For more practice using words from **Mots 1**, do Activity 46 on page H47 at the end of this book.*

Vocabulaire Mots 2

Chez le médecin

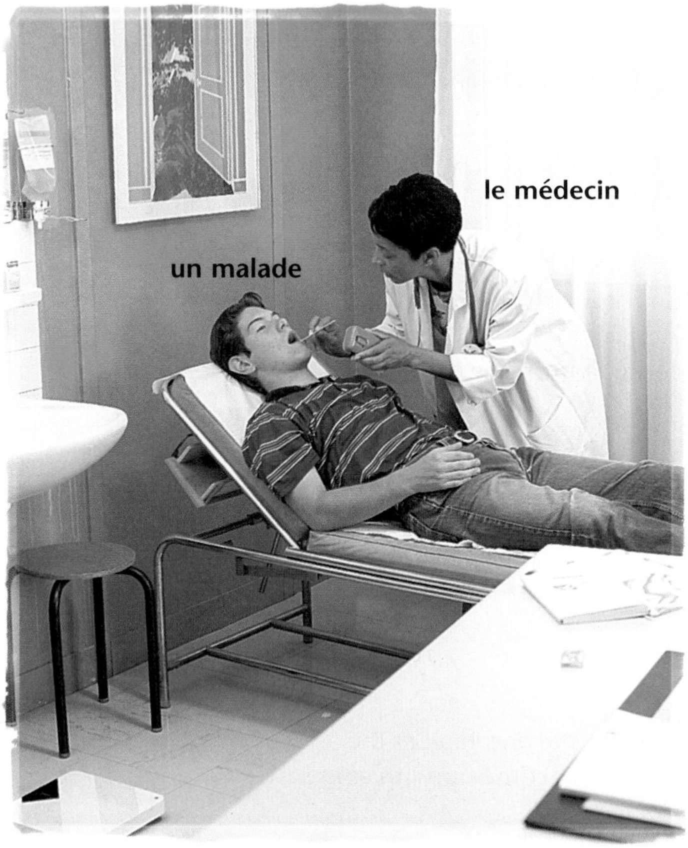

Le médecin examine le malade.
Le malade ouvre la bouche.
Le médecin examine la gorge du malade.

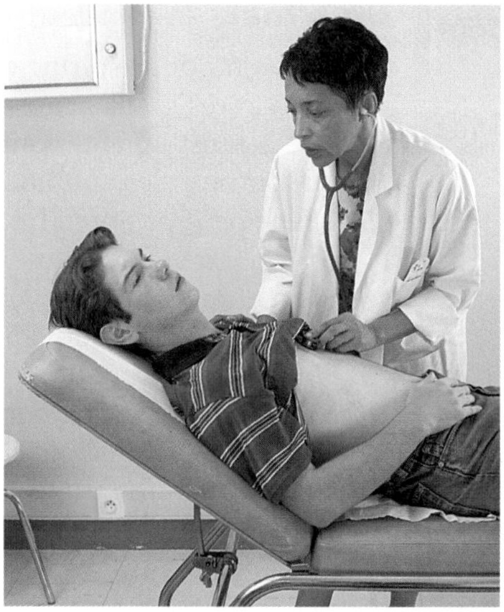

Elle ausculte le malade.
Il souffre, le pauvre.

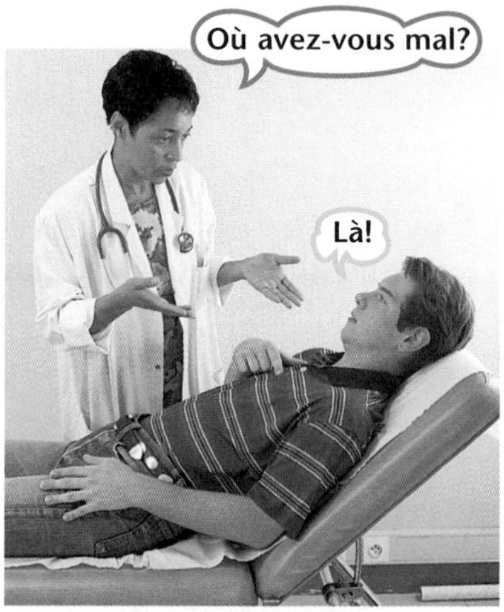

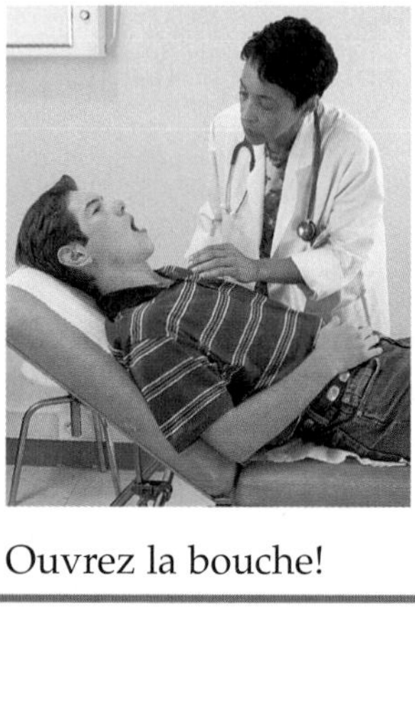

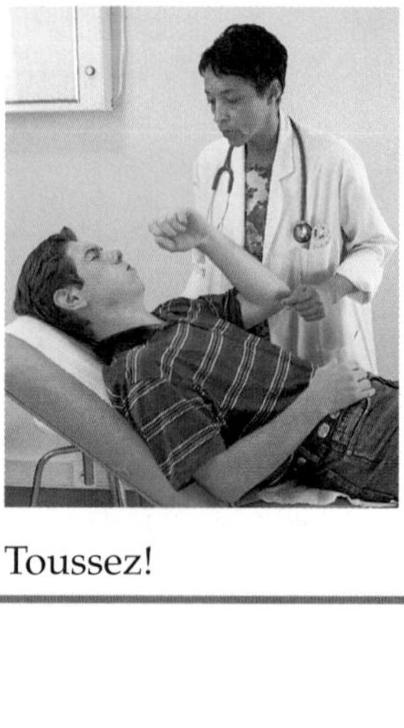

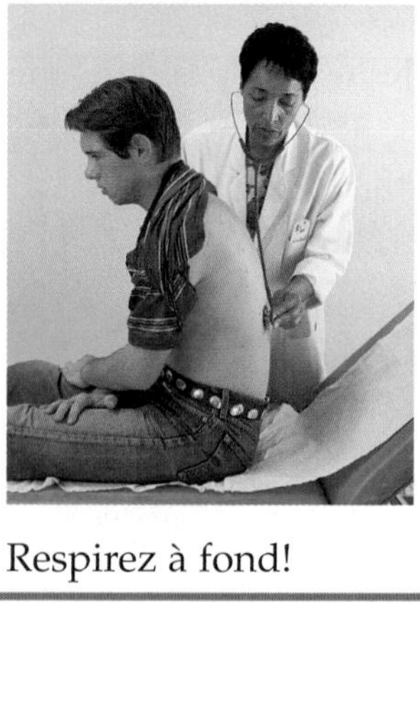

Le médecin parle. | Ouvrez la bouche! | Toussez! | Respirez à fond!

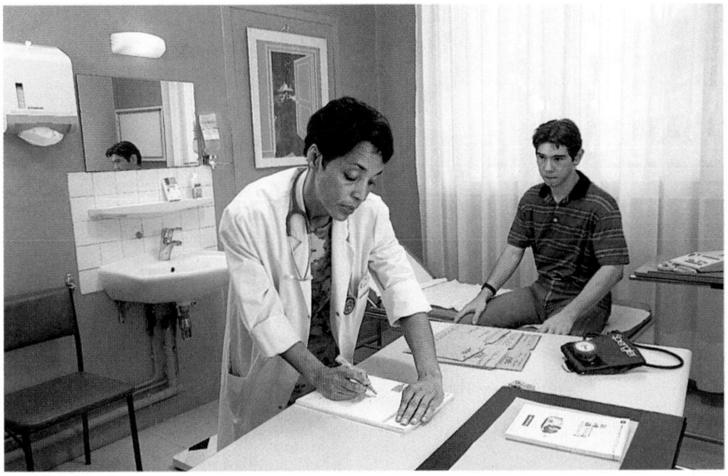

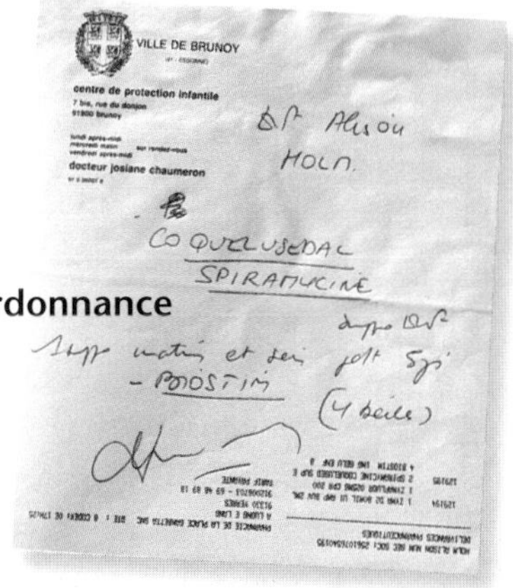

Le médecin fait un diagnostic.
Sébastien a une sinusite aiguë.
Le médecin lui prescrit des antibiotiques.
Elle lui fait une ordonnance.

À la pharmacie

Qu'est-ce que la pharmacienne donne à Sébastien?
Elle lui donne des médicaments.

Sébastien prend les médicaments.
Il va mieux.

Quel est le mot?

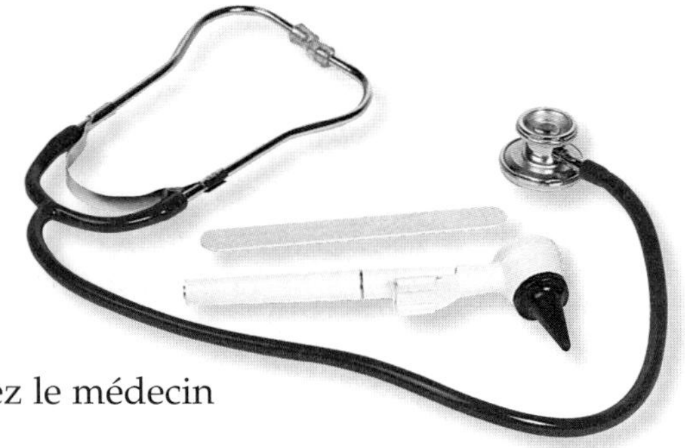

7 **Il est malade.** Choisissez.

1. Où est le malade?
   a. au travail **b.** à la crémerie **c.** chez le médecin
2. Qui souffre?
   a. le médecin **b.** le malade **c.** le pharmacien
3. Qu'est-ce que le médecin examine?
   a. la fièvre **b.** la grippe **c.** la gorge
4. Qu'est-ce que le malade ouvre?
   a. le ventre **b.** la bouche **c.** l'oreille
5. Quand le médecin l'ausculte, comment respire le malade?
   a. à fond **b.** rien **c.** bien
6. Qui est-ce que le médecin ausculte?
   a. le malade **b.** le pharmacien **c.** la pharmacienne
7. Que fait le médecin?
   a. des comprimés **b.** des médicaments **c.** des diagnostics
8. Qu'est-ce qu'il a, le malade?
   a. une cassette **b.** une sinusite aiguë **c.** un grand nez
9. Qu'est-ce que le médecin lui fait?
   a. un pharmacien **b.** une ordonnance **c.** des antibiotiques
10. Qu'est-ce qu'elle prescrit?
    a. des yeux **b.** des ordonnances **c.** des comprimés

Une pharmacie

8 **Historiette** Chez le médecin

Donnez des réponses personnelles.

1. Tu vas chez le médecin quand tu es malade?
2. Le médecin te demande où tu as mal?
3. Qu'est-ce que tu réponds au médecin?
4. Quand tu as une angine, tu as mal où?
5. Qu'est-ce que le médecin te dit quand il t'ausculte?
6. Le médecin fait un diagnostic?
7. Il te prescrit des antibiotiques?
8. Tu vas à la pharmacie pour acheter des médicaments?
9. Tu prends quelquefois de l'aspirine? Quand?
10. Pour avaler des comprimés, qu'est-ce que tu bois?
11. Après quelques jours, tu vas mieux?

9 **Je ne suis pas dans mon assiette.** Work with a classmate. Yesterday you did something that made you feel ill today. Using the first list below, tell a classmate what you did. He or she has to guess what's wrong with you, choosing from the second list.

trop regarder la télé →
—Hier, j'ai trop regardé la télé.
—Tu as mal aux yeux.

lire pendant six heures	**être enrhumé(e)**
manger trop de chocolat	**avoir mal aux yeux**
passer beaucoup d'examens	**avoir mal aux pieds**
faire une longue promenade	**être fatigué(e)**
étudier jusqu'à trois heures du matin	**avoir mal aux oreilles**
écouter de la musique trop fort	**avoir mal à la tête**
jouer dans la neige en t-shirt	**avoir mal au ventre**

10 **Qu'est-ce que tu as?** You were absent from school today. Your classmate, a French exchange student, is concerned about you and calls to find out how you are feeling. Let him or her know and tell all that you are doing to get better.

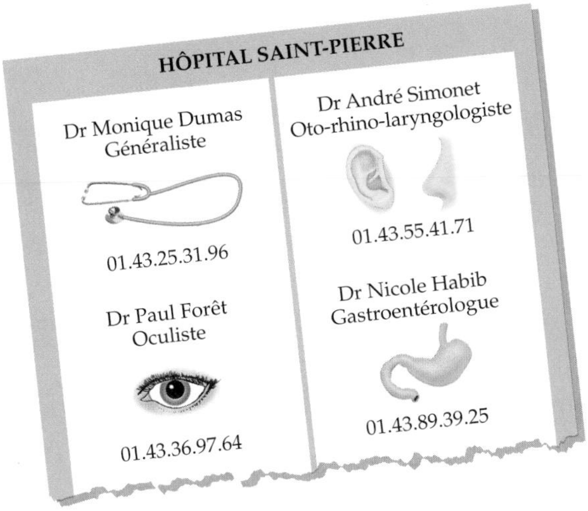

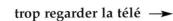

11 **Quel médecin?** While on a trip to France, you get sick. Describe your symptoms. A classmate will look at the list of doctors at the Hôpital Saint-Pierre and tell you which one to call and what the phone number is.

—J'ai mal à la gorge.
—On va appeler le docteur Simonet au 01.43.55.41.71.

12 **Au cabinet de consultation** Work with a classmate. You're sick. The doctor (your partner) will ask you questions about your symptoms. Answer the doctor's questions as completely as you can. Then reverse roles.

*For more practice using words from **Mots 2**, do Activity 47 on page H48 at the end of this book.*

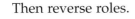

Structure

Les pronoms lui, leur
Telling what you do for others

1. You have already learned the direct object pronouns **le, la,** and **les.** Now, you will learn the indirect object pronouns **lui** and **leur.** Observe the difference between a direct and an indirect object in the following sentences.

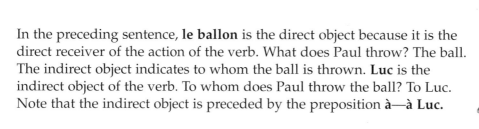

Paul lance le ballon à Luc.

Paul lance → le ballon.

Paul lance → le ballon ↗ à Luc.

In the preceding sentence, **le ballon** is the direct object because it is the direct receiver of the action of the verb. What does Paul throw? The ball. The indirect object indicates to whom the ball is thrown. **Luc** is the indirect object of the verb. To whom does Paul throw the ball? To Luc. Note that the indirect object is preceded by the preposition **à—à Luc.**

2. The indirect object pronouns in French are **lui** and **leur.** Note that the masculine and feminine forms are the same. Study the following chart.

Singulier	Le médecin parle à Pierre. Le médecin parle à Marie.	} Il lui parle.
Pluriel	Le médecin parle à ses patients. Le médecin parle à ses patientes.	} Il leur parle.

Just like the direct object pronouns, the indirect object pronouns **lui** and **leur** come right before the verb they are linked to.

Je	lui parle.
Je ne	lui parle pas.
Je veux	lui parler.
Je ne veux pas	lui parler.

Rappelez-vous que...

The object pronouns **me, te, nous, vous** are both direct and indirect.

Je te vois.
Je te parle.

Comment dit-on?

13 Historiette Une consultation

Répondez en utilisant **lui.**

1. Le médecin parle à Paul?
2. Il demande à Paul s'il a de la fièvre?
3. Paul explique ses symptômes au médecin?
4. Le médecin dit à Paul qu'il a de la fièvre?
5. Il donne une ordonnance à Paul?
6. Paul téléphone à la pharmacienne?

14 Un match de foot

Complétez avec **lui** ou **leur.**

1. Il lance le ballon à Marianne? Oui, il ___ lance le ballon.
2. Les joueurs parlent à l'arbitre? Oui, ils ___ parlent.
3. Et l'arbitre parle aux joueurs? Oui, il ___ parle.
4. L'arbitre explique les règles aux joueuses? Oui, il ___ explique les règles.
5. L'employée au guichet parle à un spectateur? Oui, elle ___ parle.

15 Personnellement

Répondez en utilisant **lui** ou **leur.**

1. Tu parles souvent à tes professeurs?
2. Tu dis toujours bonjour à ton professeur de français?
3. Tu vas téléphoner à ton copain/ta copine ce week-end?
4. Tu aimes parler à tes copains au téléphone?
5. Tu parles souvent à tes copains?
6. Tu vas écrire à tes grands-parents?

16 Des cadeaux pour tout le monde?

Work with a classmate. Describe your favorite friends or relatives. Then tell what you buy or give to each one as a gift.

ENCORE PLUS For more practice using **lui** and **leur**, do Activity 48 on page H49 at the end of this book.

Les verbes souffrir et ouvrir
Describing more activities

1. The verbs **souffrir** and **ouvrir** are conjugated the same way as regular **-er** verbs in the present.

SOUFFRIR		OUVRIR	
je	souffre	j'	ouvre
tu	souffres	tu	ouvres
il/elle/on	souffre	il/elle/on (n)	ouvre
nous	souffrons	nous (z)	ouvrons
vous	souffrez	vous (z)	ouvrez
ils/elles	souffrent	ils (z) /elles (z)	ouvrent

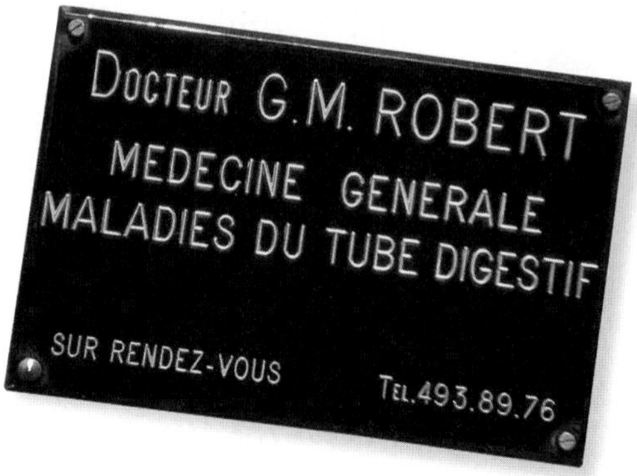

2. Note the past participles.

souffrir → **souffert** **Ils ont beaucoup souffert.**
ouvrir → **ouvert** **Il a ouvert la bouche.**

Comment dit-on?

17 Historiette Elle est malade.

Inventez des réponses.

1. Caroline souffre d'une angine?
2. Quand tu souffres d'une angine, tu as mal où?
3. Caroline va chez le médecin?
4. Quand le médecin lui examine la gorge, Caroline ouvre la bouche?
5. Le médecin lui donne une ordonnance?
6. Caroline va à la pharmacie?
7. Elle donne l'ordonnance au pharmacien?
8. Le pharmacien lui donne un paquet de comprimés?
9. Caroline ouvre le paquet?
10. Elle avale un comprimé?
11. Elle ne souffre plus?

À la pharmacie

L'impératif
Telling people what to do

1. You use the imperative to give commands and make suggestions. The forms are usually the same as the **tu, vous,** and **nous** forms. Note that the **nous** form means "Let's . . ."

PARLER	FINIR	ATTENDRE
Parle à ton prof!	Finis tes devoirs!	Attends ton ami.
Parlez à votre prof!	Finissez vos devoirs!	Attendez votre ami.
Parlons à notre prof!	Finissons nos devoirs!	Attendons notre ami.

2. Note that with **-er** verbs, you drop the final **s** of the **tu** form. The same is true for **aller** and verbs like **ouvrir.**

Regarde!
Va voir le médecin!
Ouvre la bouche!

3. In negative commands, you put the **ne... pas** or any other negative expression around the verb.

Ne respirez plus!
Ne dis rien.

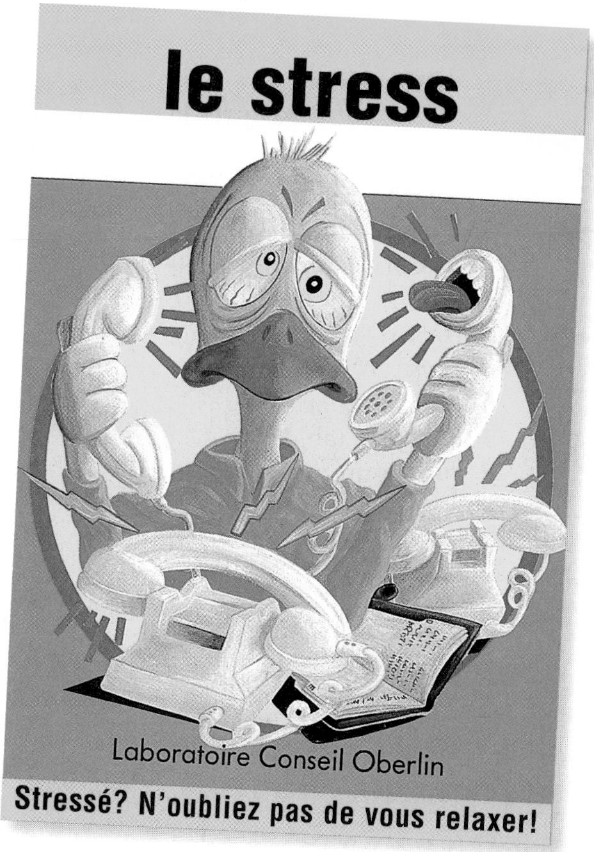
le stress
Laboratoire Conseil Oberlin
Stressé? N'oubliez pas de vous relaxer!

Comment dit-on?

18 **La loi, c'est moi!** Donnez un ordre à un copain ou à une copine d'après le modèle.

—regarder
—Regarde!

1. téléphoner à Jean
2. passer l'examen
3. parler français
4. travailler plus
5. préparer le dîner
6. ouvrir la porte
7. mettre la table
8. choisir un film
9. faire le travail
10. écrire l'exercice

Hôpitaux de Toulouse
La Santé sans tabac
Avec l'aimable autorisation de la M.N.H.
Afin de protéger votre santé et par mesure de sécurité, nous vous prions de ne pas fumer. Merci de votre compréhension
Décret n°92/478 du 29-5-92 Règlement intérieur du CHU de TOULOUSE

19 **Et vous aussi**
Donnez un ordre d'après le modèle.

—regarder
—Regardez.

1. téléphoner à Jean
2. passer l'examen
3. parler français
4. travailler plus
5. préparer le dîner
6. ouvrir la porte
7. mettre la table
8. choisir un film
9. faire le travail
10. écrire l'exercice

ENCORE PLUS *For more practice using the commands, do Activity 49 on page H50 at the end of this book.*

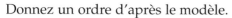

20 **Ne fais pas ça!** Donnez un ordre à un copain ou à une copine d'après le modèle.

—regarder
—Ne regarde pas!

1. lire le journal
2. écrire une lettre
3. prendre le métro
4. attendre devant la porte
5. descendre
6. aller plus vite
7. faire attention
8. entrer
9. sortir

YEUX ROUGES,
YEUX IRRITES
DÉCOUVREZ CE COLLYRE EN MONODOSES!
ANTALYRE®
Une monodose stérile, pratique, évitant la contamination
Ceci est un médicament. Lire attentivement la notice. Pas en-dessous de 36 mois. Contre-indiqué en cas de glaucome. Demandez conseil à votre pharmacien.
ANTALYRE®
Collyre en monodoses

21 **Ne faites pas ça!**
Refaites l'Activité 20 d'après le modèle.

—regarder
—Ne regardez pas!

22 **Allons-y!** Répondez d'après le modèle.

On invite Marie?
D'accord, invitons Marie!

1. On va à la plage?
2. On nage?
3. On fait du ski nautique?
4. On prend notre petit déjeuner?
5. On dîne au restaurant?
6. On sort?

23 **Jeu** **Jacques a dit...** This game is called "Simon Says" in English. Play in groups of five people or more. Give orders to your classmates. If you say **Jacques a dit** first, they have to obey the order. If you don't say **Jacques a dit** first, they should not obey your order. If they do, they are eliminated.

Le pronom en

Referring to people, places, and things already mentioned

1. The pronoun **en** is used to replace a noun that is introduced by **de** or any form of **de—du, de la, de l', des. En** refers mostly to things.

Tu as de l'aspirine?	Oui, j' en ai.
Il parle de sa santé?	Oui, il en parle.
Vous sortez de l'hôpital?	Oui, j' en sors.
Tu prends des médicaments?	Oui, j' en prends.

2. You also use the pronoun **en** with numbers or expressions of quantity. Note that in this case **en** refers not only to things but also to people.

Tu as des frères?	**Oui, j'en ai deux.**
Il prend combien de comprimés?	**Il en prend trois par jour.**
Il a combien de CD?	**Il en a beaucoup.**

3. Just like other pronouns, **en** comes directly before the verb whose meaning it is linked to.

Il en parle.
Il n'en parle pas.
Il veut en parler.
Il ne veut pas en parler.

Savez-vous que... ?

En comes after **y** in the expression **il y a.**
Il y en a deux.
Il y en a beaucoup.
Il n'y en a pas.

Comment dit-on?

24 Historiette La fête de Laurence Répondez d'après le modèle.

—Laurence sert du coca?
—Oui, elle en sert.

1. Elle sert de l'eau minérale?
2. Elle sert des sandwichs?
3. Elle sert de la pizza?
4. Elle sert de la salade?
5. Elle sert du fromage?
6. Elle sert des chocolats?
7. Elle sert de la glace?
8. Elle sert de la mousse au chocolat?

25 Dans le frigo Répondez d'après le modèle.

du coca →
—Il y a du coca dans ton frigo?
—Non, il n'y en a pas.

1. de l'eau minérale
2. de la glace
3. des légumes surgelés
4. du jambon
5. des tartes
6. de la viande

26 Historiette Tu es malade?

Répondez d'après le modèle.

Tu manges du chocolat? (trop)
Oui, j'en mange trop!

1. Tu prends combien de comprimés? (trois)
2. Tu bois de l'eau? (un litre)
3. Tu manges des fruits? (beaucoup)
4. Tu lis des magazines? (deux ou trois)
5. Tu regardes des vidéos? (trop)

27 Devinettes Devinez ce que c'est.

1. On en prend quand on est malade.
2. On en boit beaucoup quand on a de la fièvre.
3. On en utilise pour se laver les mains.
4. On en met sur une brosse à dents pour se laver les dents.
5. On en donne au vendeur quand on achète quelque chose.

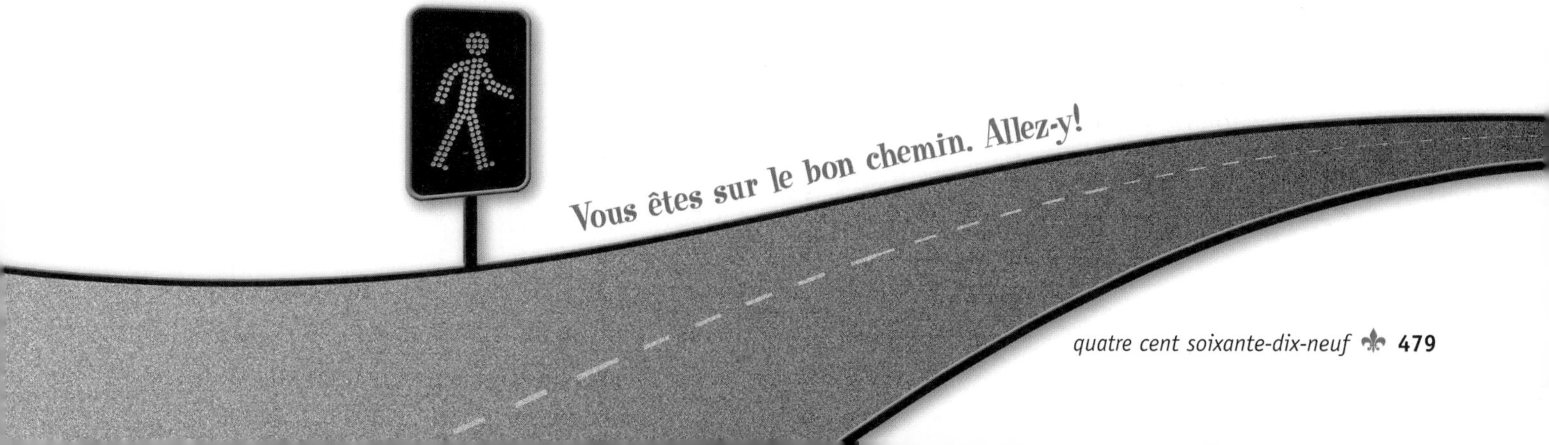
Vous êtes sur le bon chemin. Allez-y!

Conversation

Chez le médecin

Sylvie: Bonjour, docteur.
Médecin: Bonjour, Sylvie. Alors, qu'est-ce qui ne va pas?
Sylvie: Je ne sais pas… Je ne me sens pas bien du tout.
Médecin: Tu as mal où?
Sylvie: Ben, j'ai mal un peu partout, mais surtout à la gorge.
Médecin: Tu as mal à la tête?
Sylvie: Oui, à la tête aussi. Et j'ai froid, j'ai des frissons…
Médecin: Tu dois avoir de la fièvre. Ouvre la bouche, s'il te plaît. Dis «Aaa… »
Sylvie: Aaa…
Médecin: Tu as la gorge très rouge. C'est certainement une angine.
Sylvie: Une angine!
Médecin: Oui, mais ce n'est pas grave. Je vais te donner des antibiotiques. Tu vas en prendre trois par jour pendant une semaine.

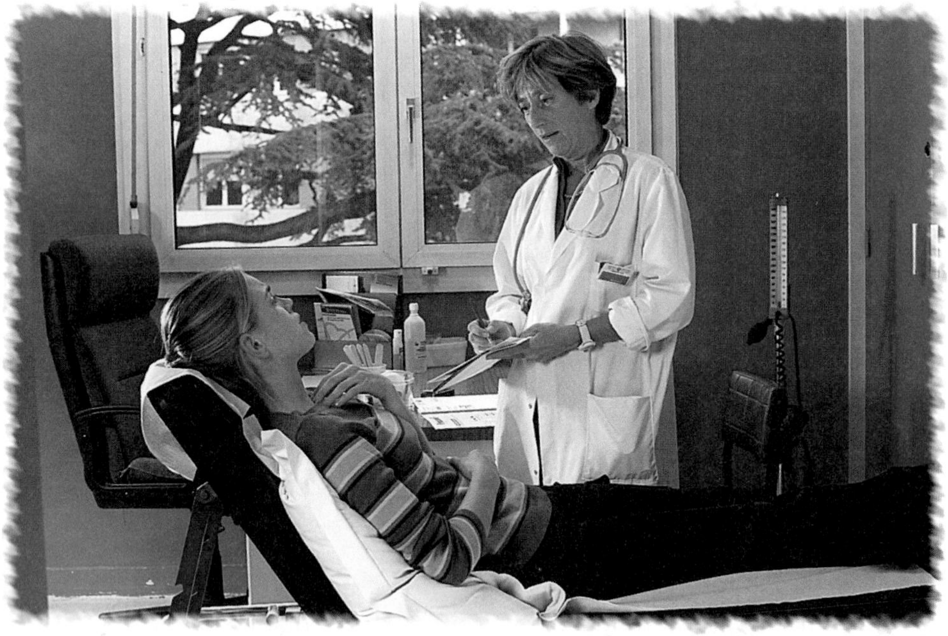

Vous avez compris?

Répondez.

1. Qui est malade?
2. Quels sont ses symptômes?
3. Elle a mal où?
4. Sylvie ouvre la bouche. Pourquoi?
5. Qu'est-ce que le médecin lui donne?
6. Sylvie doit prendre combien de comprimés par jour?
7. Pendant combien de temps?

Parlons un peu plus

A **Tu dois ou tu ne dois pas être médecin.** Work with a classmate. Interview each other and decide who would make a good doctor. Make a list of questions for your interview. One question you may want to ask is: **Tu as beaucoup de patience ou très peu de patience?**

B **Je suis très malade.** Imagine you're sick with a cold, the flu, or a sore throat. Tell the doctor (your partner) what your symptoms are. He or she makes a diagnosis and tells you what to do to get better. Use the model as a guide.

J'ai de la fièvre et des frissons.
Vous avez la grippe. Restez au lit et prenez de l'aspirine.

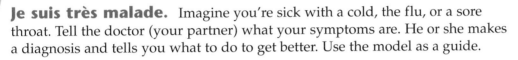

Prononciation

Les sons /u/ et /ü/

1. It is important to make a distinction between the sounds **/u/** and **/ü/,** since many words differ only in these two sounds. Repeat the following pairs of words.

   vous / vu **dessous / dessus** **roux / rue**
   loue / lu **tout / tu**

2. Now repeat the following sentences.

   Tu as beaucoup de température?
   J'éternue toutes les deux minutes.

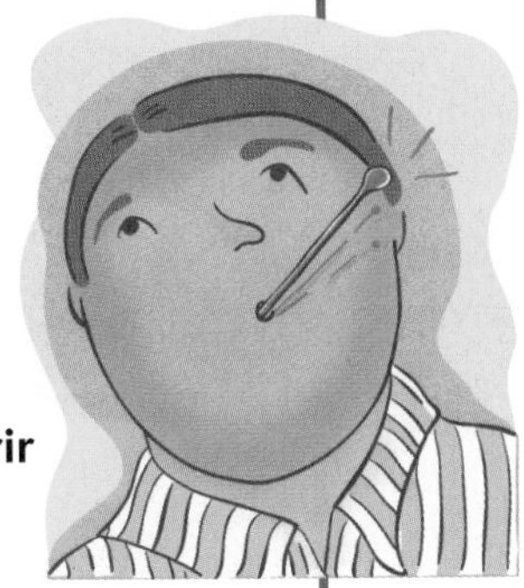

souffrir

température

Lectures culturelles

> **Reading Strategy**
>
> **Identifying important concepts**
>
> A quick way to identify the important concepts in a passage is to first read the questions that follow it. This will tell you what ideas the author is emphasizing and what type of information you should look for as you read.

Une consultation

La pauvre Mélanie. Elle est très malade! Elle tousse. Elle éternue. Elle a mal à la tête. Elle a de la température. Elle a des frissons. Elle n'est pas du tout dans son assiette. Elle veut appeler le médecin, mais c'est le week-end et son médecin ne donne pas de consultations le week-end. La seule solution, c'est d'appeler S.O.S. Médecins.

S.O.S. Médecins est un service qui envoie des médecins à domicile[1]. Un médecin arrive chez Mélanie et l'examine. Elle l'ausculte, elle lui prend sa température. Elle lui dit qu'elle a la grippe. Mais ce n'est pas grave. Elle va être vite sur pied. Le médecin lui fait une ordonnance. Elle prescrit des

[1] à domicile *to the home*

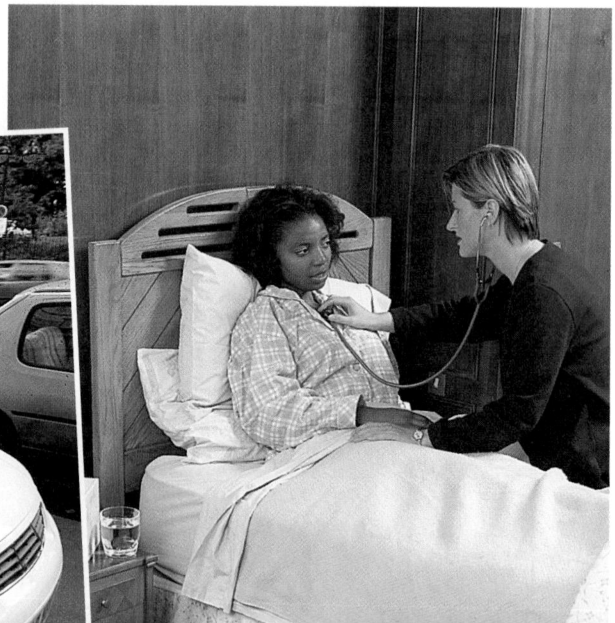

Le médecin ausculte la malade.

antibiotiques: trois comprimés par jour pendant une semaine. Mélanie va en prendre un à chaque repas.

Mélanie paie le médecin. Mais en France, la Sécurité Sociale rembourse les honoraires des médecins, c'est-à-dire l'argent qu'on donne aux médecins. Les honoraires et tous les frais[2] médicaux sont remboursés de 80 à 100% (pour cent) par la Sécurité Sociale.

[2] frais *expenses*

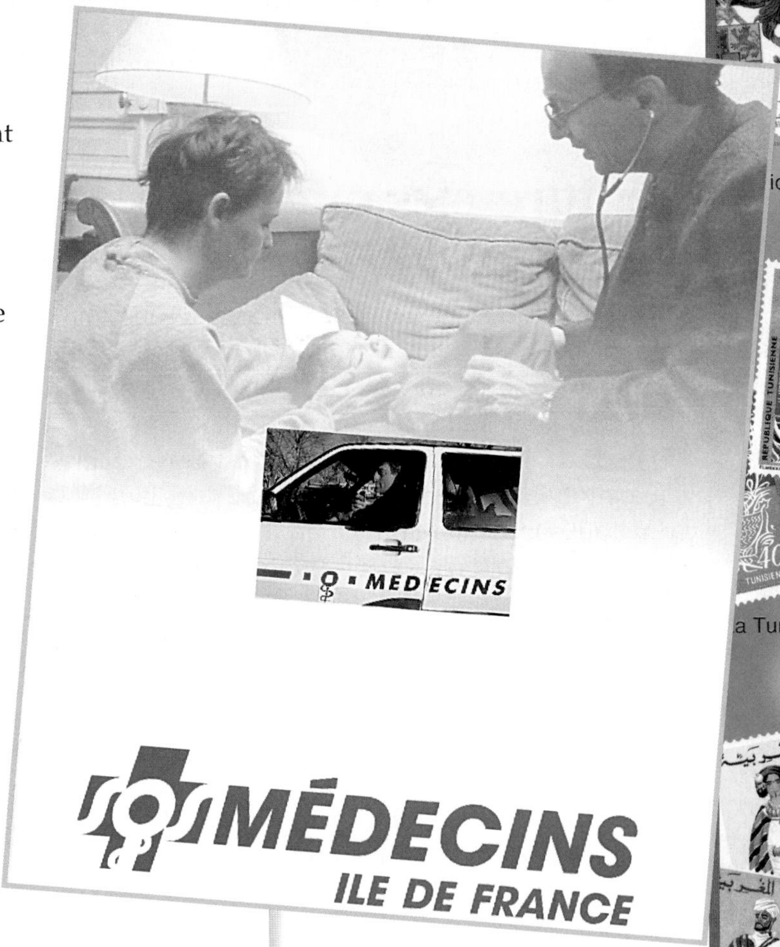

Vous avez compris?

A Autrement dit

Dites d'une autre façon.

1. Mélanie a *de la fièvre.*
2. Elle *ne se sent pas bien.*
3. Elle veut *téléphoner au* médecin.
4. Le médecin *ne voit pas de malades* le week-end.
5. S.O.S. Médecins envoie des médecins *chez les malades.*
6. Le médecin *écoute la respiration de* Mélanie.
7. La grippe n'est pas une maladie *alarmante.*
8. Mélanie va vite *se sentir mieux.*

B La pauvre Mélanie

Répondez.

1. Mélanie est très malade?
2. Elle a de la fièvre?
3. Elle a mal au ventre?
4. Elle veut appeler le médecin?
5. Son médecin donne des consultations tous les jours?
6. Mélanie téléphone à qui?
7. Le médecin lui prescrit de l'aspirine?
8. Les frais médicaux ne sont pas remboursés en France?

C En France

Qu'est-ce que vous avez appris sur les médecins et les services médicaux en France?

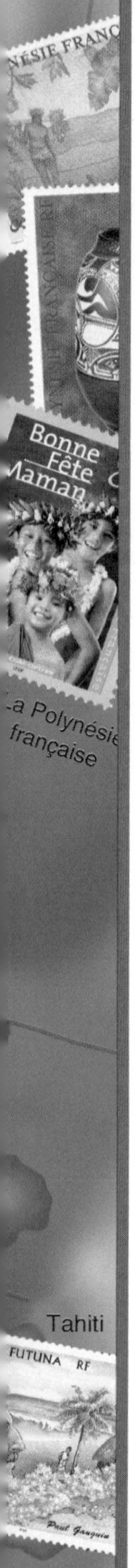

Lecture supplémentaire 1

Culture et santé

La culture influence la santé et la médecine? Certainement. Par exemple, en France tout le monde parle de son foie[1]. Les Français disent souvent, «J'ai mal au foie.» Aux États-Unis, on n'entend jamais dire ça. Pourquoi? Parce qu'aux États-Unis, une maladie du foie, c'est grave. Mais quand un Français dit qu'il a mal au foie, il veut dire tout simplement qu'il a un trouble digestif. Rien de grave. Il n'est peut-être pas dans son assiette aujourd'hui, mais il va vite être sur pied!

Aux États-Unis, par contre, on parle beaucoup d'allergies. De nombreux Américains souffrent d'une petite allergie. Les symptômes d'une allergie ressemblent aux symptômes d'un rhume. On éternue et on a souvent mal à la tête. Une allergie, c'est désagréable, mais d'habitude ce n'est pas grave. En France, on parle moins souvent d'allergies. Pourquoi? Qui sait? Vive la différence!

[1] foie *liver*

LES TROUBLES DIGESTIFS

Vous avez compris?

Des différences Répondez.

1. On dit souvent qu'on a mal au foie dans quel pays?
2. Que veut dire un Français quand il dit qu'il a mal au foie?
3. Et pour un Américain, qu'est-ce que cela veut dire «J'ai mal au foie»?
4. Qui parle souvent d'allergies?
5. Quels sont les symptômes d'une allergie?

Lecture supplémentaire 2

Les services médicaux en France

En France, il y a de grands hôpitaux avec tout l'équipement haut de gamme[1] nécessaire à la pratique d'une médecine moderne. On compte plus de 3 500 établissements de soins polyvalents[2]. Il y a à peu près 900 établissements hospitaliers publics et plus de 2 500 cliniques privées. Beaucoup de ces cliniques ressemblent à des hôtels.

En France, on fait beaucoup de recherches médicales et pharmaceutiques. C'est à l'Institut Pasteur de Paris que le docteur Montagnier a isolé le virus du sida[3]. Aujourd'hui à l'Institut Pasteur on continue à faire des recherches contre cette terrible maladie.

[1] haut de gamme *state of the art*
[2] soins polyvalents *general care*
[3] sida *AIDS*

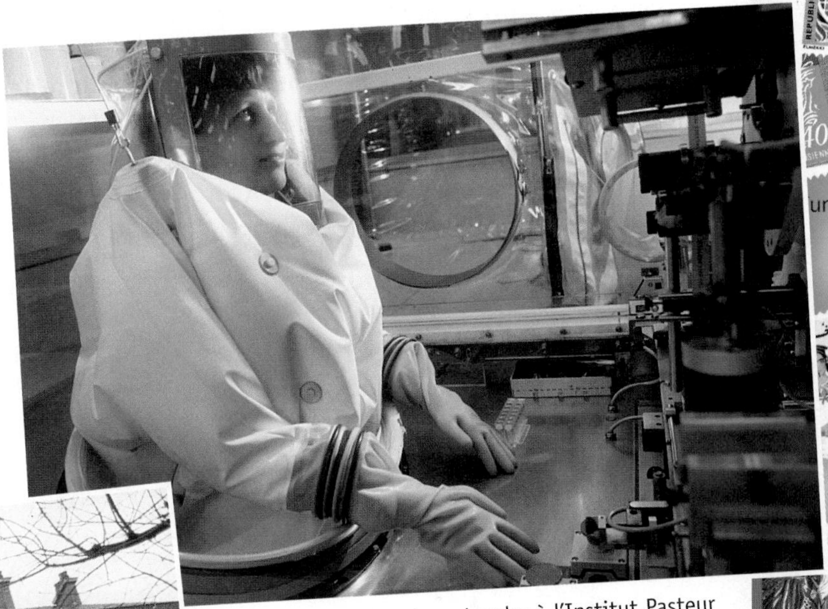

Un laboratoire de recherche à l'Institut Pasteur

L'Institut Pasteur, Paris

Vous avez compris?

Des mots apparentés Trouvez les mots apparentés dans la lecture.

CONNEXIONS

Les sciences naturelles

La diététique

Good nutrition is very important. What we eat can determine if we will enjoy good health or poor health. For this reason, it is most important to have a balanced diet and avoid the temptation to eat "junk food."

Read the following information about nutrition in French. Before reading this selection, however, look at the following groups of related words. Often if you know the meaning of one word you can guess the meaning of several words related to it.

individuel, individu
actif, activité
consommation, consommer, consommateur
adolescent, adolescence
âge, âgé

Un bon régime[1]

Il est très important d'avoir une alimentation équilibrée[2] pour être en bonne santé. Un régime équilibré comporte une variété de légumes et de fruits, des céréales, de la viande et du poisson.

Tout le monde a besoin de calories, mais le nombre idéal dépend de l'individu—de son métabolisme, de sa taille, de son âge et de son activité physique. Les adolescents, par exemple, ont besoin de plus de calories que les personnes âgées. Ils ont besoin de plus de calories parce qu'ils sont plus actifs et ils sont en période de croissance[3].

Les protéines

Les protéines sont particulièrement importantes pour les enfants et les adolescents parce qu'ils sont en pleine croissance. Les protéines aident à fabriquer des cellules. La viande et les œufs contiennent des protéines.

[1] régime *diet* [2] équilibrée *balanced* [3] croissance *growth*

Les glucides (les hydrates de carbone)

Les glucides (les pommes de terre, les pâtes comme les spaghettis, le riz[4]) sont la source d'énergie la plus efficace pour le corps humain.

Les lipides (les graisses)

Les lipides sont aussi une bonne source d'énergie. Mais pour les personnes qui ont un taux de cholestérol élevé[5], les graisses ne sont pas bonnes. Il faut faire un régime sans graisse. Il faut les éliminer.

Les minéraux

Beaucoup de minéraux sont essentiels pour le corps humain. Le calcium est absolument nécessaire pour les os[6] et les dents.

L'eau

L'eau est absolument essentielle au corps humain qui est fait de 65% d'eau.

Les vitamines

Les vitamines sont indispensables au bon fonctionnement du corps humain. Ce tableau indique la source de quelques vitamines importantes.

Vitamines	Sources
A	légumes, lait, quelques fruits
B	viande, œufs, céréales, légumes verts
C	fruits, tomates, salade verte
D	lait, œufs, poisson
E	huiles, légumes, œufs, céréales

[4] riz *rice* [5] élevé *elevated, high* [6] os *bones*

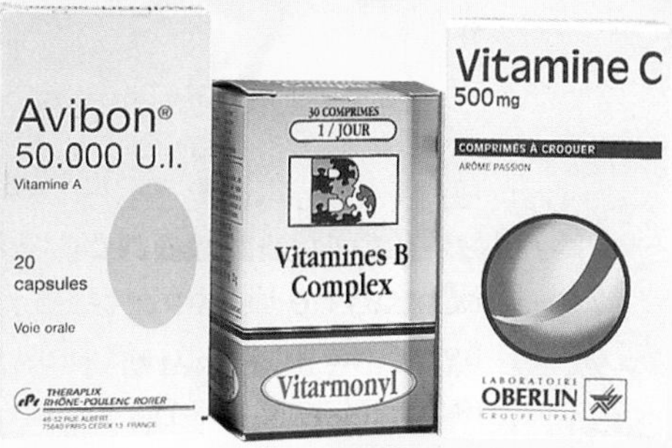

Vous avez compris?

A La diététique Répondez.

1. Qu'est-ce qu'on doit manger tous les jours?
2. Le nombre de calories pour chaque individu dépend de quoi?
3. Qui a particulièrement besoin de calories? Pourquoi?
4. Quelle est une source importante d'énergie?
5. Pourquoi faut-il contrôler la consommation de graisses?
6. Quel est un minéral important pour les os et les dents?
7. Qu'est-ce qui est indispensable au bon fonctionnement du corps humain?

B Assez de vitamines? Faites une liste de tout ce que vous avez mangé hier. Vous avez eu toutes les vitamines nécessaires?

C'est à vous

Use what you have learned

PARLER 1

Tout le monde est malade.

✔ *Describe cold symptoms and minor ailments*

Work with a classmate. Choose one of the people in the illustrations. Describe him or her. Your partner will guess which person you're talking about and say what's the matter with the person. Take turns.

1.

2.

3.

4.

PARLER 2

Une ordonnance

✔ *Discuss a prescription with a pharmacist*

You are in a pharmacy in Bordeaux. Your classmate will be the pharmacist. Make up a conversation about your prescription. Explain why and how you have to take the medicine.

PARLER 3

Jeu Je suis malade comme un chien!

✔ *Talk about how you are feeling*

Work with a partner. Make gestures to indicate how you're feeling today. Your partner will ask you why you feel that way. Tell him or her. Be as creative and humorous as possible.

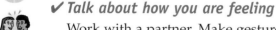

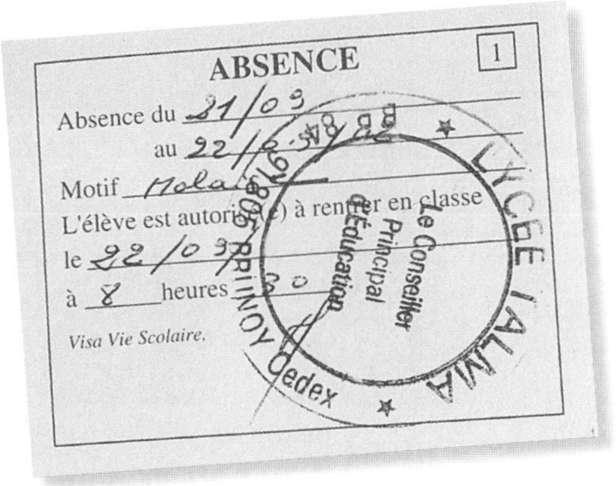
ABSENCE 1

Absence du 31/03

au 22/

Motif Malad

L'élève est autorisé(e) à rentrer en classe

le 22/03

à 8 heures

Visa Vie Scolaire.

LYCEE L'ALMA

Le Conseiller Principal d'éducation

Cedex

ÉCRIRE

4 Excusez-moi...

✔ *Write a note describing a minor illness*

You're supposed to take a French test today but you're not feeling well. Write a note to your French teacher explaining why you can't take the test, and mention some symptoms you have.

Une ambulance du SAMU

Writing Strategy

Writing a personal essay In writing a personal essay, a writer has several options: to tell a story, describe something, or encourage readers to think a certain way or to do something. Whatever its purpose, a personal essay allows a writer to express a viewpoint based on his or her own experience. Your essay will be much livelier if you choose interesting details and vivid words to relay your message.

ÉCRIRE

5 Des bénévoles

Your French club has a community service requirement. You have decided to work in the emergency room **(le service des urgences)** at your local hospital. You serve as a translator or interpreter for patients who speak only French. Write a flyer for your French club. Tell about your experience with one or more patients. Give your feelings about the work you do and try to encourage other club members to volunteer their services, too.

Assessment

Vocabulaire

To review **Mots 1**, turn to pages 464–465.

1 Choisissez.

a.

b.

c.
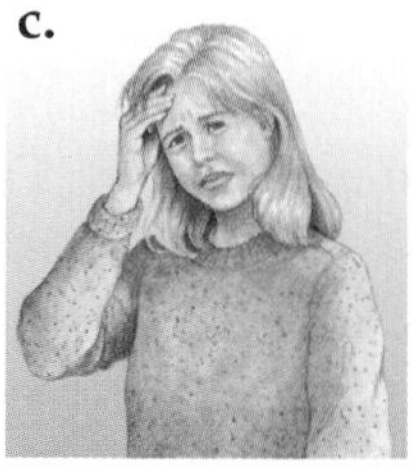
d.

1. ____ Elle a mal à la tête.
2. ____ Elle a mal au ventre.
3. ____ Elle tousse.
4. ____ Elle est enrhumée.

2 Identifiez.

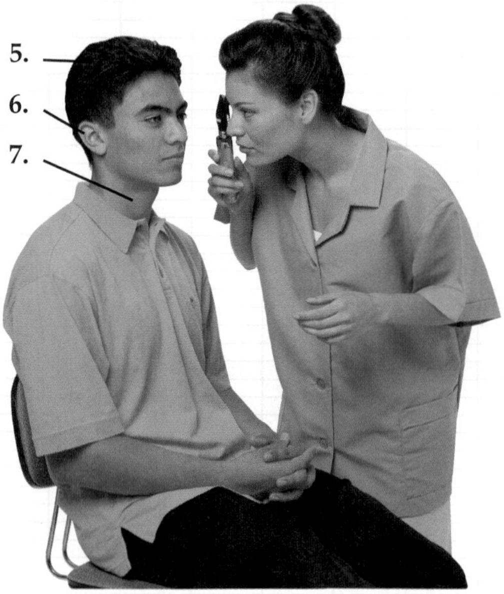

3 Complétez.

To review **Mots 2**, turn to pages 468–469.

8. Le médecin ____ le malade.
9. Le malade ouvre la ____ quand le médecin lui examine la gorge.
10. Le médecin fait un ____. Il dit que Nathalie a une sinusite aiguë.
11. Le médecin lui fait une ____ pour des antibiotiques.
12. Elle va à la ____ pour acheter ses médicaments.

Structure

4 Complétez.

13. Le médecin parle au malade?
    Oui, il ____ parle.
14. Le médecin donne une ordonnance à ses patients?
    Oui, il ____ donne une ordonnance.
15. Paul donne son ordonnance à la pharmacienne?
    Oui, il ____ donne son ordonnance.

*To review **lui** and **leur**, turn to page 472.*

5 Complétez.

16. Ils ____ beaucoup, les pauvres. (souffrir)
17. J'____ le livre à la page 100. (ouvrir)
18. Vous ____ la bouche quand le médecin vous examine? (ouvrir)

*To review **souffrir** and **ouvrir**, turn to page 474.*

6 Complétez avec l'impératif.

19. (ouvrir) Paul, ____ ton livre.
    Luc et Louise, ____ vos livres aussi.
20. (attendre) Carole, ____ un moment.
    Sandrine et Maïa, ____ avec Carole.
21. (dire) Luc, ____ au médecin où tu as mal.
    Vous deux, ____ au médecin où vous avez mal.

To review commands, turn to page 475.

7 Répondez avec un pronom.

22. Tu as de l'aspirine?
    Oui, __________.
23. Tu as douze comprimés?
    Oui, __________.
24. Tu peux sortir de l'hôpital demain?
    Oui, __________.
25. Il a beaucoup d'argent?
    Oui, __________.

*To review the use of **en**, turn to page 478.*

On parle super bien!

Tell all you can about this illustration.

Vocabulaire

Describing minor health problems

la santé
en bonne santé
en mauvaise santé
une infection
un frisson
la grippe
un rhume
une angine
une sinusite aiguë
une allergie
un mouchoir
un kleenex
se sentir bien
mal
être enrhumé(e)
tousser
éternuer
avoir mal
à la tête
au ventre
aux oreilles
à la gorge
avoir de la fièvre
le nez qui coule
les yeux qui piquent
la gorge qui gratte
malade
viral(e)
bactérien(ne)
allergique

Speaking with the doctor

le médecin
le/la malade
un diagnostic
une ordonnance
souffrir
ouvrir
examiner
ausculter
respirer
prescrire

How well do you know your vocabulary?

- Find as many cognates as you can in the list.
- Use five cognates to write several sentences.

Identifying more parts of the body

la tête
un œil, des yeux
le nez
la bouche
une oreille
la gorge
le ventre

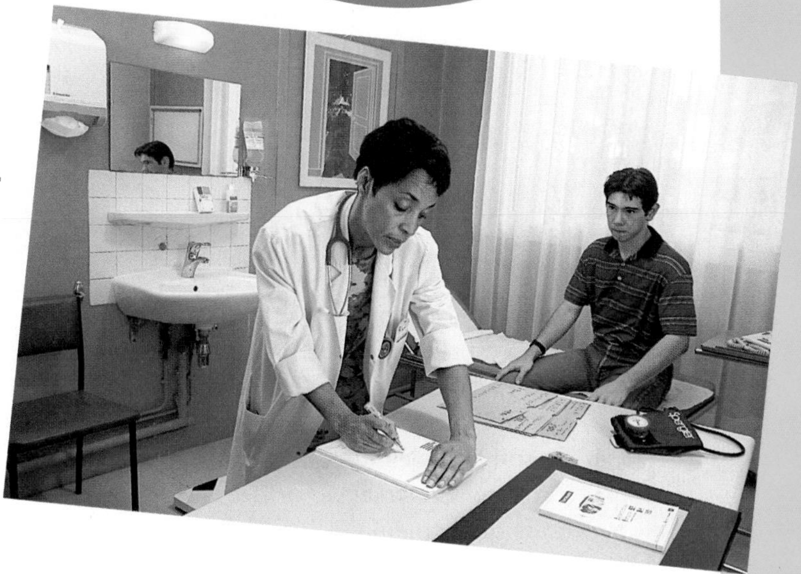

Speaking with a pharmacist

un(e) pharmacien(ne)
une pharmacie
un médicament
un comprimé
un antibiotique
un sirop
de la pénicilline
de l'aspirine *(f.)*
avaler

Other useful words and expressions

À tes souhaits!
Qu'est-ce qu'il a?
le/la pauvre
à fond

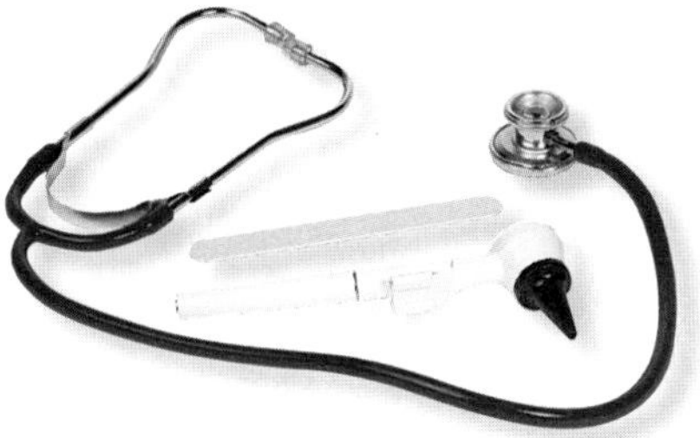

VIDÉOTOUR

Épisode 14

In this video episode, you will join Vincent as he experiences a strange nightmare. See page 539 for more information.

Révision

Conversation

On va au cinéma?

Céline: Tu as déjà vu *Autant en emporte le vent* avec Clark Gable et Vivien Leigh?

Thomas: Non, mais c'est un classique.

Céline: Tu veux le voir? On le joue au Champollion en version originale.

Thomas: Je voudrais bien, mais je ne peux pas. Je dois me coucher de bonne heure ce soir.

Céline: Pourquoi? Tu ne te sens pas bien?

Thomas: Non, pas très bien. Je ne sais pas ce que j'ai… Je suis fatigué, j'ai mal à la tête… Je crois que j'ai la grippe.

Vous avez compris?

Répondez.

1. Céline parle à qui?
2. Elle lui parle de quoi?
3. Thomas a déjà vu *Autant en emporte le vent*?
4. Il croit que c'est un bon film?
5. On joue *Autant en emporte le vent* dans quel cinéma?
6. Pourquoi est-ce que Thomas ne peut pas aller au cinéma?
7. Qu'est-ce qu'il a?

Structure

Les verbes réfléchis

1. The subject of a reflexive verb both performs and receives the action of the verb. For this reason, an additional pronoun is used. It is called a reflexive pronoun. Review the following forms.

SE LAVER		S'HABILLER	
je	me lave	je	m'habille
tu	te laves	tu	t'habilles
il/elle/on	se lave	il/elle/on	s'habille
nous	nous lavons	nous	nous‿z habillons
vous	vous lavez	vous	vous‿z habillez
ils/elles	se lavent	ils/elles	s'habillent

2. Reflexive verbs are conjugated with **être** in the **passé composé.** Note that there is no agreement when the verb is followed by a noun referring to a part of the body.

Elle s'est brossée.	**Elle s'est brossé les cheveux.**
Elles se sont maquillées.	**Elles se sont maquillé les yeux.**
Ils se sont lavés.	**Ils se sont lavé les dents.**

1 Historiette **Ce matin** Répondez que oui.

1. Il s'appelle Arnaud?
2. Qu'est-ce qu'il fait le matin? Il se dépêche?
3. Il se lève à sept heures?
4. Il s'habille vite?
5. Et toi, tu te lèves à sept heures?
6. Tu te laves les mains et la figure?
7. Tes parents se dépêchent le matin?

2 **Historiette La routine** Complétez en utilisant le passé composé.

Ce matin, je __1__ (se réveiller) tôt et je __2__ (se lever) tout de suite. Je __3__ (se laver) la figure et les mains et, après le petit déjeuner, je __4__ (se brosser) les dents.

Mes deux copains Sandrine et Sylvain __5__ (se lever) tard ce matin. Ils __6__ (se dépêcher) pour arriver à l'école à l'heure.

Et vous, vous __7__ (se lever) tard ou tôt ce matin? Vous __8__ (se dépêcher)?

Les pronoms

1. The pronouns **me, te, nous,** and **vous** can be either direct or indirect objects.

Objet Direct:	**Il me voit.**	**Elle t'invite à la fête.**
	Ils nous regardent.	**Je vous connais.**
Objet Indirect:	**Tu me parles?**	**Elle te dit quoi?**
	Il nous téléphone.	**Je vous réponds que oui.**

2. The pronouns **le, la,** and **les** are direct objects. They can replace either a person or a thing.

Jean? Je le connais.	**Son collège? Je ne le connais pas.**
Marie? Je la connais.	**Sa voiture? Je la vois.**
Tes copains? Je les connais.	**Leurs billets? Je les ai.**

3. **Lui** and **leur** are indirect objects. They replace **à** + a person.

Je téléphone à Jean.	**Je lui téléphone.**
Il lit la lettre à Anne.	**Il lui lit la lettre.**
Elle parle aux élèves.	**Elle leur parle.**

4. The pronoun **en** replaces **de (du, de la, de l', des)** + a thing.

Tu as de l'aspirine?	**Oui, j'en ai.**
Il prend des antibiotiques?	**Non, il n'en prend pas.**

Remember that with numbers and expressions of quantity **en** refers not only to things but also to people: **Tu as des frères? Oui, j'en ai deux.**

5. Object pronouns always come directly before the verb they are linked to.

Il me téléphone.	**Il va lui téléphoner.**
Elle en achète.	**Il ne va pas leur parler.**
Il ne la regarde pas.	

3 **Vraiment?** Complétez avec **me, te, nous** ou **vous.**

1. —Je vous connais, vous deux.
   —Vraiment? Tu ____ connais?
2. —On va te téléphoner.
   —Vraiment? Vous allez ____ téléphoner?
3. —Je t'aime!
   —Vraiment? Tu ____ aimes?
4. —Elle nous invite, ma sœur et moi.
   —Vraiment? Elle ____ invite?
5. —Elle t'invite aussi.
   —Vraiment? Elle ____ invite aussi?
6. —Il vous regarde fixement, ta sœur et toi.
   —Vraiment? Il ____ regarde fixement?

Musée du Louvre, Paris

4 **Jean et ses amis** Refaites les phrases en utilisant des pronoms.

1. Je connais *Jean,* mais je ne connais pas *ses amis.*
2. Je ne vois pas souvent *Caroline,* mais je parle *à sa sœur* tous les jours.
3. Jean m'invite à sa fête et je veux apporter un cadeau *à ses parents.*
4. J'aime beaucoup *Virginie et ses amis.* Je vais téléphoner *à Virginie* pour les inviter tous.
5. J'aime beaucoup *ses CD.* Je vais acheter trois CD.

5 **Questions** Répondez en utilisant un pronom.

1. Tu lis ce magazine?
2. Tu achètes les billets?
3. Tu vas voir cette pièce de théâtre?
4. Tu veux voir ces deux films?
5. Tu aimes mieux voir les films en version originale ou doublés?
6. Tu vois beaucoup de films américains?

6 **Une journée typique** Work with a classmate. Compare a typical day in your life with a typical day in your partner's life.

7 **On s'amuse.** Work with a classmate. Discuss what you do when you have free time. Do you like to do the same activities?

LITERARY COMPANION *You may wish to read the adaptation of* Le Comte de Monte-Cristo. *You will find this literary selection on page 518.*

1. La cathédrale Notre-Dame de Paris sur l'île de la Cité
2. La tour Eiffel, symbole de Paris
3. Étudiants à la terrasse d'un café au Quartier latin
4. La fontaine Stravinski près du Centre Georges-Pompidou
5. Entrée de la station de métro «Porte Dauphine»
6. La Grande Arche de la Défense, le quartier des affaires
7. Marché dans le quartier de Barbès-Rochechouart

1

2

3

4

5

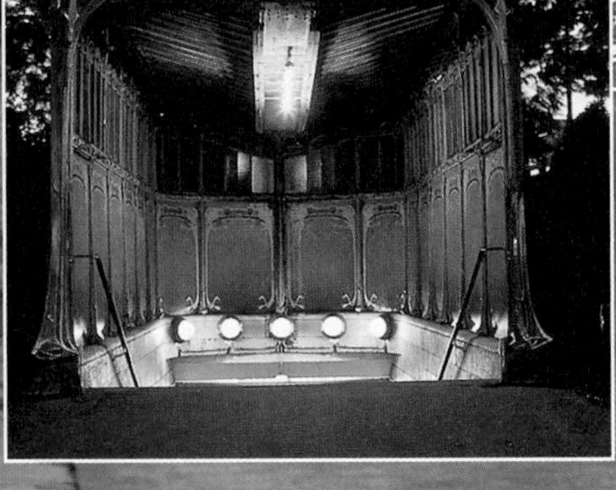

6

NATIONAL GEOGRAPHIC

REFLETS de Paris

7

8. L'Arc de Triomphe sur la place Charles-de-Gaulle
9. La pyramide du musée du Louvre
10. Horloge de l'ancienne gare d'Orsay transformée en musée
11. Petits bateaux à voiles au jardin du Luxembourg
12. Lampadaires sur le pont Alexandre III
13. Enfant avec pains
14. *La Joconde* par un jeune artiste de la rue

8

9

10

11

12

REFLETS de Paris

13

14

Literary Companion

Literary Companion

These literary selections develop reading and cultural skills and introduce students to French literature.

La petite Fadette George Sand

Vocabulaire

Les jumeaux sont semblables.
Ils ont les yeux bleus.
Ils sont forts.

Il y a deux autres garçons dans la famille.
L'aîné a cinq ans.
Le cadet a deux ans.

Il est triste. Il pleure.

Le petit garçon a peur.

Les paysans travaillent dans les champs.
La petite fille est très pauvre.

Elle est (tombe) malade.

Le Berry, France

Activités

A Historiette Les jumeaux

Répondez.

1. Les deux frères sont jumeaux?
2. Ils sont très semblables?
3. Ils ont les yeux bleus?
4. Ils sont forts ou faibles?
5. Le cadet a cinq ans ou deux ans?
6. Et l'aîné, il a quel âge?

B Quel est le mot? Complétez.

1. Des ____ sont des frères qui ont le même âge.
2. Le petit garçon est triste. Il ____.
3. Il pleure aussi quand il a ____.
4. Les jumeaux sont blonds et ils ont les yeux bleus. Ils sont très ____.
5. M. et Mme Gaillard ont deux enfants. L'____ a quinze ans et le ____ a huit ans.
6. M. et Mme Gaillard ____ dans les champs. M. et Mme Gaillard sont des ____.
7. La petite fille n'est pas riche. Elle est ____.
8. La petite fille est ____. Elle a la grippe.

INTRODUCTION Le vrai nom de George Sand (1804–1876) est Aurore Dupin. Elle est née[1] à Paris, mais elle passe son enfance à Nohant, dans le Berry. Le Berry est une région rurale.

George Sand a un mariage malheureux. Séparée de son mari, elle rentre à Paris avec ses deux enfants. Ses romans les plus connus[2] sont des romans champêtres[3]. Dans ses romans, elle montre un grand intérêt pour les paysans du Berry. *La petite Fadette* est un roman champêtre publié en 1849.

[1] née *born*
[2] romans les plus connus *best-known novels*
[3] champêtres *pastoral*

La petite Fadette

1

Le père Barbeau habite à la Cosse. Le père Barbeau est un homme important. Il a deux champs. Il cultive ses deux champs pour nourrir° sa famille. Il a aussi une maison avec un jardin. C'est un homme courageux et bon. Il aime beaucoup sa famille—sa femme, la mère Barbeau, et ses trois enfants.

C'est alors que le père Barbeau et la mère Barbeau ont deux garçons à la fois°: deux beaux jumeaux. Il est impossible de distinguer les jumeaux l'un de l'autre parce qu'ils° sont très semblables. Sylvinet est l'aîné et Landry est le cadet.

nourrir *to feed*
à la fois *at the same time*
parce qu'ils *because they*

2

Les deux garçons grandissent° sans problème. Ils sont blonds avec de grands yeux bleus. Ils parlent avec la même voix°. Ils sont très amis. Ils sont toujours ensemble.

Les enfants ont maintenant 14 ans. Le père Barbeau dit qu'ils ont l'âge de travailler. Mais il n'y a pas assez de travail pour les deux garçons chez les Barbeau. Le père décide d'envoyer° un des garçons chez un voisin, le père Caillaud. Le père Caillaud habite à la Priche.

grandissent *grow up*
voix *voice*
envoyer *to send*

Les jumeaux sont très tristes. Être séparés, c'est horrible. Sylvinet commence à pleurer et Landry pleure aussi.

—Mais, le père Caillaud n'habite pas très loin, dit Landry.

—C'est vrai. Je vais chez le père Caillaud…

—Non, Sylvinet. Pas toi, moi! Je vais chez le père Caillaud!

Donc Landry quitte la maison de son père… Maintenant, il travaille chez le père Caillaud. Le père Caillaud est content que Landry travaille pour lui. Landry est très fort.

Le père Caillaud aime beaucoup Landry. Il traite Landry comme un de ses enfants. Landry aussi aime beaucoup le père Caillaud. Il est content de travailler à la Priche. Mais Sylvinet n'est pas content. Il est jaloux de Landry.

3

Françoise Fadet est une petite fille très pauvre. Elle habite avec sa grand-mère et son petit frère handicapé. Ils habitent près de la rivière°, pas très loin de la Priche. On appelle Françoise «la petite Fadette». La petite Fadette est très solitaire. Elle n'est pas comme les autres enfants. Elle est assez différente des autres. Les autres enfants ont peur de la petite Fadette. Certains détestent la petite fille.

rivière *river*

Un jour, Landry rentre à la Priche et rencontre° la petite Fadette qui pleure.

—Pourquoi° tu pleures comme ça?

—Parce qu'on me déteste.

—C'est un peu ta faute°, Fadette.

—Ma faute? Pourquoi?

—Parce que tu es toujours très sale° et désagréable avec les autres.

rencontre *meets*

Pourquoi *Why*

faute *fault*

sale *dirty*

Émile Lambinet *Écouen, près de Paris*

Landry, lui, ne trouve° pas la petite Fadette désagréable. Il trouve même qu'elle est intelligente et intéressante. La petite Fadette trouve Landry très beau. Elle aime Landry. Landry et la petite Fadette sont souvent ensemble et Landry change la personnalité de la petite Fadette.

Le jumeau de Landry, Sylvinet, est très jaloux de Landry et la petite Fadette. Il tombe très malade. Sa famille est désespérée. Mais qui sauve Sylvinet? La petite Fadette, l'amie de son frère Landry. Maintenant, tout° est possible, même le mariage de Landry et de la petite Fadette.

trouve *finds*

tout *everything*

William Bouguereau *Jeune fille au panier de fruits*

Vous avez compris?

A **Les enfants Barbeau** Répondez.

1. M. et Mme Barbeau ont combien d'enfants?
2. Ils ont des jumeaux?
3. L'aîné, c'est Sylvinet ou Landry?
4. Et le cadet?
5. Comment sont les jumeaux?
6. Ils sont bruns ou blonds?
7. Ils ont les yeux de quelle couleur?
8. Ils ont la même voix?

B **Le père Barbeau** Décrivez le père Barbeau.

C **Les jumeaux** Décrivez les jumeaux Barbeau.

D **Séparation** Complétez.

1. Quand les enfants ont ____ ans, le père Barbeau dit qu'ils ont l'âge de ____.
2. Le père Barbeau décide d'envoyer un enfant chez un ____, le père Caillaud.
3. Le père Caillaud ____ à la Priche.
4. Les jumeaux sont très ____ parce qu'ils vont être séparés.
5. Ils sont très tristes et ils ____.
6. ____ travaille chez le père Caillaud.
7. Le père Caillaud ____ beaucoup Landry. Il ____ Landry comme un de ses enfants.

E **La petite Fadette** Répondez.

1. Avec qui habite la petite Fadette?
2. Elle habite où?
3. Comment est la petite Fadette?
4. Qui a peur de la petite Fadette?
5. La petite Fadette pleure. Pourquoi?
6. Elle parle à qui?
7. Landry trouve la petite Fadette comment?
8. Qui change la personnalité de la petite Fadette?
9. Qui tombe malade?
10. Qui sauve Sylvinet?

«Dors mon enfant» Elolongué Epanya Yondo

Vocabulaire

une revue un magazine
l'avenir le futur

Gerard Sekoto *Jeune fille à l'orange*

Activité

Un oranger Répondez.

1. Un oranger, c'est un fruit ou un arbre?
2. L'orange, c'est le fruit de l'oranger?
3. Tu aimes les oranges?
4. Tu aimes le jus d'orange?
5. Il y a des orangers dans les régions tropicales?
6. C'est beau un oranger fleuri?

INTRODUCTION La poésie africaine francophone est la poésie écrite par des Africains de langue française. La poésie africaine francophone est riche et variée. Deux écrivains de langue française célèbres sont Léopold Sédar Senghor et Aimé Césaire. Ces deux écrivains créent dans les années 30 le mouvement de «la négritude». La négritude, c'est «l'ensemble des valeurs culturelles de l'Afrique noire.»

En 1947, Alioune Diop fonde à Paris la revue *Présence Africaine.* La revue publie les œuvres[1] d'écrivains africains francophones et diffuse le concept de la négritude.

[1] œuvres *works*

Aujourd'hui, *Présence Africaine* est une maison d'édition[2] qui publie les œuvres d'écrivains africains.

«Dors mon enfant» est tiré de[3] *Kamérun! Kamérun!* du poète Elolongué Epanya Yondo. Elolongué Epanya Yondo est né au Cameroun en 1930. Il va étudier à Paris où il habite chez Alioune Diop. Elolongué Epanya Yondo veut inspirer un esprit de solidarité chez ses compatriotes pour établir un avenir[4] solide sans oublier[5] les traditions passées.

[2] maison d'édition *publishing house*
[3] tiré de *taken from*
[4] avenir *future*
[5] sans oublier *without forgetting*

«Dors mon enfant»

Dors° mon enfant dors
Quand tu dors
Tu es beau
Comme un oranger fleuri…
Dors mon enfant dors
Tu es si° beau
Quand tu dors…
Mon beau bébé noir dors

Dors *Sleep*
si *so*

Elizabeth Barakah Hodges *Madone noire*

Vous avez compris?

Dors mon enfant Répondez.

1. Qui parle dans le poème?
2. La mère trouve son enfant beau?
3. Elle compare son enfant à quel arbre?
4. Un oranger est un bel arbre?
5. Un oranger est beau surtout quand il fleurit?
6. La mère compare son enfant à un bel oranger fleuri?
7. Le petit enfant est de quelle race?
8. C'est un bébé ou un petit garçon?

La Chanson de Roland Auteur anonyme

Vocabulaire

C'est un champ de bataille.
Les deux armées ont une bataille.

Les guerriers luttent.
Un guerrier est plus fort que l'autre.
Un guerrier est blessé.

Le guerrier sonne du cor.
Ça fait du bruit.

Le guerrier frappe son épée contre le rocher.
Il veut briser son épée.

Il se couche sous un arbre.
Il cache l'épée sous lui.

une lutte une bataille, un combat
du bruit un son désagréable
la guerre Deux armées qui luttent font la guerre.
gagner la bataille être victorieux, sortir victorieux d'une bataille

Activités

A Historiette Sur le champ de bataille Répondez.

1. Il y a des guerriers sur le champ de bataille?
2. Ils luttent?
3. C'est l'armée du roi?
4. Un guerrier est plus fort que l'autre?
5. Un guerrier est blessé?
6. Il a une épée à la main?
7. Il a un cor à la ceinture?
8. Est-ce qu'un guerrier sonne du cor?
9. Ça fait du bruit quand il sonne du cor?
10. Un guerrier frappe son épée contre un rocher?
11. Il cache son épée?
12. Il cache son épée où?

B Quel est le mot? Complétez.

1. Un ____ est un ancien instrument musical.
2. Une ____ est une ancienne arme.
3. Une ____, c'est un groupe de guerriers ou de soldats.
4. Le guerrier qui ____ la bataille est victorieux.

La Chanson de Roland **Auteur anonyme**

INTRODUCTION *La Chanson de Roland* est un poème épique qui date de la fin du onzième siècle[1]. C'est le premier poème de ce genre qui est écrit en français et pas en latin. L'auteur est anonyme, c'est-à-dire qu'il est inconnu. Le poème raconte la guerre de Charlemagne en Espagne. Charlemagne passe sept années victorieuses en Espagne. Il reste une seule ville à prendre. C'est Saragosse. Roland est un chevalier[2] dans l'armée de Charlemagne. Il veut continuer la guerre pour prendre Saragosse. Mais un autre chevalier dans l'armée de Charlemagne, Ganelon, veut faire la paix[3] avec le roi de Saragosse. Il veut rentrer en France. On va voir ce qui arrive[4].

[1] siècle *century*
[2] chevalier *knight*
[3] faire la paix *make peace*
[4] ce qui arrive *what happens*

Roland et Durendal

1

Nous sommes en 771. Les Français s'appellent les Francs. Le roi des Francs, c'est Charlemagne. Il a une très grande armée composée de guerriers nobles et braves. Un de ces guerriers s'appelle Roland. Roland est le neveu de Charlemagne. Il est fort et grand comme un géant. Il est fier° et très courageux.

fier *proud*

Un jour Charlemagne donne à son neveu deux merveilleux cadeaux: un cor magique et une épée dorée°. Roland est très fier des cadeaux de son oncle. Partout où il va il garde avec lui le cor et l'épée. Il aime son épée comme une amie. Il donne un nom à son épée: «Durendal».

dorée *gilded*

Avec sa belle épée, Durendal, Roland lutte contre les ennemis de Charlemagne. Il est extraordinaire sur le champ de bataille avec son cor à la ceinture et son épée à la main. Sa belle épée dorée brille dans le soleil et protège Roland dans ses combats. Il est victorieux dans beaucoup de batailles.

Charlemagne et Roland

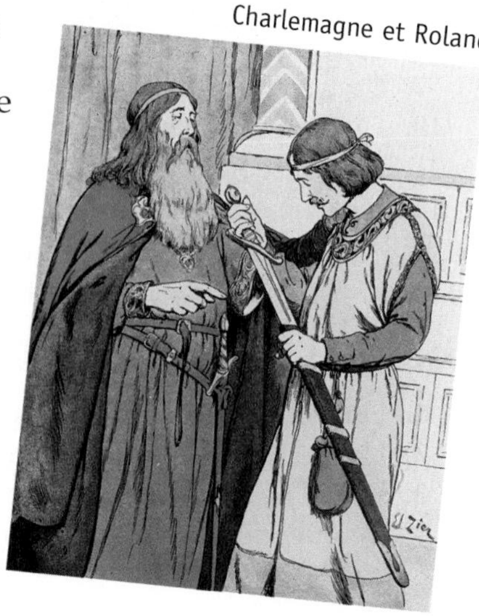

2

Un jour Roland est dans un pays étranger loin de la France. Il lutte contre un guerrier blond inconnu. Les deux guerriers sont forts et très braves. Ils luttent tous les deux avec beaucoup de courage. Leur combat commence le matin et continue toute la journée. Les deux hommes sont très fatigués. Ils sont épuisés mais ils continuent à lutter. Pendant la bataille l'épée du guerrier blond se brise°. Quand Roland voit que l'épée de son adversaire est brisée, il jette Durendal à terre°. Et la bataille continue. Les deux guerriers luttent toute la nuit. Mais le guerrier blond est blessé. Aussitôt° Roland arrête le combat et aide le guerrier blessé.

—Je m'appelle Roland et je suis le neveu de Charlemagne. On ne va pas continuer à lutter. Je veux être ton ami. Quel est ton nom?

—Olivier, répond le guerrier blond.

Les deux guerriers décident d'être amis. Désormais° ils vont toujours être ensemble. Ils ne sont plus ennemis. Ils sont comme deux frères.

se brise *breaks*
jette... à terre *throws . . . on the ground*
Aussitôt *Immediately*
Désormais *From then on*

3

778: Charlemagne et ses guerriers sont en Espagne où ils luttent victorieusement contre les Sarrasins. La bataille est presque finie. Il reste une seule ville à prendre, Saragosse. Roland veut aller à Saragosse pour prendre la ville mais un autre chevalier, Ganelon, ne veut pas y aller. Il veut faire la paix avec le roi de Saragosse, Marsile, et rentrer en France. La décision est prise. On va traverser les Pyrénées et rentrer en France. En fait, Ganelon est un traître qui veut la mort° de Roland. Il révèle aux Sarrasins le chemin° que Charlemagne va prendre pour traverser les Pyrénées.

Charlemagne s'engage dans° les montagnes à la tête de son armée. Ganelon l'accompagne. Roland et Olivier font partie de l'arrière-garde. Les soldats de Marsile sont cachés° dans les montagnes à Roncevaux. Ils laissent passer Charlemagne et les hommes qui sont avec lui. Mais quand Roland et ses hommes arrivent, ils attaquent. Ils jettent des rochers énormes sur les guerriers. Les Francs luttent avec grand courage, mais hélas, ils sont vingt mille contre cent mille. Olivier demande à Roland de sonner du cor pour appeler Charlemagne à l'aide. Mais Roland est fier, il veut lutter seul. Les Francs sont écrasés°. Seuls Olivier et Roland restent en vie°. Ils veulent continuer la bataille mais ils sont blessés et ils sont très faibles.

Roland sonne du cor.

mort *death*
chemin *route*
s'engage dans *heads into*
cachés *hiding*
écrasés *crushed*
en vie *alive*

4

Roland ne veut pas laisser Durendal aux mains de ses ennemis. Il essaie de briser son épée. Il frappe son épée contre un rocher. Le rocher est dur° mais l'épée est dure aussi. Roland frappe encore mais en vain. Il ne peut pas briser son épée.

dur *hard*

Roland va mourir°. Il se couche sous un arbre et met sa belle épée sous lui. Là, ses ennemis ne peuvent pas trouver son amie Durendal. Enfin Roland prend son cor et sonne. Il appelle Charlemagne. Il sait qu'il va mourir.

mourir *to die*

Mais Charlemagne est très loin. Il est dans une plaine en France. Il croit entendre le cor de Roland.

—Écoute! dit-il à Ganelon. C'est Roland qui sonne du cor. Il demande notre aide.

—Mais non, ce sont des bergers° qui jouent de la flûte dans la montagne, répond Ganelon.

bergers *shepherds*

L'armée de Charlemagne continue son voyage. Roland sonne encore.

—Je suis sûr que c'est le cor de Roland. On fait demi-tour° et on va à son aide, dit Charlemagne.

fait demi-tour *turn around*

—Mais Roland est brave, dit Ganelon. Il est fort et il a des hommes avec lui. Il n'a pas besoin de nous. Notre armée est fatiguée. On ne peut pas faire demi-tour.

Le pauvre Roland est désespéré et il sonne une dernière fois°.

dernière fois *last time*

—C'est Roland. C'est sûr. Il a besoin de notre aide. Demi-tour, immédiatement! crie Charlemagne.

Charlemagne et ses guerriers font demi-tour. Ils arrivent dans la vallée où est l'arrière-garde. Mais il est trop tard. Tous les guerriers francs sont morts. Charlemagne trouve les corps de Roland et d'Olivier l'un près de l'autre. Roland a sonné du cor si longtemps et si fort que les veines de ses tempes° ont éclaté°.

tempes *temples*
ont éclaté *burst*

Charlemagne et son armée attaquent l'armée de Marsile. L'ennemi est finalement écrasé. Charlemagne sort victorieux et la mort de Roland et de ses hommes est vengée.

Voilà l'histoire de Roland, le noble guerrier.

La mort de Roland

Portrait de Charlemagne

Vous avez compris?

A **Charlemagne** Répondez.

1. Qui est le roi des Francs en 771?
2. Il a une grande armée?
3. Comment sont les soldats de Charlemagne?
4. Qui est Roland?
5. Qu'est-ce que Charlemagne donne à Roland?
6. Roland donne un nom à son épée? Quel nom?

B **Un combat** Choisissez la bonne réponse.

1. Un jour Roland lutte contre ____.
   a. un ami brun **b.** un étranger blond
2. Ils luttent ____.
   a. en France **b.** dans un pays étranger
3. Pendant la bataille l'épée ____ se brise.
   a. de Roland **b.** de l'étranger blond
4. ____ jette son épée à terre.
   a. L'inconnu blond **b.** Roland
5. ____ est blessé.
   a. Roland **b.** Le guerrier inconnu
6. Roland ____ le guerrier.
   a. n'aide pas **b.** aide
7. Roland veut être ____ du guerrier blond.
   a. l'ami **b.** l'ennemi
8. Les deux vont être ____.
   a. des neveux **b.** comme des frères

Monument de Charlemagne à Roncevaux

C **En Espagne** Vrai ou faux?

1. Charlemagne et son armée luttent en Espagne.
2. Ils luttent contre les Romains.
3. Les soldats de Charlemagne prennent la ville de Saragosse.
4. Roland veut prendre la ville de Saragosse.
5. Un autre chevalier, Ganelon, veut prendre Saragosse aussi.
6. Marsile est le roi de Saragosse.
7. Charlemagne et ses guerriers décident de rentrer en France.
8. Ganelon est un ami de Roland.
9. Roland et Ganelon font partie de l'arrière-garde.
10. L'armée de Marsile attaque Roland et ses hommes.

D **Un résumé** Give a brief synopsis of the end of the story in English.

Le Comte de Monte-Cristo Alexandre Dumas

Vocabulaire

Le jeune marin va se marier.
Il regarde sa fiancée avec amour.
Ils célèbrent leurs fiançailles.

On emmène le criminel en prison.
On l'enferme dans une cellule.

Le prisonnier est désespéré.
Il frappe sur la porte.
Il crie.

Il s'est évadé de prison.

Ils ont jeté le sac à la mer.

Il a trouvé un trésor.

Activités

A Le marin Répondez d'après les indications.

1. Le jeune homme est un soldat ou un marin? (un marin)
2. Il est marié? (non)
3. Il va se marier? (oui)
4. Il adore sa fiancée? (oui)
5. Qu'est-ce qu'il a pour sa fiancée? (de l'or)
6. Qu'est-ce qu'ils célèbrent? (leurs fiançailles)

B La prison Vrai ou faux?

1. Il y a des cellules dans une prison.
2. On emmène les criminels en prison.
3. Les cellules de prison sont très belles et agréables.
4. On enferme les gardiens dans des cellules.
5. Les gardiens travaillent dans une prison. Ils surveillent les prisonniers.
6. De temps en temps, un prisonnier complètement désespéré frappe sur la porte de sa cellule.
7. Les gardiens font des trous dans les murs.
8. Pour s'évader de prison, les prisonniers creusent un tunnel.

C Un trésor Répondez que oui.

1. C'est une île?
2. Il y a une grotte sur l'île?
3. Il y a un coffre à l'entrée de la grotte?
4. Le coffre est plein d'or et de pierres précieuses?
5. Il y a un bateau dans la mer?
6. Quelqu'un jette un sac à la mer?

INTRODUCTION Il y a deux Alexandre Dumas—Dumas père et Dumas fils. Les deux sont écrivains. Le père est connu surtout pour ses romans[1] d'aventures et le fils est connu surtout pour ses pièces de théâtre.

Alexandre Dumas (1802–1870) père est né à Villers-Cotterêts dans le nord de la France. Son père est général dans l'armée française et sa mère est de Saint-Domingue dans la mer des Caraïbes. Alexandre Dumas a écrit des centaines[2] de romans. Ses romans ont procuré du plaisir à des lecteurs[3] innombrables dans le monde entier. *Le Comte de Monte-Cristo* est un de ces romans.

[1] romans *novels* [2] centaines *hundreds* [3] lecteurs *readers*

Le Comte de Monte-Cristo

1

1815: Edmond Dantès est un jeune marin marseillais. Dantès est un jeune homme honnête et courageux. Il n'est pas riche, mais il est heureux°. Il a une fiancée, Mercédès. Il travaille pour M. Morrel, un homme bon et juste qui le traite comme son fils.

Mais il y a trois hommes qui n'aiment pas le jeune marin. Ces trois hommes, Fernand Mondego, Danglars et Villefort sont des ennemis dangereux. Fernand est jaloux de Dantès parce qu'il aime Mercédès. Danglars travaille aussi pour M. Morrel. Mais Danglars falsifie les comptes° de M. Morrel et Dantès le sait. Donc Danglars veut éliminer Dantès. Villefort lui aussi veut éliminer Dantès pour des raisons politiques. Les trois hommes conspirent contre Dantès. Ils l'accusent de comploter° contre le roi° et d'être pour le retour de Napoléon sur le trône. Leur accusation est totalement fausse. Le jeune Dantès est innocent, mais il est tout de même arrêté parce que ses ennemis—et Villefort en particulier—ont beaucoup d'influence. Il est arrêté pendant une fête en l'honneur de ses fiançailles avec Mercédès. Sans explication, on l'emmène en prison sur l'île du château d'If tout près de Marseille. Là on l'enferme dans une petite cellule froide et sombre. Le pauvre Dantès ne comprend pas. Il est désespéré. Il frappe contre la porte. «Pourquoi suis-je en prison?» crie-t-il. Mais il n'y a pas de réponse. Personne ne l'entend. Chaque jour, Dantès attend sa liberté, mais en vain. Le temps passe. Pendant quatre ans, Dantès reste seul dans sa cellule.

heureux *happy*

comptes *accounts*

comploter *conspiring*

contre le roi *against the king*

Dantès en prison

Château d'If

2

Un jour, il entend un bruit° de l'autre côté du mur de sa cellule. C'est un autre prisonnier qui creuse un tunnel. Cet homme arrive à faire un trou dans le mur de la cellule de Dantès et à entrer dans sa cellule. Les deux hommes sont fous° de joie. Le nouvel ami de Dantès est un abbé°, l'abbé Faria. L'abbé Faria est un intellectuel italien d'environ soixante ans. Il raconte à Dantès ses occupations en Italie et Dantès lui raconte ses voyages. Les deux amis font le projet° de s'évader de prison. Mais l'abbé n'est pas en bonne santé. Il sait qu'il ne va pas avoir la force de s'évader avec Dantès. Il lui révèle alors l'existence d'un trésor fabuleux caché° sur une petite île de la mer Méditerranée. Cette île s'appelle l'île de Monte-Cristo. Il donne un document à Dantès qui explique comment trouver le trésor.

bruit *noise*
fous *crazy*
abbé *abbot*
projet *plan*
caché *hidden*

3

Peu de temps après les gardiens de la prison trouvent l'abbé Faria mort° dans sa cellule. Ils mettent son corps dans un sac. Il vont le jeter à la mer. Mais pendant la nuit, Dantès prend la place de Faria et se met dans le sac. Les gardiens jettent le sac à la mer et Dantès est libre! Il ouvre le sac et commence à nager. Il nage longtemps dans une mer très agitée. Finalement, il est recueilli° par un bateau. Il est sauvé!

Maintenant Dantès est un homme libre! Il part à la recherche du trésor. Après de nombreuses aventures, il arrive enfin sur l'île de Monte-Cristo. Il a quelques difficultés à trouver le trésor qui est bien caché. Finalement il découvre dans une grotte un coffre avec de l'or et des pierres précieuses—des diamants, des rubis et des perles de toute beauté. Edmond Dantès est très riche! Il change de nom. Il prend le nom de l'île où il a trouvé le trésor. Le comte de Monte-Cristo est né.

mort *dead*
recueilli *picked up*

Ils jettent le sac à la mer.

4

Le Comte de Monte-Cristo va à Paris où il achète une maison splendide. Il voyage à Rome et en Grèce. Il est invité à toutes les fêtes. Il devient° vite célèbre. Tout le monde veut faire la connaissance de cet homme mystérieux et fabuleusement riche. Mais le Comte de Monte-Cristo n'a qu'une° idée. Il veut se venger°. Il retrouve Fernand qui s'est marié avec Mercédès. Fernand est devenu très riche, lui aussi. Il a pris le nom de Comte de Morcerf. Il retrouve Danglars et Villefort. Évidemment personne ne le reconnaît. Un à un, le comte de Monte-Cristo se venge de ses ennemis. Mercédès quitte Fernand et va dans un couvent. Fernand meurt°. Danglars est ruiné et Villefort devient fou°. Mais la vengeance ne satisfait pas le comte de Monte-Cristo. Il ne se sent pas libre. Au contraire, il se sent angoissé et plein de doutes. Il décide de tout abandonner. Il laisse sa fortune à Maximilien Morrel, le fils de son ancien patron°. Puis il s'embarque sur un bateau pour une destination inconnue en compagnie d'Haydée, une très belle jeune fille.

devient *becomes*

n'a qu'une *has only one*

se venger *to get revenge*

meurt *dies*

devient fou *goes crazy*

ancien patron *former boss*

Château d'If

Vous avez compris?

A Edmond Dantès Vrai ou faux?

1. Edmond Dantès est un jeune soldat parisien.
2. Il est très riche.
3. Il va se marier avec sa fiancée Mercédès.
4. Il n'a pas d'ennemis.
5. Il y a des hommes qui sont jaloux de Dantès.
6. Ils l'accusent d'un crime.
7. Dantès n'est pas un criminel.
8. Les gardiens savent qu'ils libèrent Dantès.
9. Dantès reste longtemps en prison.

B En prison Répondez.

1. Un jour, qu'est-ce que Dantès entend?
2. Quel est ce bruit?
3. Qui est le nouvel ami de Dantès?
4. Quel projet font les deux amis?
5. Qui est malade?
6. Qu'est-ce que l'abbé révèle à Dantès?
7. Où est caché le trésor?
8. Qu'est-ce que le document de l'abbé Faria explique?

C Des années ont passé. Choisissez.

1. Les gardiens trouvent ____ mort.
   a. Dantès **b.** l'abbé Faria **c.** M. Morrel
2. Ils le trouvent dans ____.
   a. un tunnel **b.** un trou **c.** sa cellule
3. Les gardiens mettent ____ dans un sac.
   a. le document **b.** l'abbé Faria **c.** Dantès
4. Les gardiens jettent le sac ____.
   a. dans le tunnel **b.** à la mer **c.** dans une grotte
5. Dantès est sauvé par ____.
   a. un homme libre **b.** un bateau **c.** une île
6. Quand Dantès arrive sur l'île de Monte-Cristo, il cherche ____.
   a. l'abbé Faria **b.** le trésor **c.** le document
7. Il découvre le trésor ____.
   a. dans la mer **b.** dans le bateau **c.** dans une grotte
8. Des diamants et des rubis sont ____.
   a. de l'or **b.** des perles **c.** des pierres précieuses

Une cellule au château d'If

D À Paris

1. Décrivez tout ce que Dantès fait à Paris.
2. Comparez la vie d'Edmond Dantès et la vie du Comte de Monte-Cristo.

Video Companion

Using video in the classroom

The use of video in the classroom can be a wonderful asset to the World Languages teacher and a most beneficial learning tool for the language student. Video enables students to experience whatever it is they are learning in their textbook in a real-life setting. With each lesson, they are able to take a vicarious field trip. They see people interacting at home, at school, at the market, etc., in an authentic milieu. Students sitting in a classroom can see real people going about their real life in real places. They may experience the target culture in many countries. The cultural benefits are limitless.

Developing listening and viewing skills In addition to its tremendous cultural value, video, when properly used, gives students much needed practice in developing good listening and viewing skills. Video allows students to look for numerous clues that are evident in a tone of voice, facial expressions, and gestures. Through video students can see and hear the diversity of the target culture and, as discerning viewers and listeners, compare and contrast the French-speaking cultures to each other and to their own culture. Video introduces a dimension into classroom instruction that no other medium — teachers, overhead, text, Audio CDs—can provide.

Reinforcing learned language Video that is properly developed for classroom use has speakers reincorporate the language students have learned in a given lesson. In keeping with reality, however, speakers introduce some new words, expressions, and structures because students functioning in a real-life situation would not know every word native speakers use with them in a live conversation. The lively and interactive nature of video allows students to use their listening and viewing skills to comprehend new language in addition to seeing and hearing the language they have learned come to life.

Getting the most out of video The intrinsic benefit of video is often lost when students are allowed to read the scripted material before viewing. In many cases, students will have come to understand language used by the speakers in the video by means of reading comprehension, thus negating the inherent benefits of video as a tool to develop listening and viewing skills. Because today's students are so accustomed to the medium of video as a tool for entertainment and learning, a well-written and well-produced video program will help them develop real-life language skills and confidence in those skills in an enjoyable way.

On Location!

Je suis Christine. Je suis de Fort-de-France, à la Martinique.
Je suis Vincent. Je suis de Paris.
Je suis Chloé. Je suis de Lyon, en France.
Je suis Manu. Je suis algérien.
Je suis Amadou. Je suis malien.

Vidéotour
Bon voyage!

Épisode 1: Une amie et un ami

Vincent et Chloé à Montmartre

Une vue splendide sur Paris

Avant de regarder

Can you spot the following?

1. un garçon brun
2. une fille brune
3. une vue splendide sur Paris
4. une caméra
5. une fille enthousiaste

Après avoir regardé

Expansion You will be taking a video tour of Paris. As you watch, look for similarities you notice between Paris and the city or town where you live. What differences do you notice? Choose several places in Paris that you would like to visit. Do some research to find out more about Paris. Why do you find it interesting?

Vidéotour

Bon voyage!

Épisode 2: Les cours et les profs

Vincent et une amie, Élodie, au lycée Louis-le-Grand

Manu et Vincent en cours de chimie

Avant de regarder

Make an educated guess!

1. In the first photograph, what do you think Vincent is doing?
2. In the second photo, does Manu look as if he knows what he is doing?
3. How does Vincent look as he watches Manu?
4. Do you think the experiment is going to be successful?

Après avoir regardé

Expansion As you watch the video, think about whether there are any similarities between the school you see in the video and the one you attend. Do you notice any differences? Which might you prefer? Why? Do some research about schedules in French schools. Are the schedules for French students like yours?

Vidéotour

Bon voyage!

Épisode 3: Pendant et après les cours

Amadou et Christine dans la rue après les cours

Amadou et Christine dans la papeterie

Avant de regarder

Can you spot the following?

1. une papeterie
2. une calculatrice
3. une rue
4. des fournitures scolaires
5. deux amis

Après avoir regardé

Expansion You will see something in the video that Christine enjoys doing after school. Compare her likes to some of those that you may have. See whether or not you have anything in common with your new French friends. Think about the other people in the video. Knowing what you know about them, what might they enjoy doing after school?

Vidéotour

Bon voyage!

Épisode 4: La famille et la maison

Christine a une surprise pour Mme Séguin.

Christine et Mme Séguin dans la cuisine de la maison de Monet

Avant de regarder

Can you spot the following? If so, give an adjective to describe each.

1. un jardin
2. un immeuble
3. une cuisine
4. une fleur
5. une voiture

Après avoir regardé

Expansion Giverny, a charming village northwest of Paris, is a beautiful spot. Can you think of any place near where you live that could compare to Giverny? Do some research to find out more about this famous place where Monet lived and write a paragraph about it or discuss with a friend what you found out that is of interest to you.

Vidéotour

Bon voyage!

Épisode 5: Au café et au restaurant

Chloé et Christine vont dans un café.

Elles commandent une boisson.

Avant de regarder

Invent the following.

1. le nom du café
2. ce que Chloé commande
3. ce que Christine commande
4. ce que dit le serveur

Après avoir regardé

Expansion As you can imagine from what you saw in the video, café life is an important part of French culture. Do you have any cafés near where you live? If you do, do you and your friends go there often? If not, do you think you might enjoy them based on what you viewed in the video?

Vidéotour

Bon voyage!

Épisode 6: La nourriture et les courses

Vincent et Manu font les courses.

Manu «prépare» un repas fabuleux.

Avant de regarder

Answer the questions.

1. Où sont Vincent et Manu?
2. Qu'est-ce qu'ils font?
3. Qu'est-ce qu'ils achètent, d'après vous?
4. Qui va payer, d'après vous?
5. Qu'est-ce qu'ils vont manger?

Après avoir regardé

Expansion What foods that you saw in the French supermarket are similar to those found in your supermarket? Do some research on the Internet to find a French recipe that you and your family might enjoy. Then make a list of all the ingredients you need from the supermarket to prepare this recipe.

Vidéotour
Bon voyage!

Épisode 7: Les vêtements

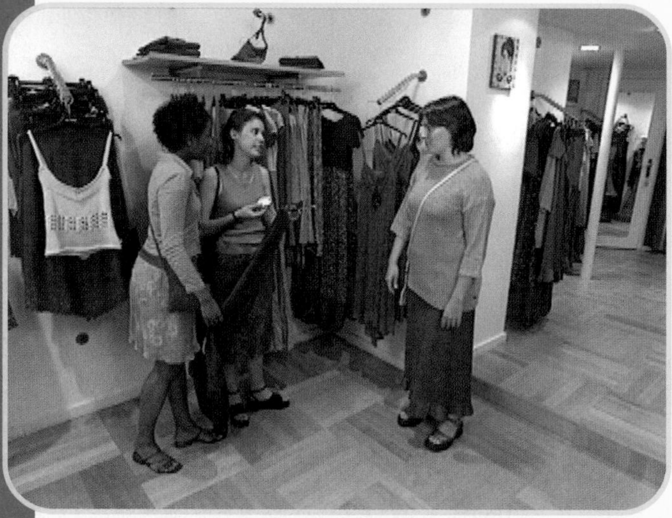

Christine et Chloé veulent acheter une robe.

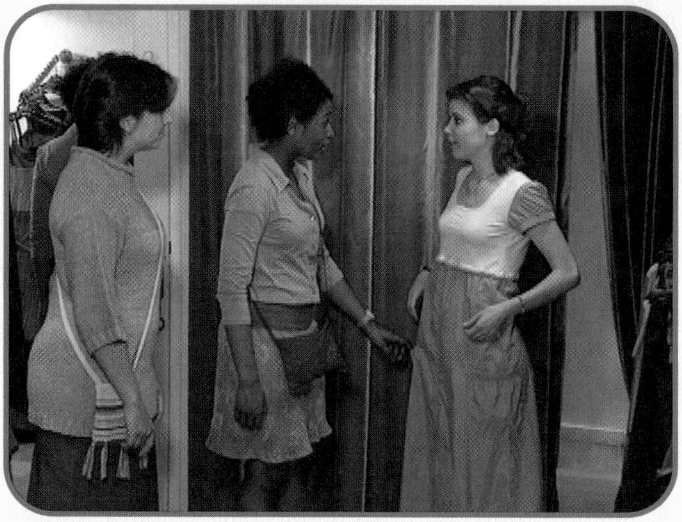

Chloé essaie une robe.

Avant de regarder

Describe the following.

1. ce que porte Christine
2. ce que porte Chloé
3. ce que porte la vendeuse
4. la robe que Christine essaie

Après avoir regardé

Expansion The world of fashion is significant in Paris and in other parts of the French-speaking world. Do some research on a famous French designer. Tell whether or not you might enjoy wearing his or her clothing. If you are artistic, draw a fashion that your designer might design.

Vidéotour

Bon voyage!

Épisode 8: L'aéroport et l'avion

Où est Christine en réalité?

Manu est à l'aéroport avec Christine?

Avant de regarder

Can you spot the following? How many of each do you see?

1. une valise
2. un passager
3. une carte d'embarquement
4. un comptoir
5. un bagage à main

Après avoir regardé

Expansion You have been exposed to many parts of the French-speaking world. Choose a place that you would most like to visit. Do some research on the Internet to plan your itinerary. Include the places you would like to visit in the city or town of your choice and explain how you would get there.

Vidéotour
Bon voyage!

Épisode 9: La gare et le train

Amadou et Chloé partent pour Lille. Ils prennent leurs billets.

Leur train part d'où?

Avant de regarder

Answer the questions.

1. Où sont Amadou et Chloé?
2. Qu'est-ce qu'ils font?
3. D'après vous, qui est l'homme avec eux?
4. D'après vous, qu'est-ce que nos amis demandent à cet homme?

Après avoir regardé

Expansion What is your favorite means of transportation for long trips. Why? Do you think most Americans would make the same choice? Survey your friends to find out their preferences.

Vidéotour
Bon voyage!

Épisode 10: Les sports

Manu joue bien au basket.

Manu est fana de basket-ball. C'est son sport favori.

Avant de regarder

Make an educated guess!

1. Où est Manu?
2. Qui joue au basket-ball?
3. Ce sont des amies de Manu?
4. Quel est le score?
5. Que fait Manu à la fin du match?

Après avoir regardé

Expansion Think of some famous French athletes and do some research to find out about them. Choose one you think is particularly good and research his or her career.

Vidéotour

Bon voyage!

Épisode 11: L'été et l'hiver

Christine «apprend» à faire du ski.

Manu est un très bon moniteur.

Avant de regarder

Can you spot the following? If so, describe each one.

1. une montagne
2. un skieur
3. une piste
4. un sommet
5. un anorak

Après avoir regardé

Expansion What fun activity do you do in the winter? And in the summer? Are video games a big part of your life?

Vidéotour

Bon voyage!

Épisode 12: La routine quotidienne

Manu se réveille.

Manu prend son petit déjeuner.

Avant de regarder

Answer the questions.

1. Que fait Manu?
2. Que lui donne Vincent dans la salle de bains?
3. Que va faire Manu avec ça?
4. Qu'est-ce que Vincent donne à Manu dans sa chambre?
5. Qu'est-ce que Manu va faire?

Après avoir regardé

Expansion Is it easy for you to get up in the morning or not? Do you go to bed early or late? Do you sleep well at night? Compare Manu's day with a typical day in your life.

Vidéotour

Bon voyage!

Épisode 13: Les loisirs culturels

Chloé visite le musée d'Orsay. Elle trouve les tableaux fabuleux.

Chloé et Vincent sur la place Igor Stravinsky

Avant de regarder

Can you spot the following?

1. une exposition
2. une danseuse
3. un tableau
4. une peinture
5. une statue

Après avoir regardé

Expansion Are you aware of your cultural heritage? Can you name some famous American painters, musicians, architects? Do some research on the Internet about the musée d'Orsay. Who are some of the artists whose art is shown there? Can you find out what special exhibitions there are currently?

Vidéotour
Bon voyage!

Épisode 14: La santé et la médecine

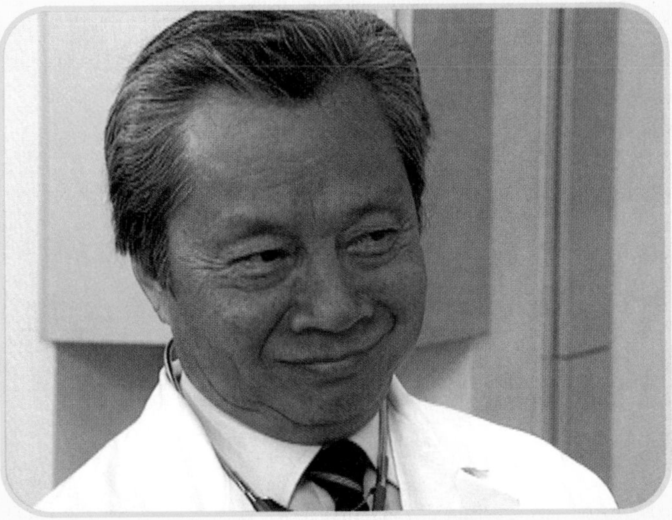

Le docteur Nguyen est très sympa.

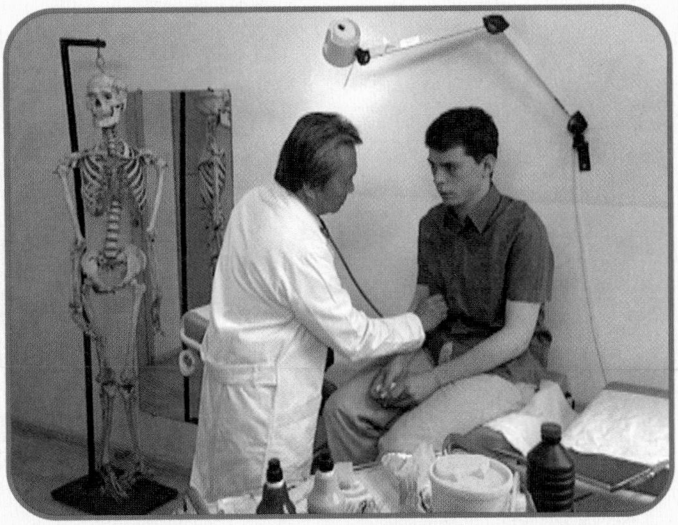

Vincent n'est pas en bonne santé.

Avant de regarder

Answer the questions.

1. Où est Vincent?
2. Pourquoi, d'après vous?
3. Vincent a un mouchoir dans la main. Pourquoi?
4. D'après vous, Vincent est très malade?
5. Que lui dit le médecin?

Après avoir regardé

Expansion Do you go to the doctor's every time something is wrong with you? Why or why not? Does your doctor make house calls? Do some research online about medical achievements and famous doctors in France. You may want to begin with an online visit to **l'Institut Pasteur**.

Handbook

Activity 1

CHAPITRE 1, Mots 1, pages 18–19

Élève A Ask your partner the following questions. Correct answers are in parentheses.

1. Comment est Sophie, petite ou grande?
   (Sophie est petite.)
2. Comment est Sylvie?
   (Elle est grande.)
3. Il est d'où, Olivier?
   (Il est de Nice.)
4. Luc est américain ou français?
   (Il est français.)
5. Comment est Olivier, brun ou blond?
   (Il est brun.)
6. Qui est de Montréal?
   (Sylvie est de Montréal.)

Élève A Answer your partner's questions based on the pictures below.

Sophie / Paris

Sylvie / Montréal

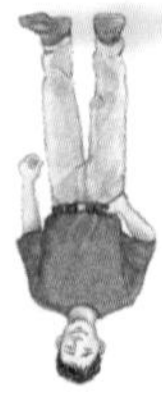
Olivier / Nice

Luc / Lyon

Élève B Answer your partner's questions based on the pictures below.

Sophie / Paris

Sylvie / Montréal

Olivier / Nice

Luc / Lyon

Élève B Ask your partner the following questions. Correct answers are in parentheses.

1. Comment est Olivier, petit ou grand?
   (Olivier est petit.)
2. Comment est Luc?
   (Luc est grand.)
3. Elle est d'où, Sophie?
   (Elle est de Paris.)
4. Qui est de Lyon?
   (Luc est de Lyon.)
5. Sophie est française ou américaine?
   (Elle est française.)
6. Comment est Luc, brun ou blond?
   (Il est blond.)

Activity 2

CHAPITRE 1, Mots 2, pages 22–23

Élève A Answer your partner's questions based on the pictures below.

Nathalie et Luc Simonet

Nathalie Simonet et Philippe Latour

Carol Smith

Bruno Lapierre

Élève A Ask your partner the following questions. Correct answers are in parentheses.

1. Qui est Luc?
   (Luc est le frère de Nathalie.)
2. Qui est Philippe?
   (Philippe est l'ami de Nathalie.)
3. Carol est élève dans une école américaine?
   (Oui, Carol est élève dans une école américaine.)
4. Bruno est élève dans un collège français?
   (Oui, Bruno est élève dans un collège français.)

Élève B Answer your partner's questions based on the pictures below.

Nathalie et Luc Simonet

Nathalie Simonet et Philippe Latour

Carol Smith

Bruno Lapierre

Élève B Ask your partner the following questions. Correct answers are in parentheses.

1. Qui est Nathalie?
   (Nathalie est la sœur de Luc.)
2. Nathalie est sympathique?
   (Oui, Nathalie est très sympathique.)
3. Carol est américaine?
   (Oui, Carol est américaine.)
4. Bruno est français?
   (Oui, Bruno est français.)

Activity 3

CHAPITRE 1, Structure, pages 26–33

Élève A Read your partner the following false statements. Correct answers are in parentheses.

1. Meg Ryan est brune.
   (Non, elle n'est pas brune. Elle est blonde.)
2. Charles de Gaulle est américain.
   (Non, il n'est pas américain. Il est français.)
3. Oprah Winfrey est timide.
   (Non, elle n'est pas timide. Elle est sociable.)
4. Napoléon est très grand.
   (Non, il n'est pas très grand. Il est assez petit.)

Élève A Correct your partner's statements based on the pictures below.

Meg Ryan

Charles de Gaulle

Oprah Winfrey

Napoléon Bonaparte

Élève B Correct your partner's statements based on the pictures below.

Meg Ryan

Charles de Gaulle

Oprah Winfrey

Napoléon Bonaparte

Élève B Read your partner the following false statements. Correct answers are in parentheses.

1. Meg Ryan est timide.
   (Non, elle n'est pas timide. Elle est dynamique.)
2. Charles de Gaulle est petit.
   (Non, il n'est pas petit. Il est grand.)
3. Oprah Winfrey est française.
   (Non, elle n'est pas française. Elle est américaine.)
4. Napoléon est américain.
   (Non, il n'est pas américain. Il est français.)

Activity 4

CHAPITRE 2, Mots 1, pages 50–51

Élève A Ask your partner the following questions. Correct answers are in parentheses.

1. Le cours de français est facile?
   (Oui, le cours de français est facile.)
2. Le prof est très sympathique?
   (Oui, le prof est très sympathique.)
3. Les élèves sont françaises ou américaines?
   (Les élèves sont françaises.)
4. Les élèves sont amies?
   (Oui, les élèves sont amies.)

Élève A Answer your partner's questions based on the picture below.

Élève B Answer your partner's questions based on the picture below.

Élève B Ask your partner the following questions. Correct answers are in parentheses.

1. Les élèves sont dans le même lycée?
   (Oui, les élèves sont dans le même lycée.)
2. Les élèves sont dans la salle de classe?
   (Oui, les élèves sont dans la salle de classe.)
3. Les élèves sont sympathiques?
   (Oui, les élèves sont sympathiques.)
4. Le cours de français est difficile?
   (Non, le cours de français n'est pas difficile.) or *(Non, le cours de français est facile.)*

Activity 5

CHAPITRE 2, Mots 2, pages 54–55

Élève A Ask your partner the following questions. Correct answers are in parentheses.

1. Guy est fort en mathématiques?
   (Oui, il est fort en mathématiques.)
2. Guy est très fort en sciences naturelles?
   (Non, il n'est pas fort en sciences naturelles.) or *(Non, il est mauvais en sciences naturelles.)*
3. Il est mauvais en géométrie?
   (Non, il n'est pas mauvais en géométrie.) or *(Non, il est fort en géométrie.)*
4. L'économie est une science naturelle?
   (Non, l'économie n'est pas une science naturelle.) or *(Non, l'économie est une science sociale.)*

Élève A Answer your partner's questions based on the report card below.

Marie Newall

Les langues:	
Le français	A–
L'anglais	B+
Les sciences sociales:	
L'histoire	D
La géographie	C+
D'autres matières:	
La musique	A

Élève B Answer your partner's questions based on the report card below.

Guy Peters

Les sciences naturelles:	
La biologie	C–
La chimie	D
Les mathématiques:	
La géométrie	A
Le calcul	B+
Les sciences sociales:	
L'économie	B

Élève B Ask your partner the following questions. Correct answers are in parentheses.

1. Marie est très forte en sciences sociales?
   (Non, elle est mauvaise en sciences sociales.) or *(Elle n'est pas forte en sciences sociales.)*
2. Le cours de français est très difficile?
   (Non, le cours de français est très facile.) or *(Non, le cours de français n'est pas difficile.)*
3. Marie est mauvaise en histoire?
   (Oui, Marie est mauvaise en histoire.)
4. L'anglais est une science sociale?
   (Non, l'anglais est une langue.) or *(Non, l'anglais n'est pas une science sociale.)*

Activity 6

CHAPITRE 2, Structure, pages 60–63

Élève A Answer your partner's questions in complete sentences, using either **Oui** or **Non.**

Élève A Ask your partner the following questions. Correct answers are in parentheses.

1. La salle de classe est petite?
   (Oui, la salle de classe est petite.) or *(Non, la salle de classe n'est pas petite.)*
2. Les élèves sont intelligents?
   (Oui, les élèves sont intelligents.) or *(Non, les élèves ne sont pas intelligents.)*
3. Le lycée est grand?
   (Oui, le lycée est grand.) or *(Non, le lycée n'est pas grand.)*
4. Vous deux, vous êtes élèves dans un lycée français?
   (Oui, nous sommes élèves dans un lycée français.) or *(Non, nous ne sommes pas élèves dans un lycée français.)*
5. Tu es fort(e) en maths?
   (Oui, je suis fort[e] en maths.) or *(Non, je ne suis pas fort[e] en maths.)*

Élève B Answer your partner's questions in complete sentences, using either **Oui** or **Non.**

Élève B Ask your partner the following questions. Correct answers are in parentheses.

1. La prof est patiente?
   (Oui, la prof est patiente.) or *(Non, la prof n'est pas patiente.)*
2. Les élèves sont sympas?
   (Oui, les élèves sont sympas.) or *(Non, les élèves ne sont pas sympas.)*
3. Le prof est intéressant?
   (Oui, le prof est intéressant.) or *(Non, le prof n'est pas intéressant.)*
4. Vous êtes copains?
   (Oui, nous sommes copains.) or *(Non, nous ne sommes pas copains.)*
5. Tu es fort(e) en histoire?
   (Oui, je suis fort[e] en histoire.) or *(Non, je ne suis pas fort[e] en histoire.)*

Activity 7

CHAPITRE 3, Mots 1, pages 82–83

Élève A Ask your partner the following questions. Correct answers are in parentheses.

1. Les élèves sont où?
   (Les élèves sont dans la cour.)
2. Ils parlent entre les cours?
   (Oui, ils parlent entre les cours.)
3. Ils étudient dans la cour?
   (Non, ils n'étudient pas dans la cour.)
4. Les copains rigolent?
   (Oui, ils rigolent.)

Élève A Answer your partner's questions based on the picture below.

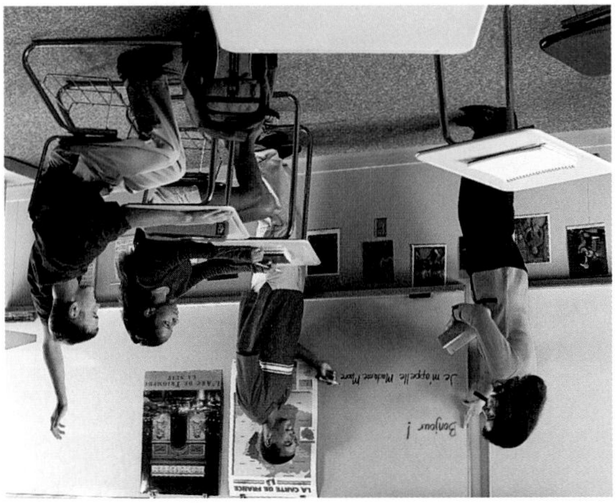

Élève B Answer your partner's questions based on the picture below.

Élève B Ask your partner the following questions. Correct answers are in parentheses.

1. Les élèves passent la journée à l'école?
   (Oui, ils passent la journée à l'école.)
2. Ils regardent la prof?
   (Oui, ils regardent la prof.)
3. Un élève pose une question?
   (Oui, il pose une question.)
4. Les élèves déjeunent pendant le cours?
   (Non, ils ne déjeunent pas pendant le cours.)

Activity 8

CHAPITRE 3, Mots 2, pages 86–87

Élève A Ask your partner the following questions. Correct answers are in parentheses.

1. Camille est à la papeterie?
   (Oui, elle est à la papeterie.)
2. Elle achète des fournitures scolaires?
   (Oui, elle achète des fournitures scolaires.)
3. Elle achète un classeur et une calculatrice?
   (Oui, elle achète un classeur et une calculatrice.)
4. Elle paie où?
   (Elle paie à la caisse.)

Élève A Answer your partner's questions based on the picture below.

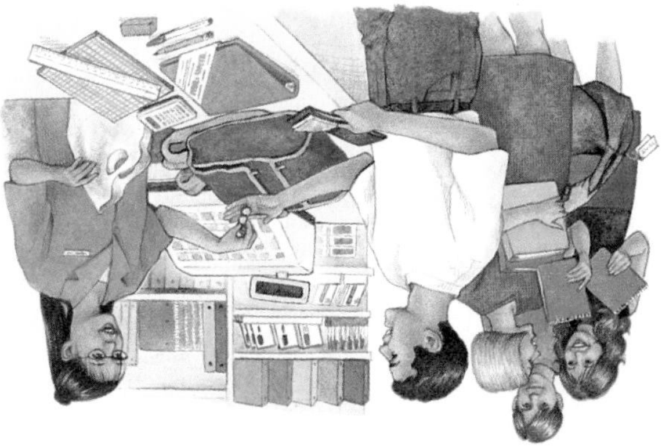

Marc Sophie

Élève B Answer your partner's questions based on the picture below.

Camille

Élève B Ask your partner the following questions. Correct answers are in parentheses.

1. Sophie travaille après les cours?
   (Oui, elle travaille après les cours.)
2. Elle travaille où?
   (Elle travaille dans une papeterie.)
3. Marc achète un sac à dos?
   (Oui, il achète un sac à dos.)
4. Il achète un classeur?
   (Oui, il achète un classeur.)

Activity 9

CHAPITRE 3, Structure, pages 90–93

Élève A Answer your partner's questions using the correct form of the verb below.

1. arriver
2. poser
3. rigoler
4. parler
5. travailler

Élève A Ask your partner the following questions. Possible responses are in parentheses.

1. Tu quittes la maison à quelle heure le matin?
   (Je quitte la maison à sept heures et demie.)
2. Qui écoute quand le prof parle?
   (Les élèves écoutent quand le prof parle.)
3. On parle français en Belgique?
   (Oui, on parle français en Belgique.)
4. Vous étudiez quelle langue?
   (Nous étudions le français.)
5. Vous détestez les examens?
   (Oui, nous détestons les examens.) or
   (Non, nous ne détestons pas les examens.)

Élève B Answer your partner's questions using the correct form of the verb below.

1. quitter
2. écouter
3. parler
4. étudier
5. détester

Élève B Ask your partner the following questions. Possible responses are in parentheses.

1. On arrive à l'école à quelle heure?
   (On arrive à l'école à huit heures.)
2. Qui pose des questions?
   (Les élèves posent des questions.) or
   (Le prof pose des questions.)
3. Vous rigolez dans la cour?
   (Oui, nous rigolons dans la cour.) or
   (Non, nous ne rigolons pas dans la cour.)
4. Tu parles beaucoup au téléphone?
   (Oui, je parle beaucoup au téléphone.) or
   (Non, je ne parle pas beaucoup au téléphone.)
5. Tu travailles après les cours?
   (Oui, je travaille après les cours.) or
   (Non, je ne travaille pas après les cours.)

Activity 10

CHAPITRE 4, Mots 1, pages 112–113

Élève A Read your partner the following statements. He or she will fill in the blank. Correct answers are in parentheses.

1. Le frère de mon père est mon ______.
   (oncle)
2. La mère de mon cousin est ma ______.
   (tante)
3. Le mari de ma mère est mon ______.
   (père)
4. La mère de mon père est ma ______.
   (grand-mère)
5. Le fils de ma tante est mon ______.
   (cousin)

Élève A Complete your partner's statements with the name of the relative.

Élève B Complete your partner's statements with the name of the relative.

Élève B Read your partner the following statements. He or she will fill in the blank. Correct answers are in parentheses.

1. La sœur de ma mère est ma ______.
   (tante)
2. La femme de mon père est ma ______.
   (mère)
3. La fille de mes parents est ma ______.
   (sœur)
4. Les parents de ma mère sont mes ______.
   (grands-parents)
5. Les enfants de mon oncle sont mes ______.
   (cousins)

Activity 11

CHAPITRE 4, Mots 2, pages 116–117

Élève A Ask your partner the following questions. Correct answers are in parentheses.

1. On regarde la télé dans la salle de bains ou la salle de séjour?
   (On regarde la télé dans la salle de séjour.)
2. On dîne dans la chambre à coucher ou la salle à manger?
   (On dîne dans la salle à manger.)
3. Le balcon donne sur la cour ou sur la cuisine?
   (Le balcon donne sur la cour.)
4. On habite au troisième étage d'un immeuble ou d'une maison?
   (On habite au troisième étage d'un immeuble.)
5. La voiture est dans la cuisine ou le garage?
   (La voiture est dans le garage.)

Élève A Now answer your partner's questions.

Élève B Answer your partner's questions.

Élève B Ask your partner the following questions. Correct answers are in parentheses.

1. On parle avec les voisins dans la cour ou la salle de bains?
   (On parle avec les voisins dans la cour.)
2. On prépare le dîner dans l'ascenseur ou la cuisine?
   (On prépare le dîner dans la cuisine.)
3. On monte à l'appartement dans le métro ou l'ascenseur?
   (On monte à l'appartement dans l'ascenseur.)
4. Les toilettes sont dans l'appartement ou dans la cour?
   (Les toilettes sont dans l'appartement.)
5. On habite dans un quartier ou dans une entrée?
   (On habite dans un quartier.)

Activity 12

CHAPITRE 4, Structure, pages 120–125

Élève A Ask your partner the following questions. Correct answers are in parentheses.

1. Marc a quel âge?
   (Il a quinze ans.)
2. Tes grands-parents ont une maison?
   (Non, ils ont un joli appartement.)
3. Tu as quel âge, toi?
   (J'ai ——— ans.)
4. Qui a deux chiens?
   (La prof de maths a deux chiens.)
5. Quel âge ont tes grands-parents?
   (Ils ont quatre-vingts ans.)

Élève A Use the chart below to answer your partner's questions. Reminder: **toi** is you.

Paul	15 ans	Une sœur
Tes grands-parents	75 ans	Un chien
Toi	?	Des profs intéressants
Tes cousines	16 ans	Deux chats
Marie	14	Une petite famille

Élève B Use the chart below to answer your partner's questions. Reminder: **toi** is you.

Marc	15 ans	Une sœur
Tes grands-parents	80 ans	Un joli appartement
Toi	?	Des profs intéressants
La prof de maths	35	Deux chiens
Sophie	14	Une petite famille

Élève B Ask your partner the following questions. Correct answers are in parentheses.

1. Qui a des profs intéressants?
   (Moi, j'ai des profs intéressants.)
2. Tes cousines ont combien de chats?
   (Mes cousines ont deux chats.)
3. Tes grands-parents ont quel âge?
   (Mes grands-parents ont soixante-quinze ans.)
4. Qui a une petite famille?
   (Marie a une petite famille.)
5. Paul a un frère ou une sœur?
   (Paul a une sœur.)

Activity 13

CHAPITRE 5, Mots 1, pages 154–155

Élève A You are the server in a French café. Ask your partner what he or she wants to order. Correct answers are in parentheses.

1. Vous désirez?
   (Un citron pressé, s'il vous plaît.)
2. Vous désirez?
   (Un croissant, s'il vous plaît.)
3. Vous désirez?
   (Une salade verte, s'il vous plaît.)
4. Vous désirez?
   (Un café, s'il vous plaît.) or *(Un express, s'il vous plaît.)*
5. Vous désirez?
   (Une tartine de pain beurré, s'il vous plaît.)

Élève A Now your partner is the server. Use the following picture menu to give your order.

1.

2.
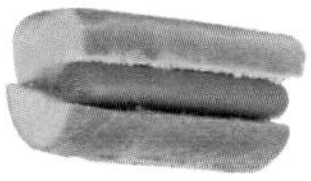

3.
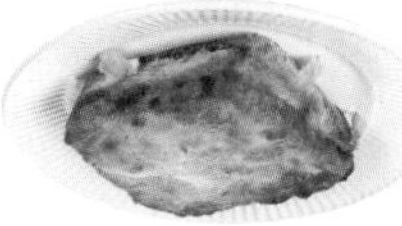

4.

5.
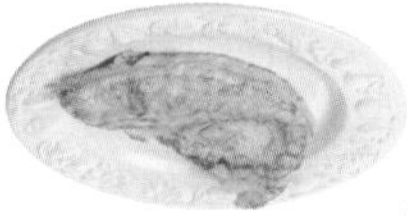

Élève B Your partner is the server in a French café. Use the following picture menu to give your order.

1.

2.

3.

4.

5.

Élève B Now you are the server. Ask your partner what he or she wants to order. Correct answers are in parentheses.

1. Vous désirez?
   (Un jus d'orange, s'il vous plaît.)
2. Vous désirez?
   (Une saucisse de Francfort, s'il vous plaît.) or *(Un hot-dog, s'il vous plaît.)*
3. Vous désirez?
   (Un croque-monsieur, s'il vous plaît.)
4. Vous désirez?
   (Une soupe à l'oignon, s'il vous plaît.)
5. Vous désirez?
   (Une omelette nature, s'il vous plaît.)

Activity 14

CHAPITRE 5, Mots 2, pages 158–159

Élève A Ask your partner the following questions. Correct answers are in parentheses.

1. Un couteau, c'est pour la soupe?
   (Non, une cuillère, c'est pour la soupe.)
2. Un verre, c'est pour le café?
   (Non, une tasse, c'est pour le café.)
3. Une soupe à l'oignon, c'est pour le dessert?
   (Non, une glace au chocolat, c'est pour le dessert.)
4. Un couteau, c'est pour le steak?
   (Oui, un couteau, c'est pour le steak.)
5. Un verre, c'est pour la limonade?
   (Oui, un verre, c'est pour la limonade.)

Élève A Use the pictures below to answer your partner's questions.

1.
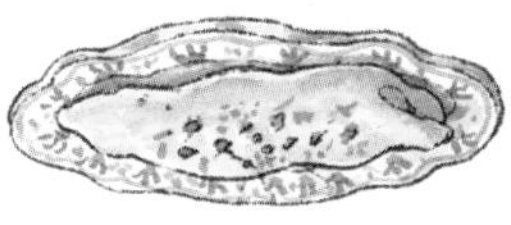

2.

3.

4.

5.

Élève B Use the pictures below to answer your partner's questions.

1.

2.

3.

4.
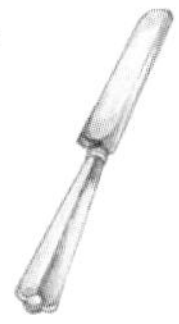

5.

Élève B Now ask your partner the following questions. Correct answers are in parentheses.

1. On prend un croissant pour le dîner?
   (Non, on prend une omelette pour le dîner.)
2. On prend une crêpe pour le déjeuner?
   (Non, on prend un sandwich au jambon pour le déjeuner.)
3. C'est un pourboire ou une fourchette?
   (C'est un pourboire.)
4. C'est un steak saignant ou bien cuit?
   (C'est un steak bien cuit.)
5. C'est une assiette ou une serviette?
   (C'est une serviette.)

Activity 15

CHAPITRE 5, Structure, pages 162–169

Élève A Ask your partner the following questions. Correct answers are in parentheses.

1. Les copains vont où?
   (Ils vont à l'école.)
2. Ils y vont comment?
   (Ils y vont en voiture.)
3. Tu vas où?
   (Je vais à la papeterie.)
4. Tu y vas à pied?
   (Non, j'y vais en bus.)

Élève A Answer your partner's questions based on the cues below.

1. l'école
2. à pied
3. le café
4. le métro

Élève B Answer your partner's questions based on the cues below.

1. l'école
2. en voiture
3. la papeterie
4. en bus

Élève B Ask your partner the following questions. Correct answers are in parentheses.

1. Vous allez où?
   (Nous allons à l'école.)
2. Vous y allez comment?
   (Nous y allons à pied.)
3. Tu vas où?
   (Je vais au café.)
4. Tu prends le bus pour aller au café?
   (Non, je prends le métro.)

Activity 16

CHAPITRE 6, Mots 1, pages 186–187

Élève A Ask your partner the following questions. Correct answers are in parentheses.

1. Pour acheter du pain, on va où?
   (On va à la boulangerie-pâtisserie.)
2. Pour acheter du lait, on va où?
   (On va à la crémerie.)
3. Pour acheter une tarte aux pommes, on va où?
   (On va à la boulangerie-pâtisserie.)
4. Pour acheter du jambon, on va où?
   (On va à la charcuterie.)
5. Pour acheter de la crème, on va où?
   (On va à la crémerie.)

Élève A Use the following pictures to answer your partner's questions.

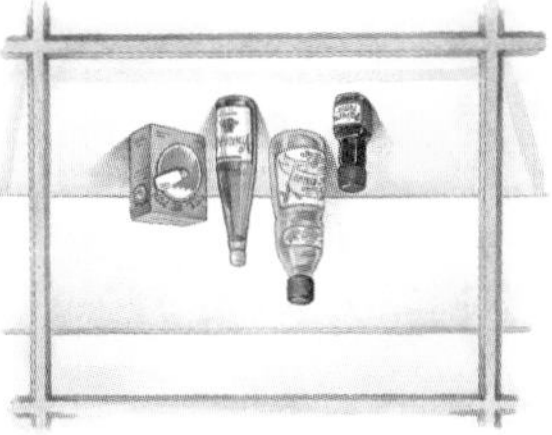

Élève B Answer your partner's questions based on the pictures below.

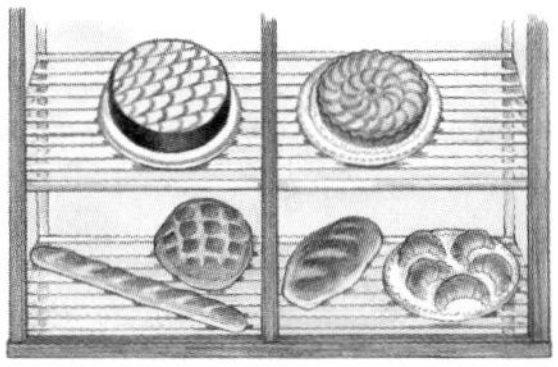

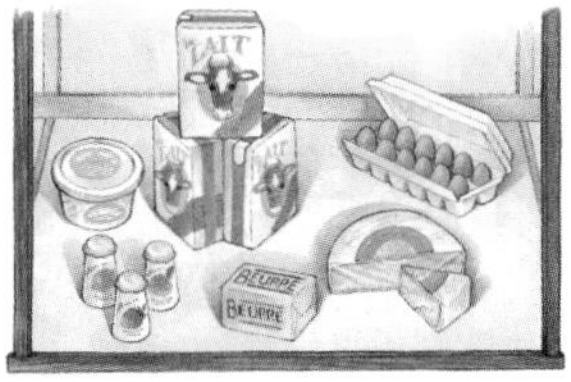

Élève B Ask your partner the following questions. Correct answers are in parentheses.

1. Pour acheter de la viande, on va où?
   (On va à la boucherie.)
2. Pour acheter du poisson, on va où?
   (On va à la poissonnerie.)
3. Pour acheter du poivre, on va où?
   (On va à l'épicerie.)
4. Pour acheter du porc, on va où?
   (On va à la boucherie.)
5. Pour acheter des crevettes, on va où?
   (On va à la poissonnerie.)

Activity 17

CHAPITRE 6, Mots 2, pages 190–191

Élève A You play the part of the vendor. Ask your partner the following questions. Correct answers are in parentheses.

1. Vous voulez de la confiture?
   (Oui, je voudrais un pot de confiture, s'il vous plaît.)
2. Vous voulez des légumes surgelés?
   (Oui, je voudrais un paquet de légumes surgelés, s'il vous plaît.)
3. Vous voulez des petits pois?
   (Oui, je voudrais une boîte de petits pois, s'il vous plaît.)
4. Vous voulez du lait?
   (Oui, je voudrais un litre de lait, s'il vous plaît.)
5. Vous voulez du jambon?
   (Oui, je voudrais une tranche de jambon, s'il vous plaît.)

Élève A Answer your partner's questions based on the information below.

un pot

250 grammes

une douzaine

une boîte

une bouteille

Élève B Answer your partner's questions based on the information below.

un pot

un paquet

une boîte

un litre

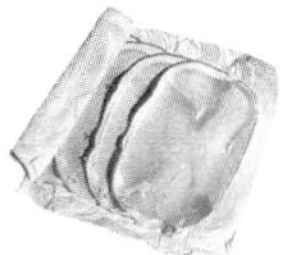

une tranche

Élève B Now you are the vendor. Ask your partner the following questions. Correct answers are in parentheses.

1. Vous voulez de la moutarde?
   (Oui, je voudrais un pot de moutarde, s'il vous plaît.)
2. Vous voulez du beurre?
   (Oui, je voudrais deux cent cinquante grammes de beurre, s'il vous plaît.)
3. Vous voulez des œufs?
   (Oui, je voudrais une douzaine d'œufs, s'il vous plaît.)
4. Vous voulez des petits pois?
   (Oui, je voudrais une boîte de petits pois, s'il vous plaît.)
5. Vous voulez de l'eau minérale?
   (Oui, je voudrais une bouteille d'eau minérale, s'il vous plaît.)

Activity 18

CHAPITRE 6, Structure, pages 194–195

Élève A Ask your partner the following questions. Correct answers are in parentheses.

1. Qui fait le déjeuner?
   (Moi, je fais le déjeuner.)
2. Qui fait du français?
   (Nous faisons du français.)
3. Qui fait des études?
   (Tu fais des études.)
4. Qui fait les exercices?
   (Alain et Eric font les exercices.)
5. Qui fait le gâteau?
   (Vous faites le gâteau.)

Élève A Use the information in the chart below to answer your partner's questions.

Qui?	**Activité**
Moi, je	(faire) les courses
Hugo et Marie	(faire) un pique-nique
Nous	(faire) de l'allemand
Vous	(faire) la cuisine
Tu	(faire) les devoirs

Élève B Use the information in the chart below to answer your partner's questions.

Qui?	**Activité**
Moi, je	(faire) le déjeuner
Nous	(faire) du français
Tu	(faire) des études
Alain et Eric	(faire) les exercices
Vous	(faire) le gâteau

Élève B Ask your partner the following questions. Correct answers are in parentheses.

1. Qui fait les courses?
   (Moi, je fais les courses.)
2. Qui fait un pique-nique?
   (Hugo et Marie font un pique-nique.)
3. Qui fait de l'allemand?
   (Nous faisons de l'allemand.)
4. Qui fait la cuisine?
   (Vous faites la cuisine.)
5. Qui fait les devoirs?
   (Tu fais les devoirs.)

Activity 19

CHAPITRE 6, Structure, pages 201–203

Élève A Ask your partner the following questions. Correct answers are in parentheses.

1. Qui veut aller au restaurant?
   (Moi, je veux aller au restaurant.)
2. Qui peut travailler après l'école?
   (Il peut travailler après l'école.)
3. Qui veut inviter des amis?
   (Tu veux inviter des amis.)
4. Qui veut manger maintenant?
   (Nous voulons manger maintenant.)
5. Qui peut regarder le film?
   (Vous pouvez regarder le film.)
6. Qui veut aller au marché?
   (Pierre veut aller au marché.)
7. Qui veut écouter des CD?
   (Eric et Michel veulent écouter des CD.)

Élève A Use the information in the chart below to answer your partner's questions.

Qui?	Activité
Moi, je	(pouvoir) regarder le film
Elle	(vouloir) aller au restaurant
Nous	(pouvoir) faire des sandwichs
Ils	(vouloir) écouter des CD
Tu	(pouvoir) manger maintenant
Alain	(pouvoir) aller au marché
Hugo et Marie	(pouvoir) inviter des amis

Élève B Use the information in the chart below to answer your partner's questions.

Qui?	Activité
Moi, je	(vouloir) aller au restaurant
Il	(pouvoir) travailler après l'école
Tu	(vouloir) inviter des amis
Nous	(vouloir) manger maintenant
Vous	(pouvoir) regarder le film
Pierre	(vouloir) aller au marché
Eric et Michel	(vouloir) écouter des CD

Élève B Ask your partner the following questions. Correct answers are in parentheses.

1. Qui peut regarder le film?
   (Moi, je peux regarder le film.)
2. Qui veut aller au restaurant?
   (Elle veut aller au restaurant.)
3. Qui peut faire des sandwichs?
   (Nous pouvons faire des sandwichs.)
4. Qui veut écouter des CD?
   (Ils veulent écouter des CD.)
5. Qui peut manger maintenant?
   (Tu peux manger maintenant.)
6. Qui peut aller au marché?
   (Alain peut aller au marché.)
7. Qui peut inviter des amis?
   (Hugo et Marie peuvent inviter des amis.)

Activity 20

CHAPITRE 7, Mots 1, pages 220–221

Élève A Ask your partner the following questions. Correct answers are in parentheses.

1. Marc porte un anorak?
   (Oui, il porte un anorak.)
2. Marc porte un blouson?
   (Non, il voit un blouson dans la vitrine.)
3. Marc porte un pull?
   (Oui, il porte un pull.)
4. Marc porte un t-shirt?
   (Non, il voit un t-shirt dans la vitrine.)
5. Marc porte une paire de chaussures?
   (Oui, il porte une paire de chaussures.)
6. Marc porte un survêtement?
   (Non, il voit un survêtement dans la vitrine.)

Élève A Use the information in the chart below to answer your partner's questions.

Elle porte…	Elle voit… dans la vitrine.

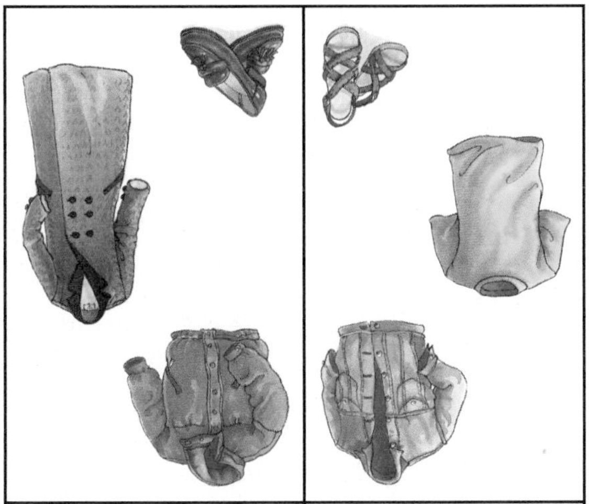

Élève B Use the information in the chart below to answer your partner's questions.

Il porte…	Il voit… dans la vitrine.

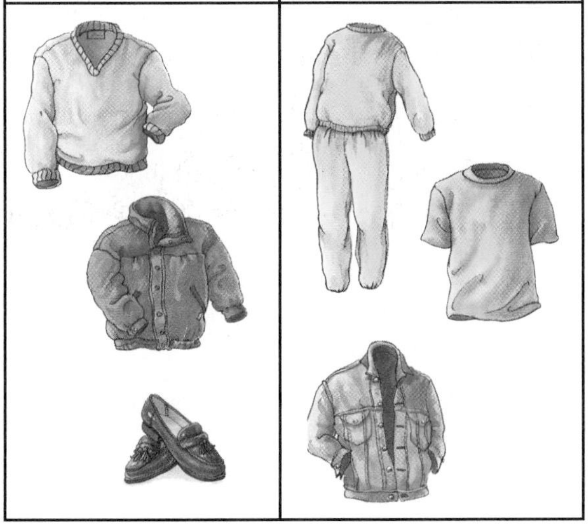

Élève B Ask your partner the following questions. Correct answers are in parentheses.

1. Chloé porte des sandales?
   (Oui, elle porte des sandales.)
2. Chloé porte un anorak?
   (Non, elle voit un anorak dans la vitrine.)
3. Chloé porte un blouson?
   (Oui, elle porte un blouson.)
4. Chloé porte une paire de chaussures?
   (Non, elle voit une paire de chaussures dans la vitrine.)
5. Chloé porte un t-shirt?
   (Oui, elle porte un t-shirt.)
6. Chloé porte un manteau?
   (Non, elle voit un manteau dans la vitrine.)

Activity 21

CHAPITRE 7, Mots 2, pages 224–225

Élève A Find out your partner's opinion of different clothing items. Correct answers are in parentheses.

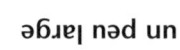

1. Il est joli, le pull bleu. Tu ne trouves pas?
   (Non, il est trop serré.)
2. Il est joli, le manteau gris. Tu ne trouves pas?
   (Non, il est trop long.)
3. Il est joli, l'anorak rouge. Tu ne trouves pas?
   (Non, il est trop cher.)
4. Elle est jolie, la jupe verte. Tu ne trouves pas?
   (Non, elle est un peu courte.)
5. Elles sont jolies, les chaussures marron. Tu ne trouves pas?
   (Oui, c'est ma couleur favorite.)

Élève A Use the information below to answer your partner's questions.

trop grand

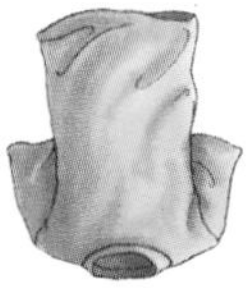

trop petit

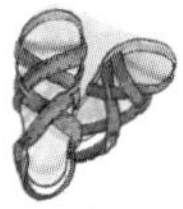

trop chères

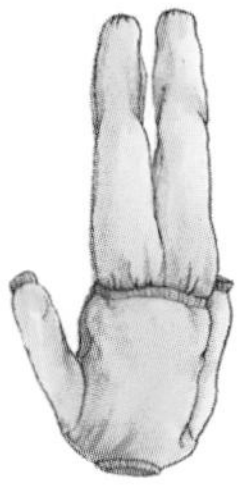

un peu large

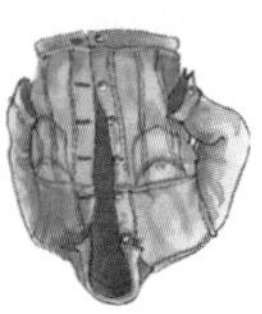

Oui, c'est ma couleur favorite.

Élève B Use the information below to answer your partner's questions.

trop serré

trop long

trop cher

un peu courte

Oui, c'est ma couleur favorite.

Élève B Find out your partner's opinion of different clothing items. Correct answers are in parentheses.

1. Il est joli, le short vert. Tu ne trouves pas?
   (Non, il est trop grand.)
2. Il est joli, le t-shirt orange. Tu ne trouves pas?
   (Non, il est trop petit.)
3. Elles sont jolies, les sandales bleues. Tu ne trouves pas?
   (Non, elles sont trop chères.)
4. Il est joli, le survêtement jaune. Tu ne trouves pas?
   (Non, il est un peu large.)
5. Il est joli, le blouson bleu. Tu ne trouves pas?
   (Oui, c'est ma couleur favorite.)

Activity 22

CHAPITRE 7, Structure, pages 228–229

Élève A Ask your partner the following questions. Correct answers are in parentheses.

1. Qui met un short?
   (Moi, je mets un short pour faire du jogging.)
2. Qui met la radio le matin?
   (Mes copains mettent la radio le matin.)
3. Qui met une cravate?
   (Mon père met une cravate pour aller au travail.)
4. Qui met la table?
   (Vous mettez la table pour le dîner.)
5. Qui met un jean?
   (Tu mets un jean pour aller au cinéma.)
6. Qui met un complet?
   (Nous mettons un complet pour aller à un mariage.)

Élève A Use the information in the chart below to answer your partner's questions.

Qui?	Activité
Moi, je	(mettre) la télé le matin
Les serveurs	(mettre) la table au restaurant
Ma mère	(mettre) une jupe pour aller au marché
Nous	(mettre) des chaussettes rouges
Tu	(mettre) des baskets pour faire du jogging
Vous	(mettre) un pantalon pour aller à l'école

Élève B Use the information in the chart below to answer your partner's questions.

Qui?	Activité
Moi, je	(mettre) un short pour faire du jogging
Mes copains	(mettre) la radio le matin
Mon père	(mettre) une cravate pour aller au travail
Vous	(mettre) la table pour le dîner
Tu	(mettre) un jean pour aller au cinéma
Nous	(mettre) un complet pour aller à un mariage

Élève B Ask your partner the following questions. Correct answers are in parentheses.

1. Qui met la télé?
   (Moi, je mets la télé le matin.)
2. Qui met la table?
   (Les serveurs mettent la table au restaurant.)
3. Qui met une jupe?
   (Ma mère met une jupe pour aller au marché.)
4. Qui met des chaussettes rouges?
   (Nous mettons des chaussettes rouges.)
5. Qui met des baskets?
   (Tu mets des baskets pour faire du jogging.)
6. Qui met un pantalon?
   (Vous mettez un pantalon pour aller à l'école.)

Activity 23

CHAPITRE 7, Structure, pages 232–233

Élève A Read the statements about clothing to your partner. Your partner does not agree with what you believe to be true. Correct answers are in parentheses.

1. Moi, je crois que le polo est plus grand que le t-shirt.
   (Non, je vois que le t-shirt est plus grand que le polo.) or *(Non, je vois que le polo est plus petit que le t-shirt.)*
2. Moi, je crois que la chemise est plus grande que le polo.
   (Non, je vois que la chemise est aussi grande que le polo.)
3. Moi, je crois que la jupe plissée est moins élégante que le chemisier.
   (Non, je vois que la jupe plissée est aussi élégante que le chemisier.)

Élève A Your partner tells you what he or she thinks about articles of clothing. Use the chart below to give your partner the correct information. Begin your response with **Non, je vois que…**

confortables	les baskets + +		les chaussures + +
cher	l'anorak $ $ $	le blouson $	le manteau $ $ $ $ $

Élève B Your partner tells you what he or she thinks about articles of clothing. Use the chart below to give your partner the correct information. Begin your response with **Non, je vois que…**

grand(e)	le t-shirt + + + + +	la chemise + + +	le polo + + +
élégant(e)	la jupe plissée + +		le chemisier + +

Élève B Read the statements about clothing to your partner. Your partner does not agree with what you believe to be true. Correct answers are in parentheses.

1. Moi, je crois que les chaussures sont moins confortables que les baskets.
   (Non, je vois que les chaussures sont aussi confortables que les baskets.)
2. Moi, je crois que le blouson est aussi cher que l'anorak.
   (Non, je vois que le blouson est moins cher que l'anorak.) or *(Non, je vois que l'anorak est plus cher que le blouson.)*
3. Moi, je crois que l'anorak est plus cher que le manteau.
   (Non, je vois que le manteau est plus cher que l'anorak.) or *(Non, je vois que l'anorak est moins cher que le manteau.)*

Activity 24

CHAPITRE 8, Mots 1, pages 260–261

Élève A Make the following statements to your partner. He or she will add the location where the activity takes place. Correct answers are in parentheses.

1. Le passager vérifie la carte d'embarquement.
   (Le passager vérifie la carte d'embarquement à la porte d'embarquement.)
2. Le passager demande une place.
   (Le passager demande une place côté couloir.)
3. Le passager vérifie son billet.
   (Le passager vérifie son billet au comptoir de la compagnie aérienne.)
4. Le passager va passer par le contrôle de sécurité.
   (Le passager va passer par le contrôle de sécurité dans l'aérogare.)

Élève A Your partner will make a statement about an activity. Tell where each activity takes place according to the chart below.

Activité	Où
prendre un vol	à l'aéroport
vérifier l'heure du départ	sur l'écran
décoller	sur la piste
faire enregistrer ses bagages	au comptoir de la compagnie aérienne

Élève B Your partner will make a statement about an activity. Tell where each activity takes place according to the chart below.

Activité	Où
vérifier la carte d'embarquement	à la porte d'embarquement
demander une place	côté couloir
vérifier son billet	au comptoir de la compagnie aérienne
passer par le contrôle de sécurité	dans l'aérogare

Élève B Make the following statements to your partner. He or she will add the location where the activity takes place. Correct answers are in parentheses.

1. Le passager va prendre un vol.
   (Oui, le passager va prendre un vol à l'aéroport.)
2. Le passager vérifie l'heure du départ.
   (Oui, le passager vérifie l'heure du départ sur l'écran.)
3. L'avion décolle.
   (Oui, l'avion décolle sur la piste.)
4. Le passager fait enregistrer ses bagages.
   (Oui, le passager fait enregistrer ses bagages au comptoir de la compagnie aérienne.)

Activity 25

CHAPITRE 8, Mots 2, pages 264–265

Élève A Ask your partner the following questions. Correct answers are in parentheses.

1. Il faut attacher sa ceinture de sécurité quand?
   (avant le décollage)
2. Qui sert les boissons?
   (le steward)
3. On peut fumer quand?
   (après le vol)
4. On ramasse les plateaux quand?
   (après le repas)
5. Il faut un passeport quand?
   (pour un vol international)
6. Il faut mettre vos bagages à main où?
   (sous le siège devant vous)

Élève A Answer your partner's questions. Choose from the answers below.

1. avant le vol / après le vol
2. le passager / le pilote
3. avant le vol / pendant le vol
4. avant le décollage / pendant le décollage
5. dans la cabine / dans le coffre à bagages
6. le pilote / le passager

Élève B Answer your partner's questions. Choose from the answers below.

1. avant le décollage / après le décollage
2. le steward / le pilote
3. pendant le vol / après le vol
4. après le repas / pendant le repas
5. pour un vol intérieur / pour un vol international
6. sous le siège devant vous / dans le couloir

Élève B Ask your partner the following questions. Correct answers are in parentheses.

1. Il faut faire ses valises quand?
   (avant le vol)
2. Qui remplit sa carte de débarquement?
   (le passager)
3. On sert un repas quand?
   (pendant le vol)
4. Il faut mettre ses bagages sous le siège quand?
   (avant le décollage)
5. Les toilettes sont où?
   (dans la cabine)
6. Qui dort pendant le vol?
   (le passager)

Activity 26

CHAPITRE 8, Structure, pages 268–269

Élève A Ask your partner the following questions. Correct answers are in parentheses.

1. Qu'est-ce que vous faites?
   (Nous remplissons la carte de débarquement.)
2. Qu'est-ce-que l'hôtesse fait?
   (Elle sert le dîner.)
3. Qu'est-ce que l'avion fait?
   (L'avion atterrit.)

Élève A Answer your partner's questions according to the illustrations.

1. 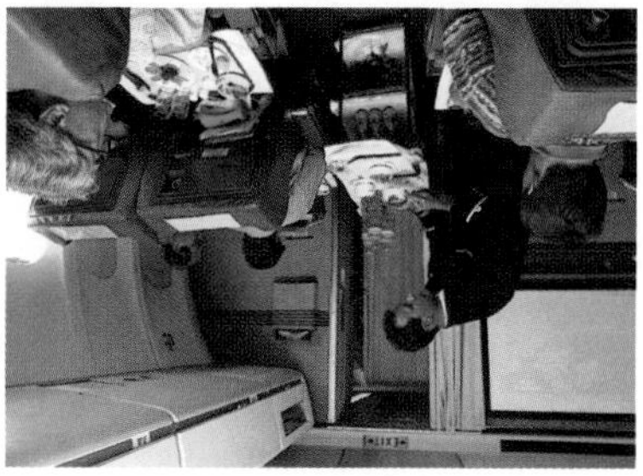

2. 

3. 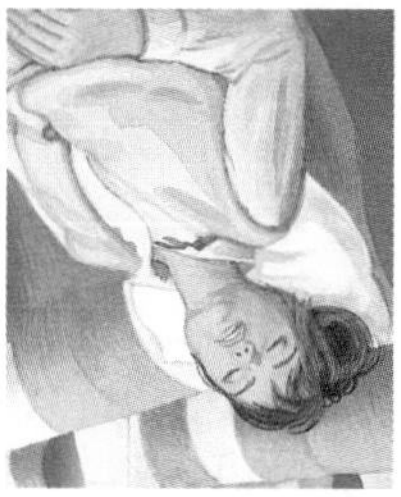

Élève B Answer your partner's questions according to the illustrations.

1. 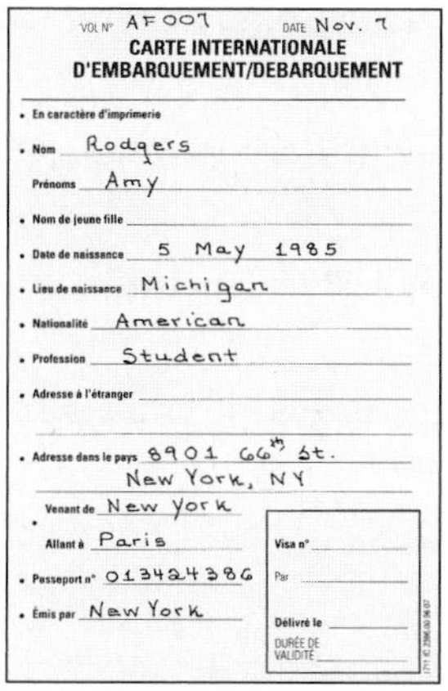

VOL N° AF007 DATE Nov. 7
CARTE INTERNATIONALE D'EMBARQUEMENT/DEBARQUEMENT

- En caractère d'imprimerie
- Nom: Rodgers
- Prénoms: Amy
- Nom de jeune fille:
- Date de naissance: 5 May 1985
- Lieu de naissance: Michigan
- Nationalité: American
- Profession: Student
- Adresse à l'étranger:
- Adresse dans le pays: 8901 66th St. New York, NY
- Venant de: New York
- Allant à: Paris
- Passeport n°: 013424386
- Émis par: New York

Visa n°:
Par:
Délivré le:
DURÉE DE VALIDITÉ:

2. 

3. 

Élève B Ask your partner the following questions. Correct answers are in parentheses.

1. Qu'est-ce que le steward fait?
   (Il sert des boissons.)
2. Qu'est-ce que le passager fait?
   (Il sort ses bagages du coffre à bagages.)
3. Qu'est que tu fais pendant le vol?
   (Je dors pendant le vol.)

Activity 27

CHAPITRE 9, Mots 1, pages 292–293

Élève A Ask your partner the following questions. Correct answers are in parentheses.

1. Que font les passagers?
   (Les passagers font la queue.)
2. Qu'est-ce que Ahmed achète?
   (un billet)
3. Il achète son billet où?
   (au guichet)
4. Tu achètes un billet Paris-Lyon-Paris?
   (Oui, un aller-retour.)
5. Tu achètes un billet Paris-Lyon?
   (Oui, un aller simple.)

Élève A Look at the picture below; then choose the best response from the options given to answer your partner's questions.

1. un journal / un billet
2. le guichet / la voie
3. au buffet / au kiosque
4. sur le quai / dans la salle d'attente
5. au buffet de la gare / au guichet

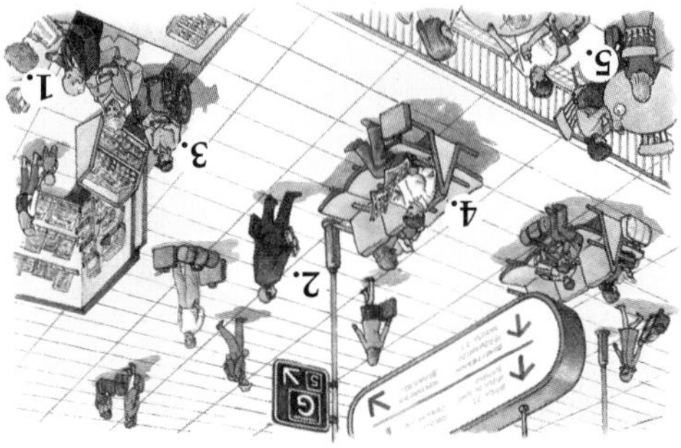

Élève B Look at the pictures below; then choose the best response from the options given to answer your partner's questions.

1. Ils attendent le train. / Ils font la queue.
2. un billet / une carte postale
3. au kiosque / au guichet
4. Oui, un aller simple. / Oui, un aller-retour.
5. Oui, un aller simple. / Oui, un aller-retour.

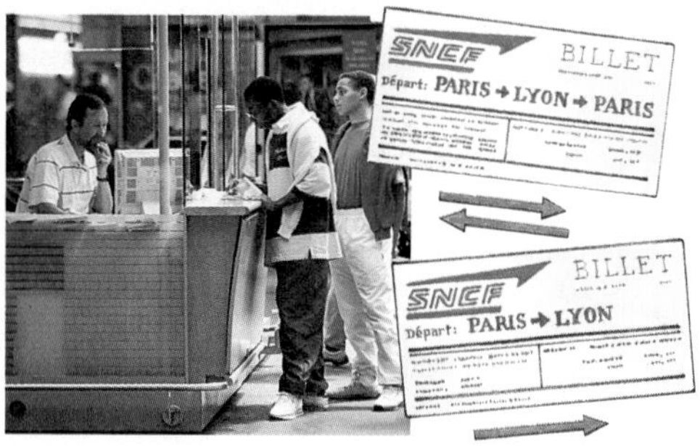

Élève B Ask your partner the following questions. Correct answers are in parentheses.

1. Qu'est-ce que Monsieur Roget achète?
   (un journal)
2. Qu'est-ce que Monsieur Laporte regarde?
   (la voie)
3. Monsieur Boucher fait la queue où?
   (au kiosque)
4. Monsieur Longtemps attend le train où?
   (dans la salle d'attente)
5. Paul prend une boisson où?
   (au buffet de la gare)

Activity 28

CHAPITRE 9, Mots 2, pages 296–297

Élève A Ask your partner the following questions. Correct answers are in parentheses.

1. Les voyageurs sont debout dans le wagon?
   (Non, ils sont assis.)
2. Anne lit le journal?
   (Non, elle écrit une carte postale.)
3. Paul et Sylvie sont où?
   (Ils sont devant la gare.)
4. Ils attendent une amie?
   (Oui, ils attendent une amie.)
5. Paul commence à perdre patience?
   (Oui, il commence à perdre patience.)

Élève A Answer your partner's questions based on the pictures below.

1–2.

3–5.

Élève B Answer your partner's questions based on the pictures below.

1–2.

3–5.

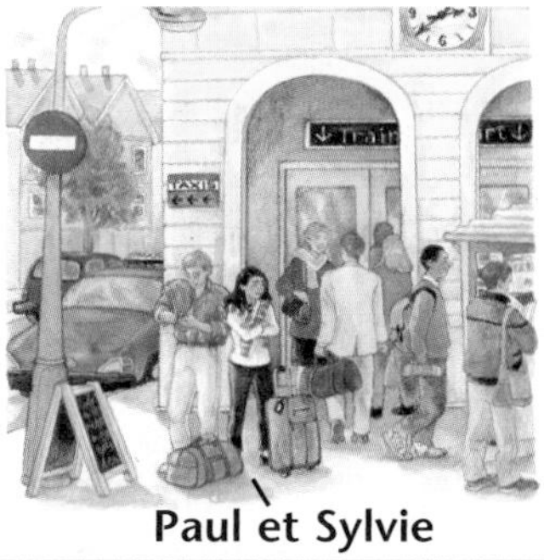

Élève B Ask your partner the following questions. Correct answers are in parentheses.

1. Madame Renoir est assise?
   (Non, elle est debout.)
2. Pierre écrit des cartes postales?
   (Non, il lit le journal.)
3. Le passager est debout?
   (Non, il est assis.)
4. Le contrôleur contrôle les boissons?
   (Non, il contrôle les billets.)
5. Toutes les places sont occupées?
   (Non, toutes les places ne sont pas occupées.)

Activity 29

CHAPITRE 9, Structure, pages 300–307

Élève A Say each of the following words to your partner. He or she will make a sentence using the word and one of the verbs listed. Possible answers are in parentheses.

1. un voyageur
   (J'attends un voyageur.)
2. les annonces
   (J'entends les annonces.)
3. un ami
   (J'attends un ami.) or
   (J'écris à un ami.)
4. des choses amusantes
   (Je dis des choses amusantes.) or
   (J'écris des choses amusantes.)
5. les bagages
   (Je descends les bagages.) or
   (J'attends les bagages.)

Élève A Your partner will say a word or phrase. Use the word with one of the verbs below to make a statement about what you do.

Example: You hear: **Le journal.**
You respond: **Je lis le journal.** *or* **Je vends le journal.**

vendre	**descendre**	**répondre**	**perdre**	**lire**

Élève B Your partner will say a word or phrase. Use the word with one of the verbs below to make a statement about what you do.

Example: You hear: **Le train.**
You respond: **J'attends le train.** *or* **Je descends du train.**

attendre	**descendre**	**entendre**	**écrire**	**dire**

Élève B Say each of the following words to your partner. He or she will make a sentence using the word and one of the verbs listed. Possible answers are in parentheses.

1. des cartes postales
   (Je vends des cartes postales.) or
   (Je lis des cartes postales.)
2. la voiture
   (Je descends de la voiture.) or
   (Je vends la voiture.)
3. la question
   (Je réponds à la question.) or
   (Je lis la question.)
4. patience *(Je perds patience.)*
5. des magazines
   (Je lis des magazines.) or
   (Je vends des magazines.)

Activity 30

CHAPITRE 10, Mots 1, pages 324–325

Élève A Ask your partner the following questions. Correct responses are in parentheses.

1. Est-ce que Rennes joue contre Auxerre?
   (Non, Rennes joue contre Lille.)
2. Il y a beaucoup de spectateurs dans le stade?
   (Oui, il y a beaucoup de spectateurs dans le stade.)
3. Le gardien de but, il bloque le ballon?
   (Non, il ne bloque pas le ballon.)
4. Le ballon entre dans le but?
   (Oui, le ballon entre dans le but.)

Élève A Answer your partner's questions based on the illustration.

Élève B Answer your partner's questions based on the illustration.

Élève B Ask your partner the following questions. Correct responses are in parentheses.

1. Un joueur a donné un coup de tête dans le ballon?
   (Non, un joueur a donné un coup de pied dans le ballon.)
2. Il y a beaucoup de places libres dans les gradins?
   (Non, les gradins sont pleins.)
3. Le gardien arrête le ballon?
   (Non, le gardien n'arrête pas le ballon.)
4. Le joueur a marqué un but?
   (Oui, le joueur a marqué un but.)

Activity 31

CHAPITRE 10, Mots 2, pages 328–329

Élève A Read the following statements to your partner, some of which are false. Your partner will correct them. The correct answers are in parentheses.

1. Le basket-ball est un sport individuel.
   (Non, le basket-ball est un sport d'équipe.)
2. Un joueur de basket sert le ballon.
   (Non, un joueur de basket ne sert pas le ballon.)
3. Les joueurs dribblent le ballon pendant un match de basket.
   (Oui, ...)
4. Une joueuse lance le ballon dans le panier pendant un match de basket.
   (Oui, ...)
5. Les joueurs de basket donnent un coup de pied au ballon.
   (Non, les joueurs de basket dribblent le ballon.)

Élève A Listen to the statements made by your partner, some of which are false. Correct the false statements.

Élève B Listen to the statements made by your partner, some of which are false. Correct the false statements.

Élève B Read the following statements to your partner, some of which are false. Your partner will correct them. The correct answers are in parentheses.

1. Le volley-ball est un sport individuel.
   (Non, le volley-ball est un sport d'équipe.)
2. Les joueurs dribblent le ballon pendant un match de volley-ball.
   (Non, les joueurs ne dribblent pas le ballon pendant un match de volley-ball.)
3. Une joueuse de volley-ball sert le ballon.
   (Oui, ...)
4. Une joueuse de volley-ball renvoie le ballon par-dessus le filet.
   (Oui, ...)
5. Le ballon doit toucher le sol pendant un match de volley-ball.
   (Non, le ballon ne doit pas toucher le sol.)

Activity 32

CHAPITRE 10, Structure, pages 332–334

Élève A Ask your partner who did the following activities. Correct answers are in parentheses.

1. Qui a joué au foot?
   (Chloé a joué au foot.)
2. Qui a perdu le match?
   (Tu as perdu le match.)
3. Qui a regardé le match?
   (Les spectateurs ont regardé le match.)
4. Qui a choisi une place?
   (Moi, j'ai choisi une place.)
5. Qui a dansé?
   (Nous avons dansé.)

Élève A Your partner wants to know who did the activities below. Answer based on the information in the chart.

Qui?	Activité
Les spectateurs	attendre longtemps
L'arbitre	voyager
Nous	gagner la coupe
Tu	finir le match
Julien	lancer le ballon

Élève B Your partner wants to know who did the activities below. Answer based on the information in the chart.

Qui?	Activité
Chloé	jouer au foot
Tu	perdre le match
Les spectateurs	regarder le match
Moi, je	choisir une place
Nous	danser

Élève B Ask your partner who did the following activities. Correct answers are in parentheses.

1. Qui a attendu longtemps?
   (Les spectateurs ont attendu longtemps.)
2. Qui a voyagé?
   (L'arbitre a voyagé.)
3. Qui a gagné la coupe.
   (Nous avons gagné la coupe.)
4. Qui a fini le match?
   (Tu as fini le match.)
5. Qui a lancé le ballon?
   (Julien a lancé le ballon.)

Activity 33

CHAPITRE 10, Structure, pages 337–339

Élève A Ask your partner who does the following activities. Correct answers are in parentheses.

1. Qui doit passer un examen?
   (Nathalie doit passer un examen.)
2. Qui reçoit le ballon?
   (Tu reçois le ballon.)
3. Qui boit de la limonade?
   (Les enfants boivent de la limonade.)
4. Qui doit être content?
   (Vous devez être contents.)
5. Qui boit du lait?
   (Moi, je bois du lait.)

Élève A Your partner wants to know who does the following. Answer based on the information in the chart.

Qui?	Activité
Rémi	boire du coca
Tu	devoir étudier
Les copains	recevoir un cadeau
Moi, je	boire de l'eau
Nous	devoir travailler

Élève B Your partner wants to know who does the following. Answer based on the information in the chart.

Qui?	Activité
Nathalie	devoir passer un examen
Tu	recevoir le ballon
Les enfants	boire de la limonade
Vous	devoir être contents
Moi, je	boire du lait

Élève B Ask your partner who does the following activities. Correct answers are in parentheses.

1. Qui boit du coca?
   (Rémi boit du coca.)
2. Qui doit étudier?
   (Tu dois étudier.)
3. Qui reçoit un cadeau?
   (Les copains reçoivent un cadeau.)
4. Qui boit de l'eau?
   (Moi, je bois de l'eau.)
5. Qui doit travailler?
   (Nous devons travailler.)

Activity 34

CHAPITRE 11, Mots 1, pages 356–357

Élève A Ask your partner the following questions. Correct answers are in parentheses.

1. Marc fait de la planche à voile?
   (Oui, Marc fait de la planche à voile.)
2. Il pleut?
   (Non, il fait beau.)
3. Sandrine fait une promenade?
   (Non, elle fait du ski nautique.)
4. Les amis sont où?
   (Les amis sont à la plage.)
5. Ils vont faire du surf?
   (Oui, ils vont faire du surf.)

Élève A Answer your partner's questions based on the picture below.

Élève B Answer your partner's questions based on the pictures below.

1–2.

3.

4–5.

Élève B Ask your partner the following questions. Correct answers are in parentheses.

1. Jeanne a passé la journée à la piscine?
   (Non, elle a passé la journée à la plage.)
2. Elle a mis un maillot de bain?
   (Oui, elle a mis un maillot de bain.)
3. Elle a mis de la crème solaire?
   (Oui, elle a mis de la crème solaire.)
4. Il a fait mauvais temps?
   (Non, il a fait beau.)
5. Elle a pris un bain de soleil?
   (Oui, elle a pris un bain de soleil.)

Activity 35

CHAPITRE 11, Mots 2, pages 360–361

Élève A Ask your partner the following questions. Correct answers are in parentheses.

1. Qu'est-ce qu'on prend pour monter au sommet?
   (On prend un télésiège.)
2. Quel temps fait-il à la montagne?
   (Il fait froid.)
3. Il y a beaucoup de neige?
   (Oui, il y a beaucoup de neige.)
4. On fait du ski à la montagne?
   (Oui, on fait du ski à la montagne.)

Élève A Answer your partner's questions based on the picture below.

Pauline

Élève B Answer your partner's questions based on the picture below.

Élève B Ask your partner the following questions. Correct answers are in parentheses.

1. Pauline a mis un anorak de quelle couleur?
   (Elle a mis un anorak bleu.)
2. Elle est bonne en ski?
   (Non, elle est débutante.)
3. Elle apprend à faire du ski?
   (Oui, elle apprend à faire du ski.)
4. Elle a eu un bon moniteur?
   (Oui, elle a eu un bon moniteur.)

Activity 36

CHAPITRE 11, Structure, pages 364–366

Élève A Read your partner the following statements. Correct responses are in parentheses.

1. Je fais un voyage en hiver.
   (J'ai fait un voyage en hiver l'année dernière.)
2. Je prends des leçons de ski alpin.
   (J'ai pris des leçons de ski alpin l'année dernière.)
3. J'apprends à faire du patin à glace.
   (J'ai appris à faire du patin à glace l'année dernière.)
4. Je dis "Merci" au moniteur.
   (J'ai dit "Merci" au moniteur l'année dernière.)
5. Je mets un bonnet.
   (J'ai mis un bonnet l'année dernière.)
6. Je lis un livre pour les débutants.
   (J'ai lu un livre pour les débutants l'année dernière.)

Élève A Your partner will tell you what he or she is doing today. Use the **passé composé** of the verb below to tell him or her you did the same thing last year **(l'année dernière).**

1. apprendre
2. prendre
3. mettre
4. faire
5. avoir
6. boire

Élève B Your partner will tell you what he or she is doing today. Use the **passé composé** of the verb below to tell him or her you did the same thing last year **(l'année dernière).**

1. faire
2. prendre
3. apprendre
4. dire
5. mettre
6. lire

Élève B Read your partner the following statements. Correct responses are in parentheses.

1. J'apprends à faire du ski.
   (J'ai appris à faire du ski l'année dernière.)
2. Je prends le télésiège.
   (J'ai pris le télésiège l'année dernière.)
3. Je mets un anorak.
   (J'ai mis un anorak l'année dernière.)
4. Je fais du ski de fond.
   (J'ai fait du ski de fond l'année dernière.)
5. J'ai un bon moniteur.
   (J'ai eu un bon moniteur l'année dernière.)
6. Je bois du chocolat chaud.
   (J'ai bu du chocolat chaud l'année dernière.)

Activity 37

CHAPITRE 11, Structure, pages 369–371

Élève A Read your partner the following statements. Correct responses are in parentheses.

1. J'arrive au bord de la mer.
   (Hier, je suis arrivé[e] au bord de la mer.)
2. Je monte dans le train.
   (Hier, je suis monté[e] dans le train.)
3. Je vais à la montagne.
   (Hier, je suis allé[e] à la montagne.)
4. Je sors de la gare.
   (Hier, je suis sorti[e] de la gare.)
5. Je tombe sur la glace.
   (Hier, je suis tombé[e] sur la glace.)

Élève A Your partner will tell you what he or she is doing today. Use the **passé composé** of the verb below to tell him or her you did the same thing yesterday **(hier).**

1. partir
2. descendre
3. rentrer
4. entrer
5. aller

Élève B Your partner will tell you what he or she is doing today. Use the **passé composé** of the verb below to tell him or her you did the same thing yesterday **(hier).**

1. arriver
2. monter
3. aller
4. sortir
5. tomber

Élève B Read your partner the following statements. Correct responses are in parentheses.

1. Je pars à l'heure.
   (Hier, je suis parti[e] à l'heure.)
2. Je descends du train.
   (Hier, je suis descendu[e] du train.)
3. Je rentre à l'hôtel.
   (Hier, je suis rentré[e] à l'hôtel.)
4. J'entre dans la classe de français.
   (Hier, je suis entré[e] dans la classe de français.)
5. Je vais à la plage.
   (Hier, je suis allé[e] à la plage.)

Activity 38

CHAPITRE 12, Mots 1, pages 400–401

Élève A Read your partner the following statements. He or she will tell you how people use the items in the daily routine. Correct responses are in parentheses.

1. Il faut une brosse à dents. Il faut du dentifrice.
   (Elle se brosse les dents.)
2. Il faut un peigne.
   (Elle se peigne.)
3. Il faut un rasoir. Il faut une glace.
   (Il se rase.)

Élève A Your partner will read you a statement about daily routine. Use the picture cues to tell him or her which products or equipment are needed.

1.

2.
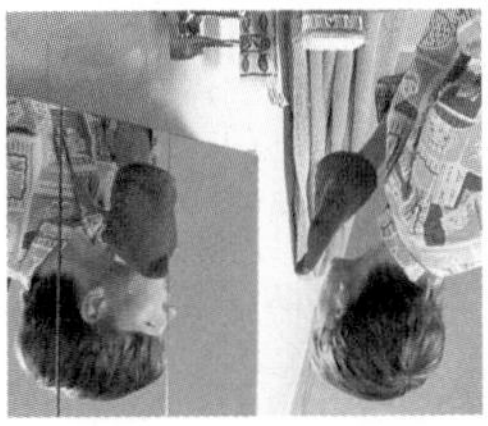

3.

Élève B Your partner will tell you which products or equipment are needed in a daily routine. Use the picture cues to tell him or her what people use the items for.

1.

2.

3.

Élève B Read your partner the following statements about daily routine. He or she will tell you what products or equipment are needed. Correct responses are in parentheses.

1. Elle se brosse les cheveux.
   (Il faut une brosse.)
2. Il se lave.
   (Il faut du savon. Il faut un gant de toilette.)
3. Il se lave les cheveux.
   (Il faut du shampooing.)

Activity 39

CHAPITRE 12, Mots 2, pages 404–405

Élève A Ask your partner the following questions. Correct answers are in parentheses.

1. Qui regarde la télé?
   (Christophe et Julie regardent la télé.)
2. Qui regarde son émission favorite?
   (Christophe regarde son émission favorite.)
3. Qui peut changer de chaîne?
   (Christophe peut changer de chaîne.)
4. Julie fait ses devoirs?
   (Non, Julie ne fait pas ses devoirs.)
5. Christophe s'est bien amusé?
   (Oui, il s'est bien amusé.)

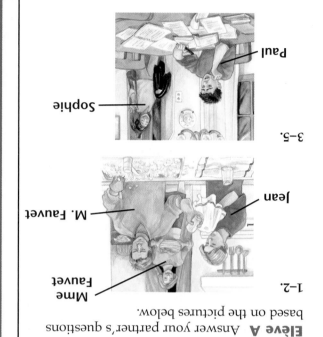

Élève A Answer your partner's questions based on the pictures below.

1–2.

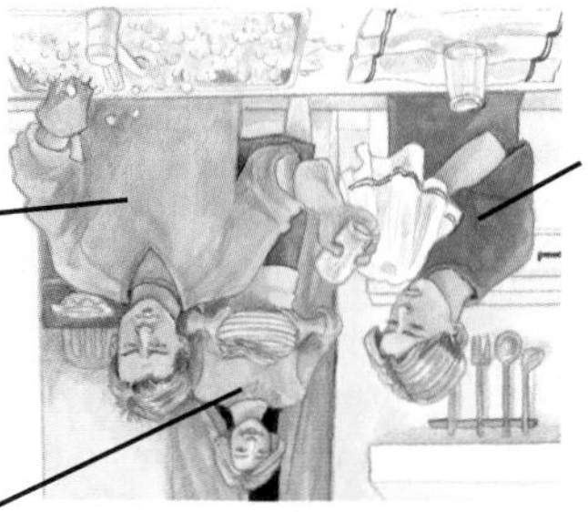

3–5.

Élève B Answer your partner's questions based on the picture below.

Élève B Ask your partner the following questions. Correct answers are in parentheses.

1. Qui débarrasse la table après le dîner?
   (Mme Fauvet débarrasse la table après le dîner.)
2. Qui fait la vaisselle?
   (M. Fauvet et Jean font la vaisselle.)
3. Qui fait ses devoirs?
   (Paul fait ses devoirs.)
4. Qui est sorti?
   (Sophie est sortie.)
5. Sophie s'est bien amusée?
   (Oui, elle s'est bien amusée.)

Activity 40

CHAPITRE 12, Structure, pages 408–412

Élève A Ask your partner the following questions. Correct answers are in parentheses.

1. Qui se maquille?
   (Sophie se maquille.)
2. Qui se réveille tôt?
   (Vous vous réveillez tôt.)
3. Qui se regarde dans la glace?
   (Moi, je me regarde dans la glace.)
4. Qui s'habille?
   (Les enfants s'habillent.)
5. Qui se promène dans le parc?
   (Nous nous promenons dans le parc.)

Élève A Answer your partner's questions based on the information in the chart below.

Qui?	Activité
Moi, je	se lever tôt
Les étudiants	se coucher tard
Paul	se raser
Nous	se brosser les dents
Tu	se peigner

Élève B Answer your partner's questions based on the information in the chart below.

Qui?	Activité
Sophie	se maquiller
Vous	se réveiller tôt
Moi, je	se regarder dans la glace
Les enfants	s'habiller
Nous	se promener dans le parc

Élève B Ask your partner the following questions. Correct answers are in parentheses.

1. Qui se lève tôt?
   (Moi, je me lève tôt.)
2. Qui se couche tard?
   (Les étudiants se couchent tard.)
3. Qui se rase?
   (Paul se rase.)
4. Qui se brosse les dents?
   (Nous nous brossons les dents.)
5. Qui se peigne?
   (Tu te peignes.)

Activity 41

CHAPITRE 12, Structure, pages 413–415

Élève A Ask your partner the following questions. Correct answers are in parentheses.

1. Qui s'est maquillé?
   (Sophie s'est maquillée.)
2. Qui s'est réveillé tôt?
   (Vous vous êtes réveillé[s] tôt.)
3. Qui s'est regardé dans la glace?
   (Moi, je me suis regardé[e] dans la glace.)
4. Qui s'est habillé?
   (Les enfants se sont habillés.)
5. Qui s'est promené dans le parc?
   (Nous nous sommes promenés dans le parc.)

Élève A Answer your partner's questions based on the information in the chart below.

Qui?	Activité
Moi, je	se lever tôt
Les étudiants	se coucher tard
Paul	se raser
Nous	se brosser les dents
Tu	se peigner

Élève B Answer your partner's questions based on the information in the chart below.

Qui?	Activité
Sophie	se maquiller
Vous	se réveiller tôt
Moi, je	se regarder dans la glace
Les enfants	s'habiller
Nous	se promener dans le parc

Élève B Ask your partner the following questions. Correct answers are in parentheses.

1. Qui s'est levé tôt?
   (Moi, je me suis levé[e] tôt.)
2. Qui s'est couché tard?
   (Les étudiants se sont couchés tard.)
3. Qui s'est rasé?
   (Paul s'est rasé.)
4. Qui s'est brossé les dents?
   (Nous nous sommes brossé les dents.)
5. Qui s'est peigné?
   (Tu t'es peigné[e].)

Activity 42

CHAPITRE 13, Mots 1, pages 432–433

Élève A Ask your partner the following questions. Correct answers are in parentheses.

1. Qu'est-ce que tu aimes comme film?
   (J'aime les documentaires.)
2. Qu'est-ce qu'on monte?
   (On monte Roméo et Juliette.)
3. Tu aimes mieux aller au cinéma ou louer des vidéos ou des DVD?
   (J'aime mieux louer des vidéos ou des DVD.)

Élève A Answer your partner's questions according to the illustrations.

1.

2.

3.

Élève B Answer your partner's questions according to the illustrations.

1.

2.
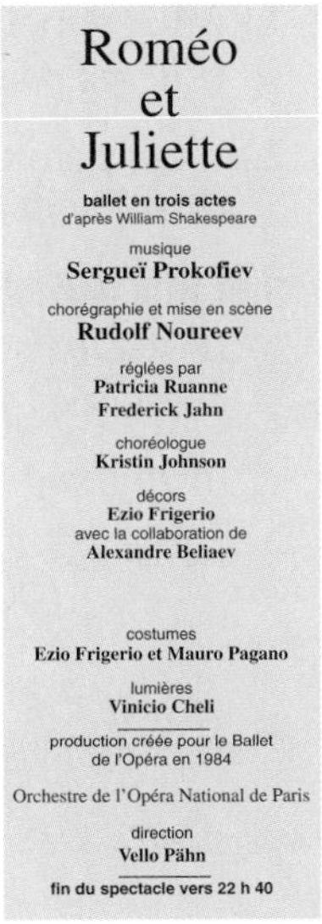

3.

Élève B Ask your partner the following questions. Correct answers are in parentheses.

1. Qu'est-ce que tu aimes comme film?
   (J'aime les dessins animés.)
2. Tu as déjà vu le chanteur?
   (Non, mais j'ai déjà vu la danseuse.)
3. Tu vas voir une pièce de théâtre?
   (Non, je vais voir un film au cinéma.)

Activity 43

CHAPITRE 13, Mots 2, pages 436–437

Élève A Ask your partner the following questions. Correct answers are in parentheses.

1. C'est un musée ou un théâtre?
   (C'est un musée.)
2. Le musée est ouvert ou fermé?
   (Le musée est ouvert.)
3. Il y a beaucoup de tableaux ou de statues au musée?
   (Il y a beaucoup de tableaux.)

Élève A Answer your partner's questions according to the illustration.

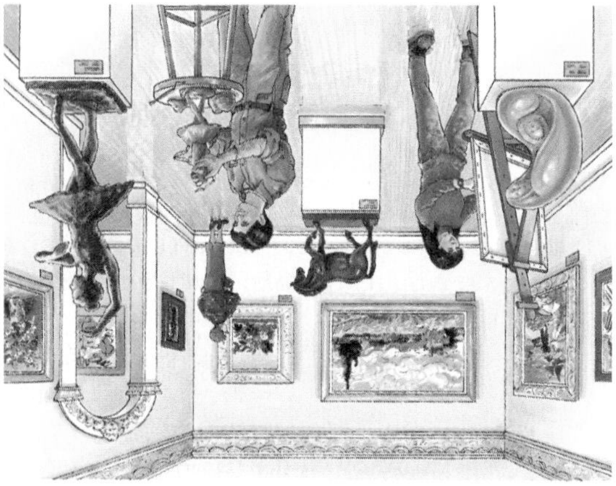

Élève B Answer your partner's questions according to the photograph.

Élève B Ask your partner the following questions. Correct answers are in parentheses.

1. Elle est peintre ou sculpteur?
   (Elle est peintre.)
2. Il est peintre ou sculpteur?
   (Il est sculpteur.)
3. Qu'est-ce qu'il y a au musée?
   (Il y a une exposition de peinture et sculpture au musée.)

Activity 44

CHAPITRE 13, Structure, pages 440–441

Élève A You are familiar with some people, places, and things, but your partner knows some facts or information he or she wants to share with you about them. Make your statement and your partner will respond. Correct responses are in parentheses.

1. Je connais Nathalie.
   (Je sais qu'elle habite à Grenoble.)
2. Je connais *Hamlet*.
   (Je sais que c'est une pièce de Shakespeare.)
3. Je connais Paris.
   (Je sais que c'est la capitale de la France.)
4. Je connais l'œuvre de Degas.
   (Je sais que Degas est un peintre français.)
5. Je connais Paul.
   (Je sais quel est son numéro de téléphone.)

Élève A Your partner and some of his or her friends are familiar with certain people, places, and things, but you and your friends have some facts or information to share. Add your comment according to the cues. Begin your statements with **Nous savons…**

1. …qu'ils sont très beaux.
2. …quelle pièce on joue en ce moment.
3. …où se trouve le théâtre.
4. …qu'elles savent danser le tango.
5. …qu'elles sont célèbres.

Élève B Your partner and some of his or her friends are familiar with certain people, places, and things, but you and your friends have some facts or information to share. Add your comment according to the cues. Begin your statements with **Je sais…**

1. …qu'elle habite à Grenoble.
2. …que c'est une pièce de Shakespeare.
3. …que c'est la capitale de la France.
4. …que Degas est un peintre français.
5. …quel est son numéro de téléphone.

Élève B You are familiar with some people, places, and things, but your partner knows some facts or information he or she wants to share with you about them. Make your statement and your partner will respond. Correct responses are in parentheses.

1. Nous connaissons les tableaux de Monet, Manet et Renoir.
   (Nous savons qu'ils sont très beaux.)
2. Nous connaissons les pièces de Molière.
   (Nous savons quelle pièce on joue en ce moment.)
3. Nous connaissons la Comédie Française.
   (Nous savons où se trouve le théâtre.)
4. Nous connaissons des danseuses.
   (Nous savons qu'elles savent danser le tango.)
5. Nous connaissons les sculptures de Rodin.
   (Nous savons qu'elles sont célèbres.)

Activity 45

CHAPITRE 13, Structure, pages 442–447

Élève A Ask your partner the following questions. Correct answers are in parentheses.

1. Tu connais les tableaux de Monet?
   (Oui, je les connais.)
2. Tu vois la sculpture moderne?
   (Non, je ne la vois pas.)
3. Tu sais le nom du film?
   (Oui, je le sais.)
4. Tu lis les sous-titres?
   (Non, je ne les lis pas.)
5. Tu veux voir la pièce?
   (Oui, je veux la voir.)

Élève A Your partner will ask a question. Respond according to the cues, using the correct object pronoun.

1. Oui…
2. Non…
3. Oui…
4. Oui…
5. Oui…

Élève B Your partner will ask a question. Respond according to the cues, using the correct object pronoun.

1. Oui…
2. Non…
3. Oui…
4. Non…
5. Oui…

Élève B Ask your partner the following questions. Correct answers are in parentheses.

1. Tu m'invites au cinéma?
   (Oui, je t'invite.)
2. Ce film te plaît?
   (Non, ce film ne me plaît pas.)
3. Je te parle au téléphone avant le film?
   (Oui, tu me parles au téléphone avant le film.)
4. Le prof nous donne beaucoup de devoirs?
   (Oui, le prof nous donne beaucoup de devoirs.)
   or
   (Oui, le prof vous donne beaucoup de devoirs.)
5. Julie vous dit quand le musée est fermé?
   (Oui, Julie nous dit quand le musée est fermé.)
   or
   (Oui, Julie me dit quand le musée est fermé.)

Activity 46

CHAPITRE 14, Mots 1, pages 464–465

Élève A Read your partner the following statements. He or she will tell you each person's symptoms. Possible responses are in parentheses.

1. Miriam n'est pas en bonne santé.
   (Elle a mal aux oreilles.)
2. Elle a besoin d'un mouchoir.
   (Elle a le nez qui coule.) or *(Elle a un rhume.)*
3. Anne est très malade, la pauvre.
   (Elle a des frissons.) or *(Elle a de la fièvre.)*
4. David ne se sent pas bien.
   (Il tousse.)

Élève A Use the pictures below to tell your partner about each person's symptoms.

1.

2.

3.
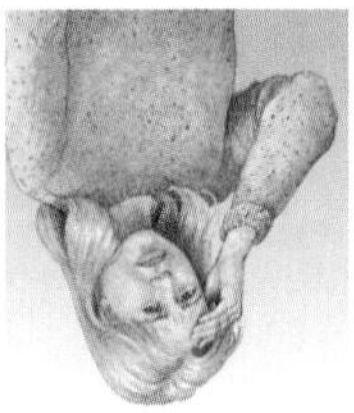

4.

Élève B Use the pictures below to tell your partner about each person's symptoms.

1.

2.

3.
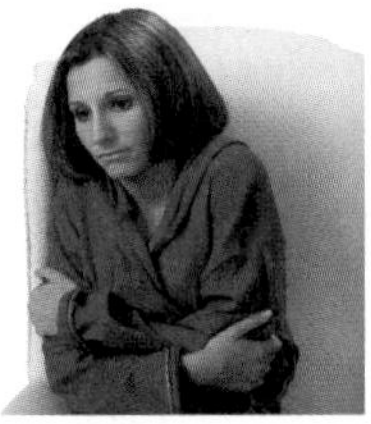

4.

Élève B Read your partner the following statements. He or she will tell you each person's symptoms. Possible responses are in parentheses.

1. Pauline est malade.
   (Elle est enrhumée.) or *(Elle éternue.)*
2. Martine est en mauvaise santé.
   (Elle a un rhume.) or *(Elle tousse.)*
3. Juliette ne se sent pas bien.
   (Elle a mal à la tête.)
4. Jeanne est très malade, la pauvre.
   (Elle a mal au ventre.)

Activity 47

CHAPITRE 14, Mots 2, pages 468–469

Élève A You are the doctor and your partner, the patient, needs help. Ask him or her the following questions.

1. Où avez-vous mal?
   (J'ai mal au ventre.)
2. Qu'est-ce que vous avez?
   (J'ai une angine.)
3. Qu'est-ce que vous avez?
   (J'ai une sinusite aiguë.)
4. Qu'est-ce que vous avez?
   (J'ai un chat dans la gorge.)
5. Où avez-vous mal?
   (J'ai mal à la tête.)

Élève A Answer your partner's questions according to the cues below.

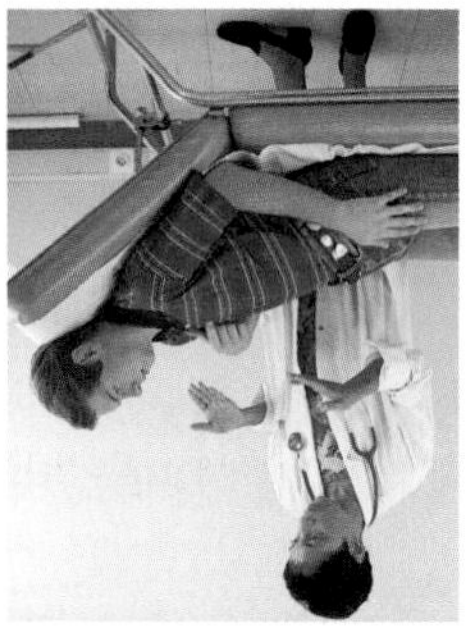

1. des frissons
2. aux oreilles
3. une allergie
4. une fièvre de cheval
5. une infection

Élève B Answer your partner's questions according to the cues below.

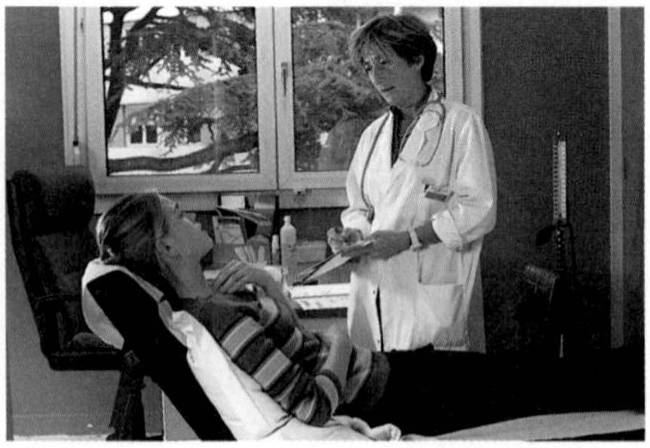

1. au ventre
2. une angine
3. une sinusite aiguë
4. un chat dans la gorge
5. à la tête

Élève B You are the doctor and your partner, the patient, needs help. Ask him or her the following questions.

1. Qu'est-ce que vous avez?
   (J'ai des frissons.)
2. Où avez-vous mal?
   (J'ai mal aux oreilles.)
3. Qu'est-ce que vous avez?
   (J'ai une allergie.)
4. Qu'est-ce que vous avez?
   (J'ai une fièvre de cheval.)
5. Qu'est-ce que vous avez?
   (J'ai une infection.)

Activity 48

CHAPITRE 14, Structure, pages 472–473

Élève A Ask your partner the following questions. Correct answers are in parentheses.

1. Tu parles souvent à ta copine?
   (Oui, je lui parle souvent.)
2. Les joueurs lancent le ballon à l'arbitre?
   (Oui, ils lui lancent le ballon.)
3. Le médecin prescrit des antibiotiques aux malades?
   (Oui, il leur prescrit des antibiotiques.)
4. Tu vas acheter un cadeau à ton frère?
   (Oui, je vais lui acheter un cadeau.)
5. Le pharmacien donne des médicaments à ta mère?
   (Oui, il lui donne des médicaments.)

Élève A Answer your partner's questions using **lui** or **leur.**

1. Oui, je ______ dis bonjour.
2. Oui, il ______ vend des billets.
3. Oui, il ______ fait une ordonnance.
4. Oui, ils ______ téléphonent.
5. Oui, elle ______ dit qu'il a de la fièvre.

Élève B Answer your partner's questions using **lui** or **leur.**

1. Oui, je ______ parle souvent.
2. Oui, ils ______ lancent le ballon.
3. Oui, il ______ prescrit des antibiotiques.
4. Oui, je vais ______ acheter un cadeau.
5. Oui, il ______ donne des médicaments.

Élève B Ask your partner the following questions. Correct answers are in parentheses.

1. Tu dis bonjour à tes amis?
   (Oui, je leur dis bonjour.)
2. L'employé vend des billets à ton père?
   (Oui, il lui vend des billets.)
3. Le médecin fait une ordonnance à Marie?
   (Oui, il lui fait une ordonnance.)
4. Les malades téléphonent au professeur?
   (Oui, ils lui téléphonent.)
5. Sa mère dit à Paul qu'il a de la fièvre?
   (Oui, elle lui dit qu'il a de la fièvre.)

Activity 49

CHAPITRE 14, Structure, pages 475–477

Élève A Ask your partner the following questions. Correct answers are in parentheses.

1. Finir les devoirs?
   (Finis tes devoirs!)
2. Préparer le dîner?
   (Prépare le dîner!)
3. Choisir un film?
   (Choisissons un film!)
4. Travailler plus?
   (Travaille plus!)
5. Dîner au restaurant?
   (Dînons au restaurant!)

Élève A Use the imperative to answer your partner's questions based on the information in the chart below.

Personne(s)	Activité
tu	prendre le métro
vous	attendre devant la porte
tu	faire du ski
tu	sortir ce soir
vous	regarder le film

Élève B Use the imperative to answer your partner's questions based on the information in the chart below.

Personne(s)	Activité
tu	finir les devoirs
tu	préparer le dîner
nous	choisir un film
tu	travailler plus
nous	dîner au restaurant

Élève B Ask your partner the following questions. Correct answers are in parentheses.

1. Prendre le métro?
   (Prends le métro!)
2. Attendre devant la porte?
   (Attendez devant la porte!)
3. Faire du ski?
   (Fais du ski!)
4. Sortir ce soir?
   (Sors ce soir!)
5. Regardez le film?
   (Regardez le film!)

For students and parents/guardians

This guide is designed to help you as students achieve success as you embark on the adventure of learning another language and to enable your parents or guardians to help you on this exciting journey. There are many ways to learn new information. You may find some of these suggestions more useful than others, depending upon which style of learning works best for you. Before you begin, it is important to understand how we acquire language.

Receptive Skills

Each day of your life you receive a great deal of information through the use of language. In order to obtain (get, receive) this information, it is necessary to understand the language being used. It is necessary to understand the language in two different ways. First you must be able to understand what people are saying when they speak to you. This is referred to as oral or listening comprehension. Oral comprehension or listening comprehension is the ability to understand the spoken language.

You must also be able to understand what you read. This is referred to as reading comprehension. Reading comprehension is the ability to understand the written language.

Listening comprehension and reading comprehension are called the *receptive skills.* They are receptive skills because as you listen to what someone else says or read what someone else has written you receive information without having to produce any language yourself.

It is usually very easy to understand your native language. It is a bit more problematic to understand a second language that is new to you. As a beginner, you are still learning the sounds of the new language, and you recognize only a few words. Throughout **Bon voyage!** we will give you hints or suggestions to help you understand when people are speaking to you in French or when you are reading in French. Following are some general hints to keep in mind.

Hints for listening comprehension

When you are listening to a person speaking French, don't try to understand every word. It is not necessary to understand everything to get the idea of what someone is saying. Listen for the general message. If some details escape you, it doesn't matter. Also, never try to translate what people are saying in French into English. It takes a great deal of experience and expertise to be a translator. Trying to translate will hinder your ability to understand.

Hints for reading comprehension

Just as you will not always understand every word you hear in a conversation, you will not necessarily understand every word you encounter in a reading selection, either. In **Bon voyage!,** we have used only words you know or can easily figure out in the reading selections. This will make reading comprehension much easier for you. However, if at some time you wish to read a newspaper or magazine article in French, you will most certainly come across some unfamiliar words. Do not stop reading. Continue to read to get the "gist" of the selection. Try to guess the meanings of words you do not know.

Productive Skills

There are two productive skills in language. These two skills are speaking and writing. They are called productive skills because it is you who has to produce the language when you say or write something. When you speak or write, you have control over the language and which words you use. If you don't know how to say something, you don't have to say it. With the receptive skills, on the other hand, someone else produces the language that you listen to or read, and you have no control over the words they use.

There's no doubt that you can easily speak your native language. You can write, too, even though you may sometimes make errors in spelling or punctuation. In French, there's not a lot you can say or write as a beginner. You can only talk or write about those topics you have learned in French class.

HINTS FOR SPEAKING Try to be as accurate as possible when speaking. Try not to make mistakes. However, if you do, it's not the end of the world. French people will understand you. You're not expected to speak a language perfectly after a limited time. You have probably spoken with people from other countries who do not speak English perfectly, but you can understand them. Remember:

- Keep talking! Don't become inhibited for fear of making a mistake.
- Say what you know how to say. Don't try to branch out in the early stages and attempt to talk about topics or situations you have not yet learned in French.

HINTS FOR WRITING There are many activities in each lesson of **Bon voyage!** that will help you speak and write in French. When you have to write something on your own, however, without the guidance or assistance of an activity in your book, be sure to choose a topic for which you know the vocabulary in French. Never attempt to write about a topic you have not yet studied in French. Write down the topic you are going to write about. Then think of the words you know that are related to the topic. Be sure to include some action words (verbs) that you will need.

From your list of words, write as many sentences as you can. Read them and organize them into a logical order. Fill in any gaps. Then proof your paragraph(s) to see if you made any errors. Correct any that you find.

When writing on your own, be careful not to rely heavily, if at all, on a bilingual dictionary. It's not that bilingual dictionaries are bad, but when you look up a word you will very often find that there are several translations for the same word. As a beginning language student, you do not know which translation to choose; the chances are great that you will pick the wrong one.

As a final hint, never prepare your paragraph(s) in English and attempt to translate word for word. Always write from scratch in French.

*In each chapter of **Bon voyage!**, you will learn how to say and write new words. In Chapter 1, you learn how to describe a person. It won't be long before you'll be able to talk about many things in French. **Bon voyage!***

CHAPITRE 1

Vocabulaire

Mots 1 & 2 *(pages 18–25)*

1. Repeat each new word in the **Mots** section as many times as possible. The more you use a word, the more apt you are to remember it and keep it as part of your active vocabulary.
2. Read the words as you look at the illustrations.
3. If you're the type who has to write something down in order to remember it, copy each word once or twice.
4. Do these activities diligently. They provide you with the opportunity to use your new words many times.
5. This may sound strange, but it's a good idea to read these exercises aloud at home or when using the CD-ROM.
6. When doing the vocabulary activities by yourself or for homework, try to do each item orally before writing the answer.
7. After doing any activity that says **Historiette,** read all the answers aloud. Each time you do this, you will be telling a story in French. It's an excellent way to keep using the material you are learning.

CLASSROOM SUGGESTION Listen to what your classmates say when they respond in class. Do not tune them out. Paying attention to them allows you additional opportunities to hear your new words. The more you hear them, the more likely you are to learn and retain them.

Structure

L'accord des adjectifs *(pages 28–30)*

Pay particular attention to the final sound of many of the descriptive words you are learning. Remind yourself that you hear the final consonant sound of many descriptive words when you are describing a girl. You do not hear the sound when describing a boy.

HINT FOR SPELLING What letter do you delete from the feminine form? Remember that you delete the **e** that follows the consonant when referring to a male.

Le verbe* être *au singulier *(pages 30–32)*

1. **Être** is the first verb you are learning in French. Throughout your study of French, you will continue to learn many more verbs. Verbs are extremely important in French. At this point, you know three verb forms:
   je suis when talking about yourself
   tu es when talking to someone
   il/elle est when talking about someone

Get off to a good start! Learn these three simple forms and remember them.

2. As you do the activities, don't try to use words you don't know in French. For example, you may want to talk about someone who is very outgoing, but you don't know a French equivalent for "outgoing." Give the message using what you do know. For example, you can say: **Jean n'est pas timide, pas du tout.** You can also say: **Marie, elle est timide? Non, pas du tout. Marie n'est pas timide.** Using **ne… pas** with a word you know, you can convey the meaning you wish even though you do not know the precise word.

CLASSROOM SUGGESTION Listen to your classmates as they respond to the structure activities. Remember, the more you hear a form, the more readily you will be able to use it.

3. After doing any activity that says **Historiette,** read all the answers aloud. Each time you do this, you will be telling a story in French. It's an excellent way to keep using the material you are learning.

Lecture culturelle

Un garçon et une fille *(pages 36–37)*

1. Always read the Reading Strategy at the beginning of the **Lecture culturelle.** Practice these strategies and try applying them to other selections you read in French. The Reading Strategy on page 36 talks about cognates and how they help you guess the meanings of words you do not know. For example, you read: **Jean est un garçon français. Il est très intelligent, très capable.** You have probably never seen or used the word **capable** in French. However, you can guess its meaning because it is a cognate of the English word *capable.*

   In addition, it is used in apposition to **intelligent.** When you see a word or expression followed by a comma and then another word (in apposition), the word in apposition almost always clarifies the precise word and has the same or similar meaning.

2. Let's look at another way to guess meaning: **Jean est intelligent et il est aussi très sage. Il est prudent.** You don't know the word **sage,** but its meaning is clarified by **prudent.** Which of the following do you think **sage** means? *Talented? Wise, smart? Nice?* Hopefully you chose *wise, smart.* Think about how and why you arrived at this correct answer.

HINTS FOR WRITING As you complete your first chapter in French, you are able to write a description of a person. At this point, you cannot tell what the person does because you don't have the necessary vocabulary. So avoid this. However, you are able to tell what he or she is like. Write down the words you know in order to write your description. Do not think of words in English. Try to think only of the words you know in French. Begin to write your description. Remember what you learned about **e** if your description is of a female.

VOCABULAIRE *(page 47)*
As you complete the chapter, look at the reference vocabulary list. If there are several words you don't remember, go back to the **Mots 1** and **Mots 2** sections and review. If there are only one or two, you can choose to look them up in the dictionaries beginning on page H72 at the end of this book.

CHAPITRE 2

Get off to a good start! Do your French homework diligently and study for a short period of time each day. Do not skip some days and then try to cram. It doesn't work when studying a foreign language.

In each lesson of **Bon voyage!** you will learn a very manageable amount of new material. Since French is a romance language, much of the new material will involve word endings. Study each small set of new endings on a daily basis, and you'll have no problem. Don't wait until you have lots of them and try to cram them in all at once.

Vocabulaire

Mots 1 & 2 *(pages 50–57)*

1. In Chapter 1, you learned that adjectives describing something feminine end in **e.** The final consonant is pronounced. The **e** is dropped and the consonant is not pronounced when describing something masculine. In Chapter 2, you have four new words that reinforce the same concept: **fort, mauvais, strict,** and **intéressant.**

   Elle est forte en maths.
   Il est fort en maths.
   La classe est intéressante.
   Le cours est intéressant.

HINT FOR PRONOUNCING NEW WORDS
Imitate the pronunciation of your teacher or the CDs to the best of your ability. Try to acquire the best pronunciation possible.

However, don't be worried if you have a slight American accent. There are three levels of pronunciation.

- **Near-native** Try to pronounce like a native. Strive for a near-native pronunciation.
- **Accented but comprehensible** Many people have an accent when they speak a foreign language. You can tell they are not native speakers, but in spite of their accent, you can understand them. If you have such an accent, don't be concerned.
- **Very accented and incomprehensible** Some people have such a strong accent that it's impossible to understand what they're saying. If you have such a strong accent, it will be necessary to repeat and imitate more carefully.

Always remember to listen carefully, repeating as accurately as possible, and you'll succeed in acquiring acceptable pronunciation.

HINT FOR SPEAKING Listen to your teacher pronounce new words or phrases and then repeat them several times. Once you know how to pronounce the words, read the words in your book. If you try to read a word in French before ever having pronounced it, the spelling will most probably interfere with your pronunciation. Always try to listen, repeat, and then read.

2. The vocabulary in **Mots 2** should be very easy to recognize and learn because many words are cognates. A cognate is a word that looks alike in both English and French and has the same meaning in both languages. In the early lessons of **Bon voyage!** we have used many cognates to help you acquire a substantial vocabulary quickly and easily. However, be careful with the pronunciation of cognates. Even though they look alike and mean the same thing in both languages, they can be pronounced very differently.

Structure

Le pluriel: articles, noms et adjectifs

(pages 58–60)

When listening, you will not hear the **s** ending for the plural of a descriptive word. When speaking, you will not pronounce the **s.** However, when writing, you have to remember to write the **s** for plural words.

Les garcons intelligents
Les filles intelligentes

Le verbe **être** *au pluriel* *(pages 60–63)*

In this lesson, you learn three new verb forms:

nous sommes when talking about yourself and someone else
vous êtes when talking to two or more people
ils/elles sont when talking about two or more people or things

Go over these three forms until you feel confident that you know them.

Conversation

(page 66)

When you listen to people speak, you will notice that they often use little words or expressions that you will never see in written form. *Yeah* and *ya' know* are examples in English. You can often guess the meaning of these expressions by the speaker's tone of voice. In this conversation, listen to the tone of voice when the young woman says **Ben oui.** Do you think **Ben oui** means *No* or *Yeah?*

Lecture culturelle

Le français aux États-Unis *(pages 68–69)*

1. Read the Reading Strategy at the beginning of the **Lecture culturelle.** Look at the title of the reading on page 68. It lets you know immediately the general topic you'll be reading about.
2. Read the three subtitles or heads in the passage. They give you a more specific idea of what you'll be reading. Without having read

the reading selection, you now have some understanding of what the reading is about. This will make comprehension much easier.

3. After looking at the title and subtitles, you may very quickly skim the reading. Rather than trying to remember all the information, look at the comprehension questions that follow it. Then go back to the reading and look for the specific factual information called for.

CHAPITRE 3

Vocabulaire

Mots 1 & 2 *(pages 82–89)*

1. Look at each photo or illustration carefully.
2. Read the labels. What does each word refer to?
3. Each word is then used in a meaningful context in a complete sentence. Repeat the individual words and then the sentences.
4. Note that in Activity 4 on page 85, the answer to the question word **qu'est-ce que (qu')** is always a thing. Therefore you should be able to guess the meaning of this question word. Does it mean *who* or *what?*
5. On page 86, after you have practiced your new words, cover up the words as you look at the drawing or photo of each classroom item. See how many you remember. If you don't remember many, you'll have to practice the words some more.

HINT Always pay careful attention to both the pronunciation and the spelling of your new words. You have now seen more than one form of certain verbs. For example: **Ils jouent. Il joue. Ils regardent. Il regarde.** Have you noticed that there is no difference in pronunciation between **regardent** and **regarde** even though they are written differently?

HINT FOR SPEAKING Whenever possible, read all the answers aloud to any activity labeled **Historiette.** Every time you do, you'll be telling a story on your own with the guidance of the activity in the text. This is an easy and useful way to get yourself speaking lots of French.

Structure

Les verbes réguliers en -er _au présent_
(pages 90–93)

1. Now that you know the word **on,** which almost always replaces **nous,** you will see that you really only have to pronounce two forms of a regular **-er** verb. When speaking, whether the subject of the sentence is **je, tu, il, on, elle, ils,** or **elles,** the verb sounds the same. Only the **vous** form has a different pronunciation. This makes spoken French quite easy.

1	2
je parle	
tu parles	**vous parlez**
il/elle/on parle	
ils/elles parlent	

2. However, when you write, remember that there are spelling changes.

je parle
tu parles
il/elle/on parle
ils/elles parlent

HINT Note that the structure activities in your book build from easy to more complex. In the beginning activities, you very often have to use only one verb form. For example, in Activity 13 on page 91, you only use the **il** form. However, in Activity 20 on page 93, you have to use all forms of the verb.

3. When doing Activity 21 on page 93, remember to use only French that you know. Refer to the list of words given here. This list will prevent you from thinking about things you cannot yet say in French.

La négation des articles indéfinis *(page 94)*
Try to condense a grammatical rule into one easy sentence that you can remember easily: **Un, une,** and **des** all become **de** after **ne... pas.**

Verbe + infinitif *(page 95)*
Note that the infinitive form of the verb used after a verb is pronounced the same as the **vous** form: **Vous travaillez.**
J'aime travailler.
Travaillez and **travailler** are pronounced the same. When writing, remember the difference in spelling:
Vous travaillez? Moi, j'aime travailler.
Vous rigolez? Moi, j'aime rigoler.

Conversation
(page 96)

1. This conversation should be very easy for you. You have already learned all the French that is used in the conversation. When practicing this conversation with a classmate, feel free to make as many changes as you want, as long as they make sense.
2. In the conversation, you hear Carol say, **C'est pas vrai.** In spoken French, **ne** is often dropped from the expression **ne... pas.**
3. Note also that Cedric says **Si, c'est vrai.** When someone tells you **no** in French and you want to contradict, you say **si** rather than **oui.**

Lecture culturelle
Une journée avec Jacqueline *(pages 98–99)*

1. Look at the photos on pages 98–99. These photos let you know the reading is about:
   a. shopping for clothes
   b. going to school
   c. making a meal
2. Skim the reading selection and look for the important information such as:
   - Who's the story about?
   - Where does she live and go to school?
   - What are her school hours?
3. Factual recall is an important reading skill. First, find the facts in the reading and then commit them to memory. Activity B tells you what factual information to look for.

VOCABULAIRE *(page 109)*
As you complete the chapter, look at the reference vocabulary list. If there are several words you don't remember, go back to the **Mots 1** and **Mots 2** sections and review. If there are only one or two, you can choose to look them up in the dictionaries beginning on page H72 at the end of this book.

CHAPITRE 4

Vocabulaire

Mots 1 & 2 *(pages 112–119)*

1. In **Mots 1**, remember to listen to the words and repeat orally before reading them. Many names for family members are cognates. Be careful to repeat them correctly.

HINT If you're the type of learner who has to write something before you can remember, copy the words in the **Mots** section once or twice. Use the following learning sequence: *listen, repeat, read, write.*

2. Activity 2 on page 114 helps you review several important question words. The answer in parentheses tells you the meaning of the question word for that sentence. Look at the following question words and answers:

Quand?	**aujourd'hui**
Qu'est-ce que?	**une fête, des cadeaux**
Qui?	**ses cousins, ses cousines**

Decide which question words mean *who, what,* and *when.*

3. Activity 4 on page 115 helps you with productive skills. Remember that when you speak or write about yourself, you must always use the masculine form if you are a male and the feminine form if you are a female.

4. After you have learned the new words in **Mots 2,** look at each illustration, cover up the sentences, and say as much as you can about the illustration. If you can describe the illustration, you know your vocabulary. If you cannot describe it, you have to study some more.

HINT Read or say aloud all the answers to the **Historiette** activities to give you practice in telling coherent stories in French.

Structure

Le verbe* avoir *au présent *(pages 120–122)*

So far, you have learned one irregular verb in French, the verb **être.** All forms of **être** are different. You will now learn your second irregular verb, **avoir**. All forms of **avoir** are also different.

1. Familiarize yourself with the forms of **avoir** as you go over the explanation in class.
2. Do the activities diligently. They give you the opportunity to use and learn the new verb forms without having to memorize them one by one.
3. Do the activities orally and in writing.
4. After doing the activities, reread the grammar explanation. See if you can give the forms of **avoir** on your own without reading them.

REVIEW You know that **un, une,** and **des** all change to **de** after **ne... pas.** The activities on pages 120–122 will help you review this point as you talk about your own home and family.

Conversation

(page 128)

Pay careful attention when you listen to the conversation on the CD-ROM or when other students are repeating it in class. The more you hear spoken French, the easier it will be for you to understand.

Lecture culturelle

Où habitent les Français? *(pages 130–131)*

1. Read the title. When you finish this reading, what will you be able to tell?
   a. where France is
   b. who the French are
   c. where the French people live
2. As you read each paragraph, draw a mental picture of what you're reading. To help you draw your mental picture, look at the photographs, too.

C'est à vous

(pages 136–137)

In Activity 5 on page 137, you are going to write about your house or a house of your dreams.

1. Picture the house.
2. In French, think of or write a list of words you can use to identify parts of the house.
3. In French, think about or write a list of words you can use to describe a house or rooms of a house.
4. Organize your story. Divide the house into parts, such as living area, sleeping area, first floor, second floor. You may even want to make a drawing of your house. Write a few sentences about each area.
5. Put the sentences in a logical order.
6. Add a few sentences to describe the area around your house.

CHAPITRE 5

Vocabulaire

Mots 1 & 2 *(pages 154–161)*

1. It can be fun to study with a classmate. You can do the following.
   - Ask one another questions in French about the illustrations.
   - Have a contest. See who can give more French words describing the illustrations in a three-minute period.
   - Tell your friend which of the items you would order if you were at a café.

2. Activity 1 on page 156 helps you reinforce the meaning of the important question words:

où	**au café**
qui	**Chantal, le serveur**
qu'est-ce que	**une table libre, une boisson**
quand	**après les cours**

3. Act out Activity 4 on page 157 with a classmate. The more you practice speaking French together, the better you'll be able to communicate.

Structure

Le verbe aller *au présent* (pages 162–164)

You will now learn your third irregular verb. Make an association with another irregular verb you have already learned. Repeat the following aloud.

je vais → **j'ai**
tu vas → **tu as**
il va → **il a**
ils vont → **ils ont**

The forms of **aller** almost sound like the forms of **avoir** with a **v** sound.

HINT The more you practice speaking French, the better. When doing your homework, go over all the activities aloud. Don't just do your French homework silently.

Aller + *infinitif* (page 165)

1. The concept of an infinitive after a verb is not new to you. You already know how to express what you like to do:
   J'aime manger.
   J'aime aller au restaurant.
2. Now, using the same type of construction, you will be able to tell what you are going to do.
   J'aime manger et je vais manger quelque chose.
   J'aime aller au restaurant et je vais aller au restaurant vendredi.

Conversation

(page 170)

Listen carefully to the conversation. You can listen to your teacher or use the CD-ROM. Listen more than once. Each time listen for a different bit of information.

- Where are Claire and Loïc?
- What do they order?
- Why is there a possible disagreement?

Lecture culturelle

Au restaurant? Vraiment? (pages 172–173)

1. Making comparisons while reading is an important reading comprehension skill. In this reading, you learned about a cultural difference that's quite interesting. What is it? You may want to share this information with family or friends who don't know any French.
2. Finding the main idea is another important reading comprehension skill. As you read, look for the main idea in the second paragraph. What is it? What is the main idea in the third paragraph?

C'est à vous

(pages 178–179)

In Activity 4 on page 179, you're going to write about a restaurant in French.

1. Get a mental picture of the restaurant.
2. Write words you know in French to describe a restaurant and restaurant activities.
3. List items that people may order.
4. Put these words into sentences. Your first paragraph will describe the restaurant. Your second paragraph will tell what your "characters" order and how they pay.

CHAPITRE 6

Vocabulaire

Mots 1 & 2 (pages 186–193)

1. Try to use your French as often as possible. When you see a food item at home or in a

store that is labeled in French, say the French word to yourself. You'll learn to identify many more food items as you continue with your study of French.

2. As you complete the activities, answer each question orally before you write the answers for homework. Try reading your written responses aloud for Activities 2 and 3 on page 188. Activity 2 reviews the question words **qui, qu'est-ce que, quand, où.**
3. On your own, review the foods you have learned by putting them with an appropriate package or container. For example:

   un paquet de fromage
   un paquet de six tranches de jambon
   un pot de confiture
   un paquet de légumes surgelés

HINTS Note that Activity 10 on page 193 points out that in spoken French, you can omit the **ne** in the expression **ne... pas.**

Be sure you understand the meaning of **pourquoi** and **parce que** when you finish this activity.

Structure

Le verbe faire *au présent* *(pages 194–195)*

1. Look at the forms of the verb **faire.** Repeat them aloud, then copy them.
2. When you complete homework activities, go back to the verb chart. Cover the verb forms and see if you can say the forms without looking at them.

Le partitif et l'article défini *(pages 196–197)*

1. Always try to make what you are learning as simple as possible. If you're talking about something in general, you use **le, la, les.** If you're talking about "some" or "any," you use **du, de la, des.**
2. When doing Activities 18 and 19 on page 197, pay particular attention to the contrast between the general sense and the partitive. You want to buy some (partitive) of the things you like (in general).

Le partitif au négatif *(pages 198–200)*

This concept of **de** is not new. Just remember **du, de la, de l',** and **des** all change to **de** after **ne... pas.** It's really simple, but you have to keep reminding yourself.

HINT Pay close attention as you and your classmates participate in each of these activities. The more you hear **j'ai du** (or **de la, des)** versus **je n'ai pas de,** the easier it will be for you to use the partitive.

HINTS FOR SPEAKING AND WRITING
Listen carefully for the difference in pronunciation between **bonne, bon,** and **gentille, gentil** as explained on page 201. Repeat the words carefully. Repeat the model sentences aloud, then copy them. Pay particular attention to the doubling of the consonant.

Les verbes pouvoir *et* vouloir *(pages 201–203)*

Pay attention to the similarity between the forms of **pouvoir** and **vouloir.**

REVIEW Using the infinitive after a helping verb is not new. Remember:

J'aime dîner au restaurant.
Je vais dîner au restaurant.

Conversation

(page 204)

1. Intonation is the melody of a language. Intonation is produced by the rise and fall of the voice. Each language has its own intonation patterns. English intonation is very different from French intonation. Pay special attention to the rise and fall of the speakers' voices as you listen to the conversations on the CD or CD-ROM.
2. Try to imitate the native speakers' intonation as accurately as possible. If you do, you'll sound much more French. Don't be inhibited. Pretend you are acting while you imitate the intonation.

Lecture culturelle

Les courses *(pages 206–207)*

You may not know the meaning of a certain word you come across in a reading selection. However, you can often guess the meaning of the word by the way it is used in the context of the sentence. A new word in this reading is **les commerçants.** Guess what it means by the context of these sentences:

Les Français aiment bien aller chez les petits commerçants du quartier—l'épicier, le boucher, le boulanger, etc.

The fact that the word **commerçants** is followed by the words **l'épicier, le boucher, le boulanger** helps you figure out the meaning of **commerçants.** What do you think the word **commerçants** means in this context?

a. office workers
b. shopkeepers
c. commercials

CHAPITRE 7

Vocabulaire

Mots 1 & 2 *(pages 220–227)*

1. Look at the illustrations in **Mots 1** and repeat each word aloud.
2. Write each word for additional reinforcement.
3. When you have finished studying the vocabulary, determine how much you remember. Say to yourself or aloud all the items you know for boy's clothing, girl's clothing, and unisex clothing. When you get dressed in the morning for school, notice how many words you know in French for those items you are wearing.
4. Before you write the answers to the vocabulary activities, work with a friend. Go over each exercise together orally. Then, each of you can write your answers. If you wish, you can check each other's work.
5. After studying the vocabulary in **Mots 2,** make a list of the things that you would most probably want to say in French to a salesperson when shopping for clothes.

REVIEW These vocabulary activities contain many adjectives, or descriptive words. Remember that many adjectives have an **e** when used with a feminine noun. They drop the **e** when used with a masculine noun.

La jupe est	**verte.** **grise.** **petite.** **grande.** **bleue.** **jolie.**	**Le blouson est**	**vert.** **gris.** **petit.** **grand.** **bleu.** **joli.**

Structure

Le verbe **mettre** *au présent* *(pages 228–229)*

1. Remember that you hear and pronounce the **t** in the plural forms of **mettre.** You do not hear or pronounce the **t** in the singular forms.
2. Do the **Attention** activity on page 229 aloud at least twice. As you do, pay very careful attention to pronunciation as well as spelling.

Le comparatif des adjectifs *(pages 230–231)*

1. Remember to make the association that **plus** (+) is more, **moins** (−) is less, and **aussi** (=) is the same. All three words are followed by **que.**
2. As you do these activities, pay particular attention to each adjective.

Les verbes **voir** *et* **croire** *(pages 232–233)*

1. Note that many forms of **voir** and **croire** are pronounced the same.

je crois	**tu crois**	**il croit**	**ils croient**
je vois	**tu vois**	**il voit**	**ils voient**

Conversation

(page 234)

This conversation should be very easy for you. You have already learned all the French that is used in the conversation. When practicing this conversation with a classmate, feel free to make as many changes as you want, as long as they make sense.

Lecture culturelle

On fait des courses où, a Paris?
(pages 236–237)

1. Look at the photos on pages 236–237. These photos let you know what the reading is about.
2. Look at the titles. They will give you an idea of what you'll be reading about.
3. Quickly scan the reading to get a general idea of what it's all about.
4. Activity A on page 237 will help you practice factual recall. To recall certain facts, it is often necessary to go back over the reading selection and look for details.
5. Drawing conclusions from a reading selection is another important reading comprehension skill. Based on what you read, draw a personal conclusion. Where would you shop in Paris? Why?

VOCABULAIRE *(page 247)*

As you complete the chapter, look at the reference vocabulary list. If there are quite a few words you don't know, go back to the **Mots 1** and **Mots 2** sections and review.

CHAPITRE 8

Vocabulaire

Mots 1 & 2 *(pages 260–267)*

1. Repeat each new word in the **Mots** sections several times. Look at the photo or illustration as you pronounce the word.
2. Some of you may remember information more easily after writing it down. Try copying each vocabulary word once or twice.
3. You may want to do the activities aloud with a friend as a paired activity. Then, individually write the answers and check each other's work.
4. Listen carefully to what your classmates say when they respond in class. The more you hear people use the new words, the more likely you are to remember them.

Structure

Les verbes en* -ir *au présent *(pages 268–269)*

The **je, tu,** and **il/elle/on** forms of many French verbs are all pronounced the same, even though they are spelled differently. The **-is** and **-it** endings are pronounced the same.

Quel *et* tout *(pages 270–271)*

In spoken French, **quel** is very easy. You pronounce all forms the same. Pay particular attention to the different spellings.

Les verbes sortir, partir, dormir *et* servir

(pages 272–275)

To learn the oral forms of many French verbs, pronounce the **ils/elles** form first. Then drop the final consonant sound and you have the pronunciation for the **je, tu, il/elle/on** forms.

ils sor~~tent~~	**je sors, tu sors, il sort**
ils par~~tent~~	**je pars, tu pars, il part**
ils dor~~ment~~	**je dors, tu dors, il dort**
ils ser~~vent~~	**je sers, tu sers, il sert**

Conversation

(page 276)

Listen carefully to the native speakers' intonation or melody on the CD, CD-ROM, or video. Then, imitate the natives' intonation as closely as you can when you repeat.

Lecture culturelle

On va en France. *(pages 278–279)*

1. To figure out the organization of this reading, scan the passage and look for the following information:
   - Who's going where and how?
   - What do they do when they arrive?
2. Sequencing events is an important reading comprehension skill. Sequence the events in this reading selection. Then see if you came up with a sequence similar to the following:

- **La classe de Madame Cadet est dans le hall de l'aérogare.**
- **Les élèves sont dans l'avion.**
- **Ils arrivent à l'aéroport à Paris.**
- **Ils visitent la belle ville de Paris.**

3. See if you can do all of Activity A on page 279 without referring to the reading for answers.
4. Activity B deals with factual recall. See how many of the facts you remember. Go back to the reading selection and find those you do not remember.

CHAPITRE 9

Vocabulaire

Mots 1 & 2 *(pages 292–299)*

1. Listen to the new words in **Mots 1** and repeat them orally before reading them.
2. Answer Activities 1 and 2 on page 294 however you wish. The more information you can give the better.
3. A good way to remember vocabulary is to group words in some meaningful way. For example, you can group cognates, synonyms, or antonyms. An antonym is a word that means the exact opposite of another. There are quite a few words in **Mots 2** for which you know the antonyms.

   Match the following antonyms.

1. **monter**	**poser une question**
2. **assis**	**descendre**
3. **lit**	**terminer, finir**
4. **répondre à la question**	**debout**
5. **commencer**	**écrit**

4. Activity 7 on page 299 helps you review the following question words: **qui, qu'est-ce que, où, quel.**

Structure

Les verbes en* -re *au présent *(pages 300–302)*

Remember to drop the final sound of the **ils/elles** form to get the pronunciation for the **je, tu, il/elle/on** forms of the verb.

ils ven~~dent~~	**je vends, tu vends, il/elle/on vend**
ils atten~~dent~~	**j'attends, tu attends, il/elle/on attend**
ils descen~~dent~~	**je descends, tu descends, il/elle/on descend**
ils enten~~dent~~	**j'entends, tu entends, il/elle/on entend**

Remember the **je, tu, il/elle/on** forms of these verbs are all pronounced the same.

HINT When doing these activities on your own, go over them first orally. Then write the answers.

Les adjectifs démonstratifs *(pages 303–305)*

Pronounce the following forms aloud and note how the final **t** sound becomes softer when used before a masculine noun that begins with a vowel sound.

cette announe	**cet horaire**	**ce train**
cette gare	**cet aeroport**	**ce billet**

***Les verbes* dire, écrire, lire** *(pages 306–307)*

1. Again remember to drop the final sound of the **ils/elles** form to get the pronunciation for **je, tu, il/elle/on.**

ils di~~sent~~	**je dis, tu dis, il dit**
ils li~~sent~~	**je lis, tu lis, il lit**
ils écri~~vent~~	**j'écris, tu écris, il écrit**

2. Pay particular attention to **vous dites.** Other similar verb forms you have learned are:
   vous faites
   vous êtes

Conversation

(page 308)

You have not learned the expression **tarif étudiant,** but it's easy to guess its meaning through association with other words. **Tarif** is a word that also exists in English. **Étudiant,** a word that is related to the verb **étudier,** is a close cognate of *student.*

Lecture culturelle

Un voyage intéressant *(pages 310–311)*
Always locate the area of the world you are reading about. Look at the map on page 310. Locate the countries of Mali and Sénégal. Locate the cities of Bamako and Dakar.

VOCABULAIRE *(page 321)*
After going over the vocabulary you need when traveling by train, think about a plane trip in French to review the words you already know about this topic.

CHAPITRE 10

Vocabulaire

Mots 1 & 2 *(pages 324–331)*

1. Look at each photo or illustration carefully.
2. Read the labels. What does each word refer to?
3. The words are then used in a meaningful context in a complete sentence. Repeat the sentence aloud as you look at the illustration.
4. To help you learn vocabulary, work with a friend or classmate. Have a contest. See who can say the most about each illustration or photo.
5. It is important to review the question words in French often. Activity 1 on page 326 reviews the following question words: **quoi, combien, qui, qu'est-ce que.**

Structure

Le passé composé des verbes réguliers
(pages 332–334)

1. The formation of the past tense, the **passé composé,** in French is very easy.
   - Review the forms of the verb **avoir.**
   - To form the past participle of all regular verbs, you only have to remember three vowel sounds: /é/, /i/, /ü/
2. Using the **passé composé** in the negative is simple. Think of **ne... pas** as the bread of a sandwich. The filling for the sandwich is the verb **avoir.**

Les verbes* boire, devoir *et* recevoir *au présent *(pages 337–339)*
Remember once again to drop the final sound of the **ils/elles** form of these verbs to get the pronunciation of the **je, tu, il/elle/on** forms.

ils boi~~vent~~	**je bois, tu bois, il/elle/on boit**
ils doi~~vent~~	**je dois, tu dois, il/elle/on dois**
ils reçoi~~vent~~	**je reçois, tu reçois, il/elle/on reçoit**

Conversation

(page 340)
The activity **Vous avez compris?** enables you to practice question words.

Lecture culturelle

Le hockey et le basket-ball *(pages 342–343)*
Before reading this selection, sit back and think for a moment about what you know concerning hockey and basketball. Make a mental picture of each game. This will help you understand the reading selection.

VOCABULAIRE *(page 353)*
Look at each word and see if you can use it in a short sentence.

CHAPITRE 11

Vocabulaire

Mots 1 & 2 *(pages 356–363)*

1. For **Mots 1**, after going over the new vocabulary, review immediately. Sit back for a moment and say aloud or to yourself five words or expressions associated with the beach.
2. Pretend you are on the beach. Think of three things you would like to do while on the beach. Start your sentences with **Je voudrais...**
3. After completing each activity on pages 358–359, read all the answers aloud or

silently. You're not only reading a story with words you know; you're also having another opportunity to use your new words.

4. In **Mots 2,** when learning the winter weather expressions, review the summer expressions on pages 356–357.
5. As you do the activities on pages 362–363, work with a classmate. Take turns asking and answering the questions orally. Then write your answers individually. Correct each other's work.

Structure

Le passé composé des verbes irréguliers *(pages 364–366)*

1. Past participles of regular verbs have only three sounds:

-er	**/é/**
-ir	**/i/**
-re	**/ü/**

2. Remember that participles of all irregular verbs, except **être** and **faire,** have only two of these sounds: **/i/** and **/ü/. /Ü/** is always spelled the same, but **i** is sometimes spelled **-is** and sometimes **-it.**
3. When reading or writing the activities on pages 365–366, pay particular attention to the spelling of past participles with the **/i/** sound.

Les mots négatifs *(pages 367–368)*

To learn the meaning of the negative words, pay particular attention to the opposites.

Oui, quelque chose.	**Non, rien.**
Oui, quelqu'un.	**Non, personne.**
Oui, toujours.	**Non, jamais.**
Oui, souvent.	**Non, jamais.**
Oui, quelquefois.	**Non, jamais.**

Le passé composé avec être *(pages 369–371)*

1. If necessary, quickly review the verb **être.**

je suis	**nous sommes**
tu es	**vous êtes**
il/elle/on est	**ils/elles sont**

HINTS FOR SPEAKING AND WRITING Past participles that end in a vowel **(/é/, /i/, /ü/)** sound the same in all forms. Even though all forms are pronounced the same, you must pay particular attention to the spelling of these past participles when writing. They add **e** for the feminine and **s** for the plural.

parti /i/
partis /i/
partie /i/
parties /i/

2. In the activities on pages 370–371, pay particular attention to the spelling of the past participle.

Lecture culturelle

Un petit voyage au Canada *(pages 374–375)*

1. Skim the selection quickly to get a very general idea of what it's about.
2. Scan the selection to look for specific information.
   - Who went where? When? How?
   - What did they see and do?
3. Which statement best summarizes the first paragraph?
   a. **C'est le mois de février.**
   b. **La classe de Madame Lebrun a pris le train.**
   c. **La classe de Madame Lebrun est allée au Canada.**
4. Which statement best summarizes the second paragraph?
   a. **Ils ont passé trois jours à Montréal.**
   b. **Ils sont allés à une très belle station de sports d'hiver.**
   c. **Ils ont mis leurs skis.**

Inference is an important reading comprehension skill. In this selection, we learn the students are really tired and they sleep like logs. The reading doesn't actually tell us why they are so tired, but you can figure it out from the information you read.

5. Why are the students so tired?
   a. They didn't sleep the night before the trip.
   b. They were anxious to get back to the dorms.
   c. They were worn out from all their activities.

CHAPITRE 12

Vocabulaire

Mots 1 & 2 *(pages 400–407)*

1. In **Mots 1,** to make it easier to remember the meaning of the new words, they are put in a logical sequence of events:
   se reveiller, se lever, se laver (la figure, les cheveux), se peigner, se maquiller, s'habiller
2. Activity 2 on page 402 helps you review the rooms of a house:
   la cuisine, la salle à manger, le salon, la chambre à coucher, la salle de bains
3. Matching synonyms and/or antonyms can often help you remember words.

   Match the antonyms *(opposites)* in **Mots 2.**

1. Il a mis la table.	**Il a débarrassé la table.**
2. Il a allumé la télé.	**Il a éteint la télé.**

   Match the synonyms.

1. un frigidaire	**mettre la télé**
2. le salon	**un réfrigérateur**
3. allumer la télé	**changer de chaine**
4. zapper	**la salle de séjour**

Structure

Les verbes réfléchis au présent
(pages 408–412)

1. Remember that if a person is doing something to or for himself or herself, the verb in French is a reflexive verb, and you must use the additional pronoun.
2. You have already learned all the verb endings that are used in these activities. The only new concept is the use of the reflexive pronoun. Pay particular attention to this pronoun as you do these activities.

Les verbes réfléchis au passé composé
(pages 413–415)

Since the past participle of almost all reflexive verbs ends in a vowel, all forms are pronounced the same. However, in writing, the plural and feminine endings must be added.

CHAPITRE 13

Vocabulaire

Mots 1 & 2 *(pages 432–439)*

1. Remember to listen to the words and repeat them orally before reading them.
2. After you have gone over the new vocabulary, see how many words you remember. Think of seven words about a movie. Think of five words about a play.
3. Go over each activity orally before you write the answers.

Structure

Les verbes savoir *et* connaître *(pages 440–441)*

1. Simplify the grammatical rule: just remember that **savoir** means to know something simple, and **connaître** means to know or be familiar with something complex.
2. When doing these activities, pay particular attention to the object of each verb to determine the use of **savoir** or **connaître.**

Les pronoms me, te, nous, vous
(pages 442–443)

Remember that the pronouns **me, te, nous,** and **vous** are part of the "filling in the sandwich." **Ne… pas** is the bread that goes around the filling.

Il ne	**me parle** **te parle** **nous parle** **vous parle**	**pas.**

Les pronoms le, la, les *(pages 444–447)*

As you do these activities, determine which word is the direct object before trying to replace it with **le, la,** or **les.** Do each activity orally before you write it.

Conversation

(page 448)

1. An important skill in understanding a foreign language is to guess the meaning of words from the context in which they occur. In this conversation, you will hear and use the expression **travailler notre espagnol.** This is new to you, but you can figure it out from the context.

   In this conversation, **travailler** means which of the following?

   a. **parler**
   b. **comprendre**
   c. **pratiquer**

2. Note how Léa says **ça me dit** in response to the question **ça t'intéresse?** Do you think **ça me dit** has the same meaning as the phrase **ça m'intéresse?**

Lecture culturelle

Les loisirs culturels en France *(pages 450–451)*

Identifying the main idea is an important comprehension skill. Read the title and subtitles. What do you think is the main idea of this reading?

a. **Il y a des musées et des théâtres en France.**
b. **Les Français apprécient les loisirs culturels.**
c. **L'entrée des musées est gratuite le premier dimanche du mois.**

VOCABULAIRE *(page 461)*

Read the list of words and determine how many you know. Many of these words are easy to remember because they are cognates.

CHAPITRE 14

Vocabulaire

Mots 1 & 2 *(pages 464–471)*

1. Whenever you have the chance to review, do so. As you do **Mots 1,** think of all the parts of the body you have learned in French.

2. To determine if you know your new vocabulary from **Mots 2,** see whether you can do the following:
   - Tell three things a patient may do in a doctor's office.
   - Tell three things the doctor may do.
   - Tell three things a doctor may say to a patient.

Structure

***Les pronoms* lui, leur** *(pages 472–473)*

Here's an easy way to tell the difference between a direct object and an indirect object. A direct object answers the question *whom* or *what.*

Whom did you see?	I saw the doctor.
What did you take?	I took the medicine.

An indirect object answers the question *to (for) whom* or *to (for) what.*

***Les verbes* souffrir *et* ouvrir** *(page 474)*

Review the forms of a regular **-er** verb. Compare them to the verb **ouvrir.**

j'écoute	**j'ouvre**
tu écoutes	**tu ouvres**
il écoute	**il ouvre**
nous écoutons	**nous ouvrons**
vous écoutez	**vous ouvrez**
ils écoutent	**ils ouvrent**

L'impératif *(pages 475–477)*

Remember, you use the command (imperative) to tell someone what to do. You merely use the **tu** or **vous** form of the verb to form the command. Just remember that you drop the final **s** from the **tu** form of regular **-er** verbs.

***Le pronom* en** *(pages 478–479)*

You will hear and use the word **en** quite frequently in French. Pay careful attention to the explanation of the use of this word.

VERBES RÉGULIERS			
INFINITIF	**parler** *to speak*	**finir** *to finish*	**répondre** *to answer*
PRÉSENT	je parle tu parles il parle nous parlons vous parlez ils parlent	je finis tu finis il finit nous finissons vous finissez ils finissent	je réponds tu réponds il répond nous répondons vous répondez ils répondent
IMPÉRATIF	parle parlons parlez	finis finissons finissez	réponds répondons répondez
PASSÉ COMPOSÉ	j'ai parlé tu as parlé il a parlé nous avons parlé vous avez parlé ils ont parlé	j'ai fini tu as fini il a fini nous avons fini vous avez fini ils ont fini	j'ai répondu tu as répondu il a répondu nous avons répondu vous avez répondu ils ont répondu

VERBES AVEC CHANGEMENTS D'ORTHOGRAPHE			
INFINITIF	**acheter**[1] *to buy*	**appeler** *to call*	**commencer** *to begin*
PRÉSENT	j'achète tu achètes il achète nous achetons vous achetez ils achètent	j'appelle tu appelles il appelle nous appelons vous appelez ils appellent	je commence tu commences il commence nous commençons vous commencez ils commencent
INFINITIF	**manger**[2] *to eat*	**payer**[3] *to pay*	**préférer**[4] *to prefer*
PRÉSENT	je mange tu manges il mange nous mangeons vous mangez ils mangent	je paie tu paies il paie nous payons vous payez ils paient	je préfère tu préfères il préfère nous préférons vous préférez ils préfèrent

[1] *Verbes similaires:* **se lever, se promener**
[2] *Verbes similaires:* **nager, voyager**
[3] *Verbes similaires:* **essayer, renvoyer, employer, envoyer**
[4] *Verbes similaires:* **célébrer, espérer, suggérer**

VERBES IRRÉGULIERS			
INFINITIF	**aller** *to go*	**avoir** *to have*	**conduire** *to drive*
PRÉSENT	je vais tu vas il va nous allons vous allez ils vont	j'ai tu as il a nous avons vous avez ils ont	je conduis tu conduis il conduit nous conduisons vous conduisez ils conduisent
PASSÉ COMPOSÉ	je suis allé(e)	j'ai eu	j'ai conduit
INFINITIF	**connaître** *to know*	**croire** *to believe*	**devoir** *to have to, to owe*
PRÉSENT	je connais tu connais il connaît nous connaissons vous connaissez ils connaissent	je crois tu crois il croit nous croyons vous croyez ils croient	je dois tu dois il doit nous devons vous devez ils doivent
PASSÉ COMPOSÉ	j'ai connu	j'ai cru	j'ai dû
INFINITIF	**dire** *to say*	**dormir** *to sleep*	**écrire** *to write*
PRÉSENT	je dis tu dis il dit nous disons vous dites ils disent	je dors tu dors il dort nous dormons vous dormez ils dorment	j'écris tu écris il écrit nous écrivons vous écrivez ils écrivent
PASSÉ COMPOSÉ	j'ai dit	j'ai dormi	j'ai écrit
INFINITIF	**être** *to be*	**faire** *to do, to make*	**lire** *to read*
PRÉSENT	je suis tu es il est nous sommes vous êtes ils sont	je fais tu fais il fait nous faisons vous faites ils font	je lis tu lis il lit nous lisons vous lisez ils lisent
PASSÉ COMPOSÉ	j'ai été	j'ai fait	j'ai lu

INFINITIF	**mettre** *to put*	**ouvrir**[5] *to open*	**partir** *to leave*
PRÉSENT	je mets tu mets il met nous mettons vous mettez ils mettent	j'ouvre tu ouvres il ouvre nous ouvrons vous ouvrez ils ouvrent	je pars tu pars il part nous partons vous partez ils partent
PASSÉ COMPOSÉ	j'ai mis	j'ai ouvert	je suis parti(e)
INFINITIF	**pouvoir** *to be able to*	**prendre**[6] *to take*	**recevoir** *to receive*
PRÉSENT	je peux tu peux il peut nous pouvons vous pouvez ils peuvent	je prends tu prends il prend nous prenons vous prenez ils prennent	je reçois tu reçois il reçoit nous recevons vous recevez ils reçoivent
PASSÉ COMPOSÉ	j'ai pu	j'ai pris	j'ai reçu
INFINITIF	**savoir** *to know*	**servir** *to serve*	**sortir** *to go out*
PRÉSENT	je sais tu sais il sait nous savons vous savez ils savent	je sers tu sers il sert nous servons vous servez ils servent	je sors tu sors il sort nous sortons vous sortez ils sortent
PASSÉ COMPOSÉ	j'ai su	j'ai servi	je suis sorti(e)
INFINITIF	**venir**[7] *to come*	**voir** *to see*	**vouloir** *to want*
PRÉSENT	je viens tu viens il vient nous venons vous venez ils viennent	je vois tu vois il voit nous voyons vous voyez ils voient	je veux tu veux il veut nous voulons vous voulez ils veulent
PASSÉ COMPOSÉ	je suis venu(e)	j'ai vu	j'ai voulu

[5] *Verbes similaires:* **couvrir, découvrir, offrir, souffrir**
[6] *Verbes similaires:* **apprendre, comprendre**
[7] *Verbes similaires:* **devenir, revenir**

VERBES AVEC ÊTRE AU PASSÉ COMPOSÉ	
aller *(to go)*	je suis allé(e)
arriver *(to arrive)*	je suis arrivé(e)
descendre *(to go down, get off)*	je suis descendu(e)
entrer *(to enter)*	je suis entré(e)
monter *(to go up)*	je suis monté(e)
mourir *(to die)*	je suis mort(e)
naître *(to be born)*	je suis né(e)
partir *(to leave)*	je suis parti(e)
passer *(to go by)*	je suis passé(e)
rentrer *(to go home)*	je suis rentré(e)
rester *(to stay)*	je suis resté(e)
retourner *(to return)*	je suis retourné(e)
revenir *(to come back)*	je suis revenu(e)
sortir *(to go out)*	je suis sorti(e)
tomber *(to fall)*	je suis tombé(e)
venir *(to come)*	je suis venu(e)

This French-English Dictionary *contains all productive and receptive vocabulary from the text. The numbers following each productive entry indicate the chapter and vocabulary section in which the word is introduced. For example,* ***2.2*** *means that the word first appeared in* ***Chapitre 2, Mots 2. BV*** *refers to the introductory* ***Bienvenue*** *lessons.* ***L*** *refers to the optional literary readings. If there is no number or letter following an entry, this means that the word or expression is there for receptive purposes only.*

A

à at, in, to, **3.1**
À bientôt! See you soon!, **BV**
à bord (de) on board, **8.2**
à cause de because of
À demain. See you tomorrow., **BV**
à destination de to *(destination),* **8.1**
à domicile to the home
à l'heure on time, **8.1**
à mon (ton, son, etc.) avis in my (your, his, etc.) opinion, **7.2**
à nouveau again
à peu près about, approximately
à pied on foot, **4.2**
à point medium-rare *(meat),* **5.2**
À tout à l'heure. See you later., **BV**
abandonner to abandon
l' **abbé** *(m.)* priest
abondant(e) plentiful
absolument absolutely
accessible accessible
l' **accessoire** *(m.)* accessory
l' **accident** *(m.)* accident
accompagner to accompany, to go with
l' **accordéon** *(m.)* accordion
l' **accusation** *(f.)* accusation
accuser to accuse
l' **achat** *(m.)* purchase
faire des achats to shop
acheter to buy, **3.2**
l' **acte** *(m.)* act, **13.1**
l' **acteur** *(m.)* actor, **13.1**
actif, active active
l' **action** *(f.)* action
l' **activité** *(f.)* activity
l' **actrice** *(f.)* actress, **13.1**
l' **addition** *(f.)* check, bill *(restaurant),* **5.2**
additionner to add
admirer to admire
l' **adolescent(e)** adolescent, teenager
adorable adorable, **4.1**
adorer to love
l' **adresse** *(f.)* address
l' **adulte** *(m. et f.)* adult
l' **adversaire** *(m. et f.)* adversary, opponent
adverse opposing, **10.1**
aérien(ne) air, flight *(adj.)*
l' **aérogare** *(f.)* airport terminal, **8.1**
l' **aéroport** *(m.)* airport, **8.1**
l' **affiche** *(f.)* poster
africain(e) African
l' **Afrique** *(f.)* Africa
afro-américain(e) African-American
l' **âge** *(m.)* age, **4.1**
Tu as quel âge? How old are you?, **4.1**
âgé(e) old
l' **agent** *(m.)* agent *(m. and f.),* **8.1**
agité(e) choppy, rough *(sea)*
l' **agneau** *(m.)* lamb, **6.1**
agréable pleasant
l' **aide** *(f.)* aid, help
à l'aide de with the help of
aider to help
aigu(ë) acute, severe, **14.2**
aimer to like, love, **3.1**
aimer mieux to prefer, **7.2**
l' **aîné(e)** older, **L1**
ainsi que as well as
l' **air** *(m.)* air; melody
avoir l'air to look
aisé(e) well-to-do
l' **album** *(m.)* album
l' **algèbre** *(f.)* algebra, **2.2**
l' **Algérie** *(f.)* Algeria
algérien(ne) Algerian
l' **aliment** *(m.)* food
l' **alimentation** *(f.)* nutrition, diet
l' **Allemagne** *(f.)* Germany
l' **allemand** *(m.)* German *(language),* **2.2**
aller to go, **5.1**
aller chercher to go (and) get, **6.1**
aller mieux to feel better, **14.2**
Allez! Come on!, **9.2**
Qu'est-ce qui ne va pas? What's wrong?
l' **aller** *(m.)* going
l'aller (simple) one-way ticket, **9.1**

le billet aller (et) retour round-trip ticket, **9.1**
l' **allergie** *(f.)* allergy, **14.1**
allergique allergic, **14.1**
allumer to turn on *(appliance)*, **12.2**
alors so, then, well then, **BV**
ambitieux, ambitieuse ambitious
l' **amende** *(f.)* fine
américain(e) American, **1.1**
l' **Amérique** *(f.)* **du Sud** South America
l' **ami(e)** friend, **1.2**
l' **amour** *(m.)* love, **L4**
ample large, full
amusant(e) funny; fun, **1.1**
s' **amuser** to have fun, **12.2**
l' **an** *(m.)* year, **4.1**
avoir... ans to be . . . years old, **4.1**
l' **analyse** *(f.)* analysis
analyser to analyse
analytique analytical
l' **anatomie** *(f.)* anatomy
ancien(ne) old, ancient; former
l' **angine** *(f.)* throat infection, tonsillitis, **14.1**
l' **anglais** *(m.)* English *(language)*, **2.2**
anglais(e) English
l' **Angleterre** *(f.)* England
l' **animal** *(m.)* animal
l' **année** *(f.)* year
l'année dernière last year
l' **anniversaire** *(m.)* birthday, **4.1**
Bon (Joyeux) anniversaire! Happy birthday!
l' **annonce** *(f.)* announcement, **8.2**
annoncer to announce, **9.1**
anonyme anonymous
l' **anorak** *(m.)* ski jacket, **7.1**
l' **antibiotique** *(m.)* antibiotic, **14.1**
Antilles: la mer des Antilles Caribbean Sea
l' **antonyme** *(m.)* antonym
l' **appareil** *(m.)* apparatus
apparenté: le mot apparenté cognate
l' **appartement** *(m.)* apartment, **4.2**
appeler to call
s' **appeler** to be called, be named, **12.1**
applaudir to applaud
apporter to bring, **11.1**
apprécier to appreciate
apprendre (à) to learn (to), **5;** to teach
apprendre à quelqu'un à faire quelque chose to teach someone to do something
après after, **3.2**
d'après according to
l' **après-midi** *(m.)* afternoon, **3.2**
arabe Arab
l' **arabe** *(m.)* Arabic *(language)*
l' **arbitre** *(m.)* referee, **10.1**
l' **arbre** *(m.)* tree, **L3**
l' **architecture** *(f.)* architecture
l' **argent** *(m.)* money, **5.2**
l' **arme** *(f.)* weapon
l' **armée** *(f.)* army, **L3**
l' **arrêt** *(m.)* stop, **9.2**
arrêté(e) arrested
s' **arrêter** to stop, **10.1;** to arrest
l' **arrière** *(m.)* rear, back, **8.2**
l' **arrière-garde** *(f.)* rear guard
l' **arrivée** *(f.)* arrival, **8.1**
arriver to arrive, **3.1;** to happen
arriver à (+ *inf.*) to manage to, to succeed in, **9.1**
l' **arrondissement** *(m.)* district (in Paris)
l' **artère** *(f.)* artery
l' **article** *(m.)* article
l' **artiste** *(m. et f.)* artiste
l'artiste peintre *(m. et f.)* painter
artistique artistic
l' **ascenseur** *(m.)* elevator, **4.2**
asiatique Asian
l' **aspirine** *(f.)* aspirin, **14.1**
assez fairly, quite; enough, **1.1**
l' **assiette** *(f.)* plate, **5.2**
ne pas être dans son assiette to be feeling out of sorts, **14.1**
assis(e) seated, **9.2**
l' **assistante sociale** *(f.)* social worker
l' **atelier** *(m.)* studio *(artist's)*
l' **athlétisme** *(m.)* track and field, **10.2**
l' **atmosphère** *(f.)* atmosphere
attaché(e) attached
attacher to fasten, **8.2**
attaquer to attack
attendre to wait (for), **9.1**
attente: la salle d'attente waiting room, **9.1**
l' **attention** *(f.)* attention
Attention! Careful! Watch out!, **4.2**
faire attention to pay attention; to be careful, **11.1**
atterrir to land, **8.1**
l' **atterrissage** *(m.)* landing *(plane)*
attraper un coup de soleil to get a sunburn, **11.1**
au bord de la mer by the ocean; seaside, **11.1**
au contraire on the contrary
au fond in the background
au revoir good-bye, **BV**
au-dessous (de) below
la taille au-dessous the next smaller size, **7.2**
au-dessus (de) above
la taille au-dessus the next larger size, **7.2**
aujourd'hui today, **BV**
auprès de with
ausculter to listen with a stethoscope, **14.2**
aussi also, too, **1.1;** as *(comparisons)*, **7;** so

l' **auteur** *(m.)* author *(m. and f.)*
l'auteur dramatique playwright
l' **autocar** *(m.)* bus, coach
automatique automatic, autonomic
l' **automne** *(m.)* autumn, **11.2**
autour de around, **4.2**
autre other, **L1**
autre chose something else
Autre chose? Anything else? *(shopping)*, **6.2**
d'autres some other, **2.2**
l'un... l'autre one . . . the other
autrement dit in other words
l' **avalanche** *(f.)* avalanche
avaler to swallow, **14.2**
avance: en avance early, ahead of time, **9.1**
avant before
avant de (+ *inf.*) before (+ *verb*)
l' **avant** *(m.)* front, **8.2**
avant-hier the day before yesterday, **10.2**
avec with, **3.2**
Avec ça? What else? *(shopping)*, **6.1**
l' **avenir** *(m.)* future, **L2**
l' **aventure** *(f.)* adventure
l' **avenue** *(f.)* avenue
l' **aviateur, l'aviatrice** aviator
l' **avion** *(m.)* plane, **8.1**
en avion by plane
l' **avis** *(m.)* opinion, **7.2**
à mon avis in my opinion, **7.2**
avoir to have, **4.1**
avoir l'air to look
avoir... ans to be . . . years old, **4.1**
avoir besoin de to need, **10.1**
avoir de la chance to be lucky, to be in luck
avoir envie de to want (to), to feel like
avoir faim to be hungry, **5.1**
avoir une faim de loup to be very hungry
avoir lieu to take place
avoir mal à to have a(n) . . . -ache, to hurt, **14.1**
avoir peur to be afraid, **L1**
avoir du retard to be late *(plane, train, etc.)*, **8.1**
avoir soif to be thirsty, **5.1**

B

le **baccalauréat** French high school exam
la **bactérie** bacterium
bactérien(ne) bacterial, **14.1**
les **bagages** *(m. pl.)* luggage, **8.1**
le bagage à main carry-on bag, **8.1**
le coffre à bagages baggage compartment, **8.2**
la **baguette** loaf of French bread, **6.1**
le **baigneur, la baigneuse** bather
le **bain** bath, **12.1**
prendre un bain to take a bath, **12.1**
prendre un bain de soleil to sunbathe, **11.1**
la salle de bains bathroom, **4.2**
le **balcon** balcony, **4.2**
le **ballet** ballet
le **ballon** ball *(soccer, etc.)*, **10.1**
la **banane** banana, **6.2**
la **banlieue** suburbs
la **base** base; basis
à base de based on
le **base-ball** baseball
basé(e) based
la **basilique** basilica
la **basket** sneaker; running shoe, **7.1**
le **basket(-ball)** basketball, **10.2**
la **bataille** battle, **L3**
le champ de bataille battlefield, **L3**
le **bateau** boat, **L4**
le **bâton** ski pole, **11.2**
bavarder to chat
beau (bel), belle beautiful, handsome, **4.2**
Il fait beau. It's nice weather., **11.1**
beaucoup a lot, **3.1**
beaucoup de a lot of, many, **3.2**
le **beau-père** stepfather, **4.1**
la **beauté** beauty
de toute beauté of great beauty
le **bébé** baby
beige *(inv.)* beige, **7.2**
belge Belgian
la **Belgique** Belgium
la **belle-mère** stepmother, **4.1**
ben *(slang)* well
ben oui yeah
le/la **bénévole** volunteer
le **berger, la bergère** shepherd, shepherdess
le **besoin** need
avoir besoin de to need, **10.1**
la **bêtise** stupid thing, nonsense
le **beurre** butter, **6.1**
le **bicentenaire** bicentennial
la **bicyclette** bicycle, **10.2**
bien fine, well, **BV**
bien cuit(e) well-done *(meat)*, **5.2**
bien élevé(e) well-behaved; well-mannered
bien sûr of course
eh bien well
bientôt soon
À bientôt! See you soon! **BV**
le/la **bienvenu(e)** welcome

le **billet** ticket, **8.1**
le billet aller (et) retour round-trip ticket, **9.1**
la **biologie** biology, **2.2**
biologique biological
le/la **biologiste** biologist
blanc, blanche white, **7.2**
blessé(e) wounded, **L3**
bleu(e) blue, **7.2**
bleu marine *(inv.)* navy blue, **7.2**
le **bloc-notes** notepad, **3.2**
blond(e) blond, **1.1**
bloquer to block, **10.1**
le **blouson** (waist-length) jacket, **7.1**
le **blue-jean** (pair of) jeans
le **bœuf** beef, **6.1**
bohème bohemian
boire to drink, **10.2**
quelque chose à boire something to drink
le **bois** wood
la **boisson** beverage, drink, **5.1**
la **boîte: la boîte de conserve** can of food, **6.2**
la boîte crânienne skull
boiteux, boiteuse lame
le **bol** bowl
bon(ne) correct; good, **6.2**
Bon! Okay!, Right!, **6.1**
bon marché *(inv.)* inexpensive
de bonne heure early
le **bonhomme de neige** snowman
bonjour hello, **BV**
le **bonnet** ski cap, hat, **11.2**
le **bord: à bord (de)** aboard *(plane, etc.)*, **8.2**
au bord de la mer by the ocean, seaside, **11.1**
la **bosse** mogul *(ski)*, **11.2**
la **botanique** botany
le **boubou** boubou *(long, flowing garment)*
la **bouche** mouth, **14.1**
le **boucher, la bouchère** butcher
la **boucherie** butcher shop, **6.1**
la **bougie** candle, **4.1**
la **boulangerie-pâtisserie** bakery, **6.1**
la **bouteille** bottle, **6.2**
la **boutique** shop, boutique, **7.1**
le **bras** arm
le **Brésil** Brazil
le/la **Brésilien(ne)** Brazilian *(person)*
la **Bretagne** Brittany
breton(ne) Breton, from Brittany
le/la **Breton(ne)** Breton *(person)*
briller to shine
la **brioche** sweet roll
briser to break, **L3**
se **briser** to break
la **bronche** bronchial tube
bronzer to tan, **11.1**
la **brosse** brush, **12.1**
la brosse à dents toothbrush, **12.1**
se **brosser** to brush, **12.1**
la **brousse** bush *(wilderness)*
le **bruit** noise, **L3**
brûler to burn
brun(e) brunette; dark-haired, **1.1**
le **buffet** train station restaurant, **9.1**
le **bungalow** bungalow
le **bus** bus, **5.2**
le **but** goal, **10.1**
marquer un but to score a goal, **10.1**

C

ça that, **BV**
Ça fait... euros. It's (That's) . . . euros., **6.2**
Ça fait mal. It (That) hurts., **14.1**
Ça va. Fine., Okay., **BV**
Ça va? How's it going?, How are you? *(inform.)*, **BV;** How does it look?, **7.2**
C'est ça. That's right., That's it.
le **cabaret** cabaret
la **cabine** cabin *(plane)*, **8.1**
la cabine d'essayage fitting room
cacher to hide, **L3**
le **cadeau** gift, present, **4.1**
le **cadet, la cadette** younger person, **L1**
le **café** café, **BV;** coffee, **5.1**
la **cafétéria** cafeteria
le **cahier** notebook, **3.2**
la **caisse** cash register, checkout counter, **3.2**
le **calcium** calcium
le **calcul** arithmetic, **2.2**
le calcul différentiel differential calculus
le calcul intégral integral calculus
la **calculatrice** calculator, **3.2**
le **calendrier** calendar, schedule
le **calligramme** picture-poem
calme quiet, calm
la **calorie** calorie
le/la **camarade** companion, friend
le/la camarade de classe classmate
le **camembert** Camembert cheese
le **camion** truck
le **camp** side *(in a sport or game)*, **10.1**
le camp adverse opponents, other side, **10.1**
la **campagne** country(side); campaign
canadien(ne) Canadian, **6**
la **cantine** school dining hall, **3.1**
capable able
la **capitale** capital
le **car** bus *(coach)*
la **caractéristique** characteristic
Caraïbes: la mer des Caraïbes Caribbean Sea
cardiaque cardiac
le **carnaval** carnival *(season)*
la **carotte** carrot, **6.2**
la **carrière** career

la **carte** menu, **5.1;** map; card
la carte de crédit credit card
la carte de débarquement landing card, **8.2**
la carte d'embarquement boarding pass, **8.1**
la carte postale postcard, **9.1**
le **carton** cardboard
la **casquette** cap, baseball cap, **7.1**
casse-pieds pain in the neck *(slang)*
la **cassette** cassette, tape **3.1**
la cassette vidéo videocassette, **12.2**
le **catalogue** catalog
catastrophique catastrophic
la **catégorie** category
cause: à cause de because of
causer to cause
le **CD** CD, **3.1**
le **CD-ROM** CD-ROM
ce (cet), cette this, that, **9**
ce soir tonight
la **ceinture** belt, **L3**
la ceinture de sécurité seat belt, **8.2**
célèbre famous
célébrer to celebrate, **L4**
la **cellule** cell, **L4**
celte Celtic
celtique Celtic
cent hundred, **2.2**
pour cent percent
les **centaines** *(f. pl.)* hundreds
le **centilitre** centiliter
le **centre** center
le centre commercial shopping center, mall, **7.1**
le **centre-ville** downtown
le **cercle** circle
les **céréales** *(f. pl.)* cereal, grains
certainement certainly
certains some
le **cerveau** brain
c'est it is, it's, **BV**
C'est combien? How much is it?, **3.2**
C'est quel jour? What day is it?, **BV**
C'est tout. That's all., **6.1**
c'est-à-dire that is
chacun(e) each (one), **5.2**
la **chaîne** chain; TV channel, **12.2**
la **chaise** chair
la **chambre à coucher** bedroom, **4.2**
le **champ** field, **L1**
le champ de bataille battlefield, **L3**
champêtre pastoral
le/la **champion(ne)** champion
la **chance** luck
avoir de la chance to be lucky, to be in luck
la **chanson** song
chanter to sing, **13.1**
le **chanteur, la chanteuse** singer, **13.1**
chaque each, every
le **char** float
la **charcuterie** deli(catessen), **6.1**
charger to load
le **chariot** shopping cart, **6.2;** baggage cart, **9.1**
charmant(e) charming
le **charme** charm
le **charpentier** carpenter
le **chasseur, la chasseuse** hunter
le **chat** cat, **4.1**
avoir un chat dans la gorge to have a frog in one's throat, **14.1**
le **château** castle, mansion
chaud(e) warm, hot
Il fait chaud. It's hot. *(weather),* **11.1**
la **chaussette** sock, **7.1**
la **chaussure** shoe, **7.1**
les chaussures de ski ski boots, **11.2**
le **chef** head, boss
le **chemin** route; road; path
la **cheminée** chimney
la **chemise** shirt, **7.1**
le **chemisier** blouse, **7.1**
cher, chère dear; expensive, **7.1**
chercher to look for, seek
aller chercher to go (and) get, **6.1**
le **chevalier** knight
les **cheveux** *(m. pl.)* hair, **12.1**
chez at (to) the home (business) of, **3.2**
le **chien** dog, **4.1**
la **chimie** chemistry, **2.2**
la **chimiothérapie** chemotherapy
chimique chemical
le/la **chimiste** chemist
chinois(e) Chinese
le **chœur** choir
choisir to choose, **8.1**
le **cholestérol** cholesterol
la **chose** thing
ciao good-bye *(inform.),* **BV**
le **ciel** sky, **11.1**
le **cinéma** movie theater, movies, **13.1**
le **circuit** circuit
la **circulation** circulation
le **cirque** circus
citer to cite, mention
le **citron pressé** lemonade, **5.1**
le/la **civilisé(e)** civilized person
clair(e) light *(color)*
la **clarinette** clarinet
la **classe** class, **2.1**
la classe économique coach class *(plane)*
la salle de classe classroom, **2.1**
le **classeur** loose-leaf binder, **3.2**
classifier to classify
classique classical
le **classique** classic
le **clavier** keyboard
le/la **client(e)** customer
le **climat** climate
climatique climatic
la **clinique** clinic
le **clown** clown

le **club d'art dramatique** drama club
le **coca** cola, **5.1**
le **code** code, **4.2**
le **coéquipier, la coéquipière** teammate
le **cœur** heart
le **coffre** chest, **L4**
le coffre à bagages (overhead) baggage compartment, **8.2**
le **coin: du coin** neighborhood *(adj.)*
la **collection** collection
le **collège** junior high, middle school, **1.2**
le/la **collégien(ne)** middle school/junior high student
le **combat** fight, battle, **L3**
combien (de) how much, how many, **3.2**
C'est combien? How much is it (that)?, **3.2**
comble packed *(stadium)*, **10.1**
la **comédie** comedy, **13.1**
comique comic; funny, **13.1**
le film comique comedy, **13.1**
commander to order, **5.1**
comme like, as; for; since
comme ci, comme ça so-so
commémorer to commemorate
commencer to begin, **9.2**
comment how, what, **1.1**
Comment ça? How is that?
le/la **commerçant(e)** shopkeeper
la **compagnie** company
la compagnie aérienne airline, **8.1**
en compagnie de in the company of
la **comparaison** comparison
comparer to compare
le/la **compatriote** compatriot
la **compétition** contest
le **complet** suit *(man's)*, **7.1**
complet, complète full, complete
le pain complet whole-wheat bread
complètement completely, totally
compléter to complete
compliqué(e) complicated
comploter to conspire
comporter to call for, require
composé(e) composed
le **compositeur, la compositrice** composer
la **composition** composition
composter to stamp, validate *(a ticket)*, **9.1**
comprendre to understand, **5**
le **comprimé** pill, **14.2**
compris(e) included, **5.2**
Le service est compris. The tip is included., **5.2**
le **compte** account
compter to count
le **comptoir** counter, **8.1**
le **comte** count, **L4**
le **concept** concept
le **concert** concert
le **concert-bal** concert and ball
le **concours** competition, contest
la **condition** condition
la **confiture** jam, **6.2**
confortable comfortable
la **connaissance: faire la connaissance de** to meet
connaître to know, **13.2**
connecter to connect
connu(e) well-known; famous, **13.1**
le (la) plus connu(e) best-known
la **conserve: la boîte de conserve** can of food, **6.2**
la **consommation** drink, beverage, **5.1**
conspirer to plot
construire to build
la **consultation** medical visit
donner des consultations to have office hours *(doctor)*
consulter to consult
le **contact** contact
la **contamination** contamination
contenir to contain
content(e) happy, glad
le **continent** continent
continuer to continue
le **contraire** opposite
contre against, **10.1**
par contre on the other hand, however
le **contremaître, la contremaîtresse** foreman, forewoman
le **contrôle** check, control
le contrôle des passeports passport check
le contrôle de sécurité security *(airport)*, **8.1**
contrôler to check; to control
le **contrôleur** conductor *(train)*, **9.2**
la **conversation** conversation
converser to converse
la **conversion** conversion
convient: qui convient that is appropriate
le **copain** friend, pal *(m.)*, **2.1**
la **copine** friend, pal *(f.)*, **2.1**
le **cor** horn, **L3**
sonner du cor to blow a horn, **L3**
la **cornemuse** bagpipes
le **corps** body
la **correspondance** correspondence; connection *(between trains)*, **9.2**
corriger to correct
cosmopolite cosmopolitan
la **côte** coast
la Côte d'Azur French Riviera
la Côte d'Ivoire Ivory Coast
le **côté** side
côté couloir aisle *(seat)*, **8.1**
côté fenêtre window *(seat)*, **8.1**

coucher to put (someone) to bed, **12**
se **coucher** to go to bed, **12.1**
la **couchette** berth *(on a train)*
couler to flow
avoir le nez qui coule to have a runny nose, **14.1**
la **couleur** color, **7.2**
le **couloir** aisle, corridor, **8.2**
le **coup: le coup de soleil** sunburn, **11.1**
donner un coup (de pied, de tête, etc.) to kick, hit (with one's foot, head, etc.), **10.1**
la **coupe** winner's cup, **10.2**
la **cour** courtyard, **3.2;** court
le **courage** courage
courageux, courageuse courageous, brave
le **coureur, la coureuse** runner, **10.2**
le coureur (la coureuse) cycliste racing cyclist, **10.2**
le **cours** course, class, **2.1**
en cours de (français, etc.) in (French, etc.) class
la **course** race, **10.2**
la course cycliste bicycle race, **10.2**
les **courses** *(f. pl.)*: **faire des courses** to go shopping, **6.1**
court(e) short, **7.2**
le **couscous** couscous
le/la **cousin(e)** cousin, **4.1**
le **couteau** knife, **5.2**
coûter to cost, **3.2**
Ça coûte combien? How much does this cost?, **3.1**
le **couturier** designer *(of clothes)*
le **couvent** convent
couvert(e) covered
le **couvert** table setting; silverware, **5.2**
couvrir to cover
le **crabe** crab, **6.1**
la **cravate** tie, **7.1**
le **crayon** pencil, **3.2**
créer to create
la **crème** cream
la crème solaire suntan lotion, **11.1**
le **crème** coffee with cream *(in a café)*, **5.1**
la **crémerie** dairy store, **6.1**
le **créole** Creole *(language)*
la **crêpe** crepe, pancake, **BV**
creuser to dig, **L4**
crevé(e) exhausted
la **crevette** shrimp, **6.1**
crier to shout, **L4**
le/la **criminel(le)** criminal, **L4**
croire to believe, think, **7.2**
la **croissance** growth
le **croissant** croissant, crescent roll, **5.1**
le **croque-monsieur** grilled ham and cheese sandwich, **5.1**
la **crosse** hockey stick
la **cuillère** spoon, **5.2**
la **cuisine** kitchen, **4.2;** cuisine *(food)*
faire la cuisine to cook, **6**
cuit(e) cooked
bien cuit(e) well-done *(meat)*, **5.2**
cultiver to cultivate
la **culture** culture
culturel(le) cultural
le **cyclisme** cycling, bicycle riding, **10.2**
le/la **cycliste** cyclist, bicycle rider
cycliste bicycle, cycling *(adj.)*, **10.2**
le coureur (la coureuse) cycliste bicycle racer, **10.2**
une course cycliste bicycle race, **10.2**

D

d'abord first, **12.1**
d'accord okay, all right *(agreement)*
être d'accord to agree, **2.1**
dangereux, dangereuse dangerous
dans in, **1.2**
la **danse** dance
danser to dance, **13.1**
le **danseur, la danseuse** dancer, **13.1**
la danseuse ballerina, **13.1**
d'après according to
la **date** date
dater de to date from
d'autres some other, **2.2**
de from, **1.1;** of, belonging to, **1.2;** about
de bonne heure early
de la, de l' some, any, **6**
De quelle couleur est... ? What color is . . . ?, **7.2**
de temps en temps from time to time, occasionally
le **débarquement** landing, deplaning
débarquer to get off *(plane)*
débarrasser la table to clear the table, **12.2**
debout standing, **9.2**
le **début** beginning
le/la **débutant(e)** beginner, **11.2**
le **décalage horaire** time difference
le **décalitre** dekaliter
le **déchet** waste
décider (de) to decide (to)
la **décision** decision
la décision est prise the decision is made
déclarer to declare, call
le **décollage** takeoff *(plane)*
décoller to take off *(plane)*, **8.1**
découvrir to discover
décrire to describe
le **défilé** parade
définir to define
la **déformation** alteration
se **dégager** to be given off

dehors: au dehors de outside
déjà already; ever; yet, **BV**
déjeuner to eat lunch, **3.1**
le **déjeuner** lunch, **5.2**
le petit déjeuner breakfast, **5.2**
délicieux, délicieuse delicious
demain tomorrow, **BV**
À demain. See you tomorrow., **BV**
demander to ask (for), **3.2**
demi(e) half
et demie half past *(time)*, **BV**
le **demi-cercle** semi-circle; top of the key *(on a basketball court)*, **10.2**
le **demi-frère** half brother, **4.1**
la **demi-heure** half hour
la **demi-sœur** half sister, **4.1**
le **demi-tarif** half price
le **demi-tour** about-face
faire demi-tour to turn around
la **dent** tooth, **12.1**
le **dentifrice** toothpaste, **12.1**
le/la **dentiste** dentist
le **déodorant** deodorant
le **départ** departure, **8.1**
le **département d'outre-mer** French overseas department
se **dépêcher** to hurry, **12.1**
dépendre (de) to depend (on)
depuis since, for, **9.2**
dernier, dernière last, **10.2**
derrière behind
désagréable disagreeable, unpleasant
descendre to get off *(train, bus, etc.)*, **9.2;** to take down, **9;** to go down, **9**
désertique desert *(adj.)*
désespéré(e) desperate, **L4**
désirer to want, **5.1**
désormais from then on
le **dessert** dessert
le **dessin** art, **2.2;** drawing, illustration
le **dessin animé** cartoon, **13.1**
la **destination** destination
à destination de to *(destination)*, **8.1**
la **destinée** destiny
détester to hate, **3.1**
déverser to spill
se déverser to be spilled
deuxième second, **4.2**
devant in front of, **8.2**
devenir to become
deviner to guess
la **devinette** riddle
devoir to owe, **10;** must, to have to (+ *verb*), **10.2**
le **devoir** homework *(assignment)*
faire ses devoirs to do homework, **12.2**
dévoué(e) devoted
d'habitude usually, **12.2**
le **diagnostic** diagnosis, **14.2**
le **dialecte** dialect
le **dialogue** dialog
le **diamant** diamond
dicter to dictate
la **différence** difference
différent(e) different, **8.1**
difficile difficult, **2.1**
la **difficulté** problem, difficulty
être en difficulté to be in trouble
diffuser to spread, to propagate
dîner to eat dinner, **5.2**
le **dîner** dinner, **5.2**
le **diplôme** diploma
dire to say, tell, **9.2**
Ça me dit! I'd like that!
directement directly
la **direction** direction
discuter to discuss
disparaître to disappear
disparu(e) disappeared, lost
la **disquette** diskette, floppy disk
distinguer to distinguish, to tell apart
divers(e) various
divisé(e) divided
diviser to divide
la **djellaba** djellaba *(long, loose garment)*
le **document** document
le **documentaire** documentary, **13.1**
le **doigt** finger
le **dollar** dollar, **3.2**
le **dolmen** dolmen
le **domaine** domain, field
le **domicile: à domicile** to the home
donc so, therefore
les **données** *(f. pl.)* data
donner to give, **4.1**
donner un coup de pied to kick, **10.1**
donner une fête to throw a party, **4.1**
donner sur to face, overlook, **4.2**
dont of which
doré(e) golden
dormir to sleep, **8.2**
le **dortoir** dormitory
la **douane** customs
doublé(e) dubbed *(movies)*, **13.1**
la **douche** shower, **12.1**
douloureux, douloureuse painful
le **doute** doubt
la **douzaine** dozen, **6.2**
le **drame** drama, **13.1**
dribbler to dribble *(basketball)*, **10.2**
le **droit** right
du coin neighborhood *(adj.)*
dur(e) hard
durer to last
dynamique dynamic, **1.2**

E

l' **eau** *(f.)* water, **6.2**
l'eau bouillante boiling water
l'eau minérale mineral water, **6.2**
l' **échange** *(m.)* exchange
échanger to exchange

s' **échapper** to escape
l' **écharpe** *(f.)* scarf, **11.2**
éclaté(e) burst
l' **école** *(f.)* school, **1.2**
l'école primaire elementary school
l'école secondaire junior high, high school, **1.2**
l' **écologie** *(f.)* ecology
écologique ecological
l' **économie** *(f.)* economics, **2.2**
économique: la classe économique coach class *(plane)*
écouter to listen (to), **3.1**
l' **écran** *(m.)* screen, **8.1**
écrasé(e) crushed
écrire to write, **9.2**
l' **écrivain** *(m.)* writer *(m. and f.)*, **L2**
efficace efficient
égal(e): Ça m'est égal. I don't care., It's all the same to me., **13.1**
égaliser to tie *(score)*
égoïste egotistical, **1.2**
égyptien(ne) Egyptian
l' **élément** *(m.)* element
l' **élève** *(m. et f.)* student, **1.2**
élevé(e) high
bien élevé(e) well-behaved
éliminer to eliminate
l' **e-mail** *(m.)* e-mail
l' **embarquement** *(m.)* boarding, leaving
embarquer to board *(plane, etc.)*
l' **émission** *(f.)* program, show *(TV)*, **12.2**
emmener to send, **L4**
l' **emploi** *(m.)* **du temps** schedule
l' **employé(e)** employee *(m. and f.)*
emprisonné(e) imprisoned
en in, **3.2;** by, **5.2**
en avance early, ahead of time, **9.1**
en avion plane *(adj.)*, by plane, **8**
en ce moment right now
en classe in class
en fait in fact
en général in general
en l'honneur de in honor of
en particulier in particular
en plein air outdoors
en plus de besides, in addition
en première (seconde) in first (second) class, **9.1**
en provenance de arriving from *(flight, train)*, **8.1**
en retard late, **9.1**
en solde on sale, **7.1**
en vain in vain
en ville in town, in the city
en voiture by car, **5.2**
encore still, **11;** another; again
s' **endormir** to fall asleep
l' **endroit** *(m.)* place
l' **énergie** *(f.)* energy
énergique energetic, **1.2**
l' **enfance** *(f.)* childhood
l' **enfant** *(m. et f.)* child, **4.1**
enfermer to shut up
enfin finally, at last, **12.1**
s' **engager dans** to head into
l' **ennemi(e)** *(m. et f.)* enemy
énorme enormous
l' **enquête** *(f.)* inquiry, survey
enregistrer to tape, **12.2**
(faire) enregistrer to check *(baggage)*, **8.1**
enrhumé(e): être enrhumé(e) to have a cold, **14.1**
enrichi(e) enriched
ensemble together, **5.1**
l' **ensemble** *(m.)* outfit; whole, entirety
ensuite then *(adv.)*, **12.1**
entendre to hear, **9.1**
enthousiaste enthusiastic, **1.2**
entier, entière entire, whole
l' **entracte** *(m.)* intermission, **13.1**
entre between, among, **3.2**
l' **entrée** *(f.)* entrance, **4.2;** admission
l' **entreprise** *(f.)* firm
entrer to enter, **7.1**
environ about
envoyer to send, **10.1**
l' **épée** *(f.)* sword, **L3**
épicé(e) spicy
l' **épicerie** *(f.)* grocery store, **6.1**
les **épinards** *(m. pl.)* spinach, **6.2**
épique epic
l' **époque** *(f.)* period, times
épuisé(e) exhausted
l' **équateur** *(m.)* equator
l' **équilibre** *(m.)* balance
équilibré(e) balanced
l' **équipe** *(f.)* team, **10.1**
l' **équipement** *(m.)* equipment
l' **escalier** *(m.)* staircase, **4.2**
l' **espagnol** *(m.)* Spanish *(language)*, **2.2**
l' **esprit** *(m.)* spirit
essayer to try on, **7.2;** to try
essentiel(le) essential
et and, **BV**
établir to establish
l' **établissement** *(m.)* establishment
l' **étage** *(m.)* floor *(of a building)*, **4.2**
l' **étape** *(f.)* stage, lap
les **États-Unis** *(m. pl.)* United States
l' **été** *(m.)* summer, **11.1**
en été in summer, **11.1**
éteindre to turn off *(appliance)*, **12.2**
éternuer to sneeze, **14.1**
étranger, étrangère foreign, **13.1**
être to be, **1.1**
être d'accord to agree, **2.1**
être enrhumé(e) to have a cold, **14.1**

ne pas être dans son assiette to be feeling out of sorts, **14.1**
l' **être** *(m.)* being
l'être humain human being
l' **étudiant(e)** *(university)* student
l' **étude** *(f.)* study
étudier to study, **3.1**
l' **euro** *(m.)* euro, **6.2**
l' **Europe** *(f.)* Europe
européen(ne) European
s' **évader** to escape, **L4**
l' **événement** *(m.)* event
évidemment evidently
l' **évier** *(m.)* kitchen sink, **12.2**
éviter to avoid, **12.2**
évoquer to evoke
exact(e) exact
exactement exactly
l' **examen** *(m.)* test, exam, **3.1**
passer un examen to take a test, **3.1**
réussir à un examen to pass a test
examiner to examine, **14.2**
excellent(e) excellent
excepté(e) except
l' **exception** *(f.)* exception
exceptionnel(le) exceptional
l' **excursion** *(f.)* excursion, outing
exécuter to carry out
l' **exemple** *(m.)* example
par exemple for example
l' **exercice** *(m.)* exercise
l' **existence** *(f.)* existence
exister to exist, to be
expert(e) expert *(adj.)*
l' **explication** *(f.)* explanation
expliquer to explain
l' **exposition** *(f.)* exhibit, show, **13.2**
l' **express** *(m.)* espresso, black coffee, **5.1**
l' **expression** *(f.)* expression
expulser to expel, banish
l' **extérieur** *(m.)* exterior, outside
à l'extérieur outside, outside the home
extraordinaire extraordinary, **13.2**

F

la **fable** fable
fabriquer to build
fabuleusement fabulously
fabuleux, fabuleuse fabulous
facile easy, **2.1**
la **façon** way, manner
faible weak, **L1**
faim: avoir faim to be hungry, **5.1**
faire to do, make, **6.1**
Ça fait mal. It (That) hurts., **14.1**
faire du (+ nombre) to take size (+ number), **7.2**
faire des achats to shop
faire attention to pay attention, **6;** to be careful, **11.1**
faire des courses to go shopping, **7.2**
faire les courses to do the grocery shopping, **6.1**
faire la cuisine to cook, **6**
faire ses devoirs to do homework, **12.2**
faire enregistrer to check (luggage), **8.1**
faire des études to study
faire du français (des maths, etc.) to study French (math, etc.), **6**
faire du jogging to jog
faire la navette to go back and forth, make the run
faire une ordonnance to write a prescription, **14.2**
faire partie de to be a part of
faire un pique-nique to have a picnic
faire de la planche à voile to windsurf, **11.1**
faire une promenade to take a walk, **11.1**
faire la queue to wait in line, **9.1**
faire du ski nautique to water-ski, **11.1**
faire du surf to go surfing, **11.1**
faire la vaisselle to do the dishes, **12.2**
faire les valises to pack (suitcases), **8.1**
faire un voyage to take a trip, **8.1**
Il fait quel temps? What's the weather like?, **11.1**
Vous faites quelle pointure? What size shoe do you take?, **7.2**
Vous faites quelle taille? What size do you take (wear)?, **7.2**
fait(e) à la main handmade
falsifier to falsify
la **famille** family, **4.1**
le nom de famille last name
le/la **fana** fan
la **fanfare** brass band
fantastique fantastic
la **farine de sorgo** sorghum flour
le **fast-food** fast-food restaurant
fatigué(e) tired
faut: il faut one must, it is necessary to, **8.2**
il ne faut pas one must not, **11.1**
la **faute** fault, mistake
faux, fausse false
favori(te) favorite, **7.2**
la **femme** woman, **7.1;** wife, **4.1**
la **fenêtre** window
côté fenêtre window *(seat) (adj.)*, **8.1**
fermé(e) closed, **13.2**

le **festival** festival
la **festivité** festivity
la **fête** party, **4.1**
de fête festive
donner une fête to throw a party, **4.1**
la **feuille de papier** sheet of paper, **3.2**
le **feutre** felt-tip pen, **3.2**
les **fiançailles** *(f. pl.)* engagement, **L4**
le/la **fiancé(e)** fiancé(e), **L4**
le **fichier** file *(computer)*
fier, fière proud
la **fièvre** fever, **14.1**
avoir de la fièvre to have a fever, **14.1**
avoir une fièvre de cheval to have a high fever, **14.1**
la **figue** fig
la **figure** face, **12.1**
le **filet** net *(volleyball, etc.),* **10.2**
la **fille** girl, **1.1;** daughter, **4.1**
le **film** film, movie, **13.1**
le film d'amour love story, **13.1**
le film d'aventures adventure movie, **13.1**
le film comique comedy, **13.1**
le film étranger foreign film, **13.1**
le film d'horreur horror film, **13.1**
le film policier detective movie, **13.1**
le film de science-fiction science-fiction movie, **13.1**
le film en vidéo movie video, **13.1**
le **fils** son, **4.1**
la **fin** end
finalement finally
finir to finish, **8.2**
fixement: regarder fixement to stare at
la **fleur** flower, **4.2**
fleuri(e) in bloom, **L2**
fleurir to bloom
le **fleuve** river
la **flûte** flute
le **foie** liver
avoir mal au foie to have indigestion
la **fois** time *(in a series),* **10.2**
à la fois at the same time
deux fois twice
la **fonction** function
le **fonctionnement** functioning
fond: au fond in the background
respirer à fond to breathe deeply, **14.2**
au fond de at the bottom of
fonder to found
le **foot(ball)** soccer, **10.1**
le football américain football
la **force** strength
la **formalité** formality
la **forme** form, shape
former to form
fort hard *(adv.)*
fort(e) strong, **2.2**
fort(e) en maths good in math, **2.2**
la **fortune** fortune
fou, folle crazy; insane
la **fourchette** fork, **5.2**
la **fourniture** supply
les fournitures scolaires school supplies, **3.2**
la **fracture** fracture *(of bone)*
frais: Il fait frais. It's cool. *(weather),* **11.2**
les **frais** *(m. pl.)* expenses; charges
la **fraise** strawberry, **6.2**
le **français** French *(language),* **2.2**
le/la **Français(e)** Frenchman (-woman)
français(e) French, **1.1**
la **France** France
francophone French-speaking
frapper to hit, **L3;** to knock, **L4**
fréquenter to frequent, patronize
le **frère** brother, **1.2**
le **frigidaire** refrigerator, **12.2**
les **frissons** *(m. pl.)* chills, **14.1**
les **frites** *(f. pl.)* French fries, **5.1**
froid(e) cold
Il fait froid. It's cold. *(weather),* **11.2**
le **fromage** cheese, **5.1**
la **frontière** border
frugal(e) light, simple
le **fruit** fruit, **6.2**
la **fumée** smoke
fumer to smoke
la **fusion** fusion
le **futur** future, **L2**

G

le/la **gagnant(e)** winner, **10.2**
gagner to earn; to win, **10.1**
le **gant** glove, **11.2**
le gant de toilette washcloth, **12.1**
le **garage** garage, **4.2**
le **garçon** boy, **1.1**
garder to guard, watch; to keep
le **gardien** guard, **L4**
le gardien de but goalie, **10.1**
la **gare** train station, **9.1**
gastronomique gastronomic, gourmet
le **gâteau** cake, **4.1**
le **gaz** gas
le gaz carbonique carbon dioxide
le/la **géant(e)** giant
geler to freeze
Il gèle. It's freezing. *(weather),* **11.2**
le **général** general, 7
en général in general
généralement generally
le **genre** type, kind, **13.1**
les **gens** *(m. pl.)* people
gentil(le) nice *(person),* **6.2**
la **géographie** geography, **2.2**

la **géométrie** geometry, **2.2**
gigantesque gigantic
la **glace** ice cream, **5.1;** ice, **11.2;** mirror, **12.1**
le **glucide** carbohydrate
la **gomme** eraser, **3.2**
la **gorge** throat, **14.1**
avoir un chat dans la gorge to have a frog in one's throat, **14.1**
avoir la gorge qui gratte to have a scratchy throat, **14.1**
avoir mal à la gorge to have a sore throat, **14.1**
le **gourmet** gourmet
grâce à thanks to
le **gradin** bleacher *(stadium),* **10.1**
la **graisse** fat
la **grammaire** grammar
le **gramme** gram, **6.2**
grand(e) tall, big, **1.1;** great
le grand magasin department store, **7.1**
de grand standing luxury *(adj.)*
la grande surface large department store; large supermarket
grandir to grow (up) *(children)*
la **grand-mère** grandmother, **4.1**
le **grand-père** grandfather, **4.1**
les **grands-parents** *(m. pl.)* grandparents, **4.1**
gratter to scratch, **14.1**
gratuit(e) free
grave serious
la **Grèce** Greece
la **griffe** label
le **griot** griot *(African musician-entertainer)*
la **grippe** flu, **14.1**
gris(e) gray, **7.2**
la **grotte** cave, **L4**
le **groupe** group
guéri(e) cured
la **guerre** war, **L3**
le **guerrier** warrior, **L3**
le **guichet** ticket window, **9.1;** box office, **13.1**
le **guide** guidebook
guillotiné(e) guillotined
la **guitare** guitar
le/la **guitariste** guitarist
la **gymnastique** gymnastics, **2.2**

H

habillé(e) dressy, **7.1**
s' **habiller** to get dressed, **12.1**
habiter to live *(in a city, house, etc.),* **3.1**
haïtien(ne) Haitian
le **hall** lobby, **8.1**
le **hamburger** hamburger
le **hameau** hamlet
handicapé(e) handicapped
le **hardware** *(computer)* hardware
les **haricots** *(m. pl.)* **verts** green beans, **6.2**
la **harpe** harp
haut: en haut de la montagne at the top of the mountain
haut de gamme state of the art
le **hautbois** oboe
l' **hectomètre** *(m.)* hectometer
l' **hémisphère** *(m.)* hemisphere
le **héros** hero
l' **heure** *(f.)* time *(of day),* **BV;** hour, **3.2**
à l'heure on time, **8.1**
à quelle heure? at what time?, **2**
À tout à l'heure. See you later., **BV**
de bonne heure early
Il est quelle heure? What time is it?, **BV**
heureusement fortunately
heureux, heureuse happy
hier yesterday, **10.1**
avant-hier the day before yesterday, **10.2**
hier matin yesterday morning, **10.2**
hier soir last night, **10.2**
l' **histoire** *(f.)* history, **2.2;** story
l' **hiver** *(m.)* winter, **11.2**
le/la **H.L.M.** low-income housing
le **hockey** hockey
l' **homme** *(m.)* man, **7.1**
honnête honest
les **honoraires** *(m. pl.)* fees *(doctor)*
l' **hôpital** *(m.)* hospital
l' **horaire** *(m.)* schedule, timetable, **9.1**
horrible horrible
hospitalier, hospitalière hospital *(adj.)*
le **hot-dog** hot dog, **5.1**
l' **hôtel** *(m.)* hotel
l' **hôtesse** *(f.)* **de l'air** flight attendant, **8.2**
l' **huile** *(f.)* oil, **6.1**
humain(e) human
l' **hydrate** *(m.)* **de carbone** carbohydrate
hyper: J'ai hyper faim. I'm super hungry.
l' **hypermarché** *(m.)* large department store/supermarket

I

idéal(e) ideal
l' **idée** *(f.)* idea
identifier to identify
il y a there is, there are, **4.1**
l' **île** *(f.)* island, **L4**
immédiat(e) immediate
immédiatement immediately
immense immense
l' **immeuble** *(m.)* apartment building, **4.2**
important(e) important
impossible impossible
les **impressionnistes** *(m. pl.)* Impressionists *(painters)*
l' **imprimante** *(f.)* printer
inaugurer to inaugurate
inconnu(e) unknown
l' **indication** *(f.)* cue

indiquer to indicate, show
indiscret, indiscrète indiscreet
indispensable indispensable
l' **individu** *(m.)* individual
individuel(le) individual
industriel(le) industrial
l' **infection** *(f.)* infection, **14.1**
inférieur(e) lower
infini(e) infinite
l' **influence** *(f.)* influence
influencer to influence
l' **information** *(f.)* information
les informations *(f. pl.)* news *(TV)*
l' **informatique** *(f.)* computer science, **2.2**
innocent(e) innocent
innombrable countless
insister to insist
inspirer to inspire
les **instructions** *(f. pl.)* instructions
l' **instrument** *(m.)* instrument
l'instrument à clavier keyboard instrument
l'instrument à cordes string instrument
l'instrument à percussion percussion instrument
l'instrument à vent wind instrument
intellectuel(le) intellectual
l' **intellectuel(le)** intellectual
intelligent(e) intelligent, **1.1**
intéressant(e) interesting, **1.1**
intéresser to interest
l' **intérêt** *(m.)* interest
intérieur(e) domestic *(flight)*, **8.1**
international(e) international, **8.1**
interne internal
l' **interprète** *(m. et f.)* interpreter
l' **interro(gation)** *(f.)* quiz
intime intimate
inventer to make up
inviter to invite, **4.1;** to pay for someone's meal, **5.2**
isoler to isolate
l' **italien** *(m.)* Italian *(language)*, **2.2**
italien(ne) Italian
l' **Ivoirien(ne)** *(m. et f.)* Ivorian *(inhabitant of Côte d'Ivoire)*

J

jaloux, jalouse jealous
jamais ever
ne… jamais never, **11.2**
la **jambe** leg
le **jambon** ham, **5.1**
janvier *(m.)* January, **BV**
le **jardin** garden, **4.2**
jaune yellow, **7.2**
le **jazz** jazz
je I, **1.2**
Je t'en prie. You're welcome. *(fam.)*, **BV**
je voudrais I would like, **5.1**
Je vous en prie. You're welcome. *(form.)*, **BV**
le **jean** jeans, **7.1**
jeter to throw, **L4**
le **jeu** game
jeune young
les **jeunes** *(m. pl.)* young people
le **jogging: faire du jogging** to jog
la **joie** joy
joli(e) pretty, **4.2**
jouer to play, **3.2;** to show *(movie)*; to perform, **13.1**
jouer à to play a sport, **10.1**
jouer de to play a musical instrument
le **joueur, la joueuse** player, **10.1**
le **jour** day, **BV**
huit jours a week
de nos jours today, nowadays
tous les jours every day, **13.2**
le **journal** newspaper, **9.1**
la **journée** day, **3.1**
Belle journée! What a nice day!, **4.2**
Joyeux anniversaire! Happy birthday!
le **jumeau, la jumelle** twin, **L1**
la **jupe** skirt, **7.1**
le **jus** juice, **5.1**
le jus d'orange orange juice, **5.1**
le jus de pomme apple juice, **5.1**
jusqu'à (up) to, until, **10.2**
juste just, **2.1**
juste à sa taille fitting (him/her) just right
juste là right there
tout juste just barely

K

le **kilo(gramme)** kilogram, **6.2**
le **kilomètre** kilometer
le **kiosque** newsstand, **9.1**
le **kleenex** tissue, **14.1**

L

là there
là-haut up there
le **laboratoire** laboratory
le **lac** lake
laisser to leave *(something behind)*, **5.2;** to let, allow
laisser un pourboire to leave a tip, **5.2**
le **lait** milk, **6.1**
lancer to throw, to shoot *(ball)*, **10.2**
le **langage: en langage courant** commonly known as
la **langue** language, **2.2**
large loose, wide, **7.2**
le **latin** Latin, **2.2**
latin(e) Latin

latino-américain(e) Latin American
laver to wash, **12**
se **laver** to wash oneself, **12.1**
le **lave-vaisselle** dishwasher, **12.2**
la **leçon** lesson, **11.1**
le **lecteur, la lectrice** reader
la **lecture** reading
la **légende** legend
le **légume** vegetable, **6.2**
la **lettre** letter
lever to raise, **3.1**
lever la main to raise one's hand, **3.1**
se **lever** to get up, **12.1**
la **liaison** liaison, linking
libérer to free
la **liberté** freedom
libre free, **5.1**
le **lieu** place
avoir lieu to take place
la **ligne** line
la **limite** limit
la **limonade** lemon-lime drink, **BV**
le **lipide** fat
le **liquide** liquid
lire to read, **9.2**
le **litre** liter, **6.2**
la **littérature** literature, **2.2**
la **livre** pound, **6.2**
le **livre** book, **3.2**
local(e) local
le **logement** housing
le **logiciel** computer program
loin far (away)
loin de far from, **4.2**
le **long: le long de** along
long(ue) long, **7.1**
longtemps (for) a long time, **11.1**
trop longtemps (for) too long, **11.1**
le **look** style
louer to rent, **13.1**
les **lunettes** *(f. pl.)* **de soleil** sunglasses, **11.1**
la **lutte** fight, battle, **L3**
lutter to fight, **L3**
le **lycée** high school, **2.1**
le/la **lycéen(ne)** high school student

M

la **machine** machine
Madame (Mme) Mrs., Ms., **BV**
Mademoiselle (Mlle) Miss, Ms., **BV**
le **magasin** store, **3.2**
le grand magasin department store, **7.1**
le **magazine** magazine, **9.1**
le **Maghreb** Maghreb
magique magic *(adj.)*
le **magnétoscope** VCR, **12.2**
magnifique magnificent
le **maillot** jersey
le maillot de bain bathing suit, **11.1**
la **main** hand, **3.1**
fait(e) à la main handmade
maintenant now, **2.2**
mais but, **2.1**
Mais oui (non)! Of course (not)!
la **maison** house, **3.1**
la maison d'édition publishing house
la **maisonnette** cottage
la **majorité** majority
mal badly, **14.1**
avoir mal à to have a(n) . . . -ache, to hurt, **14.1**
Ça fait mal. It (That) hurts., **14.1**
Où avez-vous mal? Where does it hurt?, **14.2**
Pas mal. Not bad., **BV**
malade ill, sick, **L1, 14.1**
le/la **malade** sick person, patient, **14.2**
la **maladie** illness, disease
malheureusement unfortunately
malheureux, malheureuse unhappy
malin (maligne): C'est malin! Very clever! *(ironic)*
la **maman** mom
la **Manche** English Channel
la **manche** sleeve, **7.1**
à manches longues (courtes) long- (short-) sleeved, **7.1**
manger to eat, **5.1**
la salle à manger dining room, **4.2**
la **manifestation culturelle** cultural event
le **manteau** coat, **7.1**
se **maquiller** to put on makeup, **12.1**
le/la **marchand(e) (de fruits et légumes)** (produce) seller, merchant, **6.2**
la **marchandise** merchandise
le **marché** market, **6.2**
bon marché inexpensive
le marché aux puces flea market
marcher to walk
le **mari** husband, **4.1**
le **mariage** marriage; wedding
marié(e) married
se **marier** to get married, **L4**
le **marin** sailor, **L4**
le **Maroc** Morocco
marocain(e) Moroccan
marquer un but to score a goal, **10.1**
marron *(inv.)* brown, **7.2**
marseillais(e) from Marseille
martiniquais(e) from or of Martinique
le **mat** *(fam.)* morning
le **match** game, **10.1**
les **mathématiques** *(f. pl.)* mathematics, **2.2**
les **maths** *(f. pl.)* math, **2.2**
la **matière** subject *(school),* **2.2;** matter
le **matin** morning, **BV**
du matin A.M. *(time),* **BV**
mauvais(e) bad; wrong, **2.2**
Il fait mauvais. It's bad weather., **11.1**
le **médecin** doctor *(m. and f.),* **14.2**
chez le médecin at (to) the doctor's office, **14.2**

la **médecine** medicine *(medical profession)*
médical(e) medical
le **médicament** medicine, **14.1**
la **médina** medina
le **mélange** mixture
le **melon** melon, **6.2**
même *(adj.)* same, **2.1;** *(adv.)* even
tout de même all the same, **5.2**
la **mer** sea, **11.1**
la mer des Antilles Caribbean Sea
la mer des Caraïbes Caribbean Sea
la mer Méditerranée Mediterranean Sea
merci thank you, thanks, **BV**
la **mère** mother, **4.1**
merveilleux, merveilleuse marvelous
le **message** message
la **mesure** measurement
mesurer to measure
le **métabolisme** metabolism
le **métal** metal
le **mètre** meter
le **métro** subway, **4.2**
la station de métro subway station, **4.2**
mettre to put (on), to place, **7.1;** to turn on *(appliance)*, **7**
mettre la table to set the table, **7**
les **meubles** *(m. pl.)* furniture
le **microbe** microbe, germ
microbien(ne) microbial
le **microprocesseur** microprocessor
le **microscope** microscope
midi *(m.)* noon, **BV**
mieux better, **7.2**
aimer mieux to prefer, **7.2**
aller mieux to feel better, **14.2**
militaire military
mille (one) thousand, **3.2**
le **milligramme** milligram
le **million** million
le **minéral** mineral
minuit *(m.)* midnight, **BV**
la **minute** minute, **9.2**
le **miracle** miracle
la **mi-temps** half *(sporting event)*
la **mode: à la mode** in style
le **modèle** model
le **modem** modem
moderne modern
modeste modest; reasonably priced
la **moelle épinière** spinal cord
moins less, **7.1;** minus
plus ou moins more or less
le **mois** month, **BV**
le **moment** moment, time
en ce moment right now
le **monde** world
beaucoup de monde a lot of people, **10.1**
tout le monde everyone, everybody, **1.2**
le **moniteur** *(computer)* monitor
le **moniteur, la monitrice** instructor, **11.1**
Monsieur *(m.)* Mr., sir, **BV**
le **mont** mount, mountain
la **montagne** mountain, **11.2**
monter to go up, **4.2;** to get on, get in, **9.2**
monter une pièce to put on a play, **13.1**
montrer to show
la **mort** death
le **mot** word
le mot apparenté cognate
le **mouchoir** handkerchief, **14.1**
la **moule** mussel
mourir to die, **11**
la **moutarde** mustard, **6.2**
le **mouvement** movement
moyen(ne) average, intermediate
le **moyen de transport** mode of transportation
multicolore multicolored
multiplier to multiply
muni(e) de with
municipal(e) municipal
le **mur** wall, **L4**
le **muscle** muscle
musculaire muscular
le **musée** museum, **13.2**
musical(e) musical
le/la **musicien(ne)** musician
la **musique** music, **2.2**
musulman(e) Moslem
mystérieux, mystérieuse mysterious
le **mythe** myth

N

nager to swim, **11.1**
naître to be born, **11**
la **nappe** tablecloth, **5.2**
la **natation** swimming, **11.1**
national(e) national
nationalité *(f.)* nationality
la **nature** nature
nature plain *(adj.)*, **5.1**
naturel(le) natural
la **navette: faire la navette** to go back and forth, make the run
naviguer sur Internet to surf the Net
ne: ne... jamais never, **11.2**
ne... pas not, **1.2**
ne... personne no one, nobody, **11**
ne... plus no longer, no more, **6.1**
ne... que only
ne... rien nothing, **11**
né(e): elle est née she was born
nécessaire necessary
nécessairement necessarily
négatif, négative negative
la **négritude** black pride
la **neige** snow, **11.2**
neige *(inf.* **neiger**): **Il neige.** It's snowing., **11.2**
nerveux, nerveuse nervous

n'est-ce pas? isn't it?, doesn't it (he, she, etc.)?, **2.2**
le **neveu** nephew, **4.1**
le **nez** nose, **14.1**
avoir le nez qui coule to have a runny nose, **14.1**
ni... ni neither . . . nor
la **nièce** niece, **4.1**
noir(e) black, **7.2**
le **nom** name; noun
le nom de famille last name
le **nombre** number
nombreux, nombreuse numerous
nommer to name, mention
non no
non plus either, neither
non-fumeurs non-smoking *(section)*, **8.1**
le **nord** north
nord-africain(e) North African
normal(e) normal
la **note** note; grade
nourrir to feed
la **nourriture** food, nutrition
nouveau (nouvel), nouvelle new, **4.2**
à nouveau again
la **Nouvelle-Angleterre** New England
La **Nouvelle-Orléans** New Orleans
le **nuage** cloud, **11.1**
la **nuit** night
nul(le) *(slang)* bad
le **numéro** number
le numéro de téléphone telephone number

O

ô oh
l' **objet** *(m.)* object
obligatoire mandatory
obliger to oblige, force
observer to observe
occidental(e) western
occupé(e) occupied, taken, **5.1;** busy
l' **océan** *(m.)* ocean
l'océan Atlantique Atlantic Ocean
l' **œil** *(m.)* eye, **14.1**
l' **œuf** *(m.)* egg, **6.1**
l'œuf à la coque poached egg
l'œuf brouillé scrambled egg
l'œuf sur le plat fried egg
l' **œuvre** *(f.)* work(s) *(of art or literature)*, **13.1**
officiel(le) official
l' **oignon** *(m.)* onion, **5.1**
l' **oiseau** *(m.)* bird
l' **olive** *(f.)* olive
l' **omelette** *(f.)* omelette, **5.1**
l'omelette aux fines herbes omelette with herbs, **5.1**
l'omelette nature plain omelette, **5.1**
on we, they, people, **3.2**
On y va? Let's go.; Shall we go?
l' **oncle** *(m.)* uncle, **4.1**
l' **opéra** *(m.)* opera
l'opéra comique light opera
l'opéra bouffe comic light opera
l' **opération** *(f.)* operation
opposer to oppose, **10.1**
l' **or** *(m.)* gold, **L4**
l' **orange** *(f.)* orange, **6.2**
orange *(inv.)* orange *(color)*, **7.2**
l' **oranger** *(m.)* orange tree, **L2**
l' **orchestre** *(m.)* orchestra
l'orchestre symphonique symphony orchestra
orchestrer to orchestrate
ordinaire ordinary
l' **ordinateur** *(m.)* computer
l' **ordonnance** *(f.)* prescription, **14.2**
faire une ordonnance to write a prescription, **14.2**
l' **oreille** *(f.)* ear, **14.1**
avoir mal aux oreilles to have an earache, **14.1**
l' **organe** *(m.)* organ *(of the body)*
organiser to organize
l' **organisme** *(m.)* organism
l' **orgue** *(m.)* organ *(musical instrument)*
oriental(e) eastern
originaire de native of
l' **origine** *(f.)*: **d'origine américaine (française, etc.)** from the U.S. (France, etc.)
orner to decorate
l' **os** *(m.)* bone
ôter to take off *(clothing)*
ou or, **1.1**
où where, **1.1**
d'où from where, **1.1**
oublier to forget
l' **ouest** *(m.)* west
oui yes, **BV**
ouvert(e) open, **13.2**
l' **ouvrier, l'ouvrière** worker
ouvrir to open, **14.2**
l' **oxygène** *(m.)* oxygen

P

le **pain** bread, **6.1**
le pain complet whole-wheat bread
le pain grillé toast
la tartine de pain beurré slice of bread and butter
la **paire** pair, **7.1**
la **paix** peace
le **palais** palace
le **palet** puck
le **panier** basket, **10.2**
réussir un panier to make a basket *(basketball)*, **10.2**
le **pantalon** pants, **7.1**
papa dad
la **papeterie** stationery store, **3.2**
le **papier** paper, **3.2**

la feuille de papier sheet of paper, **3.2**
Pâques Easter
le **paquet** package, **6.2**
par by, through
par exemple for example
par semaine a (per) week, **3.2**
le **parc** park
parce que because
par-dessus over *(prep.)*, **10.2**
pardon excuse me, pardon me
les **parents** *(m. pl.)* parents, **4.1**
parfait(e) perfect
parfaitement perfectly
le **parfum** flavor
parisien(ne) Parisian
le **parking** parking lot
parler to speak, talk, **3.1**
parler au téléphone to talk on the phone, **3.2**
les **paroles** *(f. pl.)* words, lyrics
la **part: de part et d'autre** on each side
de sa part on his (her) part
participer (à) to participate (in)
particulièrement particularly
la **partie** part
faire partie de to be a part of
partir to leave, **8.1**
partout everywhere
pas not, **2.1**
pas du tout not at all, **3.1**
Pas mal. Not bad., **BV**
Pas question! Out of the question! Not a chance!
le **passager, la passagère** passenger, **8.1**
la **passe** pass
passé(e) past
le **passeport** passport, **8.1**
passer to spend *(time)*, **3.1;** to go (through), **8.1;** to pass, **10.1**
passer un examen to take an exam, **3.1**
les **pâtes** *(f. pl.)* pasta
la **patience** patience, **9.2**
le **patin** skate; skating, **11.2**
faire du patin à glace to ice-skate, **11.1**
la **patinoire** skating rink, **11.2**
le/la **patron(ne)** boss
pauvre poor, **14.1, L1**
Le/La pauvre! Poor thing!, **14.1**
le **pavillon** small house, bungalow
payer to pay, **3.2**
le **pays** country, **8.1**
le **paysage** landscape
le/la **paysan(ne)** peasant, **L1**
le **peigne** comb, **12.1**
se **peigner** to comb one's hair, **12.1**
peindre to paint
le/la **peintre** painter, artist, **13.2**
la **peinture** painting, **13.2**
le **penalty** penalty *(soccer)*
pendant during, for *(time)*, **3.2**
la **pénicilline** penicillin, **14.1**
penser to think
perdre to lose, **9.2**
le **père** father, **4.1**
la **période** period
la **périphérie** outskirts
la **perle** pearl
permanent(e) permanent
permettre to permit, allow
la **personnalité** personality
la **personne** person
ne... personne no one, nobody, **11**
personnel(le) personal
le **personnel de bord** flight crew, **8.2**
personnellement personally, **13.2**
petit(e) short, small, **1.1**
le petit ami boyfriend
la petite amie girlfriend
le petit déjeuner breakfast, **5.2**
les petits pois *(m.)* peas, **6.2**
la **petite-fille** granddaughter, **4.1**
le **petit-fils** grandson, **4.1**
les **petits-enfants** *(m. pl.)* grandchildren, **4.1**
le **pétrole** oil
le **pétrolier** oil tanker
peu (de) few, little
à peu près about, approximately
un peu a little, **2.1**
un peu de a little
en très peu de temps in a short time
très peu seldom, **5.2**
peur: avoir peur to be afraid, **L1**
pharmaceutique pharmaceutical
la **pharmacie** pharmacy, **14.2**
le/la **pharmacien(ne)** pharmacist, **14.2**
le **phénomène** phenomenon
la **photo** photograph
la **phrase** sentence
le/la **physicien(ne)** physicist
physique physical
la **physique** physics, **2.2**
le **piano** piano
la **pie** magpie
la **pièce** room, **4.2;** play, **13.1**
la pièce de théâtre play, **13.1**
le **pied** foot, **10.1**
à pied on foot, **4.2**
donner un coup de pied to kick, **10.1**
être vite sur pied to be better soon, **14.1**
la **pierre** stone
la pierre précieuse gem, **L4**
le/la **pilote** pilot, **8.2**
piloter to pilot, to fly
piquer to sting, **14.1**
la **piscine** pool, **11.1**
la **piste** runway, **8.1;** track, **10.2;** ski trail, **11.2**
pittoresque picturesque
la **pizza** pizza, **BV**
la **place** seat *(plane, train, movie, etc.)*, **8.1;** place; square

la **plage** beach, **11.1**
la **plaine** plain
le **plaisir** pleasure
la **planche à voile: faire de la planche à voile** to windsurf, **11.1**
la **plante** plant
le **plastique** plastic
le **plat** dish *(food)*
le **plateau** tray, **8.2**
plein(e) full, **10.1**
pleurer to cry, **L1**
pleut (*inf.* **pleuvoir**): **Il pleut.** It's raining., **11.1**
plissé(e) pleated, **7.1**
le **plongeon** dive
plonger to dive, **11.1**
la **pluie** rain
la **plupart (des)** most (of), **9.2**
le **pluriel** plural
plus plus; more, **7.1**
en plus de in addition to
ne… plus no longer, no more, **6.1**
plus ou moins more or less
plus tard later
plusieurs several
plutôt rather
le **poème** poem
la **poésie** poetry
le **poète** poet *(m. and f.)*
le **poids** weight
point: à point medium-rare *(meat)*, **5.2**
la **pointure** size *(shoes)*, **7.2**
Vous faites quelle pointure? What (shoe) size do you take?, **7.2**
la **poire** pear, **6.2**
le **poisson** fish, **6.1**
la **poissonnerie** fish store, **6.1**
la **poitrine** chest
le **poivre** pepper, **6.1**
la **politesse** courtesy, politeness, **BV**
politique political
pollué(e) polluted
la **pollution** pollution
le **polo** polo shirt, **7.1**
la **pomme** apple, **6.2**
la tarte aux pommes apple tart, **6.1**
la **pomme de terre** potato, **6.2**
le **pont** bridge
pop pop *(music)*
populaire popular, **1.2**
le **porc** pork, **6.1**
le **port** port, harbor
la **porte** gate *(airport)*, **8.1;** door, **L4**
porter to wear, **7.1**
le/la **portraitiste** portraitist
portugais(e) Portuguese
poser une question to ask a question, **3.1**
la **position** position
posséder to possess, own
la **possession** possession
la **poste** mail
la poste par avion airmail
le **pot** jar, **6.2**
le **poulet** chicken, **6.1**
le **poumon** lung
pour for, **2.1;** in order to
pour cent percent
le **pourboire** tip *(restaurant)*, **5.2**
pourquoi why, **6.2**
pourquoi pas? why not?
pousser to push
pouvoir to be able to, can, **6.1**
pratique practical
la **pratique** practice
pratiquer to practice
précédent(e) preceding
préféré(e) favorite
préférer to prefer, **6**
le **préfixe** prefix
premier, première first, **4.2**
en première in first class, **9.1**
prendre to have *(to eat or drink*, **5.1;** to take, **5.2;** to buy
prendre un bain (une douche) to take a bath (shower), **12.1**
prendre un bain de soleil to sunbathe, **11.1**
prendre le petit déjeuner to eat breakfast, **5.2**
prendre possession de to take possession of
prendre rendez-vous to make an appointment
prendre le métro to take the subway, **5.2**
le **prénom** first name
préparer to prepare
près de near, **4.2**
prescrire to prescribe, **14.2**
présenter to present; to introduce
presque almost
prie: Je vous en prie. You're welcome., **BV**
primaire: l'école *(f.)* **primaire** elementary school
principal(e) main, principal
le **printemps** spring, **11.1**
au printemps in the spring
la **prison** prison, **L4**
le **prisonnier, la prisonnière** prisoner, **L4**
privé(e) private
le **prix** price, cost, **7.1**
le **problème** problem
prochain(e) next, **9.2**
procurer to provide
le **produit** product
le/la **prof** teacher *(inform.)*, **2.1**
le **professeur** teacher *(m. and f.)*, **2.1**
professionnel(le) professional
la **programmation** programming
le **programme** program
le **projet** plan
la **promenade: faire une promenade** to take a walk, **11.1**
promotion: en promotion on special, on sale
proposer to suggest
protéger to protect
la **protéine** protein
provenance: en provenance de arriving from *(train, plane, etc.)*, **8.1**

les **provisions** *(f. pl.)* food
public, publique public
la **publicité** commercial *(TV),* **12.2;** advertisement
publier to publish
les **puces** *(f. pl.):* **le marché aux puces** flea market
le **pull** sweater, **7.1**
pulmonaire pulmonary
punir to punish
purifié(e) purified

Q

le **quai** platform *(railroad),* **9.1**
la **qualité** quality
quand when, **4.1**
le **quart: et quart** a quarter past *(time),* **BV**
moins le quart a quarter to *(time),* **BV**
le **quartier** neighborhood, district, **4.2**
quatrième fourth
que as; that; than *(in comparisons),* **7.2**
québécois(e) from or of Quebec
quel(le) which, what
quelque some *(sing.)*
quelque chose something, **11**
quelque chose à manger something to eat, **5.1**
quelque chose de spécial something special
quelquefois sometimes, **5.2**
quelques some, a few *(pl.),* **9.2**
quelqu'un somebody, someone, **10.1**
la **question** question, **3.1**
Pas question! Out of the question! Not a chance!
poser une question to ask a question, **3.1**
la **queue** line, **9.1**
faire la queue to wait in line, **9.1**
qui who, **1.1;** whom, **10;** which, that
quitter to leave *(a room, etc.),* **3.1**
quoi what *(after prep.)*
quotidien(ne) daily, everyday

R

la **race** race
raconter to tell (about)
la **radio** radio, **3.2**
le **raisin sec** raisin
la **raison** reason
ramasser to pick up, **8.2**
le **rap** rap *(music)*
rapide quick, fast
rapidement rapidly, quickly
le **rapport** relationship; report
se **raser** to shave, **12.1**
le **rasoir** razor, shaver, **12.1**
rater to miss *(train, etc.),* **9.2**
le **rayon** department *(in a store),* **7.1**
le rayon des manteaux coat department, **7.1**
la **réalité** reality
recevoir to receive, **10.2**
la **recherche** research
à la recherche de in search of
recommencer to begin again
reconnaître to recognize
la **récré** recess, **3.2**
la **récréation** recess, **3.2**
récrire to rewrite
recueillir to pick up
le **recyclage** recycling
la **réduction** discount
refléter to reflect
le **réfrigérateur** refrigerator, **12.2**
regarder to look at, **3.1**
regarder fixement to stare at
le **reggae** reggae
le **régime** diet
faire un régime to follow a diet
la **région** region
la **règle** ruler, **3.2;** rule
regretter to be sorry, **6.1**
régulier, régulière regular
la **reine** queen
la **relation** relationship
relier to connect
religieux, religieuse religious
remarquer to notice
rembourser to pay back, reimburse
remonter to get back on
remplacer to replace
remplir to fill out, **8.2**
rencontrer to meet
le **rendez-vous: prendre rendez-vous** to make an appointment
se **rendormir** to fall asleep again
rendre to give back
rendre bien service to be a big help
renommé(e) renowned
les **renseignements** *(m. pl.)* information
rentrer to go home; to return, **3.2**
renvoyer to return *(volleyball),* **10.2**
le **repas** meal, **5.2**
répéter to repeat
répondre (à) to answer, **9.2**
le **reportage** news article
représenter to represent
réservé(e) reserved
respectif, respective respective
la **respiration** breathing; respiration
respiratoire respiratory
respirer to breathe, **14.2**
respirer à fond to breathe deeply, **14.2**
ressembler à to resemble
ressortir to leave
le **restaurant** restaurant, **5.2**
la **restauration** food service
la restauration rapide fast food
rester to stay, remain, **11.1**
il reste there remains

le **retard** delay
avoir du retard to be late *(plane, train, etc.),* **8.1**
en retard late, **9.1**
le **retour** return
la **retraite** retreat; retirement
retrouver to meet, get together with
réussir to succeed
réussir à un examen to pass an exam
réussir un panier to make a basket *(basketball),* **10.2**
réveillé(e) awake
se **réveiller** to wake up, **12.1**
révéler to reveal
la **révolution** revolution
révolutionnaire revolutionary
la **revue** magazine, **L2**
le **rez-de-chaussée** ground floor, **4.2**
le **rhume** cold *(illness),* **14.1**
riche rich
ridicule ridiculous
rien nothing
rigoler to joke around, **3.2**
Tu rigoles! You're kidding!, **3.2**
rigolo funny, **4.2**
rincer to rinse
la **rivière** river
le **riz** rice
la **robe** dress, **7.1**
le **rocher** rock, boulder, **L3**
le **roi** king, **L3**
le **rôle** role
le **roman** novel
romantique romantic
rose pink, **7.2**
rouge red, **7.2**
rouler (vite) to go, drive, ride (fast), **10.2**
la **route** road
la **routine** routine, **12.1**
royal(e) royal
le **rubis** ruby
la **rue** street, **3.1**
ruiné(e) ruined
rural(e) rural
le **russe** Russian *(language)*
le **rythme** rhythm

S

le **sac** bag, **6.1**
le sac à dos backpack, **3.2**
saignant(e) rare *(meat),* **5.2**
la **saison** season
la **salade** salad, **5.1;** lettuce, **6.2**
le **salaire** salary
sale dirty
la **salle** room
la salle à manger dining room, **4.2**
la salle d'attente waiting room, **9.1**
la salle de bains bathroom, **4.2**
la salle de cinéma movie theater, **13.1**
la salle de classe classroom, **2.1**
la salle de séjour living room, **4.2**
Salut. Hi.; Bye., **BV**
la **salutation** greeting
les **sandales** *(f. pl.)* sandals, **7.1**
le **sandwich** sandwich, **BV**
le **sang** blood
sans without
la **santé** health, **14.1**
la **sardine** sardine
satisfaire to satisfy
la **sauce** sauce
la **saucisse** sausage
la saucisse de Francfort hot dog, **BV**
le **saucisson** salami, **6.1**
sauf except, **13.2**
sauvegarder to safeguard, to save
sauver to save
le **savant** scientist
savoir to know *(information),* **13.2**
le **savon** soap, **12.1**
le **saxophone** saxophone
la **scène** scene, **13.1**
les **sciences** *(f. pl.)* science, **2.1**
les sciences naturelles natural sciences, **2.1**
les sciences sociales social studies, **2.1**
scientifique scientific
scintiller to sparkle
scolaire school *(adj.),* **3.2**
le **sculpteur** sculptor *(m. and f.),* **13.2**
la **sculpture** sculpture, **13.2**
la **séance** show(ing) *(movie),* **13.1**
sec, sèche dry
second(e) second
secondaire: l'école *(f.)* **secondaire** junior high, high school, **1.2**
seconde: en seconde in second class, **9.1**
secret, secrète secret
le **séjour** stay
la salle de séjour living room, **4.2**
le **sel** salt, **6.1**
selon according to
la **semaine** week, **3.2;** allowance
la semaine dernière last week, **10.2**
la semaine prochaine next week
par semaine a (per) week, **3.2**
semblable similar, **L1**
le/la **Sénégalais(e)** Senegalese *(person)*
le **sens** direction; meaning
se **sentir** to feel *(well, etc.),* **14.1**
séparer to separate
sérieux, sérieuse serious, **7**
serré(e) tight, **7.2**
le **serveur, la serveuse** waiter, waitress, **5.1**
le **service** service, **5.2**
Le service est compris. The tip is included., **5.2**
la **serviette** napkin, **5.2;** towel, **11.1**
servir to serve, **8.2; 10.2**
seul(e) alone, **5.2;** single; only *(adj.)*
tout(e) seul(e) all alone, by himself/herself, **5.2**

seulement only *(adv.)*
le **shampooing** shampoo, **12.1**
le **shopping** shopping, **7.2**
le **short** shorts, **7.1**
si if; yes *(after neg. question)*, **7.2;** so *(adv.)*
le **sida (syndrome immuno-déficitaire acquis)** AIDS
le **siècle** century
le **siège** seat, **8.2**
siffler to (blow a) whistle, **10.1**
le **sifsari** type of veil worn by North African women
le **signal** sign
la **signification** meaning, significance
signifier to mean
simple simple
l'aller (simple) one-way ticket, **9.1**
simplement simply
sinon or else, otherwise, **9.2**
la **sinusite** sinus infection, **14.2**
le **sirop** syrup, **14.1**
le **site** Web site
situé(e) located
le **ski** ski, skiing, **11.2**
faire du ski to ski, **11.2**
faire du ski nautique to water-ski, **11.1**
le ski alpin downhill skiing, **11.2**
le ski de fond cross-country skiing, **11.2**
le **skieur, la skieuse** skier, **11.2**
le **snack-bar** snack bar, **9.2**
sociable sociable, outgoing, **1.2**
social(e) social
la **société** company
la **sœur** sister, **1.2**
le **software** software
soi oneself, himself, herself
soif: avoir soif to be thirsty, **5.1**
le **soin** care
de soins polyvalents general care
le **soir** evening , **BV**
ce soir tonight
du soir in the evening, P.M., **BV**
le soir in the evening, **5.2**
le **sol** ground, **10.2**
le **soldat** soldier, **L3**
les **soldes** *(m. pl.)* sale *(in a store)*, **7.1**
le **soleil** sun, **11.1**
au soleil in the sun, **11.1**
Il fait du soleil. It's sunny., **11.1**
le soleil levant rising sun
la **solidarité** solidarity
solide solid
solitaire lonely
la **solution** solution
sombre dark
la **somme** sum
le **sommet** summit, mountaintop, **11.2**
le **son** sound, **L3**
le **sondage** survey, opinion poll
sonner du cor to blow a horn, **L3**
la **sorte** sort, kind, type
sortir to go out; to take out, **8.2**
sortir victorieux (victorieuse) to win (the battle)
la **souche** tree stump
dormir comme une souche to sleep like a log
souffrir to suffer, **14.2**
souhait *(m.)*: **À tes souhaits!** God bless you! Gesundheit!, **14.1**
le **souk** North African market
la **soupe** soup, **5.1**
la soupe à l'oignon onion soup, **5.1**
la **source** source
la **souris** mouse
sous under, **8.2**
les **sous-titres** *(m. pl.)* subtitles, **13.1**
soustraire to subtract
souterrain(e) underground
le **souvenir** memory
souvent often, **5.2**
les **spaghettis** *(m. pl.)* spaghetti
spécial(e) special
la **spécialité** specialty
le **spectateur, la spectatrice** spectator, **10.1**
splendide splendid
sport *(inv.)* casual *(clothes)*, **7.1**
le **sport** sport, **10.2**
le sport collectif team sport
le sport d'équipe team sport, **10.2**
les sports d'hiver winter sports, **11.2**
sportif, sportive athletic
le **squelette** skeleton
squelettique skeletal
le **stade** stadium, **10.1**
standing: de grand standing luxury
la **station** station, **4.2;** resort
la station balnéaire seaside resort, **11.1**
la station de métro subway station, **4.2**
la station de sports d'hiver ski resort, **11.2**
la **station-service** gas station
la **statue** statue, **13.2**
le **steak frites** steak and French fries, **5.2**
le **steward** flight attendant *(m.)*, **8.2**
stocker to store
la **stratégie** strategy
strict(e) strict, **2.1**
le **studio** studio (apartment)
stupide stupid
le **stylo-bille** ballpoint pen, **3.2**
la **substance** substance
le **succès** success
le **sucre** sugar
le **sud** south
suggérer to suggest
suite: tout de suite right away

suivant(e) following
suivre to follow
le **sujet** subject
super terrific, super
superbe superb
supérieur(e) higher
le **supermarché** supermarket, **6.2**
sur on, **4.2**
donner sur to face, overlook, **4.2**
sûr(e) sure, certain
bien sûr, of course
le **surf: faire du surf** to go surfing, **11.1**
le **surfeur, la surfeuse** surfer, **11.1**
surgelé(e) frozen, **6.2**
la **surprise** surprise
surtout especially, above all; mostly
surveiller to watch
le **survêtement** warmup suit, **7.1**
la **survie** survival
le **sweat-shirt** sweatshirt, **7.1**
sympa *(inv.)* nice (*abbrev. for* **sympathique**), **1.2**
sympathique nice *(person)*, **1.2**
la **symphonie** symphony
le **symptôme** symptom
le **synonyme** synonym
le **système** system
le système métrique metric system

T

la **table** table, **5.1**
le **tableau** painting, **13.2;** chart
la **taille** size *(clothes)*, **7.2**
juste à sa taille fitting (him/her) just right
la taille au-dessous next smaller size, **7.2**
la taille au-dessus next larger size, **7.2**
Vous faites quelle taille? What size do you take/wear?, **7.2**
le **tailleur** suit *(woman's)*, **7.1**
le **talent** talent
le **tango** tango
la **tante** aunt, **4.1**
tard late, **12.1**
plus tard later
le **tarif** fare
la **tarte** pie, tart, **6.1**
la tarte aux pommes apple tart, **6.1**
la **tartine** slice of bread with butter or jam
la tartine de pain beurré slice of bread and butter, **5.1**
la **tasse** cup, **5.2**
le **taux** level
la **techno** techno *(music)*
la **télé** TV, **12.2**
à la télé on TV, **12.2**
télécharger to download
la **télécommande** remote control, **12.2**
le **téléphone** telephone, **3.2**
le numéro de téléphone telephone number
téléphoner to call (on the telephone)
téléphonique telephone *(adj.)*
le **télésiège** chairlift, **11.2**
la **tempe** temple
la **température** temperature, **14.1**
tempéré(e) temperate
temporaire temporary
le **temps** weather, **11.1;** time
de temps en temps from time to time, **11.1**
l'emploi *(m.)* **du temps** schedule
en très peu de temps in a short time
Il fait quel temps? What's the weather like?, **11.1**
le **tendon** tendon
le **terme** term
le **terrain de football** soccer field, **10.1**
la **terrasse** terrace, patio, **4.2**
la terrasse d'un café sidewalk café, **5.1**
la **terre** earth, land
à terre on the ground
terrible terrible
la **tête** head, **10.1**
avoir mal à la tête to have a headache, **14.1**
le **texte** text
thaïlandais(e) Thai
le **thé** tea
le **théâtre** theater, **13.1**
la pièce de théâtre play, **13.1**
le **thème** theme
timide shy, timid, **1.2**
tirer to take, to draw
les **toilettes** *(f. pl.)* bathroom, toilet, **4.2**
le **toit** roof
le toit de chaume thatched roof
la **tomate** tomato, **6.2**
tomber to fall, **11.2**
tomber malade to get sick, **L1**
tôt early, **12.1**
totalement totally
toucher to touch, **10.2**
toujours always, **4.2;** still
la **tour** tower
la tour Eiffel Eiffel Tower
le **tour: à son tour** in turn
À votre tour. (It's) your turn.
le/la **touriste** tourist
tous, toutes *(adj.)* all, every, **2.1, 8**
tous (toutes) les deux both
tous les jours every day, **13.2**
tousser to cough, **14.1**
tout *(pron.)* all, everything
C'est tout. That's all., **6.1**
en tout in all
pas du tout not at all, **3.1**
tout(e) *(adj.)* the whole, the entire; all, any
tout le monde everyone, everybody, **1.2**
tout *(adv.)* very, completely, all, **4.2**

À tout à l'heure. See you later., **BV**
tout autour de all around *(prep.)*
tout de même all the same, **5.2**
tout près de very near, **4.2**
tout(e) seul(e) all alone, all by himself/herself, **5.2**
tout de suite right away
toxique toxic
la **tradition** tradition
traditionnel(le) traditional
la **tragédie** tragedy, **13.1**
tragique tragic
le **train** train, **9.1**
le **traitement** treatment
traiter to treat
le **traître, la traîtresse** traitor
la **tranche** slice, **6.2**
transformer to transform
transporter to transport
le **travail** work
travailler to work, **3.1;** to practice
traverser to cross
très very, **BV**
le **trésor** treasure, **L4**
la **trigonométrie** trigonometry, **2.2**
triste sad, **L1**
troisième third, **4.2**
la **trompette** trumpet
le **tronc cérébral** brain stem
le **trône** throne
trop too *(excessive)*, **2.1**
trop de too many, too much
tropical(e) tropical, **9**
le **trou** hole, **L4**
le **trouble digestif** indigestion, upset stomach
trouver to find, **5.1;** to think *(opinion)*, **7.2**
le **t-shirt** T-shirt, **7.1**
la **tunique** tunic
la **Tunisie** Tunisia
tunisien(ne) Tunisian
le **tunnel** tunnel, **L4**
le **type** type; guy *(inform.)*
typique typical
typiquement typically

U

l' **un(e)... l'autre** one . . . the other
un(e) à un(e) one by one
unique single, only one
l'enfant unique only child
uniquement solely
l' **unité** *(f.)* unit
l' **université** *(f.)* university
l' **usine** *(f.)* factory
utiliser to use

V

les **vacances** *(f. pl.)* vacation
en vacances on vacation
les grandes vacances summer vacation
la **vague** wave, **11.1**
le **vaisseau sanguin** blood vessel
la **vaisselle** dishes, **12.2**
faire la vaisselle to do the dishes, **12.2**
le **val** valley
la **valeur** value
la **valise** suitcase, **8.1**
faire les valises to pack, **8.1**
la **vallée** valley
la **vanille: à la vanille** vanilla *(adj.)*, **5.1**
varié(e) varied
varier to vary
la **variété** variety
la **veine** vein
le **vélo** bicycle, bike, **10.2**
le **vendeur, la vendeuse** salesperson, **7.1**
vendre to sell, **9.1**
vengé(e) avenged
la **vengeance** vengence
se **venger** to get revenge
le **vent** wind, **11.1**
Il y a du vent. It's windy., **11.1**
le **ventre** abdomen, stomach, **14.1**
avoir mal au ventre to have a stomachache, **14.1**
vérifier to check, verify, **8.1**
la **vérité** truth
le **verre** glass, **5.2**
vers toward
la **version originale** original language version *(of a movie)*, **13.1**
vert(e) green, **5.1**
la **veste** (sport) jacket, **7.1**
les **vêtements** *(m. pl.)* clothes, **7.1**
la **viande** meat, **6.1**
victorieux, victorieuse victorious
la **vidéo** video, **3.1**
la cassette vidéo videocassette, **12.2**
le film en vidéo movie video, **13.1**
la **vie** life
en vie alive
vieille old *(f.)*, **4.2**
vietnamien(ne) Vietnamese, **6**
vieux (vieil) old *(m.)*, **4.2**
la **villa** house
le **village** village, small town
la **ville** city, town, **8.1**
en ville in town, in the city
le **vinaigre** vinegar, **6.1**
violent(e) violent; rough
le **violon** violin
viral(e) viral, **14.1**
le **virus** virus
visionner to view
visiter to visit *(a place)*, **13.2**
vital(e) vital
la **vitamine** vitamin
vite fast *(adv.)*, **10.2**
la **vitrine** (store) window, **7.1**
vivant(e) living
Vive... ! Long live . . . !, Hooray for . . . !

voici here is, here are, **4.1**
la **voie** track *(railroad)*, **9.1**
voilà there is, there are; here is, here are *(emphatic)*, **1.2**
le **voile** veil
voir to see, **7.1**
le/la **voisin(e)** neighbor, **4.2**
la **voiture** car, **4.2**
en voiture by car, **5.2;** "All aboard!"
la **voix** voice
le **vol** flight, **8.1**
le vol intérieur domestic flight, **8.1**
le vol international international flight, **8.1**
le **volley(-ball)** volleyball, **10.2**
la **volonté** willpower
voudrais: je voudrais I would like, **5.1**
vouloir to want, **6.1**
le **voyage** trip, **8.1;** voyage
faire un voyage to take a trip, **8.1**
voyager to travel, **8.1**
le **voyageur, la voyageuse** traveler, passenger, **9.1**
vrai(e) true, real, **2.2**
vraiment really, **1.1**
la **vue** view, **4.2**

W

le **wagon** *(railroad)* car, **9.2**
le **wagon-couchette** sleeping car
le **wagon-restaurant** dining car
le **week-end** weekend
le **western** Western movie

Y

le **yaourt** yogurt, **6.1**
les **yeux** *(m. pl; sing.* **œil***)* eyes, **14.1, L1**
avoir les yeux qui piquent to have itchy eyes, **14.1**

Z

zapper to zap, to channel surf, **12.2**
la **zone** zone
la **zoologie** zoology
Zut! Darn!, **BV**

This English-French Dictionary *contains all productive vocabulary from the text. The numbers following each entry indicate the chapter and vocabulary section in which the word is introduced. For example,* ***2.2*** *means that the word first appeared in* ***Chapitre 2, Mots 2. BV*** *refers to the introductory* ***Bienvenue*** *lessons.* ***L*** *refers to the optional literary readings. If there is no number or letter following an entry, this means that the word or expression is there for receptive purposes only.*

A

a un, une, **1.1**
a week par semaine, **3.2**
a lot beaucoup, **3.1**
to **abandon** abandonner
abdomen le ventre, **14.1**
able capable
to be able to pouvoir, **6.1**
aboard à bord (de), **8.2**
about *(on the subject of)* de; *(approximately)* à peu près
about-face le demi-tour
above au-dessus (de)
above all surtout
absolutely absolument
accessible accessible
accessory l'accessoire *(m.)*
accident l'accident *(m.)*
to **accompany** accompagner
according to d'après; selon
accordion l'accordéon *(m.)*
account le compte
accusation l'accusation *(f.)*
to **accuse** accuser
act l'acte, *(m.)*, **13.1**
action l'action *(f.)*
active actif, active
activity l'activité *(f.)*
actor l'acteur *(m.)*, **13.1**
actress l'actrice *(f.)*, **13.1**
acute aigu(ë), **14.2**
to **add** additionner
address l'adresse *(f.)*
to **admire** admirer
admission l'entrée *(f.)*
adolescent l'adolescent(e)
adorable adorable, **4.1**
adult l'adulte *(m. et f.)*
adventure l'aventure *(f.)*
adversary l'adversaire *(m. et f.)*
advertisement la publicité
afraid: to be afraid avoir peur, **L1**
Africa l'Afrique *(f.)*
African africain(e)
African-American afro-américain(e)
after après, **3.2**
afternoon l'après-midi *(m.)*, **3.2**
five o'clock in the afternoon cinq heures de l'après-midi, **BV**
again encore; à nouveau
against contre, **10.1**
age l'âge *(m.)*, **4.1**
agent *(m. and f.)* l'agent *(m.)*, **8.1**
to **agree** être d'accord, **2.1**
aid l'aide *(f.)*
AIDS le sida
air *(adj.)* aérien(ne)
air l'air *(m.)*
air terminal l'aérogare *(f.)*, **8.1**
airline la compagnie aérienne, **8.1**
airmail la poste par avion
airplane l'avion *(m.)*, **8.1**
airport l'aéroport *(m.)*, **8.1**
airport terminal l'aérogare *(f.)*, **8.1**
aisle le couloir, **8.2**
aisle seat (une place) côté couloir, **8.1**
alas hélas
album l'album *(m.)*
algebra l'algèbre *(f.)*, **2.2**
Algeria l'Algérie *(f.)*
algerian algérien(ne)
alive en vie
all tout(e), tous, toutes, **2.1**
All aboard! En voiture!
all alone tout(e) seul(e), **5.2**
all around tout autour de
all right *(agreement)* d'accord, **2.1**
all the same tout de même, **5.2**
in all en tout
not at all pas du tout
That's all. C'est tout., **6.1**
allergic allergique, **14.1**
allergy l'allergie *(f.)*, **14.1**
to **allow** laisser; permettre
almost presque
alone seul(e), **5.2**
all alone tout(e) seul(e), **5.2**
along le long de
already déjà, **BV**
also aussi, **1.1**
always toujours, **4.2**
a.m. du matin, **BV**
ambitious ambitieux, ambitieuse
American *(adj.)* américain(e), **1.1**
among entre, **3.2**
to **analyse** analyser
analysis l'analyse *(f.)*
analytical analytique

and et, **BV**
animal l'animal *(m.)*
to **announce** annoncer, **9.1**
announcement l'annonce, *(f.)*, **8.2**
anonymous anonyme
another un(e) autre; encore
answer la réponse
to **answer** répondre (à), **9.2**
antibiotic l'antibiotique *(m.)*, **14.1**
antonym l'antonyme *(m.)*
Anything else? Avec ça?, **6.1;** Autre chose?, **6.2**
apartment l'appartement *(m.)*, **4.2**
apartment building l'immeuble *(m.)*, **4.2**
apparatus l'appareil *(m.)*
to **applaud** applaudir
apple la pomme, **6.2**
apple tart la tarte aux pommes, **6.1**
appointment le rendez-vous
to make an appointment prendre rendez-vous
to **appreciate** apprécier
April avril *(m.)*, **BV**
Arab arabe
Arabic *(language)* l'arabe *(m.)*
architecture l'architecture *(f.)*
arithmetic le calcul
arm le bras
army l'armée *(f.)*, **L3**
around autour de, **4.2**
to **arrest** arrêter
arrested arrêté(e)
arrival l'arrivée *(f.)*, **8.1**
to **arrive** arriver, **3.1**
arriving from *(flight)* en provenance de, **8.1**
art le dessin *(m.)*, **2.2**
artery l'artère *(f.)*
article l'article *(m.)*
artist l'artiste *(m. et f.)*; le/la peintre *(painter)*
artistic artistique
as aussi *(comparisons)*, **7;** comme
as . . . as aussi... que, **7**
as well as ainsi que
the same . . . as le (la, les) même(s)... que
Asian asiatique
to **ask (for)** demander, **3.2**
to ask a question poser une question, **3.1**
aspirin l'aspirine *(f.)*, **14.1**
at à, **3.1;** chez, **3.2**
at last enfin, **12.1**
at the home (business) of chez, **3.2**
at what time? à quelle heure?, **2**
athletic sportif, sportive
Atlantic Ocean l'océan Atlantique
atmosphere l'atmosphère *(f.)*
attached attaché(e)
to **attack** attaquer
attention l'attention *(f.)*
au pair au pair
August août, *(m.)*, **BV**
aunt la tante, **4.1**
author l'auteur *(m.)*
automatic automatique
autumn l'automne *(m.)*, **11.2**
avalanche l'avalanche *(f.)*
avenged vengé(e)
avenue l'avenue *(f.)*
average moyen(ne)
aviator l'aviateur *(m.)*, l'aviatrice *(f.)*
to **avoid** éviter, **12.2**
awake réveillé(e)

B

baby le bébé
back l'arrière *(m.)*, **8.2**
background le fond
backpack le sac à dos, **3.2**
bacon le bacon
bacterial bactérien(ne), **14.1**
bacterium la bactérie
bad mauvais(e), **2.2;** nul(le) *(slang)*
It's bad weather. Il fait mauvais., **11.1**
Not bad. Pas mal., **BV**
badly mal, **14.1**
bag le sac, **6.1**
baggage les bagages *(m. pl.)*, **8.1**
baggage cart le chariot, **9.1**
baggage compartment le coffre à bagages, **8.2**
bagpipes la cornemuse
bakery la boulangerie-pâtisserie, **6.1**
balance l'équilibre *(m.)*
balanced équilibré(e)
balcony le balcon, **4.2**
ball *(soccer, etc.)* le ballon, **10.1**
ballerina la danseuse, **13.1**
ballet le ballet
ballpoint pen le stylo-bille, **3.2**
banana la banane, **6.2**
base la base
baseball le base-ball
baseball cap la casquette, **7.1**
based basé(e)
based on à base de
basilica la basilique
basis la base
basket le panier, **10.2**
basketball le basket (-ball), **10.2**
bath le bain, **12.1**
to take a bath prendre un bain, **12.1**
bather le baigneur, la baigneuse
bathing suit le maillot (de bain), **11.1**
bathroom la salle de bains, les toilettes *(f. pl.)*, **4.2**
battle la bataille, **L3**
battlefield le champ de bataille, **L3**
to **be** être, **1.1**
to be able to pouvoir, **6.1**
to be afraid avoir peur, **L1**
to be better soon être vite sur pied, **14.1**

to be born naître, **11**
to be called s'appeler, **12.1**
to be careful faire attention, **11.1**
to be early être en avance, **9.1**
to be given off se dégager
to be hungry avoir faim, **5.1**
to be in luck avoir de la chance
to be late être en retard, **9.1;** avoir du retard *(plane, train, etc.)*, **8.1**
to be lucky avoir de la chance
to be named s'appeler, **12.1**
to be on time être à l'heure, **8.1**
to be part of faire partie de
to be sorry regretter, **6.1**
to be thirsty avoir soif, **5.1**
to be . . . years old avoir... ans, **4.1**
beach la plage, **11.1**
bean: green beans les haricots verts *(m. pl.)*, **6.2**
beautiful beau (bel), belle, **4.2**
beauty la beauté
because parce que
because of à cause de
to **become** devenir
bed: to go to bed se coucher, **12.1**
bedroom la chambre à coucher, **4.2**
beef le bœuf, **6.1**
before avant; avant de
to **begin** commencer, **9.2**
to begin again recommencer
beginner le/la débutant(e), **11.2**
beginning le début
beige beige *(inv.)*, **7.2**
being l'être *(m.)*
human being l'être humain *(m.)*
Belgian belge
Belgium la Belgique
to **believe** croire, **7.2**
below au-dessous (de)
belt la ceinture, **L3**
seat belt la ceinture de sécurité, **8.2**
berth (on a train) la couchette
better *(adv.)* mieux, **7.2**
to feel better aller mieux, **14.2**
between entre, **3.2**
beverage la boisson; la consommation, **5.1**
bicentennial le bicentenaire
bicycle la bicyclette, **10.2;** le vélo, **10.2**
bicycle race la course cycliste, **10.2**
bicycle racer le coureur (la coureuse) cycliste, **10.2**
big grand(e), **1.1**
bike le vélo, **10.2**
biological biologique
biologist le/la biologiste
biology la biologie, **2.2**
bird l'oiseau *(m.)*
birthday l'anniversaire *(m.)*, **4.1**
Happy birthday! Bon (Joyeux) anniversaire!
black noir(e), **7.2**
black pride la négritude
bleacher le gradin, **10.1**
to **block** bloquer, **10.1**
blond blond(e), **1.1**
blood le sang
blood vessel le vaisseau sanguin
bloom: in bloom fleuri(e), **L2**
to **bloom** fleurir
blouse le chemisier, **7.1**
to **blow a horn** sonner du cor, **L3**
to **blow a whistle** siffler, **10.1**
blue bleu(e), **7.2**
navy blue bleu marine *(inv.)*, **7.2**
to **board** *(plane)* embarquer
boarding l'embarquement *(m.)*
boarding pass la carte d'embarquement, **8.1**
boat le bateau, **L4**
body le corps
bohemian bohème
boiling bouillant(e)
bone l'os *(m.)*
book le livre, **3.2**
border la frontière
boss le chef; le/la patron(ne)
botany la botanique
both tous (toutes) les deux
bottle la bouteille, **6.2**
boulder le rocher, **L3**
boutique la boutique, **7.1**
bowl le bol
box office le guichet, **13.1**
boy le garçon, **1.1**
boyfriend le petit ami
brain le cerveau
brain stem le tronc cérébral
brass band la fanfare
brave courageux, courageuse; brave
Brazil le Brésil
Brazilian *(person)* le/la Brésilien(ne)
bread le pain, **6.1**
loaf of French bread la baguette, **6.1**
slice of bread and butter la tartine de pain beurré
whole-wheat bread le pain complet
to **break** briser
breakfast le petit déjeuner, **5.2**
to eat breakfast prendre le petit déjeuner, **5.2**
to **breathe** respirer, **14.2**
to breathe deeply respirer à fond, **14.2**
Breton breton(ne)
bridge le pont
to **bring** apporter, **11.1**
Brittany la Bretagne
bronchial tube la bronche
brother le frère, **1.2**

brown brun(e), marron *(inv.)*, **7.2**
brunette brun(e), **1.1**
brush la brosse, **12.1**
to **brush** *(one's teeth, hair, etc.)* se brosser (les dents, les cheveux, etc.), **12.1**
to **build** construire; fabriquer
bungalow le bungalow
to **burn** brûler
burst éclaté(e)
bus le bus; l'autocar *(m.)*
by bus en bus
bush *(wilderness)* la brousse
busy occupé(e)
but mais, **2.1**
butcher le boucher, la bouchère
butcher shop la boucherie, **6.1**
butter le beurre, **6.1**
to **buy** acheter, **3.2**
by par
Bye. Salut., **BV**

C

cabaret le cabaret
cabin *(plane)* la cabine, **8.1**
café le café, **BV**
cafeteria la cafétéria
cake le gâteau, **4.1**
calcium le calcium
calculator la calculatrice, **3.2**
calculus: differential calculus le calcul différentiel
integral calculus le calcul intégral
calendar le calendrier
to **call** appeler; *(on the telephone)* téléphoner
to call a penalty déclarer un penalty
calm calme
calorie la calorie
Camembert cheese le camembert
campaign la campagne
can pouvoir, **6.1**
can of food la boîte de conserve, **6.2**
Canadian *(adj.)* canadien(ne), **6**
candle la bougie, **4.1**
cap la casquette, **7.1**
capital la capitale
car la voiture, **4.2;** *(railroad)* le wagon
by car en voiture, **5.2**
dining car le wagon-restaurant
sleeping car le wagon-couchette
carbohydrate la glucide; l'hydrate *(m.)* de carbone
carbon dioxide le gaz carbonique
card la carte
cardboard le carton
cardiac cardiaque
care le soin
general care *(adj.)* de soins polyvalents
to **care: I don't care.** Ça m'est égal., **13.1**
career la carrière
Careful! Attention!, **4.2**
Caribbean Sea la mer des Caraïbes, la mer des Antilles
carnival *(season)* le carnaval
carpenter le charpentier
carrot la carotte, **6.2**
carry-on bag le bagage à main, **8.1**
to **carry out** exécuter
cartoon le dessin animé, **13.1**
cash register la caisse, **3.2**
cassette la cassette, **3.1**
castle le château
casual *(clothes)* sport *(adj. inv.)*, **7.1**
cat le chat, **4.1**
catalog le catalogue
catastrophic catastrophique
category la catégorie
to **cause** causer
cave la grotte, **L4**
CD le CD, **3.1**
CD-ROM le CD-ROM
to **celebrate** célébrer, **L4**
cell la cellule, **L4**
Celtic celte, celtique
center le centre
centiliter le centilitre
century le siècle
cereal les céréales *(f. pl.)*
certainly certainement
chain la chaîne
chairlift le télésiège, **11.2**
champion le/la champion(ne)
to **change** changer (de), **9.2**
channel *(TV)* la chaîne, **12.2**
to channel surf zapper, **12.2**
characteristic la caractéristique
charges les frais *(m. pl.)*
charm le charme
charming charmant(e)
chart le tableau
to **chat** bavarder
check *(in restaurant)* l'addition *(f.)*, **5.2**
to **check** vérifier, **8.1;** contrôler
to check *(luggage)* (faire) enregistrer, **8.1**
checkout counter la caisse, **3.2**
cheese le fromage, **5.1**
chemical chimique
chemist le/la chimiste
chemistry la chimie, **2.2**
chemotherapy la chimiothérapie
chest le coffre, **L4;** la poitrine
chewing gum le chewing-gum
chic chic *(inv.)*
chicken le poulet, **6.1**
child l'enfant *(m. et f.)*, **4.1**
childhood l'enfance *(f.)*
chills les frissons *(m. pl.)*, **14.1**
Chinese chinois(e)
chocolate le chocolat; *(adj.)* au chocolat, **5.1**

choir le chœur
cholesterol le cholestérol
to **choose** choisir, **8.1**
choppy *(sea)* agité(e)
circle le cercle
circuit le circuit
circulation la circulation
circus le cirque
to **cite** citer
city la ville, **8.1**
in the city en ville
civilized civilisé(e)
clarinet la clarinette
class *(people)* la classe, **2.1;** *(course)* le cours, **2.1**
in class en classe
in (French, etc.) class en cours de (français, etc.)
in first (second) class en première (seconde), **9.1**
classical classique
to **classify** classifier
classmate le/la camarade de classe
classroom la salle de classe, **2.1**
to **clear the table** débarrasser la table, **12.2**
clever: Very clever! *(ironic)* C'est malin!
climate le climat
climatic climatique
clinic la clinique
closed fermé(e), **13.2**
clothes les vêtements *(m. pl.)*, **7.1**
cloud le nuage, **11.1**
clown le clown
coach l'autocar *(m.)*
coast la côte
coat le manteau, **7.1**
code le code, **4.2**
coffee le café, **5.1**
black coffee l'express *(m.)*, **5.1**
coffee with cream le crème, **5.1**
cola le coca, **5.1**
cold froid(e) *(adj.)*; *(illness)* le rhume, **14.1**
It's cold (weather). Il fait froid., **11.2**
to have a cold être enrhumé(e), **14.1**
collection la collection
color la couleur, **7.2**
What color is . . . ? De quelle couleur est... ?, **7.2**
comb le peigne, **12.1**
to **comb one's hair** se peigner, **12.1**
Come on! Allez!, **9.2**
comedy la comédie, **13.1;** le film comique, **13.1**
musical comedy la comédie musicale, **13.1**
comfortable confortable
comic comique, **13.1**
to **commemorate** commémorer
commercial *(TV)* la publicité, **12.2**
companion le/la camarade
company la société
in the company of en compagnie de
to **compare** comparer
comparison la comparaison
compatriot le/la compatriote
complete complet, complète
to **complete** compléter
completely complètement
complicated compliqué(e)
composed of composé(e) de
composer le compositeur, la compositrice
composition la composition
computer l'ordinateur *(m.)*
computer science l'informatique *(f.)*, **2.2**
concept le concept
concert le concert
condition la condition
conductor *(train)* le contrôleur, **9.2**
to **connect** connecter; relier
connection *(between trains)* la correspondance, **9.2**
to **conspire** comploter
to **consult** consulter
to **contain** contenir
contamination la contamination
contest la compétition, le concours
continent le continent
to **continue** continuer
contrary: on the contrary au contraire
to **control** contrôler
convent le couvent
conversation la conversation
to **converse** converser
conversion la conversion
to **cook** faire la cuisine, **6**
cooked cuit(e)
cool: It's cool (weather). Il fait frais., **11.2**
correct bon(ne), **6.2**
correspondence la correspondance
corridor le couloir, **8.2**
cosmopolitan cosmopolite
cost le prix, **7.1**
to **cost** coûter, **3.2**
cottage la maisonnette
to **cough** tousser, **14.1**
count le comte, **L4**
to **count** compter
counter le comptoir, **8.1**
countless innombrable
country le pays, **8.1**
country(side) la campagne
courage le courage
courageous courageux, courageuse
course le cours, **2.1**
of course bien sûr; mais oui
of course not mais non
court la cour
courtesy la politesse, **BV**
courtyard la cour, **3.2**
cousin le/la cousin(e), **4.1**
to **cover** couvrir
covered couvert(e)
crab le crabe, **6.1**
crazy fou, folle
cream la crème

coffee with cream le crème, **5.1**
to **create** créer
credit card la carte de crédit
Creole *(language)* le créole
crepe la crêpe, **BV**
criminal le/la criminel(le), **L4**
croissant le croissant, **5.1**
to **cross** traverser
crushed écrasé(e)
to **cry** pleurer, **L1**
cue l'indication *(f.)*
to **cultivate** cultiver
cultural culturel(le)
cultural event la manifestation culturelle
culture la culture
cup la tasse, **5.2**
winner's cup la coupe, **10.2**
cured guéri(e)
customer le/la client(e)
customs la douane
cycling le cyclisme, **10.2;** *(adj.)* cycliste
cyclist *(in race)* le coureur (la coureuse) cycliste, **10.2**

D

dad papa
daily quotidien(ne)
dairy store la crémerie, **6.1**
dance la danse
to **dance** danser, **13.1**
dancer le danseur, la danseuse, **13.1**
dangerous dangereux, dangereuse
dark sombre
dark haired brun(e), **1.1**
Darn! Zut!, **BV**
data les données *(f. pl.)*
date la date
What is today's date? Quelle est la date aujourd'hui?, **BV**
to **date from** dater de
daughter la fille, **4.1**
day le jour, **BV;** la journée, **3.1**
the day before yesterday avant-hier, **10.2**
every day tous les jours
What a nice day! Belle journée!, **4.2**
What day is it today? C'est quel jour aujourd'hui?, **BV**
dear cher, chère
death la mort
decaliter le décalitre
December décembre *(m.)*, **BV**
to **decide (to)** décider de
decimal *(adj.)* décimal(e)
decision la décision
the decision is made la décision est prise
to **declare** déclarer
to **decorate** orner
delay le retard
delicatessen la charcuterie, **6.1**
delicious délicieux, délicieuse
dentist le/la dentiste
deodorant le déodorant
department (in a store) le rayon, **7.1**
coat department le rayon des manteaux, **7.1**
department store le grand magasin, **7.1**
large department store la grande surface
departure le départ, **8.1**
to **depend (on)** dépendre (de)
deplaning le débarquement
descendant le/la descendant(e)
to **describe** décrire
description la description
desert le désert; *(adj.)* désertique
designer *(clothes)* le couturier
desperate désespéré(e), **L4**
dessert le dessert
destination la destination
destiny la destinée
devoted dévoué(e)
diagnosis le diagnostic, **14.2**
dialect le dialecte
dialogue le dialogue
diamond le diamant
to **die** mourir, **11**
diet l'alimentation *(f.)*; le régime
to follow a diet faire un régime
difference la différence
different différent(e), **8.1**
difficult difficile, **2.1**
difficulty la difficulté
to **dig** creuser, **L4**
dining car la voiture-restaurant
dining hall *(school)* la cantine, **3.1**
dining room la salle à manger, **4.2**
dinner le dîner, **5.2**
to eat dinner dîner, **5.2**
diploma le diplome
direction la direction; le sens
directly directement
dirty sale
disagreeable désagréable
to **disappear** disparaître
discount la réduction
to **discover** découvrir
to **discuss** discuter
disease la maladie
dish *(food)* le plat
dishes la vaisselle, **12.2**
to do the dishes faire la vaisselle, **12.2**
dishwasher le lave-vaisselle, **12.2**
diskette la disquette
to **distinguish** distinguer
district le quartier, **4.2;** *(Paris)* l'arrondissement *(m.)*
dive le plongeon
to **dive** plonger, **11.1**
to **divide** diviser
to **do** faire, **6.1**
to do the grocery shopping faire les courses, **6.1**

doctor le médecin (*m. et f.*), **14.2**
at (to) the doctor's office chez le médecin, **14.2**
document le document
documentary le documentaire, **13.1**
dog le chien, **4.1**
dollar le dollar, **3.2**
domain le domaine
domestic (*flight*) intérieur(e), **8.1**
door la porte, **L4**
dormitory le dortoir
doubt le doute
to **download** télécharger
downtown le centre-ville
dozen la douzaine, **6.2**
drama le drame, **13.1**
drama club le club d'art dramatique
dramatic dramatique
drawing le dessin
dress la robe, **7.1**
dressed: to get dressed s'habiller, **12.1**
dressy habillé(e), **7.1**
to **dribble** (*basketball*) dribbler, **10.2**
drink la boisson; la consommation, **5.1**
to **drink** boire, **10.2**
something to drink quelque chose à boire
druid le druide
dry sec, sèche
dubbed (*movie*) doublé(e), **13.1**
during pendant, **3.2**
dynamic dynamique, **1.2**

E

each (*adj.*) chaque
each (one) chacun(e), **5.2**
ear l'oreille (*f.*), **14.1**
earache: to have an earache avoir mal aux oreilles, **14.1**
early en avance, **9.1;** de bonne heure; tôt, **12.1**
to **earn** gagner
Easter Pâques
eastern oriental(e)
easy facile, **2.1**
to **eat** manger, **5.1**
to eat breakfast prendre le petit déjeuner, **5.2**
to eat lunch déjeuner, **3.1**
ecological écologique
ecology l'écologie (*f.*)
economics l'économie (*f.*), **2.2**
efficient efficace
egg l'œuf (*m.*), **6.1**
fried egg l'œuf sur le plat
poached egg l'œuf à la coque
scrambled egg l'œuf brouillé
egotistical égoïste, **1.2**
Egyptian égyptien(ne)
electric électrique
electronic électronique
element l'élément (*m.*)
elevator l'ascenseur (*m.*), **4.2**
to **eliminate** éliminer
else: something else autre chose
Anything else? Avec ça?, **6.1;** Autre chose?, **6.2**
e-mail l'e-mail (*m.*)
emission l'émission (*f.*)
employee l'employé(e)
end la fin
enemy l'ennemi(e)
energetic énergique, **1.2**
energy l'énergie (*f.*)
engagement les fiançailles (*f. pl.*), **L4**
England l'Angleterre (*f.*)
English anglais(e)
English (*language*) l'anglais (*m.*), **2.2**
English Channel la Manche
enormous énorme
enough assez, **1.1**
enriched enrichi(e)
to **enter** entrer, **7.1**
enthusiastic enthousiaste, **1.2**
entire entier, entière
entrance l'entrée (*f.*), **4.2**
epic (*adj.*) épique
equation l'équation (*f.*)
equator l'équateur (*m.*)
equipment l'équipement (*m.*)
equivalent l'équivalent (*m.*)
eraser la gomme, **3.2**
to **escape** s'échapper; s'évader, **L4**
especially surtout
espresso l'express (*m.*), **5.1**
essential essentiel(le)
to **establish** établir
establishment l'établissement (*m.*)
euro l'euro (*m.*)
Europe l'Europe (*f.*)
European (*adj.*) européen(ne)
evening le soir, **BV**
in the evening le soir, **5.2**
in the evening (P.M.) du soir, **BV**
event l'événement (*m.*)
ever jamais
every tous, toutes, **2.1, 8;** chaque
every day tous les jours, **13.2**
everybody tout le monde, **1.2**
everyday quotidien(ne)
everyone tout le monde, **1.2**
everything tout
everywhere partout
evidently évidemment
to **evoke** évoquer
exact exact(e)
exactly exactement
exam l'examen (*m.*), **3.1**
to pass an exam réussir à un examen
to take an exam passer un examen, **3.1**
to **examine** examiner, **14.2**

example: for example par exemple
excellent excellent(e)
except excepté(e); sauf, **13.2**
exception l'exception *(f.)*
exceptional exceptionnel(le)
exchange l'échange *(m.)*
to **exchange** échanger
excursion l'excursion *(f.)*
excuse me pardon
to **execute** exécuter
exercise l'exercice *(m.)*
exhausted crevé(e); épuisé(e)
exhibit l'exposition *(f.)*, **13.2**
to **exist** exister
existence l'existence *(f.)*
to **expel** expulser
expenses les frais *(m. pl.)*
expensive cher, chère, **7.1**
expert *(adj.)* expert(e)
to **explain** expliquer
explanation l'explication *(f.)*
expression l'expression *(f.)*
exterior l'extérieur *(m.)*
extraordinary extraordinaire
eye l'œil *(m., pl.* yeux*)*, **14.1**
to have itchy eyes avoir les yeux qui piquent, **14.1**
eyes les yeux *(m. pl.)*, **L1**

F

fable la fable
fabulous fabuleux, fabuleuse
face la figure, **12.1**
to **face** donner sur, **4.2**
factory l'usine *(f.)*
fairly assez, **1.1**
fall *(season)* l'automne *(m.)*, **11.2**
to **fall** tomber **11.2**
to fall asleep s'endormir
to fall asleep again se rendormir
false faux, fausse
to **falsify** falsifier
family la famille, **4.1**
famous célèbre; connu(e), **13.1**
fan le/la fana
fantastic fantastique
far (away) loin
far from loin de, **4.2**
fare le tarif
fast *(adj.)* rapide; *(adv.)* vite **10.2**
to **fasten** attacher, **8.2**
fast-food *(adj.)* de restauration rapide
fast-food restaurant le fast-food
fat la graisse; le lipide
father le père, **4.1**
fault la faute
favorite favori(te); préféré(e)
February février *(m.)*, **BV**
to **feed** nourrir
to **feel** *(well, etc.)* se sentir, **14.1**
to feel better aller mieux, **14.2**
to feel like avoir envie de
to feel out of sorts ne pas être dans son assiette, **14.1**
fees *(doctor)* les honoraires *(m. pl.)*
felt-tip pen le feutre, **3.2**
festival le festival
festive de fête
festivity la festivité
fever la fièvre, **14.1**
to have a fever avoir de la fièvre, **14.1**
to have a high fever avoir une fièvre de cheval, **14.1**
few peu (de)
a few quelques, **9.2**
fiancé(e) le/la fiancé(e), **L4**
field le champ, **L1;** le domaine
fig la figue
fight le combat, **L3;** la lutte, **L3**
to **fight** lutter, **L3**
file *(computer)* le fichier
to **fill out** remplir, **8.2**
film le film, **13.1**
adventure film le film d'aventures, **13.1**
detective film le film policier, **13.1**
foreign film le film étranger, **13.1**
horror film le film d'horreur, **13.1**
science fiction film le film de science-fiction, **13.1**
finally enfin, **12.1;** finalement
to **find** trouver, **5.1**
fine ça va, bien, **BV**
fine l'amende *(f.)*
finger le doigt
to **finish** finir, **8.2**
firm l'entreprise *(f.)*
first premier, première *(adj.)*, **4.2;** d'abord *(adv.)*, **12.1**
in first class en première, **9.1**
fish le poisson, **6.1**
fish store la poissonnerie, **6.1**
fitting room la cabine d'essayage
flavor le parfum
flea market le marché aux puces
flight le vol, **8.1**
domestic flight le vol intérieur, **8.1**
flight attendant l'hôtesse *(f.)* de l'air, le steward, **8.2**
flight crew le personnel de bord, **8.2**
international flight le vol international, **8.1**
float le char
floor *(of a building)* l'étage *(m.)*, **4.2**

ground floor le rez-de-chaussée, **4.2**
flower la fleur, **4.2**
flu la grippe, **14.1**
flute la flûte
to **fly** *(plane)* piloter
to **follow** suivre
following suivant(e)
food la nourriture; l'aliment *(m.)*; les provisions *(f. pl.)*
food service la restauration
foot le pied, **10.1**
on foot à pied, **4.2**
football le football américain
for pour; *(time)* pendant, **3.2;** depuis, **9.2**
for example par exemple
foreign étranger, étrangère, **13.1**
foreman, forewoman le contremaître, la contremaîtresse
to **forget** oublier
fork la fourchette, **5.2**
form la forme
to **form** former
formality la formalité
former ancien(ne)
fortunately heureusement
fortune la fortune
to **found** fonder
fourth quatrième
fracture la fracture
France la France
free libre, **5.1;** gratuit(e)
to **free** libérer
freedom la liberté
freezing: It's freezing (weather). Il gèle., **11.2**
French français(e) *(adj.)*, **1.1;** *(language)* le français, **2.2**
French fries les frites *(f. pl.)*, **5.1**
Frenchman (-woman) le/la Français(e)
French-speaking francophone
to **frequent** fréquenter
Friday vendredi *(m.)*, **BV**
friend l'ami(e), **1.2;** *(pal)* le copain, la copine, **2.1;** le/la camarade
from de, **1.1**
from then on désormais
front l'avant *(m.)*, **8.2**
in front of devant, **8.2**
frozen surgelé(e), **6.2**
fruit le fruit, **6.2**
full plein(e), **10.1;** complet, complète
fun amusant(e), **1.1**
to have fun s'amuser, **12.2**
function la fonction
functioning le fonctionnement
funny amusant(e), **1.1;** rigolo, **4.2;** comique, **13.1**
furniture les meubles *(m. pl.)*
fusion la fusion
future l'avenir *(m.)*, le futur, **L2**

G

game le match, **10.1;** le jeu
garage le garage, **4.2**
garden le jardin, **4.2**
gas le gaz
gas station la station-service
gate *(airport)* la porte, **8.1**
gem la pierre précieuse, **L4**
general le général
generally généralement
geography la géographie, **2.2**
geometry la géometrie, **2.2**
germ le microbe
German *(language)* l'allemand *(m.)*, **2.2**
Germany l'Allemagne *(f.)*
Gesundheit! À tes souhaits!, **14.1**
to **get** recevoir, **10.2**
to get back on remonter
to get dressed s'habiller, **12.1**
to get married se marier, **L4**
to get sick tomber malade, **L1**
to get a sunburn attraper un coup de soleil, **11.1**
to get off *(bus, train)* descendre, **9.2**
to get off *(plane)* débarquer
to get on (board) monter, **9.2**
to get up se lever, **12.1**
giant le/la géant(e)
gift le cadeau, **4.1**
gigantic gigantesque
girl la fille, **1.1**
girlfriend la petite amie
to **give** donner, **4.1**
to give back rendre
glad content(e)
glass le verre, **5.2**
glove le gant, **11.2**
to **go** aller, **5.1**
to go (in a car, etc.) rouler, **10.2**
to go aboard s'embarquer sur
to go down descendre, **9**
to go fast rouler vite, **10.2**
to go (and) get aller chercher, **6.1**
to go home rentrer, **3.2**
to go out sortir, **8.2**
to go surfing faire du surf, **11.1**
to go to bed se coucher, **12.1**
to go through security *(airport)* passer par le contrôle de sécurité, **8.1**
to go up monter, **4.2**
to go windsurfing faire de la planche à voile, **11.1**
to go with accompagner
Should we go? On y va?
goal le but, **10.1**
to score a goal marquer un but, **10.1**

goalie le gardien de but, **10.1**
God bless you! À tes souhaits!, **14.1**
gold l'or *(m.)*, **L4**
golden doré(e)
good bon(ne), **6.2**
good in math fort(e) en maths, **2.2**
good-bye au revoir; ciao *(inform.)*, **BV**
gourmet le gourmet
grade la note
grains les céréales *(f. pl.)*
gram le gramme, **6.2**
grammar la grammaire
granddaughter la petite-fille, **4.1**
grandfather le grand-père, **4.1**
grandmother la grand-mère, **4.1**
grandparents les grands-parents *(m. pl.)*, **4.1**
grandson le petit-fils, **4.1**
gray gris(e), **7.2**
great grand(e)
Greece la Grèce
green vert(e), **5.1**
green beans les haricots *(m. pl.)* verts, **6.2**
greeting la salutation
grilled ham and cheese sandwich le croque-monsieur, **5.1**
griot le griot
grocery store l'épicerie *(f.)*, **6.1**
ground le sol, **10.2**
ground floor le rez-de-chaussée, **4.2**
on the ground à terre
group le groupe
to **grow (up)** grandir
growth la croissance
guard le gardien, **L4**
to **guard** garder
to **guess** deviner
guide(book) le guide
guillotined guillotiné(e)
guitar la guitare
guitarist le/la guitariste
guy le type
gymnastics la gymnastique, **2.2**

H

hair les cheveux *(m. pl.)*, **12.1**
Haitian haïtien(ne)
half *(sporting event)* le mi-temps
half demi(e)
half brother le demi-frère, **4.1**
half hour la demi-heure
half past *(time)* et demie, **BV**
half price le demi-tarif
half sister la demi-sœur, **4.1**
ham le jambon, **5.1**
hamburger le hamburger
hamlet le hameau
hand la main, **3.1**
handicapped handicapé(e)
handkerchief le mouchoir, **14.1**
handmade fait(e) à la main
handsome beau (bel), **4.2**
happy content(e); heureux, heureuse
Happy birthday! Bon (Joyeux) anniversaire!
harbor le port
hard dur(e); *(adv.)* fort
hardware (computer) le hardware
harp la harpe
hat *(ski)* le bonnet, **11.2**
to **hate** détester, **3.1**
to **have** avoir, **4.1;** *(to eat or drink)* prendre, **5.1**
to have a(n) . . . -ache avoir mal à (aux)... , **14.1**
Have a nice day! Belle journée!, **4.2**
he il, **1.1**
head la tête, **10.1;** *(of department or company)* le chef
to **head into** s'engager dans
headache: to have a headache avoir mal à la tête, **14.1**
health la santé, **14.1**
to be in good (poor) health être en bonne (mauvaise) santé, **14.1**
to **hear** entendre, **9.1**
heart le cœur
hello bonjour, **BV**
help l'aide *(f.)*
to be a big help rendre bien service
with the help of à l'aide de
to **help** aider
hemisphere l'hémisphère *(m.)*
here is, here are voici, **4.1;** *(emphatic)* voilà, **1.2**
hero le héros
hi salut, **BV**
to **hide** cacher, **L3**
high élevé(e)
high school le lycée, **2.1**
higher supérieur
his sa, son, ses
history l'histoire *(f.)*, **2.2**
to **hit** frapper, **L3;** donner un coup (de pied, de tête, etc.), **10.1**
hockey le hockey
hockey stick la crosse
hole le trou, **L4**
home: at (to) the home of chez, **3.2**
to go home rentrer, **3.2**
homework *(assignment)* le devoir
to do homework faire ses devoirs, **12.2**
honest honnête
horrible horrible
hospital l'hôpital *(m.)*; *(adj.)* hospitalier, hospitalière
hot chaud(e)
hot chocolate le chocolat
hot dog la saucisse de Francfort, **BV**
It's hot (weather). Il fait chaud., **11.1**

hotel l'hôtel *(m.)*
house la maison, **3.1;** la villa
publishing house la maison d'édition
small house le pavillon
housing le logement
how comment, **1.1**
How are you? Ça va? Comment vas-tu? Comment allez-vous?, **BV**
How's it going? Ça va?, **BV**
How long have you been waiting? Tu attends depuis combien de temps?
how much, how many combien (de), **3.2**
How much is it? C'est combien?, **3.2**
human humain(e)
human being l'être humain *(m.)*
hundred cent, **2.2**
hundreds les centaines *(f. pl.)*
hungry: to be hungry avoir faim, **5.1**
I'm super hungry. J'ai hyper faim.
hunter le chasseur, la chasseuse
to **hurry** se dépêcher, **12.1**
to **hurt** avoir mal à, **14.1**
It (That) hurts. Ça fait mal., **14.1**
husband le mari, **4.1**

I

I je, **1.2**
ice la glace, **11.2**
ice cream la glace, **5.1**
idea l'idée *(f.)*
ideal idéal(e)
identify identifier
if si
ill malade, **L1, 14.1**
illness la maladie
illustration le dessin
immediate immédiat(e)
immediately immédiatement
immense immense
important important(e)
impossible impossible
Impressionists les impressionnistes *(m. pl.)*
imprisoned emprisonné(e)
in dans, **1.2;** à, **3.1;** en, **3.2**
in addition to en plus de
in fact en fait
in first (second) class en première (seconde), **9.1**
in front of devant, **8.2**
in general en général
in particular en particulier
in search of à la recherche de
in vain en vain
In what month? En quel mois?, **BV**
inaugurate inaugurer
included compris(e), **5.2**
The tip is included. Le service est compris., **5.2**
to **indicate** indiquer
indigestion le trouble digestif
to have indigestion avoir mal au foie
indiscreet indiscret, indiscrète
indispensable indispensable
individual l'individu *(m.)*; *(adj.)* individuel(le)
industrial industriel(le)
inexpensive bon marché *(inv.)*
infection l'infection *(f.)*, **14.1**
infinite infini(e)
influence l'influence *(f.)*
to **influence** influencer
information l'information *(f.)*
innocent innocent(e)
inquiry l'enquête *(f.)*
insane fou, folle
to **insist** insister
to **inspire** inspirer
instructions les instructions *(f. pl.)*
instructor le moniteur, la monitrice, **11.1**
instrument l'instrument *(m.)*
keyboard instrument l'instrument à clavier
percussion instrument l'instrument à percussion
string instrument l'instrument à cordes
wind instrument l'instrument à vent
intellectual intellectuel(le)
intelligent intelligent(e), **1.1**
interest l'intérêt *(m.)*
interesting intéressant(e), **1.1**
intermediate moyen(ne)
intermission l'entracte *(m.)*, **13.1**
internal interne
international international(e), **8.1**
interpreter l'interprète *(m. et f.)*
intimate intime
to **introduce** présenter
to **invite** inviter, **4.1**
island l'île *(f.)*, **L4**
to **isolate** isoler
Italian *(adj.)* italien(ne)
Italian *(language)* l'italien *(m.)*, **2.2**
to **itch** piquer **14.1**
to have itchy eyes avoir les yeux qui piquent, **14.1**
Ivory Coast la Côte d'Ivoire

J

jacket le blouson, **7.1**
(sport) jacket la veste, **7.1**
ski jacket l'anorak *(m.)*, **7.1**

jam la confiture, **6.2**
January janvier *(m.)*, **BV**
jar le pot, **6.2**
jazz le jazz
jealous jaloux, jalouse
jeans le jean, **7.1;** le blue-jean
jersey le maillot
to **jog** faire du jogging
to **joke around** rigoler, **3.2**
joy la joie
juice le jus, **5.1**
apple juice le jus de pomme, **5.1**
orange juice le jus d'orange, **5.1**
July juillet *(m.)*, **BV**
June juin *(m.)*, **BV**
junior high student le/la collégien(ne)
just juste, **2.1**
fitting (him/her) just right juste à sa taille
just barely tout juste

K

to **keep** garder
key la clé; le demi-cercle *(basketball)*, **10.2**
keyboard le clavier
to **kick** donner un coup de pied, **10.1**
to **kid: You're kidding!** Tu rigoles!, **3.2**
kilogram le kilo(gramme), **6.2**
kilometer le kilomètre
kind la sorte; le genre, **13.1**
king le roi, **L3**
kitchen la cuisine, **4.2**
kitchen sink l'évier *(m.)*, **12.2**
knife le couteau, **5.2**
knight le chevalier
to **knock** frapper, **L4**
to **know** connaître *(be acquainted with)*; savoir *(information)*, **13.2**

L

label la griffe
laboratory le laboratoire
lake le lac
lamb l'agneau *(m.)*, **6.1**
lame boiteux, boiteuse
land la terre
to **land** atterrir, **8.1**
landing l'atterrissage *(m.)*; le débarquement
landing card la carte de débarquement, **8.2**
landscape le paysage
language la langue, **2.2**
lap *(race)* l'étape *(f.)*
large grand(e); ample
last dernier, dernière, **10.2**
last name le nom de famille
last night hier soir, **10.2**
last week la semaine dernière, **10.2**
last year l'année *(f.)* dernière
to **last** durer
late en retard, **9.1;** *(adv.)* tard, **12.1**
to be late être en retard, **9.1;** avoir du retard *(plane, train, etc.)*, **8.1**
later plus tard
See you later. À tout à l'heure., **BV**
Latin le latin, **2.2**
Latin *(adj.)* latin(e)
Latin American latino-américain(e)
to **learn (to)** apprendre (à), **5**
to **leave** partir, **8.1;** ressortir
to leave (a room, etc.) quitter, **3.1**
to leave (something behind) laisser, **5.2**
to leave a tip laisser un pourboire, **5.2**
leg la jambe
legend la légende
lemonade le citron pressé, **5.1**
lemon-lime drink la limonade, **BV**
less moins, **7.1**
less than moins de
less . . . than moins... que, **7**
lesson la leçon, **11.1**
to **let** laisser
Let's go. On y va.
lettuce la salade, **6.2**
level le taux
liaison la liaison
life la vie
light *(color)* clair(e)
like comme
to **like** aimer, **3.1**
I'd like that! Ça me dit!
I would like je voudrais, **5.1**
What would you like? *(café, restaurant)* Vous désirez?, **5.1**
limit la limite
line la ligne; *(of people)* la queue, **9.1**
to wait in line faire la queue, **9.1**
linked en liaison
linking la liaison
liquid le liquide
to **listen (to)** écouter, **3.1**
to listen with a stethoscope ausculter, **14.2**
liter le litre, **6.2**
literature la littérature, **2.2**
little: a little un peu, **2.1;** un peu de
to **live** *(in a city, house, etc.)* habiter, **3.1**
liver le foie
living vivant(e)
living room la salle de séjour, **4.2**
to **load** charger
lobby le hall, **8.1**
local local(e)
located situé(e)
lonely solitaire
long long(ue), **7.1**
(for) a long time longtemps, **11.1**
(for) too long trop longtemps, **11.1**

Long live . . . ! Vive... !
longer: no longer ne... plus, **6.1**
to **look** *(seem)* avoir l'air
to **look at** regarder, **3.1**
to look at oneself se regarder
to look at one another se regarder
to **look for** chercher
loose *(clothing)* large, **7.2**
loose-leaf binder le classeur, **3.2**
to **lose** perdre, **9.2**
to lose patience perdre patience, **9.2**
lot: a lot beaucoup, **3.1**
a lot of beaucoup de, **3.2**
a lot of people beaucoup de monde, **10.1**
to **love** aimer, **3.1;** adorer
love l'amour *(m.)*, **L4**
lower inférieur(e)
low-income housing le/la H.L.M.
luck la chance
to be in luck avoir de la chance
lucky: to be lucky avoir de la chance
luggage les bagages *(m. pl.)*, **8.1**
lunch le déjeuner, **5.2**
to eat lunch déjeuner, **3.1**
lung le poumon
luxury *(adj.)* de grand standing
lyrics les paroles *(f. pl.)*

M

ma'am madame, **BV**
machine la machine
magazine le magazine, **9.1, L2;** la revue, **L2**
Maghreb le Maghreb
magic *(adj.)* magique
magnificent magnifique
magpie la pie
mail la poste
main principal(e)
majority la majorité
to **make** faire, **6.1;** fabriquer
to make a basket *(basketball)* réussir un panier, **10.2**
to make up inventer
mall le centre commercial, **7.1**
man l'homme *(m.)*, **7.1**
to **manage to** arriver à, **9.1**
mandatory obligatoire
manner la façon
many beaucoup de, **3.2**
map la carte
March mars *(m.)*, **BV**
market le marché, **6.2**
flea market le marché aux puces
marriage le mariage
married marié(e)
to get married se marier, **L4**
marvelous merveilleux, merveilleuse
masculine masculin(e)
math les maths *(f. pl.)*, **2.2**
mathematics les mathématiques *(f. pl.)*, **2.2**
matter: What's the matter with you? Qu'est-ce que tu as?, **10**
May mai *(m.)*, **BV**
meal le repas, **5.2**
to **mean** signifier
meaning la signification; le sens
to **measure** mesurer
measurement la mesure
meat la viande, **6.1**
medical médical(e)
medicine *(medical profession)* la médecine; *(remedy)* le médicament, **14.1**
medina la médina
Mediterranean Sea la mer Méditerranée
medium-rare *(meat)* à point, **5.2**
to **meet** rencontrer; retrouver *(get together with)*; faire la connaissance de
melody l'air *(m.)*
melon le melon, **6.2**
memorable mémorable
memory le souvenir
to **mention** citer
menu la carte, **5.1**
merchandise la marchandise
merchant le/la marchand(e), **6.2**
produce merchant le/la marchand(e) de fruits et légumes, **6.2**
message le message
metabolism le métabolisme
metal le métal
meter le mètre
metric system le système métrique
microbe le microbe
microbial microbien(ne)
microprocessor le microprocesseur
microscope le microscope
middle school student le/la collégien(ne)
midnight minuit *(m.)*, **BV**
military militaire
milk le lait, **6.1**
milligram le milligramme
million le million
mineral le minéral
mineral water l'eau *(f.)* minérale, **6.2**
minus moins
minute la minute, **9.2**
miracle le miracle
mirror la glace, **12.1**
Miss (Ms.) Mademoiselle (Mlle), **BV**
to **miss** *(train, etc.)* rater, **9.2**
mistake la faute
mixture le mélange
model le modèle
modem le modem
modern moderne
modest modeste
mogul la bosse, **11.2**
mom la maman
moment le moment
Monday lundi *(m.)*, **BV**
money l'argent *(m.)*, **5.2**
monitor *(computer)* le moniteur

month le mois, **BV**
more *(comparative)* plus, **7.1**
more or less plus ou moins
more . . . than plus... que, **7**
no more ne... plus, **6.1**
morning le matin, **BV;** le mat *(fam.)*
in the morning le matin
in the morning (A.M.) du matin, **BV**
Moroccan marocain(e)
Morocco le Maroc
Moslem musulman(e)
most (of) la plupart (des), **9.2**
the most . . . le (la, les) plus...
mother la mère, **4.1**
mother tongue la langue maternelle
mount le mont
mountain le mont; la montagne, **11.2**
to (in) the mountains à la montagne
mountaintop le sommet, **11.2**
mouse la souris
mouth la bouche, **14.1**
movement le mouvement
movie le film, **13.1**
detective movie le film policier, **13.1**
movies le cinéma, **13.1**
movie theater le cinéma, la salle de cinéma, **13.1**
movie video le film en vidéo, **13.1**
science-fiction movie le film de science-fiction, **13.1**
Mr. Monsieur (M.), **BV**
Mrs. (Ms.) Madame (Mme), **BV**
multicolored multicolore
to **multiply** multiplier
municipal municipal(e)
muscle le muscle
muscular musculaire
museum le musée, **13.2**
music la musique, **2.2**
musical musical(e)
musical comedy la comédie musicale, **13.1**
musician le/la musicien(ne)
mussel la moule
must devoir, **10.2**
one must il faut, **8.2**
one must not il ne faut pas, **8.2**
mustard la moutarde, **6.2**
my ma, mon, mes, **4**
mysterious mystérieux, mystérieuse
myth le mythe

N

name le nom
first name le prénom
last name le nom de famille
My name is . . . Je m'appelle... , **BV**
What's your name? Tu t'appelles comment?, **BV**
napkin la serviette, **5.2**
national national(e)
nationality la nationalité
native of originaire de
natural naturel(le)
natural sciences les sciences naturelles *(f. pl.)*, **2.1**
nature la nature
navy blue bleu marine *(inv.)*, **7.2**
near près de, **4.2**
very near tout près, **4.2**
necessarily nécessairement
necessary nécessaire
it is necessary il faut, **8.2**
need le besoin
to **need** avoir besoin de, **10.1**
neighbor le/la voisin(e), **4.2**
neighborhood le quartier, **4.2;** *(adj.)* du coin
nephew le neveu, **4.1**
nervous nerveux, nerveuse
net le filet, **10.2**
never ne... jamais, **11.2**
new nouveau (nouvel), nouvelle, **4.2**
New England la Nouvelle-Angleterre
New Orleans La Nouvelle-Orléans
news *(TV)* les informations *(f. pl.)*
news article le reportage
newspaper le journal, **9.1**
newsstand le kiosque, **9.1**
next prochain(e), **9.2**
nice *(person)* sympa, **1.2;** aimable; sympathique; gentil(le), **6.2**
It's nice weather. Il fait beau., **11.1**
niece la nièce, **4.1**
night la nuit
last night hier soir, **10.2**
no non
no longer ne... plus, **6.1**
no more ne... plus, **6.1**
no one ne... personne, **11;** personne ne...
no smoking (section) (la zone) non-fumeurs, **8.1**
noble noble
nobody ne... personne, **11;** personne ne...
noise le bruit
nonsmoking *(section)* non-fumeurs, **8.1**
noon midi *(m.)*, **BV**
north le nord
North African nord-africain(e)
nose le nez, **14.1**
to have a runny nose avoir le nez qui coule, **14.1**
not ne... pas, **1.2;** pas, **2.1**
isn't it?, doesn't it (he, she, etc.)?, n'est-ce pas?, **2.2**
not at all pas du tout, **3.1**
not bad pas mal, **BV**

note la note
notebook le cahier, **3.2**
notepad le bloc-notes, **3.2**
nothing ne... rien, **11**
to **notice** remarquer
noun le nom
novel le roman
November novembre *(m.)*, **BV**
now maintenant, **2.2**
right now en ce moment
nowadays de nos jours
number le nombre; le numéro
telephone number le numéro de téléphone
numerous nombreux, nombreuse
nutrition l'alimentation *(f.)*

O

object l'objet *(m.)*
to **oblige** obliger
oboe le hautbois
to **observe** observer
occupied occupé(e)
ocean l'océan *(m.)*
o'clock: It's . . . o'clock. Il est... heure(s)., **BV**
October octobre *(m.)*, **BV**
of *(belonging to)* de, **1.2**
of course bien sûr
Of course (not)! Mais oui (non)!
Off (they) go! En route!
office: to have office hours *(doctor)* donner des consultations
official officiel(le)
often souvent, **5.2**
oil l'huile *(f.)*, **6.1;** le pétrole
oil tanker le pétrolier
okay *(health)* Ça va.; *(agreement)* d'accord, **BV**
Okay! Bon!, **6.1**
old vieux (vieil), vieille, **4.2;** âgé(e); ancien(ne)
How old are you? Tu as quel âge? *(fam.)*, **4.1**
older l'aîné(e), **L1**
omelette (with herbs/plain) l'omelette *(f.)* (aux fines herbes/nature), **5.1**
on sur, **4.2**
on board à bord de, **8.2**
on foot à, **4.2**
on sale en solde, **7.1**
on time à l'heure, **8.1**
on Tuesdays le mardi, **13.2**
oneself soi
one-way ticket l'aller simple *(m.)*, **9.1**
onion l'oignon *(m.)*, **5.1**
only seulement; *(adj.)* seul(e)
open ouvert(e), **13.2**
to **open** ouvrir, **14.2**
opera l'opéra *(m.)*
light opera l'opéra comique
operation l'opération *(f.)*
opinion l'avis *(m.)*, **7.2**
in my opinion à mon avis, **7.2**
opponent l'adversaire *(m. et f.)*
opponents le camp adverse, **10.1**
to **oppose** opposer, **10.1**
opposing adverse, **10.1**
opposite le contraire
or ou, **1.1**
or else sinon, **9.2**
orange *(fruit)* l'orange *(f.)*, **6.2;** *(color)* orange *(inv.)*, **7.2**
orange tree l'oranger *(m.)*, **L2**
orchestra l'orchestre *(m.)*
symphony orchestra l'orchestre symphonique
to **orchestrate** orchestrer
order: in order to pour
to **order** commander, **5.1**
ordinary ordinaire
organ *(of the body)* l'organe *(m.)*; *(musical instrument)* l'orgue *(m.)*
organism l'organisme *(m.)*
to **organize** organiser
original language version *(of a film)* la version originale, **13.1**
other autre
in other words autrement dit
on the other hand par contre
some other d'autres, **2.2**
otherwise sinon, **9.2**
our notre, nos, **4**
outdoors en plein air
outfit l'ensemble *(m.)*
outgoing sociable, **1.2**
outing l'excursion *(f.)*
outside *(n.)* l'extérieur *(m.)*; *(adv.)* à l'extérieur; *(prep.)* au dehors de
to work outside the home travailler à l'extérieur
outskirts la périphérie
over *(prep.)* par-dessus, **10.2**
to **overlook** donner sur, **4.2**
overseas *(adj.)* d'outre-mer
to **owe** devoir, **10**
to **own** posséder
oxygen l'oxygène *(m.)*

P

to **pack** *(suitcases)* faire les valises, **8.1**
package le paquet, **6.2**
packed *(stadium)* comble, **10.1**
pain in the neck *(slang)* casse-pieds
painful douloureux, douloureuse
to **paint** peindre
painter l'artiste peintre *(m. et f.)*, le/la peintre, **13.2**
painting la peinture, **13.2;** le tableau, **13.2**
pair la paire, **7.1**
pal le copain, la copine, **2.1**
palace le palais
pancake la crêpe, **BV**

pants le pantalon, **7.1**
paper le papier, **3.2**
sheet of paper la feuille de papier, **3.2**
parade le défilé
pardon me pardon
parents les parents *(m. pl.)*, **4.1**
Parisian *(adj.)* parisien(ne)
park le parc
parking lot le parking
part la partie
to be part of faire partie de
to **participate (in)** participer (à)
party la fête, **4.1**
to throw a party donner une fête, **4.1**
pass la passe
to **pass** passer, **10.1**
to pass an exam réussir à un examen
passenger le passager, la passagère, **8.1;** *(train)* le voyageur, la voyageuse, **9.1**
passport le passeport, **8.1**
passport check le contrôle des passeports
past passé(e)
pasta les pâtes *(f. pl.)*
path le chemin
patience la patience, **9.2**
to lose patience perdre patience, **9.2**
patient le/la malade, **14.2;** *(adj.)* patient(e), **1.1**
patio la terrasse, **4.2**
to **pay** payer, **3.2**
to pay attention faire attention
to pay back rembourser
peace la paix
pear la poire, **6.2**
pearl la perle
peas les petits pois *(m. pl.)*, **6.2**
peasant le/la paysan(ne), **L1**
pen: ballpoint pen le stylo-bille, **3.2**
felt-tip pen le feutre, **3.2**
penalty *(soccer)* le penalty
pencil le crayon, **3.2**
penicillin la pénicilline, **14.1**
people les gens *(m. pl.)*
pepper le poivre, **6.1**
percent pour cent
perfect parfait(e)
perfectly parfaitement
to **perform** jouer, **13.1**
period l'époque *(f.)*; la période
permanent permanent(e)
to **permit** permettre
person la personne
personal personnel(le)
personality la personnalité
personally personnellement, **13.2**
pharmaceutical pharmaceutique
pharmacist le/la pharmacien(ne), **14.2**
pharmacy la pharmacie, **14.2**
phenomenon le phénomène
photograph la photo
physical physique
physicist le/la physicien(ne)
physics la physique, **2.2**
to **pick up** ramasser, **8.2;** recueillir
picnic le pique-nique
picturesque pittoresque
pie la tarte, **6.1**
pill le comprimé, **14.2**
pilot le/la pilote, **8.2**
airline pilot le/la pilote de ligne
to **pilot** piloter
pink rose, **7.1**
pizza la pizza, **BV**
place l'endroit *(m.)*; la place
to take place avoir lieu
to **place** mettre, **7.1**
plain la plaine
plan le projet
plane l'avion *(m.)*, **8.1**
by plane en avion
plant la plante
plastic le plastique
plate l'assiette *(f.)*, **5.2**
platform *(railroad)* le quai, **9.1**
play la pièce (de théâtre), **13.1**
to put on a play monter une pièce, **13.1**
to **play** jouer, **3.2**
to play *(a sport)* jouer à, **10.1**
player le joueur, la joueuse, **10.1**
playwright l'auteur *(m.)* dramatique
pleasant agréable
please s'il vous plaît *(form.)*, s'il te plaît *(fam.)*, **BV**
pleasure le plaisir
pleated plissé(e), **7.1**
plentiful abondant(e)
to **plot** conspirer
plus plus
p.m. de l'après-midi; du soir, **BV**
poem le poème
poet *(m. and f.)* le poète
politeness la politesse, **BV**
political politique
polluted pollué(e)
pollution la pollution
polo shirt le polo, **7.1**
pool la piscine, **11.1**
poor pauvre, **L1, 14.1**
Poor thing! Le/La pauvre!, **14.1**
pop *(music)* pop
popular populaire, **1.2**
pork le porc, **6.1**
port le port
Portuguese portugais(e)
position la position
to **possess** posséder
possession la possession
postcard la carte postale, **9.1**
poster l'affiche *(f.)*
potato la pomme de terre, **6.2**
pound la livre, **6.2**

practical pratique
practice la pratique
to **practice** pratiquer; travailler
preceding précédent(e)
to **prefer** préférer, **6**
prefix le préfixe
to **prepare** préparer
to **prescribe** prescrire, **14.2**
prescription l'ordonnance *(f.)*, **14.2**
to write a prescription faire une ordonnance, **14.2**
present le cadeau, **4.1**
to **present** présenter
pretty joli(e), **4.2**
price le prix, **7.1**
priest l'abbé *(m.)*
principal principal(e)
printer l'imprimante *(f.)*
prison la prison, **L4**
prisoner le prisonnier, la prisonnière, **L4**
private individuel(le); privé(e)
problem le problème; la difficulté
product le produit
professional professionel(le)
program le programme; *(TV)* l'émission *(f.)*, **12.2;** *(computer)* le logiciel
programming la programmation
protein la protéine
proud fier, fière
public public, publique
to **publish** publier
to **punish** punir
purchase l'achat *(m.)*
purified purifié(e)
to **push** pousser
to **put (on)** mettre, **7.1**
to put on makeup se maquiller, **12.1**
to put (someone) to bed coucher, **12**
to put on a play monter une pièce, **13.1**

Q

quality la qualité
quarter: quarter after *(time)* et quart, **BV**
quarter to *(time)* moins le quart, **BV**
Quebec: from or of Quebec québécois
queen la reine
question la question, **3.1**
to ask a question poser une question, **3.1**
quick rapide
quickly rapidement
quite assez, **1.1**
quiz l'interro(gation) *(f.)*

R

race *(human population)* la race; *(competition)* la course, **10.2**
bicycle race la course cycliste, **10.2**
radio la radio, **3.2**
rain la pluie
to **rain: It's raining.** Il pleut., **11.1**
to **raise** lever
to raise one's hand lever la main, **3.1**
raisin le raisin sec
rap *(music)* le rap
rapidly rapidement
rare *(meat)* saignant(e), **5.2**
rather plutôt
razor le rasoir, **12.1**
to **read** lire, **9.2**
reader le lecteur, la lectrice
reading la lecture
real vrai(e), **2.2**
reality la réalité
really vraiment, **1.1**
rear l'arrière *(m.)*, **8.2**
rear guard l'arrière-garde *(f.)*
reason la raison
to **receive** recevoir, **10.2**
recess la récré(ation), **3.2**
to **recognize** reconnaître
recycling le recyclage
red rouge, **7.1**
referee l'arbitre *(m.)*, **10.1**
to **reflect** refléter
refrigerator le frigidaire, **12.2;** le réfrigérateur, **12.2**
reggae le reggae
region la région
to **reimburse** rembourser
relationship la relation
religious religieux, religieuse
to **remain** rester, **11.1**
remote control la télécommande, **12.2**
renowned renommé(e)
to **rent** louer, **13.1**
to **replace** remplacer
to **represent** représenter
research la recherche
to **resemble** ressembler à
reserved réservé(e)
respective respectif, respective
respiration la respiration
respiratory respiratoire
restaurant le restaurant, **5.2**
train station restaurant le buffet, **9.1**
retreat la retraite
return le retour
to **return** rentrer, **3.2;** *(volleyball)* renvoyer, **10.2**
revolution la révolution
revolutionary révolutionnaire
rhythm le rythme
rice le riz
rich riche
riddle la devinette
ridiculous ridicule
right le droit
right away tout de suite
right there juste là
to **rinse** rincer
river le fleuve; la rivière
Riviera *(French)* la Côte d'Azur
road la route; le chemin

rock le rocher, **L3;** *(music)* le rock
role le rôle
romantic romantique
roof le toit
thatched roof le toit de chaume
room *(in house)* la pièce, **4.2;** la salle
dining room la salle à manger, **4.2**
living room la salle de séjour, **4.2**
round-trip ticket le billet aller-retour, **9.1**
route le chemin
routine la routine, **12.1**
royal royal(e)
ruby le rubis
ruined ruiné(e)
rule la règle
ruler la règle, **3.2**
runner le coureur, **10.2**
running shoe la basket, **7.1**
runny: to have a runny nose avoir le nez qui coule, **14.1**
runway la piste, **8.1**
rural rural(e)
Russian *(language)* le russe

S

sad triste, **L1**
to **safeguard** sauvegarder
sailor le marin, **L4**
salad la salade, **5.1**
salami le saucisson, **6.1**
salary le salaire
sale: on sale en solde, **7.1;** en promotion
sales les soldes *(m. pl.)*, **7.1**
salesperson le vendeur, la vendeuse, **7.1**
salt le sel, **6.1**
same même, **2.1**
all the same tout de même, **5.2**
It's all the same to me. Ça m'est égal., **13.1**
sandals *(f. pl.)* les sandals, **7.1**
sandwich le sandwich, **BV**
grilled ham and cheese sandwich le croque-monsieur, **5.1**
sardine la sardine
to **satisfy** satisfaire
Saturday samedi *(m.)*, **BV**
sauce la sauce
sausage la saucisse
to **save** sauver; sauvegarder
saxophone le saxophone
to **say** dire, **9.2**
scarf l'écharpe *(f.)*, **11.2**
scene la scène, **13.1**
schedule l'emploi *(m.)* du temps; l'horaire *(m.)*, **9.1**
sports schedule le calendrier sportif
school l'école *(f.)*, **1.2;** *(adj.)* scolaire, **3.2**
elementary school l'école primaire
junior high/high school l'école secondaire, **1.2**
high school le lycée, **2.1**
school supplies la fourniture scolaire, **3.2**
science les sciences *(f. pl.)*, **2.1**
natural sciences les sciences naturelles, **2.1**
social sciences les sciences sociales, **2.1**
scientific scientifique
scientist le savant
to **score a goal** marquer un but, **10.1**
to **scratch** gratter, **14.1**
screen l'écran *(m.)*, **8.1**
sculptor le sculpteur *(m. et f.)*, **13.2**
sculpture la sculpture, **13.2**
sea la mer, **11.1**
by the sea au bord de la mer, **11.1**
seashore le bord de la mer, **11.1**
seaside resort la station balnéaire, **11.1**
season la saison
seat le siège, **8.2;** la place *(plane, train, movie, etc.)*, **8.1**
seated assis(e), **9.2**
second *(adj.)* deuxième, **4.2;** second(e)
in second class en seconde, **9.1**
secret *(adj.)* secret, secrète
security (airport) le contrôle de sécurité, **8.1**
to **see** voir, **7.1**
See you later. À tout à l'heure., **BV**
See you soon! À bientôt!, **BV**
See you tomorrow. À demain., **BV**
seldom très peu
to **sell** vendre, **9.1**
seller le/la marchand(e), **6.2**
produce seller le/la marchand(e) de fruits et légumes, **6.2**
semi-circle le demi-cercle, **10.2**
to **send** envoyer, **10.1;** emmener, **L4**
separate séparer
September septembre *(m.)*, **BV**
serious sérieux, sérieuse, **7;** grave
to **serve** servir, **8.2; 10.2**
service le service, **5.2**
to **set the table** mettre la table, **7**
several plusieurs
Shall we go? On y va?
shampoo le shampooing, **12.1**
shape la forme
to **shave** se raser, **12.1**
shaver le rasoir, **12.1**
she elle, **1.1**
sheet of paper la feuille de papier, **3.2**
shepherd le berger
shepherdess la bergère
to **shine** briller
shirt la chemise, **7.1**
shoe la chaussure, **7.1**

to **shoot** *(ball)* lancer, **10.2**
shop la boutique, **7.1**
to **shop** faire des achats
shopkeeper le/la commerçant(e)
shopping le shopping, **7.2**
to do the grocery shopping faire les courses, **6.1**
to go shopping faire des courses, **7.2**
shopping cart le chariot, **6.2**
shopping center le centre commercial, **7.1**
short petit(e), **1.1;** court(e), **7.1**
in a short time en très peu de temps
shorts le short, **7.1**
to **shout** crier, **L4**
show *(TV)* l'émission *(f.)*, **12.2**
show(ing) *(movies)* la séance, **13.1**
to **show** montrer; *(movie)* jouer
shower la douche, **12.1**
to take a shower prendre une douche, **12.1**
showing *(movies)* la séance, **13.1**
shrimp la crevette, **6.1**
shy timide, **1.2**
sick malade, **14.1, L1**
to get sick tomber malade, **L1**
sick person le/la malade, **14.2**
side le côté; *(in a sporting event)* le camp, **10.1**
sidewalk café la terrasse (d'un café), **5.1**
sign le signal
significance la signification
similar semblable, **L1**
simple simple
simply simplement
since *(time)* depuis, **9.2**
to **sing** chanter, **13.2**
singer le chanteur, la chanteuse, **13.1**
single unique; seul(e)
sink *(kitchen)* l'évier *(m.)*, **12.2**
sinus infection la sinusite, **14.2**
sir monsieur, **BV**
sister la sœur, **1.2**
to **sit: Where would you like to sit?** Qu'est-ce que vous voulez comme place?, **8.1**
size *(clothes)* la taille; *(shoes)* la pointure, **7.2**
the next larger size la taille au-dessus, **7.2**
the next smaller size la taille au-dessous, **7.2**
to wear size (number) faire du (nombre), **7.2**
What size do you wear? Vous faites quelle taille (pointure)?, **7.2**
skate le patin, **11.2**
to **skate (ice)** faire du patin (à glace), **11.1**
skating le patin
to go skating faire du patin, **11.1**
skating rink la patinoire, **11.2**
skeletal squelettique
skeleton le squelette
ski le ski, **11.2**
ski boot la chaussure de ski, **11.2**
ski cap le bonnet, **11.2**
ski jacket l'anorak *(m.)*, **7.1**
ski pole le bâton, **11.2**
ski resort la station de sports d'hiver, **11.2**
ski trail la piste, **11.2**
to **ski** faire du ski, **11.2**
skier le skieur, la skieuse, **11.2**
skiing le ski, **11.2**
cross-country skiing le ski de fond, **11.2**
downhill skiing le ski alpin, **11.2**
skirt la jupe, **7.1**
skull la boîte crânienne
sky le ciel, **11.1**
to **sleep** dormir, **8.2**
to sleep like a log dormir comme une souche
sleeping car le wagon-couchette
sleeve la manche, **7.1**
long-(short-)sleeved à manches longues (courtes), **7.1**
slice la tranche, **6.2**
slice of bread with butter or jam la tartine
slice of bread and butter la tartine de pain beurré
small petit(e), **1.1**
smoke la fumée
to **smoke** fumer
snack bar *(train)* le snack-bar, **9.2**
sneaker la basket, **7.1**
to **sneeze** éternuer, **14.1**
snow la neige, **11.2**
to **snow: It's snowing.** Il neige., **11.2**
snowman le bonhomme de neige
so alors, **BV;** donc; si *(adv.)*
soap le savon, **12.1**
soccer le foot(ball), **10.1**
soccer field le terrain de football, **10.1**
sociable sociable, **1.2**
social social(e)
social sciences les sciences sociales *(f. pl.)*, **2.1**
social worker l'assistante sociale *(f.)*
sock la chaussette, **7.1**
software le software
soldier le soldat, **L3**
solely uniquement
solid solide
solidarity la solidarité
solution la solution
some du, de la, de l', des, **6;** *(adj.)* quelques *(pl.)*, **9.2;** *(pron.)* certains
some other d'autres, **2.2**
somebody quelqu'un, **10.1**

someone quelqu'un, **10.1**
something quelque chose, **11**
something else autre chose
something special quelque chose de spécial
something to drink quelque chose à boire
sometimes quelquefois, **5.2**
son le fils, **4.1**
song la chanson
soon bientôt
See you soon. À bientôt., **BV**
sore throat: to have a sore throat avoir mal à la gorge, **14.1**
sorry: to be sorry regretter, **6.1**
so-so comme ci, comme ça
sound le son, **L3**
soup la soupe, **5.1**
source la source
south le sud
South America l'Amérique *(f.)* du Sud
spaghetti les spaghettis *(m. pl.)*
Spanish espagnol(e)
Spanish *(language)* l'espagnol *(m.)*, **2.2**
to **sparkle** scintiller
to **speak** parler, **3.1**
special spécial(e)
specialty la spécialité
spectator le spectateur, la spectatrice, **10.1**
to **spend** *(time)* passer, **3.1**
to **spill** déverser
spinach les épinards *(m. pl.)*, **6.2**
spinal cord la moelle épinière
spirit l'esprit *(m.)*
splendid splendide
spoon la cuillère, **5.2**
sport le sport, **10.2**
team sport le sport collectif; le sport d'équipe, **10.2**
winter sports les sports d'hiver, **11.2**
spring *(season)* le printemps, **11.1**
square la place
stadium le stade, **10.1**
stage *(of a race)* l'étape *(f.)*
staircase l'escalier *(m.)*, **4.2**
to **stamp** *(a ticket)* composter, **9.1**
standing debout, **9.2**
to **stare at** regarder fixement
state of the art haut de gamme
station la station, **4.2**
gas station la station-service
subway station la station de métro, **4.2**
stationery store la papeterie, **3.2**
statue la statue, **13.2**
stay le séjour
to **stay** rester, **11.1**
steak and French fries le steak frites, **5.2**
stepfather le beau-père, **4.1**
stepmother la belle-mère, **4.1**
still toujours; encore, **11**
stomach le ventre, **14.1**
stomachache: to have a stomachache avoir mal au ventre, **14.1**
stone la pierre
stop l'arrêt *(m.)*, **9.2**
to **stop** s'arrêter, **10.1**
store le magasin, **3.2**
department store le grand magasin, **7.1**
to **store** stocker
story l'histoire *(f.)*
strategy la stratégie
strawberry la fraise, **6.2**
street la rue, **3.1**
strength la force
strict strict(e), **2.1**
strong fort(e), **2.2**
student l'élève *(m. et f.)*, **1.2;** *(university)* l'étudiant(e)
studio *(artist's)* l'atelier *(m.)*
studio *(apartment)* le studio
study l'étude *(f.)*
to **study** étudier, **3.1;** faire des études
to study French *(math, etc.)* faire du français (des maths, etc.), **6**
stupid stupide
stupid thing la bêtise
style le look
in style à la mode
subject le sujet; *(in school)* la matière, **2.2**
substance la substance
subtitles les sous-titres *(m. pl.)*, **13.1**
to **subtract** soustraire
subway le métro, **4.2**
subway station la station de métro, **4.2**
to **succeed in (doing)** arriver à (+ *inf.*), **9.1**
success le succès
to **suffer** souffrir, **14.2**
sugar le sucre
to **suggest** proposer; suggérer
suit *(men's)* le complet; *(women's)* le tailleur, **7.1**
suitcase la valise, **8.1**
sum la somme
summer l'été *(m.)*
in summer en été, **11.1**
summit le sommet, **11.2**
sun le soleil, **11.1**
in the sun au soleil, **11.1**
to **sunbathe** prendre un bain de soleil, **11.1**
sunburn le coup de soleil, **11.1**
Sunday dimanche *(m.)*, **BV**
sunglasses les lunettes *(f. pl.)* de soleil, **11.1**
sunny: It's sunny. Il fait du soleil., **11.1**
suntan lotion la crème solaire, **11.1**
super super
superbe superbe
supermarket le supermarché, **6.2**

supply la fourniture
school supplies les fournitures scolaires, **3.2**
sure sûr(e)
to **surf the Net** naviguer sur Internet
surfer le surfeur, la surfeuse, **11.1**
surfing le surf, **11.1**
to go surfing faire du surf, **11.1**
surprise la surprise
survey le sondage
survival la survie
to **swallow** avaler, **14.2**
sweater le pull, **7.1**
sweatshirt le sweat-shirt, **7.1**
to **swim** nager, **11.1**
swimming la natation, **11.1**
sword l'épée *(f.)*, **L3**
symphony la symphonie
symptom le symptôme
syrup le sirop, **14.1**
system le système
metric system le système métrique

T

table la table, **5.1**
table setting le couvert, **5.2**
tablecloth la nappe, **5.2**
to **take** prendre, **5.2**
What size do you take? Vous faites quelle taille (pointure)?, **7.2**
to take down descendre, **9**
to take an exam passer un examen, **3.1**
to take off *(airplane)* décoller, **8.1**
to take place avoir lieu
to take possession of prendre possession de
to take size *(number)* faire du (nombre), **7.2**
to take the subway prendre le métro, **5.2**
to take a trip faire un voyage, **8.1**
to take a walk faire une promenade, **11.1**
taken occupé(e)
to **talk** parler, **3.1**
to talk on the phone parler au téléphone, **3.2**
tall grand(e), **1.1**
to **tan** bronzer, **11.1**
tango le tango
tape la cassette, **7.1**
to **tape** enregistrer
tart la tarte, **6.1**
apple tart la tarte aux pommes, **6.1**
tea le thé
to **teach (someone to do something)** apprendre (à quelqu'un à faire quelque chose)
teacher le/la prof *(inform.)*, **2.1**; le professeur, **2.1**
team l'équipe *(f.)*
teammate le coéquipier, la coéquipière
techno (music) la techno
teenager l'adolescent(e)
telephone le téléphone, **3.2**; *(adj.)* téléphonique
telephone number le numéro de téléphone
television la télé, **12.2**
to **tell** dire, **9.2**
to tell (about) raconter
temperate tempéré(e)
temperature la température
temple la tempe
temporary temporaire
ten dix, **BV**
tendon le tendon
term le terme
terrace la terrasse, **4.2**
terrible terrible
terrific super; terrible
test l'examen *(m.)*, **3.1**
to pass a test réussir à un examen
to take a test passer un examen, **3.1**
Thai thaïlandais(e)
than *(in comparisons)* que, **7.2**
thank you merci, **BV**
thanks merci, **BV**
thanks to grâce à
that ça; ce (cet), cette, **9**
that is c'est-à-dire
That's all. C'est tout., **6.1**
That's it., That's right. C'est ça.
thatched roof le toit de chaume
the le, la, les, **1.1**
theater le théâtre, **13.1**
their leur(s), **4**
theme le thème
then alors, **BV**; ensuite, **12.1**
there là; y, **5.2**
there are il y a, **4.1**
there is il y a, **4.1**
therefore donc
they ils, elles, **2**; on, **3.2**
thing la chose
to **think** croire, **7.2**; *(opinion)* trouver, **7.2**
third troisième, **4.2**
thirsty: to be thirsty avoir soif, **5.1**
this ce (cet), cette
thousand mille, **3.2**
throat la gorge, **14.1**
throat infection l'angine *(f.)*, **14.1**
to have a frog in one's throat avoir un chat dans la gorge, **14.1**
to have a sore throat avoir mal à la gorge, **14.1**
throne le trône
through par
to **throw** lancer, **10.2**
to throw a party donner une fête, **4.1**
Thursday jeudi *(m.)*, **BV**
ticket le billet, **8.1**
one-way ticket l'aller *(m.)* (simple), **9.1**
round-trip ticket le billet aller (et) retour, **9.1**

ticket window le guichet, **9.1**
tie la cravate, **7.1**
to **tie** *(score)* égaliser
tight serré(e), **7.2**
time *(of day)* l'heure *(f.)*, **BV;** *(in a series)* la fois, **10.2;** le temps
(for) a long time longtemps, **11.1**
at the same time à la fois
at what time? à quelle heure?, **2**
in a short time en très peu de temps
on time à l'heure, **8.1**
time difference le décalage horaire
times l'époque *(f.)*
What time is it? Il est quelle heure?, **BV**
timetable l'horaire *(m.)*
tip *(restaurant)* le pourboire, **5.2**
to leave a tip laisser un pourboire, **5.2**
The tip is included. Le service est compris., **5.2**
tired fatigué(e)
tissue le kleenex, **14.1**
to à, **3.1;** à destination de *(plane, train, etc.)*, **8.1;** *(in order to)* pour
(up) to jusqu'à
toast le pain grillé
today aujourd'hui, **BV;** de nos jours
together ensemble, **5.1**
tomato la tomate, **6.2**
tomorrow demain, **BV**
See you tomorrow. À demain., **BV**
tonight ce soir
tonsillitis l'angine *(f.)*, **14.1**
too *(also)* aussi, **1.1;** *(excessive)* trop, **2.1**
too many, too much trop de
tooth la dent
toothbrush la brosse à dents, **12.1**
toothpaste le dentifrice, **12.1**
totally complètement; totalement
to **touch** toucher, **10.2**
tourist le/la touriste
toward vers
towel la serviette, **11.1**
tower la tour
Eiffel Tower la tour Eiffel
town la ville, **8.1;** le village
in town en ville
small town le village
toxic toxique
track la piste, **10.2;** *(railroad)* la voie, **9.1**
track and field l'athlétisme *(m.)*, **10.2**
tradition la tradition
traditional traditionel(le)
tragedy la tragédie
tragic tragique
train le train, **9.1**
train station la gare, **9.1**
train station restaurant le buffet, **9.1**
traitor le traître, la traîtresse
to **transform** transformer
to **transport** transporter
traveler le voyageur, la voyageuse, **9.1**
tray le plateau, **8.2**
treasure le trésor, **L4**
to **treat** traiter
treatment le traitement
tree l'arbre *(m.)*, **L3**
trigonometry la trigonométrie, **2.2**
trip le voyage, **8.1**
to take a trip faire un voyage, **8.1**
tropical tropical(e)
trouble: to be in trouble être en difficulté
truck le camion
true vrai(e), **2.2**
trumpet la trompette
truth la vérité
to **try on** essayer, **7.2**
T-shirt le t-shirt, **7.1**
Tuesday mardi *(m.)*, **BV**
tunic la tunique
Tunisian tunisien(ne)
tunnel le tunnel
turn: It's your turn. À votre tour.
to **turn around** faire demi-tour
to **turn off** *(appliance)* éteindre, **12.2**
to **turn on** *(appliance)* mettre, **7;** allumer, **12.2**
TV la télé, **12.2**
on TV à la télé, **12.2**
twin le jumeau, la jumelle, **L1**
type le type, la sorte, le genre, **13.1**
typical typique
typically typiquement

U

uncle l'oncle *(m.)*, **4.1**
under sous, **8.2**
underground souterrain(e)
to **understand** comprendre, **5**
unfortunately malheureusement
unhappy malheureux, malheureuse
unit l'unité *(f.)*
United States les États-Unis *(m. pl.)*
university l'université *(f.)*
unknown inconnu(e)
until jusqu'à
up there là-haut
upset stomach le trouble digestif
to **use** utiliser
usually d'habitude, **12.2**

V

vacation les vacances *(f. pl.)*
on vacation en vacances
summer vacation les grandes vacances

valley la vallée; le val
value la valeur
vanilla *(adj.)* à la vanille, **5.1**
varied varié(e)
variety la variété
various divers(e)
to **vary** varier
VCR le magnétoscope, **12.2**
vegetable le légume, **6.2**
veil le voile
vein la veine
vengence la vengeance
to **verify** vérifier, **8.1**
very très, **BV;** tout
very near tout près, **4.2**
very well très bien, **BV**
victorious victorieux, victorieuse
video la vidéo, **3.1**
movie video le film en vidéo, **13.1**
videocassette la cassette vidéo, **12.2**
Vietnamese vietnamien(ne), **6**
view la vue
village le village
vinegar le vinaigre, **6.1**
violent violent(e)
violin le violon
viral viral(e)
virus le virus
to **visit** *(a place)* visiter
vitamin la vitamine
voice la voix
volleyball le volley (-ball), **10.2**
volunteer le/la bénévole
voyage le voyage

W

to **wait (for)** attendre, **9.1**
to wait in line faire la queue, **9.1**
waiter le serveur, **5.1**
waiting room la salle d'attente, **9.1**
waitress la serveuse, **5.1**
walk la promenade, **11.1**
to take a walk faire une promenade, **11.1**
to **walk** marcher
wall le mur, **L4**
to **want** désirer, vouloir, avoir envie de
war la guerre, **L3**
warm chaud(e)
warmup suit le survêtement, **7.1**
warrior le guerrier, **L3**
to **wash** se laver, **12.1**
to wash one's hair (face, etc.) se laver les cheveux (la figure, etc.), **12.1**
washcloth le gant de toilette, **12.1**
waste le déchet
to **watch** surveiller
Watch out! Attention!, **4.2**
water l'eau *(f.)*, **6.2**
to **water-ski** faire du ski nautique, **11.1**
way la façon
we nous, **2;** on, **3.2**
weak faible, **L1**
weapon l'arme *(f.)*
to **wear** porter, **7.1**
What size do you wear? Vous faites quelle taille?, **7.2**
weather le temps, **11.1**
It's nice (bad) weather. Il fait beau (mauvais)., **11.1**
What's the weather like? Il fait quel temps?, **11.1**
Web site le site
wedding le mariage
Wednesday mercredi *(m.)*, **BV**
week la semaine, **3.2**
a week huit jours
a (per) week par semaine, **3.2**
last week la semaine dernière, **10.2**
next week la semaine prochaine
weekend le week-end
weight le poids
welcome le/la bienvenu(e)
Welcome! Bienvenue!
You're welcome. Je t'en prie. *(fam.)*, **BV;** Je vous en prie. *(form.)*, **BV**
well bien, **BV;** eh bien; ben *(slang)*
well then alors, **BV**
well-behaved bien élevé(e)
well-done *(meat)* bien cuit(e), **5.2**
well-known connu(e), **13.1**
well-to-do aisé(e)
west l'ouest *(m.)*
western occidental(e)
western *(movie)* le western
what qu'est-ce que, **3.2;** quel(le), **6;** quoi *(after prep.)*
What color is . . . ? De quelle couleur est... ?, **7.2**
What is . . . like? Comment est... ?, **1.1**
What is it? Qu'est-ce que c'est?, **3.2**
What is today's date? Quelle est la date aujourd'hui?, **BV**
What's your name? Tu t'appelles comment?, **BV**
when quand, **4.1**
where où, **1.1**
from where d'où, **1.1**
which quel(le), **6**
to **whistle** siffler, **10.1**
white blanc, blanche, **7.2**
who qui, **1.1**
whole *(adj.)* entier, entière; *(n.)* l'ensemble *(m.)*
whole-wheat bread le pain complet
whom qui, **10**
why pourquoi, **6.2**
why not? pourquoi pas?
wide large, **7.2**
wife la femme, **4.1**
to **win** gagner, **10.1;** sortir victorieux (victorieuse)

wind le vent, **11.1**
window *(seat)* (une place) côté fenêtre, **8.1**
window *(store)* la vitrine, **7.1**
windsurfing la planche à voile, **11.1**
  to go windsurfing faire de la planche à voile, **11.1**
windy: It's windy. Il y a du vent., **11.1**
winner le/la gagnant(e), **10.2**
  winner's cup la coupe, **10.2**
winter l'hiver *(m.)*
with avec, **3.2;** auprès de; muni(e) de
without sans
woman la femme, **7.1**
wood le bois
word le mot
  words *(of song, etc.)* les paroles *(f. pl.)*
work le travail; *(of art or literature)* l'œuvre *(f.)*, **13.1**
worker l'ouvrier, l'ouvrière
world le monde
wounded blessé(e)
to **write** écrire, **9.2**
  to write a prescription faire une ordonnance, **14.2**
writer l'écrivain *(m.)*, **L2**
wrong mauvais(e), **2.2**
  What's wrong? Qu'est-ce qui ne va pas?
  What's wrong with him? Qu'est-ce qu'il a?, **14.1**

Y

yeah ben oui
year l'an *(m.)*, **4.1;** l'année *(f.)*
  to be . . . years old avoir... ans, **4.1**
yellow jaune, **7.2**
yes oui, **BV;** si *(after neg. question)*, **7.2**
yesterday hier, **10.1**
  the day before yesterday avant-hier, **10.2**
yogurt la yaourt, **6.1**
you tu, **1;** vous, **2**
young jeune
  young people les jeunes *(m. pl.)*
younger le cadet, la cadette, **L1**
your ton, ta, tes; votre, vos, **4**

Z

to **zap** zapper, **12.2**
zero zéro
zone la zone
zoology la zoologie

Index

Credits

Glencoe would like to acknowledge the artists and agencies who participated in illustrating this program: Meg Aubrey represented by Cornell & McCarthy; Domenick D'Andrea; Len Ebert; Judy Love; Glencoe; Fanny Mellet Berry represented by Anita Grien Representing Artists; Joseph Hammond; Studio InkLink; Carlos Lacamara; Ortelius Design Inc.; Shannon Stirnweis; Carol Strebel; Joe Veno represented by Gwen Walters; Susan Jaekel, Jane McCreary and DJ Simison represented by Remen-Willis Design Group. **COVER** (t)Rlexion Phototec/International Stock, (tc c)Oleg Cajko/Panoramic Images, (bc)David L. Brown/Panoramic Images, (b)Philippe Gontier; **i** (t)Rlexion Phototec/International Stock, (tc c)Oleg Cajko/Panoramic Images, (bc)David L. Brown/Panoramic Images, (b)Philippe Gontier; **iv** (l)Photowood Inc/U-AT/The Stock Market, (r)Mark Burnett; **v** (l)Larry Hamill, (r)Travelpix/FPG; **vi** (tl)Timothy Fuller, (tr)Jenny Andre/Photo 20-20, (b)Zephyr Images/Sunset; **vii** (l)John Evans, (r)Mark Antman/Scribner; **viii** Timothy Fuller; **ix** (tl)Explorer/Photo Researchers, (tr b)Larry Hamill; **x** (tl)Moulo/Sunset, (tr)Musee d'Orsay, Paris/Lauros-Giraudon, Paris/SuperStock, (b)PhotoDisc; **xi** Owen Franken/Stock Boston; **xii** (t)Larry Hamill, (b)David H. Endersbee/Getty Image; **xiii** (tl)Timothy Fuller, (r)Jeff Kaufman/FPG, (bl)Larry Hamill; **xiv** Tim De Waele/CORBIS; **xv** (t)Paul Hardy/The Stock Market, (b)Timothy Fuller; **xvi** (tl tr)Timothy Fuller, (b)Curt Fischer; **xvii** (l)Timothy Fuller, (r)Mark Burnett; **xviii** Timothy Fuller; **xix** (t)Massimo Listri/CORBIS, (bl br)Philippe Gontier; **xxxvi** (t)Chris Sorenson/The Stock Market, (cl)Mark Antman/The Image Works, (b)Mark Burnett; **xxxvii** (t c)Larry Hamill, (bl)Walter Bibikow/FPG, (bc)Michele Burgess/The Stock Market, (br)Alain Even/DIAF; **0** (t)Michael Krasowitz/FPG, (tc)Photobank USA/Sunset, (bc)Curt Fischer, (b)David Florenz/Option Photo; **0–1** Curt Fischer; **1** (5)Curt Fischer, (6)Robert Fried Photography, (7)Timothy Fuller, (8)Gio Barto/The Image Bank, (9)Larry Hamill; **2** Larry Hamill; **3** (tl tc bc)Larry Hamill, (tr bl)Catherine et Bernard Desjeux, (br)Timothy Fuller; **4** (l)Timothy Fuller, (r)Catherine et Bernard Desjeux; **5** Timothy Fuller; **6** Larry Hamill; **7** Mark Burnett; **8** Larry Hamill; **9** (tl)Ilico/Wallis Phototheque, (c cr)LCI/Wallis Phototheque, (others)John Evans; **11** (tl tr)Ken Karp, (bl)Jean-Daniel Sudres/DIAF, (br)Photowood Inc/U-AT/The Stock Market; **13** Mark Burnett; **14** Larry Hamill; **15** Mark Burnett; **16** Bridgeman Art Library; **16–17** Catherine et Bernard Desjeux; **18** Larry Hamill; **19** Timothy Fuller; **20** (t c br)Larry Hamill, (bl)Jill Connelly/The Image Works; **21** (tl)Pacha/CORBIS, (tr)Bettmann/CORBIS, (bl)Mitchell Gerber/CORBIS, (br)Christie's Images/CORBIS; **22** (tl tr bc)Larry Hamill, (bl)John Evans, (br)Dale Durfee/Getty Images; **23** (l)John Evans, (r)file photo; **24** (tl)Curt Fischer, (tr)Robert Fried Photography, (bl)Garufi/Wallis Phototheque, (br)Telegraph Colour Library/FPG; **25** (t)Jose Fusta Raga/The Stock Market, (c)Dannic/DIAF, (b)Goumare/Wallis Phototheque; **26** Pascal Crapet/Getty Images; **27** P. Wysocki/S. Frances/Hémisphères Images; **28** Getty Images; **30** Ken Karp; **31** (t)Peter McCabe/The Image Works, (b)Monika Graff/The Image Works; **32** (t)Larry Hamill, (b)Claudie/Sunset, (inset)Wayne Rowe; **33** Owen Franken/CORBIS; **34** (t)Travelpix/FPG, (b)Larry Hamill; **35** Bruno DeHogues/Getty Images; **36** (l)Fernand/Sunset, (r)Robert Holmes/CORBIS; **37** (t)Chris Sorenson/The Stock Market, (b)David Simson/Stock Boston; **38** (t)Brian A. Vikander, (cl)Mark Antman/The Image Works, (cr)C. Capel/Sunset, (b)Yvan Travert/DIAF; **39** (t)Private Collection/The Bridgeman Art Library International, Ltd, (b)Jean-Daniel Sudres/DIAF; **40** (t)Camille Moirenc/DIAF, (b)Sitki Tarlan/Panoramic Images; **40–41** Fototeca Storica Nazionale/PhotoDisc; **41** (t)Doug Armand/Getty Images, (b)Ric Ergenbright/CORBIS; **42** (t)Larry Hamill, (c)Peter McCabe/The Image Works, (b)Chris Duranti/Wallis Phototheque; **44** Ozu Kiki/La Phototheque/SDP-DIAF; **45** J. Brun/Explorer; **47** (t)Robert Holmes/CORBIS, (b)Larry Hamill; **48** Barnes Foundation, Merion, Pennsylvania/SuperStock; **48–49** Larry Hamill; **50** Catherine et Bernard Desjeux; **51** (t)Larry Hamill, (b)Timothy Fuller; **52** (t)Marge/Sunset, (b)Timothy Fuller; **53** John Evans; **54** Curt Fischer; **55** John Evans; **56–57** Larry Hamill; **59** Larry Hamill; **60** (tr)Gabe Palmer/CORBIS, (c)Ken Karp, (l)Monika Graff/The Image Works; **63** (t)Robert Fried Photogaphy, (b)Photobank/Sunset; **65** (tl)Zephyr Images/Sunset, (tc)Sierpinski/DIAF, (tr)Robert Fried Photography, (bl)Sylva Villerot/DIAF, (bc)Stuart Cohen/The Image Works, (br)Robert Fried Photography; **66** Larry Hamill; **68** (tl)Michele Burgess/The Stock Market, (tr)Larry Hamill, (b)Beryl Goldberg; **69** (t)David Grunfeld/The Image Works, (b)SuperStock; **70** (t)Larry Hamill, (b)Curt Fischer; **71** (tl)Larry Hamill, (tr)Stephane Cande/Mission/Wallis Phototheque, (b)Robert Holmes/CORBIS; **72** (t)Jean-Paul Garcin/DIAF, (b)Art Wolfe/Getty; **72–73** The Studio Dog/PhotoDisc; **73** (t)Beryl Goldberg, (b)Mark Burnett; **74–75** Larry Hamill; **77** Jenny Andre/Photo 20-20; **79** (t)Larry Hamill, (b)Curt Fischer; **80** Musee Du Louvre, Paris/SuperStock; **80–81** Bob Handelman/Getty Images; **82** Larry Hamill; **83** (t)Aaron Haupt, (b)Alain Le Bot/DIAF; **84** (t)R. Lucas/The Image Works, (b)Larry Hamill; **85** Ken Karp; **86** (tl)Aaron Haupt, (tr bcl bc br)Curt Fischer, (others)Amanita Pictures; **87** Larry Hamill; **88** (t c)Amanita Pictures, (b)Valerie Simmons; **89** Amanita Pictures; **91** (t)John Evans, (bl br)Ken Karp; **92** Ken Karp; **92–93** Matthieu Colin/Hémisphères Images; **94** Beryl Goldberg; **95** file photo; **96** (t)Larry Hamill, (b)John Evans; **98** (l)John Evans, (c)Hartmut Krinitz/Hémisphères Images, (r)Robert Fried Photography; **99** Larry Hamill; **100** (t)Guido Cozzi/Agence ANA, (c)Beryl Goldberg; **101** (t)Larry Hamill, (b)Christian Roger/Wallis Phototheque; **102** (t)Getty Images, (c b)Cheryl Fenton; **103** Ed Taylor Studio/FPG; **104–105** Larry Hamill; **107** Mark Antman/Scribner; **109** Curt Fischer; **110** Metropolitan Museum of Art, New York City/SuperStock; **110–111** file photo; **112** (b)PhotoDisc, (others)Larry Hamill; **113** Timothy Fuller; **114** (t)Mark Burnett, (b)Peter Marlow/Magnum Photos; **115** Giraudon/Art Resource, NY; **117** Larry Hamill; **118** Karin Ansara/Wallis Phototheque; **119** (l)Grant V. Faint/The Image Bank, (c)Stéphane Frances/Hémisphères Images, (r)Claude/Sunset; **121** (t)Michelle Chaplow, (b)Zephyr Images/Sunset; **122** file photo; **123** Michelle Chaplow; **124** Pawel Wysocki/Hémisphères Images; **125** Daniel Thierry/DIAF; **126** Walter Bibikow/FPG; **128** Larry Hamill; **129** (l)file photo, (r)Ken Karp; **130** (l)Pratt-Pries/DIAF, (r)Andrew Payti; **131** (t)Weststock/Sunset, (b)Sandra Baker/Liaison Agency; **132** (tl)SuperStock, (tr)Jean-Daniel Sudres/DIAF, (b)LCI/Wallis Phototheque; **134** (t)Lauros-Giraudon/Art Resource, NY, (b)Renunion des Musees Nationaux/Art Resource, NY; **134–135** CORBIS; **135** (t)David Noble/FPG, (c)Desvignes/Sunset, (b)Gianni Dagli Orti/CORBIS; **137** Travelpix/FPG; **139** Curt Fischer; **141** (t)Timothy Fuller, (b)Travelpix/FPG; **142** (t)Larry Hamill, (b)Mark Burnett; **143** Wayne Rowe; **144** (t)Timothy Fuller, (b)Larry Hamill; **145** R. Rozencwajg/DIAF; **147** Larry Hamill; **148** (2)Laurent Rebours, AP/Wide World Photos, (3)Bernard Boutrit/Photo Researchers, (4)Marie-José Jarry & Jean-François Tripelon/Agence Top/National Geographic Image Collection, (5)Steve McCurry/National Geographic Image Collection; **148–149** Michael Busselle/Stone; **149** (6)P. Bennett/AA Photo Library, (7)Martha Bates/Stock Boston; **150** (9)Steve Vidler/Leo de Wys Stock Photo Agency, (10)Patrick Ingrand/Stone, (11)Patrick Zachmann/Magnum, (12)Christophe Ena, AP/Wide World Photos; **150–151** Chad Ehlers/Stone; **151** (13)Craig Aurness/CORBIS, (14)Suzanne & Nick Geary/Stone; **152** Erich Lessing/Art Resource; **152–153** John Lawrence/Getty Images; **155** (orange juice, apple juice) Timothy Fuller, (fries)Aaron Haupt, (others)John Evans; **156** Timothy Fuller; **157** Gérard Gsell/DIAF; **158** Larry Hamill; **159** (l)John Evans, (c r)Aaron Haupt; **160** (t)Timothy Fuller, (b)Curt Fischer; **162** H. Gyssels/DIAF; **164** (l)Eve Morcrette/Wallis Phototheque, (r)file photo; **166** Gerard Lacz/Sunset; **167** Bill Deering/FPG; **168** James Davis/International Stock; **169–170** Larry Hamill; **172** (t)Catherine et Bernard Desjeux, (b)Timothy Fuller; **173** Wayne Rowe; **174** (t)Larry Hamill, (c)Bob Krist/The Stock Market, (b)Explorer/Photo Researchers; **175** (t)Robert Fried Photography, (c)Quinard/Wallis Phototheque; **176–177** Sami Sarkis/PhotoDisc; **178** Larry Hamill; **179** David Simson/Stock Boston; **180** Wayne Rowe; **183** (t)Gerard Lacz/Sunset, (c bl br)John Evans; **184** Musee d'Orsay, Paris/Lauros-Giraudon, Paris/SuperStock; **184–185** SuperStock; **187** (tl bl br) Larry Hamill, (tr)Curt Fischer; **188** (t)Larry Hamill, (b)Mark Burnett; **189** (t)Curt Fischer, (b)Wayne Rowe; **190** Larry Hamill; **191** (t)Timothy Fuller, (bl)Terry Sutherland, (others)Larry Hamill; **192** PhotoDisc; **193** (l)Peter McCabe/The Image Works, (r)Monika Graff/The Image Works; **194** Larry Hamill; **195** (t)Larry Hamill, (bl)Monika Graff/The Image Works, (br)Ken Karp; **197** (tl tr)Monika Graff/The Image Works, (c)J.-Ch. Gerard/DIAF, (b)Moulo/Sunset; **199** (l r)Monika Graff/The Image Works, (b)Beryl Goldberg; **200** Larry Hamill; **202** (t)Michael Busselle/CORBIS, (bl br)Ken Karp; **204** Timothy Fuller; **205** Andrew Payti; **206** (l)George Gibbons/FPG, (r)Larry Hamill; **207** (l)Michael Busselle/Getty Images, (r)Christophe Duranti/Wallis Phototheque; **208** (l)Alain Le Bot/DIAF, (r)Laurent Giraudou/Hémisphères Images; **209** (tr)Kenneth Ehlers/International Stock, (l)Andrew Payti, (br)Robert Fried Photography; **210** (tl)Charlie Abad/La Phototheque SDP, (tr)Lee Snider/The Image Works, (b)Mark Antman/The Image Works; **211** (t)Mark Antman/The Image Works, (b)Spot/SDP; **212** Larry Hamill; **213** Huet/Hoa-Qui; **215** Larry Hamill; **217** (t)Moulo/Sunset, (bl)Terry Sutherland, (bc br)Larry Hamill; **218** Werner Forman Archive/Museum fur Volkerkunde, Berlin/Art Resource, NY; **218–219** Mark Gibson/Photo 20-20; **220** John Evans; **221** Larry Hamill; **222** (tl b)Larry Hamill, (tr)Timothy Fuller; **223** Iconos/DIAF; **224** Larry Hamill; **225** (t)John Evans, (b)Timothy Fuller; **226** (t)Larry Hamill, (b)Japack/Sunset; **228** Beryl Goldberg; **231** Larry Hamill; **232** Chris/Sunset; **234** Larry Hamill; **235** Michael Dwyer/Stock Boston; **236** (l)Tim Gibson/Envision, (r)Robert Holmes/CORBIS; **237** (t)Curt Fischer, (b)Owen Franken/Stock Boston; **238** (t)H. Rogers/TRIP, (c)Gossler/Schuster/Explorer, (b)Jose Nicolas/Hemispheres Images; **239** Japack/Sunset; **240** (l)FPG, (r)Archivo Iconografico, S.A./CORBIS; **241** Bettmann/CORBIS; **242** Beryl Goldberg; **243** Getty Images; **245** Wayne Rowe; **247** (t)Larry Hamill, (b)John Evans; **248** (t)Larry Hamill, (b)Tim Gibson/Envision; **250** (t)Bertrand Rieger/Hémisphères Images, (b)Steven Needham/Envision; **252** Larry Hamill; **253** Timothy Fuller; **254** (tr)M & E Bernheim/Woodfin Camp & Associates, (cl)Bruno De Hogues/Stone, (cr)Photri/Microstock, (b)Nik Wheeler/CORBIS; **254–255** Steven Rothfeld/Stone; **255** (t)Tim Hall/Retna, (b)M & E Bernheim/Woodfin Camp & Associates; **256** (t)Bruno De Hogues/Stone, (cl)Betty Press/Woodfin Camp & Associates, (cr)Giacomo Pirozzi/Panos Pictures, (b)TempSport/CORBIS; **256–257** Kevin Schafer/CORBIS; **257** (t)Carol Beckwith & Angela Fisher, (b)Caroline Penn/Panos Pictures; **258** Private Collection/Lauros-Giraudon, Paris/SuperStock; **258–259** Tibor Bognar/The Stock Market; **260** (tl tr)Larry Hamill, (tc)Getty Images, (bl)Curt Fischer, (br)C Squared Studios/PhotoDisc; **261** (tl tr)Larry Hamill, (c)Trompas/Sunset, (b)Barret/Wallis Phototheque; **262** courtesy Air France; **263** Owen Franken/Stock Boston; **264** (t)courtesy Air France, (b)Giraudon/Wallis Phototheque; **265** (t)Stephane Frances/Hemispheres Images, (b)DeRichemond/The Image Works; **266** Barret/Wallis Phototheque; **267** Larry Hamill; **269** (l)Monika Graff/The Image Works, (r)Ken Karp; **273** Larry Hamill; **274** Oldrich Karasek/Getty Images; **275** Pictor; **276** (t)David Barnes/The Stock Market, (b)Larry Hamill; **277** Shaun Egan/Getty Images; **278** (t)Marge/Sunset, (b)Telegraph Colour Library/FPG; **279** Timothy Fuller; **281** Archive Photo/Archive France; **283** (t)ZEFA London/The Stock Market, (c)Gerard Gsell/DIAF, (b)J. Du Sordet/Agence ANA, (bkgd)Siede Preis/PhotoDisc; **284** Jose Fuste Raga/The Stock Market; **285** (l)D. Cordier/Sunset, (c)Jacques Sierpinski/DIAF, (r)David H. Endersbee/Getty Images; **287** X. Richer/Hoa-Qui; **289** courtesy Air France; **290** AKG London; **290–291** Jeff Kaufman/FPG; **292–293** Timothy Fuller; **294** (t)Wayne Rowe, (b)Larry Hamill; **295** Beryl Goldberg; **297** Timothy Fuller; **298** Photobank/Sunset; **299** Jacques Loic/La Phototheque SDP; **300** Andrew Payti; **301** The Purcell Team/CORBIS; **302** David Ball/DIAF; **303** Pascal Hinous/Top Agence; **304** (tl tr)Ken Karp, (b)Arnaud Fevrier/DIAF; **305** (t bl)Timothy Fuller, (br)Aaron Haupt; **307** (l)J. Du Sordet/Agence ANA, (r)Jose Fuste/The Stock Market; **308** Timothy Fuller; **310** Stephane Frances/Hémisphères Images; **311** (t)Henneghien/Agence ANA, (b)Alain Even/DIAF; **312** JP. Porcher/Sunset; **313** (t)John Elk/Getty Images, (b)Timothy Fuller; **314** (t)Mark Antman/The Image Works, (bl br)Larry Hamill; **314–315** The Studio Dog/PhotoDisc; **315** (t)Jeanetta Baker/Photobank/Sunset, (b)Graham Finlayson/Woodfin Camp & Associates; **316** (t)Andrew Payti, (cl)Robert Fried Photography, (cr)Beryl Goldberg, (b)P. Dannic/DIAF; **317** Camille Moirenc/Wallis Phototheque; **319** Andrew Payti; **321** (l)Timothy Fuller, (r)Arnaud Fevrier/DIAF; **322** (t)file photo, (b)Museum of Modern Art, Troyes, France/Lauros-Giraudon, Paris/SuperStock; **322–323** Tim De Waele/CORBIS; **324** (l)Ben Radford/AllSport, (r)Timothy Fuller; **325** (t)Bob Thomas/Getty Images, (b)Timothy Fuller; **326** (t)CORBIS/Temp Sport, (b)AFP/CORBIS; **328** (l r)Timothy Fuller, (c)K S Studio; **329** (t)Timothy Fuller, (bl)Bob Daemmrich/PhotoEdit, (br)Wally McNamee/CORBIS, (inset)PhotoDisc; **330** courtesy of Mini Bulldogs de Quebec; **331** (t)Gerard Vandystadt/Agence ANA, (b)AP Photo/Ryan Remiorz/Photo Archive; **333** Reuters NewMedia Inc./CORBIS; **334** Haslin/Tempsort/NewSport Photography, Inc.; **335** (l)Peter McCabe/The Image Works, (r)Ken Karp; **336** Timothy Fuller; **337** S.T.F./Sunset; **338** Monika Graff/The Image Works; **339** Claude Abron/Liaison Agency; **340** (t)Reuters/Charles Platiau/Archive Photos, (b)Larry Hamill; **342** (l)Robert LaBerge/AllSport, (r)David E. Klutho/Sports Illustrated; **343** (t)Reuters/Petar Kujundzic/Archive Photos, (b)Aaron Haupt; **344** Doug Pensinger/Allsport; **345** Tim De Waele/CORBIS; **346** (tl)M. Freeman/PhotoLink /PhotoDisc, (tr)Pictor, (br)AFP/CORBIS; **348** (l)F.Stock/Sunset, (r)Bob Martin/Sports Illustrated; **349** Simon Bruty/Sports Illustrated; **351** Curt Fischer; **353** Reuters NewMedia Inc./CORBIS; **354** Galerie Daniel Malinque, Paris, FR/The Bridgeman Art Library; **354–355** Getty Images; **356** (t)Paul Hardy/The Stock Market, (c b)Timothy Fuller; **357** (l)Laborde/Wallis Phototheque, (r)SuperStock, (cr)Timothy Fuller; **358** (t)Adina Tovy/Photo 20-20, (b)Larry Hamill; **359** (t)Timothy Fuller, (b)Jose Fuste/The Stock Market; **360** (t)Richard Lucas/The Image Works, (r)John Evans, (cl)Jonathon Rawle/Stock Boston, (cr)Bonnie Kamin/PhotoEdit, (b)Rosine Mazin/DIAF; **361** Huet/Wallis Phototheque; **364–365** S.T.F./Sunset; **365** Cosmo Condina/Getty Images; **366** Karl Weatherly/CORBIS; **367** Monika Graff/The Image Works; **368** (t)Tristian Vigouroux/Wallis Phototheque, (b)Beryl Goldberg; **370** (t)J. Sierpinski/DIAF, (b)Marge/Sunset; **371** (l)Jo Labbe/Wallis Phototheque, (r)Robert Fried Photography; **372** (t)Robert Fried Photography, (b)Aaron Haupt; **374** (l)Dave G. Houser/CORBIS, (c)Alec Ptlowany/Masterfile, (r)Patrick Frilet/Hémisphères Images; **375** Zephyr Images/Sunset; **376** (t)Marge/Sunset, (c)Nik Wheeler/CORBIS, (b)Stephane Frances/Hémisphères Images; **377** (t)Stuart Cohen/The Image Works, (c)Patrick Frilet/Hemispheres Images, (b)Mark Antman/The Image Works; **378** (t)Erich Lessing/Art Resource, NY, (b)Giraudon/Art Resource, NY; **378–379** Farinaz Taghavi/PhotoDisc; **379** Erich Lessing/Art Resource, NY; **380** (t)Marge/Sunset, (b)Picturesque/Sunset; **381** (l)Michael Buselle/Getty Images, (r)SuperStock; **383** AFP/CORBIS; **385** (t)Larry Hamill, (b)John Evans; **386** Timothy Fuller; **388** Mark Burnett; **389** Robert Fried Photography; **390** Beryl Goldberg; **392** Joachim Messerschmidt/FPG; **394** (tl)Yves Marcoux/Stone, (tr)Maggie Steber, (bl)Michael Melford, (br)George F. Mobley; **394–395** Ed

Credits

Simpson/Stone; **395** (t)Anna Clopet/CORBIS, (b)Dave G. Houser/CORBIS; **396** (t)Museé McCord, (cl)Hubert Stadler/CORBIS, (cr)Cosmo Condina/Stone, (b)AFP/CORBIS; **396–397** Chris Cheadle/Stone; **397** (t)Jocelyn Boutin, (b)Wolfgang Kaehler/CORBIS; **398** Christie's Images; **398–399** SuperStock; **400** (tcl)John Evans, (others)Timothy Fuller; **401** Timothy Fuller; **402** (t)Chris Duranti/Wallis Phototheque, (b)file photo; **403** Frederick/Sunset; **404–406** Timothy Fuller; **407** Michelle Garrett/CORBIS; **409** Andrew Payti; **411** Timothy Fuller; **412** (t)Timothy Fuller, (bl br)Ken Karp; **413** (l)Robert Fried Photography, (r)Ken Karp; **414** Timothy Fuller; **416** Larry Hamill; **418** Catherine et Bernard Desjeux; **419** (t)Philippe Moulu/Sunset, (b)Pratt-Pries/DIAF; **420** (t)Chad Slattery/Getty Images, (b)Rick Souders/Index Stock; **421** (tl)Timothy Fuller, (tc tr)Aaron Haupt, (b)Mark Burnett; **422** (t)Roy/Sunset, (b)Jonathan Blair/CORBIS; **422–423** PhotoLink/PhotoDisc; **423** (t)Martin Rogers/Stock Boston, (b)de Richemond/The Image Works; **424** (t)Mark Antman/The Image Works, (bl br) Ken Karp; **425** M. Granitsas/The Image Works; **426** (tl tc)Curt Fischer, (tr)file photo, (b)Cheryl Fenton; **427** Carton/Pitch; **429** Timothy Fuller; **430** British Museum, London/Bridgeman Art Library, London/SuperStock; **430–431** Mark Burnett; **432** Timothy Fuller; **433** (t)Timothy Fuller, (bl)SuperStock, (br)Pictor; **434** (t)Timothy Fuller, (b)Jackson Smith/ImageState/Picture Quest; **435** (t)Collections de la Comedie-Francaise, (b)Mark Burnett; **437** Timothy Fuller; **438** Giraudon/Art Resource, NY; **439** © Photo RMN - Hervé Lewandowski/Musee D'Orsay; **440** Jacques Sierpinski/DIAF; **441** Scala/Art Resource, NY; **442** Timothy Fuller; **443** (l)(file photo), (r)Monika Graff/The Image Works; **444** Yann Arthus-Bertrand/CORBIS; **445** (l)Monika Graff/The Image Works, (r)Peter McCabe/The Image Works; **446** (t)J. MarcLallemand/Wallis Phototheque, (b)© Photo RMN - Hervé Lewandowski/Musee D'Orsay; **447** Vanni/Art Resource, NY; **448** Larry Hamill; **450** Derek Croucher/The Stock Market; **450–451** Larry Hamill; **451** (t)AFP/CORBIS, (c)Ramsay/Wallis Phototheque, (b)Gérard Lacz/Sunset; **452** (t)Jason Laure, (b)Kavanah/Stone; **453** (tl)Neal Preston/CORBIS, (tr)Mark Burnett, (b)K. N'Dour/Liaison Agency; **454–455** Steve Cole/PhotoDisc; **455** (t)Robbie Jack/CORBIS, (c)Kevin Winter/Getty Images, (b)Stephane Cardinale/CORBIS/Sygma; **456** Robert Fried Photography; **457** Timothy Fuller; **459** Curt Fischer; **461** (t)Mark Burnett, (b)Robbie Jack/CORBIS; **462** Roger-Viollet, Paris/The Bridgeman Art Library; **462–463** Stefano Bianchetti/CORBIS; **464** (tr)John Evans, (l cr inset)Timothy Fuller, (br inset)Aaron Haupt; **465** Timothy Fuller; **466** Curt Fischer; **467** Mark Burnett; **468** Timothy Fuller; **469** (tr)Larry Hamill, (others) Timothy Fuller; **470** (t)John Evans, (b)Timothy Fuller; **472** (l r)Catherine et Bernard Desjeux, (c)Image Club Graphics; **474** (t)Timothy Fuller, (b)Larry Hamill; **477** Ken Karp; **479** (l)Monika Graff/The Image Works, (c)Ken Karp, (r)Thomas Marc; **480** Timothy Fuller; **481** (l)Monika Graff/The Image Works, (r)Ken Karp; **482** Timothy Fuller; **484** Timothy Fuller; **485** (l)CH. Vioujard/Liaison Agency, (r)SuperStock; **486** (cl)Curt Fischer, (cr)Mark Burnett, (br)Clasen/Wallis Phototheque; **486–487** Mitch Hrdlicka/PhotoDisc; **487** (t)Owen Franken/CORBIS, (b)Larry Hamill; **489** (t)Larry Hamill, (b)P. Wysocki/Explorer; **490** Curt Fischer; **493** (l)John Evans, (r)Timothy Fuller; **494** Everett Collection; **495** Timothy Fuller; **497** (t)Larry Hamill, (b)Owen Franken/CORBIS; **498** (t)PhotoDisc, (cl)Bob Handelman/Stone, (cr)Photri Inc., (b)Stephen Studd/Stone; **498–499** PhotoDisc; **499** (t)Chad Ehlers/Stone; (b)David Turnley/CORBIS; **500** (t)Chris Ladd/FPG, (cl)Franck Eustache/Archipress, (cr)Theo Westenberger, (b)Patrick Ingrand/Stone; **500–501** Jean-Marc Truchet/Stone; **501** (t)Harvey Lloyd/Peter Arnold, Inc., (b)Kim Hart/Black Star Publishing/PictureQuest; **502–503** Massimo Listri/CORBIS; **505** Jean-Daniel Sudres/DIAF; **506** Archiv/Photo Researchers; **507** Scala/Art Resource, NY; **508** Christie's Images; **510** Bridgeman Art Library, London; **511** (t)H. Reinhard/Sunset, (b)Elizabeth Barakah Hodges/SuperStock; **513** Giraudon, Paris/Art Resource, NY; **514** (t)Stock Montage/SuperStock, (b)AKG London; **515 516** AKG London; **517** (t)Art Resource, NY, (b)Nik Wheeler/CORBIS; **520** (t)Hulton-Deutsch Collection/CORBIS, (b)Giraudon/Art Resource, NY; **521** AKG London; **522** Franz-Marc Frei/CORBIS; **523** Marc Garanger/CORBIS; **524–539** One Nation Films, LLC; **H0–H1** Suzanne and Nick Geary/STONE/Getty Images; **H3** (tl br)Garufi/Wallis Phototheque; (tr bl)John Evans, (others)Larry Hamill; **H4** (tl br)Christie's Images/CORBIS, (tr bl)Mitchell Gerber/CORBIS, (tcl bcr)Bettmann/CORBIS, (tcr bcl)Pacha/CORBIS; **H5** Larry Hamill; **H8** John Evans; **H14** (orange juice)Timothy Fuller, (onion soup)Aaron Haupt, (others)John Evans; **H18** (mineral water)Terry Sutherland, (jelly)Timothy Fuller, (others)Larry Hamill; **H27** (t)Stephane Frances/Hemispheres Images, (b)Trompas/Sunset; **H28–H29** Timothy Fuller; **H35** (t)Adina Tovy/Photo 20-20, (cl)Laborde/Wallis Phototheque, (cr)Chris Harvey/Getty Images, (b)Timothy Fuller; **H36** Richard Lucas/The Image Works; **H39** Timothy Fuller; **H43** (t)Timothy Fuller, (c)Pictor, (b)John Evans; **H44** Timothy Fuller; **H47** (tl tr)Timothy Fuller, (bl)John Evans, (br)Aaron Haupt; **H48** Timothy Fuller.